Instructor Resources

We make the integration of our book into your course easy by providing a variety of instructor resources, overseen by the authors to ensure a consistent style and approach throughout.

- The comprehensive **Instructor's Resource Manual**, written by the book author team and revised by Dr. Mallory Malkin (Mississippi University for Women), includes chapter outlines, a concept guide that gives additional examples for each key concept, additional "Thinking Like a Scientist in Real Life" and "Research Spotlight" examples, suggestions for in-class activities, demonstrations and examples, lab/group project ideas, a feature designed to enhance psychological/information literacy, and suggestions for using end-of-chapter materials.

- Unique **Lecture Slideshows** incorporate the same active learning and hands-on approach as the textbook, with additional examples, discussion questions, demonstrations, and activities built right into the presentation to help you bring the material to life. For design chapters, we provide two sets of Lecture Slideshows: one set that incorporates the chapter's research question and a more traditional set that focuses on key concepts.

- The **Downloadable Test Bank**, powered by Diploma, includes a full assortment of test items developed by the book authors. Each chapter features over 200 multiple-choice, short answer, and essay questions, written by Dr. Sadie Leder-Elder (High Point University) and revised by Dr. Mallory Malkin, to test students at several levels of Bloom's taxonomy. This edition also features a set of data-based reasoning questions, written by Dr. Angela Sikorski (Texas A&M University, Texarkana), to test advanced critical thinking skills in a manner similar to the MCAT. Additionally, the text is supplemented by "Fix It" questions in which students identify errors in a variety of research scenarios and suggest, via short answer form, how to correct them. All the questions are written to Macmillan Learning's standards of quality and accuracy and are matched to the outcomes recommended in the *APA Guidelines for the Undergraduate Psychology Major* (APA, 2013a). The accompanying gradebook software makes it easy to record students' grades throughout a course, sort student records, view detailed analyses of test items, curve tests, generate reports, and add weights to grades.

All of these resources are available to adopters of the text for free download through LaunchPad at launchpadworks.com.

Discovering the Scientist Within

Research Methods in Psychology

Second Edition

Gary W. Lewandowski, Jr.
Monmouth University

Natalie J. Ciarocco
Monmouth University

David B. Strohmetz
University of West Florida

worth publishers
Macmillan Learning
New York

Senior Vice President, Content Strategy: Charles Linsmeier
Program Director, Social Sciences: Shani Fisher
Executive Program Manager: Daniel DeBonis
Development Editor: Katie Pachnos
Editorial Assistant: Anna Munroe
Marketing Manager: Clay Bolton
Marketing Assistant: Chelsea Simens
Director of Media Editorial & Assessment, Social Sciences: Noel
  Hohnstine
Media Editor: Stefani Wallace
Associate Media Editor: Nik Toner
Director, Content Management Enhancement: Tracey Kuehn
Senior Managing Editor: Lisa Kinne
Senior Content Project Manager: Kerry O'Shaughnessy
Project Managers: Tristann Jones and Sivaramakrishnan Velayudham,
  Lumina Datamatics, Inc.
Media Project Manager: Joe Tomasso
Senior Workflow Project Supervisor: Susan Wein
Senior Photo Editor: Robin Fadool
Director of Design, Content Management: Diana Blume
Design Services Manager: Natasha Wolfe
Cover Designer: John Callahan
Art Manager: Matthew McAdams
Composition: Lumina Datamatics, Inc.
Printing and Binding: LSC Communications
Cover Credits: otsphoto/Shutterstock

Library of Congress Control Number: 2018949731
ISBN-10: 1-319-10736-2
ISBN-13: 978-1-319-10736-9

Printed in the United States of America

1 2 3 4 5 6   23 22 21 20 19 18

Worth Publishers
One New York Plaza
Suite 4500
New York, NY 10004-1562
www.macmillanlearning.com

We dedicate this book to our students, past, present, and future, who were our inspiration as we worked on every aspect of this book. This book is also for the innovative methods professors who continually seek new ways to share science with students. Finally, we also dedicate this book to our spouses, Colleen, Dave, and June, for supporting us in our continuous pursuit of self-expansion, and to our children, Avery, Amelia, Brian, and Andrew, for helping us remember what a natural love of science and discovery looks like.

About the Authors

Avery R. Lewandowski

Gary W. Lewandowski, Jr., received his B.A. from Millersville University of Pennsylvania and his Ph.D. in social/health psychology from Stony Brook University. He is a professor at Monmouth University and director of the Relationship Science Lab. Dr. Lewandowski has published over 50 academic articles and book chapters, given over 100 conference presentations, received 12 grants, co-edited the book *The Science of Relationships: Answers to Your Questions about Dating, Marriage and Family*, and authored over 150 articles in mass media outlets, which have been enjoyed by over 2.5 million readers. His research focuses on the self and relationships, and examines ways to improve research methods and statistics instruction. In addition to being recognized by *The Princeton Review* as one of the Top 300 professors in the country, Dr. Lewandowski's work and expertise have been featured in outlets as diverse as *The New York Times*, CNN, *APA Monitor, The Washington Post, Newsweek, Business Insider, The Independent, The Atlantic*, NPR, *Time, Scientific American*, and *USA Today*. He has also given a TEDx talk titled "Break-Ups Don't Have to Leave You Broken," which has been viewed over 775,000 times.

Natalie J. Ciarocco is an associate professor of psychology at Monmouth University. She earned her B.A., M.A., and Ph.D. in experimental psychology from Case Western Reserve University. She considers herself a transformed social psychologist, as she is currently an active scholar of teaching and learning in psychology, and studies best practices for teaching research methods, as well as skill development in the psychology major. To this end, she has co-created a number of teaching resources for the scholarship of the teaching and learning community, including a resource for teaching research methods, statistics, and research writing in psychology (www.teachpsychscience.org) and a self-administered assessment of skills for students (www.employableskills.com). You can find her scholarly work in *Teaching of Psychology*, as well as *Scholarship of Teaching and Learning in Psychology*. Dr. Ciarocco is the recipient of 15 grants from organizations such as the Association for Psychological Science and the Society for the Teaching of Psychology and is an active presenter in the teaching and learning community.

Jeneanne Ericsson

Eleanor C. Swanson

David B. Strohmetz is a professor and chair of the Department of Psychology at the University of West Florida. He received his B.A. from Dickinson College and his M.A. and Ph.D. in social/organizational psychology from Temple University. He is an active contributor to the scholarship of teaching and learning, with a particular interest in assessment and the importance of skill development within the undergraduate psychology curriculum. He is a co-creator of the Employable Skills Self-Efficacy Scale (http://www.employableskills.com). Dr. Strohmetz has presented at numerous national and regional teaching conferences and authored various instructional resources to support quality teaching in the classroom, particularly in research methods courses. His other research interests include "the social psychology of the experiment," and social factors that influence people's generosity, particularly with respect to restaurant tipping behaviors.

Contents in Brief

Contents

The defining characteristic of humans is our ability to engage in rational thought, yet there are many times that we think less than rationally. For example, people engage in confirmation bias, belief perseverance, and overconfidence, and rely on anecdotal, rather than scientific, evidence. This chapter explores these forms of faulty thinking in the context of whether a person should enlist the help of psychics or palm readers, and how the characteristics of science can help you make more informed decisions. Finally, the chapter concludes with a discussion of why the skills you will acquire in a research methods course are so useful.

This chapter provides an overview of the research process so that you can think through the specific design issues in subsequent chapters in a more sophisticated way. Specifically, Chapter 2 addresses how to generate research ideas, formulate good hypotheses, conduct a background literature review, identify key design elements, incorporate open science practices, and communicate findings, as well as the need for statistics.

CHAPTER 3

Ethics: Making Ethical Decisions in Research   55

There are many ethical considerations when scientifically answering questions and disseminating research findings. This chapter discusses important ethical principles when conducting psychological research, including the treatment of participants, integrity in the treatment of data, avoidance of plagiarism and misleading graphs, and appropriate representations of research in the media.

CHAPTER 4

The Psychologist's Toolbox: Tools for Building Better Designs   85

A good scientist needs a basic set of skills before jumping into research design. This chapter prepares you to think through the issues in subsequent chapters in a more sophisticated way. Specifically, Chapter 4 introduces operational definitions, how to manipulate variables, how to measure variables, and how to recruit samples.

CHAPTER 5

Qualitative Research: Getting Into the Mind of a Serial Killer 121

Thankfully, the world is not full of serial killers. As a result, if you want to learn about how a serial killer thinks, you have to interview one. This chapter explores the mind of a serial killer through an interview, includes information on how to structure and conduct an interview, and discusses common issues in qualitative research, as well as the analysis of qualitative data.

CHAPTER 6

Observational Research: The Many Forms of Discipline in a Parent's Bag of Tricks 159

Any parent will tell you that one of their worst fears is their young child having a meltdown in a public place. This chapter examines how parents discipline their children in public settings and introduces different types of observation—including how to conduct observations, train observers, and develop coding systems—and descriptive statistics.

CHAPTER 7

Correlational Research: Is Going Greek a Great Idea? 197

The first year of college offers a number of new experiences and opportunities. One of the first decisions a new student makes is whether to join a fraternity or sorority. While there are a number of factors that play a role in that decision, this chapter explores whether a student's self-concept clarity, or how clearly and confidently one defines the self, relates to interest in "going Greek." Chapter 7 introduces correlational research, including scale construction, reliability and validity considerations, sampling options, and the strengths and limitations of correlational research.

CHAPTER 8

Two-Group Design: Texting: I Can't Get You Out of My Mind   243

Students may acknowledge that texting while driving is dangerous or that texting in class may inhibit learning, but still feel compelled to check their phones upon receiving a text. This chapter explores whether suppressing the urge to text is distracting to learning. Chapter 8 introduces the usefulness of experimental designs, establishing causality, the basics of independent and dependent variables, maintaining experimental control, the t-test for independent means, and effect sizes.

CHAPTER 9

Multigroup Design: I'm Feeling Hot, But Is the Earth Hot, Too? 283

Why do people continue to deny climate change in the face of overwhelming evidence? One reason might be that they allow personal experience to override the scientific data. This chapter explores the influence of room temperature on global warming attitudes and a person's likelihood of signing a petition for a global warming cause. Chapter 9 introduces the benefits of multigroup designs (identifying functional relationships, empty control groups, placebo groups), one-way ANOVA, and chi-square, as well as the benefits of behavioral measurement.

CHAPTER 10

Within-Subjects Design: Can Watching Reality TV Shows Be Good for Us? 317

Whether it is The Bachelor, Survivor, or The Real House-wives of (pick the nearest city), people enjoy watching reality television. This chapter explores whether watching reality TV can increase our self-esteem, and addresses how similarity affects the experience of schadenfreude (plea-sure at the misfortune of others). Chapter 10 also covers within-subjects designs, including pretest-posttest designs, repeated measures designs, and longitudinal designs. Potential threats to internal validity that are inherent to these designs—including order effects—are discussed along with potential solutions. Dependent t-tests and repeated-measures ANOVA are introduced as statistics for testing hypotheses.

CHAPTER **11**

Factorial Design: "I Lost My Phone Number, Can I Borrow Yours?" Do Pick-Up Lines Really Work?   353

Meeting someone can be intimidating. Don't just stand there—say something! But what? This chapter looks at the effectiveness of pick-up lines in terms of their humor and the attractiveness of the person saying them. Chapter 11 introduces the practical benefits of using factorial designs and the importance of interactions, the two-way ANOVA, and the hybrid design.

CHAPTER **12**

Mixed Design: Which Therapy Is Best for Treating Eating Disorders? 393

Eating disorders are a common issue for which millions of people seek therapy. This chapter examines how individuals receiving either cognitive behavioral therapy or psychodynamic psychotherapy for anorexia nervosa respond when experiencing different types of stress. Chapter 12 introduces the implementation of a mixed design and methodological issues related to clinical research, such as ethical treatment of participants, the use of double-blind procedures, and the use of appropriate control groups (e.g., waitlists and treatment-as-usual groups).

CHAPTER 13

Program Evaluation: Applying Your Skills in the Real World   435

There are many programs designed to help people, but knowing whether these programs are accomplishing their goals is not always clear. This chapter uses program evaluation to assess the effectiveness of a private addiction center, and discusses how to design a comprehensive program evaluation using focus groups and surveys, as well as how to write a thorough program evaluation report.

APPENDIX A

Statistical Tools for Answering Research Questions   477

Appendix A discusses the decision-making process when developing a data analysis plan. The focus is on a conceptual understanding of the statistical choices students need to make to test their research hypotheses, rather than the actual calculations.

APPENDIX B

Communicating the Science of Psychology   491

Appendix B provides students with some of the basics of writing an APA-style report and the other forms of communicating science, such as poster and paper presentations. This appendix emphasizes the writing process, as well as issues not covered explicitly in the design chapters (e.g., citations and references). We also include an annotated example of an APA-style report written by a student.

Preface

TO THE STUDENT

Welcome!

Most likely, you are studying psychology because you have an interest in learning about how people think, feel, and/or behave. Or, more simply, you want to figure out people. Yet you may be in this course because you are fulfilling a requirement and consider research something that you need to "get through" because it is a bit intimidating or boring. Here is a dirty little secret: most of what you have learned about psychology in your other courses relied on research to discover that new information. In your own life you have made your own guesses and created your own theories about what makes people "tick." However, only after you have acquired knowledge and skills in research methods and statistics will you be able to confidently and accurately provide answers to your questions about others' thoughts, feelings, and behavior. This knowledge and skill set will be instrumental after graduation, as they will help set you apart from other job-seekers.

While it is good to have questions about human behavior, it is often even more exciting to find out if your answers are right, and then share them with others, adding to everyone's understanding of the world. This book emphasizes this thrill of discovery and deemphasizes the simple memorization of abstract terms and concepts. Our goal is to fundamentally change the way you think about and evaluate the world around you.

We take a "learning by doing" approach, which we believe is the best way to learn almost anything. How did you learn to use Twitter or Instagram? How did you learn to use your new smartphone? We bet you didn't bother reading through an instruction manual (in fact, manuals are such a dying learning technique that you probably never even received one). Instead, you probably jumped right in by testing out different features. We believe that you can learn research skills in the same "learn by using" way. Our book will help you think like a psychologist. You will be part of the research process in which the psychologist needs to account for key issues, make decisions, and problem solve throughout the process. Along the way you'll learn lots of new concepts, but always in the context of how to use them. If you are not careful, you'll soon find yourself getting caught up in the adventure that we call research!

Best wishes for a thought-provoking course, and for all of the success that life will bring you,

Dr. L, Dr. C, and Dr. S

TO THE INSTRUCTOR

Albert Einstein once said, "The definition of insanity is doing the same thing over and over again and expecting different results." Taking this to heart, we developed a new approach to teaching research methods. This approach stays true to the course goal of covering key concepts, while placing greater emphasis on engaging students' interests and involving them in the thought process inherent in trying to answer an engaging research question. To this end, three key principles guided our writing of this textbook:

   1. **If you start with an interesting question, research design concepts become useful tools that help provide answers.**

The captivating nature of research is its ability to provide answers to some of our most perplexing questions. Yet when we teach this course, we can mistakenly put the primary focus on concepts, which are likely less interesting. Without question, we need to teach the concepts and students need to learn them, but the strong emphasis on concepts may miss the parts that make science fun and useful. In fact, research shows that students dutifully learn these concepts, but may miss out on their utility or proper implementation (Sizemore & Lewandowski, 2009). There is a better way. As Ken Bain (2004) articulates in his book, *What the Best College Teachers Do,* ". . . the best teachers often try to create what we have come to call a 'natural critical learning environment.' In that environment, people learn by confronting intriguing, beautiful, or important problems, authentic tasks that will challenge them to grapple with ideas, rethink their assumptions, and example their mental models of reality." In the "natural critical learning environment" of psychological research, we should begin with an interesting question or theory. Through the process of seeking an answer, students will become familiar with psychologists' decision-making processes in ways that will encourage them to think more like a scientist in the classroom and beyond.

   2. **The vast majority of students in this course are not going to be career researchers.**

We get it. Realistically, many, if not most, students who take a research methods course will not become career researchers or frequent writers of APA-style papers. Yet we believe that a research methods course is the most important course that every psychology major takes because it promotes scientific and psychological literacy (Halpern, 2009). Increased psychological literacy will help students learn to avoid potential biases in their decision making, as well as learn how to critically evaluate information from external sources. A research course also nurtures students' curiosity about the world. Psychologically literate students will not simply make observations about the world. Rather, they will also reflexively generate hypotheses about the nature and genesis of the observation, and will proceed to generate strategies for scientifically testing their ideas.

Finally, society seems to be experiencing a cultural movement that questions the utility of data and science in favor of going with your "gut" or relying on your own experiences. If a student needs to make a decision at some point about giving their child a vaccination, using data-based scientific evidence to guide that decision will be useful. We believe it is much easier to dismiss data as "just a bunch of numbers" if you have never had the opportunity to engage in the research process. Sadly, many students may never have the opportunity to conduct their own research study as part of their undergraduate experience. To address this, our book demonstrates researchers' careful decision making and gives a "behind the scenes" perspective on the scientific research process. By reading about this process, students will develop a deeper understanding of how a research question leads to data and findings.

3. **Design doesn't occur in a vacuum. Design, statistics, and writing are best understood through their relation to one another.**

The process of scientific discovery is an integrated endeavor. Unfortunately, many psychology curricula and textbooks treat design, statistics, and writing as distinct entities either by having separate textbooks for each, or by segregating them to different chapters. Doing so ignores the fact that each process predominantly occurs along with the other two. A psychologist rarely designs a study without analyzing the collected data. Similarly, a psychologist would not discover new information, only to avoid communicating the results. For there to be something to communicate or write about, a study has to be designed in the first place. When design, statistics, and writing are taught together, students can appreciate and benefit from their interrelations.

To address this, *Discovering the Scientist Within: Research Methods in Psychology* incorporates statistical issues and aspects of APA-style writing in conjunction with the discussion of design concepts. Because this book primarily emphasizes design, the statistics discussion focuses on why a certain statistic is appropriate for a particular design, as well as how to convey statistical results in an APA-style Results section and in tables and/or figures. We find that students commonly struggle with writing the Discussion section, which is problematic because that section focuses on applying critical thinking to the results. To address this, we model the Discussion section by explaining, interpreting, and critically evaluating our results. We also provide appendices that further reinforce statistical analyses and APA-style writing. By focusing on the basics of statistics and writing in the context of design and an interesting research question, students will be able to clearly see statistics' utility, without getting lost in the details that can cause them anxiety.

Book and Chapter Organization

We begin our text with several chapters that introduce students to the science of psychology (Chapter 1), the research process (Chapter 2), and ethics (Chapter 3). *Chapter 4: The Psychologist's Toolbox: Tools for Building Better Designs* provides a fundamental understanding of research design, the manipulation and measurement of variables, error, validity, reliability, and sampling. We believe these chapters provide students with an important foundational understanding of key research concepts that will allow them to engage more with the material in subsequent chapters. In the next set of chapters, we show how key research designs help us find answers to interesting questions.

The design chapters (Chapters 5–13) use a Socratic method that results in a less formal, more conversational writing style to lead readers through the examination of nine distinct research questions, each paired with a research design. The conversation that unfolds revolves around the thought process that a psychologist would undertake to design a study. Of course, no study is perfect and no design is infallible. Rather, our goal is to model the complicated thought process that psychologists use in pursuit of answers. In this process, readers will inevitably think of superior solutions and more elegant designs. As journal article reviewers and readers, we know that for most studies, we have ideas for improvements or other ways to do the study. In fact, we sincerely hope that our readers have this exact experience because it demonstrates that they are thinking critically about design and deeply about the topic at hand.

The design chapters follow a consistent structure where we:

1. Identify the chapter's specific student learning outcomes

2. Introduce an interesting research question

3. Model the literature review process by reviewing some of the relevant literature that piques students' interest in the topic and provides a foundational understanding of the research question, so that students have a basis for thinking through the relevant design issues

4. Discuss the operational definitions of the variables

5. Formulate hypotheses

6. Discuss ethical considerations that may influence the examination of the hypothesis

7. Discuss key design decisions (e.g., participant selection, design selection, nature of the manipulations/measures). At major decision points, we will model how a psychologist might weigh competing options

8. Discuss key issues related to data analysis (e.g., which statistic to use, the basic logic behind the statistic)

9. Demonstrate how to write an APA-style Results section and create figures and/or tables for the appropriate statistic

10. Model an APA-style Discussion section by addressing the implication and interpretation of the results, alternate explanations, and possible future directions

Finally, there are two appendices that provide more in-depth coverage of statistics and the communication of psychological science using APA style. Also included is a sample student APA-style paper, annotated with tips and tricks that students can apply to their own papers. Instructors may choose to assign the appendices as stand-alone readings, or to augment the coverage from the preceding design chapters.

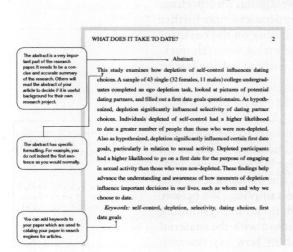

WHAT DOES IT TAKE TO DATE?   2

The abstract is a very important part of the research paper. It needs to be a concise and accurate summary of the research. Others will read the abstract of your article to decide if it is useful background for their own research project.

• Abstract

This study examines how depletion of self-control influences dating choices. A sample of 43 single (32 females, 11 males) college undergraduates completed an ego depletion task, looked at pictures of potential dating partners, and filled out a first date goals questionnaire. As hypothesized, depletion significantly influenced selectivity of dating partner choices. Individuals depleted of self-control had a higher likelihood to date a greater number of people than those who were non-depleted. Also as hypothesized, depletion significantly influenced certain first date goals, particularly in relation to sexual activity. Depleted participants had a higher likelihood to go on a first date for the purpose of engaging in sexual activity than those who were non-depleted. These findings help advance the understanding and awareness of how moments of depletion influence important decisions in our lives, such as whom and why we choose to date.

Keywords: self-control, depletion, selectivity, dating choices, first date goals

The abstract has specific formatting. For example, you do not indent the first sentence as you would normally.

You can add keywords to your paper which are used to catalog your paper in search engines for articles.

Pedagogical Features

In addition to our writing style, we have incorporated several pedagogical features to reinforce and expand our discussion of strategies psychological researchers use to answer their questions. More specifically, each chapter includes:

1. **Research Spotlight** – These boxes provide brief research summaries related to the chapter's topic that highlight studies that students should find interesting.

2. **Thinking Like a Scientist in Real Life** – These boxes describe how students can apply abstract research concepts to their everyday life by demonstrating how thinking like a scientist is useful in nonresearch contexts.

3. **Bolded Key Terms** – Good note-taking often requires students to identify key concepts and ideas as they read a textbook. To help students in this area, we bold key terms to highlight them and provide stand-alone definitions in the page margins (in addition to the in-text explanation).

4. **Your Turn** – At key points in each chapter, we provide students with an opportunity to check their progress.

5. **Chapter Review Questions** – At the end of the chapter, we provide a set of review questions to help students gauge their comprehension of key learning objectives from the chapter. Questions appear in multiple-choice and short-answer formats and test conceptual knowledge as well as students' deeper understanding.

6. **Application Exercises** – These exercises provide students with the chance to engage with the material through more hands-on experiences. These items typically ask students to apply concepts directly to their own lives, and to access an outside source (e.g., watch something on TV or read something online) to help them discover how the chapter's material has made their thinking more scientific. Two special types of application questions, THE NOVICE RESEARCHER and DIG INTO

🔍 Research Spotlight

The Upside to Video-Game Play

If you were to ask a random person on the street whether playing video games has more good or bad outcomes, most people would guess there are more negative outcomes. Like we hypothesized, there might be some real advantages to playing video games. In a year-long longitudinal study of 12-year-olds, researchers found that more time spent playing video games coincided with greater visual–spatial skills, like mentally rotating objects or solving jigsaw puzzles (Jackson, von Eye, Witt, Zhao, & Fitzgerald, 2011). This sounds promising, but 12-year-olds are not exactly surgeons. Well, it just so happens that surgeons benefit from video-game playing as well (Rosser et al., 2007). Surgeons who played video games for more than 3 hours a week made 37% fewer errors and were 27% faster in laparoscopic surgery and suturing drills compared to surgeons who never played video games. The researchers speculate that video games offer the same hand–eye coordination, timing development, sense of touch, and intuitive feel as laparoscopic surgery, giving game players a distinct advantage over non–game players.

If video games can make you a better surgeon, what other areas of your life could playing video games improve? *(Jeff Cadge The Image Bank/Getty Images)*

🧠 Thinking Like a Scientist in Real Life

How to Become More Confident

In life, when things work out a little too well, we wonder if it is a fluke. Perhaps you woke up one morning feeling the beginnings of a cold and decided to eat six oranges for breakfast. Later that afternoon you feel perfectly healthy. Fluke? Or perhaps after getting stuck in traffic on your way to work you decide to take a different way and discover that it saves you 5 minutes on your commute. In each case, you should consider whether your good fortune was simply luck. To be sure, you should attempt to replicate your past success. Eat oranges the next time you feel ill. Alternate your routes to work over several days to determine which is actually quicker. By trying to reproduce the same outcome, you work to confirm the effectiveness of the oranges or your new shortcut to see if they are consistently helpful, or if there were other reasons they worked the first time. If these experiences were lucky or random, it is hard to imagine that they would keep recurring. Achieving the same result several times will give you confidence in the outcome.

7. THE NOVICE RESEARCHER: It is important to have experimental control. Playing the role of a novice researcher, design a two-group study that has at least four problems with experimental control. At the end, identify each problem and discuss how a more experienced researcher would have handled it.

8. DIG INTO THE NUMBERS: We have provided your instructor with supplemental data for a two-group design. Analyze that data to build your skills in using the *t*-test for independent means in SPSS. Write an APA-style results section based on your analyses. If you would like even more practice, your instructor also has data that accompanies the study discussed throughout this chapter.

THE NUMBERS, challenge students to dissect the elements of a flawed study and to build their SPSS and APA-style report writing skills using provided data sets, respectively.

New to the Second Edition

Just as science is a constantly evolving enterprise, so is this textbook. Informed by valuable comments from our reviewers, plus emerging trends in psychological science, we revisited our first edition, looking for opportunities to strengthen our writing and our ability to help students become psychological scientists. Our efforts included reframing our chapter cross-references, found in the margins, as questions to increase reader engagement, and updating the text's design and photo program. More specific changes we made include:

Chapter 1: We draw new comparisons between pseudoscience and the phenomenon of "fake news," providing the reader with tools for differentiating between truths and nontruths.

Chapter 2: We now discuss APA style in the context of how to communicate our research findings as part of the research process. We now also cover programmatic research in this chapter and contextualize it as a design choice, and we expand our coverage on the value of skepticism in evaluating scientific information. Additionally, we introduce the reader to the role and importance of open science practices in psychological research, and we continue this discussion throughout each design chapter as part of the research process.

Chapter 7: We increase our emphasis on correlational research as a research design for answering research questions.

Chapters 5–13 (Design Chapters): We integrate good open science practices in our research decision process. We also summarize the final design decisions made in each chapter in the new "Our Research Plan at a Glance" feature to help students identify and review important design elements. To encourage active learning, we include chapter-specific "Dig into the Numbers" application questions to encourage students to work directly with each chapter's data (which is provided to the instructor).

Media: The second edition includes a full LaunchPad experience, including an e-book and LearningCurve, to support student learning. We have also updated the accompanying Research in Action activities to provide students with additional opportunities to think like a scientist and grapple with concepts from the book in an active way.

We recognize that there is no single best approach to teaching a research methods course. As a result, the book's format easily integrates a variety of approaches instructors take for teaching this course. For example, an instructor could elect to cover basic concepts in class before students read the book. In this approach, the book builds on class material by demonstrating how the concepts are used to answer a research question. Another strategy would be to have students read the text before class as background material. Instructors could then elect to spend class time clarifying and expanding upon the book's content. Finally, instructors can use the textbook to model their own course projects and/or labs on an entirely new research question of their choosing, or students might use the book as a model for their own project or thesis.

As William Butler Yeats said, "Education is not the filling of a pail, but the lighting of a fire." By helping students discover their inner scientist, we hope to enhance students' skills and, in the process, create a spark that will remain lit throughout their lifetime.

Media and Supplements

We make the integration of our book into your course easy by providing an unprecedented collection of high-quality instructor resources, overseen by the book's authors to ensure a consistent style and approach throughout, as well as an easy integration into your course.

First, we provide a comprehensive **Instructor's Resource Manual**, revised for this edition by Dr. Mallory Malkin (Mississippi University for Women), that includes the following resources for each chapter:

1. Chapter outline – Instructors can use the outline to organize their lectures and/or to provide to students to help them organize their notes.

2. Concept guide – To help augment the text examples, the concept guide gives additional examples for each key concept.

3. Additional "Thinking Like a Scientist in Real Life" examples – Students better understand key concepts when they are able to apply them to their own lives. Here we provide additional examples to help them practice.

4. Additional "Research Spotlight" examples – Students benefit from reading about methods in the context of interesting research. Here we provide extra opportunities for students to delve into recent studies and findings.

5. Suggestions for in-class activities, demonstrations, and examples – More so than in other courses, students must actively engage with concepts in their methods course in order to understand them. Creating new material to promote active learning can be a challenge, so we provide many suggestions.

6. Lab/group project ideas – Labs and group projects are key parts of a methods course, but finding good ideas is difficult. We provide multiple ideas, specific to each chapter, to help you out.

7. Ideas for enhancing psychological/information literacy – Becoming a better consumer of scientific information is an important learning objective for

the methods course. Here we provide opportunities to help students further develop these skills.

8. Suggestions for how to use end-of-chapter materials – Not sure how to make the best use of the end-of-chapter materials? We offer concrete suggestions.

9. Dig into the Numbers data sets – For chapters that focus on specific designs, we provide the data sets for the chapter example, as well as an entirely different, additional data set on a distinct research question.

10. Roads Less Traveled – Because each chapter is full of different design decisions, we provide thoughts on alternate directions that the chapter's study could have gone to help students consider additional options and issues.

Additionally, we provide unique **Lecture Slideshows** that incorporate the same active learning and hands-on approach as the textbook. That is, rather than creating text-dense slides that provide verbatim definitions of chapter concepts for students to copy, our slides engage students in the material. Chapter Lecture Slideshows include (directly on the slides):

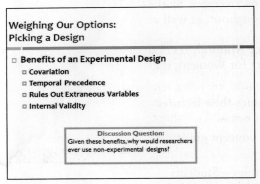

1. Additional examples – Students can always benefit from additional examples, so we have included them. This also has the benefit of allowing the slides not to be overly repetitive with the text.

2. Discussion questions – Methods courses are about getting students thinking. We provide discussion questions directly on the slides to prompt students to consider ideas in a deeper way.

3. Demonstrations – Research design is abstract, especially when you are new to it (like our students are). To make ideas more concrete, we give students a chance to be a participant in each research design (e.g., take part in a two-group design about arousal and attraction).

4. Activities – To help bring material to life, we build activities right into the presentation (e.g., having students list 20 reasons they absolutely love a movie as an explanation of the pleasure paradox). New clicker questions also provide opportunities for increased engagement.

5. Picture Suggestions – Want to include pictures/visuals in your slides, but unsure what to look for? We provide suggestions throughout the slides for keywords you can use to search in Google Images.

6. For the design chapters (Chapters 5–13), we provide two sets of Lecture Slideshows: one set that incorporates the chapter's research question and a more traditional set that focuses on key concepts. You can pick a favorite set or mix and match the slides from different sets to fit your individual style and goals.

We also provide a **Downloadable Test Bank,** powered by Diploma, which includes a full assortment of test items developed by the book's authors. Each chapter features over 200 multiple-choice, short-answer, and essay questions, written by Dr. Sadie Leder-Elder (High Point University) and revised by Dr. Mallory Malkin, to test students at several levels of Bloom's taxonomy. This second edition also features a set of data-based reasoning questions, written by Dr. Angela Sikorski (Texas A&M University, Texarkana), to test advanced critical thinking skills in a manner similar to the MCAT. Additionally, the text is supplemented by "Fix It" questions in which students identify errors in a variety of research scenarios and suggest, via short-answer form, how to correct them. All the questions are written to Macmillan Learning's standards of quality and accuracy and are matched to the outcomes recommended in the *APA Guidelines for the Undergraduate Psychology Major* (APA, 2013). The accompanying gradebook software makes it easy to record students' grades throughout a course, sort student records, view detailed analyses of test items, curve tests, generate reports, and add weights to grades.

All of these resources are available to adopters of the text for free download through the Macmillan Learning website at www.launchpadworks.com.

LaunchPad for *Discovering the Scientist Within*

For the first time, *Discovering the Scientist Within* is available with LaunchPad, a full online course space that is easily integrated with campus learning management system (LMS) platforms and built using insights from cognitive science to boost student learning. LaunchPad features an interactive e-book of *Discovering the Scientist Within* and a variety of learning and assessment tools, including the LearningCurve adaptive quizzing system and the Research in Action activities integrated throughout the text. LaunchPad is available for preview and purchase at www.launchpadworks.com.

- The **interactive e-book** allows students to highlight, bookmark, and add their own notes, just as they would in a printed textbook. The text resizes to different screen dimensions to provide a convenient and accessible reading experience on a wide range of devices.

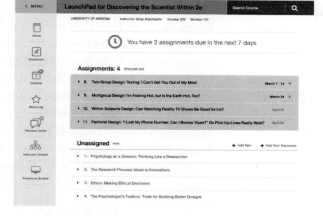

- The **LearningCurve** adaptive quizzing system is designed based on insights from cognitive research to maximize the impact of students' study time. The system engages students by adapting to their level of knowledge and challenging them as they learn more. Each question gives students immediate and valuable feedback on their performance, and when they take a break, they can study the e-book and other LaunchPad resources. Robust analytics give instructors data-driven insights into students' learning, allowing them to identify and address students' knowledge gaps.

- **Chapter Quizzes** are prebuilt for easy summative assessment. Each quiz is constructed randomly from pools of questions, so each student receives a unique selection of items.

- The **Data Visualization Activities** allow students to manipulate data from published studies in interactive graphs. Each activity includes multiple-choice questions that prompt students to investigate and interpret the data. All of the Assessments tied to the Data Visualization Activities have been tagged to APA Goals and Outcomes 2.0 as a means to help students strengthen their scientific inquiry and critical thinking skills.
- LaunchPad also includes **selections from Macmillan's video collections** to bring concepts from the research process to life.

Research in Action

You're Hired!

Because of your psychology background, you've been hired to work in a human resources department for a marketing company. The company expects you to hit the ground running, so your first job is to create a new protocol for employee-hiring interviews. Congratulations—this is a great use of your research skills!

Based on what you learned about interviews in this chapter, the online activity *You're Hired!* gives you the chance to apply your skills. In the activity, you'll identify good versus bad interview questions, develop an interview schedule, and determine the best way to conduct an interview. Being able to apply research knowledge like this is a highly valued skill. Your employer will be so impressed that you'll earn a raise in no time!

LaunchPad To complete this activity, visit LaunchPad at launchpadworks.com

Research in Action Activities

The **Research in Action** activities, created by the authors with Dr. Melanie Maggard, provide students with direct experiences in planning and designing studies. Research in Action puts users in the role of a scientific investigator and asks them to make decisions in planning and executing a study from idea to results. The authors introduce each activity in the appropriate chapter and emphasize core concepts from the text. Instructors can use Research in Action as an in-class activity or for students to get additional practice at home.

Research in Action Activities

Chapter	Activity
Chapter 1	Psychology as a Science: A Scientific Look at Psychics, **p. 20**
Chapter 2	The Research Process: Determining Key Study Elements, **p. 42**
Chapter 3	Ethics: Being an Ethical Researcher, **p. 73**
Chapter 4	The Psychologist's Toolbox: Is the Swagger-Meter 1.0 a Quality Measure?, **p. 108**
Chapter 5	Qualitative Research: You're Hired!, **p. 151**
Chapter 6	Observational Research: Is Public Affection a Public Affliction?, **p. 191**
Chapter 7	Correlational Research: Which Professor Should You Take?, **p. 216**
Chapter 8	Two-Group Design: To Multitask or Not to Multitask?, **p. 276**
Chapter 9	Multigroup Design: Dressing for Distress?, **p. 312**
Chapter 10	Within-Subjects Design: Left Out and Feeling Low, **p. 347**
Chapter 11	Factorial Design: Can the News Influence Our Implicit Prejudice?, **p. 387**
Chapter 12	Mixed Design: Do Speed Daters Become Pickier the Later It Gets?, **p. 429**
Chapter 13	Program Evaluation: Why Did You Buy THAT?, **p. 471**
Appendix B	Communicating the Science of Psychology: The Editor's Studio, **p. 496**
Appendix B	Communicating the Science of Psychology: Giving Credit Where Credit Is Due, **p. 503**
Appendix B	Communicating the Science of Psychology: The Structure of an APA-Style Paper, **p. 511**

In addition, Macmillan Learning is pleased to offer the following texts as supplements to *Discovering the Scientist Within:*

• *SPSS: A User-Friendly Approach* by Jeffery Aspelmeier and Thomas Pierce is a comprehensive introduction to SPSS that is easy to understand and vividly illustrated with cartoon-based scenarios. In the newest edition of the text for SPSS Version 22, the authors go beyond providing instructions on the mechanics of conducting data analysis and develop students' conceptual and applied understanding of quantitative techniques.

• *Psychology and the Real World: Essays Illustrating Fundamental Contributions to Society,* Second Edition, is a superb collection of essays by major researchers that describes their landmark studies. Published in association with the not-for-profit FABBS Foundation, this engaging reader includes essays that exemplify the broad scope and life-changing benefits of contemporary psychological science. A portion of all proceeds is donated to FABBS to support societies of cognitive, psychological, behavioral, and brain sciences.

• *The Worth Expert Guide to Scientific Literacy: Thinking Like a Psychological Scientist* by Kenneth D. Keith and Bernard C. Beins helps students foster habits of scientific thought, learn to apply an empirical attitude, make data-driven decisions, and see through pseudoscientific claims.

• *The Horse That Won't Go Away: Clever Hans, Facilitated Communication, and the Need for Clear Thinking* by Thomas E. Heinzen, Scott O. Lilienfeld, and Susan A. Nolan is a fascinating series of case studies in confirmation bias. The authors engage and inspire students with true stories of how psychological research methods led to some surprising truths.

Acknowledgments

The scientific process is not a solitary endeavor. All scientists depend on the wisdom, guidance, and contributions of others in their pursuit of knowledge and understanding. Writing a textbook about science is no different. We have consistently benefited from the wise counsel, advice, talents, and contributions of numerous individuals.

We are particularly indebted to Dan DeBonis, the executive program manager for psychology, who consistently challenged us, offering his sage advice as our vision for this book became a reality. Development editors Katie Pachnos and Deya Saoud Jacob were our "peer reviewers in chief" for the second and first editions, respectively, ensuring that our writing conveyed complex ideas in a clear and engaging way that would resonate with students. With the help of Stefani Wallace, the media editor for psychology, we created a variety of engaging instructor resources and media supplements to help instructors integrate this book into their course as they bring research methods to life for students. We would also like to thank Kerry O'Shaughnessy, Tristann Jones, and Sivaramakrishnan Velayudham, our content project managers, for their coordination of the book's copyediting, proofreading, typesetting, and production; Deb Heimann, copyeditor, for her careful attention to each line of the text; Susan Wein, senior workflow project supervisor, for her assistance with production scheduling; photo editor Robin Fadool, for her excellent photo research and permissions work; and design managers Natasha Wolfe and John Callahan, who worked together to create a new book design and cover that we are very proud of. In addition, we would like to thank Anna Munroe, editorial assistant, for managing our book's transmittal to production, and the leadership team at Macmillan Learning for their guidance and support.

The following individuals were also part of our writing community, contributing to the success of this book through reviews and focus groups:

Michael Amlung
University of Missouri

Stacy Andersen
Florida Gulf Coast University

Jeana Arter-Passy
California State University, Northridge

Shaki Asgari
Iona College

Paul Atchley
University of Kansas

Levi Baker-Russell
University of North Carolina, Greensboro

Michelle Bannoura
Hudson Valley Community College

Terence Bazzett
State University of New York at Geneseo

Elizabeth Becker
Saint Joseph's University

Jacob Benfield
Pennsylvania State University, Abington

Michael Biderman
University of Tennessee, Chattanooga

Miranda Bobrowski
State University of New York at Buffalo

Sister Edith Bogue
The College of St. Scholastica

Giulia Borriello
Pennsylvania State University

Candice Burkett
University of Illinois, Chicago

Natalie Ceballos
Texas State University

Bonnie Chakravorty
Tennessee State University, Nashville

Edward Chang
University of Michigan

Monali Chowdhury
Allegheny College

Kimberly Coffman
Miami Dade College

Amy Coren
Northern Virginia Community College

Patrick Coyle
Virginia Polytechnic Institute and State University

Marcus Crede
Iowa State University

Walter Curtis
University of Kentucky

Rose Danek
Columbus State University

Nikoleta Despodova
John Jay College of Criminal Justice

Michael Dudley
Southern Illinois University, Edwardsville

Kimberley Duff
Cerritos College

Amanda ElBassiouny
California Lutheran University

Carey Fitzgerald
Oakland University

Alyson Froehlich
University of Utah

Ryan Hampton
Arizona State University

Ed Hansen
Florida State University

Jessica Hartnett
Gannon University

Mahzad Hojjat
University of Massachusetts, Dartmouth

Chloe Huelsnitz
University of Minnesota

Lydia Eckstein Jackson
Allegheny College

Patricia Kahlbaugh
Southern Connecticut State University

Irina Khusid
East Stroudsburg University

Stephen Kilianski
Rutgers University

Rosalyn King
Northern Virginia Community College

Mary Kite
Ball State University

Marina Klimenko
University of Florida

Lee Kooler
Modesto Junior College

Dana Kotter-Gruehn
Duke University

Joseph Leman
Baylor University

Eliot Lopez
University of North Texas

Stella Lopez
University of Texas, San Antonio

Greg Loviscky
Pennsylvania State University

Karen Machluf
Penn State Worthington Scranton

Angie MacKewn
University of Tennessee, Martin

Francesca Manzi
New York University

Ashley de Marchena
University of the Sciences

Stuart Marcovitch
University of North Carolina, Greensboro

Brent Mattingly
Ursinus College

Ronald Miller
Brigham Young University, Hawaii

Lauren Ministero
State University of New York at Buffalo

Robert Mitchell
Eastern Kentucky University

Simon Moon
La Salle University

Keith Morgen
Centenary University

Joe Morrissey
State University of New York at Binghamton

Nora Murphy
Loyola Marymount University

Alex Nagurney
University of Hawaii, Hilo

Tess Neal
Arizona State University

Kevin O'Neil
Florida Gulf Coast University

Stephanie Payne
Texas A&M University, College Station

Zachary Petzel
University of Missouri

John Protzko
University of California, Santa Barbara

Mindi Price
Texas Tech University

Amy Przeworski
Case Western Reserve University

Cheryl Ramey
Eastern Kentucky University

Zachary A. Reese
University of Michigan

Anna Ropp
Metropolitan State University of Denver

Richard Rosenberg
California State University, Long Beach

Michelle Russell
Florida State University

Lisa Sandberg
Loyola University Chicago

Jessica Saunders
Florida International University

Pamela Schuetze
State University of New York at Buffalo

Pamela Joyce Shapiro
Temple University

Bethany Shorey-Fennell
Washington State University

Angela Sikorski
Texas A&M University, Texarkana

Megan Smith
Rhode Island College

Tamarah Smith
Cabrini College

Barbara Sommer
University of California, Davis

Charles Stangor
University of Maryland

Hilary Stebbins
University of Mary Washington

Lyra Stein
Rutgers University

Mark Stellmack
University of Minnesota

Seth Surgan
Worcester State University

Eva Szeli
Arizona State University

Heather Terrell
University of North Dakota

Sarah Thimsen
South Dakota State University

Emily Thorn
California State University, Northridge

Boyd Timothy
Brigham Young University, Hawaii

Vincent Trofimoff
California State University, San Marcos

Dunja Trunk
Bloomfield College

Nicholas Turiano
West Virginia University

Kristine Turko
University of Mount Union

Chantal Tusher
Georgia State University

Lori Van Wallendael
University of North Carolina, Charlotte

John Wallace
Ball State University

Scott Weaver
Georgia State University

Shane Westfall
University of Nevada, Las Vegas

Heather Wild
Portland State University

Darrell Worthy
Texas A&M International University

Chrysalis Wright
University of Central Florida

Marika Yip-Bannicq
New York University

Janice Yoder
University of Akron

We wish to make special note of two groups of individuals to whom we are forever indebted. Each of us had mentors who helped us to discover and nurture our own "scientist within." We have had the immense fortune to learn from these stellar teachers: Susan Luek (Millersville University of Pennsylvania), Art Aron (Stony Brook University), Kristin Sommer (Baruch College, City University of New York), Andy Skelton (Dickinson College), and Ralph Rosnow (Temple University).

Any acknowledgement would be incomplete without mentioning the group who served as our fundamental inspiration: our students. There is no greater pleasure as a professor than to influence a student's life, even in a small way. Being able to help shape how a student thinks about the world is an immense responsibility, but it is one that has led us to continually develop and improve as teachers. Along that journey we developed a sense of restlessness about the research methods course that left us resolved to find new ways to help students discover their own scientist within and experience the thrill of scientific inquiry.

Ultimately, this book represents our taking a little piece of our world and improving it. We hope that others will do the same as they use science to make the world a better place.

Psychology as a Science

Thinking Like a Researcher

Justin Lewis/Stone/Getty Images

LEARNING OUTCOMES

After reading this chapter, you should be able to:

- Describe the flaws and biases associated with thinking.

- Identify the limitations of using anecdotal evidence when evaluating claims.

- Explain how the scientific method can be used to overcome flaws and biases in our thinking.

- Describe the qualities of a good scientist.

- Differentiate between basic and applied research.

- Explain why understanding the scientific method is important for consumers of research.

- Describe career skills acquired through learning the scientific method.

Something to Think About . . .

There are times in life when knowing a person's true personality is important. If you need to pick a new roommate for the next school year, you want to get it right. After all, living with an incompatible roommate could make for a long year. However, people often alter how they present themselves in order to make a good impression, and identifying others' true characters can be difficult. To get around that, you could use graphology to analyze subtle features of a person's handwriting (e.g., the size or style of the letters) that might reveal the writer's personality. When you have narrowed down your potential roommates to the two best candidates, ask each to write a simple sentence:

1. The quick brown fox jumps over the lazy dog.

2. *The quick brown fox jumps over the lazy dog.*

If your potential roommates provided these samples, whom would you pick? And how confident should you be in your selection? These questions may be hard to answer. On one hand, you are using a systematic analysis as the basis for your evaluation. On the other hand, it is difficult to know if the handwriting you preferred belongs to the more compatible roommate. Ultimately, perceptions of graphology's accuracy may depend on who is making the judgement. If you are thinking like a scientist, you will have serious doubts in its effectiveness.

As humans, we are naturally curious about how our own and others' thoughts and behaviors influence our lives. We also like to be right. Being able to find answers and accurately separate fact from fiction are among the most important skills you will learn in college. To do these things, you must first understand possible flaws in your current ways of thinking about the world. Learning how to conduct research can help you develop new strategies for making better decisions. Our textbook emphasizes this idea by showing how research concepts apply to everyday life, and by leading you through the thought processes and decision making a researcher uses to answer questions about our world.

Why Research Methods Are Important: Thinking Differently

"Think Different." This was Apple's clarion call when Steve Jobs returned to the company in the late 1990s. And in many ways, the goal of this research methods book, and of research courses in general, is to provide you with the tools to think differently. Unlike some other psychology courses, such as introductory psychology and abnormal psychology, research methods and statistics courses focus more on "know-how" than "know-what." Research is less about memorizing concepts and more about building skills in critical thinking and using the scientific method to answer interesting questions.

How do you really know a person's personality? Though you typically would not resort to graphology, you might have a gut feeling that someone is trustworthy. But researchers do not rely on their gut instincts. They use the scientific method to find out the truth. One reason that psychology is inherently appealing is we are always curious about why we, and those around us, feel, think, or behave in a particular way. Of course, we often have our own personal answers to these questions of "why." However, those answers may not be accurate or may not have the support of strong evidence. Instead, they may be the product of flawed thinking or biased observations. Our answers may have an element of "truthiness," a term that Stephen Colbert of *The Late Show with Stephen Colbert* coined to represent our occasional tendency to accept an explanation or phenomenon simply because it feels right in our "gut." If it makes sense to us, we often do not question the correctness of our explanation.

However, if you are a psychologist who cares about finding the best treatment for a client or the best coping strategy for dealing with stress, the truth of your conclusion is crucial. And in our everyday lives, the answers we develop for our questions about the world influence how we think, feel, and behave. If our explanations have flaws, then we are likely to make poor decisions. Let's look at some of the natural flaws and biases in how we think that can prevent us from developing an accurate understanding of our world, and find out how we can minimize them.

Steve Jobs by Walter Isaacson

In what ways does Apple have you "think different" about the products you purchase and the technology you use?

(Emmanuel Dunand/AFP/Getty Images)

Natural Flaws in Thinking

As the 18th-century English poet Alexander Pope once said, "To err is human." In fact, humans' perceptions, thoughts, judgments, and decision making are all imperfect. This is not surprising given the number of decisions we constantly make, often with limited information. It is actually quite remarkable how efficient and successful we are in navigating our incredibly complex world. Without realizing it, we often fail to fully engage our thought processes and instead use mental shortcuts or heuristics to help us form impressions, make judgments, and make decisions. While these shortcuts allow us to successfully interact with our world, they are not always perfect. Imagine if weather forecasters predicted that an extremely dangerous storm was approaching and recommended that residents evacuate low-lying areas susceptible to flooding. You might rely on the **availability heuristic** in deciding whether or not to "ride out" the storm in your home. This heuristic involves judgments about the likelihood of an event or situation occurring based on how easily we can think of similar or relevant in-

At what times have you accepted an explanation or phenomenon based on "truthiness"? In what ways can this lead you to the wrong conclusion? *(Christopher Gregory/The New York Times/Redux Pictures)*

stances. If we can easily think of other times when a storm did not live up to weather forecasters' predictions, we may be more likely to ignore the current evacuation order. This can create dangerous situations for people, as recent Hurricanes Katrina, Sandy, Harvey, Irma, and Maria have demonstrated.

A related mental shortcut we use is the **representativeness heuristic,** where we determine the likelihood of an event by how much it resembles what we consider to be a "typical" example of that event. Suppose that we made a New Year's resolution to start eating healthier. We may decide what types of food to eat based on whether they seem like what we consider to be healthy foods. The problem is, although a particular food may look like it is healthy or seem representative of a healthy food, it may not actually be healthy.

Using heuristics and other mental shortcuts is not necessarily a bad thing, because they help us avoid becoming overwhelmed by our world's complexity. The problem is most people are not aware of the limitations or imperfections of these shortcuts, which can lead to incorrect conclusions about the world. You may not think this statement applies to you, but consider how you would answer the following questions: Are you a good driver? Are you a good kisser? Do you have a good sense of humor? Chances are you answered "yes" to each of these questions. Most people tend to consider themselves above average with respect to socially desirable qualities, a phenomenon referred to as the **better-than-average effect**. Although we may think that we drive, kiss, and tell jokes better than others, it is mathematically impossible for everyone to be better than average. That privilege is solely for those who are in the top 50% of performers on a task.

availability heuristic a mental shortcut strategy for judging the likelihood of an event or situation occurring based on how easily we can think of similar or relevant instances.

representativeness heuristic a mental shortcut strategy for determining the likelihood of an event by how much it resembles what we consider to be a "typical" example of that event.

better-than-average effect the tendency to overestimate our skills, abilities, and performance when comparing ourselves to others.

Many people mistakenly believe they are better-than-average drivers. In what ways do you think that you are better than average? *(Christof R. Schmidt/F1online/Getty Images)*

One reason we may think that we are indeed better than average is we tend to be overly confident in the correctness of our judgments, which is known as the **overconfidence phenomenon.** For example, low-achieving students mistakenly anticipate a much higher score on an upcoming exam than they actually receive (Miller & Geraci, 2011). Unfortunately, we often do not take the necessary steps to determine if the accuracy of our judgments matches our confidence in those judgments. If we are certain that our judgments are correct, we have little reason to investigate whether or not they are accurate. If you are overconfident in knowing that you are a better-than-average kisser, then you will likely avoid soliciting reviews from the people you have kissed.

Thinking Like a Scientist in Real Life

I'm Going to Ace That Test

There are plenty of things in our lives that evoke overconfidence. Have you ever predicted that you would get an A on a test or a paper, only to discover that you did not? It is possible that overconfidence even contributed to your less-than-stellar performance. For example, if you were overconfident in your knowledge of the test's material, you may have decided you needed to study less. Perhaps you thought you could easily craft a six-page paper in 2 hours, only to realize that the writing process was very time-consuming and really required 4 hours.

Let's consider another question: Are you a good judge of character? Again, most of us think we are good judges of other people, reflecting the better-than-average effect. But overestimating your ability to accurately evaluate people can create problems. Holding misguided beliefs about your ability to judge character could lead to mistakes such as choosing the wrong roommate, romantic partner, or even potential employee. Researchers have found that job interviews, which have the explicit goal of accurately judging a person's character, have a notoriously inconsistent track record at identifying ideal employees (Macan, 2009). Yet employers still use them.

You may be thinking, "Tell me something that I didn't already know! I've had plenty of coworkers who should never have been hired." Now you are exhibiting the **hindsight bias,** also referred to as the "I knew it all along" phenomenon. Once we learn the results of a given event, we tend to overestimate our ability to have predicted that outcome beforehand. This is an example of flawed thinking, because if we truly knew beforehand that job interviews were a poor

overconfidence phenomenon the tendency to be overly confident in the correctness of our own judgments.

hindsight bias a sense that we "knew it all along" after we learn the actual outcome.

strategy for differentiating between good and poor employees, we would not make them a central part of the hiring process.

Another problem is that when we do attempt to evaluate our judgments, we are often not impartial in the types of information we use to support our beliefs and conclusions. We generally like to be right and therefore tend to focus on information that proves that we are, thus exhibiting a **confirmation bias.** For example, if you believe that you have a better sense of humor than most people, you are more likely to notice and remember the times when you made people laugh than when your jokes fell flat. With only this select evidence in mind, it is not surprising that you confidently conclude that you possess an above average sense of humor.

To help confirm our preexisting beliefs, we often exhibit the **focusing effect,** where we emphasize some pieces of information while undervaluing others. To see how this works, think about whether those with higher incomes are happier than those with lower incomes. Because people usually focus on the benefits of having money (e.g., more vacations, a nicer house) and ignore the drawbacks (e.g., a more demanding and stressful job, less time with the family), most people mistakenly believe that more money leads to increased happiness (Kahneman, Krueger, Schkade, Schwarz, & Stone, 2006). In reality, money and happiness are only weakly related. In this case, we are focusing on the benefits of having money and overemphasizing its role in being happy.

As we seek out information to help us evaluate claims about ourselves and our world, we often utilize **introspection,** where we reflect on our own thoughts and experiences to find relevant evidence. However, it can be tricky to generalize from our own experiences. In his book *Thinking, Fast and Slow,* Nobel Laureate Daniel Kahneman (2011) suggests that we often fall prey to the **"what you see is all there is" phenomenon,** where we fail to see the limitations of our immediate experience and tend to take things at face value. Having this type of mindset predisposes us to expect the status quo and discourages us from questioning the accuracy of our beliefs, thus making it difficult to predict alternative explanations or outcomes. For example, upon meeting someone in class for the first time, you feel as though this person is studious and responsible. After the first quiz, you applaud your judgment upon discovering your new friend received an A. Incidentally, you spend very little time exploring alternative explanations, such as that many college students are studious and responsible, and it is possible most people received a good grade. But these alternative explanations take some effort to generate and may invalidate your belief about your good judgment. Hence, it is much easier to stick with your immediate impression of your new friend. Just because it is easy to form an impression does not mean your judgment is accurate, however.

To avoid some of these errors, you may decide to try to be more objective in your introspection as you draw conclusions about yourself and your world. Although this is a good plan, being objective is easier said than done. For example, suppose someone asked you to list all of the reasons why you enjoyed a particular event, such as your last birthday party. Research suggests that this

confirmation bias a bias in which we only look for evidence that confirms what we already believe, thereby strengthening the original belief.

focusing effect a bias in which we emphasize some pieces of information while undervaluing other pieces.

introspection reflecting on our own thoughts and experiences to find relevant evidence.

"what you see is all there is" phenomenon a failure to see the limitations of our immediate experience, making it difficult to predict alternative outcomes.

List all of the reasons why you love pizza. Having trouble? If so, this can make pizza seem less enjoyable, a result of the pleasure paradox. *(Betsie Van Der Meer/Taxi/ Getty Images)*

introspective analysis can actually make that event seem less enjoyable to you, a phenomenon known as the **pleasure paradox** (Wilson, Centerbar, Kermer, & Gilbert, 2005). To illustrate, think of your favorite food. Now, list all of the reasons why you like it. As much as you may love grilled cheese sandwiches, after a few seconds of analysis, it becomes clear that the reasons why you enjoy grilled cheese are elusive. Because you have trouble figuring out why you love it, you may conclude that you really do not like grilled cheese as much as you thought you did. If a more careful analysis of your favorite food can undermine your enjoyment of it, just think about what a careful analysis could do to your beliefs about yourself. If you really took the time to analyze the quality of your character judgments, you might reveal that you are not as good a judge of character as you thought.

These inherent biases in how we think reveal that we may not be as objective as we believe when evaluating claims about ourselves and our world. Even if we were able to be completely objective, we might not be willing to accept the conclusions warranted by the evidence we uncover. Suppose you had to deal with the fact that your best friend of five years was spreading lies about you on Twitter. How willing would you be to admit that you were wrong about your choice in best friends? Even in the face of clear evidence, you may exhibit **belief perseverance**, where you maintain your beliefs despite contradictory factual information. After learning about your "best friend's" malicious behavior, belief perseverance would lead you to explain away the situation (he didn't mean the nasty things he tweeted about you) and still believe that your friend is a good person. After all, you are a good judge of character. Right?

Anecdotal Versus Scientific Evidence

pleasure paradox when an introspective analysis regarding a positive experience results in it becoming less enjoyable.

belief perseverance maintaining a belief despite encountering contradictory factual information; often accomplished by interpreting information in a way that does not invalidate the original belief.

Humans have an uncanny ability to misinterpret, misperceive, and manipulate facts, all of which can lead us to mistaken conclusions. Yet we often put a premium on our own individual experiences when trying to discern truth from fiction. Perhaps, as a result, we overvalue anecdotes and others' personal experiences. According to Kahneman, this preference derives from our inclination to favor quick and simple explanations over solutions that take more conscientious thought and deliberation. As Nassim Taleb pointed out in his book *The Black Swan* (2010), "We love the tangible, the confirmation, the palpable, the real, the visible, the concrete, the known, the seen, the vivid, the visual . . . In other words, we are naturally shallow and superficial—and we do not know it" (p. 132).

Certainly, personal experiences and anecdotes can provide valuable insight, but we are often too quick to generalize beyond the specific circumstances of the experience. That is to say, individual experiences or anecdotes are often atypical or distinct. Everybody seems to know an elderly person who smokes cigarettes, never exercises, eats bacon several times a day, drinks beer for dinner, and proudly proclaims that all this healthy living stuff is nonsense. It is unlikely that such a daily regimen holds the secret to longevity. More likely, this person's longevity in spite of an unhealthy lifestyle is an anomaly that is the by-product of the law of small numbers. The **law of small numbers** states that extreme outcomes are more likely when considering a small number of cases. If you took 100, or 1,000, adults who smoked cigarettes, drank alcohol daily, never exercised, and ate poorly, it is likely that few would live to a ripe old age. Your acquaintance would be an **outlier**, a case that is distinct from the majority of other cases—the exception to the rule.

We are often quick to use a single experience or anecdote to either prove or negate a claim. However, when we hear someone else share an anecdote, we are often skeptical because it is easier to see when others are selective in their examples to prove their point. Think back to your introductory psychology class. Chances are that at some point during the semester you learned about a

Good health after eating bacon daily for 95 years is an exception to the rule, or an outlier. What is one "exception to the rule" that you have noticed in your own life? *(Jessica Rinaldi/Boston Globe/Getty Images)*

study that challenged a personal belief. Take, for example, the research on memory that shows that cramming for a test is a poor strategy and that spaced practice, or studying a little bit each day, is superior (Kornell, 2009). If you are like most students, you probably made a face and thought, "Yeah, but . . ." What follows next will vary, but your reaction will generally involve providing an example, an experience, or an anecdote about yourself or a friend that contradicts the research finding. You may think that cramming does not work for other people, but it does for you because you do your best work under pressure. Or you may think, "Yeah, but I have a friend who always crams and gets good grades." Keith Stanovich (2010) referred to this as using "person-who" statistics to support our viewpoint. That is, we will dismiss data from a research study that contradicts our existing beliefs because we can identify a "person who" seems to violate the finding. Because your "yeah, but" friend is only one example, it is hard to know if he or she is the exception or the rule.

As you might imagine, we do not generate these "yeah, buts" for all research findings. When we learn about research findings that agree with our beliefs, there is little to challenge. We tend to resist more when findings contradict our current beliefs. When it comes to study habits, by relying on anecdotal data based on one person, you run the risk of getting a poor test score after a night of cramming. And the risks can be more serious as well. For example, in the early 1970s the diagnosis of multiple personality disorder gained popularity largely based on the case of one woman, named Sybil, who described a dozen personalities emanating from experiences of childhood abuse. However, as Debbie Nathan described in her book *Sybil Exposed* (2011), the stories were just that—stories. Nevertheless, this singular case was seen as giving credence to the pervasiveness of multiple personality disorders in the population.

Given the abundant evidence for our flawed thinking and interpretations of information, you may be wondering how anyone could ever arrive at a correct conclusion. Thankfully, it is possible, but it takes a more deliberate and conscientious approach to help us avoid making these mistakes.

law of small numbers extreme outcomes are more likely when considering a small number of cases.

outlier a case or instance that is distinct from the majority of other cases; an oddball.

Need for Scientific Reasoning

In their book *Mistakes Were Made (But Not by Me)*, Carol Tavris and Elliot Aronson (2007) eloquently make the case for breaking free from our flawed ways of thinking by suggesting that "scientific reasoning is useful to anyone in any job because it makes us face the possibility, even the dire reality, that we were mistaken. It forces us to confront our self-justifications and put them on public display for others to puncture. At its core, therefore, science is a form of arrogance control" (p. 108).

Developing a strategy for discerning fact from fiction is important. One solution is to remove as many emotions and anecdotes from the decision-making process as possible. In cases where this is possible, it has been quite effective. For example, in baseball, scouts have traditionally evaluated talent based on whether or not a player has the "look" of a professional player. More recently, teams have begun to analyze players' performance stats, known as sabermetrics or a *Moneyball* approach, to objectively examine a player's potential, rather than simply relying on the impressions of the scouts (Lewis, 2003).

In the field of clinical psychology, Paul Meehl famously demonstrated the advantage of using statistical evidence rather than anecdotal evidence. In his classic 1954 book, *Clinical Versus Statistical Prediction: A Theoretical Analysis and a Review of the Evidence,* Meehl compared the accuracy of a clinician's professional judgment with judgments based on an empirically derived algorithm. His analysis revealed that the algorithm provided more reliable diagnoses than clinical judgments. For example, the algorithm would always reach the same conclusion when presented with the same facts, whereas clinicians would vary in their judgments despite using the same data. A more recent analysis of studies comparing mechanical and clinical judgments revealed that mechanical prediction was the superior method for providing higher-quality diagnoses (Grove, Zald, Lebow, Snitz, & Nelson, 2000).

Adopting a set of rules or guidelines for making judgments about our world can help us avoid the natural fallibilities in our thinking. Science can provide the answers—or at least a set of steps—that will help find the best information to address your questions. We refer to this systematic approach for addressing questions of interest as the **scientific method**, and we will talk more about those steps in Chapter 2. For now, we are going to focus on the basic characteristics that psychology shares with the scientific study of any branch of knowledge, or, what puts the "–ology" in "psychology."

scientific method a systematic approach for addressing questions of interest.

YOUR TURN 1.1

1. Michele believes her boss is an extremely difficult person. To see if her belief has merit, she asks all of her co-workers who have also had problems with him in the past if they believe the same thing. Michele's conclusion based on her "research" into this question may be erroneous because of which flaw in our thinking?
   a. Overconfidence phenomenon
   b. Focusing effect
   c. Law of small numbers
   d. Confirmation bias

2. Luke really likes the new Dodge Challenger sports car, but is undecided about whether to spend the money to buy one. To make his decision easier, he creates a list of 25 reasons why he likes the car. Is this a good idea?
   a. No. Listing so many reasons will probably be difficult and can actually make you like it less.
   b. No. If he really liked the car, he would not need a list to help him make this decision.
   c. Yes. Trying to generate 25 reasons will show Luke how much he likes the car.
   d. Yes. It shows that Luke is really putting a lot of thought into this big decision.

3. Even after having all of his arguments refuted by his girlfriend, Ryan proclaims that everyone is entitled to their own opinions and he isn't changing his. Ryan is exhibiting which flaw in our thinking?
   a. Overconfidence phenomenon
   b. Belief perseverance
   c. Hindsight bias
   d. Better-than-average effect

How did you do? Turn to the end of the chapter to check your answers.

Characteristics of a Good Scientist

All scientific endeavors start with a question and a desire to learn more about a topic. Scientists have wondered about how a pea plant inherits physical features from its predecessors, what causes a dog to salivate, and what causes illness. In some cases, scientists have questioned commonly accepted beliefs, such as when Galileo challenged the geocentric belief that the sun revolves around the Earth.

Skepticism

We are inundated with claims on a daily basis. You may have heard the claim, most likely pitched by a cartoon character, that your delicious sugary cereal is part of a balanced breakfast. As you look down at your brightly colored milk, are you skeptical about whether this claim is true? Ever wonder what they mean by a "balanced" breakfast? Just as you have a skeptical attitude in your every-day life, scientists use the same approach in research. At one time, for example, spanking was a widely accepted means of punishing children. Some researchers were skeptical of its effectiveness, and research has subsequently revealed that spanking and other forms of corporal punishment have detrimental effects on children (Gershoff & Grogan-Kaylor, 2016).

As a budding scientist, you should ask questions whenever you hear spurious claims, seemingly obvious statements, or conventional wisdom. As the medieval French philosopher Peter Abelard once wrote, "The key to wisdom is this—constant and frequent questioning, for by doubting we are led to question and by questioning we arrive at the truth." Because scientists continue to question, our knowledge about the world grows. Psychologists are no exception. Our questions just happen to focus on why people think, feel, and behave the way they do, rather than other aspects of the world.

Alfred Kinsey's open-mindedness led to the study of human sexuality. What other societal taboos do you think would cause controversy if they were studied? *(Arthur Siegel/The LIFE Images Collection/ Getty Images)*

Open-Mindedness

We must be careful to avoid being overly cynical and to balance our skepticism with an open mind. A good scientist must be willing to pursue unpopular or controversial ideas, as this helps us gain a deeper understanding about the nature of our world. A series of controversial studies on human sexuality conducted by Alfred Kinsey and his colleagues during the 1930s and 1940s serves as an example of the importance of being open-minded. Although the latest issue of *Maxim* or *Cosmopolitan* is likely to have a feature article on the sex lives of Americans, asking questions about one's sexual behavior was historically inappropriate, if not taboo. Kinsey's data collection techniques may have been flawed and his findings controversial (e.g., Dollard, 1953; Geddes, 1954), but Kinsey's open-minded line of inquiry was groundbreaking because of his willingness to scientifically pursue a highly contentious topic, leading the way for other psychologists to study human sexuality with more sophisticated techniques. Who knows—without Kinsey's open-minded approach to research, you might have fewer sex columns in your favorite magazine, and the world might know a lot less about how to lead healthy and fulfilling sex lives.

 Research Spotlight

The Future Made Me Do It

The future cannot possibly influence the present, except perhaps in science fiction movies, right? Rather than automatically dismissing seemingly farfetched ideas, good scientists try to keep an open mind as they develop scientific strategies to evaluate such claims. Daryl Bem (2011) created a stir in the scientific world by providing evidence supporting the possible validity of some types of psychic claims. Through nine separate experiments involving over 1,000 participants, Bem examined the possibility that future events can influence an individual's responses in the present. For example, in one study, 100 students engaged in a study of extrasensory perception (ESP). After a relaxation period, the participants saw 48 nouns depicting common items and were asked to visualize each one. Bem then surprised the participants by asking them to recall as many of the 48 words as they could. After they completed this recall task, participants practiced a random subset of 24 of the original 48 words by typing the words into the computer six at a time. Even though the participants did the practice task *after* they did the free recall task, they recalled more of the words that they later (and unexpectedly) typed into the computer. Although the effects Bem found were small, this suggests the possibility that participants had a psychic experience in which a future event (practicing the words) helped them with a task in the present (recalling the same words). As you can imagine, these findings are controversial, and researchers are trying to replicate Bem's findings.

Objectivity

When scientifically evaluating our ideas, we must be careful that our personal biases, feelings, beliefs, and prejudices do not get in the way of objective, empirical evidence. This is a particular challenge for psychologists because we are studying phenomena that derive from some of our own direct experiences. A chemist studying chemical reactions cannot change the way hydrogen and oxygen atoms interact based on how he or she wants things to turn out. However, a psychologist studying human nature holds a host of preconceived notions, guesses, and beliefs that can consciously or unconsciously shape conclusions. Any time you read a research finding in psychology and think, "Yeah, but I don't do that," you are letting your personal experiences override the objective evidence. Earlier in this chapter, we pointed out examples of how our thinking can be flawed or biased.

These issues are important to recognize because they can make objectivity difficult to achieve. Although it's a challenge, we do have strategies for increasing objectivity, as you will see in Chapter 2. Throughout this book you will learn a number of techniques for designing studies that minimize the biases that psychologists can unwittingly introduce into their studies. For example, we will discuss the importance of having researchers and participants "blind" or naïve to the research hypotheses under investigation. We will also stress the need to develop clear procedures for how every participant should be treated in a study. By employing sound research methods for data collection, we can be more confident that we have minimized potential biases in our study.

At times, we might not agree with the results we obtain. In a battle between objective scientific data and personal opinion, remember that the data always win. As psychological scientists, our goal is to find the best data that provide the most knowledge about the world. This means we have to be objective and open-minded enough to accept the most compelling evidence, even if it is counter to our own ideas.

Empiricism

Just like everyone else, scientists have their own opinions and speculations about the nature of the world. The difference is that scientists are willing to test their ideas and beliefs and admit when they are unsupported, which is no small feat. After all, it feels good to be right and it is easy to be right if you avoid testing your ideas. Instead, scientists purposefully evaluate the veracity of their proposed answers to their questions, even if it means finding out that their ideas were misguided.

Suppose you are skeptical about the finding we previously mentioned that cramming is not effective (Kornell, 2009). Being a scientist, you would want to evaluate this possibility through the use of **empirical research,** or the systematic use of observations and measurements. In contrast, **nonempirical research** would rely on a nonsystematic examination of personal experiences

empirical research gaining knowledge with the use of systematic observation, experience, or measurement.

nonempirical research gaining knowledge with the use of nonsystematic methods such as the examination of personal experiences and opinions.

Researchers have used hot sauce as a measure of aggression. What other creative ways could you use to measure aggression? *(Omar Torres/AFP/Getty Images)*

and opinions. For example, a nonempirical approach would rely on your own experiences or friends' experiences with cramming. In this approach, if you can think of examples of when cramming worked, it must be true. An example of an empirical approach would be to test cramming by randomly having half of your classmates cram, while the other half studies a bit each day. You would then compare the groups' scores on a test and perhaps their memory of the material several weeks later. This approach is empirical because it purposely sets up conditions for systematic comparison and better measurement of test performance.

Empirical reasoning is an important quality that differentiates science from other disciplines such as philosophy and theology, which also seek understanding and knowledge. At first, it may seem difficult to empirically investigate the questions that you have about how humans think, feel, and behave. This is why you study research methods as a psychology student. Learning how to empirically evaluate possible answers to questions of interest is vitally important to both understanding and advancing the science of psychology. As you will see, figuring out how to test your ideas may take some finesse, but the process of making decisions and solving problems along the way is what makes conducting research an exciting and personally gratifying endeavor.

Creativity

Studying human thought and behavior often requires creative or novel approaches. In the sciences, psychologists are among the most creative because, in order to truly understand human nature, we often have to simulate the world in a lab or other controlled setting. In real life, people can express aggression through profanity-laden verbal insults or physical altercations. However, researchers have to measure aggression in creative ways that do not subject participants to excess emotional or physical harm. For example, in one ingenious study, participants wrote an essay on a personally meaningful topic on which they received either insulting feedback (e.g., "I can't believe an educated person would think like this") or neutral feedback (Harmon-Jones & Sigelman, 2001). Next, ostensibly in conjunction with a second part of the study involving taste perception, participants selected a beverage that a fellow participant would have to drink. Drink possibilities included water mixed with sugar, apple juice, lemon juice, salt, vinegar, or hot sauce. Participants who received negative feedback selected more unpleasant-tasting beverages than participants who received neutral feedback. Although no one really drank the beverages, the participants' selections indicated their aggressive intent. As you read this book, you will learn how to develop your own innovative and creative strategies for testing your ideas.

Communication

Let's assume through our skepticism, open-mindedness, objectivity, and creativity that we have a new piece of empirical knowledge that the world did not know before (or at least one for which we did not have scientific evidence). For this information to benefit the world, we need to share the findings with others. A primary goal of science is to serve the common good, such that sharing research is as much a part of a scientist's job as conducting experiments and collecting data. Psychologists most often disseminate their findings through research journals. For more about communicating psychological science, see Appendix B.

Scientists share research findings for several reasons. No single person has a monopoly on truth. Only by sharing with each other what we have learned can we gain a clearer understanding of the phenomenon of interest. How does the sharing of findings accomplish this? First, we provide other scientists with the opportunity to confirm our findings by enabling them to conduct or replicate our study. **Replication** is the process of recreating another person's study to see if the findings are the same.

When we communicate our findings to others, we are also inviting critical evaluation of our ideas and conclusions. If our ideas have flaws, other scientists will address them in their own research, helping us all get closer to the truth. Finally, by sharing our work, others can build on what we already know by revisiting, refining, and extending theories. It is through the sharing of research that science advances. Just think of all the research that fills your psychology textbooks today. We have come a long way since the start of experimental psychology around 130 years ago!

 Thinking Like a Scientist in Real Life

How to Become More Confident

In life, when things work out a little too well, we wonder if it is a fluke. Perhaps you woke up one morning feeling the beginnings of a cold and decided to eat six oranges for breakfast. Later that afternoon you feel perfectly healthy. Fluke? Or perhaps after getting stuck in traffic on your way to work you decide to take a different way and discover that it saves you 5 minutes on your commute. In each case, you should consider whether your good fortune was simply luck. To be sure, you should attempt to replicate your past success. Eat oranges the next time you feel ill. Alternate your routes to work over several days to determine which is actually quicker. By trying to reproduce the same outcome, you work to confirm the effectiveness of the oranges or your new shortcut to see if they are consistently helpful, or if there were other reasons they worked the first time. If these experiences were lucky or random, it is hard to imagine that they would keep recurring. Achieving the same result several times will give you confidence in the outcome.

replication recreating another person's study to see if the findings are the same.

YOUR TURN 1.2

1. Dr. Ndukwe attends a party where several people, upon learning that she is a psychologist, offer suggestions for things she could study in her research. One person suggests, "My dog is completely neurotic. You should study whether dogs have different personalities." Although she believes this is a silly idea, Dr. Ndukwe decides to conduct a study to see if it is true. Which characteristic of science is she exemplifying?
   a. Humility
   b. Skepticism
   c. Open-mindedness
   d. Replication

2. When Samantha is told about an article in a magazine that claims listening to music on Spotify increases intelligence, she is full of questions about who was in the study, how many people were in it, and so on. What characteristic of science does this demonstrate?
   a. Humility
   b. Skepticism
   c. Objectivity
   d. Testability

3. The defining characteristic of empirical reasoning is that we use _____ in order to evaluate our ideas about the nature of our world.
   a. systematic observations
   b. introspection
   c. reliable anecdotes
   d. replication

How did you do? Turn to the end of the chapter to check your answers.

Goals of the Scientific Method

Sometimes scientists seem to pursue silly and pointless questions. But who would have thought that physicists delving into the abstract world of quantum mechanics during the early part of the 20th century would eventually lead to our having smartphones, drones, MRIs, and remote controls (Kakalios, 2010)? We have no way of knowing how the investigation of an idea today will influence something in the future. So we must embrace our ideas, knowing that the importance of discovering the fundamentals of a topic might not be immediately apparent, but that they may lead to important applications in the future.

Producing Basic and Applied Research

basic research
research dedicated to expanding the existing knowledge on a topic.

When our questioning leads to the expanding of knowledge on a topic, we are engaging in **basic research**. The goal of basic research is to build upon what we already know by developing theories to explain phenomena in our world.

When Jean Piaget developed his cognitive stages of development, he was conducting basic research that added to what was known about the intellectual development of children. Basic research often serves as the foundation for **applied research,** which usually has a more immediate goal of solving a practical problem or examining the real-world implications of a particular theory. For example, Piaget's basic research on the stages of cognitive development can be useful to an educational psychologist who is developing new strategies for helping children learn to read. But we must caution you not to view research as simply being a dichotomy between "basic" and "applied" research. Each approach stimulates research ideas for the other. What we learn from testing solutions to everyday problems can further our overall understanding of the underlying phenomena. Likewise, having a solid understanding of a phenomenon can lead to new solutions to existing problems. In the words of the famous social psychologist Kurt Lewin (1952), "There is nothing more practical than a good theory" (p. 169).

Becoming Better Consumers of Research

Aside from advancing human knowledge, there is a more practical reason for learning about the scientific method. Understanding basic research principles can help us become better consumers of research. On a daily basis, we are bombarded with information and statistics that are portrayed as "facts" despite their having very little, if any, supporting scientific evidence. For example, you may have heard people extol the virtues of graphology, feng shui, Reiki, essential oils, primal scream therapy, or conversion therapy. These are all examples of **pseudoscience** because those who believe in these concepts claim that they have been validated by substantial evidence and the scientific method, while, in actuality, they have not. People are more likely to accept such claims because they often are accompanied by numerical support, use terms or jargon such as "new scientific breakthroughs," and feature individuals associated with important-sounding schools or professions. Once we learn to carefully evaluate the evidence provided, rather than simply rely on a claim's believability or promoter, we become less susceptible to being duped by pseudoscientific claims. Ultimately, this will help us make better decisions.

When evaluating claims, you should question several facets of the information (Schmaltz & Lilienfeld, 2014). First, consider the source. Is the originator of the information impartial? Or do they have a vested interest in this information? Next, focus on what their goal may be. Would their claim help them advance a certain agenda or promote a particular viewpoint? Now, look at the information itself. What is the nature of the data? Is it from a study, or a collection of anecdotes or testimonials? Even if it looks like a scientific study, check to be sure the data is high quality. How many people were included, what were the comparison groups, and were variables defined precisely? Are the claims extraordinary, can they be disproven, and are they even testable?

For example, suppose you heard an advertisement saying that three out of four dentists recommend Sparklefresh toothpaste. Does this endorsement mean that you should immediately change your toothpaste brand to Sparklefresh? As you acquire a more sophisticated understanding of how researchers

applied research research dedicated to solving a problem and helping people by improving their quality of life.

pseudoscience claims or beliefs that are misrepresented as being derived from the use of the scientific method.

conduct high-quality science, you will learn how to more effectively question these types of claims, as well as the methods used to support them. For example, at the end of this course you will begin to ask questions like, "Is it enough to get opinions from only four dentists?" "What exactly did the dentists use as the basis for their recommendation? Was it price, quality of cleanliness, freshness of breath, amount of fluoride, or something else?" "Against what did the dentists compare Sparklefresh? Did they use other toothpastes?" "Did the dentists base their recommendation on their own use or what they saw in their patients?" "How long was Sparklefresh used before the recommendation was given?" As you can see, knowing more about research, paired with your scientific skepticism, will help you question the legitimacy of such claims and make more well-informed decisions. Whether you are making a relatively harmless decision about the best toothpaste to buy or a more important decision, such as the best way to treat your drug-dependent teenage client, your knowledge about the research process will help you become a smarter consumer of research.

The recent "fake news" phenomenon shares many characteristics with pseudoscience. Fake news, or news that is portrayed as true, yet has no basis in fact, is able to thrive when people fail to carefully evaluate the claims. People may not question fake news when they want to believe the information or do not know how to critically evaluate the claims, or when the information has an element of "truthiness" or confirms an existing belief. Recent research on discrediting misinformation reveals that people are especially likely to continue believing misinformation when they were able to think of reasons to believe it initially (Chan, Jones, Jamieson, & Albaraccin, 2017). The same questions we suggest that you ask to better evaluate pseudoscience will also help you spot fake news more easily. As fake news becomes increasingly pervasive, it is important that you hone your skills in order to be a more informed consumer of information, in this area and beyond.

Think of some ways that Facebook combines psychology, sociology, and technology. *(David Paul Morris/Bloomberg/Getty Images)*

Acquiring Career Skills

You went to college and picked a major for many different reasons, but ultimately you hope that your coursework will help you get a job after graduation. While each of your psychology classes provides useful knowledge, research methods and statistics courses help you develop an impressive set of skills useful in a wide variety of careers (**Figure 1.1**). For example, did you know that Jerry Bruckheimer, Hugh Hefner, Natalie Portman, and Jon Stewart were all psychology majors? Mark Zuckerberg was enrolled at Harvard with a double major in computer science and psychology, a combination that still influences his thinking. During a talk at Brigham Young University, in reference to the challenges of starting Facebook, Zuckerberg stated, "All of these problems at the end of the day are human problems. I think that that's one of the core insights

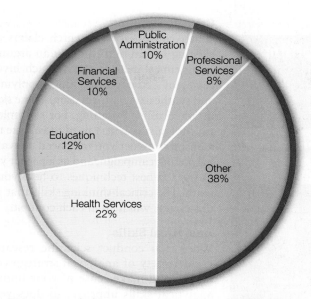

FIGURE 1.1 Industries of Full-Time Employment for Psychology Majors. This graph depicts the industries that employ bachelor-level psychology majors full-time. *(Data from Carneval, Strohel, & Melton, 2011)*

that we try to apply to developing Facebook . . . It's as much psychology and sociology as it is technology" (Larson, 2011).

Although this book is about how to conduct psychological research, we know that you may not want to become a research psychologist. In a research methods course you will specifically develop the following skills, relevant to any number of careers.

Project Management

Conducting research is a major undertaking. Each research study is a large-scale, multifaceted project that the researcher must manage. Researchers need the same planning abilities, creativity, time management, organization, and follow-through that any project manager needs. Relatedly, researchers need to be detail-oriented, paying attention to the nuances of the study that will ensure its methodological soundness. These skill sets easily transfer into the job market, as the ability to plan and carry out projects successfully is one of the expectations employers have for psychology majors (Appleby, 2014).

Problem Solving

By designing and implementing psychology studies, you will hone your ability to identify and define potential problems, generate alternatives, evaluate and select solutions, and implement these solutions. In any professional position, problems are inevitable. Thus, it is not surprising that employers list problem solving as a key skill that they expect from psychology majors in the workforce (Landrum & Harrold, 2003).

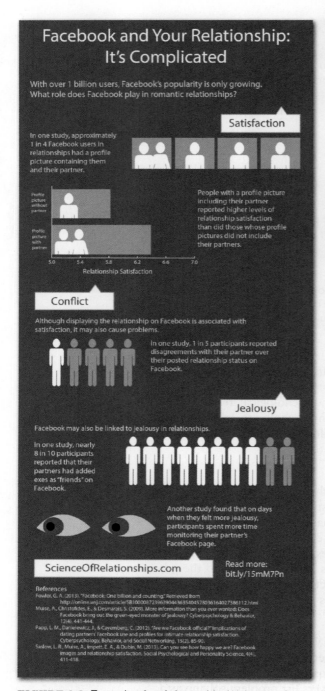

FIGURE 1.2 Example of an Infographic. Websites often use infographics to display statistical information. *(Created by Lydia Emery/ScienceOfRelationships.com)*

Critical Thinking

When you question research claims or synthesize existing literature to support an argument, you are using **critical-thinking skills,** which involve the processes of actively evaluating, applying, analyzing, and synthesizing information. These skills are useful in practically any setting. For example, as a school psychologist you may need to analyze test results, as a business owner you may need to evaluate the best marketing campaign, and as a parent you may want to use the best techniques to help your child learn math. The critical-thinking skills that you obtain in this course will help in each context.

Analytical Skills

When you conduct scientific research, you will use a variety of analytical strategies to help summarize and make sense of your findings. As your analytical skills improve, so does your ability to draw conclusions based on your data. It is difficult to imagine a career that does not rely on numerical data. Thus, by increasing your analytical skills you are increasing your value to your company.

Interpretation of Numerical Information

If you have spent any time on the Internet recently you may have seen an **infographic.** This is a chart that synthesizes statistical information with aesthetically appealing graphics (**Figure 1.2**). The popularity of infographics suggests that we are moving into a more data-conscious world. As such, it will be beneficial for employers to hire data-savvy employees who are familiar with interpreting data. Lucky for you, a research course helps make you a better consumer of research.

Communication Skills

An important aspect of science is the sharing of research findings. Many of you will likely learn how to write research reports as part of your research methods course (see Appendix B). As you will soon discover, contrary to how you write in an English class, science has its own style of written communication that involves very clear, direct, and succinct writing. This straightforward and concise form of communication will be useful when you need to write formal reports, memos, e-mails, and letters to clients.

YOUR TURN 1.3

1. Tom is investigating how different strategies for reducing anxiety can improve test performance, while Jerry is studying the impact of stress on memory recall. Even though both are studying memory, Tom's research would be considered _____ research whereas Jerry's work would be considered _____ research.
   a. pseudoscientific; scientific
   b. objective; empirical
   c. applied; basic
   d. empirical; scientific

2. The president of your company has asked you to evaluate a proposal to buy a rival business. The president gives you the proposal, which includes supporting documents such as past and projected sales of the company. Which of the following research skills do you think will be *least* helpful in this task?
   a. Analytical skills
   b. Ability to interpret numerical information
   c. Critical-thinking skills
   d. Problem-solving skills

3. While watching TV one day, you see an infomercial in which a spokesperson wearing a white lab coat starts describing a new medical breakthrough diet that helps people lose 10 pounds a week. As proof, the spokesperson interviews several clients who experienced dramatic weight loss while on this revolutionary diet. You immediately question the effectiveness of the diet because the claims being made appear to be
   a. based on empirical reasoning.
   b. pseudoscientific.
   c. examples of applied rather than basic research.
   d. supported only by infographics.

How did you do? Turn to the end of the chapter to check your answers.

Final Thoughts

Let's think back to this chapter's original question about roommate choice. After reading this chapter, you might be skeptical of graphology's ability to discern personality, and, as a better consumer of research, you may suspect graphology is a pseudoscience. As someone who now knows the value of scientific evidence, you will be interested to know that research has explored the merits of handwriting analysis. In one of the many published papers, students completed personality measures and had their handwritten responses on an exam analyzed (Furnham, Chamorro-Premuzic, & Callahan, 2003). The association between personality and a handwriting analysis focused on elements such as crossed *t*'s, width of letters, and the nature of loops, and revealed that personality and

critical-thinking skills the process of actively evaluating, applying, analyzing, and synthesizing information.

infographic a graphic that synthesizes statistical information with aesthetically appealing visuals.

handwriting were not more related than you might expect by chance. It seems you will need a better way to determine your potential roommate's personality after all.

Whether you want to work in counseling, research, human resources, social services, marketing, or a corporation, the skills you acquire from learning about research will be useful. Knowing how to find good answers to questions makes asking questions more interesting. Perhaps most important of all, learning about research will stimulate your curiosity about the world around you. As William Butler Yeats said, "Education is not the filling of a pail, but the lighting of a fire." We hope that you will feel your curiosity beginning to spark as we learn to use the scientific method to answer questions about our world.

 Research in Action

A Scientific Look at Psychics

Although many people believe that palm readers, mediums, and psychics can tell the future or "know things that no one could possibly know," psychic practices are fertile ground for a scientific approach. Even if you believe in psychics' abilities, it hardly seems fair to question psychics without having an open mind and giving them the chance to provide proof of their claims' authenticity. When testing a psychic's claims, it is important to be skeptical enough to question what is going on so that you can have faith in your own conclusions.

So, are psychics legit? That is for you to decide in the activity **A Scientific Look at Psychics,** where you will get the chance to take a firsthand look at whether psychics actually see the future—or are simply seeing something else.

LaunchPad To complete this activity, visit LaunchPad at launchpadworks.com

CHAPTER 1 Review

Review Questions

1. Santiago is applying to be a resident assistant at his college. He believes his leadership abilities are above those of typical applicants. Yet, when asked during his interview to provide examples of times he was a good leader, he cannot think of any. Which of the following explains why he struggled to answer the question?
   a. Better-than-average effect
   b. Overconfidence phenomenon
   c. Hindsight bias
   d. Belief perseverance

2. In a Theories of Personality class, you fill out a questionnaire that indicates you are an extravert. You then learn that researchers describe

extraverts as enthusiastic, talkative, and assertive. You immediately question that research because you remember several times in the past when you were not at all assertive. What has most likely led to your conclusion?

a. Relying on "truthiness"

b. Relying on self-reflection

c. Relying on scientific reasoning

d. Relying on anecdotal versus scientific evidence

3. When something happens that is the exception to the rule or distinct from the majority of other cases, it is called

a. an outlier.

b. the law of small numbers.

c. error.

d. the false uniqueness effect.

4. After seeing a scary movie, you begin to wonder how watching such a movie can influence how you feel about the people sitting nearby. For example, could being scared make you feel friendlier toward them? Since you want to test this empirically, which of the following is the best option?

a. Ask a movie usher who has worked in the theater for over 3 years what his thoughts are about scary movies' effects on friendliness.

b. Systematically observe moviegoers sitting in the same set of seats during several types of movies to see which groups act friendlier toward each other.

c. Think back to your own experiences and recall how you felt after watching scary movies and how you felt after watching funny movies.

d. Ask some of your friends what their experiences have been after watching scary movies.

5. Tia wants to determine what people find offensive. She thinks about times that other people have offended her and concludes that what is offensive to her is probably offensive to most people. In this circumstance she is using which of the following to reach her conclusion about others?

a. Introspection

b. Focusing effect

c. Hindsight bias

d. The law of small numbers

6. Which of the following is based on casual observations rather than rigorous or scientific analysis?

a. Skepticism

b. Anecdotes

c. Humility

d Focusing effect

7. A car salesperson tells Rudy that a particular model of car is the safest in its class. Rudy does not accept such claims at face value and demands to see the latest safety report. What characteristic of science is Rudy displaying?
   a. Skepticism
   b. Open-mindedness
   c. Objectivity
   d. Creativity

8. A cognitive psychologist is interested in studying memory in the context of eyewitness testimony. What type of research is this?
   a. Experimental
   b. Nonexperimental
   c. Basic
   d. Applied

9. You have just taken a job as a peer tutor for first-year students at your school. You notice that many of the students mistakenly believe that they are doing better than other students in the course, and that they will have no problem catching up if they fall behind. Which two flaws in thinking (in order) are these students expressing?
   a. Overconfidence; hindsight bias
   b. Better-than-average effect; overconfidence
   c. Hindsight bias; overconfidence
   d. Better-than-average effect; confirmation bias

10. After graduate school, you begin your career as a counselor for clients who have an eating disorder. You want to be sure to provide your clients with the best possible treatment, but are unsure whether Treatment A or Treatment B is better. To test this, you collect data that will allow you to compare the two treatment types. Which type of skills will be most important for determining the superior treatment?
    a. Analytical skills
    b. Communication skills
    c. Critical-thinking skills
    d. Problem-solving skills

11. You enter your bedroom and discover the reading light by your bed is not working. How would you use the scientific method to determine the reason the light is no longer working?

12. One skill you acquire from learning how to conduct research is problem solving. List three ways in which problem solving might help you in your future career.

13. A sports psychologist is interested in studying motivation. List one way to study motivation that is an example of applied research and one way that is an example of basic research.

14. Which characteristic of science do you think is the most important for a research study to have and why?

Applying What You've Learned

1. Now that you have read about the skills you acquire through a research methods course, update your résumé or curriculum vitae to reflect these skills.

2. Watch a 30-minute TV program for the commercials. Record how many commercials make a scientific claim as part of their persuasive appeal. For each, determine if the claim is based on pseudoscience or the scientific method.

3. Pick your favorite "as seen on TV" product. Using your critical-thinking skills, evaluate the claims associated with this product.

4. Go to: http://www.sciencedaily.com/. Check out today's "Top Science News." How does this research fit with the characteristics of science presented in this chapter?

5. Keep a diary for a week and note any instance where you or someone else (e.g., family member, friend, etc.) demonstrates a natural flaw in thinking.

6. Write a letter to students in an Introduction to Psychology class about why they should take a course in research methods.

7. Here is a citation for a study about how lowering your voice can influence how you think and feel:

   Stel, M., van Dijk, E., Smith, P., van Dijk, W., and Djalal, F. (2012). Lowering the pitch of your voice makes you feel more powerful and think more abstractly. *Social Psychological and Personality Science, 3,* 497–502. doi:10.1177/1948550611427610

   Search this study on the Web and identify all of the ways this study's results have been communicated. Critically evaluate the pros and cons of each type of communication.

Key Concepts

applied research, p. 15

availability heuristic, p. 3

basic research, p. 14

belief perseverance, p. 6

better-than-average effect, p. 3

confirmation bias, p. 5

critical-thinking skills, p. 18

empirical research, p. 11

focusing effect, p. 5

hindsight bias, p. 4

infographic, p. 18

introspection, p. 5

law of small numbers, p. 7

nonempirical research, p. 11

outlier, p. 7

overconfidence phenomenon, p. 4

pleasure paradox, p. 6

pseudoscience, p. 15

replication, p. 13

representativeness heuristic, p. 3

scientific method, p. 8

"what you see is all there is" phenomenon, p. 5

Answers to YOUR TURN
Your Turn 1.1: 1. d; 2. a; 3. b
Your Turn 1.2: 1. c; 2. b; 3. a
Your Turn 1.3: 1. c; 2. d; 3. b

Answers to Multiple-Choice Review Questions
1. a; 2. d; 3. a; 4. b; 5. a; 6. b; 7. a; 8. d; 9. b; 10. a

The Research Process
Ideas to Innovations

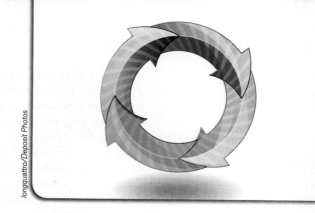

longquattro/Deposit Photos

LEARNING OUTCOMES

After reading this chapter, you should be able to:

- Develop sound empirical research questions of interest.

- Explain the role of peer-reviewed literature searches in evaluating research questions.

- Discuss strategies for generating hypotheses, and the characteristics of good hypotheses.

- Differentiate between independent and dependent variables, as well as their conceptual and operational definitions.

- Explain how experimental designs differ from nonexperimental designs.

- Discuss how between-subjects designs differ from within-subjects designs.

- Describe the purpose of the research protocol when designing a study.

- Explain why it is necessary to represent the results of a study in quantitative terms.

- Describe the various sections of an APA-style paper.

- Discuss the different ways that researchers can share their work with the scientific community.

Something to Think About . . .

According to astrophysicist and television host Neil deGrasse Tyson, "When you're scientifically literate, the world looks different to you. It's a particular way of questioning what you see and hear." Do you ever wonder about the world around you? You may not think of yourself as a scientist or psychologist, but chances are you question your experiences from time to time. For example, you might have questions about the best way to study for a test, how to know if someone is attracted to you, or why your best friend's personality differs from your own. The challenge is to develop answers to our questions while avoiding the flaws and biases in thinking that we discussed in Chapter 1. Science provides us with the best strategies for accomplishing this task.

Knowing that a scientific approach is best is the first step, but knowing how to conduct good science is equally important. Putting science into practice involves using the scientific method, a systematic approach for answering

▶ How does the scientific method help us to avoid biased thinking?
SEE CHAPTER 1, p. 8

questions that helps the questioner have more confidence in the knowledge discovered. In reality, the term "scientific method" is a misnomer in the sense that there is no one single method. Rather, this term represents many different strategies that rely on making observations to answer our questions. Although the specific strategies a scientist uses may differ, the scientific method represents a set of general steps for systematically answering questions. A wide range of scientific disciplines such as sociology, geology, and chemistry use these steps to answer questions of interest. As psychology is the science dedicated to understanding thoughts, feelings, and behavior, it uses these same steps to answer questions of interest. Throughout this book, you will learn to use the scientific method to address a variety of interesting research questions. Of course, much goes into each of the scientific method's steps, so let's explore each of them in the context of psychology.

How Do I Begin?

As Big Bird, the lovable character on Sesame Street, often reminds kids, "Asking questions is a good way to find things out." The same is true in science. For the scientific method to create new knowledge, you first need to have a question that is interesting enough to answer. You might wonder, Is it easier to read with the lights on or off? Of course, you could study this scientifically, but since the question is not terribly provocative, the answer will likely be underwhelming. Spoiler alert! Based on 3 seconds of research, the data reveal that it is easier to read when there is light.

The Research Question

Interesting questions can come from anywhere, provided you are curious, observant, and skeptical. In other words, you need to observe the world the way many comedians do. Comedians like John Mulaney, Bill Burr, and Trevor Noah build their stand-up routines around everyday observations they make about the world around them. Jerry Seinfeld, the host of *Comedians in Cars Getting Coffee*, is famous for starting his comedy bits with, "Did you ever notice . . . ?" For example, "Did you ever notice a lot of butlers are named Jeeves?" Seinfeld conjectures that one's name can have a direct impact on career choice and concludes, "I think when you name a baby Jeeves, you've pretty much mapped out his future" (*Seinfeld*, Season 4, Episode 24). Although this statement is meant to be humorous, it does raise an interesting possibility. If you had to guess, would a man named Earl be more likely to become a neurosurgeon or a cab driver? The connection between one's name and occupation feels true, but we also know that we should not rely on intuition. Instead, we should investigate, using the scientific method, the impact that one's name can have on employment opportunities.

Like many comedians, Mindy Kaling's work is rooted in observations of the world around her. *The Mindy Project*, a TV series that she writes for and stars in, was inspired by her mother's profession as an OB/GYN. How do you use the observations you make in everyday life? *(Kaling International/Universal TV/Kobal/REX/Shutterstock)*

Thinking Like a Scientist in Real Life

What's Behind a Name?

Is there any empirical evidence to suggest that a name influences your occupation? In the book *Freakonomics,* "rogue economist" Steven Levitt and journalist Stephen Dubner (2005) seek to find the hidden meaning behind everything, including the meaning behind a name. Believe it or not, the names our parents give us do not determine our occupation, but they do relate to our parents' socioeconomic status and education level. Based on more than 16 million babies born in California since 1961, the authors conclude that some names are more common among the wealthy than the poor, while other names are more common in families with high or low levels of education. For example, less-educated parents tend to give their children names with more exotic spellings (e.g., Jayne vs. Jane). While a child's first name does not directly influence life outcomes, the parental socioeconomic and educational background reflected in the name can. Ultimately, if you ever have the responsibility of naming a child, the name you choose may be more of a reflection of your background than personal preference or current cultural trends.

Often, people become interested in psychology because they want to better understand themselves or others in their lives. Embrace that feeling. We all have the ability to observe and reflect on everyday life around us. The next chance you get, take a walk across campus or down the street and try to observe the world just like a comedian would. Notice the people around you and spend some time wondering what they are thinking, why they are engaging in their behaviors, and why they might experience different emotions. Even seemingly simple questions can unlock entire fields of inquiry and knowledge. For example, much of social psychology addresses the question of how others influence us. Developmental psychologists focus on how we change over time. If you want to become a clinical psychologist, you may be interested in exploring well-being and how to help people achieve it. As you can see, even very broad or basic questions can be the start of good research questions for you to pursue.

You may be wondering how you can identify a good research question to ask. Often, the best questions are the ones you feel passionate about answering. A good research question should carry enough intrigue that you find yourself thinking about possible answers, debating the best answer with yourself or others, and thinking about how you might test your ideas. If you are not feeling a special connection to your research idea, then it may not be a good research question for *you* to explore. Leave that one for someone else, and keep looking for questions that pique your interest.

Good research questions are **empirical** in nature, which means you are able to use direct and indirect observations or experiences to test the questions. This is an important consideration because the scientific method is not appropriate for answering every question that you may have. For example, if you are wondering if falling in love is the result of being shot by a mysterious, cherubic baby

empirical an approach in which the experimenter uses direct and indirect observations or experiences to test the research question.

archer, you cannot test this question empirically to determine if you are correct. After all, Cupid is perpetually elusive and impossible to see, which means that you can never observe his existence, making it impossible to test your idea. To empirically approach answering a question, we must be able to make systematic observations that involve something we can touch, taste, hear, smell, or see.

Conducting experiments in psychology, unlike other disciplines, can be more challenging because we are not able to directly observe thoughts, emotions, and attitudes. We cannot simply open up a person's head and see what is happening inside. In order to learn about internal mental processes, psychologists need to rely on some level of inference. For example, we cannot touch, taste, hear, or smell intelligence, yet intelligence is a well-established psychological concept. There are some behaviors that we can see that help us infer intelligence, like whether or not people are willing to stick their tongue on a frozen pole in the middle of winter. Seeing this behavior might suggest lower intelligence, or at least poor judgment. Alternatively, we might try to infer intelligence by observing a person's performance on a specially designed test. For instance, when an individual takes an IQ test, we presume that answering more questions indicates greater intelligence. Not everything we want to study in psychology is directly observable, so we need to find indirect ways to assess mental processes.

The ability to empirically test a research question differentiates scientific questions from nonscientific questions. Many interesting questions we could ask are, unfortunately, outside the scope of science. For example, "Are humans inherently good or evil?" This is a great question for a philosophical debate, but it is not well-suited for the scientific method because the types of observations we would need to make are difficult to obtain. If a person were inherently good or evil, this characteristic would have to be present at birth. To empirically test this, we could observe newborns. However, it is unlikely that our observations would allow us to confidently answer our question about the intrinsic nature of humans. After all, it is impossible to know which newborn behaviors suggest inherent goodness or inherent evil, meaning this question is nonscientific because there is no way to empirically test it. While the broad question of good versus evil is difficult to test empirically, a more specific question about an individual's good behavior, such as, "Are we more likely to give money to charity when alone than in a group?", lends itself more easily to making observations that help us address a question empirically. Another example of a nonscientific question is, "What is the meaning of life?" Think about what you could possibly empirically observe to determine the answer. It would be difficult, right? A better question would be, "What gives meaning to a person's life?" With this research question, we can ask about or observe experiences of others to determine what is meaningful to individuals.

We cannot observe what someone is thinking. If you wanted to know if this person is smart, how could you tell? *(alvarez/Vetta/Getty Images)*

Once we find an interesting and empirical research question, our next step is to see if others have asked similar questions, and what they have learned.

The Literature Search

The overarching goal of science is to advance our knowledge about our world. In order to do this, we need to determine whether others have already answered our initial question. However, even if researchers have addressed aspects of our research question, it is highly unlikely that they have exhausted all avenues of inquiry. In these cases, discovering what others have learned will help us to ask a better, more specific question that will continue to advance our knowledge.

To determine what other researchers have learned, we need to search the existing literature. Books, news articles, and websites might provide this information, but it is often difficult to disentangle scientific facts from authors' personal opinions in these sources, assuming there is any scientific information in there at all. The best source for finding quality information about our question is peer-reviewed journal articles. **Peer review** is the process by which scientific experts in the field serve as reviewers who evaluate the quality of research reported in an article. To reduce potential bias, editors keep the identities of the reviewers a secret so the reviewers can feel comfortable giving honest opinions about the work. Authors submit research reports for review (this process is also often anonymous) and revise the paper multiple times based on reviewer feedback before an editor decides the work is worthy of publication. The majority of these reports never gain acceptance for publication, with the peer-review process contributing to the self-correcting nature of science.

You could think of peer review as a way of fact checking the information. As others provide feedback about how to better collect data or communicate study findings, the quality of the science improves, with only the best reports eventually gaining publication. As an example, *Psychological Science,* a monthly scientific journal of the Association for Psychological Science, only publishes around 300 of the some 3,000 reports submitted for review annually. Articles that successfully complete the peer-review process are those that ask sound research questions, use suitable methods to test possible answers to these questions, and then draw appropriate conclusions that minimize authors' personal biases. Without the peer-review process, it is difficult to know whether the information you are reading is unbiased or validated. For this reason, your professors often require that you base your papers exclusively on peer-reviewed work.

In psychology, we can find peer-reviewed scientific articles using research databases such as PsycINFO or PsycARTICLES instead of general search engines like Google or Bing. These specialized search engines help you better target your research topic. For example, PsycINFO is a database of abstracts produced by the American Psychological Association (APA). From it, you can find abstracts and descriptive information to help you locate what you need across a wide variety of scholarly publications in the behavioral and social sciences. Articles included date as far back as the late 1800s. Conducting the actual literature search is as simple as entering a few key words related to your research question, which will undoubtedly yield hundreds or thousands of related articles. For example, if you wanted to learn about research studies examining charitable giving, you could search for articles using the key words "charity" and "giving." As you reviewed your search results, you would become savvier about the terms that psychologists typically use in that

peer review the process by which other scientific experts in the field review and evaluate the quality of research before it is reported in a publication.

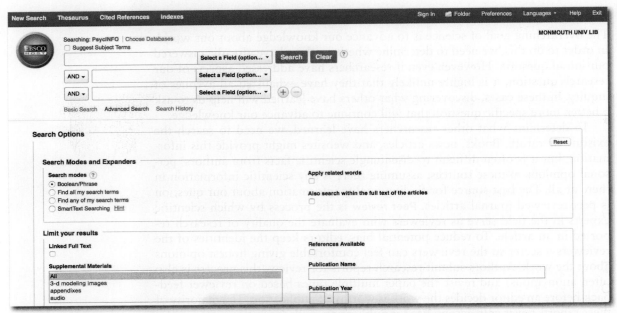

Why do psychologists prefer to use research databases when conducting literature searches? What makes these sources better than an Internet search? *(Ebsco Host)*

particular area of research. In this case, a better search term might be "altruistic behavior." As you became knowledgeable about this topic area, you would become more adept at locating pertinent studies, identifying key researchers in the field, and using the references from key published studies to help you track down additional leads.

Conducting literature searches allows us to learn what questions others have asked and the methods they used to answer them. We benefit from existing knowledge by "standing on the shoulders of giants." That is, we get to pick up where others have left off, which makes it more likely that we will be able to advance science and contribute to the world's understanding of psychological phenomena.

YOUR TURN 2.1

1. Lily is developing a research question for the study she is conducting this semester. She settles on, "What is the meaning of life?" The primary reason that the scientific method cannot be used to answer this question is

   a. it is not very interesting to most people.

   b. direct observation of this topic would be difficult.

   c. a quick search in Google indicates over 1,000 entries on this topic already.

   d. there are no peer-reviewed journal articles on this topic.

2. The key distinction between scientific and nonscientific questions is whether or not
   a. the question can be empirically tested.
   b. others have published articles on the topic.
   c. the question is of inherent interest to the researcher.
   d. the question concerns a real-world phenomenon.

3. Who are the "peers" in the peer-review process?
   a. Scientists in general
   b. People who read the journal articles
   c. The publishers of the journal articles
   d. Experts in the field

How did you do? Turn to the end of the chapter to check your answers.

Constructing a Hypothesis

Our research question leads us to search the literature, but to really put our question to the test, we will need a more specific prediction, or **hypothesis**. While a research question is what the research project generally sets out to answer, a hypothesis is a specific, educated conjecture or guess that provides a testable explanation of a phenomenon. It is a prediction that our study can test. Whenever we have questions about some phenomenon in our world, we often have some ideas about what could answer the question. These answers are the basis for the hypothesis. However, at this point, they are only possible answers. To determine if our guesses are right, we must test each hypothesis by designing a study that provides a fair test of our proposed answer.

When a large body of empirical evidence supports a hypothesis, that hypothesis may eventually become a scientific law or a theory. A **scientific law** is a statement based on repeated experimental observation that describes some aspect of the world, but makes no assumptions about why it occurs. Psychology has few laws because we often do not have enough understanding of mental processes and behavior to identify all the factors that contribute to a particular outcome. However, some laws in psychology do exist. One example is Weber's law of just noticeable difference, which states the amount by which a stimulus must change in intensity for us to perceive the change (Gescheider, 1997). We consider this a law because repeated experimental observations collected about this phenomenon have helped to describe this aspect of our world.

If empirical evidence repeatedly supports a hypothesis, it may also become a **scientific theory**, which is a well-substantiated explanation of some aspect of the natural world confirmed through repeated observation and experimentation. Rather than describing an aspect of the world, like a law, a theory is an in-depth explanation of why a phenomenon occurs. Psychology is full of theories, such as Kohlberg's theory of moral development, which argues that moral development occurs throughout the life span in six different stages. Unlike laws, which describe repeated observation, theories attempt to explain the underlying reasons for phenomena.

hypothesis an educated prediction that provides a testable explanation of a phenomenon.

scientific law a statement based on repeated experimental observation that describes some aspect of the world.

scientific theory a well-substantiated explanation of some aspect of the natural world confirmed through repeated observation and experimentation.

But let's not get ahead of ourselves. Before your ideas can become a scientific law or theory, you need to start by developing a hypothesis. For example, you may wonder whether playing video games makes someone more aggressive. A quick literature search would reveal that psychologists have generally found that exposure to violent interactive video games increases aggressive behavior, as well as cheating (Gabbiadini, Riva, Andrighetto, Volpato, & Bushman, 2014). After reading these studies and considering some of your friends who play video games, you wonder if people who play video games are happier. After conducting a literature search, you are unable to find any published studies that specifically test this idea. Therefore, you surmise the hypothesis that playing video games will lead to increased happiness. Congratulations! You have an interesting hypothesis to test that will add to our understanding about the impact of video games on behavior.

Generating Hypotheses

There are many different strategies for generating good hypotheses. In fact, McGuire (1997) describes 49 tactics for generating creative hypotheses. For this stage of your scientific career, that is about 45 too many, so here are four strategies to help you get started:

Introspection: Perhaps the most common strategy is to engage in self-observation or introspection (what some call "me" search). As we know from Chapter 1, introspection is not a good way to find answers, but it is a terrific way to formulate questions. After all, we are experts on ourselves, so starting with what you know seems like a good plan. In this approach you essentially ask, "What would I do?", "How would I feel?", or "What would I think?", and then speculate about how you would answer those questions in a particular setting. Does playing video games make *you* happier? Perhaps playing video games makes you happier under some circumstances (e.g., when you successfully catch a Pokémon), but not in others (e.g., when it takes too long to build a castle in *Minecraft*). The key is to identify the factors that might influence your happiness and use those explanations to develop a testable hypothesis.

Find the exception to the rule: Often the existing research will examine one type of outcome. For example, relationship research tends to focus on the negative effects of romantic break-ups (Lee & Sbarra, 2013). The same seems to be true of video games, with most of the research focusing on the potential negative influences (e.g., see Anderson & Bushman, 2001). In these cases, because there is virtually no outcome that is true 100% of the time, it may be more interesting to find instances that are exceptions to these well-researched outcomes. Crafting hypotheses that look at the outcomes in the opposite direction of prior research has the potential to provide new insights into the phenomenon of interest.

A matter of degree: As Shakespeare wrote in *Hamlet*, nothing is inherently good or evil. In reality, there is gray area in terms of how one factor influences another. Milk is generally good for us, but if you were to drink an entire gallon at once, you would quickly learn there are distinct downsides to excessive milk consumption. Thus, it may be that playing video games for 30 minutes a day is beneficial, while playing for 3 hours a

What Do You Think?
What other hypotheses could you generate related to playing video games?

day is not. Therefore, when you are crafting hypotheses, try to think about your variables in terms of amounts, which can take many forms, such as quantity, intensity, strength, volume, number, force, persistence, and effort.

Change the directionality: Which came first, the chicken or the egg? A classic question, for sure, but it reminds us that often there is not a set direction of how one thing influences another. Parents influence children, but children can influence their parents as well. News coverage, such as in cases of school shootings, often portrays playing video games as the cause of aggressive behavior. Yet it is equally likely that aggressive individuals gravitate toward violent video games. In our case, it could be that happy people are more likely to play video games or that playing video games makes people happier. Thinking about ideas from both directions will help you form creative hypotheses.

 Research Spotlight

The Upside to Video-Game Play

If you were to ask a random person on the street whether playing video games has more good or bad outcomes, most people would guess there are more negative outcomes. Like we hypothesized, there might be some real advantages to playing video games. In a year-long longitudinal study of 12-year-olds, researchers found that more time spent playing video games coincided with greater visual–spatial skills, like mentally rotating objects or solving jigsaw puzzles (Jackson, von Eye, Witt, Zhao, & Fitzgerald, 2011). This sounds promising, but 12-year-olds are not exactly surgeons. Well, it just so happens that surgeons benefit from video-game playing as well (Rosser et al., 2007). Surgeons who played video games for more than 3 hours a week made 37% fewer errors and were 27% faster in laparoscopic surgery and suturing drills compared to surgeons who never played video games. The researchers speculate that video games offer the same hand–eye coordination, timing development, sense of touch, and intuitive feel as laparoscopic surgery, giving game players a distinct advantage over non–game players.

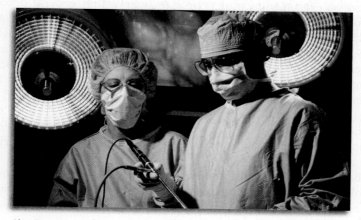

If video games can make you a better surgeon, what other areas of your life could playing video games improve? *(Jeff Cadge The Image Bank/Getty Images)*

Evaluating Hypotheses

Once you get the hang of developing hypotheses, you will need to know how to separate the winners from the losers. Good hypotheses have several characteristics. One is a high correspondence with reality. That is, your hypothesis should logically follow from what your literature search revealed on the topic. Developing a hypothesis that completely contradicts previous research findings is a bad strategy, unless there is sound justification for this prediction. For example, hypothesizing that optimal learning occurs when cramming last minute for a test contradicts decades of research on how humans learn. As a result, the chances of confirming your "cramming hypothesis" are highly unlikely.

Second, good hypotheses are simple and direct. Overly complex or wordy hypotheses make predictions unclear. **Occam's razor,** named after William of Ockham, a 14th-century English philosopher, is a phrase scientists use to refer to the idea that you should "cut away" unnecessary parts. Researchers sometimes refer to this idea as the principle of parsimony or simplicity, which suggests that if there are multiple ways of stating something, the most simple and direct way is the best.

Before we continue our discussion, consider the following: recent market testing found that psychology majors and, more specifically, readers of this textbook, tend to be fun-loving, be a little emotional, and have several loyal friends, but, at times, have doubts about their abilities and worries about the future. You are a reader of this text. Does this statement describe you? If you are like most people, you probably find this statement to be a relatively accurate description. Clearly, our market testing has perfectly matched our book with the right reader! Not so fast. As it turns out, most people (readers of this book or not) would say that this statement accurately describes them.

Psychologists call this the **Barnum effect,** named after P. T. Barnum, the founder of the Ringling Brothers and Barnum & Bailey Circus. He is often credited with saying, "We've got something for everyone." The Barnum effect refers to the tendency of people to believe that general descriptions of personality, supposedly tailored specifically for them, are highly accurate (Forer, 1949). That is, they mistakenly believe that broad statements that apply to most people are uniquely descriptive of them. These statements often seem accurate only because they are vague and nonspecific. Vague statements are so broadly applicable because there are many ways to make them seem accurate. When our market testing (which we made up for this example) says that you are a little emotional, you can certainly think of times when that was true: either when you became teary-eyed after watching a movie, or when you were overly excited about your favorite team winning a game.

The Barnum effect helps us understand why people may believe horoscopes and astrological predictions. Both consist of broad, vague statements that are difficult to refute. In reality, it is likely that even if you are a Pisces, the descriptions

Occam's razor refers to the cutting away of the unnecessary; important in hypothesis development; named after William of Ockham, a 14th-century English philosopher.

Barnum effect the tendency of people to believe that general descriptions of their personality are highly accurate and tailored specifically for them.

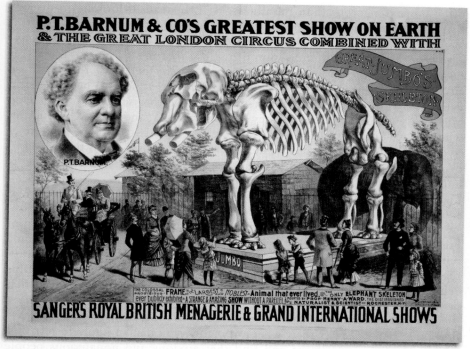

Why was the Barnum effect named after this "master of showmen"? What other examples can you think of where a Barnum effect occurs? *(Library of Congress)*

for Capricorn, Cancer, or Sagittarius would all seem similarly accurate. If, in the future, you read a horoscope or open a fortune cookie and find the descriptions to be general and dissatisfying, then chances are that you are thinking like a scientist!

The Barnum effect illustrates why good hypotheses must be specific. If our hypotheses are vague or too broadly stated, then it is unclear exactly what we are testing. Related to this idea is that good hypotheses must be falsifiable or refutable, which is to say that it must be possible to show that your hypothesis may be incorrect. This important characteristic of good hypotheses helps overcome our tendency to confirm our own ideas. Rather than trying to confirm their hypotheses, good scientists focus on trying to disconfirm them to see if they are wrong. In order to do this, it must be possible to refute one's hypothesis. A hypothesis by Benjamin Rush, a famous 18th-century American physician, illustrates why good hypotheses must be falsifiable if we wish to obtain accurate knowledge about our world. Rush hypothesized bloodletting was the best treatment for those suffering from a high fever. During the 1793 Yellow Fever epidemic in Philadelphia, Rush treated all of his patients with this technique, which, in fact, was often more dangerous than the illness itself. Instead of looking to disconfirm his hypothesis that bloodletting was beneficial, he looked to confirm it. After the epidemic was over, he focused only on the patients who recovered from the illness, thereby supporting the treatment's effectiveness. Yet he explained away those who did not recover by believing that in those situations the illness was too advanced for *any* treatment to be successful. Rush's focus on confirming evidence, as opposed to disconfirming it, made him overly confident in the efficacy of his treatment, and created a situation where it was impossible to refute his belief that his treatment was effective. If he had had the opposite, more scientific mindset—that he needed to disprove the idea that his treatment was ineffective—many more patients might have survived.

The need to disconfirm theories is equally important in psychology. If someone asked you, "Who is the most famous psychologist?" your first answer would likely be Sigmund Freud. Although very well-known, many of Freud's hypotheses about the role of unconscious processes in determining our behavior are unscientific, mainly because they are not falsifiable. That is, regardless of any experimental results, there would not be incontrovertible evidence that Freud's ideas are correct. For example, Freud suggested that people use projection as a defense mechanism when experiencing anxiety, such that people attribute their own thoughts to others (e.g., you think, "My brother's friend dislikes me," when, in reality, you dislike him). To test this, you conduct an experiment and find that anxious and nonanxious people exhibit similar levels of projection. Based on these findings, you conclude that Freud's defense mechanism hypothesis was incorrect. However, Freud would argue that the reason there was no difference was that the anxiety-ridden people used a different defense mechanism, such as repression, in that particular situation. Conveniently, this shaky explanation provides support for the role of defense mechanisms in shaping our behavior. If you have a hard time accepting this explanation, you are thinking like a scientist (although Freud would probably say that you were using the defense mechanism of denial!). Freud's theories were often not falsifiable. It is not surprising that Freud and others were so confident in his ideas, given that they were impossible to disprove.

Revisiting our research question, our literature search revealed that playing interactive violent video games can increase levels of aggression. Using the "exception to the rule" hypothesis-generation strategy, we hypothesize that people become happier the longer they play nonviolent video games. Let's check our hypothesis against our criteria for hypotheses: correspondence with reality; parsimony; specificity; and falsifiability. Connecting video games with happiness is a logical extension of the existing research into the impact of video games on behavior, so there is a correspondence with reality. We have stated our hypothesis in clear and succinct terms that make it parsimonious. We have also been specific in how we predicted game playing to influence happiness. And it is possible for us to conduct a study where we find that playing nonviolent video games actually makes people LESS happy, thus refuting our hypothesis, which means that our hypothesis is falsifiable.

YOUR TURN 2.2

1. Sitting outside the student center, Joseph sees a student with full hands drop her smartphone. As she struggles to pick it up, he wonders what would motivate him to help and realizes that he would have helped had he been closer to the student. This inspires him to hypothesize that proximity influences the willingness to help someone in need. What was his strategy for developing a good hypothesis?
   a. A matter of degree
   b. Introspection
   c. The exception to the rule
   d. Change in directionality

2. Which of the following is *not* a characteristic of a good hypothesis?
   a. Vagueness
   b. Correspondence to reality
   c. Falsifiability
   d. Parsimony

3. Which of the following characteristics of good hypotheses is important for minimizing our natural flaws in thinking?
   a. Specificity
   b. Correspondence to reality
   c. Falsifiability
   d. Parsimony

How did you do? Turn to the end of the chapter to check your answers.

Testing Your Hypothesis

As you will learn in the upcoming chapters, you have many different methods or research designs at your disposal for scientifically evaluating your hypotheses. While picking the best one to use can seem daunting, it is important to remember that no single design is inherently superior to another. Each design has its own strengths and weaknesses. The best strategy is to avoid going with your personal favorite or the one you understand the best. Instead, you should let your hypothesis guide your design decision because some methodologies are better suited than others for providing answers to certain types of research questions. For example, if you wanted to look at how a person's anxiety develops over time, you would use a different research design than if you wanted to study the effectiveness of a strategy for reducing anxiety. In order to choose the appropriate method to test your hypothesis, you will need to make a few important decisions.

Identify Key Variables

First, you must identify the key concepts or variables associated with your hypothesis. **Variables** are the factors or elements that you expect to change, vary,

variables elements that we expect to change or vary, or that can have several different values.

or have several different values. In contrast, a **constant** is a factor that does not change and remains consistent. In thinking about our hypothesis (that people become happier the more they play nonviolent video games), there are two key variables. The aspects of our hypothesis that we expect to change or vary are video-game play and happiness. A constant in our study may be the specific video game played.

As you identify your variables, you must start to consider how you will define each one, or what you mean by "happiness." Researchers often start with a **conceptual definition**, which is what the variable represents in the context of the researcher's study. In our study, we might conceptually define happiness as the variable that represents a mental state of well-being that includes positive emotions. Once we decide on a conceptual definition, we then develop an **operational definition** for the variable. The operational definition represents how we will use (or put into operation) the variables in our study. There are many different ways we could operationally define our variables. We could operationally define happiness as acing a test, or by how long a person laughs at a joke. Ultimately, we decide the best operational definitions to use for our variables by thinking about these definitions in the context of the study we are designing. The fun part about being a researcher is that you not only get to design your own study, but also to determine how you operationally define your variables. Through the process of identifying conceptual and operational definitions we connect our study to phenomena in the real world.

Choose a Research Design

Several factors influence your choice of a specific research design. The first is the nature of your research question. If your research question focuses on *why* something occurs, then you will likely use experimental methods. In **experimental designs**, the researcher manipulates at least one variable by varying or changing it in a deliberate and specific manner. The variable manipulated in an experimental design is the **independent variable (IV)** and is the variable that you believe to be responsible for influencing another variable in your study. The experimenter then measures the **dependent variable (DV)** by observing or otherwise keeping track of what happens. The dependent variable is the variable that the independent variable influences. In other words, the dependent variable represents the effect or outcome in your study. To help you distinguish between independent and dependent variables, remember that the researcher introduces or inputs the independent variable, and that changes the dependent variable, which always depends on another variable. In our case, because we predict that playing video games influences happiness, we want to know how playing a video game is responsible for influencing the outcome of happiness. Therefore, playing video games is our independent variable and happiness is our dependent variable. This process allows us to begin to answer "why" questions. The researcher's complete control of the independent variable helps to establish it as the cause of the dependent variable or measured outcome.

Once you identify the study's design and key variables, you are ready to operationally define them. If we decided to do an experiment, we could operationally

---

constant a factor that does not change and remains consistent.

conceptual definition defining a variable in theoretical terms.

operational definition determining how we will use variables in our study.

experimental design a research method in which the experimenter controls and manipulates the independent variable, allowing the establishment of cause-and-effect relationships between the independent and dependent variables.

independent variable (IV) the variable that influences the dependent variable. In experiments the researcher manipulates or controls this variable. In nonexperimental studies, it is the explanatory or predictor variable and is not manipulated by the researcher.

dependent variable (DV) the variable measured in association with changes in the independent variable; the outcome or effect. In nonexperimental studies it is referred to as the criterion or response variable.

define our independent variable (video-game play) in a number of ways by manipulating different aspects of the activity. For example, we could systematically vary the time spent playing the same video games (e.g., 1 hour, 3 hours, or 6 hours), the type of game system (e.g., Wii U, Xbox One, or PlayStation 4), or the type of game played (e.g., *Super Mario Brothers, Halo, Dance Dance Revolution,* or *Final Fantasy*). How we operationally define our variables depends on the specific research question we are trying to answer. If we want to know if the amount of video-game play increases happiness, then we should operationally define video-game play by varying how long our participants play a specific game.

We must also operationally define the dependent variable of happiness. Again, we have choices to make. We could observe the facial expressions of participants after they play the video game and record the number of times they smile as an operational definition of happiness. However, the easiest way to measure happiness would be to ask participants to self-report how they feel through a written questionnaire. If people who play the video games longer tend to be happier than those who play for less time, we can conclude that playing video games causes an increase in happiness. The ability to establish this cause-and-effect relationship allows us to identify one factor that leads to people being happy.

If you are interested in a design that describes *what* is happening, then you can use a **nonexperimental design,** also known as a **correlational design.** Researchers often employ a nonexperimental design when they want to describe a phenomenon, such as how children play during recess or how memory changes with age. In a nonexperimental design, the researcher evaluates how one variable may affect another variable, but there is no true independent or dependent variable because the researcher is not responsible for deliberately manipulating the independent variable. In nonexperimental designs, we refer to the potential causal variable as the **explanatory** or **predictor variable,** and the outcome variable as the **criterion** or **response variable.** The data collected from a nonexperimental design will tell you *what* happens to one variable when the other variable changes, but it cannot tell you *why* it happened. Because the researcher is not deliberately manipulating any variable in a nonexperimental design, you cannot conclude that one variable causes a change in another variable. Instead you can conclude that the two variables are associated or connected in some way. As in experimental designs, variables in nonexperimental designs need identification and operational definitions. Therefore, we might operationalize the explanatory variable of video-game playing by having people self-report the number of hours they spend playing a video game each day for two weeks. We might define the criterion variable of happiness by also using a self-report that measures mood each day.

Aside from addressing a "what" question, there are other reasons to utilize a nonexperimental design. One reason is that there are times when we are unsure about what causes what. In other words, we are unsure of the direction of causation. For example, you may decide that time spent playing video games can influence happiness. However, you might just as easily hypothesize that happiness influences the desire to spend more time playing video games. When we are not sure which variable causes which (i.e., the direction of causation is unclear), we use nonexperimental design to test our hypothesis. Another reason that we use nonexperimental design is because we cannot manipulate the independent

nonexperimental design a design in which there is no control or manipulation of the independent variable; cause-and-effect relationships between variables cannot be established; refer to the independent variable as the explanatory or predictor variable and the dependent variable as the criterion or response variable; also known as a correlational design.

explanatory variable a potential causal variable in nonexperimental designs; also known as a predictor variable.

criterion variable the outcome variable in nonexperimental designs; also known as a response variable.

variable for ethical or pragmatic reasons. For example, if your research question involves how the divorce of an individual's parents influences emotional stability, you cannot control whether or not participants' parents have been divorced. Similarly, if we hypothesized that people who spent more time playing nonviolent video games as children tend to be happier people, we would choose a nonexperimental design because, without a time machine, we are not able to manipulate the past.

Once you have determined whether your research question is experimental or nonexperimental, you can narrow down your design choice considerably. For nonexperimental designs, the type of information you want to obtain helps determine your final choice. If you want individuals' verbal responses and explanations for each answer, you would probably use a structured interview, while if you want individuals' written responses and ratings to many questions, a survey design would probably be best.

For experimental designs, you will need to make a few more decisions. First, you will need to decide how many different independent variables you want to manipulate in your study. This will depend on the complexity of your research question. You will also need to decide how many **levels,** or different variations of each independent variable, you want to incorporate into your study design. We could have participants play video games for 1 hour or for 3 hours before assessing happiness. Here, the two different lengths of time participants spend playing video games are the two levels for your independent variable. If you wanted to add another length of time, for example, 2 hours, then your independent variable would have three levels (1 hour, 2 hours, and 3 hours). As the researcher, you determine the types and number of levels you need in order to address your hypothesis in the best possible way.

You will also need to decide how frequently you want to gather data from the participants in your study. If you only assess participants once on the dependent variable, then you are conducting a **between-subjects design.** In this design, you might have one participant play the video game for 1 hour, and then measure the person's level of happiness. Another participant would play the video game for 3 hours before the happiness assessment. We would then test our hypothesis by comparing the responses *between* the participants who played the video game for 1 hour (one level of our independent variable) and those who played for 3 hours (the other level of our independent variable).

In some cases, you may want to expose participants to all of the levels of the independent variable. If you plan to measure the dependent variable on multiple occasions from the same participants, you are conducting a **within-subjects design.** If you carry out these measurements or observations of the participants over a period of time, we call that a **longitudinal design.** Based on our hypothesis, we could have participants play a video game for 1 hour, assess their happiness, and then have the same participants play for 3 hours and again assess their happiness. In this situation, we measure the same participants' happiness more than once and then compare differences *within* the participants based on how long they played the video game.

Pretend that you recruited six of your friends to participate in your study. If you wanted to use a between-subjects design, you would ask three of them,

levels different variations of the independent variable determined by the researcher.

between-subjects design a data collection method in which each participant or subject is only assessed on the dependent variable once.

within-subjects design a data collection method in which each participant or subject is assessed on the dependent variable more than once.

longitudinal design the collection of data on participants over a set period of time.

Ross, Chandler, and Phoebe, to play a video game for 1 hour. At the end of the hour, you would assess their levels of happiness. You would then have your other three friends, Monica, Joey, and Rachel, play the video game for 3 hours before measuring their level of happiness. To test your hypothesis, you would then statistically compare the average happiness among those playing for 1 hour with those playing for 3 hours. If you decided to use a within-subjects design, you would have all six of your friends play a video game for 1 hour, measure their happiness, and then have all six of them play a video game for 3 hours, then assess their happiness again. Unlike between-subjects designs, we test our hypothesis by essentially looking at whether or not your friends were happier when playing a video game for 1 hour or for 3 hours. You can see from the side-by-side comparison in **Table 2.1** how these two designs differ.

programmatic research
a systematic and planned sequence of related studies where subsequent studies build directly on a previous study's findings to provide a more comprehensive understanding of a phenomenon.

TABLE 2.1

Comparing Between-Subjects and Within-Subjects Designs			
Between-Subjects		**Within-Subjects**	
Level 1	**Level 2**	**Level 1**	**Level 2**
Ross	Monica	Monica	Monica
Chandler	Joey	Joey	Joey
Phoebe	Rachel	Rachel	Rachel
		Ross	Ross
		Chandler	Chandler
		Phoebe	Phoebe

Every design choice we make addresses a slightly different research question. To gain a richer understanding of the connection between video-game play and happiness, we may want to engage in **programmatic research**, which involves a systematic and planned sequence of related studies, with subsequent studies building directly on a previous study's findings. To determine if there is even a link between playing video games and happiness, we might first conduct a nonexperimental survey to assess how much time people naturally spend playing video games and their general level of happiness. If we see a connection, we may then decide to conduct a between-subjects experiment so we can manipulate the amount of time participants play video games. This will help us determine if people who play 3 hours of video games are happier than those who play for 1 hour. Based on this study's findings, we might run a second experiment using a within-subjects design to assess how levels of happiness change as each person plays for different time periods. In this study, each participant could play for 1 hour, 3 hours, and 5 hours to determine which level of time might be optimal for happiness. When engaging in programmatic research, the key is to allow the previous study's findings to inform the next study. Programmatic research provides us with a more comprehensive understanding of a phenomenon.

Most successful psychologists use programmatic research to study a specific topic in depth. Dr. Sabina Cehajic-Clancy, an assistant professor at the Sarajevo School of Science and Technology, studies intergroup reconciliation with a particular focus on the post-conflict society of Bosnia and Herzegovina. She uses both qualitative and quantitative methodological approaches to determine how in-group responsibility, emotions, and apologies all play a role in reconciliation. *(Courtesy Sabina Cehajic-Clancy)*

So far we have focused our attention on the large-scale design choices that you will need to make to test your hypothesis. It is important to reiterate that one design is not inherently better than another design. However, there are many smaller decisions that you will need to think through as you develop your specific research study. We will explore the researcher's thought process in much more detail in each of the design chapters throughout this book.

⚙️ Research in Action

Determining Key Study Elements

Once we settle on an empirical research question, we must determine how to incorporate all of the critical concepts into our research design. These decisions are up to you: You get to determine what type of design best addresses your research question and how to operationalize the variables in your study. But this can be tricky when we want to study what people think, feel, and do. You might just have to be creative.

Now that you have an understanding of how to utilize research designs to answer research questions and how to operationally define variables, see if you can identify these elements from study scenarios in the online activity ***Determining Key Study Elements.*** These scenarios may give you inspiration for how to answer your own research questions as you discover the scientist within.

📑 **LaunchPad** To complete this activity, visit LaunchPad at launchpadworks.com

Open Science Practices

The ultimate goal of science is to learn about the world. The more we learn, the better. As a result, we all have a vested interest in producing the highest-quality and most accurate science possible. To do this, you must be open and transparent about your hypotheses, how you will conduct the study, and how you plan on analyzing the results. These practices are consistent with **open science**, which involves freely sharing your scientific work along all stages of the research process.

Before researchers start data collection, they openly share their research design plans, information about their potential sample, and plans for data analysis with others on sites such as the Open Science Framework (http://osf.io). In explaining their project designs, researchers must have a clear vision for their research and be able to clearly communicate it with others. By sharing their intended project, researchers can also receive critical input and suggestions from others, potentially strengthening the research project before data collection begins. In open science, researchers share their data and analyses after study completion, as well. This provides another opportunity for fellow scientists to critique the appropriateness of the data analysis and conclusions drawn. Open science provides opportunities for peer review at all stages of the research process, not just at the final research report.

open science the practice of freely sharing our scientific work along all stages of the research process.

Practicing open science can reduce researchers' unknown biases by allowing others to point out potential flaws in data collection or analysis. Registering a study prior to conducting it provides a specific plan for data analysis before the data are even collected, which prevents the researcher from aimlessly looking for results in the data. Sharing research projects and associated data also helps other researchers replicate the results, which is an important characteristic of science. Overall, open science's goal is to facilitate carefully planned research projects that researchers conduct in a transparent way, ensuring the highest-quality and most accurate studies possible.

▶ Why is replication important for science? SEE CHAPTER 1, p. 13

Conduct the Study

Regardless of the specific research strategy we choose, we will need to test our hypothesis by putting our design into action. To do this, researchers develop a **research protocol**, which is a detailed series of steps that describes how the researcher should conduct the study, including what the researcher should say and do when interacting with the research participants. To guarantee that the researcher says the exact same thing to each participant, the protocol often includes a **script**, which is a written set of instructions that the researcher reads to each participant.

Before we actually have people participate in our study, we need to ensure that our study is safe for participants and conducted in an ethical manner. We will discuss ethical considerations in depth in Chapter 3, but, generally speaking, we will have a panel of experts conduct an ethical review of our study before we start data collection. The ethics review ensures that our research protocol will not harm our participants and that the potential benefits from our study outweigh the costs of doing it.

As part of your ethical obligations, you will start your research protocol by obtaining **informed consent** from your participants. Participants provide consent by indicating that they understand what the study expects of them, as well as the risks and benefits of participating in the study. By providing informed consent, the participant has voluntarily made the decision to take part in your study. The middle steps in a protocol all relate to the process of actually conducting your study. The last step in the research protocol is **debriefing**, where you will explain the entire purpose of the study to the participants in clear and easily understandable ways, revealing any ways in which they were misled or deceived and why this was necessary in the study. Debriefing also provides participants with the opportunity to ask any questions they may have about the study and their involvement in it.

Analyze the Data and Draw Conclusions

Your design decisions about variables, levels, and the number of times you measure participants establish the types of **data**, or distinct pieces of information, you collect. Your data, in turn, determine the analytic strategies you should use to test your hypothesis. Just as you would not use a screwdriver to hammer in a nail, you should carefully select the proper statistical tool or test to evaluate your hypothesis. If you use the wrong test, your statistical software program probably will not tell you that it is wrong and the results of that test will be meaningless.

Whoa! At this point you may be thinking that this sounds like a lot of work and that it may be easier to avoid statistics altogether. The truth is, we *need* statistics to keep us honest. As we learned in Chapter 1, humans are not entirely objective

research protocol a detailed series of steps that describes the order in which to administer the study and provides a script of what the researcher should say and do.

script a written set of instructions that the researcher reads to the participant while collecting data.

informed consent a part of standard ethical procedures at the beginning of a research study in which the participant learns about the expectations of the study, is told the risks and benefits of participating, and then freely makes the choice about whether he or she wants to be in the study.

debriefing a part of standard ethical procedures at the end of a research study; contains an explanation of the purpose of the study and disclosure of deception, and gives participants a chance to ask questions.

data distinct pieces of information.

or bias-free thinkers. Furthermore, accurately detecting patterns in data can be difficult, especially when there are several variables involved. Statistics are handy tools that simultaneously allow us to minimize our flaws and biases in thinking and empower us to see patterns in our results that we may have otherwise missed. These patterns provide the evidence to either support or refute our hypotheses.

To accomplish all of this, we first need to transform our observations into numbers, or, as statisticians might say, represent the observations quantitatively. How we accomplish this depends on how we decide to operationally define our variables. For example, how might we operationally define our dependent variable of happiness such that we can compare the happiness of our participants? We could count the number of times each participant smiles after playing the video game. We could record how much time participants spend smiling once the game is over. Another possibility is that we could ask how happy the participants are after finishing playing the video game. The challenge is asking this question in a way that allows us to compare the answers across participants. If we were to ask participants, "Are you happy right now?", we might get responses like "You bet!" "Yeah, sort of," or "Yes, but not as happy as when I aced my psychology exam." Obviously, it would be very difficult for us to compare these participants in terms of happiness. One solution would be to ask the participants to assign numbers to their own experience that reflect the magnitude or degree of happiness they experience. If you have ever been in the hospital for surgery, you know that the doctors and nurses will ask you about your current level of pain. Instead of asking, "Are you feeling pain?" (Yes!), they ask you to consider your pain level on a numerical scale. In our study, it is much easier to compare two individuals' responses to the question, "How happy are you on a scale from 1 to 9 where 1 is not happy at all and 9 is extremely happy?" than it is to ask them, "How happy are you?" and then compare potential responses of "Pretty happy" to "Mostly happy." After you obtain this information from all of your participants, you can then summarize and compare the experiences of the participants based on which level of the independent variable they experienced.

While the use of statistical analyses to test hypotheses is an important part of the scientific method, we must realize that statistical tests provide us with probabilistic conclusions about the relationships between our variables of interest, not absolute conclusions or truths. That is, statistics give us an indication of the probability or likelihood that our results are true. Typically, we need to have 95% certainty that a finding is true for us to say it actually exists. While this may seem indefinite or imprecise, we have to keep in mind that we are trying to discern the nature of the world based on a limited set of observations, which can sometimes be problematic. Because we base our conclusions on probability, researchers avoid talking about their findings in absolute terms. Instead of saying, "These findings *prove* that playing video games increases happiness," a researcher might conclude that, "These findings *suggest* that playing video games increases happiness." Good scientists recognize the limitations in their research studies and avoid overstating the conclusions based on their results.

As you progress to future chapters, we will explain how to select the proper tools to analyze your data. We also devote Appendix A to statistics and analytic strategies.

Communicate the Findings

Science cannot advance our collective knowledge if we do not share our research findings. In many ways, our study is not truly complete until we have communicated the results of our study to others. In psychology, there are several ways we can share our results.

One popular way is to present your findings at a conference where other scientists and interested observers in the field convene to learn about the latest research discoveries. A conference can be the best place to learn about cutting-edge research because the researchers often present studies that have been conducted within the last few months. The two most common conference presentation formats are posters and paper presentations. For a **research poster,** the researcher visually presents the research question and rationale for asking it, the study procedure, the findings, and what the findings mean. The poster presentation is in a written format on a large bulletin board, often in a room with dozens or hundreds of other posters, where observers can read about the study and informally discuss the study with the researcher. For a **paper presentation,** the researcher presents all of the same information in an oral presentation that is very similar to giving a speech or to teaching a class. These presentations, also known as talks, often involve the use of PowerPoint, with the researcher explaining key features of the study and the results. Audience members pose questions about the research in a group format, typically at the end of the presentation.

The other primary way psychologists communicate findings is through written research papers, also referred to as research reports or articles. To help psychologists, as well as other social scientists, report study results, psychological researchers customarily write their scientific reports using a structure established by the American Psychological Association. This format, referred to as **APA style,** is a set of rules that helps researchers standardize how they communicate their study design and describe their findings. Having a formal way to write about psychological research helps minimize potential biases due to the omission of important information. A publication called the *APA Publication Manual* (American Psychological Association, 2010) provides the formatting and stylistic guidelines. The guidelines range from how to determine authorship, to how to describe measurement tools used, to how to credit references. The APA manual also outlines the various sections to include in any research report, as well as what each section should contain.

Overview Sections of APA Style

Each APA-style report begins with a **title page** that provides the title of the work along with the names of the authors and their institutional affiliations. The next page contains the **abstract,** which is a short 120–250-word summary of the entire report. The abstract is important because it is the initial, and sometimes only, piece of information that others see about the research when they are conducting

What if scientists never presented their findings? Can science advance if we do not share it? *(Chris Spiegel/Monmouth University)*

research poster a formal visual research presentation.

paper presentation a formal oral research presentation explaining key features of the study and the results.

APA style a format for writing a research report, addressing both content and formatting, that was established by the American Psychological Association and that psychology and many other social sciences use.

APA Publication Manual a publication of the American Psychological Association that details how to write research reports in APA style.

title page the first page of an APA-style report that identifies the title of the work as well as the authors and their institutional affiliations.

abstract a short summary of an entire research report that addresses the research topic, methodology used, findings, and conclusions.

literature searches on databases such as PsycINFO or PsycARTICLES. It is your chance to convince a potential reader that your report is worth reading. Therefore, the abstract must be a brief but informative and accurate portrayal of the entire report.

After the abstract, the main body of the report begins and is broken down into four specific sections: introduction, method, results, and discussion. The first section, the **introduction,** provides background information from previous research on the topic under investigation. From the introduction, the reader should have enough information to understand the importance of the work, as well as the theoretical and empirical basis for the study's hypotheses.

Next, the **method** section describes how the researcher carried out the study. In essence, the method section is like an instruction manual for anyone who might want to conduct the same study. It describes who the participants were and how they were obtained, any materials (e.g., measurement tools) used, the design of the study, and an explanation of the procedure used to collect the data.

Following the method, the **results** section outlines the researcher's findings using a combination of statistical analyses and a narrative that explains the tests the researcher used, and what the statistical results mean in plain language. This section also refers to tables and figures, which present parts of the results at the end of the paper, after the references.

The last section of the body is the **discussion,** where the researcher discusses and interprets the research findings in the context of the research question. The goal is to explain why the research turned out as it did and how it fits with previous research findings. Additionally, the discussion includes the strengths and weaknesses or limitations of the research, along with suggestions for future research and ideas for practical applications of the findings. The report concludes with a **reference page** that provides information for any sources used within the paper. For a summary of the sections of an APA paper, see **Table 2.2.**

▶ How does APA style differ from MLA style? SEE APPENDIX B, p. 493

introduction the portion of an APA-style research report that provides background literature on the topic under investigation, as well as a justification of importance for the work and the hypotheses.

method the portion of an APA-style research report in which the researcher provides details about the sample, materials, and procedure of collecting data.

results the portion of an APA-style research report that provides information about how the hypotheses were tested, explaining through statistical language, narrative, and reference to tables and graphs.

discussion the portion of an APA-style research report in which the researcher interprets, explains, and applies the results of the study.

reference page the part of an APA-style research report in which referenced literary works are given credit.

TABLE 2.2

Sections of an APA-Style Report	
Title Page	Identifies title of the work, names of the authors, and their institutional affiliations
Abstract	A short summary of the entire report
Introduction	Provides background information from previous research on the topic under investigation and the theoretical and empirical basis for the study's hypotheses
Method	Describes how the researcher carried out the study, including descriptions of the participants, materials (e.g., measurement tools), the design of the study, and how the data was collected
Results	Outlines the study's findings using a combination of statistical analyses and a narrative that explains the tests the researcher used, and what the statistical results mean in plain language
Discussion	An analysis and interpretation of the study's findings, including strengths and weaknesses, suggestions for future research, and ideas for practical applications of the findings
References	Provides information for any sources used within the paper

At first, writing APA-style papers can seem difficult due to the rules about where different types of information should go. As you become more familiar with reading these types of reports and have more practice writing them, you will see how this standardization works to your advantage. In writing your research report, you will learn exactly what types of information you need to communicate and where you should put important details in the report. Soon enough, you will also learn how to home in on specific sections of an article you are reading to extract the particular information you need.

research journal a periodical containing articles by experts in a particular field of study.

Publish the Findings

Always remember that we ask and try to answer research questions not just for our own benefit, but to advance science. This requires that we not only conduct scientifically sound studies, but that we share them with others.

Consistent with open science practices, we submit completed research papers to a **research journal**, which is a periodical containing articles describing research studies relevant to a particular field of study. Prior to publication in a research journal, each paper has gone through the peer-review process to ensure that the research made a valid contribution to the field. Publishing one's research findings is essential to the continued advancement and openness of science. Researchers rely on studies published in journals to inform their own research and help them stay current with research in their field. For example, mental health professionals will read journal articles to inform their treatment practices. Researchers may also communicate their findings through academic books, which are publications or handbooks that cover a specific scientific area. In addition, researchers may contribute a chapter in an edited book. In this case, an editor collects chapters on the same general research subject written by various researchers. Authors from more mainstream media outlets, such as magazines, newspapers, and books, may also read and summarize the research they find in scientific journals. For example, the author Malcolm Gladwell, a self-described "cover band for psychology," is known for his ability to summarize and synthesize psychological findings so that the general public can benefit from the exciting advances in knowledge that researchers have made.

As consumers of scientific information, however, we should always read about research findings with skepticism. Websites, books, magazines, news articles, and other mass media are not peer-reviewed and may not portray the science in an accurate or unbiased way. As you read about research, consider the author's credentials, the motivation for writing about the research, if the statements reference published research, who conducted the research, and what the motivation for doing so may have been. All of this will help you determine the quality of the information so you can decide if you can trust the conclusions. The more you learn about how to conduct research yourself, the better you will be at consuming scientific information from mass media sources, and basing life choices on it.

▶ How can the skills you use when consuming mass media, such as critical thinking, help you in the future? SEE CHAPTER 1, p. 18

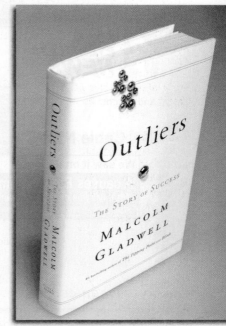

Do authors like Malcolm Gladwell, who summarize and synthesize psychological research for the general public, do more to help or hurt people's ability to learn about psychological research findings?

(Carlos Osorio/Toronto Star via Getty Images)

Why must scientists be aware of how the media presents their research findings? *("Piled Higher and Deeper"* by Jorge Cham, http://www.phdcomics.com)

YOUR TURN 2.3

1. A market researcher collects reactions to a new cookie before it hits the marketplace. The researcher tells some participants the cookie is low in calories, while other participants receive no information about the cookie. Next, each participant eats three cookies and then completes a questionnaire assessing their opinions. What is the independent variable in this study?
   a. The participants
   b. The number of cookies eaten
   c. The type of information provided about the cookie
   d. The opinions of the participants

2. A teacher wants to evaluate the effectiveness of a study strategy in helping her students learn new vocabulary words. She has some of her students learn the words using a strategy she read about in a teaching journal. She has the rest of the students study using the approach she originally taught them. The teacher then administers the vocabulary test to all of the students and compares the results of the two groups. What type of research design is the teacher employing?
   a. A longitudinal design
   b. A within-subjects design
   c. A nonexperimental design
   d. A between-subjects design

3. Which of the following is probably not very effective in helping the results from your study contribute to the scientific knowledge of psychology?
   a. Writing an APA-style paper about your study for your psychology class
   b. Submitting a paper about your study to a peer-reviewed scientific journal
   c. Giving a paper presentation on your study at a national research conference
   d. Presenting a research poster on your study at a local research conference

How did you do? Turn to the end of the chapter to check your answers.

Final Thoughts

It all starts with a question. How you answer that question is what separates the scientific thinkers from everyone else. You may or may not become a scientist one day, but the ability to use the scientific method is something that can benefit anyone. By learning the steps that scientists take to develop ideas and transform them into new and innovative findings, you will not only be able to conduct high-quality research, but will also take a more systematic approach to solving problems in your own life.

Review Questions

1. Which of the following questions is outside of the scope of science?
   a. How do parents influence their children's confidence levels?
   b. What is love?
   c. What do dreams tell us about a person?
   d. Are our lives predestined or predetermined?

2. Billy Ray is having a problem with weeds in his vegetable garden. He wants to determine the best way to control the weeds, but wants to approach it empirically. Which of the following is the best example of an empirical approach?
   a. He could go to the local home improvement store and buy whatever solution is most expensive, because if it is expensive, it must be good.
   b. He could ask his neighbor what works best in her garden.
   c. He could try out several different solutions one by one to see what works best for him.
   d. He could simply go out and pick the weeds by hand.

3. Dyala is planning her thesis and needs to generate a hypothesis. Because most people seem to think Facebook is bad for college students, she decides to study how the use of Facebook can help students' transition to college. Which of the following strategies did Dyala use to generate her hypothesis?
   a. Introspection
   b. Find the exception
   c. A matter of degree
   d. Change the directionality

4. While surfing the Internet, you come across a personality test that can determine your personality based on a combination of your favorite color, your favorite food, and your favorite hobby. Upon taking the test, you are impressed by how accurate it is. Which of the following likely explains the test's accuracy?
   a. Correspondence with reality
   b. Occam's razor
   c. Falsifiability
   d. Barnum effect

5. The owner of a coffeehouse wants to know if her customers will drink more coffee depending on the smell of the room. To test this, she hires a psychologist who sets up three similar rooms, each with its own smell (coffee, cinnamon buns, or bacon and eggs), then arranges to have 30 students spend an afternoon in each room while being allowed to drink all the coffee they like.

The amount each participant drinks is recorded for each of the three scents. What is the dependent variable?

a. Amount of coffee consumed

b. Coffee, cinnamon buns, bacon and eggs

c. Room scent

d. Time spent in each room

6. Andrea and Beau are doing a study to see if puppies and sunshine make people happy. To test this, they randomly assign 500 male and female participants to one of the following conditions: exposure to puppies and sunshine or no exposure to puppies and sunshine. Both conditions take place out on the college's quad. Participants complete measures of life satisfaction and general happiness. What is the independent variable(s)?

a. Sitting out on the quad

b. Life satisfaction

c. Happiness

d. Puppies and sunshine

7. In a study of first-year college students from a private university in California, 56 men and 88 women examined the influence of relaxation techniques on relieving anxiety associated with starting college. All students received a pamphlet containing information about good sleep habits. Next, half of the participants were taught a breathing exercise while the other half did nothing. What is the constant?

a. The sleep-habit pamphlet

b. The breathing exercise

c. Relaxation techniques

d. Anxiety

8. In an experimental design, the researcher manipulates the _____ and measures the _____.

a. criterion variable; predictor variable

b. dependent variable; independent variable

c. independent variable; dependent variable

d. experimental variable; nonexperimental variable

9. You see a video online in which a prominent businesswoman explains that her experience in a specialized kindergarten class that focused on creativity and individuality is the reason for her success. You decide to test this by following a group of children from age 5 until age 25 to see if their educational experiences correspond with their career success. What type of design would be the best way to study this?

a. Experimental

b. Longitudinal

c. Between-subjects

d. Cross-sectional

10. A psychologist was hired by a local winery to conduct a taste test of four new wines. For the taste test, the psychologist had 100 participants come into the lab, take a small sip of each wine, and rate the taste on several characteristics. Between each wine, participants ate a small cracker. What type of design did the psychologist use?

    a. Nonexperimental
    b. Longitudinal
    c. Between-subjects
    d. Within-subjects

11. Why is it important for studies to undergo peer review? What could happen if this process was not in place?

12. Describe the reasons for using a nonexperimental design.

13. What are the benefits of using statistics to help us draw conclusions?

Applying What You've Learned

1. What is your favorite topic in psychology? Conduct a literature search in PsycINFO or PsycARTICLES. Next, do the same search in Google or Bing. Compare and contrast the types of results that you get.

2. Take a walk around campus. Based on what you observe, generate 10 different research questions (e.g., Do people in expensive cars stop for less time at stop signs than people in inexpensive cars do?).

3. Generate a hypothesis using each of the following techniques: introspection; find the exception; a matter of degree; and change the directionality.

4. Here is a hypothesis from a student in Introduction to Psychology: *Kids who grow up with one father do better in life, school, overall functioning, and happiness.* Evaluate this hypothesis using each of the following: correspondence with reality; parsimony; specificity; and falsifiability.

5. The term "cheating" can have many different meanings. Provide at least three distinct operational definitions that a researcher could use for this term.

6. Read through the Method section of the following study:

   Bushman, B. J., & Anderson, C. A. (2009). Comfortably numb: Desensitizing effects of violent media on helping others. *Psychological Science, 20*(3), 273–277.

   Based on what you read, re-create the research protocol that the researchers used.

7. People love to communicate the findings of their study. Go to Google Images and search for "psychology research poster." You'll see lots of examples of research posters. What do you notice about them? How do they compare to a research journal article or to a paper presentation?

Key Concepts

abstract, p. 45

APA Publication Manual, p. 45

APA style, p. 45

Barnum effect, p. 34

between-subjects design, p. 40

conceptual definition, p. 38

constant, p. 38

correlational design, p. 39

criterion variable, p. 39

data, p. 43

debriefing, p. 43

dependent variable (DV), p. 38

discussion, p. 46

empirical, p. 27

experimental design, p. 38

explanatory variable, p. 39

hypothesis, p. 31

independent variable (IV), p. 38

informed consent, p. 43

introduction, p. 46

levels, p. 40

longitudinal design, p. 40

method, p. 46

nonexperimental design, p. 39

Occam's razor, p. 34

open science, p. 42

operational definition, p. 38

paper presentation, p. 45

peer review, p. 29

predictor variable, p. 39

programmatic research, p. 41

reference page, p. 46

research journal, p. 47

research poster, p. 45

research protocol, p. 43

response variable, p. 39

results, p. 46

scientific law, p. 31

scientific theory, p. 31

script, p. 43

title page, p. 45

variables, p. 37

within-subjects design, p. 40

Answers to YOUR TURN

Your Turn 2.1: 1. b; 2. a; 3. d

Your Turn 2.2: 1. b; 2. a; 3. c

Your Turn 2.3: 1. c; 2. d; 3. a

Answers to Multiple-Choice Review Questions

1. d; 2. c; 3. b; 4. d; 5. a; 6. d; 7. a; 8. c; 9. b; 10. d

Ethics
Making Ethical Decisions in Research

Olivier-26/Deposit Photos

BENEFITS   COST

LEARNING OUTCOMES

After reading this chapter, you should be able to:

- Provide examples of ethically questionable studies.

- Explain the meaning of "ethics" and why ethical considerations are an important part of the research process.

- Describe the important APA ethical principles that guide how scientists conduct research.

- Outline the ethical considerations and decisions associated with the planning and conducting of a research study.

- Describe the role of the Institutional Review Board and the Institutional Animal Care and Use Committee for ensuring the ethical treatment of humans and animals in research studies.

- Explain how ethical considerations are relevant to the analyses and presentation of research findings.

Something to Think About . . .

Just like that, it hit him. Research ideas really can come to you at any moment. At that particular moment, Don was sitting on the couch watching a basic cable show about war veterans' experiences in Afghanistan. On the show, Army Sergeant Huth recounted the details of a roadside bomb explosion that nearly killed several soldiers in his convoy. The show's host remarked on Sergeant Huth's impressive ability to recall everything that happened with incredible detail. Don is amazed, but also excited and intrigued. His excitement is not about the soldier's awful experiences; rather, Don is excited by the potential research possibilities. Don is actually Dr. Don Tknoethicks, a famous research psychologist who studies memory in educational settings (basically, he is an expert on improving the effectiveness of students' studying). Dr. Don wonders if Sergeant Huth remembered the events in such vivid detail because the information coincided with a traumatic experience. If Dr. Don can test this hypothesis by creating a similar extreme experience in an educational setting, he may have found the secret to improving students' performance on tests.

Dr. Don immediately starts brainstorming ways to test his research idea. His first thought is to force participants to memorize word lists at gunpoint. But he worries that is too extreme; people might honestly fear for their lives. Instead, he could ask participants to watch an extremely graphic and bloody video of a car accident. But it might be hard to obtain such a video. Dr. Don has a lot of ideas, but he needs something more practical. He then recalls research showing that you can create false memories in people (Loftus & Pickrell, 1995). The trick would be to create a false memory that would lead the participant to experience a high level of trauma. Dr. Don settles on creating the false memory that the participant had been attacked by a stray dog when he or she was 4 years old, resulting in severe injuries. He thinks this might be traumatic enough to scientifically test his hypothesis about memory improvement. Now Dr. Don needs to design a scientific approach to testing whether or not participants who "recall" this traumatic experience while engaging in a memory task remember more than those who do not recall a trauma.

Clearly, Dr. Don's research question is an interesting one, and his study may provide scientifically useful answers. However, in science, that is not the most important issue. Rather, we need to decide if the benefit of acquiring new knowledge outweighs participants' potentially negative experiences. More generally, it is an issue of whether or not there should be limits on how far scientists can go in their pursuit of knowledge. We will explore these issues in this chapter.

What Are Ethics?

Decisions about whether or not a researcher should conduct a study require ethical judgments. **Ethics** involves the application of moral principles concerning what an individual considers right and wrong to help guide one's decisions and behavior. However, when dealing with ethics, the "right" answer can often be difficult to identify. Consider the following:

> Prior to your midterm in your introduction to psychology course, the professor informs the class that a copy of the exam has mysteriously disappeared from her office. She says that if the guilty party does not come forward, all 100 students in the class will receive a zero. Due to your university's strict honor code, the dean will certainly expel the person who stole the exam. You know it was your best friend who took it.

Knowing the best course of action in this situation is difficult. On the one hand, if you stay quiet, you and your 99 other classmates will all receive a zero on the exam, which will compromise your grade in the class, your overall GPA, and possibly your chances of going to graduate school. On the other hand, you are not comfortable telling on your best friend, especially since it will result in her being kicked out of school. So, what should you do? It is this tension between potential costs and benefits that is the foundation of most ethical dilemmas, as well as ethical decisions in psychology.

Ultimately, there is no definitive right or wrong answer to ethical dilemmas. Instead, individuals develop their own personal code of ethics based on their own perspectives and experiences. For example, in the case of the psychology test, you may adopt the **utilitarian perspective** that your decision should do the greatest good for the greatest number of people. Another person may take an

ethics the application of moral principles to help guide one's decisions and behavior.

utilitarian perspective the perspective that ethical decisions should be based on doing the greatest good for the greatest number of people.

altruistic perspective, which involves helping without personal benefit. From this viewpoint, the best action is the most selfless action, although that person may have to decide whether it is more selfless to take the zero on the midterm or to sacrifice the friendship for the good of the class. Still another person may ascribe to **egoism,** which states that individuals should act in accordance with their own self-interests. Similarly, individual scientists may hold different views on ethical issues in a study. Due to the potential for individual variation, science has established a set of ethical principles to help guide decision making.

> **What Do You Think?**
> How could utilitarianism, altruism, and egoism apply to a psychologist's research process?

Important Ethical Principles

All scientists are enthusiastic about pursuing answers to their research question. They are eager to find support for their hypotheses, add to scientific knowledge, and potentially improve others' lives. However, this enthusiasm can lead to ethically questionable decisions concerning participants' treatment. In many cases, these lapses are not intentional, as potential ethical problems are often not obvious. After all, on some level, ethical decisions are subjective. What one person feels is necessary, another might find questionable. As a result, it takes standards and an outside perspective to determine whether it is ethical to pursue a particular research question.

To aid in this process, in the late 1970s the U.S. federal government published a report titled "Ethical Principles and Guidelines for the Protection of Human Subjects of Research," that later was simply referred to as the Belmont Report. The report outlines three basic ethical principles to follow when conducting research involving humans: beneficence, justice, and respect for persons. These values are reflected in three of the five General Principles underlying the American Psychological Association's "Ethical Principles of Psychologists and Code of Conduct" (APA, 2017). We will discuss the APA's other two principles, "fidelity and responsibility" and "integrity," later in this chapter.

Principle 1: Beneficence and Nonmaleficence

Because psychologists must rely on others' help to pursue knowledge, we are ethically obligated at the beginning of any research endeavor to conduct a **cost-benefit analysis** to ensure that our study's potential positive outcomes exceed potential negative experiences or risks to participants. First, we must consider the potential benefits derived from our investigation. As scientists, we value **beneficence**—acting with the purpose of benefiting others. Our research should have the potential to benefit society, the field, and/or the participants involved. At the same time, when considering benefits, researchers should not factor in potential personal benefits for themselves (e.g., getting published, obtaining fame or money, etc.).

The ethical imperative to maximize the benefits derived from our investigation is not an easy one. We do not always fully know our study's potential benefits or how the knowledge that our study contributes to science may ultimately benefit society or the lives of individuals. Still, in order to conduct the study, we must have a well-founded theoretical reason to believe that our work has the potential to benefit the psychological or larger community. At a minimum, we should maximize the benefits that our participants derive from being in our

altruistic perspective the perspective that ethical decisions should be based on helping without personal benefit.

egoism the perspective that ethical decisions should be based on acting in accordance with one's own self-interest.

cost-benefit analysis an ethical principle of research in which a researcher weighs all the potential and known benefits against all the potential and known risks before conducting a study.

beneficence actively promoting the welfare of others; an ethical obligation to maximize benefits in research studies.

nonmaleficence do no harm; an ethical obligation to mitigate or eliminate risks to study participants.

loss of confidentiality a failure to protect the privacy of individuals; a potential risk to participants.

anonymity a guarantee in research studies that individual responses cannot be linked back to individual participants.

physical harm a physical toll that study participation may have; a potential risk to participants.

A U.S. public service announcement about venereal diseases in the 1940s. The Guatemalan venereal disease studies led to a treatment plan for the army. Do you think the benefit of the treatment plan outweighed the costs of purposefully infecting participants? *(U.S. National Library of Medicine, History of Medicine Division)*

study. For example, benefits may include learning about the research process, monetary payment, or credit toward a college course assignment.

Obviously, a cost-benefit analysis is not complete without considering the potential costs of conducting the research. Here the goal is **nonmaleficence**, which means that researchers should do no harm. We must minimize or eliminate any potential risks to the participants in our study. These risks can come in many different forms. Regardless of the topic under investigation, researchers must avoid the potential risk of the **loss of confidentiality**, which involves the responses or behaviors of individual participants becoming public knowledge or the focus of public scrutiny. Assuring participants of confidentiality is not the same as promising the anonymity of their responses. **Anonymity** involves the pledge that participants' individual responses cannot be linked back to their personal identity. In many studies, researchers can assure confidentiality, but cannot guarantee anonymity. For example, if a participant provides an e-mail address, it is possible to link the data back to their name. Interestingly, research suggests that participants are more concerned about the confidentiality than the anonymity of their responses (e.g., Moore & Ames, 2002).

The work of Laud Humphreys (1975) illustrates the priority researchers place on maintaining confidentiality of participants' responses. During the mid-1960s, Humphreys, a doctoral student in sociology, was interested in learning about ostensibly heterosexual men who engaged in impersonal homosexual acts in public restrooms. Humphreys eventually garnered the trust of some of these men, who were then willing to be interviewed for his study. Given the sensitivity of his research, Humphreys was particularly diligent in protecting the confidentiality of his participants. For example, he kept the master list of potential participants locked in a safe-deposit box; no names or other identifying information appeared on the questionnaires; and he destroyed all individual interview notes. Humphreys even allowed police to arrest him rather than reveal that he was doing research on this population of men. But while he might have worked diligently to protect his participants' names, Humphreys potentially violated participants' privacy in other ways. He used false pretenses to convince people to participate, including not revealing that he was a researcher. Therefore, participants may have revealed private information to him that they would have otherwise kept to themselves. Given the maneuvers he used to pursue his research question, the issue of whether or not Humphreys invaded his participants' privacy remains.

Another potential cost of conducting research is **physical harm**. In 2010, it was revealed that during the 1940s, the U.S. government, concerned about the impact of venereal diseases on troops, oversaw a series of studies in Guatemala that involved purposefully infecting participants, sometimes without their knowledge, in an effort to test potential treatments (Walter, 2012). The researchers also exposed volunteer inmates from a federal prison in Indiana to bacteria collected from local prostitutes. In some cases, participants were encouraged to have sex with infected prostitutes so that researchers could learn how individuals naturally contract venereal diseases. Although physical harm is a much greater concern in medical research, psychologists must sometimes consider the physical toll that studies may have on research participants. For example, psychologists who study disrupted sleep patterns or sleep deprivation must be conscious of the physical risk that might be entailed.

Psychological harm—emotional suffering or mental distress such as concern, worry, and decreased self-esteem—is perhaps the most relevant risk when conducting psychological research. As such, we must be sure to eliminate or reduce any form of psychological discomfort that participation in our study might cause. Two of the most famous psychology studies—Milgram's (1974) obedience studies, in which participants were told to deliver potentially lethal shocks to other participants, and Zimbardo, Haney, Banks, and Jatle's (1973) Stanford prison study, in which participants acting as guards began to abuse other participants who were role-playing as prisoners—both involved the potential for psychological harm. You might assume that any study that causes stress or negative emotions in participants is not ethically permissible. However, ethical decisions are more complicated than that. While the ultimate goal is never to have our participants under duress, sometimes it is necessary, especially when the purpose of one's research is to study the impact of psychological stress on individuals, as was the case in the Stanford prison study.

The key issue is how to induce stress without causing harm. If psychological distress is necessary, then we must ensure that the effects are short-term and have been dispelled before the participants leave the experiment situation. That is, participants should leave the study in the same (or better) physical and psychological state that they were in at the start of the study. Ultimately, we must be confident that the potential benefits derived from our study outweigh the potential costs.

As we consider the costs of conducting our research, we must also weigh the **cost of not doing the research**. For example, perhaps you believe that you can pinpoint how various fears (e.g., spiders, dogs, clowns) develop in individuals, but you need to induce extreme fear in your participants to scientifically demonstrate your idea. Certainly, psychologists could use your study's findings to develop new treatments for phobias. However, you may decide against conducting this potentially important study because it might cause short-term stress for the participants. One could argue that not pursuing this line of research is unethical because of its potential to improve people's lives. Therefore, we must also consider the impact of not doing the research in our cost-benefit analysis.

For any study that you consider conducting, you have to weigh all the potential and known benefits against all the potential and known risks, keeping in mind that there is a cost to not doing the study, as well. Perhaps ethical decisions are not so easy after all.

Principle 2: Justice

Another ethical consideration is **justice**, which involves fairness when deciding who to use as study participants and what role they will play in

psychological harm a psychological toll that study participation may have such as stress, negative emotions, or loss of self-esteem; a potential risk to participants.

cost of not doing the research considering the potential beneficial application of study findings when doing a cost-benefit analysis.

justice fairness in selecting study participants and in determining which participants receive the benefits of participation and which bear the burden of risk.

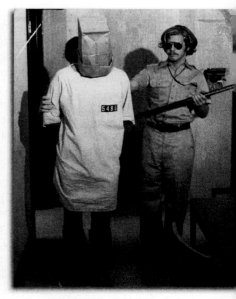

During the summer of 1971, Philip Zimbardo studied prison life by building a mock-up of a prison. This study caused psychological distress, but brought to life the complex world of prison dynamics. How do we determine the cost of not doing the research? *(Duke Downey/San Francisco Chronicle/Polaris)*

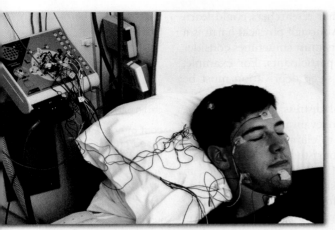

Psychologists must consider both the physical and psychological risks of their studies. What other areas of psychological research have the potential to physically harm participants? *(HANK MORGAN/Science Source/Getty Images)*

the study. First, justice in participant selection means that we choose participants equitably, such that we avoid targeting a particularly weak or vulnerable group to participate in our study, even if including them would be easy or convenient for us. This idea may seem obvious, but, historically, medical research has unfairly selected participants who were powerless in society. For example, from 1932 to 1972, the U.S. Public Health Service conducted a study on syphilis using nearly 400 low-income African American men from rural Tuskegee, Alabama, most of whom were illiterate sharecroppers. The researchers never told the participants they had syphilis, nor did they treat any participants for it because the goal of the research was to study the natural progression of untreated syphilis. Similarly, in 1939, Wendell Johnson, a speech expert and psychologist, hypothesized that stuttering was a learned behavior resulting from parental criticism. To test this, he selected 22 nonstuttering children from a local orphanage, repeatedly told them they were stutterers, and exposed them to badgering for every speech imperfection, with the goal of turning them into stutterers (Dyer, 2001). Focusing this questionable research on children from an orphanage demonstrates a lack of justice because these children probably did not enjoy the same protections as children with parents.

Current ethical standards dictate that we avoid targeting vulnerable individuals, including prisoners and other individuals in institutions such as mental hospitals, who may be at risk for coercion, and that we implement special safeguards ensuring that researchers do not exploit these populations given their inability to refuse participation in a study. However, these populations are not always off-limits. If we can show how our research question requires using a vulnerable population, and we can demonstrate the potential benefits, it may be ethical to include them as research participants.

The principle of justice mandates that there is a fair process in determining which participants receive the benefits of participation and which bear the burdens of risks. The goal is equality in the distribution of cost and benefits. For example, suppose that you wanted to evaluate the effectiveness of a new psychotherapy treatment. After recruiting participants for your study, you must decide who will receive your promising new psychotherapy technique and who will receive the current method of treatment. In this case, some participants will potentially receive the benefit of a better treatment, while others will potentially receive a less effective treatment. Because the new treatment may cost more than the regular treatment, you could assign participants with less money to the cheaper treatment, while those participants who can afford to pay for the more costly therapy receive the new treatment. However, this would be unethical because you would be depriving one group of a treatment due to factors extraneous to the study (in this example, their socioeconomic status). The ethical way to handle the distribution of costs and benefits is to assign people to groups randomly. That way, you equally distribute the burdens of risk and the benefits.

Suppose that during the course of the study it becomes clear that one particular treatment is more effective than the other treatment. Should you continue the study, depriving the group receiving the less effective treatment in order to maintain the sanctity of your original study plan? The ethical answer is no. At this point, the decision that exhibits the most justice is to end the study and make the more effective treatment available to all participants. In an experiment investigating the use of aspirin to prevent heart attacks, the researchers deemed that it would be unethical to not give aspirin to some of the participants when the benefits of aspirin in preventing heart attacks, as well as in preventing deaths from heart attacks, became clear (Steering Committee of the Physicians' Health Study Research Group, 1988). In the Tuskegee study, especially, researchers crossed an ethical line when they decided that it was more important to learn about the long-term effects of syphilis than to contribute to the well-being of those who suffered from it. Penicillin would have cured this disease, the negative symptoms of which include tumors, heart disease, paralysis, blindness, insanity, and death.

The Tuskegee syphilis study targeted a vulnerable population and involved significant deception. What changes to the research protocol could researchers have made to continue this research in an ethical way?
(Courtesy of the National Archives at Atlanta)

Principle 3: Respect for Persons

After assessing the ethical costs and benefits of your research, and ensuring that it is not unjust to any particular populations, you need to ensure that your study respects participants' **autonomy,** or has respect for persons. Autonomy is the idea that people are capable of making deliberate, informed decisions about their participation in research. That is, people should have the right to choose whether or not to be involved in your study. This principle recognizes the right of individuals to self-determination, the ability to make decisions about their own behaviors and outcomes.

You might be wondering what a participant's free choice has to do with your role as the researcher. First, participation must be voluntary. Your study must involve individuals who knowingly and willingly chose to serve as participants. As a researcher, you cannot coerce your participants in any way that could limit their freedom to consent. Sometimes coercion is obvious. For example, you cannot threaten or bribe individuals to participate in your study. Other times, coercion can be subtle, such as in situations where a researcher is also a person who has power over others. For example, in college settings, professors should not specifically recruit students from their classes for their own experiments. Doing so might make students feel compelled to participate in the study because the professor assigns the final grades in the class, or the student simply does not want to disappoint the professor. Professors can still recruit college students for their own studies; they just need to ensure that such participation is voluntary and that there are no adverse consequences if their own students decline to participate. Coercion was a distinct possibility in the famous Little Albert

autonomy freely making an informed decision about participation in research.

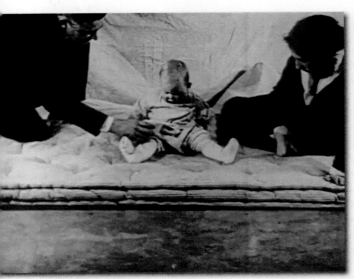

The study on Little Albert advanced the understanding of classical conditioning. But is it right for researchers to use people working for or under them as research participants?

(Penn State Media Archives)

▶ Interested in learning more about informed consent? SEE CHAPTER 2, p. 43

study, in which John Watson taught a reportedly healthy 9-month-old baby ("Albert") to fear a white rat by making a loud, startling, and unpleasant noise each time Albert saw the rat (Watson & Rayner, 1920). It was later revealed that Little Albert's mother was a low-level employee working with Watson, which suggests that she may not have been in a position to refuse such participation (Fridlund, Beck, Goldie, & Irons, 2012). This may explain why a mother would allow her baby to participate in a study designed to terrify the child.

To ensure autonomy, the researcher should obtain informed consent from each participant. This procedure involves providing potential participants with enough information about the study, including the potential risks and benefits of participation, in order for them to make an informed decision about whether or not to participate. But wait a second. What if, during a study about lying, you tell the participants exactly what the study is about? Wouldn't it be impossible to gauge their natural reactions? In cases like this, scientists cannot be completely forthcoming about the goals and purpose of their research at the start of a study. Occasionally, knowledge of this sort might prevent the participants from acting naturally during the course of the experiment itself.

In Milgram's experiments on obedience, participants believed they were actually delivering harmful shocks to the learner at the request of the researcher. In reality, the learner was part of the experiment and there were no real shocks. It is highly unlikely that Milgram would have been able to systematically investigate the impact of an authority figure on obedience if the participants had known from the beginning that the shocks were fake. Remember that, as psychologists, we are trying to understand the true nature of human behavior. However, we also have an ethical obligation to provide participants with the information they need to make an informed decision. For this reason, we must be honest about the types and number of activities participants will be asked to do, but we may not need to be completely forthcoming about why they are engaging in these tasks. Informed consent also notifies participants of their right to refuse participation or to terminate their participation at any time without penalty. That is right! A participant must be able to leave the study at any time without any negative consequences. This means that, as the researcher, you must continue to offer any promised benefits, such as a little gift or extra credit, to participants even if they decide not to complete the study.

In most studies, to obtain informed consent, a researcher has potential participants sign a form that describes the general purpose and nature of the study, the potential risks and benefits that can result from participation, and their right to terminate participation at any point during the course of the study (**Figure 3.1**).

ANYWHERE UNIVERSITY I.R.B.
INFORMED CONSENT FOR:
Problem Solving & Relationships

Researcher: Dr. Will B. Aethickle; waethick@anywhere.edu; 555-867-5309

I am engaged in a research study of how problem solving influences relationship behaviors. To help gain further insights into this topic, I will ask you to complete a number series, complete several brief questionnaires, and fill out a demographics questionnaire. This process should take approximately 20 minutes.

The data you provide will be recorded anonymously and your participation and anything you say during the session will be held in the strictest confidence. By University regulations, this informed consent statement will be filed separately from your response, so no one will know that the answers/responses you provide are yours. There are no foreseeable risks or harm for participating in the study. It is possible that participating in this study may make some people uncomfortable. This study will benefit you through providing class research credits, and by allowing you to learn about the research process.

You can ask questions about the research study or about being a participant at any time via e-mail at waethick@anywhere.edu. In addition, for any research questions, please contact the Coordinator of the Anywhere University Institutional Review Board (IRB) by phone at 555-903-5768 or via e-mail at irb@anywhere.edu.

Your participation in this study is voluntary and you may withdraw at any time. You may refuse or discontinue participation at any time without consequence or prejudice.

If your participation in our research has caused you to feel uncomfortable in any way, or if our research prompted you to consider personal matters about which you are concerned, we encourage you to take advantage of the confidential counseling services offered at Anywhere University. You can contact a counselor at 555-246-8107.

Signing your name below indicates that you have read and understand the contents of this Consent Form and that you agree to participate in this study.

Consent

I have read the above information and I fully understand the nature of my participation. I understand that my involvement in this study will be confidential, and that if a summary of the results is used for educational or publication purposes, my individual results will not be identified. I also understand that I have the right to terminate my participation at any time during the study. I understand the risks of participating in the study, including the self-consciousness I may feel while participating. Lastly, I certify that I am over 18 years of age.

_____   _____
Participant's Signature   Researcher's Signature (after reading the consent statement)

_____   _____
Printed Name   Printed Name

_____   _____
Date   Date

FIGURE 3.1 Sample Informed Consent Form.

This informed consent form should minimize scientific jargon such as "randomized experiment." It is typical to write the form at a sixth- to eighth-grade reading level so that it is easily understood by most people (Paasche-Orlow, Taylor, & Brancati, 2003). Sometimes we want to conduct our research on a group that cannot give legal consent to be in our study, such as people under 18 years of age, those with mental impairments, or psychiatric patients. In these cases, a legal guardian must provide informed consent. Additionally, the researcher, if possible, asks the participant to give **assent**, which is an active affirmation of a desire to participate that acknowledges that, at least legally, the participant is not capable of providing their own informed consent.

As you can see, the researcher plays an important role in ensuring the ethical treatment of participants. To avoid ethical violations, researchers must maximize the study's benefits while minimizing the risks, treat participants fairly and equitably, and respect participants' right to make decisions about their role in the study. See **Table 3.1** for a summary of the three basic ethical principles for human research.

TABLE 3.1

The Principles of Ethical Research	
Beneficence and Nonmaleficence	Actively promoting the welfare of others; an ethical obligation to maximize benefits in research studies while minimizing risk.
Justice	Fairness in selecting study participants and in determining which participants receive the benefits of participation and which bear the burden of risk.
Respect for Persons	Participants must freely make an informed decision about their participation in research.

 Research Spotlight

Can Voluntary Participation Be Coerced?

The Nuremberg Code for Human Experimentation is a set of research ethics principles that was developed in 1949 in response to the medical experiments performed in prison camps during World War II. It explicitly states that "the voluntary consent of the human subject is absolutely essential." However, can researchers coerce individuals to "voluntarily" participate in a research study? This is an important consideration when recruiting participants from special or vulnerable populations, such as prisoners. From the mid-1940s to 1974, researchers recruited inmates from the Holmesburg Prison in Philadelphia, Pennsylvania, to participate in medical experiments that ranged from testing the effectiveness of deodorants and foot powder to evaluating the efficacy of chemical agents for use in chemical warfare (Hornblum, 1998). The inmates could make

assent an active affirmation of a desire to participate from a person who does not have the ability to consent themselves; consent must also be sought from the legal guardian.

$300–$400 a month by participating in the ongoing medical experiments as opposed to earning 15 cents a day working in the other areas of the prison. While the prisoners received compensation, the question remains as to whether or not their participation was truly voluntary. Many repeatedly volunteered for experiments, but often without full awareness of or consideration for the potential short- and long-term consequences. Dr. Albert Kligman, a University of Pennsylvania scientist and the principal investigator, defended his practice of using paid subjects as being consistent with the ethical practices at the time (Goodman, 1998). However, today's ethical standards would suggest that he was taking advantage of this vulnerable population.

Researchers coerced prisoners from Holmesburg Prison into research participation with irresistible financial compensation. What types of benefits could researchers have offered that were less coercive? *(Photo by Michael J. Maicher, Philadelphia Evening Bulletin 2/27/66. Special Collections Research Center, Temple University Libraries, Philadelphia, PA)*

Ethics Through a Historical Lens

Looking back at some of the transgressions in the classic studies, we see that many of them seem serious and some even violate more than one ethical principle. Yet, in each case, the researchers learned information that might have been beneficial to others. Thus, it would be an oversimplification to condemn any one of these studies as being completely wrong or unethical. In fact, it was only after controversial work like Milgram's that the U.S. federal government issued ethical principles for conducting research. These now infamous studies were beneficial in the sense that they helped lead to the establishment of ethical guidelines. In retrospect, it is readily apparent that these studies are questionable, but to the researchers at the time, this may have been less obvious. The scientists responsible for these studies were most likely not purposely trying to harm participants. More likely, the types of studies and techniques they were using were so new that the scientists were not able to fully consider the ramifications of their actions.

There is also an inclination to think, "Those things happened a long time ago. Certainly, modern-day scientists know better and would never do anything like that." To some extent, that is true. As George Santayana said, "Those who cannot remember the past are condemned to repeat it." Thankfully, the field of psychology has learned from some of its mistakes, as well as from the mistakes of other scientific disciplines. In light of these experiences, scientists have refined their ethical judgments to be more aware of the issues. This awareness helps us avoid making obvious lapses in judgment, and helps guide our decision making when we consider more subtle ethical issues that can arise in research. The fact is that research involving humans and animals will always raise ethical issues. In many ways, evaluating research today can be more challenging because ethical violations are often less blatant, presenting themselves in more nuanced ways. This may help us understand why the APA bases its ethical principles on general principles instead of specific ethical standards for conducting research. These principles are intentionally aspirational, calling on researchers to engage in the highest ethical behavior.

Being mindful of ethical considerations does not mean that sensitive topics are off-limits. Rather, it means that we need to be more creative and ingenious in how we design our studies. Often this may involve a trade-off, where you study a smaller and more benign aspect of a potentially harmful issue. For example, stealing, cheating, and aggression, although important to understand, are social taboos that can be ethically challenging to study. To investigate how people might react to opportunities to be dishonest, researchers gave some participants an opportunity to cheat on a history test or steal quarters; gave some the opportunity, but later withdrew it in the middle of the study; and gave some no opportunity to cheat or steal at all (Whitaker, Melzer, Steffgen, & Bushman, 2013). Afterward, participants in each situation selected which fictitious video games they preferred to play, supposedly as part of another study. Those who had the opportunity to cheat or steal revoked midstudy were more likely to select violent video games. Withdrawing the opportunity to commit a taboo led to frustration and to selecting an outlet for aggression.

While research on sensitive topics is necessary and beneficial, you can also see the need for ethical consideration. The researchers in the cheating study were careful to test participants' desire for an aggressive outlet by using a harmless but violent video game instead of giving participants the choice to harm a real target. The researchers also minimized the social taboo by providing a controlled environment in which the infractions were minor and took place in a private lab setting. It is better to offer participants the opportunity to cheat on a fake test than to force people to cheat on their taxes or standardized tests in real life. Researchers must treat sensitive topics carefully to protect participants from harm. Like all research, the research on cheating and violent video games underwent an ethical review before data collection started. Still, research like this demonstrates how ethics is an ongoing issue in modern psychology and highlights the importance of upholding ethical principles so that history does not repeat itself.

Thinking Like a Scientist in Real Life

Keeping Things in Context

Whenever you evaluate if something is good or bad, or right or wrong, it is important to consider it in context, especially historical context. While a quick review of the classic studies may leave you with the impression that people in the "old days" were ethically challenged, you should be cautious not to condemn them too quickly. As they say, hindsight is 20/20, which is to say that it is easy to see things clearly in retrospect. For example, the soft drink Coca-Cola contained cocaine up until 1929, something we could never imagine being permissible today. Yet, at the time, it was an acceptable drink. (This might make you wonder what the future will think about the highly caffeinated energy drinks that we routinely consume today.) It is also important to recognize just how far our understanding has evolved. As recently as the 1970s, many did not understand the potentially harmful effects of smoking, and psychologists described homosexuality as a disorder in the *Diagnostic and Statistical Manual of Mental Disorders (DSM)*. When you look back on some of the classic studies and their ethically questionable procedures, you must consider their historical context and remember that our scientific understanding and ethical sensitivity were not the same as they are today. In that context, studies focused on obedience and treating venereal diseases to help troops were attempting to address highly relevant issues at the time.

YOUR TURN 3.1

1. Which of the following would *most* likely represent an ethical dilemma for a person?
   a. Obeying the speed limit
   b. Determining whether or not to report your manager at work for stealing from the register
   c. Deciding whether or not to adhere to your workplace's dress code
   d. Cheating on your income taxes

2. Selecting only homeless individuals to participate in our study even though we have no real theoretical reason to use the homeless violates which ethical principle?
   a. Beneficence
   b. Nonmaleficence
   c. Justice
   d. Autonomy

3. An informed consent form should address all of the following *except*
   a. any foreseeable risks or discomfort.
   b. that the participant's participation is voluntary.
   c. that the participant cannot quit after signing the informed consent.
   d. that the responses will be confidential.

How did you do? Turn to the end of the chapter to check your answers.

Putting Ethics Into Practice

Making ethical decisions during the planning stages of research is essential, but your ethical responsibilities do not end there. You must be mindful of ethical considerations throughout the research process. This is particularly true when researching sensitive topics like sexual conduct, risky or potentially harmful behaviors, or experiences that may threaten a participant's self-esteem. Bullying is one such topic that has become the focus of much public discussion, resulting in major educational reforms and changes in legislation. The concerns are justified, as bullying is a widespread phenomenon with serious consequences, such as low self-esteem (Callaghan & Joseph, 1995) and depression (Klomek, Marrocco, Kleinman, Schonfeld, & Gould, 2007). Bullying behavior takes many forms, such as verbal and physical intimidation, relational aggression (i.e., a deliberate manipulation of one's relationships or social status), and cyberbullying. Continued research on this sensitive topic is important as we investigate the long-term consequences bullying can have on its victims. The challenge is how to investigate this topic ethically, keeping the principles of costs and benefits, justice, and autonomy in mind.

As always, first we need to decide what aspect of bullying we want to study. Research exists on the long-term effects of bullying (e.g., Schreier et al., 2009), so our study would be most beneficial if it focused on people's immediate responses to bullying, such as isolating themselves or affiliating with others. Thus, our research question could be, "Do individuals respond to bullying by seeking out others or by seeking isolation?"

Making Ethical Decisions About Your Study

To answer this question, we will need to compare a bullied group to a nonbullied group to see if the groups respond differently. Although bullying occurs in everyday life, it is an inherently distressing experience. It is difficult to explore this topic ethically because intentionally creating a bullying experience as part of a study could potentially harm participants. However, because bullying creates distress for people, it is vital that research help us better understand the topic. That is, we must do our cost-benefit analysis and consider the ethical ramifications of conducting the research, but also the ramifications if we do not conduct the research.

Sensitive research like this requires us to think through our various options, weighing the potential benefits and risks involved. Remember that our first ethical principle requires that the potential benefits of our study outweigh any risks it may pose. To accomplish this, we must be sure to eliminate or reduce any form of psychological distress or discomfort our study might cause, while collecting data in the way that is most beneficial to understanding the real experience. You might be wondering what our options are for studying bullying. Here are a few thoughts:

1. The first, most obvious option would be to have one group experience actual, real-life bullying from a **confederate**, or an accomplice, of the experimenter. While this would closely approximate a real-life bullying experience, it may be too emotionally or psychologically stressful to the participants and, therefore, ultimately have too much risk.

confederate an accomplice of the experimenter.

2. Another option is to study bullying in a natural setting with no interference from the researchers. For example, we could spend time on local playgrounds in order to identify bullying that is already occurring, and monitor children's responses (e.g., if they find a new group to play with or play alone after bullying). Although this seems simple, the ethical obligations in this scenario are complex. For instance, once we identify a bully, we would have an ethical obligation to intervene and reduce suffering.

3. One low-risk way to conduct this research is to ask one group of people to read a story in which a peer bullies the participant, while another group reads a neutral story. This method would mitigate the risk, but it also would have fewer benefits. How participants react after reading a story about bullying may be very different from their reaction to a true experience, so the results may not be as useful.

4. Instead of reading about someone else's experiences, we could ask people to write a story about their own personal experiences with bullying. This method might cause some people to temporarily experience sadness, anger, or embarrassment as they relive their experiences, but this should be milder than the emotion experienced in the original situation. The data gathered using this method would more closely relate to real-life experiences of bullying and, therefore, would be more applicable to real-world bullying. The limitation with this approach is that we would be relying on the participants' potentially flawed memories.

As you can see, we have several options from which to choose. Some options carry too much risk to the participants, while the less risky options do not seem to fully address the research question. In these types of cases, the best way to ethically study a topic is often by examining a less potentially harmful form of the behavior. So while we may not be able to study bullying directly, we can study social rejection, which is one component of bullying (Steinberg, 2008).

To do this, we could ask a group of participants to work on a collective ice-breaking activity in the lab, where everyone takes M&Ms and then shares something personal about themselves for each M&M they took. Next, we could separate the participants into two different groups. We could individually tell the participants assigned to one group that everyone in the group said nice things about them and reported wanting to work with them again. For individuals in the second group, we could tell them that the others in the group gossiped about them and did not want to work with them again. Neither set of feedback would actually be true. After receiving this feedback, each participant would have the option of completing the follow-up measures alone (i.e., social isolation) or with others (i.e., social affiliation). This version of the study has the benefit of realistically mimicking a key feature of bullying (social rejection), but lessens the impact and potential harm by having the message delivered indirectly by the experimenter. As a result, the data we collect from this method should more closely resemble responses in the real world. However, this method is not without risk, so we must add a number of steps to mitigate these risks. Our goal, to understand how people respond to bullying in a situation we can control, has potential risk, but has a greater potential reward.

> **What Do You Think?**
>
> In what other ways could you ethically study bullying? What other responses to bullying might you investigate (e.g., cognitive, emotional, behavioral)?

Conducting Your Study Ethically

The cost-benefit analysis we used to determine our study's design is merely the first step in ethically testing our research question. Next, we must make sure we conduct our study ethically. In our study, we will be careful to uphold justice by not targeting participants who are particularly weak, vulnerable, or susceptible to coercion (e.g., children, prisoners, the mentally ill or disabled, etc.). We will offer study participation to adults at a local recreation center or to students on a college campus. Once we have a sample, we will exercise fairness by randomly assigning participants to study groups so that each participant is equally likely to take on the risks and receive the benefits of participation. To accomplish this, before a participant arrives for our study, we will pull a group name out of a hat to determine whether or not that participant will be in the social exclusion/ bullied group.

For our data collection, we will be mindful of the principle of autonomy by providing an environment in which people can freely choose to partici-pate. Therefore, we should not bribe (e.g., "If you participate, we will pay you a thousand dollars") or threaten (e.g., "If you don't participate, you will fail your psychology course") people in order to convince them to par-ticipate in our study. Likewise, we should not invoke any power we have to coerce them into participating in the study (e.g., "You must participate because your professor says you should"). Ultimately, participation should be a choice made solely by the participant after learning about the nature of the study.

We can accomplish this by obtaining informed consent from every research participant. In a study like ours, where we are trying to re-create a real-world experience, deciding which information to provide for informed consent, and how to explain it, is a delicate matter. We need participants to have enough information to make an informed decision and to feel comfortable partici-pating, but we must also be careful not to undermine natural reactions by revealing too much. If participants know exactly what we are studying, they will be more likely to give unnatural responses, which will make our study results less useful. To ensure natural reactions from our participants, we will provide a cover story that tells participants the study is about responses to group interactions, which is entirely true. By taking this approach, combined with acknowledging the study's risks in the informed consent form, we are truthfully informing participants of the nature of their participation without possibly influencing their responses. Our informed consent forms will also alert participants to their right to refuse or terminate participation at any time without penalty. In all cases, we will write our informed consent using plain, nonscientific language that our participants can easily understand. Once our participants have provided consent, we can expose them to our social exclu-sion procedure, which we are using as a proxy for bullying, and observe their subsequent behavior.

Regardless of the topic under investigation, the researcher must protect the privacy of individuals to reduce the threat of loss of confidentiality. This involves actions like separating consent forms (which contain signatures) from the data and using a coding system so no one can link responses to specific participants. These safeguards ensure that a researcher cannot discuss an individual's data in resulting presentations or publications.

Our study involves **deception**, which is the purposeful misleading or misdirection of participants, both in our cover story (i.e., giving participants misleading information about the impression they made on others) and through the false feedback (i.e., giving participants misleading results about their performance). Our study also has the potential risk of temporary psychological distress. As a result of the deception and potential for distress, we need a thorough debriefing. Although not every study requires debriefing (such as those that involve no known or potential risks or deception), debriefing can help to minimize any potentially lasting effects from participating in the study, and provides the opportunity to teach participants about the scientific process, which can be beneficial to their lives. For our study, the researcher will read a debriefing script and will encourage participants to ask questions about the study. The script will explain that there was deception in our study via the cover story and false feedback, and will indicate why the deception was necessary. In addition, the debriefing will tell participants that any emotional responses they had during the study are natural and common to this type of research. Finally, we will provide participants with contact information for free counseling services in case the study causes any later emotional distress.

It is also imperative that participants act ethically, providing honest and truthful responses to the questions in a study. This expectation begins from the moment a researcher recruits a participant. Sometimes it is critical to a study's validity that all of the participants share a common characteristic. However, if some potential participants are dishonest, they may participate in a study for which they are not qualified. For example, suppose a researcher was recruiting college students for a study that required participants to have been in a serious, committed romantic relationship for at least 2 years, and some of the students decided to lie about their relationship status in order to participate. These students might try to justify their dishonesty by saying that they needed the credit for class, or that the study was not that important. However, the researcher both assumed that participants had behaved ethically and trusted the participants' integrity. Unfortunately, these participants would have harmed the cause of science, because if the researcher published these potentially inaccurate results, others might make important, potentially consequential decisions based on untrustworthy data.

Ethical decisions are not always easy to make. Our goal is to study bullying in a meaningful way that protects our participants. While the principles covered provide some ethical standards for research, each study is different and may present unique challenges. Thankfully, you are not entirely on your own in making these decisions. Most colleges and universities have governing bodies that provide the ultimate ethical approval for any proposed research studies that involve the use of humans or animals. These committees are an important safeguard, ensuring psychological research is ethical and does not pose a risk to study participants or subjects.

deception intentionally misleading participants in some fashion.

Institutional Review Board (IRB) a board that reviews the ethical merit of all the human research conducted at an institution.

The Institutional Review Board

Every institution that receives federal funding must have an **Institutional Review Board (IRB)** to review the ethical merit of all the human research conducted at the institution, including any research conducted by faculty members or students. The mission of the IRB is to provide ethical oversight of research projects. IRB members include faculty or staff at the institution who have expertise in research and people from the community, such as physicians, scientists, or clergy. Researchers must complete an IRB proposal for every research study they wish to conduct. In this proposal, the researcher explains any and all benefits, risks, and procedures associated with the proposed study, as well as any forms and questionnaires to be used in the study, including consent forms and debriefing scripts. The proposal must also explain how the researcher will maintain confidentiality. The IRB classifies the proposed research study based on the level of potential risk and participants involved. For example, a research project that entails less than minimal risk (i.e., when there is no physical, emotional, or psychological harm involved) and does not involve a vulnerable population (e.g., children, the elderly, pregnant women, prisoners, or mentally disabled people) will receive a different level of review or scrutiny than a study that has higher risks or includes vulnerable populations. Still, the IRB reviews each proposal using principles from the Belmont Report and from the federal regulations on the "Protection of Human Subjects" (U.S. Department of Health and Human Services, 2009) to determine whether or not the study meets all ethical guidelines. **Table 3.2** summarizes how the IRB classifies research reviews.

TABLE 3.2

Levels of IRB Review		
Classification	**Description**	**Process**
Exempt	The research poses less than minimal risk (i.e., no known physical, emotional, psychological, or economic risk) and includes a nonvulnerable population.	Reviewed by the chair of the IRB.
Expedited	The research poses minimal risk typically encountered in daily life, such as moderate exercise or minor stress from testing or surveys, and includes a nonvulnerable population.	Reviewed by the chair or by a qualified member of the IRB committee.
Full Review	The research poses a greater than minimal risk typically encountered in daily life, such as maximal exercise, stressful psychological tests, or questions about illegal activities, *or* includes a vulnerable population (e.g., children, elderly, prisoners, pregnant women, or mentally disabled persons).	Reviewed by a committee of at least five members of the IRB.

Research in Action

Being an Ethical Researcher

We always need to be able to justify how our proposed research will advance science without causing harm to or placing undue burden on our participants. To help us with this task, we present our research studies for ethical review to the Institutional Review Board (IRB). But what does the IRB look for to determine if a study is ethical?

In the online activity *Being an Ethical Researcher,* you will have the opportunity to role-play as the member of an IRB tasked with reviewing various research study proposals. You will decide if each proposal meets the ethical standards for conducting quality science and, if not, which ethical principles are being violated. Learning to identify potential ethical problems in proposed research studies will ensure that you will always be an ethical researcher!

LaunchPad To complete this activity, visit LaunchPad at launchpadworks.com

Institutional Animal Care and Use Committee (IACUC) a board that reviews the ethical merit and research procedures for all animal research conducted within an institution and ensures research animals have proper living conditions.

The Institutional Animal Care and Use Committee

Psychologists do not just study humans. For many reasons, some psychologists use animals to address their research questions. For example, those studying the impact of genetic factors on behavior conduct animal research because animals such as mice can be bred to be genetically identical. Researchers in animal labs can also completely control the experiences of animals in a way they cannot with humans. This helps to identify the impact of a particular factor more easily. In addition, researchers can evaluate animals 24 hours a day. Because animals do not have the ability to provide informed consent, however, there is an entirely different process for assessing the ethics of animal research. Every institution that has animal research must have an **Institutional Animal Care and Use Committee (IACUC).** This committee reviews all animal research procedures to ensure that researchers follow U.S. laws on animal research, and requires that the researchers' laboratories be inspected every 6 months to confirm adherence to all regulations regarding the proper care and treatment of the animals. For example, they make sure the animals have proper housing, sufficient food, health care, and clean conditions. The IACUC must consist of at least five members, including a veterinarian and a practicing scientist experienced in animal research. As with the IRB processes, researchers must have IACUC approval before conducting their research.

For a variety of reasons, psychologists study animals to better understand human behavior. However, animals do not have the ability to provide informed consent. Does this mean it is unethical to conduct animal research? *(Science Source/Inc-Photo/Getty Images)*

Researchers, along with the IRB and IACUC, try to weigh the benefits of the research against the risk to the participant or subject. The right choice is not always clear, but society puts its utmost faith in science and expects us to conduct ourselves ethically. As there are potential costs to participants, there are potential social costs if we fail to uphold these ethical principles. The discovery of unethical behavior results in a loss of trust in the field of psychology, and in the scientific community as a whole.

YOUR TURN 3.2

1. A marriage counselor wants to evaluate the efficacy of a new approach to help couples communicate better in public settings and among strangers. Before this study can be conducted, approval is needed from all of the following groups *except*

   a. the female participants in the study.

   b. the Institutional Review Board.

   c. the Institutional Animal Care and Use Committee.

   d. the male participants in the study.

2. Suppose that you are a psychology professor who wants to recruit research participants from your class. Which of the following strategies would be best for ensuring that you are preserving your students' autonomy while recruiting them for your research study?

   a. Offer research participation in your study as one of the options for fulfilling a course requirement

   b. Require your students to participate in the study as part of their educational experience

   c. Suggest to students that they may not do as well in your course if they fail to participate in your study

   d. Offer to exempt any students who participate in your study from the final exam

3. To ensure confidentiality during a study, the researcher would do all of the following *except*

   a. assign code numbers to the data.

   b. keep the participants' informed consent forms separate from the participants' data.

   c. have participants submit completed surveys in a sealed envelope.

   d. highlight an individual's responses by name in a conference presentation.

How did you do? Turn to the end of the chapter to check your answers.

Scientific Integrity

It is clear that a scientist has ethical responsibilities in planning and carrying out a study. This is so important that the APA (2017) included the general principles of "fidelity and responsibility" and "integrity" in its code of ethics. Fidelity and responsibility reminds researchers that they must never engage in behaviors that violate the trust others have in the scientific process, while integrity highlights scientists' ethical responsibility to be forthright and honest as they analyze, interpret, and share the findings from their studies. The goal of science is to provide new knowledge that may ultimately improve our everyday experience. Just as a medical doctor relies on the reported findings from drug studies to know the best medicine to prescribe for the treatment of heart disease or cancer, a clinical psychologist relies on others' research to learn the best way to treat a client with posttraumatic stress disorder. Similarly, a parent will rely on published research to know the best way to discipline their child, and a schoolteacher will read an educational psychology journal to identify the best way to teach students how to read. As you can see, scientists are not merely conducting studies to satisfy their own curiosity about the world. Rather, science has a relationship with society. The world relies on scientists to provide information to help solve real problems and trusts that the information provided is accurate.

For this reason, it is imperative that scientists uphold a high degree of **scientific integrity,** by maintaining an open and honest approach to science while adhering to ethical principles throughout the research process. This includes researching important topics that may be socially or politically unpopular. In maintaining scientific integrity, we must also be aware that researchers may study certain topics more often because the government and corporations provide research funding for those topics. This means to some extent (or to the extent that researchers pursue this money) that the government and corporations may prioritize the research conducted, which can potentially place important topics on the backburner.

The Ethical Treatment of Data

One way that a scientist can compromise scientific integrity is by falsifying or faking data. A dishonest researcher can accomplish this by changing a few numbers, or even fabricating all the data, so that the results provide support for the researcher's hypotheses. Although this type of conduct may seem outlandish, there have been two high-profile examples of falsifying data. In one case, the research assistants of Marc Hauser, a Harvard professor and director of the Cognitive Evolution Lab, accused him of reporting falsified data (Bartlett, 2010). The data in question was from a study of pattern recognition in monkeys in which two observers coded the monkeys' reactions. An analysis of one coder's observations revealed that the monkeys did not detect any pattern changes while an analysis of Professor Hauser's coding of the observations showed that the monkeys were able to recognize a pattern change. An investigation revealed that Professor Hauser had committed at least eight instances of scientific misconduct.

In a higher-profile case, Dutch researcher Diederik Stapel admitted to fabricating entire experiments, many of which top journals in the field had published (Carey, 2011). Many, if not all, of the journals have since retracted these papers. Worse, Stapel's misconduct occurred over a period of 10 years. The "findings" from several of his studies captured the public's interest, as they were widely reported by newspapers, magazines, and blogs. Stapel's studies

scientific integrity a commitment to intellectual honesty and adherence to ethical principles in scientific research.

Diederik Stapel admitted to fabricating his provocative research. How might the actions of unscrupulous researchers undermine the public's trust in science?

(Reyer Boxem/Hollandse Hoogte/Redux)

gathered much publicity because his findings were seemingly groundbreaking, thought-provoking, and provocative—all things that the popular media desires in a good story. For example, one of Stapel's studies allegedly demonstrated that meat-eaters were more selfish than vegetarians, while another showed that messy and unorganized environments led White people to discriminate more against Black people. The problem was that Stapel's "studies" were just stories. They had no scientific merit. It is impossible to know how many people altered their own behavior or gave others bad advice based on what they believed were accurate findings from Stapel's research. As Stapel himself said in light of the scandal, via a statement in the Dutch newspaper *Brabants Dagblad,* "I failed as a scientist. I adapted research data and fabricated research. Not once, but several times, not for a short period, but over a longer period of time."

Fabricating data about meat-eaters' selfishness may not seem like a major transgression. But what if the reported findings suggested seemingly better ways to treat someone with suicidal ideation or an eating disorder? As you can imagine, the consequences of fabricating an entire data set related to these topics could be severe. However, falsifying, modifying, or omitting data from just some of the participants can be equally unethical. This practice is referred to as "massaging the data" (or data trimming, cooking data, or mining data) because it does not involve the blatant falsification or altering of data. For example, the researcher may choose, without sufficient justification, to drop certain participants from the analyses until the hypotheses have support. The researcher may focus on reporting the findings that back the overall hypotheses while ignoring or downplaying those that do not.

Another example of data massaging is picking and choosing the variables to include in one's analyses, ignoring other potentially important variables. In these cases, researchers make their decisions based on the ability to confirm the hypotheses and not based on theoretical considerations. These researchers may even go so far as to include a wide range of variables in their study, but then fail to mention their inclusion when they fail to yield hypothesized results. Likewise, it is problematic to keep running analyses, regardless of your initial hypotheses, until you find something significant to report. Essentially, in this situation, researchers report only the "hits" and hide all of the "misses." Simmons, Nelson, and Simonsohn (2011) have suggested that this type of "flexibility" in data analytical decisions can easily increase the likelihood that a study will support the scientist's hypotheses, even if unwarranted. It is unclear how often these unethical practices occur or if they do at all. The problem is that no one can really be sure if scientists adhere to an ethical code of conduct when analyzing and reporting the results of a study. This problem emphasizes the value of replication for increasing confidence in the integrity of a researcher's findings. If independent researchers obtain similar results as the original study, it is less likely that the findings are the result of either falsified data or data massaging.

To help promote the ethical treatment of data, Simmons and his colleagues (2011) provide researchers with a suggested list of rules or best practices to help decrease the temptation to falsify data. Among their many suggestions for scientists and for those who review scientists' results, they suggest that researchers decide how many participants they will collect data from before the study starts (e.g., "We will collect data from 120 participants"). By doing this, scientists must adhere to the predetermined number and avoid the temptation to end data collection once they believe their hypotheses have support. Another suggestion is that researchers report all of the different groups and variables they used in the study. By doing this, scientists avoid reporting only the pieces that worked, and readers of the research learn which analyses failed and which did not. In each case, these practices should help minimize data massaging and should result in more accurate reporting of findings.

The Ethical Presentation of Findings

A scientist could carry out each part of a study and data analysis to the highest ethical standards, but if the findings are not reported clearly and accurately, the study's scientific integrity will still be compromised. The most common way this happens is when a study's findings are misrepresented, or even overstated. Suppose a study has data showing there is an association between two factors, A and B. However, when the study's findings are reported, they are portrayed as factor A causing factor B. For example, in the fall of 2011, the University of Notre Dame issued a press release describing research by a Notre Dame economics professor that showed a link between the number of years there are between siblings and their academic achievement. The more spaced out siblings were, the higher their reading and math scores, particularly for the older siblings. Clearly, these factors were associated with one another. However, the press release was titled "Want Smarter Children? Space Siblings at Least Two Years Apart, Research Shows." Well, not exactly. That title implies that the two-year space causes the difference and that if you space your children out by at least two years, they will be smarter. The actual research study did not make this causal claim because it is possible that other factors help account for the finding. For example, it could be that parents are more likely to space their children out when they have high-paying jobs, have more education, or generally have higher socioeconomic status, all of which could help children's test scores. To be fair, it is often not the scientist who makes these types of mistakes, but, rather, media outlets seeking to make a study's findings as provocative as possible. Nevertheless, misrepresenting or overstating conclusions drawn from one's study is an ethical issue.

Another way to make a study's findings look more impressive than they really are is by creating a figure that misrepresents the results. Typically, this occurs when someone mislabels an axis on a figure or diagram by not starting the scale on the y-axis at zero. For example, suppose that a researcher conducted a study using 10,000 students to examine the effect of memory boosters in smoothies

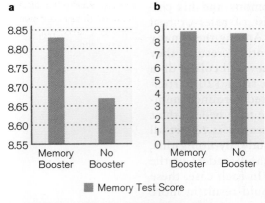

Memory Test Score

FIGURE 3.2 Misrepresenting Data Through Figures. Researchers can easily misrepresent statistical findings in graphs.

and found that those taking the memory booster had better performance on a 10-question memory test. Now, take a look at the two charts in **Figure 3.2**, both of which represent the same study results.

In Part a, the results look much more impressive. The difference in the height of the bars is dramatic. In contrast, the bars in Part b appear to be nearly identical. So, what gives? The only difference is in how the figure scales the data on the y-axis. In Part a, the y-axis starts at 8.55 and extends to 8.85, which results in the small mean difference between conditions (0.16 points on the 10-point memory test) appearing to be very large. However, starting at 0 and extending to 9 results in a more appropriately scaled y-axis, which results in the relatively small 0.16-point difference appearing small (rightfully so).

The issue of ethics in the reporting of results even extends to the decisions made by scientific journals concerning which studies to accept for publication. Journals are much more likely to publish a study in which the results support the hypotheses. Studies in which the results are inconclusive or do not support the researcher's hypotheses are much more likely to be rejected or ignored and subsequently never shared with the scientific community. In a study of over 4,600 research articles from a variety of scientific disciplines, Fanelli (2012) not only found a bias toward publishing papers that support the researcher's hypothesis, but also found that this bias has increased by 22% over time. The nonpublication of research findings is often referred to as the **file drawer problem** in that many studies that may be important for advancing scientific knowledge are simply filed away and never published because they do not conclusively support the hypotheses of interest.

You might be wondering if this is really a problem. After all, we typically want to know what works, not what doesn't. However, unsupported hypotheses can also provide important information. Suppose that 10 researchers were independently examining the effect of eating chocolate on nighttime sleep quality. Each researcher runs essentially the same study, where each member in a group of participants is given a 3-ounce milk chocolate bar with a glass of milk right before bedtime. The comparison group receives only a glass of milk. They then all measure for how long the participants sleep and their alertness upon waking up in the morning. Of the 10 researchers, only one finds that chocolate helps quality of sleep, while nine find that it has no effect. Given the file drawer problem, only one of these studies, the one demonstrating the power of chocolate, is likely to get published. In reality, there are nine studies showing the opposite effect, which suggest that the one positive result might be a fluke. But the world may never know the full story because those nine studies will get filed away and never published in the pages of scientific journals.

Finally, when researchers write about their study's findings, they should be sure to do so ethically. The primary ethical issue when describing a study is **plagiarism.** As you probably know, plagiarism involves representing others' ideas as your own, or without providing the proper credit. The most blatant, and clearly

file drawer problem a bias in the scientific community to only publish findings that confirm a researcher's hypothesis.

plagiarism representing others' work or ideas as our own, or without giving proper credit.

unethical, form of plagiarism involves overtly copying from a source and portraying it as your own work. To avoid this, the author should **paraphrase**, or put the original sources' information into his or her own words. Good paraphrasing captures the same overall meaning, but varies sentence structure and word choice from the original version in a way that often leads to a more concise version of the author's statement. Learning how to paraphrase takes practice and requires a clear understanding of the source so that you are able to retain the original meaning. However, that is just the start. Since many of the ideas and background information you provide a reader when writing a research paper are not your own original ideas, as the author, you must acknowledge the source or multiple sources used. In psychology, we do this by providing APA-style citations.

paraphrase summarizing others' ideas in our own words while providing a proper citation.

YOUR TURN 3.3

1. A researcher notices that several participants do not appear to be carefully reading the questions on her survey. She decides not to include these participants' data in her study so that she has a "better" test of her research hypothesis. This behavior is problematic because of its
   a. unethical treatment of the participants.
   b. unethical treatment of the data.
   c. unethical treatment of the results.
   d. unethical presentation of the findings.

2. A researcher demonstrating scientific integrity would do all of the following *except*
   a. share only significant findings in the write-ups of their studies.
   b. determine criteria for terminating data collection prior to starting the study.
   c. properly label the y-axis on figures and charts in order to avoid exaggerating small differences.
   d. carefully describe findings such that correlational findings would not imply cause and effect.

3. A journal editor decides to accept for publication only research studies in which the results are statistically significant. All of the following are potential ethical problems resulting from this decision *except*
   a. there is an increased potential for a file-drawer problem.
   b. researchers may be more likely to alter their data to ensure their results are statistically significant.
   c. authors are more likely to plagiarize from other statistically significant studies.
   d. authors may take more liberties in how they present the results to make them appear more impressive.

How did you do? Turn to the end of the chapter to check your answers.

Final Thoughts

Based on what you have learned in this chapter, if you were sitting on an IRB, would you approve Dr. Don's false-memory study? On the one hand, there are potential risks. Although the memories are false, participants may believe the memories are real, even after debriefing, and they may experience extreme emotional reactions. On the other hand, his study could reveal a way to greatly improve students' memory. Because it is impossible to know if the study will actually work, the decision that best protects human participants is to not do the study. However, if Dr. Don is willing to compromise, he could still examine his hypothesis. For example, Dr. Don could create a milder form of trauma or discomfort by having participants drink a mixture of hot sauce and water, or repeatedly experience a loud, uncontrollable noise blast. Both hot sauce (Harmon-Jones & Sigelman, 2001) and noise blasts (Twenge, Baumeister, Tice, & Stucke, 2001) have been used in previous research, which helps us have greater confidence that we can use them as an approximation of trauma, and that we can do so without participants experiencing excessive harm.

As you can see, there are many ethical decisions that a researcher must account for when planning and conducting a study. At all times, researchers must make sure that participants are the ones determining their role in the study, that participants receive fair and equal treatment, that every precaution has been taken to ensure that there is minimal harm to participants, and that the benefits of the study outweigh the costs. As Dr. Will B. Aethikle might say, "The process of scientific discovery and answering one's own research questions is exciting because of the potential for new knowledge, but it is imperative that such advances do not come at the expense of the participants that we rely upon."

CHAPTER 3 | Review

Review Questions

1. As a financially challenged college student, you see a flyer on campus about a research study on the impact of sunburns. The advertisement says you will be paid $500 to have a 1 inch by 1 inch square of skin on your forearm severely burned with ultraviolet light. You know that sunburns can have long-term consequences (e.g., skin cancer). However, you desperately need the money for textbooks, so you seriously consider participating. What ethical line has this research study violated?

   a. The defilement of justice
   b. The failure to determine assent
   c. The coercion of voluntary participation
   d. The failure to provide informed consent

2. Cyrus is reading an article and believes that he cannot articulate the topic better than the researcher already has. However, his professor said students could not use quotes in their APA-style introductions. Instead of using quotes, Cyrus takes the researcher's sentence and changes one word of it by replacing the word with a synonym. Which of the following is true?

    a. Because one word is changed, this is not a case of plagiarism.

    b. As long as Cyrus cites the researcher, this is not a case of plagiarism.

    c. The only way for this not to be a case of plagiarism is for Cyrus to paraphrase instead.

    d. The only way for this not to be a case of plagiarism is for Cyrus to replace at least two words with synonyms.

3. If an experimental psychologist studies learning in pigeons, which of the following oversight groups would ethically approve the research?

    a. Institutional Review Board (IRB)

    b. Institutional Animal Care and Use Committee (IACUC)

    c. Psychology Ethics Committee (PEC)

    d. People for the Ethical Treatment of Animals (PETA)

4. Chauncey wants to conduct an experiment on the impact of negative feedback on concentration. As part of the procedure, some participants "overhear" another participant, who is actually a confederate, say something negative about them. Which ethical principle should Chauncey be most concerned about?

    a. Beneficence

    b. Justice

    c. Respect for persons

    d. Privacy

5. Deidra needs just one more participant to complete her data collection for her undergraduate thesis. The last participant signs the consent form, but halfway through the study, the participant wants to leave. Deidra tells her that she must stay and finish the study, and the participant complies. What ethical principle has Deidra violated?

    a. Beneficence

    b. Justice

    c. Respect for persons

    d. Privacy

6. If a study you conduct involves the purposeful misleading or misdirection of participants, when and how do you notify participants of the deception?

    a. You explain the nature and necessity of the deception in the debriefing at the end of the study.

    b. You notify participants of the deception in the consent form before each participant agrees to participate.

    c. As long as the participants leave the study happy, you never have to tell them.

    d. You only tell participants about deception if it involves confederates.

7. Which of the following would most likely represent an ethical dilemma for a person?
   a. Cheating on an exam
   b. Not paying a parking ticket
   c. Reporting one's professor to the head of the department for cancelling too many classes due to personal reasons
   d. Downloading pirated music from the Internet

8. Marc wants to do a study on the influence of energy drinks on motivation. After conducting a literature search on PsycINFO for published research on this topic, Marc cannot find any research and concludes that this topic has never been studied. However, what else could explain this?
   a. Nonresponse bias
   b. Lack of reliability
   c. The use of poor sources
   d. File drawer problem

9. Teagan finishes up her thesis, but finds that her hypothesis was not supported. She looks at the data and finds that if she omits the data from three participants, her results work out as she predicted. Which unethical practice has she engaged in?
   a. Stapeling the data
   b. Massaging the data
   c. Plagiarism
   d. Analysis falsifiability

10. All of the following are forms of deception *except*
    a. false feedback.
    b. cover story.
    c. confederates.
    d. imprecise informed consent.

11. If you had to do away with any of the ethical principles, which one would you remove? Why?

For questions 12–15, imagine that a researcher plans to conduct research using the procedures listed below. For each proposed procedure:

    a. Indicate whether you would approve or reject the study on the basis of ethical issues.

    b. If you disapprove of a procedure, indicate the ethical principle(s) that cause you concern (i.e., beneficence, justice, respect for persons). If there is no cause for concern, indicate that.

12. A researcher randomly assigns some, but not all, low-income students to an experimental program designed to help improve college acceptance rates.

13. A researcher instructs participants to say insulting things to another participant while this other participant tries to complete a task.

14. With the parents' permission, but without the children's awareness, a researcher videotapes 4-year-old children during cooperative play.

15. A researcher exposes male college students to a sexually explicit video for 10 minutes and measures their physiological arousal in response.

Applying What You've Learned

1. The Tuskegee syphilis study was a clear violation of the ethical standards we have today. Write a letter to the researcher of this study explaining what ethical violations occurred. Additionally, suggest changes to the procedure that would allow researchers to study the impact of syphilis in a more ethical way.

2. Both the lay press and the scientific literature regularly report on events relevant to the discussion of science and research ethics. Find a relevant news article, blog posting, video clip, or book that addresses ethics in science. The item you select should be current (i.e., published no earlier than 12 months ago). Identify the ethical issue and discuss potential outcomes.

3. You want to conduct a study on a weight-loss program in which you assign half of your participants to a "mental exercise" that you predict will lead to weight loss and the other half to a control condition that you predict will lead to no weight change. However, you know you need to get your study approved by the IRB. Explain how you will handle each issue below to adhere to the ethical principles required by the IRB.

   a. Identify and explain any potential psychological and physical risks of participating in your study. Additionally, identify and explain any potential psychological or physical benefits the participants might receive from participation.

   b. Given the principle of beneficence, how will you guarantee that the potential benefits outweigh the costs?

   c. Given the principle of justice, explain how you will select participants for your study. In addition, explain how you will determine which participants do the "mental exercise" and which do not.

   d. What actions will you take to safeguard the privacy of those who participate in your study?

   e. What steps will you take to respect the autonomy of the participants in your study? Keep in mind the ideas of consent and coercion.

4. Read the article "Hey, Everyone, Don't Fall for This Misleading Graph About College Costs" found here: http://www.theatlantic.com/business/archive/2012/06/hey-everyone-dont-fall-for-this-misleading-graph-about-college-costs/258299/. Why is this presentation of data potentially problematic?

5. Obtain a copy of your school's IRB or ethics committee application. On the application, identify the sections where they address the general principles of the APA code of ethics.

Key Concepts

altruistic perspective, p. 57

anonymity, p. 58

assent, p. 64

autonomy, p. 61

beneficence, p. 57

confederate, p. 68

cost-benefit analysis, p. 57

cost of not doing the research, p. 59

deception, p. 71

egoism, p. 57

ethics, p. 56

file drawer problem, p. 78

Institutional Animal Care and Use Committee (IACUC), p. 73

Institutional Review Board (IRB), p. 72

justice, p. 59

loss of confidentiality, p. 58

nonmaleficence, p. 58

paraphrase, p. 79

physical harm, p. 58

plagiarism, p. 78

psychological harm, p. 59

scientific integrity, p. 75

utilitarian perspective, p. 56

Answers to YOUR TURN

Your Turn 3.1: 1. b; 2. c; 3. c

Your Turn 3.2: 1. c; 2. a; 3. d

Your Turn 3.3: 1. b; 2. a; 3. c

Answers to Multiple-Choice Review Questions

1. c; 2. c; 3. b; 4. a; 5. c; 6. a; 7. c; 8. d; 9. b; 10. d

The Psychologist's Toolbox

Tools for Building Better Designs

maxyustas/Deposit Photos

LEARNING OUTCOMES

After reading this chapter, you should be able to:

- Differentiate between true experiments and quasi experiments.
- Describe multiple methods for measuring a variable.
- Identify potential sources of error in data collection.

- Explain the importance of validity and reliability when choosing a measurement.
- Outline the various methods of creating a sample from a population.
- Identify potential sampling problems.

Something to Think About . . .

At some point, when you embark on your career with college degree in hand, you will be responsible for a major project. Before your supervisor gives you this responsibility, he or she will explain what you need to do, establish a set of guidelines or rules for you to follow, and provide you with the fundamental pieces of information you will need to successfully complete the project. However, beyond these basics, you will likely be on your own in terms of making specific decisions along the way.

Conducting a research study requires the same steps as any project. To prepare you to manage a research project, we have explained the basics of the research process (Chapter 2) and the ethical guidelines to follow when conducting psychological research (Chapter 3). Although there are a variety of research designs, each one helps us use science to answer interesting questions about the world. Before you jump into your first project, we want to provide a few additional basic research design concepts that you need to know (**Figure 4.1**). Think of these concepts as building blocks that provide the foundation on which you build most research designs. In this chapter, we introduce many of the key concepts that you will need in order to work through the research design decisions in the remaining chapters of the book. Master the basics in this chapter, and you will have an opportunity to explore each research design in more depth in later chapters. After all, it will be easier to understand more specific concepts in the

FIGURE 4.1 **Research Process Overview.** Every study starts with a question, and then uses design to help find the answers.

context of answering a specific research question. Every research design includes the same basic steps: choose the right research design for your goal, determine the best measures, and recruit research participants (**Figure 4.2**). In this chapter, we will guide you through how to best navigate each of these steps and design the best research project possible.

Choosing the Right Design for the Job

As you will see in the upcoming chapters, researchers have a variety of research designs available to them. Each design has the potential to help you find the answer to your research question. You may be thinking, "Just tell me which design is the best and I'll learn that one. No need to waste my time on other designs." This attitude makes sense to some degree, because everyone wants to use the "best" design to find answers. The problem is that there is no one "best" design. Rather, the optimal design to use is the one that best addresses your research question. You do not choose the design; the design chooses you. While you may develop an affinity for a particular design, such as a survey, it is much more important to use the design that provides you with the best test of your hypothesis or research question. Science focuses on quality, not convenience. If you have to drive a nail, you will need to use a hammer, even if your favorite tool is a screwdriver. For this reason, you will want to learn about various designs so that you are always prepared to use the most effective approach for answering your research question.

As you think about how to answer your research question, you will have a few basic designs that you can employ. Sometimes the study's goal is simply to describe a behavior, something we need to do before we set out to understand why that behavior occurs. As discussed in Chapter 2, there are designs that help answer the question, "What takes place?" and designs that answer, "Why does it take place?" To answer "what" questions, as well as questions about "who," "how much," and "how often," we use nonexperimental research designs, which do not involve the researcher changing or manipulating any of the variables. Instead, the researcher simply measures or assesses the variables. Examples of nonexperimental designs that you will learn about in later chapters include interviews, observations, and survey research. To answer "why" questions, or questions about how one variable influences another, we use experimental research designs, which involve the researcher changing or manipulating at least one variable. Examples of experimental designs that you will learn about in later chapters include two-group, multigroup, repeated-measures, factorial, and mixed designs.

When the researcher manipulates all of the independent variables, the design is a **true experiment**. What we mean by "manipulate" is that the researcher creates

true experiments
designs in which the researcher manipulates all of the independent variables and randomly assigns participants to groups.

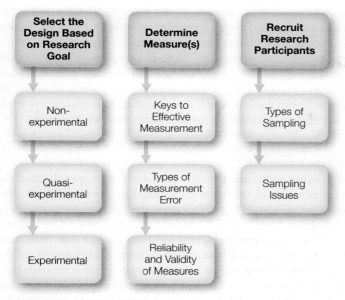

FIGURE 4.2 The Basic Steps to Designing a Research Project.

experiences for one group of participants that differ from another group's. If you were conducting a study on stress, you could manipulate stress by asking one group to complete a complex task in a short period of time under noisy conditions, while asking another group to complete the same task during a much longer time period and in a quiet room. In true experiments, the researcher also assigns participants to different experimental conditions in an unbiased manner.

Sometimes it is not feasible or ethical for a researcher to randomly assign participants to different experimental conditions. Suppose you wanted to know what impact relationship status might have on one's happiness. We cannot ethically require some participants to be in a relationship simply to learn how it influences their happiness. Gender is another common example of a variable we cannot manipulate. We refer to these types of variables as **quasi-independent variables** because we treat them *as if* they were independent variables in the experimental design even though the researcher does *not actually* manipulate them. We refer to designs where we cannot manipulate the independent variable or cannot randomly assign participants to groups as **quasi-experimental designs** (Shadish, Cook, & Campbell, 2002). For example, imagine you are interested in the difference between the games boys and girls play on the playground. Although we use gender to create groups, we cannot manipulate who is a boy and who is a girl because they are preexisting groups. You may also want to look at the effectiveness of a treatment or intervention (e.g., a type of therapy or medication). In some cases, such as if you wanted to test the long-term effects of marijuana use on memory, it is not possible to ethically manipulate the independent variable and randomly assign participants to smoking or nonsmoking

▶ Interested in learning more about how researchers manipulate variables, use random assignment, and help rule out alternate explanations? SEE CHAPTER 8, p. 250

quasi-independent variables variables treated as if they were independent variables in the experimental design even though the researchers did not manipulate them.

quasi-experimental designs designs in which the researcher cannot manipulate the independent variable or use random assignment.

conditions. When you want to investigate cause and effect and which specific variable leads to changes, a true experiment is the way to go. However, some situations do not lend themselves to manipulating variables and randomly assigning participants to groups. In these cases, quasi-experimental designs are the best option. Regardless of the design you choose, you will need to make decisions concerning how you will measure your variables and recruit participants for your study. These decisions will have important implications for the quality of your study and your ability to answer your research question.

Measuring Variables

Compared to other scientists, psychologists have a tough job. Studying thought and behavior presents us with unique challenges. Consider love. How do you know if someone is in love? How in love is the person? Are some people "really in love" and others "just a little"? How can you know? The answers to these questions are not straightforward, and some may argue that truly assessing love is impossible. However, this is one of the exciting challenges of conducting psychological research. Galileo once wrote, "Measure what is measurable, and make measurable what is not so." Make no mistake: Being able to measure complex psychological variables is important. For example, measuring love is critical to understanding why people fall in and out of love, a topic of great importance to couples in counseling. As Lord Kelvin said, "If you cannot measure it, you cannot improve it." For psychologists, the ability to measure psychological concepts such as love, depression, stress, anxiety, loneliness, happiness, body image, and self-esteem means that we can study strategies for improving peoples' lives in these areas. The foundation for any research design is our ability to measure participants' experiences in a way that provides useful information to answer our question. To accomplish this, there are two main types of measurement we can use: self-report and behavioral.

Self-Report

Every study requires measuring some aspect of the participant. Sometimes you want to assess the actual behavior of the participant, and other times you want to learn about internal events, such as what the participant is thinking or feeling. Unfortunately, there is no easy way for us to observe these "private events." In these cases, the appropriate measurement tool is the **self-report**, which involves directly asking participants to express how they feel or what they think about a particular topic. The most common examples of self-report measures are interviews, and surveys or questionnaires.

Advantages of Self-Report

On the practical side, some types of self-reports are useful measurement tools because they are relatively cheap and easy to administer. For example, it is much quicker and easier to ask participants to complete a self-report survey than any other data collection strategy. However, the biggest potential advantage to using self-reports is that you receive first-hand information from the source. If we wanted to know how happy you are right now reading this book, you would

self-report any measurement technique that directly asks the participant how they think or feel.

be in the best position to answer that question. You could just tell us! You have a unique perspective that others do not have because you have self-knowledge regarding your internal thoughts and memories (Sedikides & Spencer, 2007), as well as your feelings and desires (Hofstee, 1994), and specific abilities (Zell & Krizan, 2014). As an alternative to self-report, we could secretly observe you reading the book and notice that you are starting to smile. From this behavior, we could assume that you like what you are reading. However, only you know why you are smiling. You might be smiling because you like our book, or you could be smiling because the book is so boring that your mind has wandered to something funny that your roommate said last night. Due to the privileged position that your "self" has regarding your thoughts and feelings, self-report measures are one of the most common measurement tools, particularly in fields such as personality psychology (Hofstee, 1994).

social desirability the tendency for respondents to give answers that make them look good.

Disadvantages of Self-Report

Relying on a person's self-knowledge and self-perceptions can also be problematic. Participants may not have enough self-knowledge to provide accurate answers (Baldwin, 2000; Nisbett & Wilson, 1977), or may not be able to accurately describe their past and future behavior (e.g., Wilson, 2002). For example, we are prone to engage in self-enhancement such that we believe we are much stronger, smarter, more attractive, and generally better than we really are (Shepperd, Malone, & Sweeny, 2008). We come to these types of conclusions because we engage in self-deception, where we try to convince ourselves about what we think is true, in part by seeking out favorable information and discounting contrary evidence (Hofstee, 1994). So, if we asked participants in our study, "To what extent are you a kind person?", they would likely inflate their responses because they would have forgotten, discounted, or rationalized several instances where they were less than kind. Research also demonstrates that we have "blind spots" that result in an inability to accurately assess how others perceive us (Gallrein, Webels, Carlson, & Leising, 2016). In these cases, as much as participants would attempt to report what they believed to be true, their assessments would unfortunately be less than 100% accurate.

It is also possible that participants are inaccurate or misleading on purpose. They could decide to doodle on their answer key, or purposefully give a wrong response in an attempt to be funny (e.g., "Age: ___19___ Sex: ___yes, please___"). In other instances, participants may simply lie to disguise their true feelings. For example, sometimes a lack of honesty is an attempt to maintain **social desirability**, or the desire to give answers that make the participant look good to others. Participants can give socially acceptable answers by underreporting undesirable behavior, such as the amount of pornography they view, or overreporting desirable behavior, such as how much money they donate to charity. When participants provide socially desirable responses, they are attempting to portray themselves in a particular way to the researcher, but this hinders the researcher's ability to measure the truth.

Would you be completely honest in a face-to-face interview about your sex life? Adding anonymity to a research study helps reduce the need for people to represent themselves in a way that makes them look good, allowing them to be more honest. *(Hill Street Studios/Blend Images/ Getty Images)*

demand characteristic
a cue that potentially
makes participants aware
of what the experimenter
expects.

To minimize socially desirable responses, we can ensure confidentiality so participants know that others will not see their individual responses. We can also ensure the anonymity of the participants' responses. If their identity is unknown, there will be no reason for participants to worry about looking good. To accomplish this, you can institute additional steps into your procedure, such as asking participants to seal their responses in an envelope to help them feel unidentifiable and reduce their concerns about social desirability.

Participants may also succumb to **demand characteristics,** or cues that potentially make participants aware of what the experimenter expects. Then they may try to help the researcher by giving responses that they believe the researcher wants (Orne, 1962; Strohmetz, 2008). With self-report measures, this is especially likely when the researcher asks questions that reveal the true purpose of the study. For example, if you asked people coming out of a yoga class, "Please indicate your current level of stress," they may determine that you are researching the benefits of yoga and decide to help you by reporting an exaggeratedly low level of stress because they believe that yoga helps reduce stress. Although participants may believe exaggerating is helpful, it makes it difficult for the researcher to know if yoga really does reduce stress.

To minimize this problem, the researcher can make the real purpose of the study difficult for the participant to figure out. Researchers often misdirect participants about the goal of the research study or the purpose of a particular self-report measure completed by the participants. For example, we might tell participants we are administering a self-report that will assess their "current state of affect." We then administer a self-report that asks a variety of questions that mix the topic we are interested in (i.e., stress) with a number of other filler items (e.g., happiness, fear, sadness). Later, we will only analyze the questions that relate to our variables. Of course, we will need to reveal any misdirection used in our studies during debriefing. If your participants do not know what the study is really about, then they are more likely to respond in a natural way.

▶ Wondering if it is okay to mislead participants like this? SEE CHAPTER 3, p. 71

 Thinking Like a Scientist in Real Life

Who Loves Purple Sweatpants?

People frequently succumb to demand characteristics in life. In your classes, you have likely been asked to provide your opinion about the course or the teacher. When that happened, were you tempted to write what you thought your teacher wanted to hear? If you thought it might help you receive a better grade or spare the teacher's feelings, you probably did. Have you ever received a really nice outfit as a present from your grandmother? Think: purple sweatpants with a paisley shirt. What did you say when you opened the gift? Chances are that you probably said something like, "Thanks, Grandma! These are exactly what I wanted and I can't wait to wear them!" In each example, you are crafting your reply to match what you think the other person wants to hear. While these types of responses are examples of being polite, the social skill of giving a response the other person wants to hear is the essence of a demand characteristic.

Sometimes, self-report measures provide low-quality answers through no fault of the participant. The researcher may simply be asking questions that participants cannot accurately answer, even if they wanted to. This can occur when asking participants to answer questions related to past events. In these cases, participants may exhibit a **retrospective bias** where they view or interpret past events in an inaccurate way. For example, if you ask participants how they felt upon graduating from high school, they may have a more favorable recollection than what their experience actually was at the time. One reason for this is that the way individuals generally think about an event ("graduations are celebrated events") influences how they remember it. At the time, they might have been quite apprehensive about starting college, moving out, or finding a job, but as they reflect back on that event, they focus on the expectation that the event should be a happy one, leading them to remember graduation as a more positive experience than it actually was. Similarly, despite their best intentions, participants may not be able to accurately provide answers to questions about the future. People are notoriously bad at accurately predicting their own future behavior and emotional responses (Gilbert, 2006), so researchers should be cautious when asking participants to self-report anticipated future thoughts or behaviors. Although participants will likely provide a response, it may not be very accurate or informative.

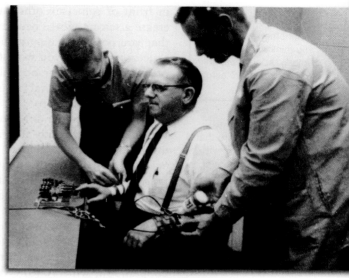

If you had been a participant in Stanley Milgram's obedience studies, would you have shocked others to the point of really hurting them just because the experimenter told you to? Asking people to self-report about hypothetical behavior like this does not always reflect actual behavior because we have a hard time truly envisioning ourselves in the situation.

(From the film Obedience © 1968 by Stanley Milgram, © renewed 1993 by Alexandra Milgram; and distributed by Alexander Street Press.)

Behavioral Measures

What you say does not always match up perfectly with what you do. Ask a young child, "Are you tired?" The response is almost invariably, "No." Rather than rely completely on the child's self-report, wise parents will look at the child's behaviors, such as their amount of whining and crankiness, in order to determine if it is naptime. Good researchers take a similar approach. In addition to asking participants to self-report their thoughts or feelings, researchers will observe participants' behaviors in that situation. A **behavioral measure** assesses the actions a person takes, how the person responds to a request, the person's decisions, or simply what some researchers call "actual behavior" (Knee, Lonsbary, Canevello, & Patrick, 2005).

To properly measure actual behavior, the researcher needs to identify or create a situation in which he or she can observe the behavior and a way of quantifying or measuring that behavior. For example, suppose you want to learn if a person experiences more embarrassment when spilling food or making a mess

retrospective bias when participants view or interpret past events in an inaccurate way.

behavioral measure a measure of participants' actions in a research design.

What Do You Think?
What other ways can you think of to set up an embarrassing situation in which to measure actual behavior?

behavioral trace a behavioral measure that relies on evidence left behind by a participant who is no longer present.

in front of same-sex others or opposite-sex others. First, you would need to create a setting where people typically spill food or make a mess, but in a way that you control (e.g., you rig a ketchup bottle to splatter whenever someone squeezes it). Next, you would need to have this embarrassing act occur in front of either same-sex or opposite-sex people. Finally, you would have to decide what type of behavioral measure you will use to assess your participants' level of embarrassment.

There are several different ways that you can measure a person's behavior within a research study (Lewandowski & Strohmetz, 2009). One way to measure behavior is by being like an investigator on the television show *CSI: Crime Scene Investigation,* using evidence left behind by a person who is no longer present to determine if a behavior occurred. This type of measure is a **behavioral trace** (Fritsche & Linneweber, 2006; Webb, Campbell, Schwarz, Sechrest, & Grove, 1981). For example, by examining the playlists someone has on their phone, you can develop a good idea about that person's musical tastes and perhaps even their personality (Gosling, 2008; Rentfrow & Gosling, 2003). One advantage of using behavioral traces is that it does not require participants' cooperation, which allows the researcher to avoid issues such as social desirability and demand characteristics. A disadvantage is that the interpretation of a behavioral trace's meaning depends on the researcher to draw inferences (Aronson, Wilson, & Brewer, 1998). For example, Michael Crichton, the creator of television's *ER* and the author of *Jurassic Park,* writes in his book *Travels* about how he would work on stories by taping story sections around the room, leaving scraps of tape behind when he was finished. After doing this once while staying at a high-end hotel that prided itself on catering to its guests, he was surprised the next time that he stayed there to find the hotel had placed pieces of tape around the room for him. In this case, the hotel found a behavioral trace (the tape), but misinterpreted its meaning. They believed it was an eccentricity, while, in reality, its placement during Crichton's previous stay was specific to his working on his book.

Despite the need to make an interpretational leap, researchers are able to use behavioral traces in their research. In a study of relationship satisfaction, couples wrote down all of the items they displayed in their home in areas where visitors might see them, such as the living room (Lohmann, Arriaga, & Goodfriend, 2003). For example, a couple might display some pictures of themselves, or a painting they purchased together while on vacation. These objects represented behavioral traces, left behind by the couple, that the researchers interpreted as the couple's desire to affirm the relationship. Other objects, like a recent magazine or the furniture,

How much do you think you can learn about one of your classmates simply by looking at their dorm room or apartment? What behavioral traces would be most informative? Which ones would be least informative? What would someone learn by looking at your room?

(Greg Friedler/Photolibrary/Getty Images)

were not considered relationship affirming. Their analysis revealed that couples with more relationship-affirming behavioral traces reported higher levels of closeness and relationship satisfaction.

To learn about how much a person enjoys reading, a researcher could look at behavioral traces such as the participant's library card activity or account history at an online bookseller. However, in each case, the researcher may not know why there was more or less activity. A person could take out numerous library books because they love to read, or because several people share the same card. Rather than looking for evidence that a behavior has occurred, you could simply observe the behavior as it happens by noting how many books a person checks out at the library. A **behavioral observation** is a measure that relies on directly seeing or observing behavior as it occurs. The advantage of behavioral observation is that it allows you to see the behavior in its entirety as the person actually engages in it. This provides us with more information about the behavior, resulting in less of a need to make guesses about the meaning behind the behavior.

If a behavior is laden with social desirability, behavioral observation also may reveal responses that are more genuine, provided the person does not know they are being observed. For example, several researchers wanted to determine peoples' attitudes toward the homeless (Van den Bos, Euwema, Poortvliet, & Maas, 2007). Certainly, they could have asked participants, "How do you feel about the homeless?" However, it is hard to imagine that anyone would willingly share an unfavorable attitude, because such an attitude would display an undesirable lack of empathy. In a clever design, the researchers asked participants to enter a room containing a row of eight chairs. In the very last chair, the researchers placed several items allegedly left behind by a homeless person who had momentarily stepped out of the room. The experimenter asked the participant to take a seat, and then noted where the participant sat. The implication was that those with less-favorable attitudes sat farther from the homeless person's chair. By taking this approach, the researchers were more likely to determine the participants' true attitudes, rather than the ones they wanted the world to see.

While direct observation provides more information, social desirability and demand characteristics may still prove problematic if participants know they are under observation. Observation also requires some degree of inference. Even if you observe how many books a person checks out from the library, you cannot be sure who will read all of the books. This highlights the difficulty in finding behaviors that accurately reflect how a person thinks or feels. When your professor returns graded papers, some of your classmates spend more time looking over the feedback than others. Why? Researchers suggest that those with artificially inflated self-esteem may be more defensive, leading them to quickly dismiss threatening feedback (Schröder-Abě, Rudolph, Wiesner, & Schütz, 2007). Although this interpretation seems plausible, the researchers cannot definitively know why some students review feedback more quickly than others based on observing the behavior alone.

In addition to observing actual behavior, we can observe our participants' physiological state. Suppose we were interested in how stressed students are

behavioral observation
a behavioral measure that relies on directly seeing or observing behavior.

when taking a high-stakes exam such as the SAT. We could use number of teeth marks made in the wooden pencil used during the exam as a behavioral trace of stress. We could do a behavioral observation by counting the frequency and rate at which participants tap their pencil while looking at the exams, inferring that participants under more stress tap their pencil more frequently and more rapidly. We could also measure physiological changes, such as each student's heart rate, blood pressure, or respiratory rate, before, during, and after the exam period. We could even look at changes in the hormone cortisol in our participants, as the experience of stress influences our endocrine system. Behavioral observations can go beyond what we observe with our eyes. For instance, researchers determined that fetuses in utero can recognize their mothers' voices (Kisilevsky et al., 2009). Obviously, you cannot ask a fetus if the voice they just heard belonged to their mother, but you can make a behavioral observation based on heart rate. When the fetuses heard their own mothers reading to them through an audio recording, their heart rates got faster. Researchers also use techniques such as electroencephalography (EEG), positron emission tomography (PET), and functional magnetic resonance imaging (fMRI) to make observations of brain activity in an effort to learn about participants' thought patterns.

Another specific behavioral measurement that researchers might use involves people's **behavioral choices,** or purposeful selections from several options. People make numerous decisions every day: large or extra-large coffee, Lucky Charms or Cheerios, boxers or briefs, go to the gym or take a nap, go to a party or study for an upcoming exam. These decisions reveal information about an individual's internal state. A person who chooses to go to the gym and eat Cheerios is likely more health conscious, while the person who chooses to go out to a party and eat Lucky Charms is likely less health conscious.

To employ a behavioral choice measure, the researcher creates a situation where participants must choose between several predetermined options (e.g., pick which food you would like to eat) or have the choice of whether or not to engage in a behavior (e.g., will you sign a petition to prevent tuition increases?). Behavioral choice was used in a series of studies examining how culture and previous success influence whether a person would choose a novel activity or an activity in which they had already experienced success (Oishi & Diener, 2003). In the first study, Asian American and European American students worked on solving word puzzles, while in the second study, the participants shot basketballs. In both studies, participants recalled their performance on the original task a month later, and then had the choice of doing a word puzzle or word completion (Study 1), or shooting basketballs or throwing darts (Study 2). Across both studies, European American students who did well on the task previously were more likely to choose to solve word puzzles or shoot basketballs again, whereas for Asian American students, past performance did not relate to their subsequent activity choice. These results show how participants' cultural backgrounds may influence the role of past performance in decision making.

behavioral choice a behavioral measure involving participants making a purposeful selection from several options.

For a summary of the types of behavioral measures, see **Table 4.1**.

TABLE 4.1

Types of Behavioral Measures		
	Definition	**Example**
Behavioral trace	A behavioral measure that relies on evidence left behind by a participant who is no longer present	Determining how worn out the floor is in front of the exhibit as a measure of exhibit popularity
Behavioral observation	A behavioral measure that relies on directly seeing or observing behavior	Timing how long a person will work on an unsolvable puzzle as a measure of motivation
Behavioral choice	A behavioral measure involving participants making a purposeful selection from several options	Giving a person the option to work in a group or alone on the next task in a study as a measure of group affiliation

Advantages of Behavioral Measures

Examining participants' behavior is important because what people think they will do may not always coincide with what they actually do. Have you ever said that you were going to start a major paper or project early, only to end up working on it at the last minute? If so, you have first-hand experience with the discrepancy between self-report and behavior. By including behavioral measures, researchers can evaluate whether participants' self-reports are consistent with their actual behavior. This may make it easier to identify potential biases in participants' self-reports, or may make people's behaviors easier to interpret. Suppose you were interested in voters' attitudes toward different political candidates. Using a self-report, you find that voters view one candidate more favorably. By observing whether or not voters are more likely to discard the flyers of the less preferred candidates, you will have more confidence in the conclusions that you draw from your study (e.g., Cialdini & Baumann, 1981).

By seeing what people do, it is easier for a researcher to minimize issues with lying, social desirability, and demand characteristics, particularly if participants do not know you are measuring their behavior. Further, when a study uses a behavioral measure, the results and the study itself become more accessible to nonscientists (Cialdini, 2009; Taylor, 2009). Rather than talking about survey responses regarding candidate preferences on a self-report scale, it is often more interesting to discuss a behavior that can demonstrate how a person truly feels. Think of the study that assessed voters' attitudes toward political candidates by looking at how likely they were to throw an opposing candidate's flyer on the ground (Cialdini & Baumann, 1981). As expected, those who found a flyer on their car for a candidate they did not vote for were more likely to litter by leaving

participant reactivity
participants act differently or unnaturally because they know someone is watching them.

unobtrusive measures
strategies that allow for observation and assessment without the participant's awareness.

the flyer behind. Despite these advantages, researchers have lamented the fact that overall, but especially in social and personality psychology, researchers have been increasingly moving away from measuring behavior (Baumeister, Vohs, & Funder, 2007; Patterson, 2008).

Disadvantages of Behavioral Measures

One reason for the move away from behavioral measures is their disadvantages, such as being time-consuming, expensive, and cumbersome to use. We can potentially survey 100 participants in just 10 minutes, provided that they all self-report at the same time. This level of efficiency is not necessarily possible for behavioral observations. Let's look again at the example about social embarrassment. A lot of planning must go into orchestrating a situation to measure behavior in a scientific way. At a minimum, we are only able to observe one participant at a time, not to mention the time it takes to set up the study. Also, there is the risk of **participant reactivity**, where participants may act differently or unnaturally if they know someone is watching them. For example, participants may work longer on a boring task, such as counting the dimples on a golf ball, in an experiment than they would at home because they know an experimenter is watching them. Because the researcher assigns the participants the boring task, it may also serve as a demand characteristic that cues the participants about how to behave. They may believe that the experimenter is studying task endurance, and so they will persist at completing this task. In either case, the participant's behavior is not natural, which hurts the results. One way to reduce these problems is by using nonreactive or **unobtrusive measures.** These are strategies that allow researchers to make measurements outside of the participant's awareness. We could secretly monitor their behavior (e.g., through a one-way mirror), or we could observe them in a setting where the behavior naturally takes place. If participants do not know researchers are watching or that they are even part of a study, it is highly unlikely that they will purposely behave differently than usual.

For a summary of self-report measures versus behavioral measures, see **Table 4.2**.

TABLE 4.2

Summary of Self-Report and Behavioral Measures		
	Advantages	**Disadvantages**
Self-report	• Cheap and easy to administer • Provides first-hand information about internal processes (thoughts and feelings)	• Accuracy of self-knowledge is questionable • Social desirability bias • Demand characteristics • Retrospective bias
Behavioral	• Provides information about what people actually do • More engaging for participants • Findings may be more relatable to the general public	• Expensive and time-consuming to administer • Demand characteristics • Participant reactivity

Thinking Like a Scientist in Real Life

You're on Camera! Act Natural?

Suppose researchers selected you to participate in a study in which you were asked to live in a house on a New Jersey beach. In this study, multiple TV cameras follow you 24 hours a day, just waiting for you to do something interesting. You know that if you come across as boring, you will not be able to continue participating in a study that is paying you a lot of money. How will you behave? Will you act normally in various situations, or will you change your behavior? Participant reactivity is a problem when people know that they are being observed and their behavior is being scrutinized. Under these circumstances, it is difficult to know if a person's behavior is authentic or contrived as they encounter various situations. This is something to think about as you watch "reality" TV shows like *Keeping Up With the Kardashians* and *Project Runway*.

Determining Which Measure Is Best

As you can see, self-report and behavioral measures both have their own strengths and weaknesses. The reality is that no one type of measure is perfect and researchers should use multiple types of measures. By incorporating several ways of measuring the variables into your study, the advantages of one measurement type can compensate for the disadvantages of another (Rosenthal & Rosnow, 2009). Suppose you wanted to study patriotism. The inherent potential for social desirability responding with this variable may make self-report problematic ("Of course I'm patriotic, I love my country"). A good decision would be to utilize behavioral measures that are less prone to social desirability concerns, such as behavioral traces (e.g., how many U.S. flags participants own) or behavioral choices (e.g., when given a choice of bumper stickers, will participants choose a patriotic one?). However, if you wanted to study how much a person loves his or her parents, a self-report is better because any behavior the researcher could measure introduces unnecessary inference (e.g., if people hug their mother, does it mean they love her, or is it a social obligation?). To truly learn how a person feels in a given situation, it may be best to ask the person who knows that answer. However, by using additional measures, you can have increased confidence in the study's conclusions.

YOUR TURN 4.1

1. Audrey, a senior thesis student, is interested in views on parenting. Specifically, she is interested in whether frequent moving from one home to another as a child influences trust as an adult. She asks participants to self-identify whether they moved often as a child or not and then complete questionnaires about trust. Later, she compares the responses of those who moved with those who did not. What type of design is Audrey using?
   a. Nonexperimental
   b. True experimental
   c. Quasi-experimental
   d. Qualitative research

2. A researcher wants to conduct a study on college students' conscientiousness and study habits. To measure conscientiousness, the researcher examines students' dorm rooms to see how organized the rooms are, how neat their desks appear, and how orderly they keep their closets. What type of measure is the researcher using for conscientiousness?

   a. Behavioral traces
   b. Self-reports
   c. Behavioral observations
   d. Behavioral choices

3. You notice that the participants in your study are agreeing with everything that you ask them on a questionnaire even if the answer they give is unflattering. Which of the following biases may be a potential problem in your study?

   a. Retrospective bias
   b. Participant reactivity
   c. Demand characteristics
   d. Social desirability

How did you do? Turn to the end of the chapter to check your answers.

Types of Measurement Error

As we construct our research studies and make decisions about how to collect data and measure variables, we need to recognize that, regardless of our decisions, our measurements will not be perfect. Do not despair; any time a scientist attempts to measure something that happens in the natural world, there is some degree of error. When you step on a scale, the number it displays is not your true weight, but, rather, a close approximation. It will overestimate or underestimate your weight to some degree. The degree to which the measurement differs from your true weight could be due to a poorly constructed scale, an uneven floor, the temperature or humidity in the room, the clothes you are wearing, or the meal you just enjoyed. The same is true for psychological variables. Even if you measure your research participants' general anxiety level using a well-established anxiety scale, their scores will represent their true anxiety level as well as extraneous factors such as how much sleep they got the night before, how they interpreted the questions, or even their plans for the next day.

Many of you took the SAT or ACT test to assess your academic ability when you were applying for college. While no one really likes taking these exams, they are useful in the college admission process because they provide a standardized way to compare college applicants. If you took this exam more than once, your scores were probably similar, but not identical, because your actual score, or **raw score**, contains two things: your true score and error. The **true score** is an accurate depiction that represents your actual ability, or what your score would be on a perfect test, free of extraneous factors. **Error** represents those extraneous influences that cause the raw score to deviate (up or down) from the true score.

raw score the actual score, comprised of a true score and error.

true score what the score would be if the test were a perfect measure of the attribute being tested and were uninfluenced by any extraneous factors.

error extraneous influences that cause the raw score to deviate from the true score.

Suppose you did poorly on the exam. There are two possible reasons why this occurred. First, you may not be very bright, meaning that the raw score was a perfect reflection of your true score on the test. However, your raw score may have been lower than your true academic ability due to unrelated factors. Perhaps you broke up with your significant other the night before the test, overslept the morning of the test, forgot to have breakfast, and received a traffic ticket on the way to the testing site. Certainly, these factors have very little to do with your academic ability, but may affect how well you did on the test. Perhaps you prepared for the exam by taking a course in test-taking strategies, had plenty of sleep the night before the test, had a good breakfast, and happened to make some lucky guesses on the questions that you did not know. In this case, your raw score may have been higher than your actual ability because of these other factors. Obviously, the goal is to have a measure in which error is minimized so that the raw score is more similar to the true score. In order to achieve this, we must recognize that there are two types of measurement error: random error and bias.

Random Error

Random error is variation from one's true score due to unsystematic or chance factors that occur in a haphazard, disorganized, or arbitrary way. You can think of random error as glitches in your Netflix streaming or static on a radio. In this second example, the static gets in the way of the true signal you are looking for (the song), but the static noise is unpredictable in the parts of the song it interrupts. In the example of weighing ourselves, we can determine if our measurement tool (the scale) introduces random error by checking our weight several times. If we get a different reading (sometimes higher, sometimes lower) over repeated measurements, then random error is present. In psychological research, random error can exist for a variety of reasons. As researchers, we might carelessly record or code some of the raw scores (e.g., mistyping a *4* when we intended a *7*). Sometimes odd events, like a fire alarm going off, might occur during a testing session, possibly influencing participants' responses. Some participants may misread a question and answer inappropriately or carelessly. In each case, the error is non-systematic and occurred in an unpredictable way that affects our results.

Due to random error's unpredictability, we cannot eliminate it. However, we can assume that these errors tend to cancel themselves out over the long run, which is why collecting data from a large number of individuals is a good idea. Think of it this way: If you have one person in your study and the fire alarm goes off while that person completes your measures, 100% of your measurements contain this piece of random error. But if you had collected data from 99 additional participants at other times, the fire alarm will create random error for only 1% of your sample. With more measurements, problematic measurements become less influential. Even so, fluctuations in raw scores due to random error can make it difficult to evaluate how one variable influences another variable. Thankfully, we use statistics to evaluate our results. Statistics are the ideal tool for addressing random error because they enable us to estimate what the true score for our participants is amid the random error. Without delving into the math involved, statistics help us identify consistent patterns in our measurements despite differences that may be due to random error.

random error variation from the measure's true score due to unsystematic or chance factors.

bias error that consistently pushes scores in a given direction; also known as systematic error.

Bias

The much more problematic form of error is **bias** or **systematic error.** This is error that varies systematically or consistently pushes scores higher or lower in a way that leads to inaccurate or misleading conclusions. Suppose you like to adjust your bathroom scale so that you always weigh 5 pounds more than you actually do in order to motivate you to stay on your diet. Your scale will never actually indicate your true weight. If we measure a group of individuals using your scale, all of our measurements will overestimate the true weight of the group. A song on the radio that has certain words bleeped out is also an example of bias because there is a consistent pattern to the missing parts of the song.

Measurement bias can have important societal implications. The SAT test has been criticized for being biased against specific subgroups in the population (Santelices & Wilson, 2010). Although unintentional, recent research suggests that one's racial background may influence how one answers questions on the SAT, even after controlling for academic ability. Specifically, many of the questions on the verbal section of the SAT involve cultural expressions that are more familiar to those immersed in White society (Santelices & Wilson, 2010). This suggests that the SAT may systematically underestimate the academic ability of certain minority groups, putting them at a disadvantage for admission to college. Although the SAT creators did not design the test to discriminate, this bias may result in just that.

Bias can also occur if the participants placed in the experimental group receive preferential treatment while the control group does not. For example, a memory researcher who gives one group more time to memorize a list of words than the other group is biasing the results. Unfortunately, statistics cannot address bias, but good research practices can help eliminate unintended systematic differences. While we cannot eliminate random error, we can estimate or control for biases with good experimental design. As you design your study, you will need to choose data collection strategies that minimize random error and prevent the introduction of bias.

Keys to Effective Measurement

There is more to measuring a variable than the measurement tool itself. In order to minimize error, we must consider the setting or administration of the measure as well. There are ways to set yourself up for success, and there are pitfalls you should be sure to avoid.

Setting the Stage

The researcher creates the context or setting in which measurement occurs, establishes the instructions participants receive, and dictates the manner in which to give these instructions. Deviations in the data collection setting such as room appearance, presence of noise, or variations in the researcher's treatment of participants can introduce measurement error.

Suppose we are doing a study on optimism and memory to see if people who feel optimistic remember more than those who are less optimistic. Unfortunately, we have to conduct the study in two different rooms. One lab room is spacious and painted in a bright color, with a large window that looks out over a beautifully landscaped lawn. The other room is very small and painted gray, and has poor artificial lighting. If you can imagine yourself feeling more optimistic in one room than the other, then you can see the problem. The lack of consistency between the two spaces creates the potential for random error or bias. The room introduces random error if the big bright room makes some participants more optimistic, but others less optimistic in an inconsistent way. However, if the big bright room consistently makes participants more optimistic, the room has created bias.

To avoid this problem, you should incorporate **standardization** by keeping the experimental situation the same for everyone and as free from variation as possible. To accomplish this, researchers need to develop and adhere to an identical research protocol for all participants. As you may recall from Chapter 2, a research protocol outlines the order in which the steps in the study should happen, as well as a script of exactly what the experimenter should say to the participants. The protocol and script help ensure that the researcher treats everyone the same and minimizes error. Standardized tests like the SAT often have highly detailed administration protocols. The protocol may require proctors administering the test to start at a specific time, read a specific set of instructions that tell you when to grab a pencil and when to rip open the exam, and time exactly how many minutes you get on each section. This seemingly overly strict protocol is a nationwide attempt to ensure standardization. After all, you would not be happy if students at another location received extra time or were allowed to use a dictionary. Standardization helps minimize bias, but it cannot remove random errors such as a distracting noise outside the testing room. While there is no perfect solution to these random errors, having a large sample and taking multiple measurements will help.

standardization keeping the experimental situation the same for everyone and as free from variation as possible.

Can you see how your responses to research questions might differ depending on the room in which you are sitting? We must be sure to keep each context or setting in which measurement occurs as standardized and free of variation as possible. *(Jo-Ann Richards/First Light/Getty Images; Tim Macpherson/Photodisc/Getty Images)*

If you were asked to observe people's friendliness in the dining hall, in what ways might you display observer bias? *(Frank and Helena/Cultura RM Exclusive/Getty Images)*

observer or scorer bias misinterpreting an observation based on the researcher's existing beliefs, previous experiences, or expectations.

sensitivity the range of data a researcher can gather from a particular instrument.

Building the Better Measurement

In an ideal world, we have error-free measurement tools. When studies use a behavioral measure, that measurement tool is often the researcher or observer. Because observers are human, they are prone to **observer or scorer bias**, which involves misinterpreting an observation based on one's existing beliefs, previous experiences, or expectations. The observer is not doing something intentionally wrong. In most cases, observers mean well but interpret the world through their own experiences. Imagine you have joined the local police force for the day and are responsible for catching people speeding. As you sit in your cruiser, something on the radio distracts you, causing you to accidentally drop the radar gun on the floor. As you look up, you see two vehicles speeding down the road. One vehicle is an older minivan complete with wood-grain paneling down the side, while the other vehicle is a shiny, cherry red sports car. Which would you pull over? It probably would not be the "wood-paneled wonder" because that vehicle is likely inconsistent with your previously held beliefs or experiences with fast cars. In this case, your beliefs about sports cars and minivans may bias how you observe their behavior, leading you to be more likely to assume the sports car is speeding.

Removing observer bias completely is difficult, but it is important to minimize it by extensively training any observers ahead of time. If you are completing a study where the observer needs to code children's aggressive behavior on a playground, you will want to minimize any biases the observers may have. For example, it is possible that observers could interpret boys wrestling as "boys being boys" and not aggression, while observers who see girls doing the same thing could label it aggression. Similarly, if observers witness kids verbally teasing one another, depending on their personal definitions of aggression (e.g., "aggression is always physical"), they may not register this behavior as aggressive.

It is also important to avoid bias in self-report measures like surveys. One way to do this is to make sure your measure has proper **sensitivity,** or that the response options fully capture all of the participants' possible responses. If a measure has too few options, it is not sensitive enough and does not assess the exact magnitude of a response. For example, on his show *The Colbert Report,* comedian Stephen Colbert would measure his guests' attitudes toward then President George W. Bush by asking, "George W. Bush: Great President or the Greatest President?" (Colbert, 2008). What if someone did not like President Bush? The measure is not sensitive enough to capture that. When a measure fails to gauge the full breadth of a respondent's true feelings, it has a restricted range. To increase the range and the measure's sensitivity, a researcher could have a scale with many options: "Please rate how you feel about George W. Bush using the following scale: 1 = worst president ever; 1,000 = best president ever." Certainly, you now have a wider range, but these response options are overly sensitive, such that differences between responses are not very meaningful. If one respondent gives a rating of 765, while another says 759, a 6-point difference on a 1,000-point scale is not likely to indicate a meaningful difference in opinion. To strike the right balance between overly sensitive and not sensitive enough, many self-report measures use 5 to 9 response options (**Figure 4.3**).

Lack of Sensitivity

To what extent do you enjoy the food at the dining hall?

1   2

Not at   Very
All   Much

Ratings on this scale are too restrictive and do not allow respondents to express their true feelings.

Overly Sensitive

To what extent do you enjoy the food at the dining hall?

1.........10.........20........30........40.........50.........60........70.......80.......90........100

Not at   Very
All   Much

Ratings on this scale are not likely to indicate a meaningful difference in opinion.

Optimum Sensitivity

To what extent do you enjoy the food at the dining hall?

1   2   3   4   5   6   7

Not at   Average   Very
All   Much

Ratings on this scale grant respondents enough range to express their feelings while still providing meaningful data.

FIGURE 4.3 Not So Sensitive, Overly Sensitive, and Optimally Sensitive Scales.

ceiling effect occurs when the upper boundary of a measurement tool is set too low, leading most to select the highest response.

floor effect occurs when the lower boundary of a measurement tool is set too high, leading most to select the lowest response.

This provides participants with enough flexibility to select a number that closely fits how they feel, but does not overwhelm them with so many options that the numbers lose their meaning.

When a measure does not have appropriate sensitivity, the vast majority of participants might have similar responses. If you were to ask participants their annual income, but the highest level they could select was "$35,000 per year," you might get a **ceiling effect**, in which participants would tend to provide responses at the top end of the scale. Because the highest option is $35,000, every person with this salary and higher would be forced to answer the same. A ceiling effect occurs when a measurement tool's upper boundary is set too low, leading everyone to select the highest response, which provides an imprecise and inaccurate representation of the information we hope to gather. Adding income categories up to "$200,000 or above" would make the measure more sensitive and reduce the likelihood of a ceiling effect. It is also possible to have a ceiling effect, or piling of scores on the high end of a scale, if a test is too easy. In addition, a ceiling effect may occur if the independent variable is unable to affect the dependent variable. For example, if you hope to boost children's self-esteem by exposing them to a treatment, but all the participants already have high self-esteem, the treatment can have no further impact on their already high self-esteem. A **floor effect** is the opposite outcome, in which all of the responses are at the low end of the scale, which would happen if you asked, "How likely would you be to go skydiving without a parachute? 1 = not at all likely; 7 = very likely." In this case, the vast majority of participants (or all of them, we hope) would not skydive without a parachute, so they would all answer a "1." With so many scores on the low end of the scale, the measure essentially becomes useless.

As we set out to answer questions we have about the natural world, we must remember that no measure is perfect. By knowing the various sources of bias and random error, we can take steps to eliminate or reduce error and improve the effectiveness of our measure.

YOUR TURN 4.2

1. If the speedometer in your car consistently shows that you are going more slowly than you actually are, it has which type of error?
   a. Random error
   b. Nonstandardization error
   c. Bias
   d. Nonsystematic error

2. You ask 100 history majors how interesting they find World War I, and notice that almost everyone chooses either a 6 or 7 on your 7-point measurement scale. Which of the following may be a problem with your measurement?
   a. Scorer bias
   b. Ceiling effect
   c. Systematic error
   d. Floor effect

3. Which of the following measurement problems is beyond your control?
   a. Measurement sensitivity
   b. Observer bias
   c. Random error
   d. Bias

How did you do? Turn to the end of the chapter to check your answers.

Reliability and Validity of Measures

In life, quality matters. A quality diamond is admired more and worth considerably more than a diamond full of flaws. To evaluate a diamond's quality, a jeweler will direct you to the 4 Cs: carat, color, clarity, and cut. In research design, quality matters as well. While researchers lack a fancy mnemonic like the 4 Cs, we do have two ways to assess a measure's quality: reliability and validity.

Before discussing these concepts, it is important to note that there are many different types of reliability and validity. Chapter 4 focuses on the most general differences to provide an introductory overview. We will discuss many other types of reliability and validity in subsequent chapters, where you will learn about these concepts in the context of a study. This approach will help bring these terms to life and allow you practice thinking like a scientist while making decisions about a study.

▶ Curious about the specialized types of reliability and validity and how we use them in research?
SEE CHAPTERS 6 AND 7, pp. 164, 177–178, 212–215

Reliability of a Measure

Reliability refers to consistency. You have a reliable car if each time you step on the brakes, it slows down. Similarly, your best friend is reliable if he or she dependably helps you when you need it. In research, a measure's reliability depends on whether it minimizes error and routinely provides a similar or consistent measurement each time we use it on the same target. For example, a ruler is a highly reliable measurement tool. If we use the same ruler to measure the same item (e.g., the span of a person's palm), we should have minimal error and will get the same answer each time we take that measurement. While there is variability from person to person in palm width, each time we use the ruler to measure the same palm, we will obtain a consistent result. A ruler is reliable because its measurements are stable (e.g., the length and markings do not change). As long as the human user avoids error and always reads it perfectly, any difference in measurement is due to the variation in width from palm to palm and not due to the measure itself. But while a measure might be reliable, we must remember that humans are not always perfectly consistent. We have certain aspects that are relatively stable, like personality. If you are a conscientious person, then you are likely organized and self-disciplined in most environments. However, humans are highly variable in other aspects. Although researchers change over time, they can still reliably measure their variables in a moment of a research study. We must avoid overextending our findings by mistakenly portraying a snapshot as indicative of a larger pattern.

reliability the stability or consistency of a measure.

Ideally, we want our measurement tools in psychology to be as reliable as a ruler. Human behavior, emotion, and thought are more complex concepts to measure than length, so without reliable behavioral measures, we cannot have any confidence in our findings. Suppose that after catching a few of your friends lying, you want to study dishonesty. Reviewing past research, you learn that researchers have measured dishonesty by seeing whether or not participants cheat by looking at the answers to problems on which they are working, or overpay themselves for completed work (Vohs & Schooler, 2008). In addition to measuring dishonesty by looking at a person's actions, you can also measure dishonesty physiologically via pupil dilation. Human pupils dilate due to a variety of experiences: during cognitive difficulty (Beatty, 1986), when viewing sexual images (Finke, Deuter, Hengesch, & Schächinger, 2017), in response to angry faces (Feurer, Burkhouse, Siegle, & Gibb, 2017), and under stress (Baltaci & Gokcay, 2016). Using a physiological response like pupil dilation as a measure might be a good choice because participants cannot fake it, thus reducing the potential for social desirability responses, which seems important when measuring dishonesty. Still, to use pupil dilation as a measure of dishonesty, we would need to find a way to consistently measure how dilated one's pupil has become.

Validity of a Measure

▶ What are the types of validity, and how do we use them in research? To learn more about external validity, SEE CHAPTER 6, p. 164. For more on internal validity, SEE CHAPTER 8, p. 250. You can learn more about specialized types of validity in CHAPTER 7, pp. 214–215.

While consistency is one indication of a measure's quality, by itself it is an incomplete indicator. Thinking back to the ruler, if its numbering happened to skip from 1 to 4 (i.e., it was missing 2 and 3), the ruler would reliably and consistently provide a measurement. However, that measure would be wrong because it would give a measurement of 4 inches when the actual length is really 2 inches. Similarly, if you decided to measure a person's dishonesty by asking, "Are you always honest? Yes or No," you may consistently and dependably get the same answer, "Yes!" Yet, despite the participant reliably giving the same response, it may not be accurate. Certainly, a dishonest person could also consistently say, "Yes!" In this case, the measure is reliable, but it is reliably measuring the wrong thing. It is hard to have any confidence in your findings if aspects of your study are consistently wrong. In addition to consistency, we also need to consider the accuracy or **validity** of our measurements. When we have validity, we are confident that we are measuring what we believe we are measuring.

What Do You Think?

Is your GPA a valid measure of your performance in college? Why or why not?

We might also question the idea that pupil dilation is a valid measure of dishonesty. As cognitive and emotional stresses are both known to cause pupil dilation, it is reasonable to assume that people feel stress when they are being dishonest and therefore will display pupil dilation (Janisse & Bradley, 1980). Perhaps poker players are wise to wear sunglasses to hide when they are bluffing. However, in cases where people are comfortable lying and do not feel any stress, their pupils will not dilate and our honesty measure will be inaccurate. To ensure that pupil dilation can validly measure lying, we would have to be sure that participants' pupils consistently dilate in situations where they are lying and are in a comparatively constricted state when they are telling the truth. It is also possible that pupil dilation may simply measure cognitive and emotional stress, rather than lying. This may not seem like an important difference, but it would be if you were falsely accused of committing a serious crime and forced to take

validity the degree to which a tool measures what it claims to measure.

a lie detector test based on pupil dilation. If the thought of being falsely accused causes you any cognitive or emotional stress, your pupils may dilate, leading to the inaccurate and mistaken conclusion that you are a liar.

The Interplay Between Reliability and Validity

To construct the best research design possible, we need to use measures that are high in both reliability and validity. While the two are related, they may not perfectly coincide with one another. If you fail to establish reliability, you cannot have validity. But once you have reliability, your measure can either be reliably wrong, making it invalid, or reliably right, making it valid. Suppose that you wanted to measure extraversion, or the extent to which a person prefers social gatherings and interacting with others. To do this, you decide to have participants carry around a recorder so that you can analyze their conversation. Unfortunately, because participants do not always place their recorders in a good spot, the recordings are often hard to understand. As a result, it is difficult to consistently hear what they say well enough to code the conversations reliably. While conversations may theoretically be a valid measure of extraversion, until we are able to measure them consistently, we cannot know for sure.

Let's try again. This time, because eyes are allegedly windows to the soul, you decide to measure participants' iris radius as an indicator of extraversion. You know that you can consistently take this measurement, which will make it reliable. Despite the fact that you have a reliable measurement, you will not learn anything meaningful about extraversion because there is no evidence that iris circumference portrays anything about your personality. As such, the measurement tool, though reliable, lacks validity because it fails to accurately measure the intended variable.

YOUR TURN 4.3

1. You are convinced that an exam was unfair because none of the questions even remotely resembled what was taught in the class. In this case, you are questioning the exam's
   a. reliability.
   b. reactivity.
   c. validity.
   d. sensitivity.

2. A researcher asks participants to complete a personality measure. Two weeks later, the researcher asks the same participants to complete the same personality measure. The researcher then compares the two scores for consistency. What is the researcher trying to evaluate?
   a. The reliability of the measure
   b. The validity of the research findings
   c. The validity of the measure
   d. The sensitivity of the measure

3. Whenever you choose a measurement tool, you need to first determine if the instrument has acceptable
   a. reactivity.
   b. validity.
   c. nonbias.
   d. reliability.

How did you do? Turn to the end of the chapter to check your answers.

 Research in Action

Is the Swagger-Meter 1.0 a Quality Measure?

Psychologists use a wide variety of measures in research to learn about their participants. Individuals also like to learn about themselves and see how they "measure up" on a variety of traits. Companies are keenly aware of this and seek to provide a variety of metrics, scores, and measurement opportunities for their customers. Now that you know more about what goes into a quality measurement, you are better able to critically evaluate those things that you see in the world.

Let's see if you can help evaluate a new measure for a psychological quality you may not have thought about—swagger. What is swagger, you ask? Can you even measure something like that? Well, that's for you to decide. YOLO Inc. has developed the Swagger-Meter 1.0, which "provides user-specific, science-based insights into a key aspect of young adults' personality." Their business plan involves placing the Swagger-Meter in malls across the country to target the key young adult demographic. YOLO Inc. wants you to get in on the ground floor as an investor. Using what you know about validity, reliability, demand characteristics, and standardization, determine whether the Swagger-Meter is going to be "Swagtastic" or "Meh" in the online activity, *Is the Swagger-Meter 1.0 a Quality Measure?*

🔲 **LaunchPad** To complete this activity, visit LaunchPad at launchpadworks.com

Recruiting Research Participants

Choosing your measurement tools is not the only important decision you will make as you construct your study. You are going to need to decide who the best participants are to help you answer your research question. If your research question concerns how 6-year-olds engage in perspective taking during play, you obviously need children as your participants. That means that recruiting participants from the campus student center and local retirement village are out. Local day-care centers, schools, or playgrounds would be better options. Next, you will need to determine if you want your study's findings to apply to all 6-year-olds or to a specific subgroup, such as males or inner-city residents. In either case, the overall goal is to research a relatively small set of people and apply what you learn about them to a larger group.

Sampling the Population

Suppose you wanted to learn more about how students at your institution view a proposed tuition increase. In an ideal world, you would simply ask every single student on campus his or her opinion. If you are able to gather responses from every possible person in the group you are studying, you have measured the **population**. Unfortunately, questioning an entire population is usually impractical. First, you may not be able to identify all of the members of the population, particularly if the population of interest is extremely large. Even if you were able to identify the entire population, some may not be available or want to participate in your study. Including the entire population in your study may not be possible for other practical (Do you really have time to do it?) or economic (Will you have money to travel so that you can ask everyone your questions?) reasons as well.

Luckily, researchers have a solution to this problem. Rather than question everyone in the entire population, we simply study a subset, or a **sample,** of this population. Using what we learn from this smaller group, we make inferences concerning the nature of the larger population. We often use this strategy in our daily lives to help us make decisions. Have you ever stood in front of an ice cream counter, unable to decide which flavor to order? Sometimes we will ask for just a "taste" or a "sample" of the different ice creams to help us make our final decision. The underlying assumption is that the small sample (i.e., spoonful) is representative of the larger population (i.e., the entire container), and that by taking a small taste of the ice cream, you will be able to make judgments about the overall flavor of the ice cream in that container. This is the same premise behind sampling in the social sciences. By studying a smaller sample or subset of a population, we should be able to gain accurate insights into the nature of the population itself. However, the degree to which we can make this leap of faith depends on our **sampling plan,** the explicit strategy we use for recruiting participants from the population we want to study.

In any sampling plan, the goal is to make sure your participants represent the specific characteristics of the group to which you hope the findings will apply. A **representative sample** is one that shares specific characteristics with the population you want to study. If you want to learn more about the attitudes of students at your school, you should not simply collect data on your friends or classmates, and then automatically assume that most students at your institution hold similar attitudes. In this case, your friends may not accurately represent all of the students at your school. It is better to collect data on a variety of students on campus, such as those with different majors, commuter and residential students, and four-year and transfer students. There are several approaches you can use to obtain a representative sample.

population the entire group of interest in a research study from which the researcher draws the sample.

sample a subset of the population from which the researcher collects data.

sampling plan the explicit strategy used for recruiting participants from the population.

representative sample a sample with specific features that characterize the population of interest.

Will a sample-sized spoonful of ice cream always accurately portray how the entire "population" of the container tastes? What if we sample cookie dough or rocky road ice cream? What is the solution? *(Clark Brennan/Alamy)*

Types of Sampling

One general approach to sample selection is **probability sampling,** which means everyone in a given population has an equal chance of selection for participation. Perhaps the most common strategy used for probability sampling is **simple random sampling,** in which the researcher uses chance to select a subset of individuals from a population. In this method, each member of the population has the same probability of selection for the sample (e.g., your friends are no more likely to be in the sample than another person's friends). The selection of any one population member into the sample does not affect the probability of selecting the remaining members (e.g., your friend's selection for a study does not impact your chances of selection). To effectively select a simple random sample, you must have access to the entire population, which is often difficult to do.

To illustrate, suppose you decide to randomly sample students at your school. To start, you list every student at your school (population) in alphabetical order, and then roll dice to select the sample. If you get a *3,* you will take the third person on the list. If you then roll an *8,* you will move eight spots down the list to select the next person and so on until you have a sample of 50 people. Using this strategy, you may have 50 participants before you reach the end of the list, which means that those at the end of the alphabet did not have the same chance for inclusion in the sample as those in the beginning of the alphabet (e.g., Amelia Adams is more likely to be in the sample than Zach Zukalow). Additionally, selecting participants early in the alphabet decreased the probability of selecting others. To obtain a true simple random sample, you could put everyone's names individually in a large lottery-like tumbler, and then pull each name out one by one until you have a big enough sample.

There are several other sampling strategies that utilize probability sampling. In **stratified random sampling,** the researcher divides the population into strata or subpopulations. Then the researcher uses simple random sampling to select participants from each stratum, making sure the sample represents the population at large. For example, if you know the population comprises 60% Democrats and 40% Republicans, for every 10 participants, you randomly select 6 from the Democrat stratum and 4 from the Republican stratum. **Cluster random sampling** uses a similar strategy, where you divide the total population into groups (or clusters) and you use simple random sampling to select which clusters will participate in your study. The sample includes all participants from the selected cluster. For example, suppose a school board would like to survey their teachers about the effectiveness of their classroom resources. The board might divide or cluster the school district by individual schools and then use simple random sampling to select 15 schools to survey. Each teacher at those selected schools would receive the survey to complete.

Random sampling makes the assumption that although your sample will not be identical to the population of interest, there should be no biases in the participants you pick. Therefore, the sample will be representative of the population. Unfortunately, it is difficult to test this assumption. Further, meeting the criteria of random sampling may be difficult if the population is extremely large or if it is difficult to identify every member of the population.

---

probability sampling a sampling approach in which everyone in a given population has an equal chance of selection for participation.

simple random sampling a probability sampling method in which a subset of individuals are randomly selected from population members.

stratified random sampling includes dividing the population into strata or subpopulations and using simple random sampling to select participants from each strata in proportion to the population at large.

cluster random sampling dividing the total population into groups (or clusters), then using simple random sampling to select which clusters participate; all observations in a selected cluster are included in the sample.

Due to the inherent difficulties in random sampling, researchers use other methods to obtain a sample. Another general sampling approach is **nonprobability sampling**. Nonprobability sampling comes in various shapes and sizes, but essentially it means that everyone does not have an equal chance of being sampled, thereby creating a bias in your sample. Using a nonprobability sample makes it harder to apply the results you get from the sample to the general population.

Perhaps the most common form of nonprobability sampling is **convenience sampling**. Convenience sampling involves nonrandomly recruiting participants from a known, readily available population. For example, suppose you wanted to learn about the opinions of the students at your school regarding a proposed tuition hike. To make life easy, you decide to sample the students in your classes to gauge the attitudes of the entire student body. While this sample is certainly convenient, it may not reflect how most of the students at your institution feel. First, if you take mostly psychology classes, psychology majors will probably be overrepresented in your sample. If you only attend day classes, then evening students will be underrepresented in your study.

Although this may seem like a minor issue, given that older students may be more likely to take evening classes to accommodate their work schedules, you could have an age bias in your sample. In both cases, your sample fails to accurately represent the entire population. When television shows, radio hosts, or websites use opinion surveys on issues like celebrity divorces, they use convenience sampling. It is important to acknowledge that different types of people listen to certain radio stations, so any one station's listeners are not necessarily reflective of Americans in general. In addition, the listeners who responded to the poll are probably not even representative of all the station's listeners. Rather, the respondents are likely individuals who have very strong opinions and care enough to want their opinion known. Thus, it is possible that the same exact poll on another radio station would yield drastically different results. This highlights the limited nature of any conclusions drawn from nonprobability sampling.

A convenience sample is not the only strategy for nonprobability sampling. In **quota sampling**, researchers decide ahead of time that they want their sample to hold certain characteristics (e.g., 70% Christian). They are then free to choose any participant they want as long as the final sample meets this quota. In **purposive sampling**, the researcher chooses the sample based on predetermined qualities that they think make someone appropriate for the study. Researchers primarily use purposive sampling when there are a limited number of people that have expertise in the area under investigation. For example, if you wanted to understand key personality traits of high-performing CEOs from successful companies, you would need to establish what qualifies as

nonprobability sampling everyone in the population does not have an equal chance of being sampled, therefore creating a bias in the sample.

convenience sampling nonrandom selections of participants who are readily available to the researcher to serve as the sample.

quota sampling freely choosing any participant as long as they help meet predetermined targets for the sample's characteristics.

purposive sampling the researcher chooses the sample based on who they think would be appropriate or qualified for the study; used when a limited number of people have expertise in the area under investigation.

Do you think television shows such as *American Idol* rely on random sampling to determine who their viewers believe is the most talented or best performer? *(FOX/Getty Images)*

snowball sampling
existing study participants recruit future participants from among their acquaintances.

"high-performing" and what makes a company "successful." Then, you would intentionally sample only those who meet your criteria.

A researcher might also use **snowball sampling**. In this strategy, existing study participants recruit future participants from among their acquaintances. The first few participants refer a friend. The friends also refer a friend, and so on. Samples selected with this method may have bias because they give people with more social connections a higher chance of selection (Berg, 2006). Remember that bias is likely in any sample selected through nonprobability sampling techniques, as everyone does not have an equal chance of inclusion. Although at times easier, nonprobability sampling hinders your ability to apply the results of your study to the general population.

For a summary of the types of sampling, see **Table 4.3**.

TABLE 4.3

Types of Sampling			
Probability		**Nonprobability**	
Simple random sample	Randomly selecting a subset of individuals from the population	*Convenience sample*	Nonrandomly selecting participants who are readily available to the researcher
Stratified random sample	Dividing the population into strata or subpopulations and using simple random sampling to select participants from each strata in proportion to the population at large	*Quota sample*	Freely choosing participants as long as the sample meets an already established quota
Cluster random sample	dividing the total population into groups (or clusters), then using simple random sampling to select which clusters participate; all observations in a selected cluster are included in the sample	*Purposive sample*	Choosing the sample based on who is thought to be appropriate for the study; used when a limited number of people have expertise in the area under investigation
		Snowball sample	Existing study participants recruiting future participants from among their acquaintances

Sampling Issues

A sound sampling plan is an important first step in gaining confidence that your sample will help you draw meaningful conclusions about the population of interest. However, even the best sampling plan can produce a flawed sample. By understanding how biases can be introduced into your sampling plan, you can take appropriate steps to maximize the generalizability of your conclusions.

Nonresponse Bias

In random sampling, there is no guarantee that we can contact all the individuals whom we randomly selected for our study, despite repeated attempts to do so. In addition, as we learned in Chapter 3, we cannot ethically compel individuals to participate in our study. As a result, our sample may contain a **nonresponse bias** such that those who refused to participate in our study may systematically differ in meaningful ways from those who did. This will reduce confidence in our ability to generalize the results from the sample to the targeted population.

One of the problems with the nonresponse bias is that it is a largely silent problem. It is difficult to determine the nature of this bias, or its extent, given that, by definition, the researcher has no information about the nonparticipating subset of the sample. Sometimes a little detective work can help infer the potential for nonresponse bias. During World War II, Abraham Wald, a statistician, worked on strategies for improving the survivability of military aircraft (Wainer, 1999). As aircraft returned from their missions, Wald carefully recorded which parts of the plane had bullet holes versus which parts were in pristine condition to determine where to put additional armor. Based on these data, where would you put the extra armor? At first, it may seem obvious to reinforce the areas with holes. But remember, the planes Wald examined were the ones that made it back safely. Wald, thinking like a scientist, recommended reinforcing the areas of the planes that appeared to have little damage. Why? Wald reasoned that his sample's nonresponders, those he was unable to examine, failed to return because they were hit in vulnerable areas. The returning aircraft, however, made it back because they were not hit in these vulnerable areas. The only way to determine if Wald was correct would have been to recover the downed aircraft and compare the damage on those planes to the planes that survived. In the case of the planes, there was a systematic difference between the surviving planes that made it into his sample and those that did not survive to make it into his sample.

You may be able to infer the direction of a potential nonresponse bias by making multiple attempts, rather than just a single attempt, to recruit individuals from the sample. By specifically comparing the responses of individuals who refused at first but subsequently agreed to participate after additional solicitations, you may be able to gain insight into how nonrespondents may differ from respondents. The key point is that if we want to have increased confidence that the conclusions we draw from our study generalize to the population of interest, we need to employ a random sampling plan and be wary of the potential for a nonresponse bias.

The Volunteer Subject Problem

Imagine that a researcher asked individuals to participate in an in-depth study about their sexual attitudes and experiences. Would you volunteer for this study? You may or may not volunteer, but chances are that those who would be reluctant and politely decline differ in some meaningful way from those who

nonresponse bias a potential systematic difference between those who refused to participate in a study and those who participated.

would be quite eager to volunteer to share their sexual exploits. During the 1930s and 1940s, Kinsey and his colleagues conducted such a study in which they interviewed approximately 12,000 men and 8,000 women about their sexual practices (Kinsey, Pomeroy, & Martin, 1948; Kinsey, Pomeroy, Martin, & Gebhard, 1953). Their results were surprising and controversial because they found that almost half of the males and over a quarter of the females had engaged in homosexual behavior by the time they were middle-aged. Despite the large number of individuals who participated in these interviews, many criticized Kinsey's conclusions because his sample was composed solely of volunteers, which could bias the results. For example, the people who volunteered for the Kinsey interviews tended to be higher in self-esteem than those who refused, and people with higher self-esteem tend to have more unconventional sexual attitudes (Maslow & Sakoda, 1952). This suggests that the conclusions made by Kinsey and his associates may have been overstated with respect to actual practices in American society simply because of who volunteered to be in the study.

This example raises the question as to the extent to which research conclusions based on volunteer research participants can truly generalize to others because volunteers can differ from nonvolunteers in meaningful ways (Rosenthal & Rosnow, 2009; Rosnow & Rosenthal, 1997). For example, people who volunteer to participate in research studies tend to be better educated, higher in social class, higher in intelligence, and higher in need for social approval compared to nonvolunteers. The volunteer status of your participants may exaggerate differences between the various groups or conditions in your study. Suppose you wanted to test how an emotionally persuasive message can impact a person's willingness to make a charitable donation. Given that volunteers tend to be higher in social approval than nonvolunteers, individuals who volunteered to be in your study may be more susceptible to persuasive messages, which could lead you to overstate the impact of persuasion on people's general behavior.

Fortunately, there are recruiting strategies you can use to reduce the possibility for a volunteer bias (Rosenthal & Rosnow, 2009). For example, if you would like people to volunteer for your study, you should make it as interesting and nonthreatening as possible. When you ask for volunteers, explain why your study is important and how it may potentially benefit others. By minimizing potential biases in your sample, you can have increased confidence in the generalizability of your research conclusions.

The "College Sophomore Problem"

The problem here is not college sophomores themselves. They really are nice people. The problem starts with researchers' use of convenience sampling and the implicit assumption that random sampling is not necessary because psychological processes are universal to all humans. If this assumption is true, psychology's heavy reliance on undergraduate research participants is justifiable because their thought processes mimic other older and/or less-educated adults. However, researchers have increasingly questioned this assumption. As a classic paper stated, "The existing science of human behavior is largely the science of the behavior of sophomores. Too much research effort is expended on college students with subsequent waste of journal space devoted to speculation concerning whether the findings hold for mankind in general" (McNemar, 1946, p. 333).

Similarly, others expressed concern that by focusing on American college students, psychologists bias their conclusions concerning the universal nature of psychological processes (Sears, 1986). More recently, a study found that the research published in the six premier journals of the American Psychological Association used research participants who were mainly American, particularly of European American descent (Arnett, 2008). The conclusion is that psychological researchers have overrelied on samples of WEIRD (Western, educated, industrialized, rich, and democratic) participants (Henrich, Heine, & Norenzayan, 2010a). Given the increasing cross-cultural evidence that basic cognitive and motivational processes are not necessarily universal, researchers need to consider the degree to which their findings can generalize to other populations (Henrich, Heine, & Norenzayan, 2010b).

For what types of research topics might a WEIRD sample give you nonrepresentative results?
(DreamPictures/Getty Images)

One alternative to using undergraduates as research participants is to use Internet sites as a way to recruit participants. Tools like Amazon's Mechanical Turk (MTurk: http://www.mturk.com) serve as a go-between for researchers and potential participants. MTurk provides a forum for data collection and arranges compensation for participants (about 5–10 cents or more for a 5–10 minute study). Although MTurk is subject to the volunteer bias, these participants are significantly more diverse than typical American college samples, providing a more representative sample of the population at large (Buhrmester, Kwang, & Gosling, 2011). Ideally, every study would use a sound sampling plan that maximizes the generalizability of the conclusions, but often that is not the case. Because many psychology studies, including those that likely take place at your school, use a convenience sample, this may inconveniently hurt our ability to relate our findings to populations outside college students. Luckily, when researchers write about their study, part of the process involves being clear about the sample and its potential limitations.

YOUR TURN 4.4

1. A researcher notices that mostly males have signed up for his study on changes to reaction times while skydiving. Which of the following may be a problem with the researcher's sample?

   a. There may be a volunteer subject problem.

   b. There may be a nonresponse bias.

   c. Random sampling has biased the study.

   d. College sophomores may be overrepresented in the sample.

2. Drew wants a representative sample for his research study. He identifies the entire population and subdivides it. He then uses simple random assignment to see which members of each given subpopulation will be a part of the sample. Drew is using which sampling strategy?
   a. Convenience sampling
   b. Stratified random sampling
   c. Quota sampling
   d. Snowball sampling

3. Students will often use websites like Rate My Professors to help them select the best classes to take. Critics point out that ratings on the site only capture the most extreme responses and that those with more moderate viewpoints do not bother to post their ratings. What problem does the site suffer from the most?
   a. College sophomores may be overrepresented in the sample.
   b. There may be a nonresponse bias.
   c. Random sampling has biased the study.
   d. There may be a problem with purposive sampling.

How did you do? Turn to the end of the chapter to check your answers.

Final Thoughts

Any time you set out to accomplish a goal, it is impossible to know every single piece of information that you will need along the way. But knowing a few basics will provide you with the foundation to get started and then fill in the blanks in your understanding as you go. You have now learned a few of the building blocks of psychological research. Regardless of which research design ends up being the best choice for answering your question, you will need to measure variables, recruit participants, and communicate your findings to others. You will also need to make wise choices to minimize potential sources of bias so that your hard work will add to our scientific knowledge. Using the skills you learned in this chapter, you are now ready to use research design to help answer research questions like, "What is the nature of a serial killer's thought patterns?", "Is there a relationship between students' sense of self and their interest in joining a fraternity or sorority?", and "Can trying to ignore a text message lead to distraction?" We will ask these questions in upcoming chapters.

CHAPTER 4 Review

Review Questions

1. Marcus and Lilja both want to study how stress influences the likelihood of getting sick. Marcus plans on measuring life stress and splitting participants into two groups: high and low. Lilja plans on manipulating stress by exposing one group to a snake and the other to a guinea pig. Marcus' a design is a _____ and Lilja's design is a _____.

   a. quasi experiment; quasi experiment

   b. true experiment; true experiment

   c. true experiment; quasi experiment

   d. quasi experiment; true experiment

2. Corrin works at a clothing store in the mall. After a staff meeting where the employees learn sales are declining, she notices that some days the music in the store is really loud, while other days it is impossible to hear. She decides that the store manager is changing the music to see if it influences sales, and decides to try harder to sell clothes on days the music is loud. What problem does this exemplify?

   a. Social desirability

   b. Demand characteristics

   c. False consensus effect

   d. Retrospective bias

3. In high school, Raul was involved in a terrible car accident when his friend fell asleep at the wheel. Despite the fact that Raul was in the hospital for a month in a full-body cast due to a broken back, when talking about the experience, Raul recalls that time very fondly and says that "it wasn't so bad." What problem does this exemplify?

   a. Social desirability

   b. Demand characteristics

   c. False consensus effect

   d. Retrospective bias

4. Darius wants to measure conscientiousness to determine whether it varies depending on students' majors. Rather than asking participants how conscientious they are, he decides to ask to look at each participant's calendar and planner. What type of measurement is Darius using?

   a. Behavioral trace

   b. Behavioral observation

   c. Behavioral choice

   d. Self-report

5. Norah wants to videotape her roommate Joanne for a class project on sleeping behaviors. However, because Joanne knows she is being videotaped, she has trouble sleeping. This illustrates which potential problem when conducting research?

   a. Participant reactivity
   b. Retrospective bias
   c. Social desirability
   d. Demand characteristics

6. Felicia wants to measure the true number of miles her car gets per gallon of gas (the MPG) to determine if it is worthwhile to get a new car. During a summer road trip where she drove 300 miles after buying 12 gallons of gas, she determines that she gets 25 miles per gallon. During this trip, she had the air conditioner on most of the time and was driving in the mountains. Which of the following may be contributing to the error in this measurement?

   a. The amount of gas she purchased
   b. How she calculated the miles per gallon (MPG)
   c. The fact that she used the air conditioner and drove in the mountains
   d. The number of miles she drove

7. _____ is a form of systematic error, while _____ is nonsystematic. Of these two, _____ is more problematic.

   a. Random error; bias; bias
   b. Bias; random error; random error
   c. Random error; bias; random error
   d. Bias; random error; bias

8. _____ is synonymous with accuracy. _____ is synonymous with consistency.

   a. Reliability; Validity
   b. Sensitivity; Lack of bias
   c. Validity; Reliability
   d. Lack of bias; Sensitivity

9. For her study on females' music preferences, Quinn decides to interview the girls in her residence hall because all of the girls happen to be from very different parts of the country. What type of sampling is Quinn using?

   a. Snowball sampling
   b. Convenience sampling
   c. Representative sampling
   d. Random sampling

10. Dr. Smokey is conducting a study on the effects of marijuana use on memory. Upon posting the study to recruit participants, 100 people sign up within the first 10 minutes. Dr. Smokey's sample most likely suffers from which issue?

    a. Response bias
    b. Nonresponse bias
    c. Volunteer subject problem
    d. The "college sophomore problem"

11. Compare and contrast the advantages and disadvantages of self-report and behavioral measures.

12. What is more important, reliability or validity? Why?

13. You are interested in comparing the sharing habits of boys and girls. Several local preschools have agreed to let you collect data at their facilities. Name at least three ways to standardize your study setting in an attempt to reduce bias.

Applying What You've Learned

1. Take a look at the subjects included in the American Community Survey from the U.S. Census Bureau (http://www.census.gov/programs-surveys/acs/). What type of measurement is this? How might social desirability influence participants' responses?

2. Over the next week, keep a behavioral diary. In that diary, note behaviors that you see people exhibit with notes about what you think is taking place psychologically that has led that person to behave that way.

3. Read the following study and identify how the researchers used both self-report and behavioral measures. Which do you think is better? Why?

   Holland, R. W., Hendriks, M., & Aarts, H. (2005). Smells like clean spirit: Nonconscious effects of scent on cognition and behavior. *Psychological Science, 16*, 689–693. doi:10.1111/j.14679280.2005.01597.x

4. Look around where you live and find something that provides a measurement. In that measurement, distinguish between the raw score, true score, and error.

5. Watch the news tonight. Pick one story and identify how it could contain bias and how it could contain random error.

6. For each of the following terms, provide your own example of how they can apply to your everyday life: social desirability, demand characteristics, validity, reliability, and sampling.

7. How could you measure *vanity* using each of the following:
   a. a behavioral trace
   b. a behavioral observation
   c. a behavioral choice

8. How could you also measure *anxiety* using all three methods?

Key Concepts

behavioral choice, p. 94

behavioral measure, p. 91

behavioral observation, p. 93

behavioral trace, p. 92

bias, p. 100

ceiling effect, p. 104

cluster random sampling, p. 110

convenience sampling, p. 111

demand characteristic, p. 90

error, p. 98

floor effect, p. 104

nonprobability sampling, p. 111

Answers to YOUR TURN

Your Turn 4.1: 1. c; 2. a; 3. c

Your Turn 4.2: 1. c; 2. b; 3. c

Your Turn 4.3: 1. c; 2. a; 3. d

Your Turn 4.4: 1. a; 2. b; 3. b

Answers to Multiple-Choice Review Questions

1. d; 2. b; 3. d; 4. a; 5. a; 6. c; 7. d; 8. c; 9. b; 10. c

Qualitative Research

Getting Into the Mind of a Serial Killer

lightsource/Deposit Photos

LEARNING OUTCOMES

After reading this chapter, you should be able to:

- Identify the difference between qualitative and quantitative research.
- Identify the difference between bottom-up and top-down approaches to qualitative research.
- Differentiate between various types of interviews.
- Explain how interviewer bias and interviewer characteristics may influence an interviewee's responses.

- Describe the characteristics of a good interviewer.
- Create an effective interview schedule.
- Recognize the ways that bias can influence a small sample.
- Explain how researchers use grounded theory in qualitative data analysis.
- Identify the types of coding used in content analysis.

Something to Think About . . .

"*I am the most cold-blooded son of a bitch you'll ever meet. I just liked to kill, I wanted to kill.*" Who would say something like that? A serial killer, that's who. In this case, that serial killer was Ted Bundy. Criminal behavior represents an interesting psychological phenomenon. The perpetrator of a premeditated crime knowingly and willingly breaks established standards that govern society's behavior. This is notable because most people tend to adhere to society's laws and expectations. You have no trouble following basic rules, such as driving on the proper side of the road, paying taxes, and refraining from robbing people at gunpoint. Then again, you are not a serial killer. (Note: We can say this with a certain level of confidence because, thankfully, there are very few serial killers in the world. The best current estimate is that serial killers make up less than 0.000001% of the United States' population.) Whether due to their rarity or due to the audacity of their criminal acts, people often find serial killers intriguing.

Have you ever wondered what goes on in the mind of a serial killer like Ed Gein (the inspiration for *The Silence of the Lambs* and Alfred Hitchcock's *Psycho*)? What can we learn about psychology and deviant behavior from a serial killer's thoughts? *(Francis Miller/The LIFE Picture Collection/Getty Images)*

Introduction to Our Research Question

As a student in a psychology course, you likely find serial killers fascinating and wonder what sort of thought processes lead to such deviant behavior. Or, to put that in the form of a general research question:

RESEARCH
? **What is the nature of a serial killer's thought patterns?**

Given our research question, we will want to educate ourselves in a few important topics. First, we will want to know some background information about serial killers. Next, we will want to learn what researchers and experts have already learned about serial killers (e.g., their personal history) and the techniques they have used to gather their information. Because our research topic touches on several areas of the social sciences (e.g., psychology, sociology, and criminology), we will avoid limiting our literature review to only psychology journals. We need to have a broader understanding of serial killers.

Reviewing the Literature: What Do We Already Know About This Topic?

It is always a good idea to do some background research on your topic before you start to think about your design. Given our focus on serial killers, we should look for relevant research in a few key areas: What are common background characteristics of serial killers? How do researchers elicit information from serial killers? What psychological and situational factors influence serial killers' behavior? We saved you some time by using PsycINFO, Sociological Abstracts, and JSTOR to find several sources that will provide insight into these questions. We also provide summaries so that you can familiarize yourself with the literature in order to start thinking about our study more concretely.

Characteristics of Serial Killers

Ressler, R. K., Douglas, J. E., Groth, A. N., & Burgess, A. W. (2004). The men who murdered. In J. H. Campbell and D. DeNevi (Eds.), *Profilers: Leading investigators take you inside the criminal mind* (pp. 73–81). Amherst, NY: Prometheus Books.

Based on interviews with incarcerated male serial murderers, results indicated that half had families with psychiatric problems, half had families with criminal histories, a majority had alcohol abuse, most had an older brother, a third lived in one location growing up, most had little connection with the community, a majority had the father leave home before age 12, and a majority considered the mother to be the primary parent, though most considered the maternal relationship to be uncaring and reported inconsistent or abusive discipline.

Eliciting Information From Serial Killers

Campbell, J. H., & DeNevi, D. (2004). Interviewing techniques for homicide investigations. In J. H. Campbell and D. DeNevi (Eds.), *Profilers: Leading investigators take you inside the criminal mind* (pp. 109–114). Amherst, NY: Prometheus Books.

In an analysis of serial killer interviews, several recommendations emerged. Interviewers should establish motive in the "pre-crime phase," identify details of the act during the "murder event," identify associated fantasies during the "disposal of the body," and determine killer reflections and behavior in the "post-crime phase."

Ressler, R. K. (2004). How to interview a cannibal. In J. H. Campbell and D. DeNevi (Eds.), *Profilers: Leading investigators take you inside the criminal mind* (pp. 135–177). Amherst, NY: Prometheus Books.

This chapter discusses the importance of establishing rapport to uncover details, and how acknowledging absurd behavior can facilitate disclosure. In an in-depth interview, serial killer Jeffrey Dahmer discussed victim selection based on opportunity rather than race/ethnicity, inducing a zombie state in victims through drugs, drilling holes in victims' skulls, and pouring in acid or injecting them with boiling water. Dahmer mentioned his admiration for the Emperor from the *Star Wars* series, and that he had a big blue globe light that he was going to pair with skeletons to recreate scenes from the Jedi movies. Dahmer also described aspects of his cannibalism, body disposal, and several close calls in which he was nearly detected.

The Psychology of Serial Killers

Knight, Z. G. (2006). Some thoughts on the psychological roots of the behavior of serial killers as narcissists: An object relations perspective. *Social Behavior and Personality, 34,* 1189–1206. doi:10.2224/sbp.2006.34.10.1189

The author explores serial killers as pathological and destructive narcissists who cope with feelings of conflict with close others by attacking and torturing strangers. The primary issue is lack of parental interest and support, as well as the presence of abuse. As a result, the child feels helplessness, inadequacy, and shame that contrast with feelings of grandiosity, and later engages in aggression, cruelty, sadism, and violent crime.

LaBrode, R. (2007). Etiology of the psychopathic serial killer: An analysis of antisocial personality disorder, psychopathy, and serial killer personality and crime scene characteristics. *Brief Treatment and Crisis Intervention, 7,* 151–160. doi:10.1093/brief-treatment/mhm004

This article examines how research on violent criminals often confuses antisocial personality disorder (ASPD) and psychopathy. Psychopaths will have most characteristics of ASPD (e.g., lack of remorse, manipulation, cold affect), but are also "predators" who use their personal attributes (e.g., charisma) to achieve goals. All psychopaths have ASPD, but not all ASPD cases are psychopaths, just as all psychopaths are not serial killers. However, psychopathy is seen in serial killers such as Ted Bundy, Ed Gein, and Dennis Rader (aka the BTK killer).

Broader Influences on Serial Killers

Haggerty, K. D. (2009). Modern serial killers. *Crime, Media, Culture, 5,* 168–187. doi:10.1177/1741659009335714

This article explores phenomena that help construct society's image of serial killers, including mass media, the rise of celebrity culture, and the modern society of strangers. The media's fascination with serial killers provides killers with celebrity status that may help shape a killer's identity or help the killer to relive the event. Modern urbanization also creates a greater sense of anonymity, such that a person encounters many more strangers (the typical prey of a serial killer).

From Ideas to Innovation

As you can see, previous researchers have learned a lot about serial killers and have already analyzed possible psychological influences, such as family upbringing, mental illness, and substance abuse. One study took a slightly different approach by suggesting that broader social influences may play a role (Haggerty, 2009), which is an interesting angle to examine. Certainly, there are many possibilities, which is why we need time to develop a systematic approach to studying our question. Otherwise we run the risk of heading off in several scattered directions.

Defining Key Terms: What Do You Mean By ___?

▶ Want a refresher on how to develop conceptual definitions? SEE CHAPTER 2, p. 38

Looking back at our general research question, "What is the nature of a serial killer's thought patterns?", our first step is to provide conceptual definitions in which we clearly and specifically state what we mean by "serial killer" and "thought patterns." Although there are times when you define key concepts on your own, in most cases it is better to leave it to the experts. You will find that when you look for definitions in the research literature, there is some variety in their presentation, so you are free to pick the definition that most closely resembles how you view the term. Here are two definitions of "serial murder" from the literature:

1. "The unlawful killing of two or more victims by the same offender(s), in separate events." (FBI, 2008)

2. "Serial murder is the killing of three or more people over a period of more than 30 days, with a significant cooling-off period between the murders." (Holmes & Holmes, 2009)

In this case the definitions are quite similar. Because cases with three victims sound more serious than those with two, let's go ahead and use the second definition.

Next, we need to decide which types of "thought patterns" interest us. As we saw in our literature search, one potential thought pattern involves the serial killers' fantasies related to the murders (Ressler, 2004). We can look at other thought patterns as well. For example, it may be interesting to obtain killers' explanations of their motives, thoughts regarding victim selection, reflections on the murder acts, or subsequent thoughts seeking to justify their actions. As with the definition of a serial killer, we could pick one aspect that fits our plan most closely. However, in this case we may be getting ahead of ourselves. Given that serial killers are likely to display a variety of interesting thoughts, we may be better off leaving this as a broad definition rather than providing a specific operational definition. This broadness will give us the opportunity to see what types of thought patterns might emerge.

Weighing Our Options: Qualitative or Quantitative Research?

▶ Why should you allow the research question to determine the design? SEE CHAPTER 2, p. 26

As we mentioned in Chapter 2, a good researcher avoids picking the design ahead of time. Rather, as the research question develops, the question dictates the design that will best answer it. Although we were able to define a serial killer, we realized that, given our research question, we did not want to define "thought patterns" specifically. Rather, our research question focuses on understanding serial killers' unique experiences and perspectives.

There are two general approaches to research. In **qualitative research**, researchers focus on gaining in-depth information on a few individuals with the goal of developing a more thorough understanding of their perspectives and life experiences. In **quantitative research**, researchers use statistics and numbers to summarize how large groups of people think or behave, collecting less detailed information from more people, with the goal of extending these conclusions to others. Although we distinguish between these types of research, they are not completely dichotomous or distinct (Allwood, 2012). Often, researchers use **mixed methods research**, which is a blend of qualitative and quantitative methods that capitalizes on the strengths of each to examine a research question from multiple perspectives. For example, a researcher may collect information using qualitative methods, then later quantify responses (e.g., the number of hostile thoughts expressed). Or a researcher may conduct a series of studies in which an initial qualitative study provides information that forms the basis of subsequent quantitative research.

Given its emphasis on acquiring more detailed information, qualitative research is an ideal approach to answering our research question. Qualitative research is a generic term for a variety of methods that focus on getting more in-depth information from participants about their own world and how they experience events (Willig, 2008). To better describe participants' experiences, qualitative research typically favors studying participants in naturally occurring settings in "the field," rather than in a more structured or laboratory setting. However, qualitative research is flexible enough to work in many types of settings, including a laboratory. Although qualitative research methods favor detailed description (e.g., "I'm happy today because I feel accomplished") over numbers (e.g., "I'm a 5 out of 7 on a happiness scale"), qualitative research can incorporate numbers as well (Marecek, 2003). Basically, a qualitative researcher believes we gain more understanding from the participant's explanation than from a number. Qualitative research, as a result, tends not to use statistics to test hypotheses, but will use numbers to help describe a phenomenon (e.g., how frequently a person feels happy), and does not try to make predictions or establish cause-and-effect relationships. Rather, the original research question is merely a target that a qualitative researcher pursues with minimal guidance about the direction it may lead. Thus, our question, "What is the nature of a serial killer's thought patterns?" fits well with a qualitative approach.

In contrast, quantitative research would be a better fit if we had asked, "What causes serial killers' behavior?" Quantitative research is any method (e.g., surveys, experiments) that tries to determine how variables relate, predict outcomes, or make comparisons (Smith, 1983). A complex phenomenon such as serial murder probably will not have an easily identifiable cause, which makes our question better suited for a qualitative approach. This further demonstrates why it is best to let the research question determine design choice. For a direct comparison between qualitative research and quantitative research, see **Table 5.1.**

qualitative research a generic term representing a variety of methodologies that focus on obtaining an in-depth account of participants' perspectives on their own worlds and their experiences of events.

quantitative research a generic term for methods that seek to objectively examine associations between variables, predict outcomes, and make comparisons.

mixed methods research a blend of qualitative and quantitative methods that capitalizes on the strengths of each to examine a research question from multiple perspectives.

TABLE 5.1

Key Features of Qualitative Versus Quantitative Research Approaches	
Qualitative Research	**Quantitative Research**
• Focuses on obtaining in-depth information from fewer participants	• Focuses on obtaining specific pieces of information from more participants
• Strongly values each participant's perspective and insight into their own experience	• Generally places less emphasis on participants' subjective interpretation
• Favors studying participants in naturally occurring settings	• Favors studying participants in well-controlled laboratory settings
• Favors detailed description over reliance on numbers	• Favors using numbers to describe participants' thoughts and behavior
• Very little hypothesis testing	• Emphasis on hypothesis testing
• Generally does not seek to establish cause and effect	• Seeks to establish cause and effect when possible
• Generally does not seek to generalize to broader populations	• Seeks to generalize study's findings to broader populations
• Researcher provides very little guidance or structure to the study; more participant-defined than researcher-defined	• Researcher provides high degree of structure and guidance in the study to keep participants' experiences as similar as possible; researcher-defined rather than participant-defined
• Avoids summating, categorizing, or reducing the data in any way during data collection	• Provides conclusions using summaries, categories, and generalizations over groups of people, rather than focusing on individual responses
• Researcher has a larger influence in the research process and acknowledges that role	• Researcher attempts to minimize his or her influence in the research process and rarely seeks to assess any potential influence

What Do You Think?

What aspects of serial killers would be useful to quantify?

A criticism of quantitative approaches is their focus on numbers, such as average scores, to represent an entire group (e.g., collectively, everyone in your research methods course has an average IQ of 125). The problem is that while the average score represents the overall group well, it does a poor job of characterizing any one individual's score (e.g., everyone does not have an IQ of 125). Critics point out that a mean score undermines any one person's contributions and misses valuable information (Willig, 2008). To address this, qualitative approaches attempt to capture participants' thoughts "in their own words." Thus, when collecting data, a qualitative researcher avoids summating, categorizing, or reducing the data in any way.

Qualitative research shares some of the typical concerns associated with self-report, such as the amount of time and energy it takes to collect information and the possibility that the participant may lie or provide inaccurate information due to social desirability concerns or demand characteristics. Qualitative research also relies on small samples of participants, which raises questions about the study's generalizability, or ability to apply to broader populations. Typically, qualitative researchers are not trying to achieve reliability or consistency in their findings because the primary goal is to look at individuals in a specific context (Willig, 2008). For similar reasons, representativeness or generalizability is also not a key goal. Instead, qualitative researchers often focus on a specific or relatively rare phenomenon that is not common in the general population, a goal that fits our study on serial killers perfectly. Qualitative research seeks to increase reliability through techniques such as **triangulation**, which involves using multiple techniques and/or samples to assess the same information and provide a more comprehensive examination. For example, a researcher who wanted to identify the best educational practices in preschools would use a mix of in-depth interviews and general surveys, and would gather information from children, parents, and educators. This technique allows researchers to "double-check" their findings, and, if all methods reveal the same conclusion, increase confidence in their conclusion.

Qualitative research can have fewer concerns related to the validity or the accuracy of the conclusions because the researcher can ask the participants to clarify what they meant, and can give participants the chance to correct any of the researcher's assumptions. Often, the researcher will share the findings directly with the participants to make sure the researcher made accurate conclusions. Contrast this situation with a quantitative response on a survey item, where a participant indicates a 5 out of 7 on a happiness scale, but we cannot be sure what this means to the participant or what factors contributed to that score. Finally, qualitative research encourages investigators to take an active role in the data collection and acknowledges their subjective influence. Although this could potentially bias the findings (e.g., two different researchers could draw different conclusions from the same information), qualitative research does encourage **reflexivity,** in which the researcher monitors and records his or her role in the data collection on a continuous basis during the study, allowing for a more accurate assessment of the researcher's influence (Berger, 2015). As a researcher of serial killer's thought patterns, for example, you would want to keep track of your own feelings and reactions during data collection to minimize potential interference.

Qualitative Research Approaches

When you are starting research on a topic and considering a new angle within that area, it can be hard to know where to start. Thankfully, a central feature of qualitative research is learning about a phenomenon through a **bottom-up approach** (Camic, Rhodes, & Yardley, 2003). Here, the researcher uses an information-first or inductive approach by engaging in a participant-led exploration of a topic, where the information provided from the participant's direct experiences guides the researcher's development of a theory. In essence, the researcher gathers information before forming concrete ideas about how things work.

▶ Curious about the advantages and disadvantages of self-report? SEE CHAPTER 4, p. 88

triangulation a research strategy that involves using multiple techniques and/or samples to assess the same information to provide a more comprehensive examination.

reflexivity a practice through which the researcher monitors and records his or her role in the data collection on a continuous basis during the study, which allows for a more accurate assessment of the researcher's influence.

bottom-up approach an approach where the researcher develops a theory by exploring a topic using information provided from participants' direct experiences.

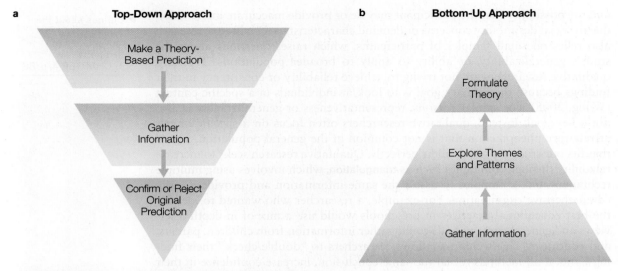

FIGURE 5.1 Top-Down Versus Bottom-Up Approaches.

This is the opposite of a **top-down approach,** where the researcher uses a theory-first or deductive approach to test preconceptions and previously established theories with the collected data. You can remember that top-down is theory-first because both words ("theory" and "top") begin with the letter *t.*

It is easy to see how early on in a research project, or when researching a novel area, gathering information and building a theory from direct in-depth interactions with participants can be especially valuable. For our research question, it seems that killers' thought processes have not received ample attention, so it is unclear what to expect. In this case, we should use the bottom-up approach, letting our serial killer guide the development of our theory. For a visual representation of top-down versus bottom-up approaches, see **Figure 5.1.**

In order to capture information in a more authentic way, qualitative research strives to provide a **situated analysis,** in which the researcher examines a topic within its naturally occurring context. In other words, researchers try to study phenomena where they happen. For example, if you wanted to learn about how dental patients experience stress, you would interview them in the dentist's office ahead of a procedure. When researchers embed themselves within the context under examination, they capture information that provides a more "pure" look at the phenomenon. In our research, we would ideally have the opportunity to explore a serial killer's thoughts leading up to, during, and immediately following a murder. Aside from obtaining a serial killer's diary, or accompanying a serial killer during murders, obtaining perfectly situated information about a serial killer's thoughts would be difficult.

A qualitative approach also allows you to see how a variety of smaller pieces fit together within the larger picture (Camic et al., 2003). In the case of serial killers, it may be that a seemingly random anecdote about a childhood experience

top-down approach a deductive approach where the researcher tests preconceptions and previously established theories with the collected data.

situated analysis an approach where the researcher examines a topic while it is embedded within its naturally occurring context.

with a parent relates to victim selection later in life, or that a recollection of peer interactions during high school contributes more to a killer's perceptions of others' feelings than the researcher originally anticipated. Without the very detailed data that a qualitative approach can provide, it may be impossible for researchers to study behaviors that fall well outside the norm. Thus, for our purposes, we will strive for a **holistic analysis**, which allows the researcher to examine how numerous properties contribute to patterns within the larger and more complex system. There are many factors that contribute to any particular outcome, and a holistic analysis attempts to take as many of them into account as possible.

What Do You Think?
What other behaviors may be well suited to a holistic analysis?

 Thinking Like a Scientist in Real Life

How Do You Form Impressions?

As you met new people during your first year in college, you likely formed impressions of them. Were they cool? Smart? Funny? Someone who could be your friend, or someone to avoid? In general, there are two ways you approached forming these impressions: top-down or bottom-up. If you used a top-down approach, you had some preconceived notions about the person that you then tested out as you got to know him or her. For example, if you tend to believe that you are smart and everyone else is dumb, when you met others, you were probably on the lookout for anything that might indicate lack of intelligence. In contrast, if you used a bottom-up approach, you waited to form an impression until you had enough time to get to know them. That is, you allowed what others said and did to form the basis of your impression. So, upon meeting fellow first-year students, you waited for them to say something stupid before labeling them as such. Of course, this approach also increased the chance that you noticed the smart things they said, and allowed you to form an entirely different first impression.

Weighing Our Options: Picking the Best Data Collection Technique

Within qualitative research, there are a variety of techniques and approaches. Because this chapter's goal is to provide an introduction to qualitative methods, we have provided an overview of its different types in **Table 5.2**. When choosing the data collection technique for the study, we must be careful to focus on what is most appropriate for our research question. Because the world is (thankfully) not full of serial killers, we should avoid designs that require large samples. We also want to gather in-depth information about how a serial killer thinks, which requires specific data collection techniques. Given our research question, it seems best to use a **phenomenological approach** that seeks to understand a human experience and the meaning of experiences based on how those involved view that situation. To obtain first-hand accounts of our participants' thoughts and behaviors, we will want to use self-report, rather than focusing on behaviors, which could be dangerous when dealing with a serial killer.

holistic analysis an approach where the researcher examines how numerous properties contribute to patterns within the larger and more complex system.

phenomenological approach an approach that seeks to understand a human experience and the meaning of experiences based on how those involved view that situation.

TABLE 5.2

Types of Qualitative Methods	
Method	**Description**
Action Research	A research design that explicitly involves participants in the research and tries to change some aspect of the research's focus
Case Study	A comprehensive description of a specific organization, group, or person studied over a period of time that contains information from a variety of sources
Content Analysis	A systematic analysis of written work that allows researchers to organize and summarize the substance of the communication
Conversation Analysis	An analysis technique that involves an examination of the natural patterns of dialogue, focusing on features such as turn taking, gaze direction, and how speakers sequence speech
Ethnography	A design that uses detailed and typically long-term observations or interactions to situate a phenomenon in the proper cultural context of those being studied
Focus Group	A data collection format where several participants, typically strangers, gather together to discuss a topic
Grounded Theory Technique	An approach where the researcher does not have any explicit theories or hypotheses to test prior to the research, but instead uses information from participants to generate the categories and build a theory
Interview	A data collection technique that can mimic a conversation, where the researcher elicits self-report data directly from the participant
Narrative Analysis	An examination of first-person stories or descriptions of one's life that the researcher analyzes from the storyteller's point of view
Phenomenological Approach	An approach that seeks to understand a human experience and the meaning of experiences based on how those involved view that situation
Postmodern Approach	A perspective that explicitly questions basic assumptions about the nature and capabilities of research (e.g., Is it possible to truly understand another person's experience?)
Visual Ethnography	A type of ethnography that combines observations and interactions with visual media such as photographs or videos

One potential source of self-report information would be the killer's personal diary or journal. This type of data is **archival** because the data have already been collected in a naturally occurring setting. Examples of other archival data sources include newspapers, magazines, books, health records, public records, and Internet sources such as online dating websites, Facebook profiles, or Twitter feeds. A major benefit of archival research is that it can enable the study of otherwise impossible or difficult to study variables. In our case, there is the potential that a serial killer's journal could reveal the killer's thoughts leading up to and immediately after the murders. Unfortunately, if we relied on this method, we would be limited to researching only those killers who kept a journal, and it is unlikely that one of our areas of interest (societal influences) would find its way onto the pages of a journal.

Instagram posts can serve as archival records for researchers. What types of research questions could you answer by examining participants' Instagram accounts? *(Karly Domb Sadof/AP Images.)*

The most common strategy to elicit self-report is to ask a series of questions in a pen and paper or online format. However, for our purposes, this approach may not be ideal. For a serial killer to truly open up and feel comfortable discussing his crimes—and especially his thoughts—it seems likely that the researcher would need to establish rapport with the killer. Simply handing him a packet of questions to complete seems unlikely to accomplish that goal. Gaining rapport would most likely involve meeting face to face with the killer over prolonged periods of time, which would have the added benefit of allowing the researcher to collect data on the killer's nonverbal forms of communication. A set of questions would not accommodate changes in expression, tone of voice, and mannerisms that might yield valuable information about the killer's thoughts. In addition, answers to predetermined items would not be open and flexible enough to adequately answer our research question.

Thus, it would be better to meet with our participants in person. However, meeting with a serial killer one on one can be time-consuming. If we wanted to gather information from multiple serial killers, and wanted to increase efficiency, we could consider running a **focus group**. This format involves several participants, typically strangers, gathering together to discuss a topic (Krueger & Casey, 2008). Groups commonly start with an icebreaker activity to encourage members' contributions, and then proceed to the key topic, which researchers later analyze. Focus groups have the benefit of providing more information about how group members interact, agree or disagree, and resolve conflict. Researchers commonly use focus groups in political research to gather feelings about candidates, and in consumer research to reveal product preferences. But what may be a good idea to use with voters and consumers may not be the best technique to use with serial killers. For

▶ In what situations might self-reports be more useful? SEE CHAPTER 4, p. 88

▶ What are the pitfalls of self-report strategies? SEE CHAPTER 4, p. 89

archival data data that have already been collected in a naturally occurring setting, such as newspapers, health records, or social media.

focus group a data collection format where several participants, typically strangers, gather together to discuss a topic.

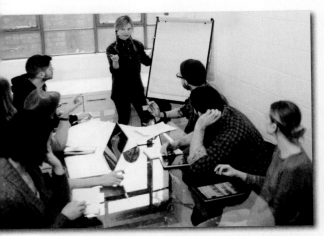

What other research topics do you think would be well-suited for a focus group? *(Mike Harrington/Iconica/Getty Images)*

our research, we should seriously consider whether we want to assemble several serial killers in a room where we lead a discussion to see how killers interact, agree, disagree, and resolve conflict. When considered further, it seems like a terribly unsafe idea. More importantly, our research question emphasizes an individual's thoughts, rather than interactions between serial killers.

Due to our focus on a single individual's thoughts and experiences, the best strategy for obtaining our objective is an interview. An **interview** is a data collection technique that can mimic a conversation, where the researcher elicits self-report data directly from the participant (Kvale & Brinkmann, 2008). The major advantage for our study is that an interview would allow us to build a relationship with our participant in such a way that may encourage greater disclosure, providing richer insight into the killer's thoughts. Perhaps more importantly, it gives us greater control over the wording and sequence of questions, as well as the ability to ask follow-up questions if one of the killer's answers requires additional clarification. The disadvantage of interviews is their artificial and contrived format (Potter & Hepburn, 2005), although, in the case of serial killers, it would be impossible to study them in a more natural setting.

An interview would help us answer our research question most directly. However, it is possible that another researcher may include our interview as part of a larger **case study**, which is a comprehensive description of a specific organization, group, or person studied over a period of time that contains information from a variety of sources. There are various kinds of case studies; for more information, see **Table 5.3**. Along with the interview, a serial killer's case study, for example, might contain newspaper clippings, crime scene reports, interviews with victim's families, interviews with law enforcement, and forensic evidence. Case studies are an important method because they allow us to study phenomena that are rare or unethical to study experimentally, and yet, at times, have the ability to generalize to a larger sample.

Weighing Our Options: Planning the Interview

Prior to meeting with the serial killer, we must determine what type of interview we want to conduct, as that decision will influence the type of questions we will eventually ask. First, we should determine the interview format. Common options include face-to-face, telephone, e-mail, texting, and direct or instant message interviews. Given their sensitive nature, our questions would probably be best asked in person, and conducting the interview in person would provide more data regarding the killer's mannerisms and other forms of nonverbal communication.

interview a data collection technique that can mimic a conversation where the researcher elicits self-report data directly from the participant.

case study a comprehensive description of a specific organization, group, or person studied over a period of time that contains information from a variety of sources.

TABLE 5.3

Types of Case Studies	
Method	**Description**
Case Study	A comprehensive description of a specific organization, group, or person studied over a long period of time that contains information from a variety of sources
Collective (or Multiple)	A comparison of multiple case studies
Descriptive	A case study that seeks information about how an intervention operates in a real-life context in order to provide a more complete portrayal of the subject matter
Explanatory	A case study focusing on the reasons why an intervention produces a certain outcome
Exploratory	A case study that seeks to outline the potential outcomes of an intervention
Instrumental	A case study designed to serve a specific purpose, such as theory building, or as an example of a particular issue
Intrinsic	A case study where the researcher has a direct interest in a particular case

Interview Types

Although there are many specific interview types that researchers can use (Madill & Gough, 2008), there are three general interview formats that we should consider:

- **Structured interview** The researcher prepares specific questions prior to the interview and asks them in a standardized, fixed order with little or no probing.

- **Unstructured interview** The researcher anticipates potential topics, but does not plan specific questions or the order of topics. This format is more conversational and allows participants to describe their own views, share stories, and determine the interview's structure as the interviewer probes to promote elaboration.

- **Semistructured interview** A combination approach where the interviewer preplans some questions and the order of some of these questions, but remains flexible to probe via additional questions that allow the participant to provide further information.

Typically, researchers use structured interviews for quantitative approaches where the focus is on mapping out the specific extent of a problem. As a result, predetermined questions, response options, categories, and interview structures help keep things consistent across many participants. Unstructured interviews are useful for qualitative approaches where the researcher wants to understand the nature of the problem by asking a few participants in-depth questions that allow individuals to fully describe their unique perspectives.

structured interview an interview style where the researcher prepares specific questions prior to the interview and asks them in a standardized, fixed order with little or no probing.

unstructured interview an interview style where the researcher may anticipate potential topics but does not plan specific questions or the order of topics so that the interview is conversational and allows participants to describe their own views, share stories, and determine the interview's structure; allows the interviewer to probe to promote elaboration.

semistructured interview a combination of structured and unstructured interview approaches where some questions and portions of the order are preplanned, but the interviewer remains flexible to probe via additional questions that allow the participant to provide further information.

Compared to a self-report or the different types of interviews, what are the benefits of having an entire case study at hand? *(Melanie Stetson Freeman/Christian Science Monitor/Getty Images)*

For our research question, it is not feasible for us to fully anticipate topics a serial killer may want to discuss. Thus, a structured interview may be too restrictive and may prevent us from extracting the full meaning of the killer's descriptions. An unstructured interview, on the other hand, may give the killer too much control over the conversation, which could lead to undesirable and uninformative tangents. The topics a serial killer wants to talk about the most may be quite different from our topics of interest, though they may be useful. As a result, to answer our research question, a semistructured approach is best because it will allow us to focus on relevant topic areas, but will also give the killer enough flexibility to discuss valuable topics we do not anticipate. The ability of semistructured interviews to accomplish both goals helps make them the most popular data collection technique in qualitative psychology research (Madill, 2007).

Within our semistructured interview, we may want to incorporate a **critical incident technique**, which involves purposefully asking the interviewee to focus on a key event or specific behavior. For our research, we might focus on the four main phases or events in serial killings: the precrime phase, murder event, disposal of the body, and postcrime phase (Campbell & DeNevi, 2004).

Weighing Our Options: What Do We Want to Know?

Now that we have established the general format of our interview, we will want to keep in mind that interviews should not be too long (approximately one hour) in order to prevent interviewee fatigue. As a result, we will want to select our questions judiciously. We will also want to avoid long questions; good interviewers use short questions that provoke longer answers (Kvale, 1996). We value longer answers from the participant because qualitative research emphasizes the participant's subjective experience and allows the participant to establish the central themes (Camic et al., 2003). To uncover these themes, we should plan our interview accordingly.

One way to approach this is by avoiding specific questions and establishing topic headings (Willig, 2008). These are a set of guiding topics that we would use to generate questions during the interview. The benefit of this approach is that we can directly incorporate the interviewee's answers and specific phrasings into our questions (Willig, 2008). For example, we could use the four main phases in serial killings—precrime phase, murder event, disposal of the body, and postcrime phase—as our topic headings (Campbell & DeNevi, 2004). However, it can be difficult to pay complete attention to the interviewee's responses while simultaneously formulating our questions, which may result in low-quality questions and therefore low-quality data. Thus, we are probably better off determining our questions ahead of time. Of course, as the interview progresses, we should still look for opportunities to incorporate the killer's own comments, examples, or phrasings to show that we are fully engaged in the conversation. We should also remember to remain flexible enough to ask follow-up questions in response to particular answers.

critical incident technique an interview technique where the researcher purposefully has the interviewee focus on a key event or specific behavior.

YOUR TURN 5.1

1. Jen and Angelina are roommates who are both planning a senior thesis. Jen wants to determine how students' general feelings about conservatism or liberalism influence their choice of major. Angelina wants to determine the characteristics of a successful college president. To best answer these research questions, Jen should take a _____ approach, while Angelina should take a _____ approach.
   a. situated analysis; holistic analysis
   b. holistic analysis; situated analysis
   c. quantitative; qualitative
   d. qualitative; quantitative

2. Roger is an incoming first-year student who isn't sure what major to pick. Rather than just picking something to see if it is a good fit, Roger collects information on every major and uses what he learns to make a decision. What type of approach is Roger taking?
   a. Bottom-up
   b. Top-down
   c. Quantitative
   d. Deductive

3. Juanita is applying for a job at a substance abuse treatment center. As part of the hiring process, she has an interview that is more like a casual conversation that focuses on topics as they arise. What type of interview did Juanita most likely have?
   a. Structured
   b. Unstructured
   c. Semiregulated
   d. Semistructured

How did you do? Turn to the end of the chapter to check your answers.

Design in Action

There is no standard procedure for conducting an interview, but generally we need to do the following: (1) state our purpose; (2) identify potential participants; (3) determine the questions we want to ask; and (4) determine the question order (Kvale & Brinkmann, 2008). We established our purpose earlier with our research question. Along with stating our purpose, we need to determine a **unit of analysis**, or the type of data we want to learn about. Possible units of analysis could be one individual, several individuals, a group, a town, or a phenomenon (e.g., divorce). Focusing our analysis on an individual killer will provide us with the information we need to address our research question. Next, we can identify potential participants by obtaining a list of incarcerated serial killers from national authorities, such as the Federal Bureau

unit of analysis major entity under investigation or type of data (e.g., individual or group, etc.) that is the focus of the study of Investigation (FBI) in the United States. Let's assume we have done this and determined that Reid Hickernell, an infamous (and fictitious) killer, at the Attica Correctional Facility in New York, is willing to participate. We have identified him as the interviewee. In cases where the interview subject is not already well known, the researcher can assign a pseudonym to the participant to maintain confidentiality.

Based on a review of Reid Hickernell's case file, we know a few details about him and his crimes. Growing up, Reid's father was abusive and his mother was described by a family member as unsupportive, unpredictable, and abusive. Reid had several arrests and a classmate described Reid as "full of himself, but likable. . . . You didn't mess with him because he could be downright cruel. He once put a disemboweled cat in a guy's locker. It wasn't proven, but we all knew Reid did it." Reid dropped out of school, obtained a GED, and served in the Navy from ages 18–23. Upon his return, Reid worked at a used bookstore. Over the next several years, Reid Hickernell (aka "The Vampire of Rochester") murdered 10 victims (9 females and 1 male) aged 16–28. A psychiatric evaluation diagnosed Reid with antisocial personality disorder (ASPD) and mild to moderate psychopathy and described his demeanor as distant, but charismatic. The FBI classified Reid as an "organized" killer due to his careful disposal of the bodies in remote areas. All 10 of his known victims had bite marks on their necks, with a majority fully drained of blood, with no murder weapon or other obvious evidence present. To find out more, we will we need to carry out the interview.

Focus on Ethics: Should We Really Do That?

Before we proceed, it is worth examining the ethical issues involved with interviewing prisoners. As we learned in Chapter 3, prisoners constitute a protected population because the conditions of their incarceration may prevent them from making a truly voluntary decision regarding participation. Their imprisonment also means that researchers must not offer benefits (e.g., better living conditions or other privileges) that the prisoner views so favorably that he or she cannot objectively weigh the risks of participation and provide truly informed consent. Generally, the prisoner cannot feel coerced into participation (by the researcher or any prison official) and can only assume the same level of risk that a nonprisoner volunteer might experience.

▶ Why is voluntary participation so important? SEE CHAPTER 3, p. 61

Given the heinous nature of a serial killer's past transgressions, it may seem odd to worry about risk. However, the general guideline of not exposing a participant to greater risk than normally encountered does provide some flexibility in this case. While it may be overly traumatic to discuss gruesome details of rape, murder, and assault with most of the general population, doing so with a serial killer would not qualify as excessive risk. All psychological researchers must follow ethical guidelines, but qualitative research generally extends the ethical responsibility of the researcher by having an explicit goal of benefitting the participants, rather than simply avoiding any harm to them (Willig, 2008). In our case, considering that Reid Hickernell is a prisoner, participating in an interview may be a welcome break from his typical daily activities and thus beneficial to him.

The Role of the Interviewer

As is true for most qualitative research, as the researcher, you will play a central role in the study. This is perhaps truer for interviews than for any other research design. As a result, we must account for how we might unwittingly influence the interview.

Interviewer Bias

The interviewer should monitor for potential **interviewer bias,** which is any way that the interviewer influences the participant's responses. To avoid this bias, we should question our motivations for pursuing this particular research question and how those motivations (e.g., personal, political, or professional gain) may influence follow-up questions during the interview or our interpretations of responses. Some argue that objectivity in science is a myth (Camic et al., 2003), so rather than assume objectivity, researchers should actively monitor their subjective biases to assess their influence on their research. As the interviewer, you should clarify the respondent's answers and your interpretations to minimize your influence (Kvale, 1996). For example, if Reid says, "So many of these people were just asking for it," you might ask, "When you say 'asking for it,' what do you mean?" rather than assuming you know what he means.

A researcher may also influence the interview in more subtle and uncontrollable ways. For example, your personal qualities can affect the interview (Willig, 2008). Prior to the interview, consider how your demographic characteristics (e.g., socio-economic status, gender, ethnicity, age, religious views, nationality, etc.) or physical appearance (e.g., your style of dress) may influence the participant's responses. In the 1991 movie *The Silence of the Lambs,* the interactions between Hannibal Lecter (played by Anthony Hopkins) and Clarice (played by Jodie Foster) would likely have been different if the interviewer were male. In your case, you would want to carefully consider your attire for the interview and how being a college student might lead to the impression that you are naïve and inexperienced. You will also want to be sure that you are the best interviewer you can be.

Qualities of a Good Interviewer

Given the central role of the researcher in qualitative research, you will want to be prepared. First, make sure you are fully knowledgeable about the interviewee. For Reid's interview, you should thoroughly review his case file so you can probe more effectively and identify any lies. You should also practice so you can ask your questions clearly, without sounding rushed or nervous. A good interviewer is attentive and focused, displays sensitivity and tolerance, segues appropriately between topics, and is highly organized.

Creating an Interview Schedule or Agenda

To facilitate organization, you should create an **interview schedule** or **interview agenda,** which is a type of protocol that guides the interview. In structured or semistructured

interviewer bias any way that the interviewer influences the participant's responses (e.g., leading questions).

interview schedule a type of protocol that includes the questions to ask and anticipated order in which the interviewer should ask them; also called an interview agenda.

interview agenda see *interview schedule.*

How might your personal qualities influence an interview? What about an interview with a serial killer in particular? *(Image Source/Getty Images)*

interviews, the interview schedule outlines the questions to ask and the anticipated order in which the interviewer should ask them. Interviews can be unpredictable, so having an agenda helps the interviewer focus on the original research question, while also providing the latitude to explore unanticipated responses or topics that may arise (Willig, 2008).

Determining Our Questions

A researcher can ask many types of questions, and, because serial killers are so interesting, you likely have many that you want to ask. But, consistent with the goals of qualitative research, we want Reid to establish his own themes (Eisner, 2003), which means that the critical incident technique probably is not best. Rather, we want him to select the key incident, so you should ask general questions. Since you are new to the world of serial killer interviews, it is a good idea to consult previous research. For example, you should be aware of the various phases of serial murder (Campbell & DeNevi, 2004), but should inquire about them more generally by asking Reid, "Which aspect of the killings would you like to discuss?" Similarly, based on our literature search, you know that much research has focused on psychological influences on serial killers (Knight, 2006; LaBrode, 2007). However, one study suggests that research may want to focus more on outside influences (Haggerty, 2009). Thus, you could ask, "What types of outside factors influenced your actions?"

In the interview, Reid will inevitably describe certain events in shocking detail. Normally the interviewer should remain neutral and avoid any overt reactions that may influence the participant's responses. However, for serial killer interviews, openly acknowledging strange details can be helpful (Ressler, 2004). Thus, we can prepare for that possibility ahead of time with a leading question such as, "Surely you would say that your behavior wasn't normal, right?" In certain contexts, such as political polls or eyewitness testimony, interviewers should generally avoid *leading questions* in which the wording of the question influences the nature of the response (e.g., "Candidate A is clearly better than Candidate B, don't you think?"). However, in a qualitative interview, leading questions help the interviewer "fact-check" (Kvale, 1996).

You will also want to plan a few potential follow-up questions. For example, if Reid mentions a key detail that you want him to talk more about, you could ask, "Can you give other examples of when this happened?" If there is a moment where his thoughts might be of particular interest, you can ask, "When you did that, what were you thinking?" Finally, you should also have a few transition phrases prepared, such as, "Let's introduce a new topic . . ." or "Moving on to another aspect . . ." Now that you have your set of questions planned, you will want to obtain IRB approval prior to conducting your study.

Sequence of Questions

In planning the interview schedule, the questions are important, but the order in which you ask questions can also influence responses, especially when asking general questions, which is commonly the case in qualitative research (Schuman & Presser, 1996). That is, you want to be mindful of what you ask

▶ Not sure why you need approval from an Institutional Review Board (IRB)? SEE CHAPTER 3, p. 72

first and last, and the order of the questions in between. When you start the interview, the first question you may want to ask is, "Do you have any weapons, and do you plan on trying to kill me?" However, realistically it is more appropriate to start with "warm-up" type questions that are more general and less sensitive to help encourage the participant to talk. Thus, you could start off by asking Reid about the public details of his arrest and trial, but, to sustain the interviewee's interest, avoid stringing together long lists of fact-based questions. You should also save the most sensitive or difficult questions for the end, after you have established a rapport. That way, if Reid bails on the interview because he does not like a question, you will still have some information that you can use.

Conducting the Interview

At the actual interview, following informed consent, you will want to establish rapport early by being conversational and not acting in a way that makes the situation feel like an interview (Kvale, 1996). One way of doing this is to avoid using any audio or videotaping devices in favor of handwritten interview notes. The major disadvantage, however, is that you will inevitably omit information by missing things that were said or because your note-taking distracted the interviewee. Because they are your notes, there is a greater chance of interviewer biases (e.g., you may only note comments that confirm your initial impressions). A better option would be to use audio or videotaping equipment after all, allowing you to transcribe the interview afterward, and providing you with a richer data source. A video camera may feel too invasive or unnatural, so an audio recording is probably the best idea because it captures Mr. Hickernell's own words in a minimally invasive way.

During the interview, stick to your interview schedule as much as possible and allow Reid to talk. Even when he seems to have completed a thought, remain silent for just a bit to see if he expands upon his answer. He may view you as naïve or inexperienced, but you can use this to your advantage to get him to more fully describe some key aspect or to explicitly recount his thoughts. At the end, you will thank Mr. Hickernell for his time and debrief him. Finally, you will ask if it is okay to contact him again once you have your results, so that he can corroborate your interpretations and conclusions.

YOUR TURN 5.2

1. Camden is a vegan who is interviewing the owner of a butcher shop about the ethics of the business. Which of the following is the greatest threat to the objectivity of the interview?

   a. Question reactivity

   b. Volunteer bias

   c. Reflexivity

   d. Interviewer bias

2. All of the following are qualities of a good interviewer *except:*
   a. sensitive and tolerant.
   b. well prepared.
   c. organized.
   d. does not point out inconsistencies in responses.

3. Jayna wants to interview several posttraumatic stress disorder patients. During her interview, she wants to ask them about the traumatic experience itself, their childhood, their friendships, and their personality. Which of the following is the best question order for Jayna to use?
   a. Personality questions; childhood; friendships; traumatic experience
   b. Friendships; childhood; traumatic experience; personality questions
   c. Childhood; friendships; personality questions; traumatic experience
   d. Traumatic experience; childhood; personality questions; friendships

How did you do? Turn to the end of the chapter to check your answers.

In Search of Answers

In any research investigation, the goal is to pose a question, collect information that can potentially answer the question, examine that information to see if answers emerge, and then present the answers in some type of summarized format that others can easily understand and use. In quantitative research, statistics are the primary way that researchers summarize information and draw conclusions. In qualitative research, although researchers use numbers on occasion, the focus is not on generating numbers to show where a person falls on a particular quality or on using statistics to test specific hypotheses (Marecek, 2003). Rather, qualitative analysis focuses on uncovering the participant's real-life subjective perspectives and experiences.

If you had actually had a conversation with Reid Hickernell, you would first need to transcribe the interview in order to reveal themes (see the example transcription starting on p. 152) and provide a written account of the interview, either verbatim or in a condensed format, often including indications of nonverbal behavior. Performing a highly detailed transcription can be extremely time-consuming, so for your purposes, a summarized transcription that relies primarily on the audiotape, along with major nonverbal events (e.g., long pauses, sighs, laughter) will suffice.

Selecting the Proper Tool

The data you collect always dictate the analysis strategy. For example, if you only have written interviewer notes, you cannot do a **conversation analysis**, which examines natural dialogue patterns by focusing on features such as turn taking, gaze direction, and how speakers sequence speech (Willig, 2008). However, since you have an audio recording of a semistructured interview, you can use several strategies. One strategy, **content analysis**, systematically examines data

conversation analysis an analysis technique that involves an examination of the natural patterns of dialogue and focuses on features such as turn taking, gaze direction, and how speakers sequence speech.

content analysis an analysis technique that involves the systematic examination of communication where researchers organize responses in order to summarize the substance of the communication.

so that researchers can organize and summarize the substance of the communication. Researchers use content analysis on a variety of data formats, including verbal formats such as speeches and interviews, or written formats such as magazines and advertisements (Harwood & Garry, 2003). There are several approaches to conducting a content analysis. Since we are not testing an explicit theory, we can use a **grounded theory technique,** which uses information from participants to generate categories, establish themes, and build a theory (Glaser & Strauss, 1967). To develop a coding scheme, the researcher first skims the data and identifies major concepts. Next, the researcher arranges concepts into groups or themes that highlight interrelationships or associations between categories. Finally, the researcher picks a core concept or storyline to tie together the various concepts. According to Kvale (1996), following your analysis, ideally you should re-interview the participant for

Considering all the feature articles and advertisements in magazines, what types of research questions might you be able to answer with a content analysis of a magazine? *(Tom Cockrem/Lonely Planet Images/Getty Images)*

clarification, elaboration, and accuracy. Unfortunately, this is not a viable option because, a few weeks after your interview, Reid Hickernell was killed by another inmate, who stabbed Reid in the chest with a wooden shard.

 Research Spotlight

Content Analysis of Disney Princess Films

Content analyses are useful for capturing themes in a variety of contexts, including pop culture. Disney princesses appear in wildly popular movies and products that the company markets to young girls (England, Descartes, & Collier-Meek, 2011). But many wonder how these portrayals may affect children. To determine whether princesses and princes portrayed in these movies exhibit stereotypical gender roles and traits, researchers conducted a content analysis of Disney princess films (e.g., *Snow White, Beauty and the Beast, The Princess and the Frog*). Using predetermined codes based on several previous studies, the researchers coded princess and prince characters on masculine qualities (e.g., curious to explore, physically strong, assertive, unemotional) and feminine qualities (e.g., weak, submissive, emotional, nurturing). As expected, princes were more masculine and princesses were more feminine. The three most common codes for princes were: shows emotion; affectionate; and physically strong. For princesses, they were: affectionate; assertive; and fearful. Although assertive is a masculine characteristic, princesses most often expressed assertiveness toward children or animals. The three least common codes for princes were: collapses crying; ashamed; and focuses on their physical appearance. For princesses, they were: leader; inspires fear; and unemotional. By completing a content analysis of these movies, the researchers revealed that the Disney princess movies they examined did not provide the most positive portrayal of female roles and traits.

grounded theory technique an approach where the researcher does not have any explicit theories or hypotheses to test prior to the research, but instead uses information from participants to generate the categories and build a theory.

Writing the Results in APA Style: Content Analysis

Now that you have collected all of this information, you will want to put the findings in the format that will benefit others the most. In this section, we provide an example APA-style "results" section so that you can see how researchers might write up their interview results based on a content analysis of the transcribed interview. In a qualitative research study like ours, we want to identify several central themes that reoccur throughout the interview, followed by examples from the interview that illustrate these themes. As you read through, notice the types of information provided, how we present them, and the nature of the conclusion.

Results

A complete copy of the interview transcript is available upon request from the author. A summary of key features of Reid Hickernell's crimes appears in Table 5.4. Findings related to the coding categories and themes appear in Table 5.5.

Fantasy Thought

Like many serial killers, Reid Hickernell's motivations had elements of fantasy. These thoughts are not based in reality and largely focus on his belief that he is a vampire. Consistent with this belief, Reid engaged in several "vampire-like" behaviors with his victims, including neck biting, drinking blood, trying to create his own hunting coven, and believing in his own immortality. He mentioned, "I tried with the first half dozen or so to have them join my coven," and, "As a vampire I prefer to exsanguinate my prey."

He seemed to truly believe he was a vampire, to the point that he explained away obvious inconsistencies: "A true vampire can will himself to be in the sun, no problem. But it takes practice. Mind over matter." He also appeared to believe he was immortal. When talking about his eight consecutive life sentences in prison, he calmly remarked, "Since I'm immortal, I'll be out again."

Controlled/Calculated Thought

Although Reid Hickernell brutalized and killed 10 innocent people, his thoughts were not exclusively based in his fantasy world.

At many points Reid demonstrated a great deal of clarity, rationality, and control in his thoughts. For example, he explained, "I was in control all the time. Plotting, planning, covering my tracks. I studied up," and, "That stuff about new vampires being mindless killing machines is garbage. It may be true for others, but I controlled my thirst. I figured if I wasn't careful, I'd get sloppy and then get caught."

He was obviously able to calculate risk and demonstrated some awareness of his actions, though this mainly took the form of avoiding detection so that he could continue his "quest." As he said, "I was careful, smart, and patient about it . . . I gave it the time it deserved," and, "Ain't no coincidence that my entire house was floored in all plain, ordinary tile. No carpet, no carpet fibers. You have to plan ahead."

Media Influences

At several different points during the interview, Reid made references to forms of media. He mentioned books ("[I] read a lot of James Patterson and John Sandford books") and comics ("I thought it was cool to use the same gun Batman used in his early comics"). He also mentioned television shows like *CSI: Crime Scene Investigation,* saying, "But really, how could these idiots mess up and leave evidence behind when there are shows out there like *CSI?* I mean, that show is basically a 'how-to' manual for not leaving evidence behind," and, "I studied up . . . watched a lot of *CSI.*"

Reid mentioned these without prompting, and then acknowledged some direct influences when asked about media directly: "I was aware of these things, and watched them all the time. . . . Some of it is ridiculous. Sparkling in the sun? C'mon, who believes this Hollywood nonsense?" and, "The vampire books, shows, and movies . . . helped create easy prey. I mean, I told my recruits I was a vampire and what I planned to do . . . and they just thought it was cool and fed right into it."

Superiority

If there is a central theme or core concept that unites the various pieces of Reid's interview, it is his felt superiority. Reid's strong narcissistic tendencies and elevated view of himself permeated his fantasy and rational thought. For example, "I realized that none of them were truly worthy of joining me . . . no one was good enough. . . . These people should have been thankful . . . honored really . . . that I selected them." His beliefs were so grandiose that he thought the media was under his control, stating, "Vampire books, shows, and movies became popular just for me to enjoy."

Part of his perceived superiority emanated from his belief that, as a vampire, he was naturally intelligent and cunning. For example, he explained his capture by saying, "It was really the only way the police could have ever dreamed of catching someone as smart as me . . ." and, "It's the great thing about being so smart . . . it helps with everything."

 Research Spotlight

Identifying a Serial Killer May Be a Matter of Speaking

Psychopathic killers are clearly a bit different from the rest of us. In fact, research suggests that the way killers speak, specifically in the words that they use, may differ in identifiable ways, ways that quantitative analyses may not reveal (Hancock, Woodworth, & Porter, 2013). To test this, researchers asked two groups, one with 14 male psychopathic murderers and the other with 38 nonpsychopathic murderers, to each tell stories. Researchers then subjected the stories to a linguistic analysis that looked for both word choice and usage patterns. Compared to nonpsychopaths, the psychopaths spoke with more "uh's" and "um's" (known as disfluencies), and focused more on the need for food and money and less on the need for relationships or religion. The more frequent use of past tense in psychopaths' language also suggested less of a connection with the murders. Finally, psychopaths' language contained words such as "since" and "because," which may indicate that the speakers felt their actions were at least partly inevitable. These findings suggest another data analysis tool that researchers can use to uncover serial killers' thought patterns.

Don't Just Tell Me, Show Me: Using Tables

Along with presenting their qualitative information in the text of a research report, researchers also report the results of their content analysis in tables and figures. These visuals provide a different way to summarize the data, with **Table 5.4** listing Reid Hickernell's victims and crimes, and **Table 5.5** containing a content analysis of his thoughts.

TABLE 5.4

Summary of Reid Hickernell's Victims and Crimes					
Victim	Sex	Age	Cause of Death	Condition of Body	Items Taken
1	F	17	Asphyxiation	Multiple neck bites	ID
2	F	22	Stabbing (Dalton Cupid Automatic Knife)	Multiple neck bites, body positioned with arms crossed	Purse
3	M	16	Stabbing (Dalton Cupid Automatic Knife)	Body positioned with arms crossed	Wallet
4	F	19	Asphyxiation	Single neck bite, body drained of blood, body positioned with arms crossed	None
5	F	24	Asphyxiation	Single neck bite, body drained of blood, body positioned with arms crossed	Jewelry (cross necklace)
6	F	18	Asphyxiation	Single neck bite, body drained of blood, body positioned with arms crossed	Cell phone
7	F	23	Stabbing (Dalton Cupid Automatic Knife)	Single neck bite, body dismembered and drained of blood	Jewelry (cross necklace)
8	F	20	Gun shot (Colt .45)	Single neck bite, body dismembered and drained of blood	ID, cell phone
9	F	28	Gun shot (Colt .45)	Multiple neck bites, body dismembered and drained of blood	None
10	F	19	Gun shot (Colt .45)	Single neck bite, body dismembered and drained of blood	ID, purse

TABLE 5.5

Summary of Coding Categories and Related Themes	
Coding Categories and Retrieval Information	**Themes and Exemplars**
Fantasy Thoughts (50/94)*	**Vampire Behavior** *"As a vampire, I prefer to exsanguinate my prey."* *"A true vampire can will himself to be in the sun, no problem. But it takes practice. Mind over matter."* **Immortality** *"Since I'm immortal, I'll be out again."* *"They were to be chosen for the chance to be immortal."*
Controlled/Calculated Thoughts (26/94)	**Exercising Control** *"I was careful, smart, and patient about it."* *"I controlled my thirst. I figured if I wasn't careful, I'd get sloppy and then get caught."* **Purposeful/Planned Behavior** *"Ain't no coincidence that my entire house was floored in all plain ordinary tile. No carpet, no carpet fibers. You have to plan ahead."* *"I was in control all the time. Plotting, planning, covering my tracks. I studied up."*
Media Influence (18/94)	**Books/Comics** *"I thought it was cool to use the same gun Batman used in his early comics."* *"Read a lot of James Patterson and John Sandford books."* **TV Shows** *"But really, how could these idiots mess up and leave evidence behind when there are shows out there like CSI? I mean, that show is basically a 'how-to' manual for not leaving evidence behind."* *"I studied up . . . watched a lot of CSI."* **Awareness of Vampire Fad** *"I was aware of these things, and watched them all the time. . . . Some of it is ridiculous. Sparkling in the sun? C'mon, who believes this Hollywood nonsense?"* *"It was like the vampire books, shows, and movies became popular just for me to enjoy. It also helped create easy prey. I mean, I told my recruits I was a vampire and what I planned to do . . . and they just thought it was cool and fed right into it."*

Superiority (44/94)   Perceived Intelligence

> "It was really the only way the police could have ever dreamed of catching someone as smart as me."

> "It's the great thing about being so smart . . . it helps with everything."

Grandiosity

> "These people should have been thankful . . . honored, really . . . that I selected them."

> "I realized that none of them were truly worthy of joining me . . . no one was good enough."

*Represents the number of times mentioned out of the total categories coded. Please note that some excerpts could fall under multiple categories.

Our Research Plan at a Glance

What Is Our Research Question? What is the nature of a serial killer's thought patterns?

What Is Our Design? Semistructured interview with critical incident technique.

Why Are We Using This Design? We want an in-depth look into thought patterns and the flexibility to ask about key topic areas, but also enough flexibility to gain insight into unanticipated areas.

What Are Our Variables? Because of the type of design we are using, there are no true independent or dependent variables.

What Are Our Hypotheses? With this design, we do not have pre-established hypotheses to test. We take a bottom-up approach and allow the information that we collect to inform our conclusions. However, we do establish a set of guiding topics to ensure we cover all of the areas we are interested in.

Who Are Our Participants? Reid Hickernell, an infamous (and fictitious) killer at the Attica Correctional Facility in upstate New York.

What Ethical Considerations Do We Need to Keep in Mind?
- Incarcerated individuals may not be able to make a truly voluntary decision to participate.
- We must be sure not to over-incentivize participants by making the benefits of participation so great that the prisoner cannot objectively weigh the risks of participation and provide truly informed consent.
- The risk that the prisoner assumes must not exceed what a nonprisoner volunteer might experience.
- In qualitative research, there is an explicit emphasis on providing benefits. In this case, a break from his typical daily routine.

What Is Our Data Analysis Plan? We perform a content analysis of the interview transcripts using a grounded theory technique that allows us to generate categories, establish themes, and build a theory.

Let's Discuss What Happened

▶ Want to know more about the process of writing a discussion section? SEE APPENDIX B, p. 509

After a researcher learns the results of the study, the next step is to write an APA-style "discussion" section, where the researcher puts the results in context by showing how they compare to previous research. Here the researcher also offers thoughts on why the findings came about, and any potential issues or limitations with the study. We model these features below so that you can see how a researcher might try to make sense of the findings. As you read through, notice how we use previous research to explain our present findings and how we critically evaluate our own research design to identify possible flaws. The process of reflecting on one's own research is a valuable way to gain insight into the research topic and to help think of future research questions.

In this chapter, the purpose of our study was to answer the question, "What is the nature of a serial killer's thought patterns?" based on a semistructured interview with convicted serial killer Reid Hickernell. Following a grounded theory technique, we found that several themes emerged from our interview, including fantasy thought, controlled and calculated thought, media influences, and superiority.

Why These Findings?

Consistent with common characteristics of serial murderers, Reid is a physically attractive and highly intelligent White male (Ressler et al., 2004). Contrary to previous research, Reid did not indicate that his actions related to any previous childhood transgression, or from a desire to enact revenge on someone, although this is impossible to rule out. Reid's behaviors were clearly indicative of antisocial personality disorder (ASPD) due to his failure to express any type of remorse, as well as his manipulation, sense of entitlement, and cold affect. Although ASPD and psychopathy can coincide, this is not always the case (LaBrode, 2007). In Reid's case, it is less clear whether or not he was a psychopath. He did have the key characteristic of being predatory toward his victims, and, since he mentioned that he often told his victims that he was a vampire, it seems that he used his personality to help procure his victims.

Reid Hickernell displayed tendencies of a mission-oriented type of serial killer who seeks to remove certain individuals from society or to improve society or a group of people in some way (Holmes & DeBurger, 1985), which is consistent with Reid's goal of recruiting new members for his coven. Reid's belief in his own superiority and status as a vampire also suggested a power/control-oriented type of serial killer who likes to dominate victims and instill fear in them, typically for erotic reasons. In Reid's case, he felt a need to dominate and viewed himself as having an elevated status. However, based on his descriptions, there did not seem to be any overt sexuality to his quest. As is often the case when using typologies that attempt to categorize human behavior, Reid showed a few characteristics of each type, but did not fit into either type neatly or perfectly.

Reid seemed to manage his fantasy thoughts by purposefully engaging in controlled planning. Some consider it a myth that serial killers are highly intelligent or "evil geniuses" (FBI, 2008). Reid Hickernell, however, seemed highly intelligent and used his intelligence to avoid detection, which is consistent with an "organized" killer (Canter, Alison, Alison, & Wentink, 2004). Serial killers commonly display traits such as a grandiose sense of self-worth, selfishness, and a casual attitude toward their crimes (FBI, 2008; Knight, 2006), a description that is consistent with Reid's strong feelings of superiority and illusions of grandiosity (e.g., he thought he was immortal).

As suggested by Haggerty (2009), the broader social and cultural context may influence serial killers' behaviors. The interview did not suggest any direct causal link between the media and Reid's actions. Reid never blamed or directly implicated the media as a reason for killing, but he did acknowledge that the media had a role. This was similar to Jeffrey Dahmer's affinity for the Emperor from *Return of the Jedi* (Ressler, 2004). As is common with a qualitative approach, through the interview process, Reid gained new insight into his own behaviors. Reid's new perspective on the media's role was similar to that of another serial killer: "He begins to search out newer and more sophisticated imagery to play out in his mind. This imagery—which he obtains from books, magazines, movies, or any other sources depicting new examples and new methods of violence" (Anonymous, 1998, p. 128).

Although Reid did not acknowledge any sexual component to his killings, there may have been an underlying eroticism to his quest that he has not fully acknowledged. Reid mentioned his fixation on the song "Love Bites" by Judas Priest. The lyrics to that song strongly suggest an eroticized component of vampire-like acts (e.g., "Gently you moan, lust's in the air"). In fact, unbeknownst to Reid, that song contains the hidden lyric, "In the dead of the night, love bites," which can be heard when playing the song backward (Associated Press, 1990). Although some have suggested that listeners can obtain information from these backward or "backmasked" messages (Vokey & Read, 1985), more recent research refutes this claim (Kreiner, Altis, & Voss, 2003).

What Could Be Improved?

In retrospect, there were aspects of the interview that we could have improved. Looking at the transcript, it was probably a mistake for us to have labeled thoughts as "patterns." As is often the case in qualitative research, after the study, the researcher will discover a better research question to pursue (Willig, 2008). In future research, it would be better to ask about thoughts in general, and then allow the subject to define the nature of them on his own. There were also several times when more probing for information would have helped. This

Despite there being little evidence to suggest that backmasking influences our thoughts, why do you think so many people believe that it does have an influence? *(Flashpop/Iconica/Getty Images)*

is a natural by-product of having a limited interaction. In a one-hour interview, it is impossible to discuss everything, and the researcher is only privy to what the interviewee wants to share. Thus, it is possible that Reid omitted potentially useful information that he considered unremarkable.

We also have to be careful about generalizing too broadly from our single interview. Due to the nature of serial killers, we will have a nonresponse bias because we can only ever talk to the serial killers who have been caught. Thus, it is possible that serial killers who remain uncaught or undetected exhibit different characteristics. Similarly, there is a volunteer bias or volunteer subject problem because we are only able to interview killers who want to talk. Those who prefer to avoid being interviewed may be different in some important and unknown way. Finally, it is important to acknowledge how characteristics of the interviewer may have influenced Reid Hickernell's responses. For example, as novice interviewers, it is possible that we were not able to elicit as much detailed information as a more experienced interviewer would have. However, it is also possible that our inexperience helped Reid feel comfortable and led him to tell us more.

▶ Wondering how sampling problems influence findings? SEE CHAPTER 4, p. 112

What Do You Think?

How might serial killers who avoid interviews be different from those who are willing to be interviewed?

YOUR TURN 5.3

1. Anita completed an analysis of several celebrity Twitter feeds in which she identified a central theme (vanity) that was common across many areas. What type of analysis is this?
   a. Thematic
   b. Content
   c. Conversation
   d. Grounded theory

2. Which of the following did the "discussion" section identify as a weakness of the research interview with Reid Hickernell?
   a. The findings from the single interview may not generalize to other serial killers.
   b. The interview provided evidence to support that Reid Hickernell had antisocial personality disorder.
   c. The interview identified Reid Hickernell as a mission-oriented type serial killer.
   d. There were several missed opportunities for obtaining more information.

3. Nolan is interested in studying shopping addiction, so he posts an advertisement online soliciting participants on several online retailers' sites. In his interviews, he discovers that his participants are very proud of their addiction. Which of the following is most likely influencing his conclusion?
   a. Volunteer bias
   b. Interviewer bias
   c. Response bias
   d. Experimenter bias

How did you do? Turn to the end of the chapter to check your answers.

🔧 Research in Action

You're Hired!

Because of your psychology background, you've been hired to work in a human resources department for a marketing company. The company expects you to hit the ground running, so your first job is to create a new protocol for employee-hiring interviews. Congratulations—this is a great use of your research skills!

Based on what you learned about interviews in this chapter, the online activity *You're Hired!* gives you the chance to apply your skills. In the activity, you'll identify good versus bad interview questions, develop an interview schedule, and determine the best way to conduct an interview. Being able to apply research knowledge like this is a highly valued skill. Your employer will be so impressed that you'll earn a raise in no time!

LaunchPad To complete this activity, visit LaunchPad at launchpadworks.com

Final Thoughts

In this chapter, you have seen how qualitative research can help us learn about the mind of a serial killer. Because qualitative research focuses on providing an in-depth look at individuals in a specific context, it is well suited for serial killer research. By taking a bottom-up approach and using a semistructured interview, we were able to touch on key topics while providing our participant with enough flexibility to tell his own story. Using a grounded theory technique, we were able to analyze the data in a way that allowed several key themes to emerge. Ultimately, allowing participants to fully explain their own thoughts and feelings is one of the key benefits of qualitative research. It is possible that if we had taken another approach, we may have never thought to ask about all of the ways that media influenced Reid's behavior.

After hearing Reid Hickernell's cold-blooded and casual description of his murders, along with his vampire-inspired explanations, it is hard to find serial killers any less intriguing than when we started. Certainly, there are many more questions we could ask about how media may have influenced his vampire quest, probably in ways he has not considered. It would also be interesting to learn more about why he picked certain victims and how his relationships with others may have influenced his actions (oddly, he never mentioned interactions with anyone other than his victims). One thing that remains unclear is whether Reid Hickernell's personality led him to interpret media messages in a unique way, or if those messages can influence anyone in a similar way. Chances are that Reid was uniquely influenced; otherwise, there would be many more supposed vampire killers on the hunt. The only way to know for sure is through further research.

Excerpt of Interview Transcript

INTERVIEWER (I): Hello. My name is Taylor and as part of my research class I'd like to interview you. [Interviewee extends hand to shake, interviewer declines] Specifically, I'd like to ask questions about why you are in jail, your background, and your experiences, in hopes of writing up what I find and submitting it to a journal for potential publication. In that publication, with your permission, I would identify you as the interviewee. To make sure I don't miss anything, I will audiotape the interview, if that is okay with you. The interview should take about an hour, though you are welcome to quit at any point.

REID HICKERNELL (RH): That all sounds okay. Shoot. . . . I've got time to kill.

I: Thanks. First I'd like you to read this informed consent. If you agree to participate, please say that you agree out loud.

RH: I guess. Sure, I mean, why not? I'll play along.

I: Great. Thank you. First, can you tell me what you were arrested for?

RH: [suppresses a laugh] Well, I'd have to say it was mainly for killing a bunch of people and for being unlucky enough to get caught. I was way too smart for it to be anything but luck.

I: Okay.

RH: Really, it was bad luck. I'm minding my own business, and get stopped at a DUI checkpoint. I think, no problem, I'm totally sober . . . just out cruising the highways. But of all the dumb luck things, this cop fancies himself as some type of classic car fan, and likes my car enough that he wants to look around. I mean, I drive a 1972 Camaro, which isn't exactly a collectable, but I get stopped by this wannabe expert who starts poking around, asking me questions about what was original on the car. I tell him "everything" just to get him to send me on my way, but then deputy do-gooder notices that the back seat wasn't original. He starts asking more questions, sticks his head in the passenger side window, and notices the smell. [sighs loudly]

I: Smell?

RH: Ya know . . . death. Well, actually, it wasn't really death as much as it was the smell of bleach, hydrogen peroxide, and a fancy enzyme solution. I guess after all this time I was used to it. The problem was that I tried to introduce a girl to immortality back there, but it turned into that scene from *Pulp Fiction*. Blood squirting everywhere, and impossible to really get out of the seats, so I reupholstered it myself. Did a damn good job, too, but apparently not good enough for classic car nerd. The thing is, it wasn't even the smell, or that he saw blood, it was just that the seat cover was different . . . dumb friggin' luck. It really was the only way the police could have ever dreamed of catching someone as smart as me . . . and the only way I was ever going to stop.

I: Um . . .

RH: So they got lucky this time, but the joke's on them. Sure, I'm locked up for eight consecutive life sentences, but since I'm immortal, I'll be out again, and they won't get so lucky the next time.

I: You'll kill again?

RH: Whoa . . . now, now. I would never conceive of doing such a thing. I'm reformed, [waves both hands up in the air] and have no intention of harming anyone ever again, and I'm sure the parole board will see it that way soon enough. . . . I'm being cooperative with you, aren't I?

I: Yes, thanks. So . . . which aspect of the killings would you like to discuss?

RH: I don't know if I want to discuss it the most, but the part that disappoints me the most is that I spent so much time selecting my recruits, and yet, in the end, none were truly worthy.

I: Recruits or victims?

RH: They weren't victims at all. . . . They were recruits, one of the chosen. I mean, these people should have been thankful . . . honored, really . . . that I selected them. Every one of them should have thanked me for how lucky they were to be chosen for the chance to be immortal . . . because not everyone was. I specifically looked for recruits who were healthy . . . ya know, took care of themselves, didn't smoke, didn't have that fake tan nonsense. These things were important because I was recruiting them to be fellow vampires who would join my hunting coven. The stakes were high, so I had to take the time to properly select them, watch them for a while . . . then find the right opportunity to bring them home. I was careful, smart, and patient about it . . . I gave it the time it deserved. Despite all of my efforts, I realized that none of them were truly worthy of joining me. Sure, I tried with the first half dozen or so to have them join my coven, but it was useless. No one was good enough, which is why I started tearing them to pieces after feeding.

I: What do you think goes through other serial killers' heads when they select a victim?

RH: Honestly, I think most of them are hacks who weren't capable of developing intricate enough procedures to avoid detection, probably due to some sort of grandiose sense of their own ability. But really, how could these idiots mess up and leave evidence behind when there are shows out there like *CSI*? I mean, that show is basically a "how-to" manual for not leaving evidence behind. Ain't no coincidence that my entire house was floored in all plain ordinary tile. No carpet, no carpet fibers. You have to plan ahead.

I: Can you describe in detail what a typical killing was like?

RH: I'd love to.
. . .

[Reid spends the next 30 minutes providing a step-by-step description of each murder]
. . .

I: You mentioned that you drained each victim's blood. Surely you would say that your behavior wasn't normal, right?

RH: What's not normal about it? As a vampire, I prefer to exsanguinate my prey. The only odd part, I suppose, was that I used milk jugs to save some for drinking later. I probably should have used different containers. Milk jugs have such an oddly small opening that I spilled a lot.

I: Moving on to another aspect . . . you used weapons sometimes? I thought vampires didn't do that.

RH: Ahhh, you are naïve and have much to learn. Of course, as a vampire I don't need to use weapons, but I thought it was cool to use the same gun Batman used in his early comics. The knife was one the Joker used in *Dark Knight,* which I thought was ironic. I'm a pragmatist. I used whatever got the job done best at the time.

I: What was the nature of your thought patterns during the killings?

RH: Patterns? Hell, there wasn't anything patterned about it, well, unless you consider chaos a pattern. Yup, a regular ol' Ian Malcolm chaos theory pattern. My own little *Jurassic Park* in upstate New York. [laughter]

I: I see. But what do you mean by chaos?

RH: Boy, are you dense or something? So, here you go . . . real slooowwwww [he draws out the word in deliberate way] so you can keep up. My brain, my mind, they are filled with turbulence. My thoughts are nonlinear, almost like Ping-Pong balls in a lottery machine. That stuff about new vampires being mindless killing machines is garbage. It may be true for others, but I controlled my thirst. I figured if I wasn't careful, I'd get sloppy and then get caught. Sure, most of my thoughts were hyperfocused on my next feeding. But I also had to keep myself under control, so that I wouldn't slip up. Cause man, that would've been counterproductive to my quest.

I: Can you give other examples of this?

RH: [pfft] Easily. I was in control all the time. Plotting, planning, covering my tracks. I studied up . . . watched a lot of *CSI,* read a lot of James Patterson and John Sandford books. I was smart enough to know how to get rid of the leftovers.

I: Leftovers?

RH: The bodies. Like the pizza crust you don't want after you're done.

I: When you disposed of bodies, what were you thinking?

RH: Mainly about not getting caught. Early on I used bleach, but then got concerned that someone would start tracking my purchases. It sorta draws attention when you buy 5 or 10 gallons at a time [chuckles], and buying some here and there is tedious. I considered setting the bodies on fire, but since I was disposing of them at night I didn't want to draw attention to it. If I've learned anything, the longer the leftovers are out in the elements, the less evidence there is for the lab techs to use. It is even better if the local wildlife got to it first . . . so after driving bodies all the way out to the Adirondacks, I smeared bacon grease on the bodies to help attract the local black bears. It's the great thing about being so smart . . . it helps with everything.

I: Let's introduce a new topic. What types of outside factors influenced you?

RH: What do you mean, like aliens or people controlling my thoughts? Cuz, I'm not crazy like that.

I: More like things other than your childhood that may have influenced your actions.

RH: Well, because of my job and all, I read a lot. When it was dead in the store, I'd read the latest stuff that came in.

I: Did you like anything in particular?

RH: I liked the murder mystery books. I also read those trashy teenage vampire books because so many people made a fuss about them. Dumb story, but it had a lot of vampire stuff in there . . . even had some of it right. From there I watched the movies, then started watching all of the vampire shows on TV. So yeah, I was aware of these things, and watched them all the time. As for their influence . . . I suppose they influenced me in an inspirational type of way, and helped me relive some of my own feedings. But they certainly didn't control me or cause me to do anything. I'm above that. Some of it is ridiculous. Sparkling in the sun? C'mon, who believes this Hollywood nonsense? A true vampire can will himself to be in the sun, no problem. But it takes practice. Mind over matter. More than anything it was like the vampire books, shows, and movies became popular just for me to enjoy. It also helped create easy prey. I mean, I told my recruits I was a vampire and what I planned to do . . . and they just thought it was cool and fed right into it.

I: Anything else?

RH: I never really thought about it before, but during the same time I really got into the song "Love Bites" by Judas Priest. There was just something about it . . . [breaks into song]. It played on continuous loop in my head.

[knock on door to signify time is up]

I: That's for you. Thanks for talking to me today.

RH: Away I go, gliding on mist . . .

CHAPTER 5 Review

Review Questions

1. Tosha is interested in understanding the culture of "hooking up." She decides to gather in-depth information on a few individuals so she can have a more thorough understanding of their perspectives and experiences concerning hooking up. Which of the following research approaches is Tosha using?
   a. Quantitative
   b. Qualitative
   c. Bottom-down approach
   d. Top-down approach

2. Shantel believes that her boyfriend is about to propose. She hunts around in his bedroom and finds a receipt from a jewelry store and a note regarding a dinner reservation at a fancy restaurant. Shantel believes this evidence confirms her prediction. Which of the following approaches in Shantel using?
   a. Quantitative
   b. Qualitative
   c. Bottom-up approach
   d. Top-down approach

3. Hugo's research methods professor gives him an assignment to create an interview. As it is his first time serving as an interviewer, he prepares 10 specific questions prior to the interview and asks all his questions in a specific order. What type of interview is Hugo creating?

   a. A structured interview
   b. An unstructured interview
   c. A semistructured interview
   d. An unbiased interview

4. Which of the following is part of developing an interview schedule?

   a. Determining where the interview will take place
   b. Rehearsing the questions
   c. Deciding the sequencing of the questions
   d. Determining the day and time of the interview

5. Which of the following is a weakness of qualitative designs?

   a. They focus on obtaining in-depth information.
   b. They involve a small sample.
   c. They often involve collecting data in naturally occurring settings.
   d. They are more participant-defined than researcher-defined.

6. As a research project in his U.S. history class, Mack reads a number of case files from adults immigrating to the United States over the last 100 years. He wants to focus on reasons for immigrating. From the interviews, he generates categories and establishes themes (e.g., religious freedom, better opportunity, poverty, safety). Which of the following best describes what Mack is doing?

   a. He is engaging in conversation analysis.
   b. He is employing the use of content analysis.
   c. He is developing a grounded theory.
   d. He is systematically coding the data.

7. An interview schedule is most like which of the following concepts that was discussed in a previous chapter?

   a. Establishing validity
   b. Protocol
   c. Operational definitions
   d. Conceptual definitions

8. Jose is doing a study about students' likelihood to cheat on an online test. He has questions about their demographic characteristics, how often they have cheated in the past, their intrinsic and extrinsic motivations, and their grades. Which questions should Jose ask first?

   a. Their grades
   b. Their past cheating behavior
   c. Their demographics
   d. Their intrinsic and extrinsic motivations

9. Rick is interested in examining obituaries from the post–World War II era. After reading through several, he establishes general concepts that frequently occur, and then settles on one (patriotism) that is most common. What type of analysis is this?
   a. Grounded theory
   b. Conversation
   c. Content
   d. Thematic

10. As a researcher in the Health Department, Stella has the task of identifying strategies for lowering her city's obesity rate. She invites a dozen residents to her office to discuss their lifestyle. Through those conversations, she identifies several small factors (e.g., consuming artificial sweeteners, watching reality TV, exposure to the sun) that seem to contribute to the larger problem. What type of analysis is Stella doing?
   a. A holistic analysis
   b. A situated analysis
   c. A conversation analysis
   d. A content analysis

11. List the characteristics of a good interviewer. Which characteristics do you think you need to better develop if you want to become an effective interviewer?

12. In what ways can a researcher bias the findings in a qualitative study?

13. What are some of the strengths and weaknesses of qualitative designs?

Applying What You've Learned

1. What are three topics in psychology that you would like to study? For each, identify whether a qualitative or quantitative approach would be more effective. Support your conclusion for each.

2. You may never interview a serial killer, but you may need to conduct an interview at other times in your life. List several examples of when you might use an interview.

3. You plan to conduct an interview on campus about the quality of campus dining because you think the food is low quality. What can you do to reduce any potential interviewer bias and ensure you obtain objective data?

4. Assume the role of hiring manager for a Fortune 500 company. Plan out an interview for a managerial candidate with at least 10 questions, then devise an interview schedule, keeping in mind what you learned about question order.

5. Develop three research questions that would be ideally suited for each of these data collection methods: archival, focus group, and case study.

6. Watch an interview that lasts at least 20 minutes from a news program such as *20/20*. Identify the interview type, as well as what good interviewer characteristics you observed. Explain how the interviewer did or did not display bias during the interview.

7. THE NOVICE RESEARCHER: Conduct a very brief, 3–5-minute interview with a friend, roommate, or classmate about his or her career goals. With his or her permission, record the interview and transcribe it. Identify any areas where your transcription failed to fully capture the nature of your original conversation. Would a video recording have helped? Why or why not?

Key Concepts

archival data, p. 131

bottom-up approach, p. 127

case study, p. 132

content analysis, p. 140

conversation analysis, p. 141

critical incident technique, p. 134

focus group, p. 131

grounded theory technique, p. 141

holistic analysis, p. 129

interview, p. 132

interview agenda, p. 137

interviewer bias, p. 137

interview schedule, p. 137

mixed methods research, p. 125

phenomenological approach, p. 129

qualitative research, p. 125

quantitative research, p. 125

reflexivity, p. 127

semistructured interview, p. 133

situated analysis, p. 128

structured interview, p. 133

top-down approach, p. 128

triangulation, p. 127

unit of analysis, p. 135

unstructured interview, p. 133

Answers to YOUR TURN

Your Turn 5.1: 1. c; 2. a; 3. b

Your Turn 5.2: 1. d; 2. d; 3. c

Your Turn 5.3: 1. b; 2. a; 3. a

Answers to Multiple-Choice Review Questions

1. b; 2. d; 3. a; 4. c; 5. b; 6. c; 7. b; 8. d; 9. c; 10. a

Observational Research

The Many Forms of Discipline in a Parent's Bag of Tricks

Jamie Grill/The Image Bank/Getty Images

LEARNING OUTCOMES

After reading this chapter, you should be able to:

- Identify when and why to use observational methods.
- Articulate the various types of observational methods.
- Develop a coding system and protocol for collecting observational data.
- Determine the appropriate procedures and training for recording observations.
- Identify the proper statistics to use for observational research.
- Write a results section involving descriptive statistics.

Something to Think About . . .

Have you ever been out at a store, walking through a park, or eating at a restaurant when a child starts having a tantrum? We have all seen it, and many parents will say that their young child having a disruptive meltdown in a public place is one of their worst fears. The next time you see this happen, notice how others, particularly other adults, react to the situation. Some give a supportive "I've been there" look, while others watch with a scornful facial expression that clearly says, "Control your child." The parent obviously wants to end the child's tantrum as quickly as possible, but how?

Parents have a few techniques in their tantrum response arsenal. For example, the parent could ignore the tantrum, allow the child to cry it out, threaten to punish the child, bribe the child with candy to get him or her to stop, or use corporal punishment like spanking to really give the child "something to cry about." Although each parent tends to have his or her own style or preferred way of handling these incidents, what parents actually do in a tantrum situation may depend on who is around and who they believe is watching. That is, parents may not normally spank their child at home, but may feel compelled to do so when others are present in order to end a tantrum quickly. Or they may spank their child at home, but think better of it when others are watching. Regardless of who is watching, a parent should always do what is best for the child. But what a parent should do and what a parent actually does are not always the same thing. This seems like an idea worth investigating.

How do you react when you see a child crying in a public place? Might your reactions influence how and if a parent disciplines their child? *(kirin_photo/E+/Getty Images)*

Introduction to Our Research Question

We could reframe this idea more formally by phrasing it as a research question:

RESEARCH **?** What forms of discipline do parents use when others are around?

There are two general types of research questions we can ask: "what" and "why." The type of question we ask leads us to the general research design. "What" questions are about detailing phenomena and lead to **descriptive research.** We use this research approach to label the nature of *what* is happening, such as what a person feels, thinks, or does. In contrast, research questions that seek to explain *why* a phenomenon occurs lead to **experimental research,** which helps us explore why a person feels, thinks, or does something in particular. We will talk much more about experimental research in future chapters. Given that our current idea focuses on *what* forms of discipline parents use, not *why* they use them, our research approach is descriptive. Before jumping in and starting to collect data, we need to learn more about what researchers know about discipline strategies, and if researchers have already explored our research question.

Reviewing the Literature: What Do We Already Know About This Topic?

▶ Not sure how to conduct a literature search or find background sources to help you design your studies? SEE CHAPTER 2, p. 29

As we did in the previous chapter, we saved you some time by finding several research studies that provide the necessary background to help develop our study. Before testing if the presence of others influences parents' reactions to misbehaving children, we must search the literature to determine what is already known about the types of discipline that parents use and the factors that influence each parent's discipline style. Below we summarize several studies that are relevant to our research question.

Types of Parental Discipline

Gershoff, E. T., Grogan-Kaylor, A., Lansford, J. E., Chang, L., Zelli, A., Deater-Deckard, K., & Dodge, K. A. (2010). Parent discipline practices in an international sample: Associations with child behaviors and moderation by perceived normativeness. *Child Development, 81,* 487–502. doi:10.1111/ j.1467-8624.2009.01409.x

descriptive research
a research design that describes what is happening.

experimental research
a research design that explores why a phenomenon occurs.

Parental discipline involves any action intended to change a child's behavior. In this study, researchers categorized parental discipline into 11 different actions: talking to the child about good and bad behavior, asking the child to apologize, putting the child in a time-out, taking away privileges, spanking or using other forms of corporal punishment, expressing disappointment in the child, telling the child he or she should be ashamed, scolding the child in a loud voice, telling the child that the parent will no longer love the child if the child does it again, threatening some punishment if the child performs the behavior again, and promising to give the child something rewarding if the child behaves appropriately (i.e., a bribe). The researchers then linked each type of discipline to aggression and anxiety in the child. Using corporal punishment, expressing disappointment, and yelling all significantly related to child aggression, and giving a time-out, using corporal punishment, expressing disappointment, and shaming all significantly related to greater anxiety.

Gershoff, E. T. (2002). Corporal punishment by parents and associated child behaviors and experiences: A meta-analytic and theoretical review. *Psychological Bulletin, 128,* 539–579. doi:10.1037/0033-2909.128.4.539

Corporal punishment is the deliberate infliction of pain by physical force for the purpose of disciplining. Although it is still commonly used in the United States, corporal punishment is, arguably, damaging. In this study, the researcher examined the impact of corporal punishment by reviewing the findings of 88 different studies over a 62-year time span. Although the use of corporal punishment resulted in immediate compliance, it also resulted in more aggression and lower levels of moral internalization and mental health. In addition, it hurt the quality of the parent–child relationship by invoking fear, anxiety, and anger in the relationship.

Influences on Discipline Style

Lopez, N. L., Schneider, H. G., & Dula, C. S. (2002). Parent discipline scale: Discipline choice as a function of transgression type. *North American Journal of Psychology, 4,* 381–393.

These researchers examined when parents used specific types of discipline. They categorized discipline into three types: induction, nonaggressive power assertion, and aggressive power assertion. Induction is a disciplinary tactic in which the parent communicates the rationale for a rule and the consequences of the child's actions. Power-assertive tactics use power to enforce rules, including aggressive forms, such as spanking, and nonaggressive forms, such as a time-out. The researchers also categorized the transgression committed by the child into categories of aggressive and nonaggressive social violations and aggressive and nonaggressive safety violations. Overall, parents were more likely to use all types of discipline interventions when addressing aggressive violations as opposed to nonaggressive violations. However, when comparing violations of safety with social norm violations, parents used higher levels of both aggressive power assertion and induction with safety violations. Overall, the types of transgression linked to specific types of disciplinary action.

Fletcher, A. C., Walls, J. K., Cook, E. C., Madison, K. J., & Bridges, T. H. (2008). Parenting style as a moderator of associations between maternal disciplinary strategies and child well-being. *Journal of Family Issues, 29,* 1724–1744. doi:10.1177/0192513X08322933

Parenting style influences the types of discipline that parents use. In this study, researchers categorized mothers into one of four parenting styles based on how demanding the mother was of her child and how responsive she was to the child's needs. Parenting style categories included authoritative (parents who are both responsive and demanding of their children), indulgent (parents who are highly responsive but not demanding), authoritarian (parents who are highly demanding but nonresponsive), and indifferent (parents who are not responsive or demanding). Indifferent mothers were the most likely to use punitive discipline such as yelling, spanking, and withholding privileges. Authoritative parents were the least likely to use these methods.

From Ideas to Innovation

Clearly, parental discipline and spanking, in particular, are important topics among developmental psychologists. They have also studied some of the factors that influence discipline styles. What appears to be missing is how the immediate environment, like the presence of others, plays a role in discipline. This seems like a good area to investigate because it is possible that how we behave in the privacy of our own home is not always how we behave in the presence of others.

Defining Key Terms: What Do You Mean By ___?

Given our research question, "What forms of discipline do parents use when others are around?", we need to determine conceptual definitions for "discipline" and "when others are around." To conceptually define discipline, we do not have to work too hard. We know from our literature search that parental discipline is any action taken by a parent to change a child's behavior (Gershoff et al., 2010). This includes a few broad types of discipline and specific tactics that will help us decide how we will measure it later. We should note that using previously existing definitions from the literature is not cheating or being lazy. Rather, it is better to use something that other researchers have used successfully than to try to create your own definition that may have unanticipated flaws. Still, as a researcher, you should consider whether the definition provided in others' research is accurate and believable before making a final decision. Next, we need to conceptually define "when others are around." This could mean any time that another person is present, but that may be a bit too broad because, in a parenting context, another person could be the other parent, siblings, or other children. Thus, we should focus on situations that involve the presence of unfamiliar adults outside of one's own private residence. Later, we will decide how to use these concepts in our study.

▶ What is a conceptual definition? SEE CHAPTER 2, p. 38

Weighing Our Options: Picking the Best Design

Now that we have a clear sense of our research question, we need to determine the best way to answer it. For example, within descriptive research, we could interview parents or ask them to complete a survey about their discipline tactics in various settings. But wait—a self-report measure may not be ideal because our research question focuses on actual observable behavior, not data obtained through introspection. In addition, parents may not really know how they would discipline their child when others are present. People are often inaccurate in their predictions about their own future behaviors (Gilbert, 2006), and their reflections on past behavior may be susceptible to retrospection bias.

▶ Do you remember the pros and cons of using self-report? SEE CHAPTER 4, p. 88

▶ How can retrospective bias hurt the research process? SEE CHAPTER 4, p. 91

We have an interest in how parents discipline their children when others are present because we think that there may be something unique about how that situation influences parents' behavior. Parents may handle a misbehaving child differently in front of others because they are worried about how others will judge them. Similarly, social desirability concerns may influence how parents answer vital questions on a self-report measure, leading them

▶ Under what circumstances do people try to maximize their social desirability to researchers? SEE CHAPTER 4, p. 89

to underreport their use of spanking or overreport their use of more socially acceptable disciplinary tactics so that they look like good parents to the researchers.

For these reasons, we should use a behavioral measure. One option would be to identify evidence that different types of discipline may leave behind. However, it is unlikely that many types of discipline will produce these types of behavioral traces (e.g., there is no behavioral trace for ignoring). Abuse is one exception, but since abuse is not the focus of our research question, behavioral traces are not the best option for us. Instead, we could wait for a time when a child misbehaves and then ask a parent to choose which type of discipline she or he wants to use from a list of choices. However, providing this type of behavioral choice would mean artificially limiting the discipline tactics to a relatively small number of behaviors and requiring parents to choose only one of them. As it turns out, real-life parenting does not occur in a multiple-choice format. Behavioral choice also restricts participants to making a single choice when they may naturally use a combination of tactics.

Remember our research question: "What forms of discipline do parents use in the presence of others?" This question requires that we use a public setting where others are present. We also want to provide an environment that allows parents to engage naturally in discipline. Essentially, we want to see parental discipline in its entirety, live as it occurs, like a real-life reality television show. Therefore, given our focus, the best behavioral measure for us to use is behavioral observation, which relies on directly seeing or witnessing behavior as it occurs.

While observation is the best method to answer our research question, there are other reasons to engage in observational research. In its early stages, observational research can help identify the key factors that relate to a phenomenon, and we may identify connections that will help us form theories for further research. For example, if we wanted to investigate how product placement impacts the sale of jeans, we might start with an observational study at a clothing retailer where we note patterns we see, such as if people more often purchase jeans featured on an unrealistically skinny or a realistically full-sized mannequin. This might lead us to design an experimental study where we systematically present the same jeans on different mannequins to determine if size really plays a role in our desire to purchase a product. Second, some phenomena are impossible to study experimentally, for practical or ethical reasons. For instance, it would be unethical for us to force some children, but not others, to misbehave just so we can see how parents respond.

Weighing Our Options: Picking an Observational Method

When we are out in public, most of us "people watch" by making casual observations of others in a haphazard way. But when we do this for fun, we may only pay attention to some behaviors, like a child crying, while largely ignoring other children who are quietly playing. Or we might note the outrageous mannerisms of one person without noticing the more subdued mannerisms of others. Our casual, everyday observations have no specific

What Do You Think?
Most research on parental discipline uses self-reports. Why would researchers use self-reports to document this type of behavior?

focus or goal. As researchers, however, we want to make purposeful and specific observations based on our research question. That is, instead of casual or haphazard observations, we want to conduct **systematic observational research,** in which we view and note the occurrence of predetermined behaviors in an organized way.

For our research question, we need to methodically observe and record parental discipline in the presence of others. Not only does a systematic observation fit the needs of our research question, it has the added advantage of having high **external validity,** meaning we can apply or generalize the study findings beyond the data collection setting. If we systematically observe behavior, we can be reasonably sure that the behavior will look the same in other similar settings, persons, or places. Assuming we can find patterns in how people discipline in the presence of others at the mall, we have high external validity if those same discipline patterns also appear in other public locations, like playgrounds, churches, or stores, and with other types of people, like children of different ages or people of different ethnicities. We know that systematic observation is the way to go, but we still need to make some decisions about which type will be best for addressing our research question: laboratory, participant, or naturalistic observation.

Laboratory Observation

To make our lives easy, we could use **laboratory observation,** where we bring participants into a controlled setting on campus and watch their behavior under different conditions or situations. To explore our research question in this manner, we could create a large playroom where several sets of children play simultaneously while we observe the nature of parents' discipline tactics. With this method, we have more control over factors such as the environment (e.g., the types of activities and toys that are present), as well as the people who participate (e.g., the types of parents or number of kids), which would result in greater confidence that one variable is the cause of change in another variable. Conversely, because the participants know the researcher is observing them, laboratory observations are prone to both demand characteristics and social desirability. Parents in our study might want to spank their children or scream at them, but knowing they are being watched might cause them to alter their behavior in order to please us or to look like good parents. Both are substantial concerns, because we want parents' natural behavior.

All laboratory settings also have some degree of artificiality. After all, participants know that they are in a study and that the researcher has designed the study setting. This can hurt a study's **ecological validity,** or the degree to which the research situation re-creates the psychological experiences that participants would have in real life. In other words, we need our participants to forget that they are in a study so that they will feel and act the same way they would in a similar real-life situation. To do this, the method, materials, and setting of the study must be similar to the real-life situation under investigation. If we use a laboratory playroom that does not mimic how a parent experiences the presence of others in a real way, ecological validity will suffer, the results will be less meaningful, and our generalizability will suffer. In each decision you make about how to collect your data there will be trade-offs. Given our particular research question and the poorer ecological validity of laboratory studies, studying our topic outside the laboratory is a much better choice. Our original inspiration for the study was how parents discipline their child in public; therefore, the best place to gather data will be out in the real world.

Participant Observation

Participant observation, where the researcher actively interacts with those being studied while systematically noting their behavior, is one way to observe parents in a natural environment where they may need to discipline their child. Instead of remaining an outside, unengaged observer, the researcher seeks to gain a close familiarity with the group or persons under observation through intense involvement in their natural environment. The researcher essentially becomes a part of the action by observing it from the inside.

Laboratory studies are notoriously poor in ecological validity. If you were participating in this study, do you think you could eventually forget you were behaving within the context of a study and act naturally? *(Photo by John-Abbott, Courtesy Vassar College)*

To study parental discipline, we could become a regular at the local playground and jump into the action by pushing kids on the swings or helping them across the monkey bars while we observe the parent–child interactions. Using this approach makes us more likely to experience events the same way as the parents we want to study. However, the close familiarity gained with the group under observation could make objectivity extremely difficult, which is a limitation of participant observation. Rather than objectively seeing things as they occur, researchers may introduce their own subjective feelings or interpretations. In particular, researchers may succumb to observer biases in that they begin to see what they want or expect to see, leading to systematic overestimation or underestimation of events and erroneous conclusions. For example, as you get to know the other parents at the playground, you may become more inconsistent in your interpretations of what constitutes physical discipline. If your favorite parent, Karen, lightly slaps her child Mikey's hand as he reaches for another child's toy, you might not rate that correction as physical discipline. However, if Karen were a stranger, you might rate the same behavior as an example of physical discipline. While bias can undermine any observation, it is more difficult to overcome in participant observations because when we become too involved in the situation, we are at risk of losing the objectivity we need.

In addition to their own observational biases, participant observers can influence the participants in unintentional ways. Being a part of the action means the participants under observation will naturally interact with the researcher, which may unintentionally change the participants' behavior. In pushing one child on

---

What Do You Think?

If you could infiltrate any group to study how it works from the inside, what group would it be and why?

▶ What can we do to prevent observer bias?
SEE CHAPTER 4, p. 102

participant observation
an observational data collection technique in which the researcher interacts with those being studied while systematically recording their behavior.

Does this person blend into the environment? Successful participant observations require inconspicuous interactions with participants.
(Virginia Star/Moment/Getty Images)

a swing, we might inadvertently prevent another child from getting a turn, leading to a temper tantrum that might not have occurred if we were not there. Another possibility is that our subtle facial expressions while watching the parent might encourage or discourage how the parent responds to the child's tantrum. While participant observation could be a useful way to answer our research question because we already anticipate that the presence of others plays a role in parental discipline, we may not want to use this method for more practical reasons. Participant observation requires finding places where we can immerse ourselves in situations involving parent–child interactions without being too conspicuous. Blending in at a playground or toy store might be difficult to do without a child in tow (and, if you do not have a child, you might need to find one to help you out). If we hang out watching children play in a public area for too long, kids might start yelling "stranger danger," which could lead to an adult calling the cops! Perhaps most importantly, our research question focuses on how having others around, in general, influences discipline. Thus, if we actively participate in the situation, we may end up learning about how the presence of a researcher can influence parental behaviors rather than answering our research question.

Naturalistic Observation

Instead of being an active participant, we could remain an outsider, carefully observing parental discipline without interacting with parents or their children. **Naturalistic observation** involves systematically noting behavior outside the laboratory, within the environment in which it typically occurs, while taking great care to avoid interfering with the behavior under investigation. In this method, the researcher unobtrusively collects data on regularly occurring behaviors, does not become an active part of the research setting, and has virtually no direct influence on the people under observation. While remaining an outside observer does not eliminate all potential observer biases, it minimizes them to some degree. Because the researcher does not interact with participants while observing them, the researcher can remain more objective in his or her observations and interpretations of events. For example, you will be more likely to record that little hand slap Mikey receives from his mom as an act of physical punishment.

The downside to naturalistic observation is that the observer is not immersed in the situation and therefore cannot experience the event as the participants do. Considering our research question, this is not a major concern. Even if we involved ourselves in the situation as a participant observer, we would never really experience events the same way as the participants (e.g., we would never be in a situation in which we could know what it was like to be Mikey's parent). Given the benefits of naturalistic observation and the fact that the possible negatives are less applicable to our research question, it seems that we have found the best design to answer our research question!

When we engage in naturalistic observations, we can become overwhelmed because most settings are too complex for us to accurately and reliably record

naturalistic observation an observational data collection technique in which the researcher witnesses and systematically records behaviors as they occur in their original, unaltered setting.

everything involved. To avoid this problem, researchers tend to narrow the scope of their observations to key behaviors they want to observe and record. Before we visit a local playground or amusement park to observe parents' discipline behaviors, we need to operationally define both "parental discipline strategies" and "the presence of others." We also have to decide whether we should hide our observations from our participants or let them know that we are observing them as part of a study. **Table 6.1** reviews the three types of observations researchers can use.

TABLE 6.1

Types of Observational Research	
Laboratory	Observational research conducted in a controlled setting
Participant	Observational research in which the researcher actively interacts with those being studied while systematically recording their behaviors
Naturalistic	Observational research in which the researcher systematically records events as they occur in the real world without interfering in any way

Weighing Our Options: To Conceal or Not to Conceal

Whether an observation is laboratory, participant, or naturalistic, we must decide whether to tell participants that we will observe them as part of a research study. This decision depends on both ethical concerns and the nature of the phenomenon under investigation. In **nonconcealed observations,** the researcher informs participants that they will be observed, though the disclosure is often partial. That is, participants know that they are under observation as part of a study, but they do not know what behaviors the researcher is observing.

Even if participants are not aware of the research purpose, the knowledge that they are being observed may interfere with participants' natural tendencies. The worry with nonconcealed observation is potential participant **reactivity,** where individuals alter their behavior when they become aware that they are under observation. For example, do you become self-conscious about your appearance or behavior when someone points a camera in your direction? Reactivity can be a problem in any observational study, thus leading to potential biases. We can imagine that parents might become harsher or more lenient in how they discipline a child when under the watchful eye of others, especially researchers whom they may perceive as having some level of expertise on parenting. Over time, reactivity diminishes as those under observation tend to forget that someone is watching. This helps to explain why people on reality shows sometimes behave in embarrassing ways even when a camera is filming them. In fact, the slogan of MTV's *The Real World,* which premiered in 1992, was "when people stop being polite and start getting real." With enough time, we become accustomed to the observation and start to act naturally again. But in our case, we probably do not have enough time to let this happen. We want to know what parents would typically

nonconcealed observation an observational data collection technique in which participants know that their behaviors are being recorded.

reactivity when individuals alter their performance or behavior due to the awareness that they are under observation.

do if no one were watching, so the potential problems associated with reactivity are a concern.

We could, however, conduct a **concealed observation**, in which the observer never reveals to the participants that they are under observation. The observation happens without the knowledge or consent of the participants, which can dramatically reduce or potentially eliminate reactivity, as well as concerns about social desirability and demand characteristics. Given the advantages of concealed observation, it seems best that we use it for our study. However, can we really systematically observe people without their knowledge?

 Research Spotlight

Life as a Freshman

What are today's undergraduates like? To answer this question, a 52-year-old cultural anthropologist took a hiatus from being a college professor in order to live undercover as a student. To perform her participant observation, Cathy Small enrolled as a college freshman at a large state university, where she spent a year living in a residence hall, taking classes, and playing pickup volleyball games. She even got in trouble with a resident assistant for drinking beer. During her time as a student, Small secretly gathered data in the form of daily observations, interviews, and conversations with peers, professors, and university employees. Small reported her findings in the book *My Freshman Year: What a Professor Learned by Becoming a Student* under the pseudonym Rebekah Nathan to protect the identity of all involved. In completing a concealed participant observation, Small was able to observe behaviors that students were unlikely to report to researchers due to social desirability concerns. For example, Small found that when students talked about assignments, they tended to focus on the grades associated with the assignments rather than the substance of the assignments themselves. These types of observations gave Small a better understanding of the student perspective and shifted how she teaches her courses.

Focus on Ethics: Should We Really Do That?

While concealed observation would be best for our study because it can minimize reactivity problems, the ethics of this approach are questionable. Imagine how you would feel if the person sitting next to you in your math class all semester, a person with whom you shared details about your life, turned out to be a researcher recording your behavior. You might feel tricked, deceived, or even violated. We can certainly argue that concealment provides better data because people are unaware that they are being observed, meaning our data will more accurately reflect real life. Nonetheless, what may be best for the researcher is not always best for the participants. This is especially a concern when concealed participant observations include infiltrating a group and becoming familiar with research participants through intensive involvement. Doing this requires the

concealed observation an observational data collection technique in which participants do not know that their behaviors are being recorded.

extensive use of deception, or deliberately misleading our participants. This deception must be justifiable and handled with care.

Imagine instead that you find out that someone in your math class has been observing you all semester, but this person always sat at the back of the room and was someone you never talked to, much less noticed. In this situation, you would likely be much more comfortable with the observations made. What you don't know won't kill you, right? In concealed naturalistic observations, the researcher avoids the deceit of becoming involved in the situation under false pretenses. Participants remain unaware of the observation, which has the benefit of eliminating reactivity, demand characteristics, and social desirability problems, without adding deception.

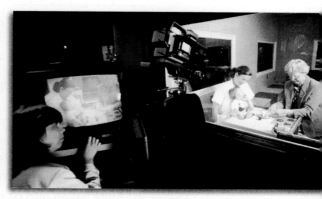

Would you be upset to discover that a researcher was secretly observing you? Researchers must be careful to justify the need for concealed observations with the IRB. *(Richard T. Nowitz/Science Source)*

▶ How can you ethically use deception in human research? SEE CHAPTER 3, p. 71

To be ethically sound, a researcher must demonstrate that concealment is necessary in order to conduct the research study (i.e., the researcher could not obtain the necessary information through nonconcealment). In our case, the nature of our research question suggests that the presence of others plays a role in parental discipline. Because we think this is a behavior that is sensitive to social settings, there is reason to believe that parents would not behave the same way if they knew of the observation. Therefore, we must conceal our naturalistic observation to help minimize potential reactivity issues.

Unlike in most other psychological research designs, when utilizing concealed observations, we do not first obtain informed consent from potential participants. Doing so would defeat the purpose of not telling participants that they are part of a study. Likewise, debriefing does not usually occur. However, this does not absolve us from our ethical obligations. We must be reasonably sure that participants would consent to participate in our observational study if they had the option. In our case, people routinely discipline their children in public settings where they know others could be watching. Thus, it is reasonable to assume that they would consent to having that behavior observed, since we would be just one more person in a public setting who could potentially watch the parents' behavior. There are limits, though. We could not hide under a bed in someone's home or install hidden cameras in an apartment to make our observations, as these are not public spaces. Nor could we eavesdrop in a public location where someone expects privacy, such as a bathroom stall or fitting room. To further support the ethical merit of a concealed observation in this case, parents have consented to have their discipline tactics observed in previous laboratory studies (e.g., Verschueren, Dossche, Marcoen, Mahieu, & Bakermans-Kranenburg, 2006). Even under such circumstances, we should only undertake the research if it involves no more than minimal risk to the research participants. As always, we cannot determine whether our own study is ethical, so we will need approval from an Institutional Review Board.

YOUR TURN 6.1

1. Johan wants to study how the placement of products in a store impacts consumer purchases. He decides to go to the grocery store and record the position of particular items as they already are and the frequency in which they are purchased. Which of the following methods of data collection is he using?
   a. Nonconcealed participant observation
   b. Concealed participant observation
   c. Laboratory observation
   d. Naturalistic observation

2. Anita has an interest in how temperature influences worker productivity in a car manufacturing facility. She establishes a baseline for productivity based on previous records. Every two days she changes the temperature of the factory by 5 degrees, starting with 65 degrees and continuing to 95 degrees. She records productivity on the days she changes the temperature by openly watching the workers and counting how many pieces they assemble each day. To her surprise, productivity goes up each day no matter what the temperature is. What is the most likely cause of these findings?
   a. Reactivity
   b. Laboratory observation
   c. Ecological validity
   d. Concealment

3. To study the aspects of being a fraternity member, Chong joins a pledge class without telling anyone the real reason he wants to be a part of the fraternity. This data collection method is which of the following?
   a. Nonconcealed participant observation
   b. Concealed participant observation
   c. Concealed laboratory observation
   d. Naturalistic observation

How did you do? Turn to the end of the chapter to check your answers.

Defining Key Terms: What Do You Mean By ___?

▶ Unsure about the difference between conceptual and operational definition? SEE CHAPTER 2, p. 38

Now that we have determined what, conceptually, we want to study and the best overall design, we need to figure out how to make it all happen. We want to know what forms of discipline that parents use in the presence of others, but this research topic is still very broad. The lack of any specific direction in our research question will likely lead to vague, nonspecific answers. To avoid this problem, we should make decisions about our observation's focus.

Operational Definition: Parental Discipline

To start, we need to operationally define what we mean by parental discipline. We want to keep our operational definition comprehensive to avoid missing anything in our observations, as no one has ever done a study exactly like ours. Still, if others have already defined some aspect of our question for us, we should use it. Thus, we will follow the lead of Gershoff et al. (2010) and define parental discipline as threatening, bribing, reasoning, and spanking. However, for each behavior, we need to more specifically determine what we mean and provide a clear definition.

- Threatening is defined as a verbal promise of punishment, such as a time-out, loss of a privilege (e.g., a toy), or a spanking, if the child performs the behavior again or does not stop the unacceptable behavior.

- Bribes are verbal promises to give the child something rewarding, such as a treat, if the child behaves appropriately.

- Reasoning involves talking to the child about good and bad behavior (e.g., defining acceptable and unacceptable behavior).

- Spanking is the act of striking the bottom of another person with an open hand.

There may be some debate about what constitutes spanking and what does not, such as an open-hand strike on the hand or face, which is why operational definitions are so important. As the researcher, you need to use the literature to help you clearly define how you will categorize each behavior in your study. There is one additional behavior tactic that might also be important for us to include in our definition of discipline: ignoring. If a parent strategically ignores the child's behavior in an attempt to potentially change that behavior, this is technically a form of discipline. Therefore, we will define ignoring as the conscious nonacknowledgment of a child's behavior in an effort to change it. The coding of this behavior will be tricky, as we must be able to distinguish between intentional ignoring and simply the failure to notice the child's undesirable behavior, but we can address that in a bit. We now have a much clearer idea of what we mean by discipline, but have not yet determined how to operationalize "when others are around."

Operational Definition: When Others Are Around

Who are the "others"? To answer this, we should carefully consider whether just anyone can influence parents, or if there are particular types of people who may have more influence. We have already decided that we are interested in strangers who are unfamiliar with our target parent–child dyad. Certainly, we could observe their behavior when a number of other children are present. However, other children are also just learning social norms, and they would be unlikely to judge an unfamiliar parent's behaviors. Their presence will not pressure the parent of a misbehaving child to correct the behavior. Rather, the most pressure is likely to come from adults who do not know the parent or the child well, as other adults are fully aware of social norm violations and the parental obligation to teach these norms. There is some support for the idea that adults can influence one another's discipline styles. For example, we know that the discipline practices of mothers influence how the corresponding fathers discipline their children (Capaldi, Pears, Kerr, & Owen, 2008). This provides initial

What Do You Think?
What other observable factors in the environment might influence the discipline choices a parent makes?

support for the idea that one adult can influence the parenting of another. Given this idea, our best operational definition of "when others are present" is when and how many unfamiliar adults are present when a child breaks a social norm.

Influences on Parental Discipline

Remember that parental discipline is any action a parent takes to change a child's behavior (Gershoff et al., 2010). Two major reasons to change a child's behavior are to keep them safe and to teach them social norms or rules for how to behave in specific situations (Myers, 2013). When parents use discipline in response to their child's taking another child's toy, staring at a stranger, or not waiting patiently for his or her turn, they are attempting to teach social norms. When our behavior is inconsistent with social norms, we often feel pressured to correct our behavior to better align with expectations (Asch, 1951; Miyajima & Naito, 2008). Parents may also perceive pressure when their child is breaking a social norm, and feel an obligation to make their child comply, particularly when in the presence of others. This added pressure may lead parents to discipline the child differently than they might without this perceived pressure from others.

Many things can influence how parents discipline, so we need to determine what, specifically, might influence disciplinary behaviors in the presence of others. For example, we could focus on demographic characteristics of the parents, such as ethnicity or socioeconomic status. We could also focus on situational factors, such as the setting in which the discipline is occurring (e.g., a store versus a playground) or the number of other adults and children present at the time. An easy way to narrow down the possibilities is to identify factors supported by past research that fit well with our research question. We could focus on the socioeconomic status of the parents, but this is not particularly novel. Prior research has already investigated the role of income on disciplinary practices and found that low-income parents tend to endorse the use of harsher discipline overall (Pinderhughes, Dodge, Zelli, Bates, & Pettit, 2000). To create new knowledge, we will want to focus on a factor that researchers have yet to explore. Besides, because we are using a naturalistic observation, we cannot ask parents to self-report their income, so we would have to determine their socioeconomic status based on observation of visual cues such as brands of clothing or shoes. This is not easy to do. Even if you train observers to identify designer labels, clothes may not accurately reflect income or status because research has shown that people living in poverty pay for designer labels for the symbolic status they portray (Van Kempen, 2004). Given these issues, socioeconomic status may not be well suited for a naturalistic study. More importantly, socioeconomic status is a factor for the parent, not for the situation.

Because our research question focuses on the presence of others, it implies there is something situational influencing behavior. If we further explore the literature, we will find that there is evidence that situational aspects do influence parental discipline practices. For example, we know family stress plays a role in the choice of discipline strategies (Pinderhughes et al., 2000). While stress is a temporary mental state, this finding does indicate that temporary factors can influence disciplinary behavior. Still, we need to focus on temporary factors directly related to having others around, so we should look at research on how the presence of others can influence our behavior. For example, we know that the mere physical presence of others can alter how we perform on a task (Strauss, 2002; Zajonc, 1965) and can influence our decision to intervene and help others (Darley & Latané, 1968; Song & Oh, 2018). If knowing that others are around can influence our behavior, that same pressure might lead parents to behave differently depending on the number of others present.

Now that we have operational definitions to help focus our observations on specific forms of discipline and factors of the situation related to others being present, the next step is to develop a system that specifies how to observationally identify and record these behaviors.

Developing a Coding System: What and How to Observe

We also need to define the type of discipline scenario we want to observe. To observe parental discipline strategies, we will need to observe children in a context where they can break a social norm or are in some other way able to misbehave. We already know that parents have different disciplinary responses to the type of transgression the child commits (Lopez, Schneider, & Dula, 2002), so it would be best for us to record only acts of discipline in response to the same violation. One norm violation we can always count on from a preschooler is a good old-fashioned tantrum. By tantrum, we mean an emotional outburst that typically includes crying, screaming, shouting, and/or physical behaviors such as hitting and stomping, as well as defiance (Goodenough, 1931; Potegal & Davidson, 2003). Tantrums are loud and potentially disturbing to those around them; they are certainly a norm violation that others will notice. Moreover, parents may be particularly eager to stop a tantrum in the presence of others, as it may provoke feelings of embarrassment. Therefore, we will focus our observations on children having a tantrum.

Next, we need to decide how we want to record our observations. For example, we could record the number of times parents use a particular disciplinary tactic, how long they use it, or the tactic's effectiveness. Regarding the presence of others, we could classify the overall number of other adults witnessing the child's tantrums and subsequent parental behavior, or we could simply categorize the situation as having either "high" or "low" numbers of others present. To address these types of issues, a researcher must develop a **coding system** to measure the variables of interest. This is a set of rules to help guide how the researcher classifies and records various observations. In our study, we want to create a classification system that categorizes specific types of disciplinary behaviors into broader units, as well as a protocol for deciding what behaviors count as instances of a given category.

We must first decide how we will determine the number of unfamiliar adults present during a child's tantrum. If we record this variable by counting the number of other adults in the immediate vicinity of the tantrum, defining "immediate vicinity" as anyone who can potentially see or hear the tantrum taking place, we could theoretically have values ranging from 0 to over 100. However, our goal is to provide a meaningful description of parental discipline when others

coding system a set of rules to help guide how the researcher classifies and records behaviors under observation.

are around. Trying to report parents' use of discipline while each specific number of people watched would be time-consuming and not result in very useful information. A better way to categorize the event would be as a "high" or "low" in the presence of others based on a standard we set ahead of time. For example, when a social norm violation occurs, we could look at the number of unfamiliar adults present. If four or fewer other adults are present while the tantrum is occurring, we could code that event as a "low" presence event. If five or more are present, we could classify it as a "high" presence event. However, without any previous research to guide us on the presence of others and how it relates to parenting, setting four as the cutoff would be arbitrary. For now, we will record the actual number of parents present and determine our cutoff for high and low levels later.

For discipline, we have to decide what aspect we want to code most. For example, we could record the duration of time between the onset of a child's tantrum and the parent's strategy for stopping this behavior. This would give us valuable information about how public pressure may influence the speed of the discipline response. This approach is an example of **duration recording,** which researchers use in several ways, such as the elapsed time during which a particular behavior occurs (e.g., how long a child cries), as well as the length of time elapsed between behaviors (e.g., passage of time between the tantrum onset and parental action). However, our research question focuses on *what* disciplinary behaviors parents use, not how long they occur or how quickly a parent responds. Thus, we could record each time a specific disciplinary tactic such as bribing occurs, a strategy known as **frequency-count recording.** Frequency-count recording is useful when target behaviors are short-lived and when the behaviors' duration is not of particular importance. For our research question, we just want to know what discipline strategies parents use, rather than how many times they use each in a single incident (e.g., it could become difficult to count the number of times a parent ignores a child). Therefore, we will record whether a parent uses or does not use a particular form of discipline as they deal with the tantrum. For example, let's say a 3 year-old throws a tantrum over wanting another juice box. At first, Mom offers her a bribe, saying that she will let her stay and play for a little longer if she stops crying. Then Mom ignores her before bribing her again, this time with the promise of a new toy. When the child continues to cry, she forcefully picks her up and gives her a swat on the bottom. The child cries a little longer before settling down. Based on our operational definitions, the observer would record the occurrence or absence of each disciplinary tactic that the parent used to resolve the tantrum. Our record for an observation of this parent's behaviors during a tantrum might look as follows:

Bribing: *Used*

Reasoning: *Not used*

Physical punishment: *Used*

Threats: *Not used*

Ignoring of behavior: *Used*

duration recording documenting the time elapsed during which a behavior occurs.

frequency-count recording documenting each time a target behavior occurs.

Because we will be making many observations, we will need a strategy for systematically recording them. This involves developing an **observation schedule,** which is a paper-and-pencil or electronic form where the observers note the particulars of the behaviors or phenomena they observe. If you cannot identify an existing form from past research, you can create one. You will refine the observation schedule, along with your coding definitions and categories, when you train your research observers.

Design in Action

We have made many important decisions about what to observe and how to record it, but we still have a few more decisions to make before we can actually begin our data collection. Specifically, we need to identify our sample, train people to conduct systematic observations, and devise a procedure for collecting the data.

Weighing Our Options: Finding a Sample

Before we can conduct our observation, we need to determine exactly whom we want to observe and where we can find this target sample. In a naturalistic observation like ours, our participants do not come to us; instead, we must find our participants. We know our naturalistic observations need to occur in a place where parents and children interact among other unfamiliar adults. We also know that for ethical reasons, our observations should take place in a public venue where people are willing to have their behavior observed. We could head to the playground at a local park. In this setting, children will most likely be accompanied by their parents. While this location could work, there are a couple of practicalities to keep in mind that may impact our ability to draw useful conclusions based on our observations. For one thing, there are many days and, depending on region, even seasons, when outdoor playgrounds will be empty due to bad weather. Similarly, overly hot days may significantly alter parent and child behavior because people tend to behave more aggressively (Anderson, Anderson, & Denser, 1996) and react more negatively (Cohen & Krueger, 2016) in hot weather.

Another important consideration is that people generally only go to parks near their own neighborhood. Although this might not seem like a major limitation, remember that we want a sample that is as representative as possible of the population or the larger group to which we want our findings to apply. Because parks represent local neighborhoods, and neighborhoods represent socioeconomic standing and often race or culture, using a neighborhood park may not provide us with the diverse sample we hope to attain, potentially hurting the external validity of our study.

Instead, we might look for an indoor shopping mall that features stores for shoppers at a variety of economic levels. This option prevents weather problems while providing multiple places to do observations on many different groups of people within a confined space. We could use practically any location in the mall (e.g., food court, toy store, or thoroughfare), as long as

▶ Why is finding a representative sample so important to researchers? SEE CHAPTER 4, p. 109

observation schedule a paper-and-pencil or electronic form in which the observers note the particulars of the behavior or phenomenon that they observe.

we remember that being ethical in our research means that we cannot invade anyone's privacy while collecting data. Even if a parent takes a child into a public restroom, into a dressing room, or out to their car for punishment, that parent has a reasonable expectation of privacy. As ethics are always a part of the decision-making process, we need to stick to locations that are clearly public.

Before we can finalize our decision about mall location, we should also consider who we want to observe the most. We know we want to observe parent–child interactions, so we want to exclude anyone who is with a child but does not seem to be a parent. A stroller and a diaper bag may seem like good indicators of parent status, but they are not perfect predictors. Plus, in a naturalistic observation, we cannot ask adults what role they play in a child's life, so we will train our observers to recognize a parent, perhaps based on how the adult interacts with the child. That leaves us with the decision of which parents we should observe—moms, dads, or both. We can certainly observe both, but there may be systematic differences in how fathers versus mothers discipline their children, and this would complicate our study. Past research is helpful here because most discipline research focuses on mothers (Berlin et al., 2009; Lansford, Wager, Bates, Pettit, & Dodge, 2012; Verschueren et al., 2006), as well as children ages 2–5 (Berlin et al., 2009; Capaldi et al., 2008; Pinderhughes et al., 2000).

To build on this research, we should keep our observations on interactions between a mother and her preschool age child. Again, we will have to train our observers to recognize this age group for inclusion in our study. Keeping all these things in mind, the perfect location in the mall to do our observation might be the play area. These are areas where parents often bring their young children, and they provide a ripe atmosphere for tantrums. After all, what preschooler wants to leave when mom says it is time to go? There are also likely to be other unfamiliar adults around to observe the tantrum. To be sure the mall play area is suitable for our study, we should spend some time at this location to determine whether all the elements we need to make our observation (i.e., parents, young children, tantrums, and other adults) are present. We should also be sure to seek permission from the mall to conduct our observational study there. After all, we do not want mall security to become concerned about observers loitering around the mall playground.

Observer Training

Now that we have developed a coding system and identified a suitable location to conduct our study, we are ready to start making observations. We developed the coding scheme, so we are obviously the best people to make the observations for our study, right? Actually, the opposite is true. Our planning of the entire study may compromise our ability to be objective, making observational biases more likely. Our investment in the research question might lead us to see what we want or expect to see, preventing us from seeing things as they really are.

This means we need help, lots of help. We need to train others to identify and code the targeted behaviors using our system, which, unfortunately, is not a simple process. Observers are human. They have memories and opinions that can make maintaining objectivity difficult. For example, you might personally find spanking to be a barbaric form of discipline, but, as an observer, you cannot allow this opinion to influence your ratings such that you overreport the frequency of the spanking observed in the field. As you can see, objectivity is not easy. We must work hard to keep observational biases from happening, so that our data is as accurate and objective as humanly possible. Our coding system will help maintain accuracy by providing objective ways to identify the spanking (striking with an open hand on the child's bottom), so that there is no room for a biased interpretation. Training minimizes the potential biases by teaching observers how to identify appropriate situations to observe and how to record what they observe, bias-free, using the coding system.

Are these two people acting aggressively? How might your personal beliefs about aggression alter your interpretation of this event? *(Scott Olson/Getty Images)*

Another factor that might bias an observation is awareness of the overall goal of the research study. If our observers are aware of the study's purpose, then they are less likely to be objective in watching and coding an event. Luckily, we can eliminate this problem by conducting **blind observations**, in which we train observers to look for particular behaviors, but keep them uninformed about the overall purpose or hypothesis of the investigation. This "blindness" helps to keep the observers objective because if they do not know what the study is about, they cannot possibly bias their ratings in a way that "helps" the researcher.

For these reasons, training good observers takes a lot of time and effort, but it is necessary to ensure that we get accurate data. The goal of this training is to teach our observers to conduct consistent, accurate, and objective observations. After all, observers are essentially the measurement tool when conducting observational research. So, like any measurement tool, we need them to provide both reliable and valid observations. For the sake of reliability, we need our observers to be consistent within their own codings, known as **intra-observer reliability.** When our observers see a disciplinary action taken by a parent, we need to know that each observer rates the behavior the same way today as they will tomorrow, and that they categorize the same action by a different parent the same way. Their codings must be consistent over time and from situation to situation. This is where an established coding system and training come into play. For example, if a parent grabs the child by the shoulders, is that physical discipline? We need to have a clear definition of physical discipline and how to categorize it so our observers can know how to consistently code that behavior. For the sake of validity, we must be confident that our observers are accurately coding what we intended them to code. Therefore, we must train observers to correctly identify acts of discipline objectively.

▶ Why are reliability and validity so important to research projects?
SEE CHAPTER 4, p. 105

blind observation an observational data collection technique in which observers are trained to look for particular behaviors, but are uninformed about study expectations or the overall purpose of the research investigation.

intra-observer reliability the extent to which an observer consistently codes a phenomenon.

Good training is time-consuming because observers learn best through practice. After we give them some basic training on our target behaviors and coding system, we might take our observers out into the field to practice, or we might have them rehearse using video recordings that mimic the types of settings our study requires. Essentially, the observers are engaging in **pilot testing**, a trial run used to test and refine the design, methods, and instruments of a study prior to carrying out the actual research. Observers can pilot test the coding system to make sure it works for the study, making any necessary adjustments as they arise, as well as discovering any uncertainties they may have about how to do the coding.

Another way to improve the quality of our observations and to control for biased individual opinions is to have multiple observers. These observers practice as a team and collect data as a team, making independent observations simultaneously. If we have two people coding the same event, we can systematically compare their recorded observations against each other to determine their inter-observer reliability. **Inter-observer reliability**, also known as inter-rater reliability, indicates how much consensus there is between two observers' ratings of the same event. In preparation for our study, we might have observers-in-training watch the same video of a 15-minute interaction between a parent and child and then examine whether they coded the same number and types of disciplinary actions during the observation. Ideally, we want the different observers to provide similar observations. Inter-observer reliability can help you evaluate the effectiveness of your training, as knowing which ratings do not match up can help you identify inconsistency between the observers, potential biases, or problems with the coding system before data collection actually begins. Strong inter-observer reliability is an expectation of any observational research published. Having consensus among your observers during the data collection process indicates that biases were unlikely in your study. This is necessary for anyone to trust your results.

 Thinking Like a Scientist in Real Life

Good/Bad Call, Ref!

You and your best friend attend a football game between your schools, whose teams are archrivals. Your team is down by three points with 30 seconds left on the clock. Your quarterback throws a pass to the receiver, and, just before he can catch it, a player from the opposing team attempts to get in front of him, running into the receiver, who ends up dropping the ball. Is this pass interference? You may think so, but your best friend may believe otherwise. We all have our own opinions that can make remaining objective difficult in certain circumstances. For example, our fan loyalty can influence how we interpret a play. You may undoubtedly believe the referee should call the pass interference, while your friend may watch the exact same play and firmly believe that the play was fair. As sports announcers are fond of saying, "We sometimes see with our hearts and not our heads." The same lack of objectivity that biases the observation of everyday events can also bias observational research. But with training and practice, we can become aware of biases so that we can learn to overcome them.

pilot testing a trial run used to refine the design, methods, and instruments for a study prior to carrying out the actual research.

inter-observer reliability the level of agreement between two observers' coding of the same phenomenon; also known as inter-rater reliability.

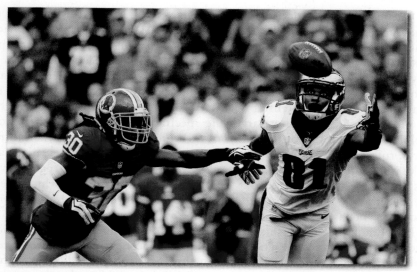

Should a penalty be called on this play? Your interpretation may depend on your team loyalty, or personal biases. *(Rich Schultz/Getty Images)*

Collecting Data

Our observers have only one set of eyes each and many potential observations to make. We still need a procedural plan for how much time and attention each parent in our observational setting will receive. One way we could execute our observations is to take a specific observation period (e.g., an hour) and break it down into equal, smaller time periods or intervals (e.g., 5 minutes). Observers would then indicate if the target behavior—in our case, a particular form of discipline—occurred or did not occur during each interval. This procedural method is **interval recording**. However, this method does not really work with the type of data we hope to record. We are not looking to see whether or not discipline occurred within a particular time frame. Instead, we are interested in waiting for a specific circumstance (i.e., a tantrum) and recording all the disciplinary ways a parent responds.

Another option is **continuous recording**. This method involves recording all of a target individual's behaviors during a specified observation period (e.g., 10 minutes). In its strictest sense, this would involve recording all the behaviors that one child–parent dyad engages in during that particular period of observation. That is closer to what we need, but not exactly what we want to do, either. In our case, a modified version of continuous recording is best. Once a tantrum starts, that child and mother will be the target, and we will continuously observe the various actions the parent takes in disciplining the child. Once that interaction resolves, our observers will wait for the next tantrum to start the next continuous observation.

interval recording breaking down an observational period into equal, smaller time periods and then documenting whether a target behavior occurred during each time period.

continuous recording documenting all of the behaviors of a target individual during a specified observation period.

We must also decide if we want to make our observations while the behaviors actually occur, or through video recordings of the behaviors. Most likely there are video cameras throughout the mall for security purposes. We could ask for permission to view the camera recordings from the play area. If we gained access to this footage, we could review the tapes as often as we liked, rewatching and recoding the data. That would certainly help minimize potential reactivity concerns, but the downside is that the video cameras may not target the specific behaviors we want to code. A child may walk out of the range of the video camera just as the tantrum starts, ruining our ability to code that event. The camera angles might also make it hard for us to code how many other adults are in the area. To avoid this problem, we should do our observations as they occur, which means we need to rely on well-trained observers who can quickly and efficiently record key behaviors.

If we think that witnessing a tantrum will be rare during our observations, we could artificially induce a tantrum. Perhaps someone from our research team could pass out lollipops under the premise that they are a promotional item from one of the stores. Surely, some parents will tell their children they cannot have the candy, which might start a tantrum. Or we could send in a clown to make balloons and have him suddenly run out of time, leaving many kids wanting one. That might start a few tantrums! Artificially introducing a variable that we are interested in and then unobtrusively observing what happens is a **contrived observation.**

Since our goal has always been to describe discipline in the presence of others in a naturalistic way, we will hold off on contriving tantrums during our observation. Luckily, we did some scouting of the location ahead of time. Based on the preliminary observations we did at the mall, we know that moms and young children tend to be at the play area on weekdays between 10 a.m. and 3 p.m. We also know that two or three different tantrums tend to occur during this time frame, with more tantrums happening later in the day, presumably closer to nap time. On average, parent–child dyads stay in the play area for 22 minutes. Preliminary observations conducted on the weekends indicate that whole families are often present (i.e., mom and dad) and that the play area is too crowded for quality observations, so we will avoid collecting data then. Based on this information, we decide to send our observers to the mall Tuesday through Thursday from 11 a.m. to 3 p.m. for 3 weeks.

To address our research question, we will carry out a study where we sample children, aged 2 to 5, and their mothers at the public play area inside a mall. We will conduct a concealed naturalistic observation in real time with multiple trained observers who will code both the presence of adults unfamiliar to the target dyad and the parental discipline used when a child has a tantrum. To avoid tipping potential participants off to our concealed observation, we will not debrief our participants. Using this observational method, we can collect data on actual behavior with strong ecological validity and good external validity.

contrived observation an observational data collection technique in which the researcher artificially introduces a variable of interest and unobtrusively records what happens.

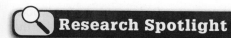
Research Spotlight

Contrived Observations

How much do we believe in the idea of honor, or that honor may influence how we react to an insult? To study this idea, researchers did a contrived observation on a local train between Amsterdam and Rotterdam in the Netherlands (IJzerman, van Dijk, & Gallucci, 2007). To make sure an insult took place, a confederate stood up, bumped into a male passenger, and said, "Hey, watch it!" (well, actually, it was more like, "*Hey, kijk eens uit joh!*") to half the participants in the study. The confederate bumped the other half of the participants without an insult. Immediately after the bumping incident, observers rated the participants' emotional reactions, including anger, irritation, joy, happiness, nervousness, fear, and resignation. Afterward, participants completed a questionnaire that assessed their belief in honor, which included questions about family honor, respect, reputation, and humiliation in public. Insulted participants with a stronger belief in honor were angrier, less joyful, less fearful, and less resigned than insulted participants with weak beliefs in honor. This study shows how a contrived observation may be necessary to study participants' natural reactions in real-world settings. Otherwise, these participants would not only have had trouble knowing what they would have actually done in this situation, but they may have not wanted to admit that they would react negatively.

Description Versus Prediction

In our research study, we are interested in what forms of discipline parents use in the presence of other parents. When we developed our coding, we determined how to quantify our behavioral observations, but decided to use them as a way to describe events. Because we are the first that we know of to study the impact of the immediate situation on parental discipline, our study is exploratory in nature. Our objective is to make systematic observations that describe the event, with the hope that our observations will help us make more specific predictions in the future. For now, we will just record how many other adults are present at the tantrum, as well as the forms of discipline used. Therefore, our research study is descriptive in nature and not predictive. We will make objective interpretations of events with no working hypothesis. We are not predicting how these observations might relate to one another; we are purely documenting their occurrence.

> **What Do You Think?**
> Based on the observations we will record in our study, what specific predictions would you make about the presence of others and discipline?

Focus on Open Science: Preregistering Your Hypotheses, Materials, and Data Analysis Plan

Finally, before collecting our data, we should be sure to preregister our study details on an open science website (e.g., http://osf.io). There we will share how we operationally defined our variables, the descriptive nature of our study, our intended participants, our observational method, and our coding system for recording observations, including copies of any measures or materials we used. Once we determine the analyses we need to conduct to answer our research question, we should also preregister our data analysis plan. This will make data analysis much more straightforward because the plan will outline the exact tests we need to run and will help

▶ Why is open science important to the research process? SEE CHAPTER 2, p. 25

us avoid the temptation of conducting analyses until we find something that works. For this study, we need to describe and summarize our data, as well as determine the inter-observer agreement between our two observers. Once we collect all of the data, we can make the data set available to other researchers via an open science website.

YOUR TURN 6.2

1. Astrid and Josette are collecting observational data on the impact of window displays on sales. They separately record the length of time a person looks at a display in the store window, as well as whether or not that person purchases the item. To ensure their observations are consistent, they should do which of the following?
    a. Employ the use of only blind observations.
    b. Use continuous rather than interval recording.
    c. Examine their study's inter-observer reliability.
    d. Include a contrived observation in the study.

2. Lachlan is a market researcher for a major cosmetic company. He wants to know which beauty products are naturally most appealing to the adult females he has recruited for his study. Different types of beauty products are located on various tables around a room and participants can examine and use any product they see at their leisure over a 30-minute period. Every 5 minutes, Lachlan records which product the participant is examining or using. What type of recording is he using?
    a. Continuous recording
    b. Interval recording
    c. Duration recording
    d. Frequency-count recording

3. A professor trains an undergraduate researcher to simply identify and code "rude behavior" unobtrusively and sends her to a retail store on December 24th. What type of observation is the undergraduate conducting?
    a. A blind observation
    b. A participant observation
    c. A laboratory observation
    d. A contrived observation

How did you do? Turn to the end of the chapter to check your answers.

Statistics: In Search of Answers

We want to know what forms of discipline parents use when others are around. Now that we have collected data, we need to figure out how our data can answer our research question. Currently, we have a number of behaviors observed for each parent. Our goal is to summarize what we observed across all parents so we can describe what forms of discipline parents used in the presence of other parents. Later, we will use those summaries to explain what we observed at the mall.

Before we can examine our research question, we need to enter our data into a statistics program, as shown in **Figure 6.1**. In that data set, each row will

Observation_number	Obsv1_people	Obsv2_people	Obsv2_ignore	Obsv1_ignore	Obsv1_threat	Obsv2_threat	Obsv1_bribe	Obsv2_bribe	Obsv1_spank	Obsv2_spank	Obsv1_reason	Obsv2_reason
1	2	2	used	used	used	used	not used	not used	used	used	used	used
2	4	4	not used	not used	not used	not used	not used	not used	used	used	used	used
3	6	6	not used	not used	used	used	used	used	not used	not used	not used	used
4	0	0	used	used	not used	not used	used	used	used	used	not used	not used
5	1	1	used	used	not used	not used	not used	not used	used	not used	not used	not used
6	3	4	not used	not used	not used	not used	not used	not used	not used	not used	not used	not used
7	4	5	not used	not used	used	used	used	used	not used	not used	not used	not used
8	5	5	used	used	used	used	used	used	not used	not used	used	used
9	2	2	used	used	used	used	not used	not used	used	used	used	used
10	6	6	used	used	not used	not used	used	used	not used	not used	used	used

FIGURE 6.1 Example of SPSS Data Spreadsheet. *(SPSS)*

contain all of the information from one observation. Along that row we should include columns for the observation number (Variable name = Observation_ Number), as well the details of that particular observation. Remember that we had two observers recording each tantrum, so we must have a place for each of their observations in our data set, and we need to indicate which observer provided that piece of data. To make it clear in our data set which observer recorded that particular piece of data, we will add prefixes to each variable (Obsv1_ and Obsv2_). Each observer recorded the number of unfamiliar adults present (people), and whether, as well as the number of times, each of the five discipline behaviors (ignore, threat, bribe, spank, and reason) was used for each tantrum. Each of these six variables will have two columns, one for each observer, for a total of 12 columns of data in addition to the observation number.

Selecting the Proper Tool

In observational research, just as in any other type of research, the tools we use to analyze our data depend on the design and the answers we hope to obtain. Remember that our research question is descriptive so that we can determine "what" is happening, not "why" it is happening. We want to figure out if there are patterns in how parents discipline their children. Because our goal is to describe behavior, we will use **descriptive statistics**, which describe or summarize quantitative data in meaningful ways, allowing for simpler interpretation of the data. In order for us to make meaningful statements about parental discipline in the presence of other parents, we need to organize our variables (i.e., observations of the number of other adults around and types of discipline used) and express them as quantities. Descriptive statistics will help us do this. If we present our raw data (e.g., what form of discipline each individual parent used) as a simple list of all our observational recordings, it will be hard to comprehend what all of the data shows. Descriptive statistics do not, however, allow us to draw conclusions beyond the data we have analyzed or reach conclusions regarding any hypotheses we might have made. (If that was our goal, we would use inferential statistics to test specific predictions we might have made for our study.)

We need to determine across all of the observations how often parents used each of five specific disciplinary tactics in response to the child's tantrum. When

▶ What if our goal is to draw conclusions beyond our data using inferential statistics?
SEE APPENDIX A, p. 486

descriptive statistics statistics that describe or summarize quantitative data in meaningful ways.

researchers measure a variable using distinct groupings, like we did with each discipline tactic, they are using a **categorical variable.** We want to determine how many times our participants used each discipline tactic, so we can use a **frequency distribution,** which is a summary of how often the individual values or ranges of values for a variable occur. Because discipline tactic is categorical in our study, we will display the number of times each tactic occurred. The simplest distribution would list every value of a variable (e.g., ignoring, spanking, reasoning, threats, and bribes) and the frequency of its occurrence. **Table 6.2** provides an example of the frequency distribution we might create for our study.

► Why is classifying the types of variables we use in our research so important to data analysis? SEE APPENDIX A, p. 478

TABLE 6.2

Example of a Frequency Distribution
Discipline Types
These are the types of discipline recorded by observers over 10 hours of observation:
ignoring, reasoning, ignoring, threats, bribes, threats, bribes, bribes, ignoring, ignoring
To make the frequency distribution, count how many times each discipline type occurred and record it:

Discipline Types	Frequency
Bribes	3
Ignoring	4
Reasoning	1
Spanking	0
Threats	2

categorical variable a way to classify data into distinct groupings.

frequency distribution a summary of how often the individual values or ranges of values for a variable occur.

continuous variable a variable with an infinite number of different values between two given points.

central tendency a value that summarizes all of the other obtained measurements or values for a particular variable.

mode (*Mo*) the most frequently occurring value in a set of scores; a measure of central tendency.

mean (*M*) the mathematically calculated average of a set of scores; a measure of central tendency.

We have yet another piece of information to summarize: the presence of others. Our observers measured this variable by noting the number of other adults present when each tantrum occurred. We assessed the number of adults present using a **continuous variable,** which is a variable that can have an infinite number of different values between two given endpoints. To summarize the presence of others, we want to know, across the entire sample, generally how many other adults were typically around during the tantrum and subsequent discipline. To do this, we calculate the **central tendency** of a distribution, which is a value that summarizes all of the obtained measurements or values for a particular variable. There are several ways you can indicate the central tendency of data. The way that is most often used with categorical data is the **mode** (symbolized as *Mo*), or the most frequently occurring value in a set of observations. The mode will tell us what number of others present occurred most frequently (e.g., among our 20 observations, the most common number of others around was 3). We could also summarize number of others present by determining an average. We do this by calculating the arithmetic **mean** (symbolized as *M*), which determines central tendency by summing a collection of numbers and dividing by the size of the collection (e.g., add up all 20 observations, and then divide by 20).

As we were collecting data, we made the decision to record the exact number of adults present at each tantrum so that we could then categorize the presence of others into "high" and "low" groups. We did not want the cutoff point to be arbitrary (e.g., ≤ 5 = low; ≥ 6 = high), so to get a meaningful cutoff point, we can use the **median** (symbolized as *Mdn*), or the score found at the exact middle of the set of values. One way to compute the median is to list all 20 scores in numerical order, and then locate the score in the center of the sample. We will use the exact midpoint as the cutoff point for our categories, labeling everything below the midpoint as "low" and everything above it as "high." **Table 6.3** reviews these three measures of central tendency.

TABLE 6.3

Measures of Central Tendency			
Mean	M	The mathematically calculated average of a set of scores	The mean will tell us the average size of group around during our observation (e.g., the average number of people present over 20 observations was 4.67 people).
Median	Mdn	The value found at the exact middle of a set of scores	The median will tell us the exact midpoint of group size over our 20 observations. From this number, we know that in half of the observations there were fewer people present and in half of the observations there were more people present.
Mode	Mo	The most frequently occurring value in a set of scores	The mode will tell us the most commonly occurring number of others present (e.g., among our 20 observations, the most common number of others around was 3 people).

We also need to determine whether our two observers had similar observations of the discipline witnessed by calculating inter-observer reliability, which indicates the agreement between the observers' coding of the same behavior. There are a number of ways to calculate inter-observer reliabilities based on the types of variables in your study. The resulting calculations range from 0 to 1, where 0 means that there is absolutely no agreement and 1 means perfect agreement. Researchers generally want the reliability of their observations to be 0.7 or higher. In the data set, we recorded whether each of our two observers indicated the discipline type was "used" or "not used," resulting in categorical data. When you have categorical data from two raters, and want to determine inter-observer reliability, Cohen's kappa is the appropriate statistic. **Cohen's kappa coefficient** is a statistical measure of inter-observer agreement between two observers for categorical items. It is a better measure of agreement than simply determining the percentage of overlap between two observers because it takes into account the agreement occurring by chance. If our observers do not agree, either our coding is defective or the observers need to be retrained. Without reliably collected data, our results will be meaningless; therefore, we need high levels of observer agreement to proceed with our data analysis.

median (*Mdn*) the value found at the exact middle of the set of scores; a measure of central tendency.

Cohen's kappa coefficient a statistical measure of inter-observer agreement between two observers for categorical items.

After we determine there is good consensus between observers, we must still decide what to do with both sets of data. If possible, we will combine and average the multiple observations of the same situation. That is not easily done with categorical data such as discipline tactics, so instead we must decide at random which observer's rating to use by flipping a coin. You will find a formal summary of our findings below in the format of an APA-style results section and several figures.

Writing the Results in APA Style: Descriptive Statistics

Results

Inter-observer Reliability

We conducted inter-observer reliabilities on the number of times each of the five discipline tactics occurred during the tantrums witnessed. Each test revealed substantial to almost perfect agreement. Cohen's kappa (K) for each of the five disciplines ranged from 0.79 to 0.97. Due to the high level of consensus between our observers, we randomly selected the data from observer 1 for our subsequent analyses.

Presence of Others

The number of other unfamiliar adults present during a tantrum ranged from 0 to 6. Overall the modal number of people present was 4, the mean number of people present was 3.25, and the median was 3.50.

Overall Discipline Use

In total, our observers collected data on 20 tantrum incidents involving mothers and their young children. Overall, in response to a tantrum, parents engaged in each discipline tactic with the following frequency: ignoring, 55%; threatening, 45%; bribing, 45%; spanking, 40%; and reasoning, 55%.

Discipline Use in the Presence of Others

The low presence of others group included 10 observations. When there were few other adults around, the most commonly used tactic was ignoring, which participants used in 80% of these observations, followed by spanking (70%), reasoning (30%), threatening (20%), and bribing (20%). The high presence of others group also included 10 observations. When the number of other adults around was high, parents engaged in reasoning the most (80%) followed by threatening (70%) and bribing (70%). Participants only used ignoring 30% of the time, while spanking was only used 10% of the time.

bar chart a figure with rectangular bars that represent the values of a variable.

Don't Just Tell Me, Show Me: Using Graphs

Frequency distributions are great ways to visually display the overall findings of your research. **Figure 6.2** shows the frequency distribution with all five categories of discipline defined. This figure uses percentages to represent how often parents used each discipline tactic overall. Because the discipline tactics we coded are categorical, the best way for us to graphically depict our results is with a **bar chart,** which is a figure with rectangular bars that represent the values. The bar lengths are proportional to the values that they represent, which is to say longer bars

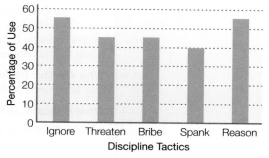

FIGURE 6.2 Overall Use of Discipline.

represent more of the value (e.g., higher frequency or greater percentage), and shorter bars indicate less. In this figure, each bar represents one of the five disciplinary tactics coded. The length of the bar represents the percentage of our parent sample who used that tactic.

Figure 6.3 represents parents' use of each disciplinary tactic when the presence of others was low, or when the number of other adults was 3 or fewer. On the other hand, **Figure 6.4** represents parents' use of each disciplinary tactic when the presence of others was high, meaning 4 or more. Looking at these two figures gives us a visual representation of how parents' use of discipline tactics differs based on the presence of other adults.

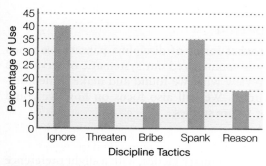

FIGURE 6.3 Use of Discipline When Presence of Others Was Low.

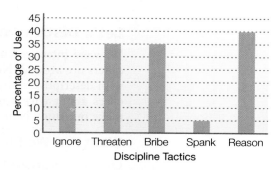

FIGURE 6.4 Use of Discipline When Presence of Others Was High.

Our Research Plan at a Glance

What Is Our Research Question? What forms of discipline do parents use when others are around?

What Is Our Design? We are using a naturalistic concealed observation.

Why Are We Using This Design? This design allows us to study a phenomenon in the real world in a context that provides good ecological validity and minimizes reactivity.

What Are Our Variables? Because of the type of design we are using, there are no true independent or dependent variables. However, we are recording the frequency of parental discipline (i.e., ignoring, bribing, reasoning, spanking, and threatening) and the presence of other adults to categorize later as high and low.

What Are Our Hypotheses? With this design, we do not have pre-established hypotheses that we are testing. We are making objective interpretations of events with no working hypothesis. We are not predicting how these observations might relate to one another; we are purely documenting their occurrence.

Who Are Our Participants? Mothers and their preschool-aged children at the play area inside a shopping mall.

What Ethical Considerations Do We Need to Keep in Mind?
- In making a concealed observation, we must collect data in a public location where people expect that others may observe them.

What Is Our Data Analysis Plan?
1. **Evaluate inter-observer reliability.** Using Cohen's kappa coefficient, we evaluate the inter-observer reliability of the raters' coding for each of the discipline tactics. Based on this evaluation, we determine the ratings to be used for subsequent analyses.
2. **Describe our data.** We summarize and compare the use of the different discipline tactics using a frequency distribution, and we summarize the presence of others by using measures of central tendency.

Want to practice the analyses for this research yourself? Ask your instructor about the data set that accompanies this study.

Let's Discuss What Happened

We were interested in determining what forms of discipline parents use when others are around. Now that we have summarized our systematic observations with descriptive statistics, we will review what we found and make some inferences about why it may have occurred. We will also focus on how we could make our study better and ideas for future studies.

What Did We Find?

Overall, parents used each of the five disciplinary tactics, with a slight preference for ignoring and reasoning over the other tactics. Although we cannot make any statements about cause and effect, there seems to be a distinct pattern in parents' use of discipline based on the number of unfamiliar adults around. When there were few other adults around, participants more frequently used the tactics of ignoring and spanking. However, when there were many other adults around, parents used bribes, reasoning, and threats more frequently.

Why These Findings?

When a child has a tantrum in public, the parent must consider the best way to discipline the child and the reaction of others present. The social pressure that the presence of others creates may influence the way parents discipline their children. Parents may discipline more by ignoring and spanking when there are fewer people around due to less social pressure. Tantrums are often disruptive to those around the child. While ignoring a child during a tantrum may be one strategy to use (Luangrath & Hiscock, 2011), it is not always a convenient one because others might perceive ignoring the tantrum as the parent being selfish or neglecting the situation. Therefore, a parent may reserve ignoring for times when fewer people are around to experience the disruption or to judge the parent's perceived lack of response.

Similarly, parents may use spanking more when fewer people are present because there is less social pressure and less potential for others to pass judgment on the parent. Spanking remains common in the United States, with 80% of parents still using it (Gershoff, 2008). However, despite its prevalence in the United States, 24 countries have banned the use of physical punishment, such as spanking, on moral grounds, and research clearly demonstrates that physical punishment leads to a number of negative outcomes. The issue of spanking is a polarizing one for many parents. Although a parent may personally believe in spanking's effectiveness, he or she may also be aware that this discipline tactic could be offensive to others and reserve this tactic for use when relatively few people are around to witness it. Because ignoring a tantrum is disruptive to others and spanking is controversial, parents may rely on alternative discipline tactics when situations are highly public.

Using reasoning, bribes, and threats of punishment are all more socially desirable and publically sanctioned discipline tactics to get the child back in line with social norms. These strategies communicate to others that the parent is actively working to end the tantrum, but in a less controversial manner, hence their more frequent use when a tantrum occurs in the presence of other people.

What Could Be Improved?

Our study was a great first step in exploring this research question. Still, there are a few changes to the methodology that could strengthen the study. For example, we based our coding of discipline on just five discipline tactics, four of which we adapted from past literature. However, in reality, researchers have expanded lists to include up to 11 discipline tactics (Gershoff et al., 2010). Including all 11 tactics may give us a fuller understanding of our research topic. We also limited the coding of physical punishment to just spanking, which means that we did not include other physical actions meant to correct behavior (e.g., jerking a child by the elbow, pushing, etc.) in our coding. Finally, our coding did not allow us to record the frequency at which each discipline tactic occurred. That is, we recorded if it occurred, but not if a parent used that particular strategy more than once to resolve the tantrum. A larger and more comprehensive coding of discipline tactics would give us a clearer and more realistic picture of parenting.

What's Next?

Our naturalistic observation study was a great first step in exploring parental discipline. We now have some initial evidence to help us develop future studies on this topic. For example, we could do a contrived observation study where we experimentally manipulate the number of people present to help establish cause and effect. We could also build on our current study by examining the effectiveness of various discipline strategies. Instead of recording the use of each strategy, we could record which strategy is the most effective at resolving the tantrum (i.e., which tactic ends the tantrum the most quickly).

What Do You Think?
Based on what we now know about discipline in the presence of others, what study would you conduct to further explore this topic?

YOUR TURN 6.3

1. Grace wants to determine which dining hall food stations (i.e., pizza, pasta, salad bar, deli) the student body prefers at lunch time. She collects data as a participant observer by walking around with a tray of food. Grace is most interested in determining which food station is most commonly used. What statistic should she use?
   a. The mode
   b. The median
   c. The mean
   d. The range

2. Sam wants to describe the frequency at which a typical student checks his or her cell phone throughout class. He recorded the number of times each student in his Introduction to Psychology class checked phones during one class meeting. If Sam wants to know how often the average student checks his or her phone, which form of central tendency should Sam use?
   a. The mean
   b. The median
   c. The mode
   d. The range

3. What was the biggest weakness of our methodological design and procedure?
   a. We had a biased sample.
   b. We had poor inter-observer reliability.
   c. We conducted the study in a natural environment.
   d. Our coding of discipline was not comprehensive.

How did you do? Turn to the end of the chapter to check your answers.

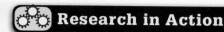 **Research in Action**

Is Public Affection a Public Affliction?

When making observations in everyday life, one of the most basic questions you may ask is how common or rare a behavior is. Just because you observe something does not mean that it happens all the time. Take, for example, public displays of affection, aka PDA. Ever notice how many couples walk around holding hands, hugging, or kissing in full view of the rest of the world? You might notice these couples more often because you find these behaviors romantic, because you find them irritating, or simply because you have a low threshold for what counts as PDA.

These potential biases present a perfect opportunity for you to use your knowledge of observational research. See if public displays of affection really are all around you in the online activity *Is Public Affection a Public Affliction?*

LaunchPad To complete this activity, visit LaunchPad at launchpadworks.com

Final Thoughts

You now see how researchers can use systematic observations to explore a research question. Although developing a detailed and comprehensive coding system and training observers can be difficult, observational methods are a good way to identify the key factors related to a phenomenon. Naturalistic observation allows for the unobtrusive examination of psychological phenomena in a real-world setting, which increases the external validity of our findings. As a result, we can be reasonably sure that what we observed in our mall will generalize to other people and places.

There are many factors that play a role in how parents discipline their children, such as parenting style, ethnicity, and their own experiences with punishment as children (Berlin et al., 2009; Fletcher et al., 2008; Simons & Wurtele, 2010). It is also possible that other situational factors, in addition to the number of others present, influence discipline tactics. For example, what if the grandparents are present? What if the parent is sleep-deprived, hungry, or in a bad mood? The next time you hear a child crying and throwing a fit, instead of feeling irritated or overly sympathetic, pause for a moment to think about how your presence might influence the parent's way of handling the situation. The strategy the parent uses when you are there may not be the same strategy that she or he would use in private.

Review Questions

1. Sheila is concerned about reactivity and wants to use an unobtrusive research technique to examine her research question. Which of the following should she use?
   a. Participant observation
   b. Naturalistic observation
   c. Survey
   d. Experiment

2. Hiram wants to study how product placement in a grocery store influences buying behaviors. To be sure his study re-creates the psychological experience of a grocery store, Hiram re-creates four aisles in the lab just as they appear at his local grocery store and has participants use an actual shopping cart. Which aspect of the study is Hiram strengthening?
   a. Ecological validity
   b. Internal validity
   c. Demand characteristics
   d. Social desirability

3. Jaye's goal is to observationally study the bonds that form between sorority members through the rush process. To do this, Jaye pledges a sorority and grows close to her pledge class and her big sister, all the while making her research observations. What form of observation is Jaye using?
   a. Unbiased observation
   b. Naturalistic observation
   c. Nonconcealed observation
   d. Participant observation

4. To study how people place blame for failure, Takahiro brings groups of participants into the lab and gives them an unsolvable task to work on collaboratively. He informs the participants that he will observe them, but does not tell them what specific behaviors he plans to observe. Which of the following observational methods is he using?
   a. A naturalistic observation
   b. A concealed laboratory observation
   c. A nonconcealed laboratory observation
   d. A blind observation

5. Which of the following is a major concern with nonconcealed observations?
   a. Participant reactivity
   b. Biased observations
   c. Poor inter-observer reliability
   d. Poor intra-observer reliability

6. Jack and Jill are trained research observers for a study on pretend play in children. Jack and Jill are very consistent in their own independent coding. However, when comparing their ratings of the same event to each other's, their consensus or agreement is poor. Which of the following is correct?

   a. They have good intra-observer reliability and good inter-observer reliability.

   b. They have poor intra-observer reliability and good inter-observer reliability.

   c. They have good intra-observer reliability and poor inter-observer reliability.

   d. They have poor intra-observer reliability and poor inter-observer reliability.

7. Jannette plans to observe children on the playground for a total of 2 hours on a given day. She breaks down the 2 hours into eight 15-minute time periods and then indicates whether or not a particular behavior occurs during each time period. Jannette is using which of the following recording strategies?

   a. Interval recording

   b. Continuous recording

   c. Duration recording

   d. Optimal recording

8. Clint predicts that extreme temperatures will influence aggressive behavior. He trains two research observers on how to identify and record "aggressive behaviors," along with the current weather conditions, but never lets them know his prediction. This observation is which of the following?

   a. A contrived observation

   b. A naturalistic observation

   c. A blind observation

   d. A participant observation

9. If your research question is a "what" question, which of the following statistical analyses should you use to examine your data?

   a. Inferential statistics

   b. Inductive statistics

   c. Practical statistics

   d. Descriptive statistics

10. Verla, Santa's second cousin twice removed, wants to know if weight plays a role in jolliness. If her variables are weight measured in pounds and jolliness measured by the number of belly laughs, what type of variable is weight?

   a. Range variable

   b. Modal variable

   c. Continuous variable

   d. Categorical variable

11. What are some of the advantages and disadvantages of conducting an observational design?

12. Describe the various types of observational methods, including naturalistic, laboratory, concealed, and participant.

13. List and describe each measure of central tendency.

Applying What You've Learned

1. A manager wants to know if her employees are satisfied in their current job positions, but she fears they might not respond honestly if she asks them directly. To help her out, develop a behavioral trace, a behavioral choice, and a behavioral observation to assess the job satisfaction of her employees. Be sure to develop a conceptual definition for job satisfaction, as well as an operational definition for each type of behavioral measure.

2. In the book *A Glasgow Gang Observed*, a 26-year-old schoolmaster went undercover with the help of one of his students to study teenage gang violence in Glasgow, Scotland. Explain the ethical implications of both conducting and not conducting this research.

3. To better understand the world of law enforcement, use one segment (~7 minutes) of the TV show *COPS* to practice a continuous recording. Remember this involves recording all of the target individual's (i.e., the law enforcement officer's) behaviors during a specified observation period. Along with your observations, comment on the benefits and drawbacks of this observational method.

4. Based on what you have learned from your continuous recording in #3, develop a coding system that includes the types of behaviors you expect to see from a suspect during a law enforcement encounter. Pilot your coding system by watching a new segment of the TV show *COPS*, and use your observation schedule to record the frequency of each behavior listed. Along with your observations, note what behaviors were missing or were useless in your coding system and create a revised version.

5. As a researcher, you are in charge of training several students to be observers for your observational study on the eating behaviors of students in the dining hall. Develop an agenda for this training that includes important topics to cover and activities to do in the training.

6. Using the Research Spotlight on contrived observations in this chapter as inspiration, design a contrived observation that you could do on your campus. Start with a specific research question to address, then develop a methodology and coding system for your research. Collect data using at least two observers. Use your data to create a bar chart representing your findings. What conclusions can you draw based on your observations?

7. THE NOVICE RESEARCHER: At your next social gathering (e.g., holiday celebration, birthday party, or family dinner), conduct your own participant observation study of your friends and family. Explain how your prior knowledge of those you were observing might have influenced the observations you made. Were you looking for evidence that would confirm what you already believed about your friends and family?

8. DIG INTO THE NUMBERS: We have provided your instructor with supplemental observational study data. Analyze that data to build your skills in using descriptive statistics in SPSS. Write an APA-style results section based on your analyses. If you would like even more practice, your instructor also has data that accompanies the study discussed throughout this chapter.

Key Concepts

bar chart, p. 187

blind observation, p. 177

categorical variable, p. 184

central tendency, p. 184

coding system, p. 173

Cohen's kappa coefficient, p. 185

concealed observation, p. 168

continuous recording, p. 179

continuous variable, p. 184

contrived observation, p. 180

descriptive research, p. 160

descriptive statistics, p. 183

duration recording, p. 174

ecological validity, p. 164

experimental research, p. 160

external validity, p. 164

frequency-count recording, p. 174

frequency distribution, p. 184

inter-observer reliability, p. 178

interval recording, p. 179

intra-observer reliability, p. 177

laboratory observation, p. 164

mean (*M*), p. 184

median (*Mdn*), p. 185

mode (*Mo*), p. 184

naturalistic observation, p. 166

nonconcealed observation, p. 167

observation schedule, p. 175

participant observation, p. 165

pilot testing, p. 178

reactivity, p. 167

systematic observational research, p. 164

Answers to YOUR TURN

Your Turn 6.1: 1. d; 2. a; 3. b

Your Turn 6.2: 1. c; 2. b; 3. a

Your Turn 6.3: 1. a; 2. a; 3. d

Answers to Multiple-Choice Review Questions

1. b; 2. a; 3. d; 4. c; 5. a; 6. c; 7. a; 8. c; 9. d; 10. c

Correlational Research

Is Going Greek a Great Idea?

BrianAJackson/Deposit Photos

LEARNING OUTCOMES

After reading this chapter, you should be able to:

- Differentiate between a correlational and experimental study.
- Describe how to test a research question using a survey.
- Describe the purpose of a scale.
- Identify good practices when writing quality scale items.
- Discuss potential biases that influence how people respond to scale items, and discuss how to minimize these biases.

- Explain how psychologists assess the reliability of a measure.
- Describe the different types of validity used to evaluate the accuracy of a scale.
- Discuss how researchers summarize a set of measurements.
- Explain how associations between variables are measured.
- Write a method and results section for a correlational study using a scale.

Something to Think About . . .

When you first decided to go to college, you might have had some expectations about the types of experiences you might have: meeting new friends, living with a quirky roommate, having a curmudgeonly professor, staying up late, avoiding the "Freshman 15," and getting involved in campus life. While there are many groups you can join in college, the ones that often come to mind first are fraternities and sororities. The decision of whether or not to "go Greek" can be a difficult one. While fraternities and sororities provide plenty of opportunities to socialize, it is also fair to wonder why college students would want to join an organization that requires specific initiation rituals, demands secrecy, and involves many hours of their time. Throughout your life, you have encountered many different groups, some that you wanted to join, others that you did not. Have you wondered what makes some people want to join some groups, like fraternities and sororities, while other people avoid these affiliations?

Among the many decisions students may have to make in college is whether or not to join a fraternity or sorority. What types of students do these organizations attract?

(Steve Skjold/Alamy)

Introduction to Our Research Question

We are social creatures who have a fundamental need to associate with others (Baumeister & Leary, 1995). However, we do not seek out just anyone; some groups of people are more attractive to us than others. This seems particularly true when we think about college fraternities and sororities. For some students, these Greek organizations epitomize the excitement of college life, while other students view them as cultlike groups that promote conformity and eliminate individuality. Some might think that those who "go Greek" are self-assured individuals who know who they are, whereas others might believe that joining a fraternity or sorority indicates a sense of personal weakness or insecurity.

You could probably make compelling arguments for both possibilities, which is a clear sign of a good research question! To determine which answer is best, we could debate both sides of the issue using our own thoughts and experiences. But we know better than that by now. Instead, we will use the scientific method to ask the research question:

RESEARCH **Is there an association between students' sense of self and their interest in joining a fraternity or sorority?**

As is true for most research questions, the best place for us to start is by searching the literature so we can learn what others have already discovered.

Reviewing the Literature: What Do We Already Know About This Topic?

As we consider our literature search strategy, we need to identify the key parts of our research question. First, we should learn if those who join Greek organizations differ from those who do not. If those groups are not really different, our question has less support. If there are differences, we should pay special attention to whether or not these differences existed before members joined their respective groups, as these differences may influence the decision to "go Greek." Our question also suggests that people differ in terms of what psychologists refer to as self-concept, which is essentially their sense of who they are or how they define the self (Kassin, Fein, & Markus, 2017). You may have noticed that when asked the question, "Who are you?" some people seem to have no problem rattling off a list of personality traits, whereas others look dumbstruck. While everyone can describe his or her self to some degree, some people seem to have greater certainty in their description of who they are. This characteristic, known as self-concept clarity, reflects how clearly, confidently, and consistently people describe their sense of self (Campbell, 1990).

As we have done for other chapters, we have already found some articles relevant to our research question. Because our question involves experiences

▶ How do you conduct a quality literature search?
SEE APPENDIX B, p. 497

related to college life, we should not limit our search to psychology-specific databases such as PsycINFO and PsycARTICLES. This is a good opportunity to talk to a librarian at your school. Librarians are experts in helping students identify additional databases to use when searching the literature. A particularly good education-specific database to use for our research question is ERIC (Education Resources Information Center, http://www.eric.ed.gov/). We can use this database to explore the literature on differences between Greek and non-Greek college students. Here are summaries of some articles we found that are relevant to our research question.

Differences Between Greek and Non-Greek College Students

Atlas, G., & Morier, D. (1994). The sorority rush process: Self-selection, acceptance criteria, and the effect of rejection. *Journal of College Student Development, 35,* 345–353.

In this study, one of the questions examined was how women who want to join a sorority might differ from those who do not. One hundred and nine female first-year students were surveyed during the first week of school, then again two months and seven months later. Approximately half of these students rushed at least one sorority. Those who wanted to rush a sorority tended to have a higher need for exhibitionism (e.g., be the center of attention, like having an audience), but not a higher need for affiliation (e.g., enjoy being around people). They were more willing to attend parties where they did not necessarily "fit in" with the crowd. These women had higher social self-esteem, but not higher overall self-esteem.

Park, A., Sher, K. J., & Krull, J. L. (2008). Risky drinking in college: Changes as fraternity/sorority affiliation changes: A person-environment perspective. *Psychology of Addictive Behaviors, 22,* 219–229. doi:10.1037/0893/0893-164X.22.2.219

Part of this study examined initial individual differences between college students who did and did not join a Greek organization. Researchers surveyed over 3,700 first-time students during the summer college orientation and again at the end of the fall and spring semesters. Students who joined a fraternity or sorority during their first year of college were higher in extraversion and placed greater importance on partying and having fun in college. They were more likely to engage in risky behaviors involving substance use. The researchers suggest that fraternities and sororities may be attractive to some types of students because these organizations help to fulfill their social needs and need for sensation-seeking.

Thompson, J. G, Jr., Oberle, C. D., & Lilley, J. L. (2011). Self-efficacy and learning in sorority and fraternity students. *Journal of College Student Development, 52,* 749–753. doi:10.1353/csd.2011.0078

This study compared Greek and non-Greek students on self-efficacy and academic performance. Self-efficacy is an individual's belief that he or she can achieve a desired outcome. One hundred and eighty-six students (140 women; 32 Greek and 154 non-Greek) participated in this experimental study involving a learning task. As part of the procedure, all participants completed a self-efficacy scale. Researchers found that self-efficacy was significantly higher for Greek students.

Wilder, D. H., Hoyt, A. E., Surbeck, B. S., Wilder, J. C., & Carney, P. I. (1986). Greek affiliation and attitude change in college students. *Journal of College Student Personnel, 27,* 510–519.

This study examined how Greek membership may influence changes in students over the four years of college. Students (2,178) completed a survey right before they started their first year in college and then again later, the semester they graduated. These students were categorized as being "Greek," "ex-Greek" (i.e., joined a Greek organization as freshmen but were no longer involved by senior year), or independent. Among the various findings, the researchers found that the Greek students were less autonomous or independent in relation to their family and peers. This difference was greater among freshmen, indicating that these differences existed before the students made the decision of whether or not to join a Greek organization. The researchers concluded that initial differences, not the values associated with Greek organizations, account for how students change while in college.

Self-Concept Clarity

Campbell, J. D. (1990). Self-esteem and clarity of the self-concept. *Journal of Personality and Social Psychology, 59,* 538–549. doi:10.1037/0022-3514.59.3.538

The researchers posit that low self-esteem people also have low self-concept clarity, or less well-defined self-beliefs. In Study 1, low self-esteem participants were not as extreme in their self-descriptions as high self-esteem participants. They were also less confident about their self-ratings. This suggests that they had less certainty or clarity of their self-concept. In Study 2, participants rated themselves on 20 social adjectives (10 positive; 10 negative) at two different times, 8–9 weeks apart. The low self-esteem participants were less consistent in their self-ratings between testing sessions, suggesting that their self-descriptions are less stable over time. Study 3 found that low self-esteem participants had less consistency in their self-descriptions when comparing general and situation-specific ratings of their behavior. Finally, Study 4 found that low self-esteem participants showed less internal consistency in their self-descriptions. Collectively, these studies support the notion that self-concept clarity is an individual difference related to self-esteem. Low self-esteem individuals tend to have a less clearly defined self-concept.

Campbell, J. D., Trapnell, P. D., Heine, S. J., Katz, I. M., Lavallee, L. F., & Lehman, D. R. (1996). Self-concept clarity: Measurement, personality correlates, and cultural boundaries. *Journal of Personality and Social Psychology, 70,* 141–156. doi:10.1037/0022-3514.70.1.141

In a set of studies, the researchers demonstrated that the Self-Concept Clarity Scale (SCC Scale) is a reliable and valid self-report measure of self-concept clarity.

Lewandowski, G. W., Jr., & Nardone, N. (2012). Self-concept clarity's role in self-other agreement and the accuracy of behavioral prediction. *Self and Identity, 11,* 71–89. doi:10.1080/15298868.2010.512133

The researchers explored the idea that those with greater self-concept clarity have greater accuracy in self-knowledge. Studies 1 and 2 assessed accuracy by looking at the level of agreement between participants' self-ratings and ratings by others of the participants' personality traits and frequency of everyday behaviors. Both studies found that those with higher self-concept clarity had greater agreement. Study 3 extended these findings by demonstrating that those with high self-concept clarity were more accurate in predicting their actual behavior on a novel task. Collectively, these studies demonstrate that self-concept clarity is an individual difference variable that can be used to explain differences in the accuracy of self-knowledge and predictions of future behavior.

Lewandowski, G. W., Jr., Nardone, N., & Raines, A. J. (2010). The role of self-concept clarity in relationship quality. *Self and Identity, 9,* 416–433. doi:10.1080/15298860903332191

The researchers looked at the relation between self-concept clarity, relationship satisfaction, and relationship commitment. Study 1 found that those with higher self-concept clarity reported greater satisfaction with and commitment to their relationships. Manipulating self-concept clarity, Study 2 found that those in the self-concept clarity condition reported greater relationship satisfaction and commitment than those in the self-concept confusion condition. Overall, these studies demonstrate that self-concept clarity is related to the quality of romantic relationships.

From Ideas to Innovation

College students who decide to join a fraternity or sorority differ in meaningful ways from other students, according to the research. Some of these differences relate to personality traits (e.g., Atlas & Morier, 1994; Park, Sher, & Krull, 2008; Wilder, Hoyt, Surbeck, Wilder, & Carney, 1986); others relate to the self (e.g., Thompson, Oberle, & Lilley 2011). There is also evidence that these differences existed before the students actually joined a Greek organization (Wilder et al., 1986), suggesting that these individual differences may help explain the decision to "go Greek."

We are most interested in whether a sense of self, or self-concept clarity, helps explain this decision. The research suggests that some people have clearer and more accurate beliefs about themselves compared to others (Campbell et al., 1996; Lewandowski & Nardone, 2012). It also appears that self-concept clarity relates to relationship satisfaction and commitment (Lewandowski, Nardone, & Raines, 2010). If we think about belonging to a group as a type of relationship, we might begin to wonder if self-concept clarity relates to the types of groups people want to join. However, we did not find any research specifically examining this question. While this may seem frustrating, it is really an opportunity because it suggests that we are asking a question that researchers have not yet pursued.

Defining Key Terms: What Do You Mean By ___?

Our research question focuses on the relationship between self-concept clarity and interest in joining a fraternity or sorority. Our first task is to conceptually define these two variables. As we learned during our literature search, psychologists define self-concept clarity, our first variable, as how clear and certain a person is about who he or she is. Individuals with high self-concept clarity are able to give clearer and more confident self-descriptions than those with low self-concept clarity (Campbell, 1990). Our second variable is interest in joining a fraternity or sorority. We will conceptually define "interest" as a positive attitude toward joining a Greek organization.

Weighing Our Options: Picking the Best Design

Now that we have conceptually defined our variables, we need to choose the best strategy for answering our research question. We are wondering if there is an association between students' sense of self and their interest in joining a fraternity or sorority. Associations are systematic

Some people have a clearer sense of who they are, or self-concept clarity, than others. How might this sense of clarity affect one's thinking and behavior when interacting with others? *(Tara Moore/Stone/Getty Images)*

patterns that we find in data. For example, are the students most interested in going Greek the ones with the greatest self-concept clarity? Or is it the students with the least self-concept clarity who find joining a fraternity or sorority most attractive? The best strategy for testing associations or relationships between two variables is a **correlational study,** which is any study that allows us to evaluate if changes in one variable correspond in a predictable way with changes in another variable.

▶ Want to refresh your memory of descriptive research? SEE CHAPTER 6, p. 160

You will remember that in descriptive research we are only able to summarize what happened. Correlational studies enable us to go one step further in our conclusions by revealing how these things relate to each other. If we conducted a purely descriptive study, we could only provide information like the percentage of college students who want to join a Greek organization or the percentage of students who have high self-concept clarity. Correlational studies allow us to draw conclusions about the connections between variables we are studying, such as, "Higher self-concept clarity is associated with lower interest in joining a fraternity or sorority." Notice that we did not say that self-concept clarity level determines or causes one's interest in joining a Greek organization. Correlational studies do not allow the drawing of any cause-and-effect conclusions. They only enable us to explore how two variables relate to each other. If we wanted to say that changes in one variable *cause* changes in another variable, we would have to do an experimental study. (We will learn more about experimental studies, which involve manipulating or controlling one variable to see if it has an impact on another variable, in future chapters.) Before we can start making causal claims about how self-concept clarity influences the decision to "go Greek," we need to establish the link between the two. This is the value of correlational research.

Now that we know that a correlational study is the best design to address our question, we need to decide how to collect information about students' sense of self and their interest in joining a fraternity or sorority. We could conduct in-depth interviews with a few college students and ask about these topics. While this qualitative research approach might help us understand the individual decision-making processes, it would likely limit our ability to identify relationships between the variables. Besides, as we learned in Chapter 5, qualitative research is particularly useful when we do not have a specific question to test. In our case, we do have a specific question, so another approach would be best. Another option, conducting observations, is not ideal either, as it would be difficult to observe someone's "self-concept clarity" or to determine what a "positive attitude toward joining a Greek organization" looks like.

correlational study a research approach that focuses on how variables relate to one another.

survey a quantitative research strategy for systematically collecting information from a group of individuals; the information is then generalized to a larger group of interest.

Because we want to know about students' perceptions of their own selves and their own attitudes toward "going Greek," we will have to use self-report measures. Rather than collecting information from a few people, we will want to obtain self-reports from many individuals, as this will best allow us to see if self-concept clarity and college students' interest in joining a Greek organization are related. To accomplish this, our best strategy is to use a **survey,** which is a quantitative research strategy in which we systematically collect information from a group of individuals in order to apply our findings more generally to other, larger groups (de Leeuw, Hox, & Dillman, 2008). In our case, we could ask a group of college students about their self-concept clarity and interest in joining a Greek organization. Using their responses, we could then evaluate the degree of association between the two variables.

▶ Why does correlation prevent us from making causal claims? SEE CHAPTER 8, p. 249

 ## Research Spotlight

Are All College Professors the Same?

We have all heard blanket statements about college professors' political preferences. When one professor takes a stance or makes a political statement, media pundits are quick to assume that all professors have the same political leanings. But is this fair? To test this idea, two researchers used a web-based survey to ask social-personality psychologists about their political ideology in three different areas: social issues, economic issues, and foreign policy (Inbar & Lammers, 2012). In this survey, they found that psychologists had similar political leanings on social issues, but their viewpoints in the areas of economic issues and foreign policies were more diverse than previously believed, refuting the idea that all professors have the same political biases. Studies such as this one show the importance of using science and research strategies such as surveys to evaluate our assumptions about the world.

Weighing Our Options: Using a Scale to Measure Our Variables

Our first step before we design our actual study is to decide how to measure our two variables. Because we are using self-report, we need to decide what to ask participants. We could ask participants **open-ended questions,** which they would answer using their own words. Qualitative researchers usually use open-ended questions in their investigations. Example questions include, "How clear is your self-concept?" and "Are you interested in joining a fraternity (or sorority)?" However, imagine the types of answers we might get: "Crystal clear and you bet!" "Kind of hazy and no way!" "Well, my self-concept is sort of clear, I guess, and it depends on the fraternity." Most likely we will receive such a wide range of responses that it will be difficult to answer our research question. To solve this problem, we need a way for participants to provide more systematic responses. A good solution might be using **closed-ended questions,** where we provide participants with a predetermined set of response options to answer the questions. For our study, we could ask participants, "On a scale from 1 to 7, where 1 means 'not at all' and 7 means 'extremely,' how clear is your self-concept? How interested are you in joining a Greek organization?" While this may seem rather straightforward, remember that we want to collect accurate information. Asking a person a single question is not always the best option for accomplishing this goal because other factors may be influencing the person's response. For example, the person may have misunderstood the question and given an inaccurate answer. Another possibility is that a single question does not adequately capture the complexity of the measured variable.

One solution to our problem is to use a **scale** to measure our variables. A scale usually consists of a series of closed-ended questions. The researcher sums

▶ Want to learn more about open-ended questions, including their role in interviews? SEE CHAPTER 5, p. 133

open-ended question a question that participants answer using their own words.

closed-ended question a question that participants answer using a predetermined set of response options.

scale a measurement strategy for assigning a number to represent the degree to which a person possesses or exhibits the target variable.

the participant's responses to these questions to create a single score representing the degree to which the participant possesses or exhibits the target variable. This score provides us with a more precise measurement of the variable than any single question because the random error associated with any single item tends to cancel out when using multiple items.

We will need two different scales for our study: one that measures self-concept clarity and another that measures interest in joining a Greek organization. As we were conducting our literature review, we noticed that researchers routinely used the Self-Concept Clarity (SCC) Scale to measure a person's clarity of self-concept (Campbell et al., 1996). As we learned in Chapter 4, it is important to have reliable and valid measures. Using a published scale such as the SCC Scale, shown in **Figure 7.1**, is a wise decision because researchers have already

---

INSTRUCTIONS: Answer each question according to the way you personally feel, using the scale. Please place your answer in the space next to each item.

1	2	3	4	5
Strongly Disagree	Disagree	Neither Agree Nor Disagree	Agree	Strongly Agree

_____ 1. My beliefs about myself often conflict with one another.*

_____ 2. On one day I might have one opinion of myself and on another day I might have a different opinion.*

_____ 3. I spend a lot of time wondering about what kind of person I really am.*

_____ 4. Sometimes I feel that I am not really the person that I appear to be.*

_____ 5. When I think about the kind of person I have been in the past, I'm not sure what I was really like.*

_____ 6. I seldom experience conflict between the different aspects of my personality.

_____ 7. Sometimes I think I know other people better than I know myself.*

_____ 8. My beliefs about myself seem to change very frequently.*

_____ 9. If I were asked to describe my personality, my description might end up being different from one day to another day.*

_____ 10. Even if I wanted to, I don't think I could tell someone what I'm really like.*

_____ 11. In general, I have a clear sense of who I am and what I am.

_____ 12. It is often hard for me to make up mind about things because I don't really know what I want.*

* Item is worded in the opposite direction and should be reverse-coded

SOURCE: Copyright ©1996 by the American Psychological Association. Reproduced with permission from Campbell, J. D., Trapnell, P. D., Heine, S. J., Katz, I. M., Lavallee, L. F., & Lehman, D. R. (1996). Self-concept clarity: Measurement, personality correlates, and cultural boundaries. *Journal of Personality and Social Psychology, 70*, 141–156.

FIGURE 7.1 Self-Concept Clarity Scale.

established the scale's quality and reliability. Although we found the SCC Scale through our literature search, there are other sources to identify potentially useful scales. For example, there are books that describe published scales, along with information about their reliability and validity (e.g., Robinson, Shaver, & Wrightsman, 1991; Shaw & Wright, 1967). Your library may have online or print access to the *Mental Measurements Yearbook* (http://buros.org), which is a comprehensive guide to over 2,700 different measures. Sometimes researchers will provide an overall description of a scale they used in their study without providing the actual scale. In these cases, you can e-mail the first author of the article to ask if you can be sent a copy of the scale, using Google to confirm the author's contact information in case he or she has moved to another institution. For our study, we can use the SCC Scale to measure self-concept clarity. Because there does not seem to be an existing scale that measures interest in joining a fraternity or sorority, we can develop our own reliable and valid scale.

Our first decision is the type of scale we should create. Similar to how our research question helps determine our study design, what we want to measure influences our scale choice. We want to use a scale that measures one's attitude toward joining a fraternity or sorority. Psychologists often measure attitudes using a **summated ratings scale** (Spector, 1992), more commonly referred to as a **Likert scale** after its original developer, Rensis Likert (1932). On a Likert scale,

Not at All Interested	Not Very Interested	Neutral	Somewhat Interested	Very Interested
1	2	3	4	5
Not at All	Not Really	Undecided	Somewhat	Very Much
1	2	3	4	5
Not at All Like Me	Not Much Like Me	Neutral	Somewhat Like Me	Very Much Like Me
1	2	3	4	5
Not at All Happy	Not Very Happy	Neutral	Somewhat Happy	Very Happy
1	2	3	4	5
Never	Rarely	Every Once in a While	Sometimes	Almost Always
1	2	3	4	5

Likert scales are commonly used to measure people's attitudes. A person evaluates a series of statements using a predetermined set of response options. The researcher then sums these responses to represent the person's measurement on the variable.

summated ratings scale a scale where a participant evaluates a series of statements using a set of predetermined response options, and the responses are summed to represent the overall measurement for the variable; commonly referred to as a Likert scale.

Likert scale another name for a summated ratings scale.

participants evaluate a series of statements using a predetermined set of response alternatives. These judgments could involve level of agreement (e.g., how much participants agree/disagree with the item), frequency of occurrence (e.g., how often the item occurs), or overall evaluation (e.g., how good/bad the item is). Each response alternative has a descriptor label such as "not at all" or "strongly agree" that corresponds to a numerical value. The researcher sums the numerical values of all the chosen response alternatives to represent a participant's measurement on that variable. Looking back at our literature review, you will notice that the Self-Concept Clarity Scale is an example of a Likert scale (Campbell et al., 1996). Because we want our new scale to measure participants' attitudes as well, we can create our own Likert scale to measure interest in joining a Greek organization. Using a Likert scale for both of our variables is a good idea because participants will make responses on the same scale, which avoids unnecessary confusion.

Writing High-Quality Items

Now we are ready to start writing the individual items. For a Likert scale, we phrase items as statements to be judged rather than questions to be answered. The best starting point is to brainstorm by writing down as many items as possible to use in our scale to reflect our desired variable. If we want to be confident that our own preconceived notions or stereotypes about Greek organizations do not bias our brainstorming, we should collect some qualitative data from other students about possible reasons for joining a fraternity or sorority and incorporate them into our list. Here are some potential items we came up with for our scale:

1. Belonging to a Greek organization increases my chances of being successful.
2. Greek life is an important part of the college experience.
3. The best way to meet other students is to join a fraternity or sorority.
4. To become active in the social life on campus, I should join a fraternity or sorority.
5. Belonging to a Greek organization can be personally fulfilling.
6. Joining a fraternity or sorority will help me meet my academic goals and meet others with similar goals.
7. Pledging a fraternity or sorority can be a rewarding experience.
8. Rushing a fraternity or sorority will help me make friends.
9. I will feel more "at home" on campus if I go Greek.
10. I need to join a Greek organization to build my résumé.
11. Being involved in a fraternity or sorority will make college more fun.
12. I can be a major part of change on campus by getting involved in Greek life.
13. Being a member of a fraternity or sorority will help me develop leadership skills and the ability to work in groups.
14. Joining a fraternity or sorority will help my future job prospects.
15. Joining a Greek organization will help me make friends.

16. Joining a fraternity or sorority will help me be cool.
17. Fraternities and sororities offer a good way to spend time.
18. Fraternities and sororities are for obtuse students who distinctly lack erudite qualities.
19. Pledging a Greek organization can be a self-actualizing experience.

Next, we need to identify the best items to include in the final scale. We must confess, writing a quality scale item is much more challenging than it seems, so some of our items may be imperfect. One criterion for a quality item is that it should be clear and unambiguous. If an item confuses participants, we are almost sure to obtain confusing data. As computer programmers say, "Garbage in, garbage out." Let's go back and review our list of potential items to see if any are not as clear as we might think. For example, look at item #1: "Belonging to a Greek organization increases my chances of being successful." It may sound like a good item, but, if you examine it more closely, it is not clear whether "being successful" refers to academic success (e.g., better grades), social success (e.g., having many friends), or even success after graduation (e.g., better job opportunities). Each item needs to be as precise as possible, and we can develop parallel or similar items referring to other types of possible successes.

Original Item:

Belonging to a Greek organization increases my chances of being successful.

Better Items:

1. Belonging to a Greek organization increases my chances of being academically successful.
2. I am more likely to be socially successful by belonging to a fraternity or sorority.
3. Being a member of a Greek organization will help me become successful after graduation.

If we are trying to be clear, take a look at item #6: "Joining a fraternity or sorority will help me meet my academic goals and meet others with similar goals." Notice anything? In this item, we are really asking about two different things at the same time—academic goals and meeting other people. This is an example of a *double-barreled* item because it prompts participants to provide a single response to an item that asks two separate questions. Participants will not know how to respond if they disagree with one part of the statement but agree with the other part. They may just give a midpoint answer as a compromise, which leaves us with the problem of not knowing if the participant's midpoint answer means that he or she agrees with one part of the statement and disagrees with the other part or that the participant felt neutral about the entire statement. Participants may also just focus on one part of the question and ignore the rest. The best thing for us to do is to separate this item into two different items.

Original Item:

Joining a fraternity or sorority will help me meet my academic goals and meet others with similar goals.

What Do You Think?
What other statements might we consider for our scale?

What Do You Think?
What other statements from our list do you believe are unclear or confusing?

What Do You Think?
Are there any other double-barreled items in our list?

Better Items:

1. Joining a fraternity or sorority will help me meet my academic goals.
2. Belonging to a fraternity or sorority will help me meet other students with similar goals to mine.

In order to make our items clear, we should avoid using jargon or overly complex or specific terms that some participants may not know. For example, look at item #8: "Rushing a fraternity or sorority will help me make friends." We cannot be sure that every participant will know what the phrase "rushing a fraternity or sorority" means. Are these students especially speedy? Is it a running exercise? Or is it merely another term for "planning to join"? This possible uncertainty in understanding the item's meaning may lead to a less precise measurement, as some participants may guess how they should respond. As you write your items, always ask yourself if what the item asks will be clear to everyone.

What Do You Think?
Do any of the other items in our list contain jargon or phrases that not everyone may be familiar with?

Original Item:

Rushing a fraternity or sorority will help me make friends.

Better Item:

Going through the fraternity or sorority selection process will help me make friends.

Similarly, we must be aware of our participants' reading level and use vocabulary they will understand. This may be a problem with item #18: "Fraternities and sororities are for obtuse students who distinctly lack erudite qualities." If participants do not know what the words "obtuse" and "erudite" mean, they may not ask the researcher for either clarification or a dictionary. Instead, they may randomly choose a response and move on to the next item, or they may just leave the item unanswered. Either way, we now have the potential for an imprecise measurement. It is better for us to reword the item to avoid the issue of using unfamiliar jargon and uncommon language.

What Do You Think?
Are there any other items that use uncommon language or may be inappropriate for the reading level of our intended participants?

Original Item:

Fraternities and sororities are for obtuse students who distinctly lack erudite qualities.

Better Item:

Fraternities and sororities are for simple-minded students who distinctly lack intellectual qualities.

Looking at our list of potential scale items, we notice that we phrased almost all of them so that participants with a positive attitude toward joining a Greek organization will agree with the statement. While our intent is to have higher scores represent a more positive attitude, this consistent phrasing may be a problem. Imagine yourself as a participant. After you answer the first few items, you will probably "catch on" or develop an idea of what the scale asks, and then become tempted to answer all of the items the same way without reading or really thinking about each item. That is, some participants may agree (or disagree) with every item regardless of what it asks, leading to inaccurate measurements.

Psychologists refer to a response bias as a **response set**. An **acquiescent response set** (or yea-saying) is a response bias where the person tends to agree with every statement, regardless of the item's content. The potential for this bias leaves us with the dilemma of never being sure whether high scores on our scale are the result of participants' positive attitudes toward joining a Greek organization or an acquiescent response set. The best way to avoid this bias is to have some reverse-coded items, where high scores have a different meaning. On our scale, reverse-coded items will require participants to disagree with them if they have a positive attitude toward joining a fraternity or sorority. To accomplish this, we can rephrase some of our items. For example:

Original Item:

Fraternities and sororities offer a good way to spend time.

Better Item:

Fraternities and sororities are a waste of time.

As we rephrase some of the items, we need to avoid simply including a negative word such as "not" in the statement. For example, it would be a poor idea to rephrase item #15 so that it becomes "Not joining a fraternity or sorority will not help me make friends." Frankly, this type of double negative makes the item confusing and

> **What Do You Think?**
> What other items can we reword in the opposite direction to minimize the possibility of an acquiescent response set biasing our measurements?

Does this person really feel strongly about each item, or is the person just exhibiting the acquiescent response set? It is hard to tell without using strategies such as the inclusion of reversed items in the scale.

response set a response bias where a participant tends to give the same answer to most, if not all, of the items on a scale, regardless of what questions are asked.

acquiescent response set a response bias where a participant tends to agree with most, if not all, of the items on a scale, regardless of what questions are asked.

difficult to answer. To minimize the potential influence of this bias on our measurement, it is a good idea to have around half of a scale's items stated in the opposite direction (Ellard & Rogers, 1993).

We originally created 19 statements for our scale. Obviously, they were not all high-quality "keepers." After reworking our original items, correcting the problems, and incorporating the suggestions we discussed, we chose the following items for our scale. Just for our own reference, we will mark the items using opposite direction wording with an asterisk. These asterisks will not appear on the version of the scale given to our participants.

Attitude Toward Greek Organizations Scale

1. Being a member of a Greek organization will help me become successful after graduation.
2. Fraternities and sororities are a waste of time.*
3. Belonging to a fraternity or sorority will help me meet others.
4. Belonging to a Greek organization will hurt my chances of being academically successful.*
5. Greek life is a trivial part of the college experience.*
6. To become active in the social life on campus, I should join a fraternity or sorority.
7. Pledging a fraternity or sorority is a meaningless experience.*
8. Going through the fraternity or sorority selection process will help me make friends.
9. I need to join a Greek organization to build my résumé.
10. Fraternities and sororities are for simple-minded students who distinctly lack intellectual qualities.*
11. Being involved in a fraternity or sorority will make college more fun.
12. I can be a major part of change on campus by getting involved in Greek life.
13. Joining a fraternity or sorority will hurt my future job prospects.*

Response Alternatives

Next, we need to choose the number of response alternatives participants will use. This decision influences our measurement's sensitivity. We could simply provide only two response alternatives, such as True and False. This would be an example of a **forced choice scale** because participants must choose between one of only two response options. However, there are several problems with this option. Participants may not respond to an item if they truly cannot decide which option to choose. Using only two items means that our scale will have minimal sensitivity in differentiating between respondents' interest in joining a fraternity or sorority. That is, if someone responded that an item is "true," we cannot know if this person believes the item is just sometimes true or always true. We could add a third response option such as "sometimes true, sometimes false." However, participants may simply select this middle option because it seems less extreme or closer to the average rating on the scale. This bias, also known as the **error of central tendency**, reflects some participants' tendency to avoid the

▶ What do we mean by measurement sensitivity? SEE CHAPTER 4, p. 102

forced choice scale a scale where a person must choose between only two response alternatives for each item.

error of central tendency a response bias where a participant tends to avoid using the extreme response alternatives on a scale.

highest and lowest ends of the response alternatives whenever making judgments. This bias may mean that while we think participants are thinking about all three points on a scale, some are actually thinking about only one point on the scale.

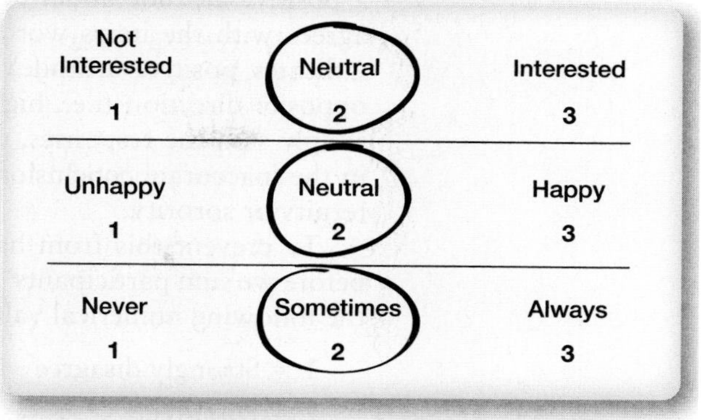

One way to improve our scale's precision as well as minimize the error of central tendency is to use more response alternatives. The question is, how many? We could use a 100-point scale, but that would probably be overkill and give the illusion of false precision (e.g., the difference between a measurement of 67 and one of 69 would not be very meaningful). It will also be difficult to provide verbal descriptors for that many response alternatives (e.g., if 2 = somewhat disagree, what would we put to describe what a score of 67 or 69 represents?). To address this issue, Likert scales typically include five to nine response alternatives with verbal descriptors such as strongly disagree, disagree, neither agree nor disagree, agree, and strongly agree (Spector, 1992). To avoid confusing our participants by changing how they make their judgments of each item, we will use the same response options used for the Self-Concept Clarity Scale in **Figure 7.2**.

Why are only the middle response options selected? We do not know if these responses reflect the person's true evaluations or simply his or her tendency to avoid using the extreme points on a scale. By including more response options, we can minimize this error of central tendency.

Calculating the Participant's Score

As we discussed earlier, we are using scales to measure our two key variables because they provide us with more precision than if we used single-item questions for each variable. When we use a Likert scale, we determine our variable's measurement by summing the responses to all of the individual items on the scale. For our scale, we want higher total scores to indicate that the participant has a more positive attitude toward joining a Greek organization. But we must be careful because we worded some of the items in the opposite direction (e.g., "Fraternities and sororities are a waste of time."). Participants who are very interested in "going Greek" will tend to disagree with the opposite direction items, meaning that they will choose response alternatives associated with lower numerical values, not higher ones. Suppose we have a participant with such

1	2	3	4	5
Strongly Disagree	Disagree	Neither Agree Nor Disagree	Agree	Strongly Agree

FIGURE 7.2 Response Options for the Self-Concept Clarity Scale.

a positive attitude about joining a Greek organization that he or she strongly agrees with the items worded in the positive direction (i.e., higher agreement indicates positive attitude) and strongly disagrees with those worded in the opposite direction (i.e., higher agreement indicates a negative attitude). If we simply sum the responses, they will essentially cancel each other out, resulting in the inaccurate conclusion that the person is ambivalent about joining a fraternity or sorority.

To prevent this from happening, we use a technique called **reverse-coding** before we sum participants' responses on the scale. To accomplish this, we assign the following numerical values to our positive direction items:

1 = Strongly disagree
2 = Disagree
3 = Neither agree nor disagree
4 = Agree
5 = Strongly agree

However, for the items worded in the opposite direction, we re-assign the numerical values this way:

5 = Strongly disagree
4 = Disagree
3 = Neither agree nor disagree
2 = Agree
1 = Strongly agree

As you can see, we assign the higher numerical values to the low end of the response alternatives for items worded in the opposite direction. By doing this reverse-coding, when we sum the participants' responses, we can be certain that higher scores represent a more positive attitude toward joining a fraternity or sorority. Now we know that higher scores indicate what we hoped (i.e., a more positive attitude toward joining a Greek organization).

Weighing Our Options: Is Our Scale Reliable and Valid?

When developing a scale, we need to make sure it works properly before including it in our study. If our Attitude Toward Greek Organizations Scale actually measures attitude toward college in general, our study will be useless. That is, we need to have a quality measure. As you recall from Chapter 4, reliability refers to the measure's consistency while validity is concerned with the measure's accuracy. There are several different ways we can examine our scale's reliability and validity.

Reliability

We should first evaluate our scale's reliability because an unreliable scale cannot be valid. There are several ways to evaluate our scale's consistency. One way is to look at the scale's **internal consistency reliability,** or the degree to which individual items in the scale interrelate or connect with one another. If the items all measure the same underlying variable, namely one's attitude toward joining

reverse-coding a scoring strategy where more negative response alternatives are assigned higher numerical values and more positive response alternatives are assigned lower numerical values; used to minimize the potential for an acquiescent response set.

internal consistency reliability the degree to which the individual items in a scale are interrelated.

a Greek organization, then participants should respond consistently and similarly to the scale's individual items. For example, if a person agrees with the statement, "Belonging to a fraternity or sorority will help me meet others," the person should also agree with the scale item, "Going through the fraternity or sorority selection process will help me make friends." If participants tend to agree with the first item but disagree with the second, then there would be low internal consistency reliability, suggesting that our questions are not consistently measuring their attitude towards "going Greek."

Another way to evaluate our scale's consistency is to see if we obtain essentially the same measurement after administering the scale to the same participant on two different occasions. If a person has a positive attitude toward Greek organizations one week, we would expect them to have the same positive attitude the following week. This type of consistency is **test-retest reliability,** which refers to the measure's temporal stability, or ability to produce similar measurements across different time periods. We evaluate test-retest reliability by looking at the **correlation,** or degree of association between the Time 1 and Time 2 scale scores. We will discuss correlations in depth when we analyze our study's results. Ideally, we want our participants to give the same exact responses both times they complete the scale so that we have perfect test-retest reliability. However, this will rarely, if ever, happen in the real world. Participant scores can vary between Time 1 and Time 2 simply because of random error or chance fluctuations that have nothing to do with the scale. For example, participants may become distracted when completing the scale a second time, leading to a slight variation in their responses. Or a participant may have just had an argument with a friend concerning the value of Greek organizations, which could affect his or her responses when completing the scale again.

Other more systematic factors or biases can also lead to differences in scores between testing administrations, thus affecting the scale's test-retest reliability. For example, participants may become wiser or better at completing the scale the second time, therefore providing different answers. Another possibility is that if you measure participants too soon the second time, you may be measuring how well they remember their previous responses rather than the variable itself. On the other hand, if you wait too long, then the participants may have naturally changed on variables the scale measures. For instance, attitudes toward Greek life might change if participants complete the scale before the Greek organizations start to recruit new members and then again after the organizations have selected their new members, leading to some elated and some disappointed participants. Generally, to properly evaluate test-retest reliability, one to two weeks between scale administrations is sufficient (Constantine & Ponterotto, 2006).

To avoid some of the problems associated with test-retest reliability, researchers will sometimes evaluate a scale's **alternative-form** (or **equivalent-form) reliability** by asking participants to complete two different versions of the same scale or an equivalent scale. If the scale is a reliable measure, then participants should respond similarly on both scales. You may have experienced this if your professor has ever given the class two different versions of the same exam. Your professor is assuming that students who do well (or poorly) on one version of the test will perform similarly on the other version of the test. If students who do well on one version of

test-retest reliability the temporal stability of a measure.

correlation a measure of the linear relationship between two variables; can range from -1.0 to $+1.0$; typically represented by the symbol r.

alternative-form reliability a form of reliability that evaluates how well a measure correlates with a similar, but different, measure of the same variable.

equivalent-form reliability another name for alternative-form reliability.

the test do poorly on another version of the same test, then the test is not a reliable measure of what they have learned.

See Table 7.1 for a review of types of reliability.

TABLE 7.1

Review of Types of Reliability	
Type of Reliability	**Type of Consistency Examined**
Internal consistency reliability	How interrelated are the individual items in the scale?
Test-retest reliability	How consistent is the scale over time?
Alternative-form (or equivalent-form) reliability	How consistent is the scale with other comparable measures of the variable?

▶ Why are demand
characteristics and social
desirability potential
concerns in self-report
measures?
SEE CHAPTER 4, p. 89

face validity the degree
to which a scale appears,
on the surface, to measure
the intended variable.

content validity
the degree to which the
items on a scale reflect
the range of material
that should be included
in a measurement of the
target variable.

construct validity the
degree to which the
scale actually measures
the desired construct;
established by evaluating
the convergent and
discriminant validity of
the measurement.

convergent validity the
degree to which scores
on a measurement
correspond to measures
of other theoretically
related variables; used
to help establish the
construct validity of a
measurement.

Validity

Once we determine that our scale provides consistent measurements, we will want to make sure it is valid, or actually measures what we claim it measures. We can evaluate our scale's validity in several different ways. Look at our final scale items again. If you think anyone reading the questions could guess they gauge one's interest in Greek life, then the scale has strong **face validity**, or degree to which the scale *appears* to measure such interest. However, one of the problems with assessing face validity is its subjectivity, such that it depends on what the observer perceives (Sartori, 2010). In addition, if the scale makes too obvious to participants what you are trying to measure, it may introduce demand characteristics and the potential for social desirability bias.

Have you ever taken a test that you believed was unfair because it did not cover much of the material that you had learned in class? If so, that test had poor **content validity**, which rates the degree to which the items reflect the range of material that should have been covered (Carmines & Zeller, 1979). A scale with good content validity covers the basic aspects associated with the measured variable. Looking at our scale, we can see that we have statements about how Greek organizations may affect one's social life success, academic success, and success after graduation. That seems to do a pretty good job of covering the basics. However, if all of our items focused on how Greek organizations might affect a person's social life, we would have had more concerns about content validity.

We want a scale that assesses attitude toward joining a fraternity or sorority. Thus, we should make sure that it does not actually measure something different, such as attitude toward partying in general or succeeding in college. We are now considering our scale's **construct validity**, or the extent to which the scale actually measures the construct we want (Carmines & Zeller, 1979). To establish a scale's construct validity, we evaluate two specific types of validity (Campbell & Fiske, 1959; Cronbach & Meehl, 1955). First, we look at the scale's **convergent validity**, or the degree to which scores on the scale correlate with participants' scores on measures of other theoretically related variables. For example, because Greek organizations are opportunities for extracurricular involvement, participants' attitudes toward joining a fraternity or sorority should correlate with attitudes toward becoming involved in campus life in general. If they do not correlate, then we will need to question our scale's convergent validity. Second, we should establish the scale's **discriminant validity**, which is basically the opposite of convergent validity. For a scale to have high discriminant validity, it should not correlate with measures of unrelated variables. We would have concerns about the discriminant validity if we found that scores on our scale were highly correlated with a scale measuring interest in joining a church. In practice, to establish convergent and discriminant validity, we would include additional measures with our items. If our scale *converges* with measurements of similar variables and *diverges* from measurements of dissimilar variables, our scale has high construct validity.

Finally, our attitude scale should correlate with the person's likelihood of actually engaging in the behavior of seeking out membership in a fraternity or sorority. That is, it should have high **criterion validity**, which is how strongly the scale relates to a particular outcome or behavior. If people score high on our scale, they really should be more likely to join a Greek organization. We can evaluate criterion validity in two ways. First, we can use a criterion that is present at the same time we measure the participants' attitudes. In this case, we can establish criterion validity by examining the scale's **concurrent validity**. For example, we can record the number of Greek organizations participants speak with at an information session once they have completed our scale. Our scale will have strong concurrent validity, and therefore high criterion validity, if participants with higher scores tended to talk with more Greek organizations about possibly joining them. The second way we can establish the criterion validity of our scale is to use a criterion that will occur at some later time. We can have our participants complete the scale and then observe the number of Greek events they attend over the next 6 months, as this may reflect their interest in joining a Greek organization. This allows us to assess our scale's criterion validity by looking at its **predictive validity**, or how our scale coincides with a criterion that occurs in the more distant future.

See **Table 7.2** for a review of types of validity.

discriminant validity the degree to which a measurement does not correspond to measures of unrelated variables; used to help establish the construct validity of a measurement.

criterion validity the degree to which a measurement relates to a particular outcome or behavior; established by evaluating the concurrent and predictive validity of the measurement.

concurrent validity the degree to which a measurement corresponds with an existing outcome or behavior; used to establish the criterion validity of a measurement.

predictive validity the degree to which a measurement corresponds with a particular outcome or behavior that occurs in the future; used to establish the criterion validity of a measurement.

TABLE 7.2

Review of Types of Validity	
Type of Validity	**Type of Accuracy Examined**
Face Validity	Does the scale appear to be measuring the variable?
Content Validity	Do the items on the scale represent the various aspects of the variable being measured?
Construct Validity	Does the scale actually measure the intended variable?
Convergent Validity	Does the scale relate to other measures of the variable?
Discriminant Validity	Does the scale relate to measures of unrelated variables?
Criterion Validity	Does the scale relate to a relevant outcome or behavior?
Concurrent Validity	Does the scale relate to a relevant outcome or behavior that was measured at the same time?
Predictive Validity	Does the scale relate to a relevant outcome or behavior that occurs in the future, after the scale is completed?

What Do You Think?

How would you evaluate our scale on the different types of validity? Are there other types of items we should have included to improve its overall validity?

Pilot Testing

We do not need to specifically evaluate the reliability and validity of the Self-Concept Clarity Scale because our literature search revealed that other researchers have already done this (Campbell et al., 1996). We do need to determine whether or not our measure of attitude toward Greek organizations will be a good tool to use. To do this, we need to pilot test our scale by giving it a trial run, where we ask a group of people from the target population (i.e., college students) to complete the scale. The pilot testers will let us know if there are any confusing items or items they did not know how to answer. Pilot testing also gives us an initial opportunity to evaluate the reliability and validity of our scale.

We conducted a ministudy to specifically pilot test our Attitude Toward Greek Organizations Scale. From this pilot data, we learned that many of the students found item #10, "Fraternities and sororities are for simple-minded students who distinctly lack intellectual qualities," to be confusing. Because this item was low quality, we decided to simply drop that item, leaving us with a final 12-item scale. Next, we evaluated the test-retest reliability of our final scale by having many of the same students complete the scale a week later. The correlation between the two administrations of the scale was .84, which is acceptable for test-retest reliability (Carmines & Zeller, 1979). We found satisfactory internal consistency reliability for our scale of 12 items. Reviewing the final items, we concluded that the scale had satisfactory face validity and content validity. To evaluate the construct validity, when we had students complete our scale a second time, we also asked them to answer questions related to their interest in becoming involved on campus and in the local community. Scores on our scale strongly correlated with responses to the campus involvement questions, demonstrating convergent validity. Conversely, these scores were unrelated to expressed interest in becoming involved in the local community, thus providing evidence for our scale's divergent validity. Collectively, these findings provide support for the construct validity of our scale. Now that we know we have good measurement tools, we can start formulating our hypothesis and designing our study.

Research in Action

Which Professor Should You Take?

Each semester, you are tasked with choosing a professor for each of your classes. Should you take a class with Professor Sandman, or will you learn more from Professor DeBestie? Your friends will have their own opinions, but how can you be certain that their advice is not biased? Are ratings of professors posted on the Internet any better? How should you obtain the information you need to make your decision?

As scientists, we seek objective information in order to draw reliable conclusions. In the online activity *Which Professor Should You Take?,* you will have the opportunity to develop your own objective measure of professor quality with the "Rate-A-Prof Scale." Creating a quality scale is not an easy task, but, with practice, you might just become "de bestie" at survey construction!

LaunchPad To complete this activity, visit LaunchPad at launchpadworks.com

Our Hypothesis

Now that we have established how we are going to measure our variables, we should formally state our hypothesis, or prediction about the study's outcomes, before we decide upon our actual procedures for conducting our study. Being clear in our research hypothesis will not only help us design our study, but will determine which statistical test we should use and the types of conclusions we can draw based on our data. Given our research question, it makes sense for us to hypothesize that there is an association between self-concept clarity and interest in joining a fraternity or sorority. This would be an example of a **nondirectional hypothesis,** as we are not specifying the nature, or direction, of this relationship. We could take this prediction a step further by hypothesizing how the two variables may be related. For example, we could predict a positive relationship where those with *higher* self-concept clarity also hold *more* positive attitudes toward joining a Greek organization. This seems rea-

Sometimes we know exactly where we want to go. The same is true in research: Sometimes we know the specific type of prediction we want to make, so we make directional hypotheses. When we are not so certain, we make nondirectional hypotheses. *(ra2studio/ Deposit Photos)*

sonable because those who know themselves better may want to seek out other like-minded people, and could choose a Greek organization that is a good fit. Conversely, we could just as easily predict a negative relationship where those with *higher* self-concept clarity also have a *less* positive attitude about joining fraternities and sororities. In this case, perhaps individuals who know themselves very well view Greek organizations as groups that help members define their sense of self. Since a person with high self-concept clarity would already have a highly defined self, membership in that group would be unnecessary. These are both examples of a **directional hypothesis** that predicts the exact nature of the relationship between the two variables. However, given that we can think of reasons for different patterns of association between our two variables, we will stick with a nondirectional hypothesis and simply predict that self-concept clarity relates to interest in joining a Greek organization.

nondirectional hypothesis a hypothesis that does not make a specific prediction as to how two variables are related.

directional hypothesis a hypothesis that makes a specific prediction as to the exact nature of the relationship between two variables.

> **YOUR TURN 7.1**

1. Devon wants to measure students' attitudes toward a controversial building project on campus. She has students indicate how much they agree or disagree with a series of statements about the project and then sums their responses to obtain an overall attitude scale. What is Devon using to measure students' attitudes?

   a. A Likert scale

   b. A survey

   c. An interview

   d. An experimental study

2. Ivan notices that many of his participants tended to agree with all of the items in his Likert scale. Which of the following may be a problem with his scale?
   a. The construct validity of the scale
   b. The error of central tendency
   c. The random error in his scale
   d. The acquiescent response set

3. Allyson wants to establish the construct validity of her scale. Which of the following pieces of information will she need?
   a. The scale's internal consistency reliability
   b. The scale's content validity
   c. The scale's divergent validity
   d. The scale's concurrent validity

How did you do? Turn to the end of the chapter to check your answers.

Design in Action

We now have the necessary pieces in place for our study. Our next steps are to finalize our survey, decide on our participants, and determine how we want to administer our survey.

Weighing Our Options: Finalizing Our Survey

In addition to our scales, we will want to collect information about our participants, such as their age, gender, and ethnicity. This information will allow us to describe our sample. It is often best to include basic demographic questions toward the end of our survey. This way, if a participant decides to complete only half of our survey, he or she will most likely have answered the questions that deal more directly with our research question.

Because our survey consists of two scales and a few demographic questions, it should not take participants very long to complete. While this is good because it will help our participants stay focused, it also makes it easier for them to figure out the purpose of our study. For example, it may be clear from our scale that we want to know the participants' views on fraternities and sororities.

We now have the potential for demand characteristics and social desirability, as participants will try to guess what we are "really looking for" in our study. This speculation may even lead participants to experience **evaluation apprehension**, as they could become anxious or concerned about how their answers or behaviors during the study will make them appear to the researcher (Rosenberg, 1969/2009). To minimize these potential problems, we should include other items in our scale that will mislead participants into thinking that the purpose of our survey is something else. These items, called **distractor items**, seem related to the "real" scale items but are not actually what the scale truly measures. When we determine our participants' score on the scale, we simply ignore the responses to these distractor items.

evaluation apprehension anxiety or concern that participants may experience about how their answers or behaviors appear to the researcher.

distractor items items included in a scale to mislead participants as to the real purpose of the scale.

For our survey, we can easily incorporate distractor items into the attitude scale by having participants make judgments about other extracurricular activities in college that are unrelated to Greek organizations. Here are some distractor items that we will intersperse among the "real" items in our attitude scale:

- Being a member of the student government will help develop my leadership skills.
- Joining intramural sports is a good way to meet new people on campus.
- Participating in an academic club will help me achieve my academic goals.
- I need to be involved in extracurricular activities to strengthen my résumé.
- The best way to make friends in college is to avoid joining student groups.
- I will feel more "at home" on campus if I get involved in student activities.
- Being involved on campus will help me be academically successful.

See **Figure 7.3** for the Attitude Toward Greek Organizations Scale, including the distractor items, that we will use in our survey.

We will want to add one last set of questions to our survey. As we discussed earlier, we want to evaluate our attitude scale's validity. One of the ways we can do this is by demonstrating its criterion validity. If high scores on our scale do reflect greater interest in joining a fraternity or sorority, then those participants with high scores should be more proactive in seeking out information about Greek life on campus. We can assess our scale's criterion validity by providing participants with the opportunity to sign up to receive e-mails from the different fraternities and sororities on campus. At the end of our survey, we will list each of these organizations with a very brief description. Participants can select which (if any) of the fraternities or sororities they would like to learn about through a follow-up e-mail. Presumably, the more fraternities or sororities they sign up to receive e-mails from, the greater their interest in joining a Greek organization.

Focus on Ethics: Should We Really Ask Them That?

Earlier we mentioned that we could collect additional information beyond our key scales. For example, we may want to include questions about the participants' partying behaviors by asking things like, "How many times have you tried heroin?", "How many times have you smoked marijuana?" and, "Have you ever used ecstasy?" However, these questions may ask participants to confess to illegal behaviors. We could ask about less incriminating behaviors such as, "How often do you get drunk?" But, given that we are surveying college students in our study, drinking alcohol under 21 years of age will also be an illegal behavior for many. In either case, this raises the question of whether researchers are ethically responsible for reporting illegal behavior, especially potentially dangerous behavior, to authorities. Remember, ethics are not about what we can do, but rather what we should do. While there are researchers who study drug and alcohol use among undergraduate students who ask these types of questions in their studies, they do so because the questions directly pertain to their research question and their research has clear benefits for understanding those behaviors. In our case, these potentially illegal behaviors are not central to our research question and there is no clear benefit to including them. As researchers, we must

What Do You Think?
What other distractor items might we add to our scale?

INSTRUCTIONS: *Answer each question according to the way you personally feel, using the scale. Please place your answer in the space next to each item.*

1	2	3	4	5
Strongly Disagree	Disagree	Neither Agree Nor Disagree	Agree	Strongly Agree

_____ 1. Participating in an academic club will help me achieve my academic goals.+

_____ 2. Being a member of a Greek organization will help me become successful after graduation.

_____ 3. Joining intramural sports is a good way to meet new people on campus.+

_____ 4. Fraternities and sororities are a waste of time.*

_____ 5. Belonging to a fraternity or sorority will help me meet others.

_____ 6. Belonging to a Greek organization will hurt my chances of being academically successful.*

_____ 7. Being a member of the student government will help develop my leadership skills.+

_____ 8. I need to be involved in extracurricular activities to strengthen my résumé.+

_____ 9. To become active in the social life on campus, I should join a fraternity or sorority.

_____ 10. Greek life is a trivial part of the college experience.*

_____ 11. Being involved on campus will help me be academically successful.+

_____ 12. Pledging a fraternity or sorority is a meaningless experience.*

_____ 13. I will feel more "at home" on campus if I get involved in student activities.+

_____ 14. Going through the fraternity or sorority selection process will help me make friends.

_____ 15. The best way to make friends in college is to join a student group.+

_____ 16. Being involved in a fraternity or sorority will make college more fun.

_____ 17. I need to join a Greek organization to build my résumé.

_____ 18. I can be a major part of change on campus by getting involved in Greek life.

_____ 19. Joining a fraternity or sorority will hurt my future job prospects.*

NOTE: *indicates that the item is worded in the opposite direction and should be reverse-coded; + indicates that the item is a distractor and should be excluded when calculating the total scale score

FIGURE 7.3 Attitude Toward Greek Organizations Scale.

be mindful of asking things only when the information will provide use and not simply because we would like to know.

Similarly, in our study, asking about participants' sexual orientation can be ethically questionable unless we have a clear reason to believe that sexual orientation relates to self-concept clarity or interest in joining a Greek organization. In either case, if we ask participants to disclose personal or sensitive information about themselves or their behaviors, we must be able to defend this decision to our Institutional Review Board (IRB). If we cannot justify our use of the questions, we should not ask them. For our study, it is clear that we should leave these questions out and stick with measuring self-concept clarity and interest in joining a Greek organization, and obtain only the demographic information that we need to adequately describe our sample.

As we put together our final survey, we should consider which scale participants will complete first. Sometimes the questions participants initially answer on a survey can influence how they interpret and answer later questions. It is possible that asking participants to first reflect upon their self-concept may influence their interest in extracurricular activities such as fraternities and sororities. Or, if it does not influence participants' actual attitudes, it could influence their willingness to report their interest. In these situations, researchers will use two or more versions of the survey where they vary, or counterbalance, the order of the scales. Because we do not know if answering questions about self-concept clarity can influence interest in joining a fraternity or sorority, we will use two versions of the survey in our study. Half of our participants will first complete the Self-Concept Clarity Scale and then the Attitude Toward Greek Organizations Scale. For the other half, we will reverse this order, thereby minimizing this potential source of bias. We will then have participants select fraternities or sororities on campus, if any, from which they wish to receive e-mails. The last few questions on the survey will ask about participants' age, gender, and ethnicity so that we can adequately describe our sample.

Weighing Our Options: Selecting Our Sample

With our survey finalized, our next step is to develop a sampling plan that describes how we will obtain our participants. Given our desire to measure interest in joining a Greek organization, we certainly do not want to survey students who have already had the opportunity to choose whether to "go Greek." The ideal participants are students just beginning college who still need to make this decision. To catch them in time, we should survey participants early in the fall semester before the Greek organizations start to recruit new members.

Now that we know we are going to target new students, we need to decide how to recruit them to be participants in our study. We could survey the entire population (i.e., new first-year students). However, this could become quite cumbersome and probably is not necessary if we use good sampling strategies. For example, we could use convenience sampling by distributing our survey to first-year students in the dining hall during breakfast. But that may raise concerns about our sample's representativeness because it is highly unlikely that first-year students who get up to have breakfast before their early morning classes are typical or representative of most first-year students. A better choice would be to use simple random sampling by choosing study participants using chance alone from the entire population of first-year students. This way, each first-year student has the same probability of being selected for our study. However, it is possible that some subgroups may be over- or underrepresented in our sample. For example, suppose we know that 60% of first-year students are female. It is quite possible that simple random sampling can result in a sample that has only 35% females. In this case, our sample would underrepresent females, which would limit our ability to generalize our findings to the population.

▶ What are some good sampling strategies we could use?
SEE CHAPTER 4, p. 109

Whenever we know a particular population characteristic is important for our study, it is wise to use a stratified random sampling plan (Kalton, 1983). To do this, we first split our population into two or more subgroups and then use simple random sampling within each group, making sure that the number of participants we select from each group matches the proportion of the size of that group within the population. For example, if 60% of first-year students were female, we would divide the population into two groups: females and males. Then we would randomly select enough participants from each subgroup so that our final sample is 60% females and 40% males. Stratified random sampling helps increase the probability that our sample is representative of the population, particularly when certain subgroups are rather small, such as underrepresented ethnic groups at a school.

A variation on stratified random sampling is **area probability sampling**, where, rather than dividing our population based on some known characteristic, we separate the population into subgroups based on geographic area and then randomly sample from each area. In our case, we could sample from the first-year residence halls. However, because some residence halls are much bigger than others, we might want to random sample proportionately from each residence hall (i.e., more from the larger halls and less from the smaller halls). For our study, this is not practical because some first-year students (e.g., commuters) do not live in the residence halls. To address this, we could include commuters as another geographic subgroup to make sure that we adequately represent this group in our sample.

As we decide on which sampling plan will be best for our study, we will want to consider how to administer our survey. Remember that the better our sample represents the population from which it is drawn, the more confident we will be in generalizing our study's findings. Thus, some sampling plans may be preferable depending on how we decide to actually collect our data.

See **Figure 7.4** for a review of the three types of random sampling.

area probability sampling a sampling strategy where the researcher first divides the population into subgroups based on geographic area and then randomly selects participants from each geographical subgroup.

FIGURE 7.4 Three Types of Random Sampling. (a) Simple Random Sampling; (b) Stratified Random Sampling; (c) Area Probability Sampling

Weighing Our Options: How Should We Administer Our Survey?

An important decision we need to make is how to actually administer the survey. We could conduct the survey by reading each question to each participant, either in-person or over the telephone. A major advantage of reading each question is that it is easier to detect whether the participant misunderstood any of the items. We saw how this can be important when we discussed qualitative research designs in Chapter 5. However, this approach is very time-consuming. If it took 15 minutes to complete our survey, and we had 200 participants in our study, it would take us 50 hours to collect our data! We could save some time by giving each participant a paper version where the participant would read each question and indicate his or her answer directly on the survey. In either case, we could inadvertently introduce demand characteristics into the situation because of our presence. As you can imagine, if we wore a "Greek Life Rules, Dude" T-shirt, participants might respond differently, but it is also possible our presence could influence participants in more subtle or unknown ways.

A more efficient way to conduct our study would be to administer a paper survey to groups of participants. If we were able to get 200 participants in the same room at the same time, we could have all of our data collected within 15 minutes. Of course, there are always trade-offs with this efficiency. Administering surveys to groups is less personal than the individual approach. This means that it may not be as easy to detect whether or not participants clearly understood each item on the survey.

An increasingly popular strategy is to administer surveys over the Internet (Dillman, Smyth, & Christian, 2009). For example, we could post our survey on our school's website or on social media, inviting visitors to complete it. However, this would not be a very good decision, as we have no control over who completes the survey or even how many times they complete it. This haphazard sample would undermine our ability to generalize our findings. A better option would be to randomly select students for our sample and send them an e-mail invitation to participate in the study via a direct link to our web-based survey. This approach allows us to control who participated in our study and how often they completed the survey.

Researchers are increasingly using the Internet to conduct survey studies, as there appears to be little difference in the quality of the data collected compared to more traditional survey strategies (Gosling, Vazire, Srivastava, & John, 2004) and because they are a cost-effective way to obtain large numbers of participants. In fact, rather than randomly sampling participants, we could easily just invite all first-year students to participate in our study. We could even ask new students at other institutions to be in our study. This would allow us to compare our findings across campuses, increasing our confidence in the external validity of our study. However, if we want to invite students from other campuses to participate in our study, our institution's IRB may require us to obtain permission from the other institution's IRB before contacting their students.

Despite their cost-effectiveness and efficiency, web surveys do have some drawbacks. First, these types of surveys are rather impersonal, which may decrease the **response rate,** or the likelihood that those invited to complete the survey will actually do so. That would raise concerns about whether we can

response rate the proportion of the invited sample that actually completes a survey.

generalize our findings. The concern is that there could be a nonresponse bias such that those who choose to complete the survey differ from those who decline participation in meaningful ways related to our hypothesis. For example, if students who are uncertain about their sense of self or who are anti-Greek are less willing to complete our survey, we will have a serious flaw in our sample.

▶ Want to learn more about nonresponse bias? SEE CHAPTER 4, p. 113

Thankfully, these problems are surmountable. When we invite students to participate in our study, we should make the study as appealing and nonthreatening as possible. To do this, we could offer an incentive for agreeing to participate in our study, as long as the incentive does not become coercive and is not contingent on the actual completion of the survey. For our study, anyone who accesses our survey, regardless of whether they complete it, will receive a coupon for a free drink at the student café. Finally, to reduce a potential nonresponse bias, we will encourage any nonresponders by sending one or two follow-up e-mail invitations (Dillman et al., 2009). Participants have the right to refuse participation, so we will never get a 100% response rate. As with any survey study, we will need to examine how well our final sample represents the population. The more representative the sample, the more confidence we can have in generalizing our findings and conclusions.

 Thinking Like a Scientist in Real Life

Tell Us How We're Doing!

It seems that every time we visit a store, a restaurant, or even a website, someone asks us to complete a survey. These surveys may ask about the quality of the experience we just had, the level of customer service provided, or suggestions for improving the company itself. While it is certainly important for organizations to receive feedback if they wish to improve, we cannot help but wonder about the quality of the data generated by these surveys. Who takes the time to complete them? Most likely, survey respondents are those people who had some type of extremely positive or negative experience that prompted them to make the effort to complete the survey. If this is true, then we must question how representative the survey is. If a business collects biased data, their conclusions will contain bias as well, which is a recipe for making poor decisions. While surveying people is very easy if we want to learn about their thoughts, feelings, or behaviors, survey designers must always consider how best to obtain a representative sample. Simply asking customers at the bottom of their receipt to go online to complete a survey may not be enough. Always remember that high-quality data is best for helping you to make good decisions, and that high-quality data starts with a high-quality sample.

Based on these considerations, we decide to use a web survey for our study. Rather than using a random sampling plan, we will invite the entire population of new first-year students to complete our survey titled "Campus Life and You." We will send each new student up to three e-mail invitations, and, to encourage participation, we will emphasize that completing the survey will help us better understand differences in how people view campus activities. By clicking on the "begin survey" link, participants will be providing their informed consent to participate in the study with the following description: "The survey asks participants to indicate their level of agreement with various statements about how they view themselves and different extracurricular activities available on campus." After participants either complete the survey or indicate that they no longer wish to participate in the study, a "thank-you" webpage will appear to debrief our participants. The debriefing webpage will provide a fuller description of the purpose of our study, whom they should contact if they have further questions, and a coupon for a free 20-ounce fountain drink from the student café. We will also remind participants that all survey responses are confidential and that their names will not be added to any e-mail lists.

Focus on Open Science: Preregistering Your Hypotheses, Materials, and Data Analysis Plan

Finally, before collecting our data, we will preregister our correlational study on an open science website (e.g., http://osf.io). We will upload the actual scales we are using and describe our sampling plan. Once we determine the analyses we need to conduct to answer our research question, we should also preregister our data analysis plan. Because we are doing a correlational study, we will need to do several things. First, we will describe how we are calculating participants' overall scores on both scales. Second, we will assess the internal consistency reliability of our scales. Finally, we will not only describe and summarize our data, but also test our specific hypothesis. Because our data analysis plan will outline the exact tests we need to run, it will be easier for us to avoid the temptation of conducting analyses until we find something that works. Once we collect all of the data, we can make the data set available to other researchers via an open science website.

▶ Why is open science important to the research process? SEE CHAPTER 2, p. 25

YOUR TURN 7.2

1. As Allan begins to complete a study habits survey for his professor, he notices that if he answers the questions truthfully, he may not look like a particularly conscientious student. Which of the following concerns may be creating a bias in this survey?
   a. Social desirability
   b. Demand characteristics
   c. Acquiescent response set
   d. Evaluation apprehension

2. Erika wants to conduct a survey to compare how students with different majors feel about the reduction in library hours on campus. Which type of sampling plan would be the best way to increase the representativeness of her survey sample?
   a. Convenience sampling
   b. Simple random sampling
   c. Stratified random sampling
   d. Area probability sampling

3. If Tyrone wants to reduce the likelihood that his participants will be able to guess the purpose of his survey, what should he include in this survey?
   a. Open-ended items
   b. Distractor items
   c. Forced-choice items
   d. Alternative form items

How did you do? Turn to the end of the chapter to check your answers.

Statistics: In Search of Answers

Let's assume that we conducted our survey over the first 3 weeks of the fall semester, resulting in 474 completed surveys. One of the benefits of using a web-based survey is that as soon as participants finish the survey, their responses are automatically added to a spreadsheet with the responses of the other participants. The typical format of this data spreadsheet, which we access through our survey software, is that each column represents a survey item and each row represents a single participant. In **Figure 7.5**, if we look at the data along any row, we will know that participant's response to each survey item. If we look at the data in any one column, we can see all of the responses to that particular survey item. With our data collection completed and entered into a spreadsheet, we are almost ready to see how self-concept clarity relates to interest in joining a fraternity or sorority.

However, we are not there just yet. Remember that we are operationally defining self-concept clarity as one's overall score on the Self-Concept Clarity Scale, while interest in joining a fraternity or sorority is operationally defined as the total score on our Attitude Toward Greek Organizations Scale. For both scales, higher scores mean either greater self-concept clarity or a more positive attitude. Before we can actually calculate these total scores, we will need to account for participants' responses to the reversed-coded scale items. As we discussed earlier, we worded reverse-coded items in the opposite direction of the other scale items to minimize a potential acquiescent response set bias. The first thing we need to do is identify which scale items need to be reverse-coded. To remind ourselves, we marked each of these items with an asterisk. The first item

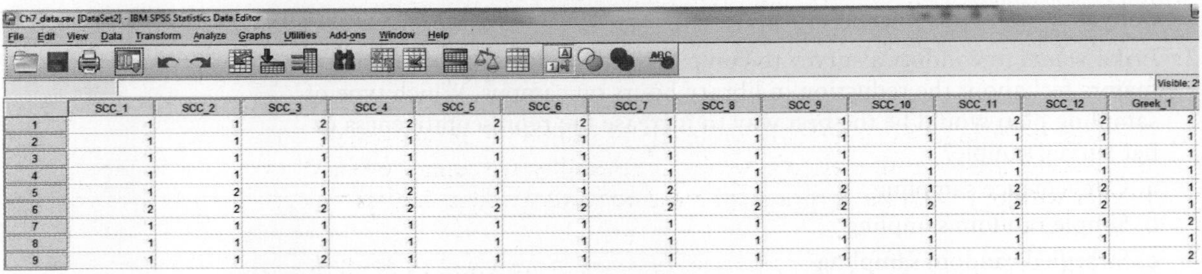

	SCC_1	SCC_2	SCC_3	SCC_4	SCC_5	SCC_6	SCC_7	SCC_8	SCC_9	SCC_10	SCC_11	SCC_12	Greek_1
1	1	1	2	2	2	2	1	1	1	1	2	2	2
2	1	1	1	1	1	1	1	1	1	1	1	1	1
3	1	1	1	1	1	1	1	1	1	1	1	1	1
4	1	1	1	1	1	1	1	1	1	1	1	1	1
5	1	2	1	2	1	1	2	1	2	1	2	2	1
6	2	2	2	2	2	2	2	2	2	2	2	2	1
7	1	1	1	1	1	1	1	1	1	1	1	1	2
8	1	1	1	1	1	1	1	1	1	1	1	1	1
9	1	1	2	1	1	1	1	1	1	1	1	1	2

FIGURE 7.5 Example of SPSS Data Spreadsheet. *(SPSS)*

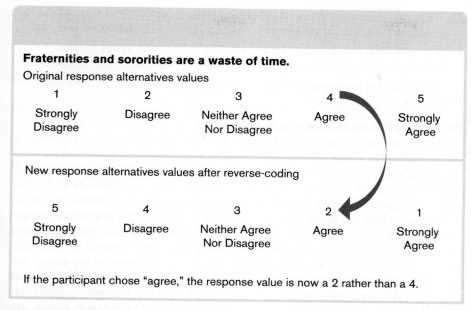

Fraternities and sororities are a waste of time.

Original response alternatives values

1	2	3	4	5
Strongly Disagree	Disagree	Neither Agree Nor Disagree	Agree	Strongly Agree

New response alternatives values after reverse-coding

5	4	3	2	1
Strongly Disagree	Disagree	Neither Agree Nor Disagree	Agree	Strongly Agree

If the participant chose "agree," the response value is now a 2 rather than a 4.

FIGURE 7.6 Example of Reverse-Coding.

that requires reverse-coding on the Attitude Toward Greek Organizations Scale is #4: "Fraternities and sororities are a waste of time."

If we want to have higher scores mean the participant is higher on that variable, we need to use reverse-coding before we sum the items to determine the participants' overall scale score. Looking at our spreadsheet, we find the column that contains all of the responses to that item. Going down the column, whenever we see a "1," we change it to a "5." If it is a "2," we make it a "4." "4s" become "2s," and "5s" become "1s." "3s" remain as is, as shown in **Figure 7.6**. We then sum the responses on each scale (ignoring the distractor items, which are also included in our spreadsheet) to establish our measurement of the participants' self-concept clarity and their attitude toward joining a Greek organization. Fortunately, our spreadsheet program can quickly do this reverse-coding and summing, minimizing the possibility of our making any errors in our calculations. Adding up the number of fraternity or sorority e-mail lists participants checked off provides us with a behavioral measurement of interest in joining a Greek organization.

Selecting the Proper Tool

We are now ready to use statistics to accomplish four tasks:

1. We need to evaluate the internal consistency reliability of our two scales. If our scales are poor in internal consistency reliability, we cannot proceed further with our analyses. Inconsistent measurements are meaningless measurements.

2. We want to summarize and describe the responses we received from all of the participants on each of our variables.

3. We want to measure to what extent self-concept clarity and interest in joining a Greek organization are related to each other based on our data.

4. We need to decide whether we believe this association exists in the population as a whole, not just among the participants in our sample.

Fortunately, there are enough tools in our statistical toolbox to easily accomplish these tasks.

Evaluating Internal Consistency Reliability

The literature has already established the internal consistency reliability of the Self-Concept Clarity Scale (Campbell et al., 1996), but it is always wise to check if the scale is also reliable for the population we are testing. We certainly need to look at the internal consistency reliability for our attitude scale. One common strategy for assessing the internal consistency of a scale is calculating a statistic called **Cronbach's alpha** (Cronbach, 1951). This statistic evaluates how well the individual scale items "hang together," or are consistent with each other. The values for Cronbach's alpha can range from 0 to 1.0. Zero means that there is no internal consistency among the items in the scale; they are essentially measuring completely different things. Conversely, 1.0 means that all of the items measure the same exact thing. While this may sound ideal, it really is not because it implies there is complete redundancy among the items. In effect, you are asking the same exact question, just in slightly different ways. For acceptable internal consistency reliability, you ideally want your Cronbach's alpha to be at least .70 (Streiner, 2003). We found that, for our data, Cronbach's alpha for the Self-Concept Clarity Scale was .95. Cronbach's alpha for our attitude scale was lower, at .82, but still in the acceptable range. We do not compute Cronbach's alpha for the behavioral measures, as they are not scale items.

Summarizing Our Measurements

Our next task is to get a general idea of how our participants tended to respond to our scales. That is, we want to summarize our variables' measurements using the descriptive statistics we introduced in Chapter 6. Frequency distributions can summarize our demographic variables, gender and ethnicity, as they are categorical variables. The three other variables are continuous variables, so we should use a measure of central tendency to summarize these measurements. Although we could use the mode, which is the most frequently occurring score, or the median, which is the midpoint score for our set of measurements, the arithmetic mean is the preferred measure of central tendency to use with continuous variables.

While knowing that the arithmetic mean is important for summarizing our data, the mean does not tell us the full story about each measurement. For example, based on our output, the mean number of fraternities or sororities our participants checked off in our behavioral measure was approximately 2. However, this number does not indicate that all of the participants only wanted their names added to two different fraternity or sorority e-mail lists. Rather, there are likely differences among the participants' responses, though it is unclear

▶ What are the different ways we can summarize our measurements? How might we create a single score to represent a group of scores? SEE APPENDIX A, p. 483

Cronbach's alpha
a statistic used to evaluate the internal consistency reliability of a scale; can range from 0 to 1.0.

how much difference there is, and measures of central tendency cannot help us determine this information.

To determine how much participants' measurements differ, we need another statistic that allows us to summarize the **variability** of our data, which is how far or close individual scores are from the mean. When we have continuous variables, the statistic we use to express variability is the **standard deviation**, represented with the symbol SD. The standard deviation represents how much, on average, an individual participant's score differs or varies from the mean of all the scores. The larger the standard deviation, the greater the variability there is among the scores in a data set (i.e., scores are more spread out). The smaller the standard deviation, the more homogeneity, or similarity, there is among the measurements (i.e., scores are more packed in). If the standard deviation for our behavioral measure was 0, then we would know that all of the participants selected exactly two Greek organizations. However, the actual standard deviation for this variable was 1, so now we know there were differences among the respondents. If the standard deviation had been 2, then we would know that there was much more variation in the number of organizations participants selected. See **Figure 7.7** for an example of two sets of data with differing variability.

variability the degree to which individual measurements of a variable differ from one another.

Measuring Associations

Finally, we need to quantify the degree to which two variables are associated with or related to one another. A correlation is a statistic that does this by representing the degree to which two variables are linearly related. By linear relationship, we mean the extent to which we can predict the measurement on one variable if we know the measurement on another variable. We can then use this statistic to answer our research question. For example, if our hypothesis is correct, knowing someone's degree of self-concept clarity will be a good indication of that person's interest in joining a Greek organization. Similarly, you will recall that we used a correlation to assess

standard deviation a statistic used to indicate how much, on average, an individual score differs from the arithmetic mean of the scores; represented with the symbol SD.

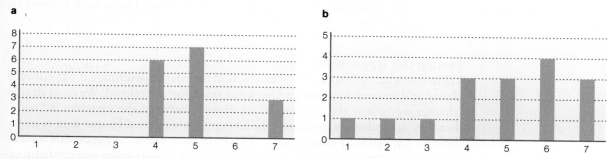

FIGURE 7.7 Two Sets of Data With Differing Variability. While the means may be the same for both sets of data, the variability tells us something important. Most of the participants responded similarly in the first group, but there was much more disagreement in the second group. It is always important to look at both the central tendency and the variability of a set of data.

statistical hypothesis testing a procedure for evaluating the probability of obtaining one's results given the researcher's prediction; this probability is represented with the symbol *p*.

statistically significant the conclusion a researcher makes when the probability is that one's hypothesis is likely to be correct given the data collected.

test-retest reliability earlier to allow us to examine how well participants' initial scores on our scale predicted their scores after completing the scale a second time.

As shown in **Figure 7.8**, we typically represent a correlation with the symbol *r*. The value of a correlation can range from -1 to $+1$. This value actually contains two important pieces of information about the nature of the association between the two variables. First, ignoring the sign, the value indicates how *strongly* related the two variables are. A correlation with a value of 0 means that the two variables are completely unrelated. A value of 1 (regardless of sign) tells us that the two variables relate perfectly such that by knowing the measurement for one variable, we can perfectly predict the measurement on the other variable.

The correlation value's sign ($+$ or $-$) is the second important piece of information, as it tells us the direction of the association. A positive sign indicates that higher measurement values on one variable correspond to higher measurements on the other variable (i.e., they have a positive relation). Likewise, a positive sign indicates lower measurements on a variable are associated with lower measurements on the other variable (also a positive association). Essentially, the variables move in the same direction. In our study, we are assessing interest in joining a Greek organization with both an attitude scale and a behavioral measure. We would expect that participants who score high on our scale should also sign up for more fraternity or sorority e-mail lists. Similarly, those who score low on the scale should sign up for fewer Greek e-mail lists.

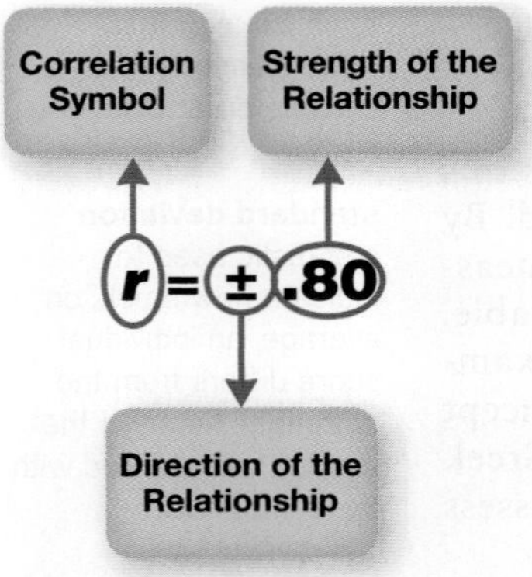

A negative sign with the correlation value indicates that higher measurements on one variable correspond to lower measurements on the other variable, and vice versa (they have a negative or opposite relation). If there is a negative relation between self-concept clarity and interest in going Greek, then those with high self-concept clarity would have low interest in joining a Greek organization. Similarly, those with low self-concept clarity would have high interest in Greek life.

FIGURE 7.8 Anatomy of a Correlation.

Testing Our Hypothesis

There is one last statistical tool that we need in order to determine if self-concept clarity and interest in joining a Greek organization are related. We must decide whether we believe the association we observe between the variables is "real," that they are indeed related, or if the association suggested by our data is just a fluke, or happened by chance alone. This leads us to **statistical hypothesis testing**, where we evaluate the likelihood of obtaining our results given our predictions. We use the symbol *p* to indicate this probability level. We will save you the longer explanation for now, but suffice it to say that if the probability (*p*) is less than 5%, we conclude that our finding is **statistically significant**, which means that the association we found is probably not a simple chance occurrence. Thus, we can conclude that our hypothesis is supported given the data we collected.

▶ Want to learn more about statistical hypothesis testing? SEE APPENDIX A, p. 486

Writing the Method Section in APA Style

Method

Participants

Four hundred and seventy-four new first-year students at a comprehensive university in the Midwestern United States completed our web-based survey, entitled "Campus Life and You." Sixty-one percent of the participants were female. Fifty-nine percent were White (non-Hispanic), 18% Black or African American, 9% Hispanic or Latino, and 9% Asian, Asian American, or Pacific Islander. We provided all participants with a certificate for a free fountain drink at the university's student café for taking part in the study. Both the gender and ethnic composition of the sample were comparable to the overall population of incoming students at this university.

Measures

Self-Concept Clarity Scale (Campbell et al., 1996). This measure assessed how confidently and clearly participants defined the self. This 12-item Likert scale consists of items such as, "In general, I have a clear sense of who I am and what I am," and, "I spend a lot of time wondering about what kind of person I really am." Participants indicated how much they agreed or disagreed with each statement using a five-point scale (1 = strongly disagree; 5 = strongly agree). For the current study, Cronbach's alpha was .95.

Attitude toward Greek organizations. We developed a 12-item Likert scale to measure each participant's attitude toward college fraternities and sororities. Participants responded to statements such as, "To become active in the social life on campus, I should join a fraternity or sorority," and, "Fraternities and sororities are a waste of time" using a five-point scale (1 = strongly disagree; 5 = strongly agree). We included seven additional distractor items that we discarded when determining the participant's overall attitude score. Pilot testing indicated that the test-retest reliability of the scale was satisfactory, $r = .84$, $p < .01$. Cronbach's alpha for the present study was .82.

Behavioral measure of Greek interest. Depending on their gender, we gave participants descriptions of the university's five fraternities or five sororities. We told participants, "Please check off for which of these fraternities or sororities, if any, you want to be notified about upcoming new member recruiting events." The total number of fraternities or sororities participants selected served as our behavioral measure of interest in joining a Greek organization.

Procedure

We created two versions of our survey using web-based survey software. In one version, participants first completed the Self-Concept Clarity Scale and then the Attitude Toward Greek Organizations Scale. We reversed this order for the second version. All participants then completed the behavioral interest measure followed by the demographics section. The web survey software randomly determined which version of the survey participants received.

All new first-year students at the institution received an e-mail along with a link to the survey during the second week of the fall semester, inviting them to participate in a survey about their views on their selves and campus life. We sent two follow-up reminder e-mails, approximately 1 week apart, to those students who had not yet completed our survey. Students were able to opt out of receiving any reminder e-mails by clicking on the "I do not wish to participate" button on the initial page of the survey. Participants provided informed consent by clicking on the "begin survey" button. Of the approximately 1,200 new students initially invited to participate in the study, 474 completed the survey for a 40% response rate.

Writing the Results in APA Style: Correlational Statistics

> ### Results
>
> The mean score on the Self-Concept Clarity Scale was 35.20 (SD = 12.60). For the Attitude Toward Greek Organizations Scale, it was 41.70 (SD = 8.00). Participants signed up for an average of 2.10 (SD = 1.0) fraternities or sororities.
>
> There was a statistically significant, positive relation between one's self-concept clarity and one's attitude toward Greek organizations, r = .64, p < .001. Participants with higher self-concept clarity tended to have a more positive attitude toward Greek organizations. Our behavioral measure of interest, however, was not significantly correlated with self-concept clarity, r = .04, p = .37. Likewise, this behavioral measure was not significantly correlated with attitude toward Greek organizations, r = .07, p = .14.

Don't Just Tell Me, Show Me: Using Tables

Sometimes, numerical information provided within the text of a paragraph can be overwhelming or difficult to follow. In addition to graphs (see Chapter 6), psychologists use tables to display their data. **Table 7.3** provides a summary of both the descriptive statistics associated with our three variables and the correlations between each of them.

TABLE 7.3

Correlations and Descriptive Statistics for the Three Study Measures				
	M (SD)	Self-Concept Clarity	Attitude Toward Greek Organizations	Behavioral Interest
Self-Concept Clarity	35.2 (12.6)		.64*	.04
Attitude Toward Greek Organizations	41.7 (8.0)			.07
Behavioral Interest	2.1 (1.0)			

* p < .001.

Our Research Plan at a Glance

What Is Our Research Question? Is there an association between students' sense of self and their interest in joining a fraternity or sorority?

What Is Our Design? We are engaging in a correlational design using a self-report, web-based survey.

Why Are We Using This Design? Correlational designs allow us to measure how strong of a relation or association there may be between two variables. We are using self-report measures, as one's sense of self and attitude toward Greek organizations are introspective and hard to observe.

What Are Our Variables? We have two variables in our study, neither of which we are manipulating: one's sense of self and one's attitude toward Greek organizations. We are measuring sense of self using the already established Self-Concept Clarity Scale. We are using our self-developed Attitude Toward Greek Organizations scale to assess interest in joining a fraternity or sorority. We are also measuring this interest behaviorally by asking participants which fraternities or sororities, if any, they would like to learn more about.

What Are Our Hypotheses? As we do not have a specific prediction, we are making a nondirectional hypothesis that there is an association between one's sense of self and one's interest in joining a fraternity or sorority.

Who Are Our Participants? Rather than use a sampling plan, we send all incoming first-year students at our university an e-mail invitation to complete our web-based survey. We offer an incentive for participating in our study.

What Ethical Considerations Do We Need to Keep in Mind?
- We do not ask participants questions that might be overly sensitive, invasive, or irrelevant to our research question.
- Respondents must provide informed consent when they click on the link to begin the survey.
- We are using an incentive to participate that is not excessive or seemingly coercive.

What Is Our Data Analysis Plan?
1. **Calculate our data.** We reverse code the appropriate items from the scales, and sum the responses to the reversed coded and nonreversed coded items to create the overall score for each scale. Then we calculate Cronbach's alpha to evaluate the internal consistency reliability for each scale.
2. **Test our hypothesis.** We compute the descriptive statistics for each scale, calculating the correlations between the scales and determining which correlations are statistically significant.

Want to practice the analyses for this research yourself? Ask your instructor about the data set that accompanies this study.

Let's Discuss What Happened

Our study set out to determine if greater self-knowledge relates to interest in joining a Greek organization in college. Using data collected from a web-based survey, we calculated a correlation to test our hypothesis. We are now ready to review and try to explain what we found in terms of our research question. We will reflect on how this new knowledge contributes to our understanding of self-concept clarity and suggest future directions this research can take.

What Did We Find?

We found that participants with higher self-concept clarity had a more positive attitude toward Greek organizations in college. However, self-concept clarity was not associated with the number of fraternity or sorority e-mail lists that participants wanted to be added to. Similarly, attitude toward Greek organizations on the Likert scale was not associated with the behavior of signing up on the e-mail list. This lack of concurrent validity raises concerns about the criterion validity of the scale we developed. It appears that our attitude scale and our behavioral measure may have been assessing different things.

Why These Findings?

We did find that people with greater self-concept clarity had a more positive attitude toward Greek organizations. One possible explanation is that individuals with high self-concept clarity do not believe Greek organizations threaten one's sense of self. This could be the result of high-clarity individuals having so much certainty about who they are that their sense of self is not easily threatened. It could also be that rather than seeing a Greek organization as a threat to their personal identity, those with high clarity have an easier time seeing how the organization can add to their social identity. Whether self-concept clarity influences one's actual decision to join a fraternity or sorority is unknown.

Psychologists have long recognized that people's attitudes do not necessarily correspond with their behavior (Ajzen & Fishbein, 2005). Attitudes are more predictive of actual behavior when they are specific to that behavior. Looking back at the Likert scale we developed, our items involved one's attitude toward Greek organizations in general, not the specific fraternities and sororities at the university where we collected our data. In addition, the items on our scale did not necessarily gauge one's actual interest in joining a Greek organization, unlike our behavioral measure. This may explain why our scale's measurement of attitude toward Greek organizations did not significantly relate to actual expressed interest in joining the specific fraternities or sororities on campus.

What Could Be Improved?

We thought that our Likert scale measured interest in joining a Greek organization, but it now appears it has assessed attitude toward fraternities and sororities in general. This issue points out the importance of developing a conceptual definition of a variable before creating a scale to measure that variable. If we had a clearer conceptual definition of "interest in joining a Greek organization," we would have better guidance in the types of items we should develop for our scale. While pilot testing helped to establish the reliability of our scale, the current findings are useful for evaluating the validity of our scale. What we have learned will help us make changes in our scale for future research in this area.

The present study asked participants if they wanted to receive information about Greek recruiting events. This may not have been the best way to determine whether or not students wanted to actually join a fraternity or sorority.

For example, students may sign up for information to appear social or to learn more about who joins those organizations, without any actual intention of joining themselves.

Nevertheless, we did learn that self-concept clarity and attitude toward Greek organizations are significantly related. Because the demographics of our participants generally reflect the students initially invited to participate in our study, we do not believe a nonresponse bias represents a serious threat to the external validity of our findings. However, we need to replicate our study at other institutions to increase our confidence in this conclusion.

What's Next?

While self-concept clarity may not relate to students' actual desire to join a Greek organization in college, in light of previous research on self-concept clarity (e.g., Lewandowski et al., 2010), future research should look at self-concept clarity's role in students' subsequent satisfaction with and commitment to their fraternity or sorority. It is also possible that self-concept clarity is more closely related to desired membership in other types of groups. For example, if students view academics as more central to their sense of self in college, self-concept clarity may be more relevant for groups or activities that directly relate to students' majors or future careers.

YOUR TURN 7.3

1. Researchers use Cronbach's alpha to evaluate the _____ of a scale.
   a. internal consistency reliability
   b. test-retest reliability
   c. alternative-form reliability
   d. construct reliability

2. To determine the likelihood that your hypothesis is correct given your data, you should
   a. calculate the correlation between the measurements of your two variables.
   b. calculate statistical significance.
   c. assess the variability of the two sets of measurements.
   d. compare the mean, median, and modes of the measurements.

3. What was a major problem with our study that limited the conclusions we could draw?
   a. We were only able to get 40% of our invited participants to complete the survey.
   b. Social desirability concerns may have influenced the participants' responses.
   c. There was too much variability for one of our measurements.
   d. One of our measurements may not have been a valid measure.

How did you do? Turn to the end of the chapter to check your answers.

Final Thoughts

In this chapter, we conducted a correlational research study examining the association between self-concept clarity and attitude toward Greek organizations, and using self-report scales, as these variables are not easily observable. Because a measure of attitude toward Greek organizations did not exist, we created a scale and took steps to demonstrate its reliability and validity. To efficiently collect data from a large sample, we incorporated our scales into a web-based survey. We learned that psychologists use correlations as their statistical tool for evaluating associations between two variables. Identifying such associations is important for adding to our understanding of the world. However, our knowledge becomes limited if we focus on how just two variables relate to each other. Ultimately, we want to identify causal relationships in our world. Fortunately, as we will learn, experiments are very useful in helping us accomplish this important scientific goal.

CHAPTER 7   Review

Review Questions

1. Darren and his friends are arguing about who has the worst part-time job. They decide to create a scale to assess how "bad" a job is so that they can objectively compare their different places of employment. This means that Darren and his friends will be doing what to settle their argument?

   a. They will be creating a standardized measure to quantify their workplace experiences.

   b. They will be conducting a correlational study of their workplace experiences.

   c. They will be developing open-ended questions to compare their workplace experiences.

   d. They will be creating a plan for systematically observing one another's workplaces.

2. Whenever he is asked a closed-ended question, Julio refuses to use the endpoints in the provided set of response options. Julio is exhibiting which response bias?

   a. The acquiescent response set

   b. The error of central tendency

   c. Participant judgment bias

   d. Random response bias

3. Tyrone believes his psychology test was unfair because the questions did not appear to reflect what was discussed in class or in the textbook. Tyrone is upset because he believes the test has poor

   a. internal consistency reliability.

   b. construct validity.

   c. criterion validity.

   d. content validity.

4. As a restaurant server, Lonnie notices that his customers always say that their meal was "fine" whenever he asks them. Wanting to get a more accurate understanding of his customers' satisfaction with their dining experience, Lonnie decides to survey each of his dining parties. What is the best way for him to minimize potential yea-saying?

   a. Include some reverse-coded items in the survey

   b. Extensively pilot test his survey to establish its reliability

   c. Use a forced choice scale

   d. Avoid asking double-barreled questions

5. A college director of admissions is wondering if a new measure of college preparation will effectively identify students who will be successful in college. Which type of validity should the director consider in order to answer this question?

   a. Construct validity

   b. Content validity

   c. Criterion validity

   d. Face validity

6. Working as an intern for a political campaign, Fernando needs to develop a sampling plan for surveying potential voters' candidate preference. If Fernando wants to make sure his sample is representative of potential voters across the congressional district, he should use

   a. random assignment.

   b. simple random sampling.

   c. area probability sampling.

   d. stratified random sampling.

7. While reading a description of a scale in a research paper, you notice that the author includes the scale's Cronbach's alpha. The author is providing the scale's

   a. test-retest reliability.

   b. statistical significance.

   c. convergent validity.

   d. internal consistency reliability.

8. Clinton finds that the results in his study are statistically significant. This means that his results

   a. have practical significance.

   b. are of significant importance.

   c. are unlikely the result of bias.

   d. are unlikely to have occurred by chance alone.

9. To evaluate how similar individual measurements are to one another, one should look at the
   a. Cronbach's alpha associated with the measurement.
   b. standard deviation of the measurement.
   c. correlation between the measurements.
   d. reliability of the measurement.

10. Earnestine finds that there is a positive correlation between one's score on a sensation-seeking scale and one's attitude toward amusement parks. This means that
    a. those higher in sensation-seeking tend to like amusement parks.
    b. those higher in sensation-seeking tend to have a negative attitude toward amusement parks.
    c. the sensation-seeking scale and the attitude scale have satisfactory alternative-form reliability.
    d. both measures have good convergent validity.

11. What is the difference between reliability and validity of a measurement?

12. How are simple random sampling, stratified random sampling, and area probability sampling similar? How do they differ?

13. What is the difference between nondirectional and directional hypotheses? When would you use each?

Applying What You've Learned

1. Develop an open-ended question and a closed-ended question that address the same issue. Have several of your friends answer both questions and then compare the types of information each question provides. How might using each type of question be beneficial for answering your research question? What are the limitations associated with each type?

2. Find five simple poll questions from a variety of websites. Evaluate the quality of the questions using what you learned about writing quality survey items.

3. Go to http://www.quibblo.com/take/survey and find a survey of a psychological construct that interests you. Create a new and improved set of questions to measure the same construct.

4. Find another survey at http://www.quibblo.com/take/survey that interests you. How might you assess the content validity of that survey? Its construct validity? Its criterion validity?

5. Summated ratings scales (also known as Likert scales) are just one type of scale used by psychological researchers. Other types of scales include

Thurstone scales, Guttman scales, and semantic differential scales (see http://changingminds.org/explanations/research/measurement/measurement.htm for information about these scales). How do these different scale types differ from Likert scales? What types of research questions would you use each type of scale to answer?

6. Review all of your Facebook, Instagram, or Snapchat connections and calculate the percentage that are "single," "married," "in a relationship," or "other." Then use simple random sampling to choose 20 of these people and calculate the percentages that are in each relationship category. Do the same using stratified random sampling with gender as your two subgroups. Finally, draw a sample of 20 of these people using area probability sampling based on whether or not the person currently lives in the same state as you. Again, calculate the percentage of this sample in each relationship category. Compare the results from the three different random samples to the actual relationship statuses of your social media connections. Which random sampling plan resulted in percentages that were closest to the actual percentages? Which plan yielded the least accurate results?

7. THE NOVICE RESEARCHER: Have a group of your friends complete the Rosenberg self-esteem scale at http://www.wwnorton.com/college/psych/psychsci/media/rosenberg.htm, as well as provide you with the number of Instagram followers that they currently have. Enter the data into an SPSS spreadsheet or another similar statistical software program. After reverse-coding the relevant scale items, calculate the mean scale score for each participant. Calculate the Cronbach's alpha associated with your scale. Finally, correlate the participants' mean scale score with the number of followers that they have. Is this correlation positive or negative? What does this mean? Is this correlation statistically significant? If so, what does that mean?

8. DIG INTO THE NUMBERS: Analyze the supplemental correlational study data provided to your instructor using a Cronbach's alpha, descriptive statistics, and a correlation in SPSS. Based on the example provided in this chapter, write an APA-style results section based on your analyses.

Key Concepts

acquiescent response set, p. 209

alternative-form reliability, p. 213

area probability sampling, p. 222

closed-ended question, p. 203

concurrent validity, p. 215

construct validity, p. 214

content validity, p. 214

convergent validity, p. 214

correlation, p. 213

correlational study, p. 202

criterion validity, p. 215

Cronbach's alpha, p. 228

directional hypothesis, p. 217

discriminant validity, p. 215

distractor items, p. 218

equivalent-form reliability, p. 213

error of central tendency, p. 210

evaluation apprehension, p. 218

Answers to YOUR TURN

Your Turn 7.1: 1. a; 2. d; 3. c

Your Turn 7.2: 1. d; 2. c; 3. b

Your Turn 7.3: 1. a; 2. b; 3. d

Answers to Multiple-Choice Review Questions

1. a; 2. b; 3. d; 4. a; 5. c; 6. c; 7. d; 8. d; 9. b; 10. a

Two-Group Design

Texting: I Can't Get You Out of My Mind

Ariel Skelley/DigitalVision/Getty Images

LEARNING OUTCOMES

After reading this chapter, you should be able to:

- Provide operational definitions for key variables.
- Identify key design issues with two-group research.
- Identify factors involved in establishing causation.

- Explain how control is established in an experiment.
- Discuss the importance of group independence and random assignment.
- Write a results section for an independent samples *t*-test.

Something to Think About . . .

You have probably found yourself sitting in class dutifully trying to pay attention, but distracted by a window, people passing by the door, someone tapping a pen, a classmate with a cold, or some idiosyncrasy of the professor. (Really, how many times can a person say "alrighty then" in one class?) While these are surely all distractions, many people view technology as the biggest distraction of all. At this point, it is common knowledge that texting while driving is dangerous. If your syllabi are any indication, it seems professors are equally concerned about how technology can distract your learning. Whether you are checking Facebook on your laptop, tweeting from your tablet, texting from your smartphone, or doing all three, your professor probably does not condone this behavior. If you think about it, you can understand your professor's perspective. These forms of technology can lead you to miss course material, or, worse, distract other students, leading them to miss things. Then again, it is all too easy to blame technology for an age-old problem. You play with your smartphone; your parents passed notes. Technology-based classroom distractions are not a "new" problem, but, rather, the latest version of a long-standing issue. Besides, before we worry too much about smartphones' potential classroom harm, we need to see some proof that smartphone use is actually distracting.

In order to combat the perceived evils of technology, many professors craft highly restrictive course policies that treat using portable technology as a form of high treason. However, is it possible that by invoking an absolute ban, these professors are creating more of a distraction? We will answer that question with another question: Have you ever been hungry and tried to avoid thinking about food? As soon as you tell yourself not to think about being hungry, what do you feel? Hungry. Clearly, this method does not work very well. By trying to avoid thinking about food, you tend to think about that exact thing even more. Are you still not a believer? Try this: Right now, no matter what, do *not* under any circumstance think of Donald Trump naked.

Yikes! See that? You thought about exactly what we asked you *not* to think about. Sorry about that! Next, we'd like you *not* to think about a cute puppy playing with a ball. That image should make it all better. This little exercise helps us demonstrate a point: Not thinking about something is really hard. If we are truly "addicted" to our technology, or just really attached to it, a rule that forbids us from using our devices essentially asks us not to think about them. Ironically, this could create a major distraction. It would be great if someone could design a study to test if well-intentioned, antitechnology professors are actually inhibiting your learning. That someone could be you.

Introduction to Our Research Question

Before we design a study to test our idea, we should state our key question a bit more clearly. Although smartphones allow us to do many different things, we will focus on texting because that seems to be the number one offender on professors' lists. We want to answer the general question:

RESEARCH ? Can trying to ignore a text message lead to distraction?

Compared to our research questions from previous chapters, this question seems to make a more specific prediction about a type of behavior that leads to a specific outcome. Our focus has moved beyond merely describing what is taking place, to identifying how one factor (ignoring text messages) can lead to changes in another factor (distraction). To answer this type of question, we will need to use experimental research to determine cause and effect. But let's not get too far ahead of ourselves just yet. If professors have antitexting classroom policies, there must be research on the detrimental effects of using technology. Let's see some evidence.

▶ What is the difference between experimental and nonexperimental designs? SEE CHAPTER 2, p. 38

Reviewing the Literature: What Do We Already Know About This Topic?

If we are going to conduct a well-designed study, we should familiarize ourselves with the existing research. It would be useful to know the answers to a few key questions: How prevalent is student texting in class? Does texting have any detrimental effects? What is the evidence that texting is distracting while driving? What about for learning or thinking, in general? Are there any benefits to texting? Has anyone looked at the consequences of preventing texting? Based on a literature search and reading through several articles, we have taken notes and written our own summaries of a few relevant studies that will help us understand the research in this area.

▶ Curious about how best to take notes on research articles? SEE APPENDIX B, p. 498

Prevalence of Texting

Tindell, D. R. (2012). The use and abuse of cell phones and text messaging in the classroom: A survey of college students. *College Teaching, 60,* 1–9. doi:10.1080/87567555.2011.604802

This study examined 269 college students to determine the extent to which students used their cellular devices in class. An overwhelming majority (95%) of students brought their cellular devices to lectures on a daily basis, though 91% said they had it set on "vibrate." Of these students, most (92%) used their cellular devices in order to send SMS (short message service) messages during lectures at some point, 97% said they were aware of other students doing it, and a small number (10%) reported that they used their cellular device during a test. A majority of students (61.6%) agreed with the statement, "Yes, I see no problem with using a cell phone to text in class as long as I am not disturbing other students," while some (31.5%) believed that sending texts negatively influenced students "through loss of attention and/or poor grades."

The Influence of Texting on Driving

Wilson, F. A., & Stimpson, J. P. (2010). Trends in fatalities from distracted driving in the United States, 1999 to 2008. *American Journal of Public Health, 100,* 2213–2219. doi:10.2105/AJPH.2009.187179

Researchers studied data on driving fatalities in the United States from 1999 through 2008 to determine how they related to texting and cell phone use. Their analysis indicated that distracted driving fatalities decreased from 1999 to 2005, but rose (up 28%) from 2005 to 2008. The researchers' analyses led them to conclude that texting was responsible for an additional 16,000 fatalities over a 6-year period from 2001 to 2007.

The Negative Impact of Technology on Learning and Cognition

Rosen, L. D., Lim, A. F., Carrier, M., & Cheever, N. A. (2011). An empirical examination of the educational impact of text message-induced task switching in the classroom: Educational implications and strategies to enhance learning. *Educational Psychology, 17,* 163–177.

To determine whether texting has an effect on memory recollection of classroom material, researchers assigned 185 undergraduate students to one of three groups: no texting, medium texting (8–15 texts), and excessive texting (16 texts or more). Researchers manipulated texting by sending messages to participants while participants watched a 30-minute video of a class, and then gave participants a memory test based on the video. The excessive-texting group had the worst test scores of the three experimental groups. Those who typed more in their text messages and received longer messages also did worse than those sending/receiving shorter messages.

Smith, T., Isaak, M. I., Senette, C. G., & Abadie, B. G. (2011). Effects of cell-phone and text-message distractions on true and false recognition. *Cyberpsychology, Behavior, & Social Networking, 14,* 351–358. doi:10.1089/cyber.2010.0129

This study tested if distractions from a cellular device and texting could inhibit college students' ability on a cognitive identification task (i.e., memory of words). Researchers randomly assigned 64 college students to one of three groups: no distraction, distraction (answered their phones if they rang), or different distraction (answered their phones using a text message). Groups reviewed two sets of 24 related words (e.g., diaper, crib), then took an identification exam to test their recall of the words. Results indicated that participants in the no-distraction group performed best, while both distraction groups had worse performance.

Potential Benefits of Texting

Brett, P. (2011). Students' experiences and engagement with SMS for learning in higher education. *Innovations in Education & Teaching International, 48,* 137–147. doi: 10.1080/14703297.2011.564008

It might be possible that text messages can promote students' learning in educational settings through texting with tutors. To test this, researchers asked 1,121 students questions about texting behavior, then transcribed their responses. Students viewed text messages from tutors as intrusive, mainly because they viewed cell phones as being used for primarily personal reasons (i.e., texting friends and family). Students did acknowledge that texting kept them in constant contact with the tutor, which they saw as beneficial if it was consistent with students' perceived needs.

Drouin, M. A. (2011). College students' text messaging, use of textese and literacy skills. *Journal of Computer Assisted Learning, 27,* 67–75. doi:10.1111/j.1365-2729. 2010.00399.x

To determine if texting and the use of textese (e.g., "LOL" or "IMO") hindered literacy skills, researchers had 152 undergraduate students take literacy (reading and spelling) tests, then answer questions about texting behavior and use of textese. Students reported frequent use of texting and use of textese, though use was primarily in the context of texts or e-mails to friends, not professors. Results of the analysis showed that, contrary to previous studies, more self-reported texting was associated with greater literacy. However, participants who reported using more textese in e-mails to professors or on social networking sites had poorer reading accuracy scores.

The Consequences of Preventing Texting

Skierkowski, D., & Wood, R. M. (2012). To text or not to text? The importance of text messaging among college-aged youth. *Computers in Human Behavior, 28,* 744–756. doi:10.1016/j.chb.2011.11.023

This study examined texting behaviors, including the restriction of texting, among 23 psychology students (age 18–23). Results found that texting was the most frequent way students kept in touch. Both frequent and infrequent texters reported difficulty with limiting their texting and higher levels of anxiety when cell use was restricted. The researchers suggested that texting is a norm for this age group, and having texting limited throughout the day may hinder social relationships.

From Ideas to Innovation

We have to hand it to the antitexting professors of the world: Although it may be tough to admit, they seem to be right about texting's negative consequences. However, just because texting on the road can make you a worse driver (Benedetto, Calvi, & D'Amico, 2012) and texting in class can lower test scores (Rosen, Lim, Carrier, & Cheever, 2011) does not mean that a total classroom texting ban is best. Remember that researchers have a number of strategies for coming up with interesting research ideas and hypotheses, one of which is looking for the exception to the rule. Texting has negative consequences, but a complete ban on texting in classrooms may introduce problems as well. In spite of the downsides to texting, there is some research showing that texting may lead to greater literacy (Drouin, 2011), that it can have benefits in an academic context (Brett, 2011), and that restricting texting may provoke anxiety in some students (Skierkowski & Wood, 2012). Our literature search did not reveal any studies that directly examined how trying to ignore text messages may create a distraction, suggesting that our research question may be onto something new. The next time your professor gets annoyed by in-class texting, it would be nice to be able to provide scientific evidence that completely banning smartphone use can have negative consequences, too.

▶ Interested in learning strategies for developing better research questions? SEE CHAPTER 2, p. 26

 ## Research Spotlight

Are Smartphones Good for Friendships?

Smartphones have revolutionized the ways we stay in touch with other people. But have you ever wondered how they can affect our relationships, even when we are not using them? Recent research suggests that the mere presence of a cell phone can undermine relationships. In two studies, researchers asked randomly assigned pairs of strangers to have a conversation in a room with either a nondescript cell phone or an old-fashioned pocket notebook on a nearby desk (Przybylski & Weinstein, 2013). The presence of the cell phone (vs. the notebook) led participants to report less closeness with the partner and lower relationship quality following their conversation. Even when the researcher encouraged participants to talk about a meaningful topic, having a phone nearby still undermined the relationship by evoking less empathy and trust between the partners.

Defining Key Terms: What Do You Mean By ___?

Before we can develop a study, we need to define the key parts of our research question. Specifically, we should determine what we mean by "trying to ignore" and "distraction." While at least one previous study looked at not using one's cell phone (Skierkowski & Wood, 2012), that may not be the same as ignoring it. We all know the concept of ignoring something, but we need to determine how psychologists define "trying to ignore something."

One way to ignore something is to engage in selective attention, where you purposefully focus on important information while screening out distractions (e.g., Wolfe, 2014). Selective attention is responsible for what psychologists call the "cocktail party effect," or the ability to focus on one conversation in a noisy environment while ignoring everything else taking place (Bronkhorst, 2000). Selective attention requires something to focus on and some ongoing distraction to ignore. In a classroom setting, selective attention would involve your ability to pay attention to a lecture amid ongoing distractions. Receiving a text message does not really qualify as an ongoing distraction. Rather, it is an intrusion that enters your awareness when you hear a "ping" or feel a vibration. These experiences are short-lived, but they may trigger a cascade of thoughts about the text message. In this

Take a moment to think about these white bears. Visualize what they are going to do next. Now, for the next 30 seconds, think about anything you want *except* the white bears. Go! Suppressing behaviors and thoughts can be difficult to do. *(Ralph Lee Hopkins/Getty Images)*

context, to effectively ignore the text requires thought suppression, the process of deliberately trying to stop thinking about certain thoughts (Najmi, 2013). At the beginning of the chapter, when we asked you to avoid thinking about President Trump naked, we activated a thought-suppression scenario.

This conceptualization fits in with our original idea about the distraction of ignoring texts. When we try to ignore a text message, we must suppress a variety of thoughts surrounding the text, such as who sent the text, if it is about an important matter that needs a response, or if the sender will be angry if we do not respond. And there is more to ignoring a text than simply not thinking about it. We have to avoid acting on it, too. Psychologists call this impulse control, a process that involves any attempt to suppress a desired but inappropriate behavior (Baumeister, Bratslavsky, Muraven, & Tice, 1998). When you receive a text in class or while driving, you need to suppress the urge to pick up the phone and read the message. Based on what we were able to dig up from the psychological literature, we can combine existing conceptual definitions of thought suppression and impulse control to create the definition for "trying to ignore."

We also need to determine a conceptual definition for "distraction." Obviously, we are not the first to explore the topic of distraction, so again the literature can help us clarify what we mean in terms that concur with other psychologists. Distraction occurs when something captures our attention, drawing us away from the focal task or any task that requires our full attention (Parmentier, Elsley, & Ljungberg, 2010). Typically, we are trying to focus on one focal event or object (e.g., a class lecture), when another event or object (e.g., a text, phone call, etc.) grabs our attention and then requires us to divide our attention between the two. We could get distracted either because the focal event is not sufficiently interesting, or because the distractor is especially intriguing. This explanation of distraction fits perfectly with the notion that ignoring a text may be a distraction. After all, the sound or buzz of an incoming text can pull your attention from focal tasks, like listening to a dull professor, because the distracting text is potentially more appealing.

Weighing Our Options: Picking a Design

Next, we need to choose our study's design. We should let our research question guide our design choice, so let's refer back to our question: "Can trying to ignore a text lead to distraction?" From Chapter 2, we know that there are two main design types: nonexperimental designs, which focus on determining what happens, and experimental designs, which focus on determining why something happens. In our case, the research question makes a prediction about how one factor causes the other, rather than merely trying to describe what takes place. As a result, the nonexperimental research designs (e.g., interviews, observations, and surveys) are not appropriate ways to answer this particular question. (If we wanted to know whether or not people believe they get distracted by texts, or if we wanted to watch them in class to see the extent to which a text might distract, those designs would work.) Our question requires an experimental design.

Benefits of Experimental Designs

A major benefit of experimental designs is their ability to identify cause-and-effect relations between variables. That is, we can infer that one variable actually creates or enacts a change in another variable. For an experiment to establish causation, it must meet three specific criteria.

Let's assume that you want to determine whether different body postures or poses can change levels of hormones, such as testosterone or cortisol (Carney, Cuddy, & Yap, 2010). To establish causation, you must first establish that body posture relates to hormone levels, or that there is **covariation** between these two variables. For covariation to exist, two variables must vary or change together in a systematic way. If participants' body poses varied, but you found no difference in hormonal levels, then you would not have covariation. If hormonal levels systematically varied with changes in participants' body positions (e.g., participants' testosterone levels were higher when standing in a dominant position and lower when standing in a submissive position), then you would have covariation. A correlational study cannot establish causation, but it can establish covariation.

Covariation tells us that two variables relate to each other, but, unfortunately, does not tell us the direction of this relation. That is why we have the mantra that correlation does not equal causality. While it is possible that people have higher levels of testosterone after standing in a dominant position, it is also possible that having higher testosterone levels leads people to stand in a dominant position. If you believe that body posturing causes a change in hormone levels, you have to establish that body posture changes occur before hormone level changes. That is, you must demonstrate **temporal precedence** by showing that changes in the suspected cause occur before the changes in the effect or outcome. Correlational designs often cannot establish temporal precedence because both variables occur at the same time. However, it is easy to establish temporal precedence in an experimental design because you dictate the study's order and can manipulate your independent variable (body posturing) before you measure the dependent variable (hormone level). Without temporal precedence, you cannot determine which variable is the cause and which is the effect.

▶ In what other circumstances would it be better to use a nonexperimental design? SEE CHAPTER 2, p. 39

▶ Want to review why correlational studies cannot establish causation? SEE CHAPTER 7, p. 202

covariation when changes in one variable are associated with changes in another variable; part of determining causality.

temporal precedence when changes in the suspected cause (treatment) occur before changes in the effect (outcome).

Research shows that parental support and grades covary (Hamilton, 2013). When parents give more financial support to their college-enrolled children, students' grades are lower, while students who receive less help have higher grades. Although there is covariation between parental support and grades, we cannot say that receiving more financial help from parents causes lower grades. *(fstop123/iStock/Getty Images)*

The final step of establishing causality is showing that covariation between variables is only due to the independent variable and not due to an **extraneous variable,** which is any factor separate from the independent variable that could account for variations in the dependent variable. To determine causality, you need to eliminate or control any extraneous variables that could serve as an alternative explanation for the observed changes in the dependent measure. The extent to which you can do this has implications for the **internal validity** of your experiment. Internal validity refers to the degree to which you can rule out other possible or alternate causal explanations for an association between the independent and dependent variables in your experiment. To show that body posturing causes changes in hormone levels, you must demonstrate that everything except for body posture is the same throughout your experiment.

Ensuring that our text-messaging study has good internal validity may be challenging. The fact is that some things may vary in a study even when we identify and subsequently attempt to control them. Fortunately, a strong experimental design and procedures can eliminate most of the problems with extraneous variables and help us establish a cause-and-effect relationship.

Operationally Defining the IV: Manipulating Ignoring Text Messages

As we design our text-messaging experiment to establish cause and effect, we should figure out which of our key concepts, "trying to ignore" or "distraction," causes the other. Our research question implies that we want to see how ignoring a text message impacts our ability to avoid distraction. Therefore, trying to ignore the text is our independent variable (IV), as we want to examine if ignoring texts causes or alters the outcome. The result or outcome of ignoring the text is our dependent variable (DV), or, in this case, the amount of distraction. Based on this, we will eventually want to manipulate the independent variable and measure the dependent variable. Now that we have clearly defined both of our key concepts ("trying to ignore" and "distraction") and identified our independent and dependent variables, we are ready to operationalize each variable in our study.

When you set out to define variables in an experiment, you can operationally define either the independent or dependent variable first. As the researcher, it is your judgment call based on what you learned from your literature search or how you approach the research question (e.g., which variable feels like the most natural place to start for you?). In our case, our research question emanates from our interest in the potential consequences of professors forcing students to ignore text messages. These consequences are a good place to begin. Based on the conceptual definition we established earlier, ignoring should involve deliberately trying to suppress thoughts about texting.

Because ignoring texts is our independent variable, we will need to devise a way of manipulating the "ignoring" part of our experiment. We ignore smartphones

▶ What types of things can threaten the internal validity of a study? SEE CHAPTER 9, p. 292

What Do You Think?

Can you think of a nonexperimental way to determine if there is a connection between ignoring a text and distraction?

▶ What is the difference between an independent and dependent variable? SEE CHAPTER 2, p. 38

extraneous variable a factor other than the intended treatment that might change the outcome variable.

internal validity the degree to which we can rule out other possible causal explanations for an observed relationship between the independent and dependent variables.

all the time, whether we are ignoring others' use of their phones when they are texting or when we hear others' phones signaling an incoming call or text. While these are potential distractions, trying to ignore our own phone can be more distracting. Whenever our phone makes a noise, we cannot help but wonder who is trying to contact us and why. However, we also know that there are some situations in which it is not permissible to check our phone, such as while driving or sitting in a classroom. In fact, we know that many professors are not pleased when they see students texting during class and that some have course policies that strictly forbid phone usage during lectures.

The easiest way to manipulate our independent variable may be to mimic the types of policies professors use to restrict phone use in their courses. That is, we can create a "forbidden phone checker" group in which we force participants to ignore their phones by strictly forbidding them to check their phones. Mimicking actual course policies with our manipulation has the benefit of increasing our study's **mundane realism,** or how closely our study parallels the real world. The goal will be to make the participants' task in our experiment as similar to a classroom experience as possible.

Experiments are essentially about comparing sets of participants to determine how these groups may differ. For our study, we need to identify another group to which we can compare our "forbidden phone checker" group. Given that we are one of the first studies (or perhaps *the* first) to examine this research question, we should keep things simple. Although it may be tempting to design a study that tests many factors at once, it is often better to start with a more focused study. That way we can see if ignoring one's phone has any effect on learning before we devote additional time and energy (our own and our participants') to studying how other factors may relate to this research question. We will use a **two-group design,** or **simple experiment,** which is an experimental design that compares two groups or conditions and is the most basic way to establish cause and effect.

Weighing Our Options: Identifying the Best Groups for Our Study

Next, we need to determine the best two groups to use for our simple experiment. We refer to these groups as the experimental and control groups. The **experimental group** is whichever group gets the key treatment, and the **control group** is the comparison group that gets less of the treatment. When creating groups, we can start with the most obvious comparison, which is an *all-or-nothing* comparison. Think of this as a comparison where in one group a light switch is on (all) and in the other group the light switch is off (nothing).

mundane realism
the degree to which a study parallels everyday situations in the real world.

two-group design an experimental design that compares two groups or conditions and is the most basic way to establish cause and effect; also known as a simple experiment.

experimental group
the group or condition that gets the key treatment in an experiment.

control group any condition that serves as the comparison group in an experiment.

We cannot ethically allow participants to drive on real roads while doing something potentially dangerous, like texting or checking their phones. However, we can increase the mundane realism of lab studies by making the testing situation as real to life as possible. *(narvikk/E+/Getty Images)*

In the context of our study, we could have a high-restriction group, which is strictly forbidden to use or check their phones in any way, while the no-restriction group has free and complete use of their phones.

However, this all-or-nothing approach can lead to several differences between the groups. For example, compared to those in the high-restriction group, participants in the no-restriction group have full use of their phones and may keep them in view, respond to text messages or e-mails, check Twitter, use Snapchat, book a trip for spring break . . . you get the idea. In fact, there are so many differences between the two groups that if we were to compare groups and find that the no-restriction group was more distracted, we would not know why. Was it because their phones were visible and usable, because they sent more messages, or because they received more messages? With these two groups, it is impossible to know, which makes it difficult to have any confidence in a conclusion. Ultimately, the quality of the manipulations we use to create groups plays a major role in determining the quality of our study.

To create quality groups, we want to be sure we have a high degree of **experimental control,** or the ability to keep everything between groups the same except for the one element you want to test. This element, sometimes called the treatment, is the factor you think makes a difference in the outcome variable. This approach makes intuitive sense. For example, if you want to determine if 8 hours of sleep helps students' alertness the next morning, you would tell one group to go home and sleep 8 hours that night, and tell the other group to sleep 5 hours. Although the groups certainly seem similar, with 3 hours of sleep being the only difference, assuring experimental control is harder than it seems. If you allowed participants to sleep at home, there could be a near endless number of differences in the study that could affect alertness, besides number of hours slept. For example, the participants' beds and pillows might be different, some might have roommates while others do not, and some might sleep in a warm room while others prefer cold, not to mention that what the participants do before going to bed would vary considerably. For instance, even if everyone watches TV, what they watch might be different and might influence sleep and next-day alertness. The most common solution to these types of issues is to bring participants into a laboratory where experimenters can control many factors to help keep participants' experiences similar.

Rather than strictly forbidding participants to look at their phones, we could allow participants to have their phones out, face down, and in "silent" mode, where they would not make any noise or vibration. Participants would not be allowed to use their phones or pick them up to check them. We could keep the same "no restriction" control group. Although this scenario is better because we have now controlled the presence of the phones across groups, the groups are still different in a way that makes it difficult for us to draw conclusions about distraction. Compare the two groups:

experimental control
the ability to keep everything between groups the same except for the one element we want to test in an experiment.

Group A: *Not allowed* to know about incoming messages; *Not allowed* to use the phone

Group B: *Allowed* to know about incoming messages; *Allowed* to use the phone

In this setup, we have two key differences between the groups: knowing about incoming messages and being allowed to use the phone to respond to the messages. However, our research question focuses more on the implications of participants ignoring their phones and less about participants' use of their phones. Consequently, these two groups are too dissimilar. As we said, the goal of experimental control is to have only one element vary between groups, and that element should be whatever the researcher considers the "key ingredient," the factor the researcher wants to test.

a

b

If these two pictures were stimuli for two different conditions, what did the experimenter control? What did the experimenter fail to control? *(a: Ondine32/Getty Images; b: Fuse/Getty Images)*

 ## Thinking Like a Scientist in Real Life

Determining the Quickest Way to Go

In your commute to school or to work, you likely have several possible routes you could take. After narrowing down all of the possibilities to the two quickest routes, you could just flip a coin to determine your way. Yet, as a scientist, you know the best method to making a final choice involves scientific testing. The easiest test would be to take Route A one day and Route B the next, while timing how long it takes each day. However, even in that simple comparison there are many factors that could vary from day to day, such as the weather, the time of day, and the day of the week. To test the difference between Routes A and B fairly, you should keep everything else as similar as possible by controlling these other factors. For example, you would want to make sure that you leave at exactly the same time and on the same day of the week, always drive the speed limit, and travel in similar weather conditions. Only once you have utilized these types of experimental controls and replicated your findings can you be confident that one route is truly faster than the other.

We see now that the differences between groups in an all-or-nothing approach can be drastic. To have more control in our study, we can use the *a-little-more-versus-a-little-less* approach, in which the experimental group gets a little bit more of the treatment (in our case, smartphone restrictions), while the control group gets a little less. Before we set up these groups, we should consider whether our groups will vary by the "key ingredient" according to our research question. We want to know whether trying to ignore text messages creates a distraction in the classroom. Thus, the key factor to manipulate is the degree to which participants have to ignore text messages on their smartphones. We will require one group to ignore their phones by forbidding them to check their phones when they hear a text, while the other group can check their phones to see who the text is from and what the message says. Ultimately, we will operationally define our groups to have the following differences:

> High-Restriction "Forbidden Phone" Group: *No Phone Checking, No Phone Use*
>
> Low-Restriction "Phone Checker" Group: *Phone Checking Allowed, No Phone Use*

Our groups will vary in terms of phone checking, but we must make sure these groups are otherwise similar. We already decided that both groups of participants should have the phones out of sight and set on silent. Students use their phones for other potentially distracting things, like e-mail, games, calls, and checking social media. Although these are potential distractions, they are not our central interest at this point. Yet, we cannot ignore them. We will keep these aspects consistent in both groups by telling everyone those uses are not allowed and that the only notification they should enable on their phones is the vibration for texts.

Ultimately, there should only be one key difference: phone checking forbidden versus allowed. In looking at our groups, the experimental group should be the one that we think will be more distracted. Our exploration of this topic started with the premise that overly restrictive classroom phone policies are actually more distracting than less restrictive policies. Based on this, the "forbidden phone" group is more restrictive, and since we think being overly restrictive is the key factor in distraction, that makes it the experimental group, while the less restrictive "phone checker" group is our control group.

Operationally Defining the DV: Measuring Distraction

We think that overly restrictive phone policies can create distraction, but we still need to determine how we will know whether a participant becomes distracted. That is, we need to find a way to capture or measure our dependent variable. It sounds simple, but distraction is a mental process that we cannot see directly. Because the participant is the only person privy to that information, we could ask our participants to self-report their levels of distraction. Although there are many times when a self-report is appropriate, this is not one of them. Due to social desirability concerns, participants may be reluctant to admit to succumbing to distraction.

What Do You Think?
What other groups could you compare to test the influence of smartphone restrictions?

It is also possible that part of experiencing distraction is not realizing you are distracted. Even if we could ensure that participants were completely forthcoming and accurate about their levels of distraction, asking them to reflect on their distraction might lead them to wonder why we are asking about distraction, all of which might ultimately make them less distracted. Given the limitations of self-report for this particular dependent variable, we need to consider alternatives. As we discussed in Chapter 4, mental processes can have behavioral manifestations. Feeling sad coincides with certain facial expressions and, on occasion, crying. Similarly, feeling distracted will manifest in certain behaviors, so it is possible that a behavioral measure is more appropriate for our study.

◀ Why do researchers use both self-report and behavioral measures? SEE CHAPTER 4, p. 88

Research Spotlight

Driven to Distraction

Driving is full of distractions. There are pedestrians, other drivers, music, and making sure we finish our drive-thru fries before they get cold. Then there are cell phones. Nearly every American driver owns one and can be distracted from the roadway. While some states have yet to pass any laws about cell phone use, others have restricted cell phone use to situations that are "hands free." These laws imply that the danger of cell phone use while driving is more about not having your hands on the wheel and less about the distraction of talking. Does hands-free cell phone use eliminate the danger of using your phone while driving? To find out, researchers had 30 participants use a driving simulator (Benedetto et al., 2012). During the simulated driving experience, participants used a cell phone while encountering a critical stopping decision. Participants repeated each road scenario four times without calls and while answering a call in one of the following ways: hands-free voice activated device, hands-free cell phone, or handheld cell phone. The conclusion was that using a cell phone of any kind slowed drivers' reaction times and decreased driving performance equally across all cell phone modes. States that encourage the use of hands-free phones may not be making their roads any safer than those without cell phone restrictions.

Weighing Our Options: Identifying Key Behaviors

If we are going to examine behaviors that indicate distraction, we need to be relatively sure that the behavior actually indicates distraction and not some other mental process. Otherwise we run the risk of inferring too much based on the observed behavior. For example, if a participant plays with her hair, is that an indicator of distraction? It could just as easily indicate nervousness or boredom. The easiest way to avoid inferring too much is to use previous research to identify behaviors that other researchers have already used as indicators of distraction. By mirroring previous research as much as possible, we will have more confidence in our measurement.

Since our goal is to test the idea that bans on texting can be as distracting as texting, showing similar effects on measures used in texting studies would be convincing. Although previous research has not focused specifically on distraction resulting from restrictive phone policies, texting research has examined behaviors that texting influences. As we learned from our literature review, texting can influence driving ability (Benedetto et al., 2012), memory of a video (Rosen et al., 2011), and memory for a word list (Smith et al., 2011). Of these, the studies on memory are most similar to the type of distraction students might experience in class.

Memory tests relate to learning in a classroom, but we may be able to improve on them. We could, for example, measure distraction by observing students' natural reactions in class. However, it would be hard to know exactly what we observe. Some people might stare or appear to "zone out" when distracted, while others might do the exact same thing when they are thinking deeply about a difficult problem. Our measure of distraction should be more direct. Given that other research used tests to measure distraction, we could use students' test performance as our measure, under the assumption that greater distraction will lead to poorer performance.

What Do You Think?

What other behaviors could be used as indicators of distraction?

Focus on Ethics: Should We Really Do That?

There are both practical problems and ethical issues to consider with this proposed measure of distraction. If our study undermines students' learning or their actual quiz or test performance in the class, there are ethical implications. In fact, our literature search revealed that cell phone use while studying can undermine performance (Rosen et al., 2011; Smith et al., 2011). As a result, we should not expose our participants to a potentially harmful situation. In a real classroom setting, poor test performance could hurt students' overall course grade, which could then hurt their GPA, which could then influence their acceptance into a desired graduate school, and so on. While this may sound extreme, we need to consider the ethical implications of our design decisions when conducting research in a real-life setting.

Even if we are able to effectively resolve these ethical issues, there are too many factors in a natural classroom environment that are out of our control. These include things like the day's lecture topic, where the student sits, other students' behaviors that day, and so on. Any of these could lead to more or less distraction in a way that would make it hard to tell what type of influence a phone policy would have. Because these factors are not part of our intended manipulation, we will control them by keeping them constant across our two groups. To do that, we will want to measure distraction in a way that parallels how it occurs in a classroom setting, increasing our study's mundane realism. We will also want to conduct our study in a laboratory setting where we can minimize outside influences. Thus, to assess participants' distraction, we can measure test performance on material presented via a video lecture and a reading in a controlled situation. This exercise addresses the ethical issues we identified, closely parallels a classroom setting, and borrows methods from previous research.

If our dependent variable is test performance, we want to be sure that we have a good way to measure it. Our test should be long enough that we can collect a variety of scores. That is, if we only have 5 questions, the top and bottom scores will only differ by 5 points, but if we have 40 questions (20 for the video and 20 for the reading), scores will be more varied. This feature makes our measure more sensitive, which means we will be more likely to see potential differences between the two groups. We can also help ensure variation in our scores by making our questions moderately difficult. If the questions are too easy, we may have a problem with a ceiling effect, in which most participants get high scores regardless of whether or not the phones were distracting. Finally, we need to determine the quiz format. Should we use multiple-choice or short-answer questions? Although the latter may provide more information, multiple-choice questions are more objective (i.e., it is easier to identify correct and incorrect answers), and it is more likely that participants will have had previous experience with multiple-choice questions. To keep our testing situation controlled, we will have participants record their answers on a Scantron bubble sheet. To make sure we have a high-quality test, we will pilot test the questions ahead of time. Ultimately, we will operationally define distraction as participants' performance on the 40-question multiple-choice test, with lower scores indicating more distraction.

▶ What is measurement error?
SEE CHAPTER 4, p. 98

▶ Why might a researcher conduct pilot testing?
SEE CHAPTER 6, p. 178

Our Hypothesis

Our original research question has led us to think through a variety of issues in order to identify the best way to test our idea that overly restrictive smartphone-use policies may be a distraction. While others may choose to tackle this question in a different way (which is the beauty of science), we have settled on a simple experiment where we will manipulate our independent variable of smartphone use policy. We will have two groups, as detailed in **Table 8.1**. The experimental group will have a high level of restriction. Participants in this "forbidden phone" group cannot use their phones in any way. The control group, or "phone checkers," will have restrictions but will still be able to check their phones. To compare how distracting these two policies are, we will measure our dependent variable of distraction by examining test performance.

TABLE 8.1

Our Two-Group Design	
Smartphone Policy	
High Restriction	Low Restriction

Based on these, we can formally state our **experimental hypothesis**, where we make a clear and specific prediction of how the independent variable will influence the dependent variable. We could test the following hypothesis:

Those in the highly restricted smartphone-use group will perform differently on the test than those in the group who are allowed to check their phones.

With this prediction, we are making a nondirectional hypothesis that we expect the groups to differ, but without saying how they will differ. We make this type of prediction when we think that restricted smartphone use will cause a difference in how well one does on the test compared to the nonrestricted group, but we are unsure if the restriction will improve or hurt test performance.

Based on what we already know about impulse control and thought suppression, we have a theoretical reason to believe that restricting smartphone use will be more distracting than allowing phone checking. Therefore, we do not

▶ How do nondirectional and directional hypotheses differ?
SEE CHAPTER 7, p. 217

experimental hypothesis a clear and specific prediction of how the independent variable will influence the dependent variable.

just want to predict a difference between our groups; we want to predict the direction of that difference. Specifically, we will test the following hypothesis:

Those in the highly restricted smartphone-use group will perform worse on the test than those in the group who are allowed to check their phones.

You will notice that we predicted a specific outcome by stating which of the two groups would perform worse. This is called a directional hypothesis because we specified which group would have higher (or lower) scores on the dependent variable.

Before we move on, let's be sure we understand the experimental hypothesis, because it seems a bit counterintuitive. One group is not allowed to check their phones, while the other group is. Common sense would suggest that the phone checkers would be more distracted. However, science suggests that trying to suppress or ignore thoughts (in this case, thoughts about whether you are missing messages on your phone) is distracting. Thus, our experimental hypothesis predicts that being forced not to think about a smartphone will leave participants more distracted than if they were allowed to check it. This, in turn, will impede learning as measured by performance on the test.

YOUR TURN 8.1

1. Professor Dunphy conducts a study where two groups listen to a 50-minute audio recording of a lecture. The first group listens to a lecture on art history and the second group listens to a lecture on Greek philosophy. After the lecture, each group completes a questionnaire that measures intellectual curiosity. In this study, the independent variable is _____, while the dependent variable is _____.
   a. length of the lecture; lecture topic
   b. length of the lecture; intellectual curiosity
   c. lecture topic; intellectual curiosity
   d. intellectual curiosity; lecture topic

2. A school psychologist believes that preschoolers who eat chicken nuggets in the shapes of letters show a greater interest in books. For the experimental group, preschoolers will eat five chicken nuggets shaped like the letters *A*, *E*, *I*, *O*, and *U*. What would be the best control group to test the school psychologist's belief?
   a. A group that eats 5 ounces of macaroni and cheese with noodles shaped like the letters *A*, *E*, *I*, *O*, and *U*.
   b. A group that eats a bowl of cereal with alphabet-shaped bits.
   c. A group that eats five chicken nuggets shaped like the letters *D*, *N*, *R*, *S*, and *T*.
   d. A group that eats five regularly shaped chicken nuggets.

3. Cognitive-behavioral therapist Dr. Johnson believes her type of therapy is best for treating nocturnal enuresis (nighttime bed-wetting). To test her assumption, she assigns one group of bed-wetters to cognitive-behavioral

therapy for 3 months, while the other group undergoes psychodynamic therapy for the same time period. Both groups' therapy sessions are led by an independent therapist, Dr. Jack, who is not aware of Dr. Johnson's prediction. At the end of treatment, Dr. Johnson has a neutral therapist assess symptoms in both groups. In this study, the experimental group is the _____, while the control group is the _____.

a. cognitive-behavioral therapy group; psychodynamic therapy group

b. psychodynamic therapy group; cognitive-behavioral therapy group

c. group led by Dr. Jack; group led by Dr. Johnson

d. therapist; symptoms

How did you do? Turn to the end of the chapter to check your answers.

Design in Action

We know what we want to have in our study in terms of the manipulation and measures. We even have some of the basics in place for establishing experimental control and using appropriate measurements. Next, we need to turn our attention from the "what" of our study to the "how," as in, "Just how are we going to carry out the study in a way that meets our goals?" The first decision we have to make is from where to gather our participants.

Weighing Our Options: Obtaining Participants

Generally speaking, it is best to use a random sample of the overall population as the participants in an experiment. In our case, that would mean randomly selecting from the entire population of college students who have smartphones. In practice, obtaining a sample of that entire population is nearly impossible, not to mention prohibitively expensive. Instead, a convenience sample of students at our own school makes the most sense. Convenience sampling has the benefit of being easier to carry out, and, since students may need to participate in research as part of their classes, the sample is not expensive to obtain. Although we may lose some ability to generalize to other populations if students at our school react differently than students at another school would, we need to remember that no study is perfect. Your job as the researcher is to know enough about the relevant issues to make the choices that will best answer your research question. First, we need to figure out whether or not restrictive smartphone policies actually create distraction. If we establish that this happens, then we can conduct follow-up studies to see if we can replicate our result in other groups of students.

Next, we need to determine how we will obtain our convenience sample. We only want students who regularly use smartphones, so we should be sure to screen out those who may not have a phone or may not use their phone often. Thus, when we recruit participants, we will tell them, "We are conducting a study of smartphone habits," and then ask them to text us to set up an appointment. This method will ensure that the participants are highly familiar with texting, and will allow us to ask them to bring their phones to the study without arousing suspicion.

▶ What other sampling strategies can researchers use? SEE CHAPTER 4, p. 109

What Do You Think?
Is sampling only college students and not sampling other parts of the population, such as older people who are not in college, a problem? Why or why not?

▶ Why is replication an important part of science? SEE CHAPTER 1, p. 13

Weighing Our Options: Placing Participants in Groups

We want to make sure we have enough participants to reasonably determine whether or not the smartphone restrictions make a difference, given all the other random factors that may influence their ability to concentrate. Based on our previous planning, we know that we will have two groups (the "forbidden phone" group and the "phone checkers" group), and we should aim for about 50 participants in each group. Collecting data from 100 participants will definitely be time-consuming.

The Importance of Independent Groups

One way to speed up data collection is by testing several participants at a time. Our room holds up to eight people, so we can sign up that many participants for each of the study's time slots. Once the eight participants arrive, we can tell them all which group they are in, making sure that we have equal numbers in each group. But this approach has a downside. It is possible that participants will stop acting like eight individuals and start behaving as a single group. In research terms, this can compromise our study's **independence**, which is the assumption that each participant represents a unique and individual data point. As we know from social psychology and the minimal groups paradigm (Struch & Schwartz, 1989; Tajfel, 1970), as soon as people know they are part of a particular group, they favor that group. As a result, in our study, participants in Group 1 will like their fellow Group 1 members more than they like those in Group 2, behaving less like autonomous individuals. Participants may even take cues from other group members in ways that make each individual participant act less naturally. For example, the behavior of others in the room may have more influence than experimental manipulation over whether or not participants look at their smartphones. In addition, those in the experimental condition may start complaining to each other about being forbidden to use their smartphones. Thus, it is important to minimize interactions between the participants. The simplest way to solve this problem is to test one participant at a time. Although this approach will take up more time, it minimizes the possibility that interactions between participants will undermine our study.

Problems with Nonrandom Assignment

Even when collecting data from one participant at a time, we need to be careful about how we assign each participant to the experimental or control group. We could place participants in either group simply by allowing them to decide whether they prefer the high-restriction or low-restriction group. However, doing this creates two problems. First, in order to choose, participants will need to know what both groups will do in the study, which increases the chances that participants will accurately guess the purpose of the study and the researcher's hypothesis. Second, participants who pick the high-restriction group may do so because they naturally care less about monitoring their smartphones. Thus, if we found that high restriction led to less distraction, it would be impossible to know if the finding was due to the restrictive policy or if it was due to the high-restriction group having more participants who cared less about monitoring their smartphones.

independence the assumption that each participant represents a unique and individual data point.

There is danger in allowing the individuals in your study to think of themselves as a group. In doing so, individual participants may not represent their unique thoughts or behaviors, thus compromising the independence of the study. *(The Catcher Photography/Getty Images)*

Perhaps it would be better if you, the researcher, placed participants in groups. As the person who knows the study best, you seem like a natural choice. However, although you may believe you are assigning groups in a fair and ethical manner, there is always the chance that you may bias your assignments. For example, what if you unknowingly tend to put participants with iPhones in the low-restriction group? That may not seem like a big deal, but it is possible that iPhone users are more addicted to their phones. If this were the case, you could find differences between your two groups that had nothing to do with your restriction manipulation.

The Importance of Random Assignment

To avoid these problems, we need to eliminate human choice and potential bias from the group assignment process. We can do this by using **random assignment**, which is any method of placing participants in groups that is nonsystematic and nonbiased, and that ensures each participant has an equal chance of being in any group. We could determine random assignment with a simple flip of a coin. When the coin is heads, we could assign that participant to our "forbidden phone" group. When it is tails, we could assign the participant to the "phone checkers" group. We could roll a die and designate odd rolls as one group and even rolls as the other. Or, we could place the name of each group into a hat and draw one out each time we have a new participant in our study. Better yet, we could use an online resource. There are websites such as http://www.randomizer.org that generate random numbers we could use to assign participants to groups.

Now you may be thinking, "What if there are some participants who are complete texting addicts, while there are others who just got their first smartphone?" As the researcher, you would want to ensure that all of the texting

random assignment any method of placing participants in groups that is nonsystematic and nonbiased, and that ensures each participant has an equal chance of being in any group.

addicts are not in one group, with all of the novices in the other, which theoretically could happen through random assignment. In cases where you can easily identify important differences like this, you can use a **matched-pair design,** in which you create a set of two participants who are highly similar on a key trait (e.g., two texting addicts), then randomly assign one to the experimental group and the other to the control group. Doing so makes sure that both groups have participants who are similar, or matched, on that important trait. This technique can work well if there are participant characteristics that you as the researcher know are important and can measure in a reliable and valid way. The problem is that researchers cannot possibly know every variable that can influence the dependent variable. Thus, a matched-pair can sometimes create a false sense of security where you think you have your groups matched and highly similar, when, in reality, some other unmatched participant trait influences the outcome.

The list of potential influences in any study is endless. For example, in our study, participants' age, sex, ethnicity, socioeconomic status, past experience with a smartphone, data plan, number of friends, and so on might influence how our restriction manipulation affects participants. It is also possible that what happened earlier that day, current mood, typical attention span, tiredness, general disinterest, and so on can influence the participant's distraction level. Thankfully, random assignment accounts for all of these potential influences, plus all of the ones we did not think of. Notice that we say "accounts for" and not "eliminates." There will always be factors that are unaccounted for that may have an influence, so the best we can do in an experiment is have these factors influence both groups similarly. Provided you have enough participants (which is why we want 100 participants in our study rather than 10), random assignment will even out any variable's influence. Because participants have an equal chance of being in any group, one group should not end up with a disproportionate number of tired, disinterested, or text-obsessed participants.

So, we will randomly assign our participants to either the "forbidden phone" group or the "phone checkers" group. Because we want to know how these two groups compare on test performance, we will use a between-subjects design, where we expose our participants to only one of the two groups. This means we will also only assess the dependent variable of test performance once for each participant.

Developing a Protocol

Now that we know how we are going to find participants and assign them to either the experimental or control group, we can make decisions about our procedure. As we do, we will want to maintain experimental control by keeping the procedure identical for everyone. We know that using a protocol will help us accomplish that goal. We decided earlier that having participants come to a controlled, "laboratory" setting would be better than using an actual classroom setting, so we will plan on collecting data in a small classroom on campus.

When they arrive for the study, we will first ask our participants to read an informed consent form. Our informed consent will include enough information for our participants to make an educated decision about whether they want to be

---

What Do You Think?
What important traits would you match participants on, given our research question?

▶ How do between-subjects and within-subjects designs differ?
SEE CHAPTER 2, p. 40

▶ Why is a consistent research protocol important?
SEE CHAPTER 2, p. 43

matched-pair design
a design in which one creates a set of two participants who are highly similar on a key trait and then randomly assigns individuals in the pair to different groups.

in our study, without revealing too many details that could cause participants to act unnaturally. In our case, we will tell participants, "We are conducting a study of smartphone habits that will require participants to watch a video, read a short passage, and complete a brief quiz."

Following informed consent, we will direct each participant to sit at a desk in the middle of the room. Once the participant takes a seat, we will explain that his or her task is to watch a 30-minute video lecture on the nature of clouds. The participant will then read a text-book chapter section that is not too long or boring on the same topic. (Clouds are a good topic because they should interest participants, while likely not being a topic that they are extremely familiar with.) Prior to putting on the video, we will ask the participant to switch his or her smartphone to vibrate and place it out of sight in a metal basket under the desk. This instruction might seem silly to add to the protocol, but smartphones can vary in terms of their vibration intensity, which makes some easier to hear than others. A metal basket will ensure that the vibration is consistently audible. Never underestimate the importance of these types of details when designing a study!

Everything up to this point has been the same for all of our participants. Now we need to manipulate our independent variable, giving participants slightly different instructions so that they know which "smartphone policy" to follow (allowed to check their phones vs. not allowed to look at them). Remember, we want to keep our instructions as similar as possible. As a result, everyone will hear the same first part of the instructions:

> Please adjust your smartphone settings so that all sound effects are off. In case you receive any texts, please leave your phone on vibrate for texts only. Once you have the settings adjusted, please place your smartphone out of sight in the basket below your desk. You should not, under any circumstances, use your smartphone to make a call, check e-mail or social media, play games, or send any text messages.

Virtual reality experiences attempt to influence people to "lose themselves" in the experience of the virtual world. In our experiments, we should also strive to recreate the experiences we want to study. If we want to know about reactions to fear, then our participants need to be afraid. *(Russell Curtis/Science Source/Getty Images)*

These instructions help ensure participants all set up their phones the same way, and ensure that they all know not to actually use their phones. The second part of the instructions will vary depending on which group the participant is in:

High-Restriction "Forbidden Phone" Group: If your phone vibrates, you must ignore it and not think about it. Do not pick up your phone to check who the message is from or read the message. Leave your phone in the basket.

Low-Restriction "Phone Checker" Group: If your phone vibrates, you can check to see who the message is from and read the message. Once you are done, return your phone to the basket.

It is the second part of the instructions that establishes the key "ingredient," or difference, between the groups: *No Phone Checking* versus *Phone Checking Allowed.*

We want to be sure the study feels as real as possible. In other words, we want to ensure that our study has **experimental realism**, such that participants become engrossed in the manipulation and feel like it influences them. Rather than having participants sit at a desk by themselves, we could have others sitting at desks as well. Certainly, in a class environment, there are other people sitting near you, but where are we going to find the extra people? One option would be to have other participants sitting in surrounding desks. But in this scenario, we will have less control over the situation. Participants may know each other, and different combinations of participants (e.g., all males or all females) may lead to different dynamics. A better solution would be to use confederates, or accomplices of the study, who will know to treat all participants the same. When the participant enters the room, we can have five confederates already sitting at other desks. We can be sure that our confederates always sit in the same spots and act in the exact same way for every participant.

► What is a confederate? SEE CHAPTER 3, p. 68

In order to have participants either ignore their phones or check them, we need to be sure that the phones actually vibrate during the study session. The only way to ensure that each participant receives a text is for us to be the ones who send it. To do this, we will need the participant's cell phone number. Since participants signed up for the study via text message, we can ask participants, following informed consent, to provide their phone numbers so that we can allegedly check off who showed up to the study from our list of numbers.

During the 30-minute video lecture and subsequent reading, we will text the participant several times. In order to standardize the experience for everyone, we will text a total of eight times, spaced out in a preplanned way. We could space the texts out so that we send one every 6 minutes, but that may seem too obvious. Instead, we will plan on sending a text at the following minute marks during the video: 2, 9, 15, 20, and 26. We will then text participants three additional times while they are doing the reading, at the 1-, 3-, and 4-minute marks. When we send the texts, the participant should not know it is us, which means they will not recognize the sender. Rather than sending the participant five texts from the same unknown number, we should mix it up by sending texts from three different phone numbers. The content of our texts should be general so that it applies to all participants (e.g., "heyyy how are you?? :)"), should be informal in terms of grammar and punctuation in order to seem more authentic, and should be the same for each person in our study.

There is one potential problem: Some participants may get real texts while watching the video or reading the selection. Because we cannot do much about this problem, we will keep **researcher notes**, in which we keep track of anything out of the ordinary that happens during the study. For example, we would note if any of the participants in the high-restriction/forbidden smartphone group looked at their phone in violation of our "policy."

After watching the video, the participant will start the reading portion of the lesson. To be sure that this portion of the procedure is also controlled, we will give all participants 5 minutes to read the short selection. If they finish early, the researcher will ask them to reread the passage until the 5 minutes are up. As we walk away, we will start a timer and stop the participants after 5 minutes. Once the participants complete the reading, we will administer the knowledge test.

experimental realism the degree to which a study participant becomes engrossed in the manipulation and truly influenced by it.

researcher notes a place to keep track of anything out of the ordinary that happens during a study.

Following the test, we will give each participant a **manipulation check,** which is a measure that helps determine whether the manipulation effectively changed or varied the independent variable across groups. Because we were manipulating whether participants could check their smartphones, we need to see if the two groups differed in their perceptions of the permissiveness to check their phones during the study. We can simply ask them to rate on a scale of 1 to 7 how permissible it was to check their phones. If we find that there is no difference between the high-restriction and low-restriction groups on this question, then we cannot be certain we adequately manipulated our independent variable. This is important information to have if we find no differences between the experimental and control groups on our dependent variable. It may help us decide whether a smartphone ban is distracting or whether there was a flaw in our study because the manipulation did not work. We will also want to check if participants noticed the phones vibrating by asking them to report the number of times they detected it going off. This is important because if participants in the highly restricted group did not hear the phones, then they were not actually ignoring them as we hoped.

Next, we will ask participants to answer a few demographic questions and several additional questions related to our study's topic. For example, we should ask questions about the participant's typical smartphone use, texting habits, GPA, and knowledge about clouds prior to the study. In each case, these variables may help us understand potential results. Finally, we will debrief participants and thank them for participating. Because we are using a number of different materials in our study (i.e., Scantron testing sheet, demographic sheet, manipulation check), we want to be sure that we place a participant number on each piece of material. That way we can easily match all the materials associated with a particular participant when it comes time to enter our data.

Focus on Open Science: Preregistering Your Hypotheses, Materials, and Data Analysis Plan

Before we collect any data, we will be sure to preregister our study on an open science website (e.g., http://www.socialscienceregistry.org). There, after our study, we will share study details such as how we manipulated our independent variable (including the exact instructions participants heard) and our study materials, including the video participants saw, the article they read, and the quiz they completed. Based on our hypothesis, we will also preregister our plan for analyzing the data we will collect. For this study, we will want to make sure our manipulation worked by seeing if our two groups ("Forbidden Phone" and "Phone Checker") differ on how permissible it was to check their phone, as well as their self-reported distraction. We will also test our hypothesis by comparing the two groups' test scores to see if the "Forbidden Phone" group had lower test scores. By having a preregistered plan, we can focus only on the analyses that help us test our preregistered research hypotheses. Once we have collected all of the data, we will post the data set on an open science website where other researchers can conduct their own analyses.

▶ Why is open science important to the research process? SEE CHAPTER 2, p. 42

manipulation check a measure that helps determine whether the manipulation effectively changed or varied the independent variable across conditions.

> **YOUR TURN 8.2**

1. Murray, a server in a restaurant, wonders if writing a simple "thank you" on the check before he delivers it will increase his tips compared to not writing anything at all. What he is most worried about is the individual difference between his patrons in tipping habits, as some people naturally tip at a higher percentage than others. How can Murray reduce this concern?
   a. By having patrons report their average tipping tendencies
   b. By using random assignment
   c. By using random sampling
   d. By only using patrons that are known to be bad tippers

2. Emily wants to know if mood impacts cooperation. She has half of her participants watch a slide show that shows sad images and half watch a slide show of neutral images. Afterward, she gives each participant the opportunity to cooperate on a game with a player in another room. At the end of the study, she collects demographic information and administers a measure of mood. Which element of her study was included as a manipulation check?
   a. The sad slide show
   b. The neutral slide show
   c. The opportunity to cooperate
   d. The mood measure

3. As an animal trainer, Melaine wants to test which type of reward (crab vs. fish) will work best in training otters for her new amusement park show. She creates sets of subjects based on both age and the level of previous training before she begins the training. What technique is Melaine using?
   a. random assignment
   b. random sampling
   c. matched pairs
   d. independence

How did you do? Turn to the end of the chapter to check your answers.

Statistics: In Search of Answers

After we have run the study and collected information from 100 participants, we need to enter our data into the computer for analysis. Because we conducted an experiment, it is crucial that we identify each participant's group or condition prior to entering their test scores, manipulation checks, and demographics. In our researcher notes, we should have a list of participant numbers that includes their groups and any notes that we made regarding each participant's experience.

Researcher Notes

Participant Number	Condition	Notes
1	low	participant was 5 min late, received 3 real texts
2	low	none
3	high	had trouble finding cell phone, received 2 real texts
4	low	none
5	high	asked for clarification on 2 mc questions
6	high	received 1 real text
7	low	none

FIGURE 8.1 Example of Researcher Notes.

(See **Figure 8.1** for an example of researcher notes.) Prior to entering data, we will need to have the Scantron sheets scored so that we have the participants' test scores. Once we have all of the information, we can enter the data into a statistical computer program, as shown in **Figure 8.2**. Even though participants will be in different groups, any time we enter data, each participant's information must appear on one row. The key difference with an experiment compared to a survey is that in one column we will have a variable for the independent variable ("Condition") with numbers identifying each group (1 = Experimental Condition, 2 = Control Condition).

Ch8_TwoGroup_t-test_Data.sav [DataSet3] - IBM SPSS Statistics Data Editor

File Edit View Data Transform Analyze Graphs Utilities Add-ons Window Help

	Participant	Condition	quizscore	permissible	timesheardphone	distraction	Sex	Age	SchoolYear	Ethnicity	typicalcelluse	textingexpertise	gpa	cloudknowledge	realtexts
1	1.00	Low Rest...	39.00	7.00	7.00	4.00	Fem...	20.00	Freshman	African A...	5.00	6.00	3.49	3.00	3.00
2	2.00	Low Rest...	40.00	6.00	8.00	3.00	Fem...	27.00	Freshman	Caucasian	6.00	6.00	2.88	1.00	.00
3	3.00	High Res...	40.00	2.00	7.00	7.00	Fem...	18.00	Freshman	Caucasian	5.00	6.00	2.82	4.00	2.00
4	4.00	Low Rest...	18.00	7.00	7.00	5.00	Fem...	18.00	Sophomore	Caucasian	7.00	7.00	3.95	4.00	.00
5	5.00	High Res...	30.00	1.00	8.00	6.00	Fem...	24.00	Freshman	Caucasian	7.00	5.00	1.78	3.00	.00
6	6.00	High Res...	31.00	2.00	7.00	4.00	Fem...	18.00	Freshman	African A...	6.00	6.00	3.44	3.00	1.00
7	7.00	Low Rest...	36.00	7.00	7.00	4.00	Male	21.00	Freshman	African A...	7.00	7.00	3.66	6.00	.00
8	8.00	Low Rest...	36.00	7.00	10.00	6.00	Fem...	19.00	Freshman	African A...	7.00	5.00	2.42	9.00	2.00
9	9.00	Low Rest...	36.00	6.00	10.00	3.00	Fem...	18.00	Freshman	Caucasian	4.00	7.00	3.60	8.00	2.00
10	10.00	High Res...	32.00	1.00	7.00	6.00	Male	18.00	Freshman	Multiracial	4.00	7.00	3.66	9.00	.00

FIGURE 8.2 Example of SPSS Data Spreadsheet. *(SPSS)*

With the data entered, we can focus on answering our research question, "Can trying to ignore a text message lead to distraction?" Given our design, we will want to see if our high-restriction group had test scores that were significantly lower than the low-restriction group. Did the participants in the high-restriction group do worse on the test as hypothesized, and did they do worse enough for us to be relatively certain that it did not happen by chance?

Selecting the Proper Tool

To answer our research question, we need to accomplish three tasks during our data analysis:

1. Make sure our groups were similar on variables that may provide alternate explanations.

2. Make sure our manipulation was effective.

3. Test our hypothesis.

Our first set of analyses should focus on making sure that alternate explanations (e.g., number of actual texts received, GPA, familiarity with clouds, etc.) are not responsible for any potential findings. Random assignment should have ensured that those variables were controlled for or kept similar in both groups, but, as the saying goes, "Trust, but verify." We can verify that our two groups are similar by using statistics, and we can determine the right statistic to use by considering key features of our study. We have a between-subjects design, two levels of the independent variable, and a continuous dependent variable. Based on these qualities, we should run a ***t*-test for independent means** (also known as an **independent samples *t*-test**), which is, generally speaking, a test to see if the two groups or conditions are different. The *t*-test, the anatomy of which is shown in **Figure 8.3**, determines this by comparing each group's mean to see if they differ from one another

***t*-test for independent means** a statistical test comparing groups' means to see if the groups differ to a degree that could not have happened accidentally or by chance; also known as an independent samples *t*-test.

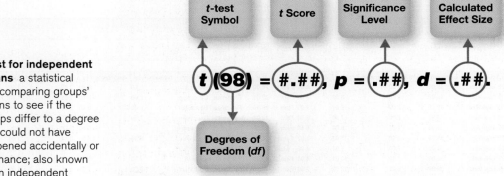

FIGURE 8.3 Anatomy of a *t*-test for Independent Means.

to a degree that could not have just happened accidentally. Remember here that statistical significance (represented by p) is the probabilistic indication (really just a percent likelihood) of how much confidence we have that the two groups differ. If the t-test for independent means is significant ($p < .05$), we can be fairly confident that our results represent a real difference between the groups. If the t-test for independent means fails to reach significance ($p > .05$), there is not enough evidence to suggest that the groups are different.

A t-test only indicates the likelihood of there being a difference. Regardless of whether the difference is significant, we often want to know the **effect size** (represented by d), or the magnitude of the difference, between the groups. The effect size allows us to evaluate the practical significance of our findings. For example, suppose we find that forbidding smartphone checking leads to students performing significantly worse on a test. Before we start advocating for large educational reforms, we should evaluate how large of an impact this policy has on test performance. If the effect is small, we might want to direct our efforts to improve student learning elsewhere. If it is large, we will want to consider how to minimize such distractions in the classroom.

Second, in order to be sure our manipulation did what we intended it to do, we need to make sure participants knew the instructions. We can do this by comparing the two groups on whether they thought smartphone checking was permissible. Related to the effectiveness of our manipulation, we should also verify that participants heard the texts, because if they did not hear the texts, there would not have been any thoughts for them to suppress. Similarly, we should verify that the high-restriction group reported more distraction, because the logic of our hypothesis depends on restriction creating more distraction. We can run another set of t-tests for independent means to see if the groups were different in how well they heard the texts and in how much they felt distracted by their smartphones.

Finally, we need to test our hypothesis that those in the highly restricted smartphone-use group will have worse test performance than those in the group who can check their phones. Since we are looking for differences in a between-subjects design with two groups on a continuous dependent variable, we will again use a t-test for independent means. Also, because we have a directional hypothesis, we are predicting how our groups will differ. In experiments, we rarely predict that there will be no difference. A "no difference" hypothesis, also known as a **null hypothesis,** is most often the hypothesis that we are trying to statistically reject. That is, we start out with the assumption that there is no difference between groups. Our goal is then to show that there is a difference between groups, by demonstrating that the assumption of no difference is unlikely given our results. The null hypothesis is an important part of the logic behind the statistics we use to test or analyze our hypothesis, but it is something that researchers naturally assume, and thus do not explicitly state when writing up the results.

▶ How do you select the proper statistic for answering your research question?
SEE APPENDIX A, p. 481

▶ How do you interpret *p*-values?
SEE CHAPTER 7, p. 230

▶ How do we statistically test our hypothesis?
SEE APPENDIX A, p. 486

effect size a statistical measure of the magnitude of the difference between groups.

null hypothesis the hypothesis of no difference; usually the hypothesis the researcher is trying to statistically reject.

Writing the Results in APA Style: *t*-test for Independent Means

Results

Means and standard deviations for the two experimental groups on key variables appear in Table 8.2 (all analyses are two-tailed).

Alternate Explanations

To determine if the high- and low-restriction groups differ on several variables that could potentially serve as alternate explanations when testing our hypothesis, we conducted a series of *t*-tests for independent means. The results of those analyses were as follows: typical smartphone use, $t(98) = 1.31$, $p = .19$, $d = .27$; texting expertise, $t(98) = 0.29$, $p = .78$, $d = .16$; number of real texts during the study, $t(98) = 0.31$, $p = .75$, $d = .06$; grade-point average (GPA), $t(98) = 0.18$, $p = .86$, $d = .04$; and previous cloud knowledge, $t(98) = 0.67$, $p = .50$, $d = .14$. These analyses suggest that our two groups were not significantly different on these variables.

Manipulation Check

To determine if the high- and low-restriction groups differed on how permissible it was to check their smartphones, we conducted a *t*-test for independent means comparing the groups. The analysis was significant and had a moderate effect size—$t(98) = 51.19$, $p < .001$, $d = 10.34$—suggesting that the manipulation was effective.

We also wanted to see if smartphone restriction influenced participants' self-reported distraction. To do this, we conducted a *t*-test for independent means comparing the high- and low-restriction groups on distraction scores. The analysis was significant and had a moderate effect size: $t(98) = 4.72$, $p < .001$, $d = .95$. This suggests that those in the high-restriction group were significantly more distracted than those in the low-restriction group. We also conducted another *t*-test for independent means to determine if the groups differed on how often they heard the smartphone ring. Results of that analysis, $t(98) = 0.98$, $p = .33$, $d = .20$, suggest that the groups were not significantly different.

Hypothesis 1

To determine if smartphone restriction influenced participants' quiz scores, we conducted a *t*-test for independent means comparing the high- and low-restriction groups on quiz scores. The analysis was significant and had a moderate effect size: $t(98) = 2.32$, $p = .022$, $d = .47$. As hypothesized, those in the high-restriction group had significantly lower quiz scores (an average of 28.88 points out of 40 total points, or 72.20% correct) than those in the low-restriction group (an average of 32.10 points out of 40 total points, or 80.25% correct). Results also appear in Figure 8.4.

Don't Just Tell Me, Show Me: Using Tables and Figures

In addition to presenting their findings in the text of a research report, researchers also depict the results of their experiment in tables and figures. These visuals provide another way to summarize the data. **Table 8.2** shows the differences between our restriction conditions on key variables, and **Figure 8.4** displays the differing quiz percentages between our high- and low-restriction participants.

TABLE 8.2

Differences Between Restriction Conditions on Key Variables					
Variable	**High Restriction**	**Low Restriction**	***t***	***p***	***d***
Typical Smartphone Use	6.12 (0.82)	6.34 (0.85)	1.31	.19	.27
Texting Expertise	6.36 (0.69)	6.32 (0.71)	0.29	.78	.16
Real Texts During Study	1.18 (1.24)	1.26 (1.31)	0.31	.75	.06
GPA	3.27 (0.58)	3.29 (0.64)	0.18	.86	.04
Cloud Knowledge	5.04 (2.59)	4.68 (2.76)	0.67	.50	.14
Distraction	5.54 (1.47)	4.08 (1.61)	4.72	< .001	.95
Times Heard Phone	7.52 (1.07)	7.28 (1.37)	0.98	.33	.20
Quiz Score	28.88 (7.12)	32.10 (6.74)	2.32	.02	.47

Note: $n = 100$. Higher scores indicate a greater magnitude of each variable. All analyses are two-tailed.

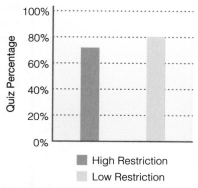

FIGURE 8.4 Percentage of Points on Quiz by Condition.

Our Research Plan at a Glance

What Is Our Research Question? Can trying to ignore a text message lead to distraction?

What Is Our Design? We are using a two-group between-subjects experimental design.

Why Are We Using This Design? This design allows us to establish causality by manipulating one variable (ignoring text messages), while keeping other factors controlled (i.e., the same) so that we can determine how it affects outcomes (distraction).

What Are Our Variables?

Independent Variable(s): Ignoring Text Messages

High-Restriction "Forbidden Phone" Group: If your phone vibrates, you must ignore it and not think about it. Do not pick up your phone to check who the message is from or read the message. Leave your phone in the basket.

Low-Restriction "Phone Checker" Group: If your phone vibrates, you can check to see who the message is from and read the message. Once you are done, return your phone to the basket.

Dependent Variable(s): Distraction

Participants watch a video lecture and complete a short reading about clouds, followed by a 40-question multiple-choice test. Test performance (score out of 40) serves as an indicator of distraction (lower test performance = more distraction).

What Are Our Hypotheses? Those in the highly restricted smartphone use group will perform worse on the test (i.e., display signs of more distraction) than those in the group who are allowed to check their phones.

Who Are Our Participants? Convenience sample of college students who regularly use a smartphone.

What Ethical Considerations Do We Need to Keep in Mind?

- Since smartphone use could potentially hurt actual test performance, we would not want to run this study in a real class where it could lower students' actual test scores.

What Is Our Data Analysis Plan?

1. **Make sure our groups are similar on variables that may provide alternate explanations.** We compare the two conditions (Experimental/"Forbidden Phone" vs. Control/"Phone Checker") on variables such as number of actual texts received, GPA, and familiarity with clouds using a *t*-test for independent means.

2. **Make sure our manipulation is effective.** We compare both groups to see if they report a difference on how permissible it was to check their smartphones and self-reported distraction using a *t*-test for independent means.

3. **Test our hypothesis.** We compare the two conditions (Experimental/"Forbidden Phone" vs. Control/"Phone Checker") of our independent variable with a *t*-test for independent means, this time to determine if the groups had different quiz scores. If the data support the hypothesis, the "Forbidden Phone" group will have lower quiz scores, indicating more distraction.

Want to practice the analyses for this research yourself? Ask your instructor about the data set that accompanies this study.

Let's Discuss What Happened

Our experiment attempted to determine how course policies concerning students' smartphone use influence students. Based on the premise that trying not to think about something makes you think about it more, we hypothesized that overly restrictive smartphone policies may create more distraction and undermine student learning. To test this, we conducted a two-group experiment where we randomly assigned students to a group that was forbidden to check their phones or to a group that was allowed to check their phones. With the results of our experiment in hand, we must now interpret our findings. As we do this below, notice how we place our findings in the context of previous research and theory, and how we identify the limitations of our design and make concrete suggestions for future research.

What Did We Find?

A series of analyses testing potential alternate explanations found no significant differences between the groups on typical smartphone use, texting expertise, the number of real texts the participant received during the study, grade point average (GPA), or previous cloud knowledge. The results of our study suggest that our manipulation was effective. Participants in both groups were aware of their group's restrictions, both groups heard the smartphone a similar number of times, and, most importantly for the assumption underlying our hypothesis, the high-restriction group reported feeling more distracted than the low-restriction group. The test of our hypothesis revealed a significant difference, such that participants in the high-restriction group had test scores that were 8% (nearly a full letter grade) lower on average than participants in the low-restriction group.

Why These Findings?

Participants who were forbidden to check their phones performed worse on the test and reported experiencing more distraction. Although people believe they have the ability to control their thoughts, our findings are consistent with previous research on thought suppression showing that attempting to control or suppress a thought is futile (Najmi et al., 2010). In the context of a restrictive smartphone policy, the participant needs to enact a negative implementation intention or plan not to act (e.g., "If I get a text, I will not check my phone") in order to follow the restriction (Adriaanse, van Oosten, de Ridder, de Wit, & Evers, 2011). However, research on these strategies shows that planning not to act on a habit can actually strengthen the habit by increasing thoughts of the target behavior, which is consistent with Wegner's (1994) ironic process theory. By asking our high-restriction group to plan on not checking their phones (a negative implementation intention), we likely led them to think about their phones more than they would have.

These thoughts are likely distracting because the person receiving the text wonders about the message's content (e.g., "Is it important?" "Is there something wrong?"). Ironically, the text's actual content is probably much more benign. In fact, teens tend to text others for mundane reasons like wanting to say hi or to chat rather than for important personal matters (Lenhart, Ling, Campbell, & Purcell, 2010).

Rather than restricting smartphone checking, which conjures anxiety (Skierkowski & Wood, 2012) and thoughts the student futilely tries to suppress, having course policies that permit students to check their phones is not only something students want (Tindell, 2012), but may be something that allows them to spend more time focusing on class material.

What Could Be Improved?

A major benefit of the present study was that we looked at participants' actual behavior rather than self-report, which is important since previous research shows that self-reported smartphone use and actual smartphone use are not significantly correlated (Underwood, Rosen, More, Ehrenreich, & Gentsch, 2012).

There are a few potential limitations to our study. First, our sample focused entirely on college students, ignoring older segments of the population and those who do not attend college, which could undermine generalizability. However, given the nature of our research question (how course policies affect college students), we must have a target population of college students. Some may also question whether participants in our study really cared about the texts since they came from us. Although this limits realism to some degree, many of our participants still received "real" texts during the study, it would not have been immediately obvious that the texts were from us, and responding to texts may be such an automatic response that the sender's identity is not a key influence (and definitely was not for those in the group who were not allowed to check their phones). We cannot rule out the possibility that the lack of realism influenced the results, but the fact that we got an effect with this limitation suggests that in real-life settings, texts may be even more distracting.

In any simple experiment, there is always room for improvement, especially in terms of measuring additional factors that contribute to the dependent variable. In our case, though we found that placing restrictions on phone checking was problematic, we cannot be sure if students who could respond to texts (i.e., an even lower level of restriction) would do better or worse on the test. The truth is that there are numerous other variables that a researcher could test or additional factors that a researcher could control. In each case, it will become useful to add additional groups to the research design, a technique we will discuss more in Chapter 9.

What's Next?

Importantly, our study is silent in terms of how checking one's phone can potentially distract others. Thus, future research could use our same paradigm, but have a confederate be the person with the phone and see how others nearby react. It is also possible that the difficulty of the lesson or course content influences the smartphone's ability to distract a student. Research on cognitive load, the extent to which a person has working memory available, suggests that in more demanding classes where load is higher, smartphone use could make it more difficult for students to pay attention and ignore their smartphone (Lavie, 2010).

The present findings can also apply to the workplace in terms of how interruptions influence job performance. Given the present findings regarding the negative effects of trying to ignore an interruption, it may be best to allow employees to check their smartphones. In fact, research shows that interruptions hurt task performance, but that there is a learning effect that takes place such that later interruptions are less damaging (Altmann & Trafton, 2007). Research on restrictive smartphone policies in workplace settings would help establish the true cost of smartphone use on worker productivity.

> **What Do You Think?**
> Given the research findings, what study would you conduct next to continue our understanding of smartphone use in classrooms?

YOUR TURN 8.3

1. Fernando wants to determine if a person's mood influences belief in God. He randomly assigns participants to either a positive or negative mood group, then administers a "Belief in God" measure, along with several demographic questions. To see if there is a difference between groups, which statistic should he use?
   a. t-test for dependent means
   b. Pearson r
   c. Effect size
   d. t-test for independent means

2. Amie reads a magazine story that says that people who undergo life coaching are more successful than those who do not. As a savvy statistics and research student, Amie wants to know the study's _____, which will tell her whether the difference is significant, and the _____, which will tell her how large the difference was between the means.
   a. t score; degrees of freedom
   b. p level; t score
   c. p level; effect size
   d. effect size; p level

3. In the discussion, we noted that several variables that could serve as potential alternate explanations did not differ between the groups. Based on this, which of the following statements is true?
   a. Participants' GPA and cloud knowledge did not have any influence on test performance.
   b. The groups were relatively similar on these variables, meaning that we kept them relatively controlled.
   c. Random assignment was not effective.
   d. All students who were participants in our study had a high degree of texting experience.

How did you do? Turn to the end of the chapter to check your answers.

Research in Action

To Multitask or Not to Multitask?

Do you ever feel like your to-do list just keeps getting longer and longer with no end in sight? What is the best way to get everything done on your list? Should you go through the list item by item, or would it be better to do several things at once? Maybe you should first study for your exam, then do your laundry, and then text your friends to confirm your weekend plans. Alternatively, you could do these three things at the same time. After all, it could be just as effective as completing one task before moving on to the next.

Fortunately, we can rely on science rather than intuition to see which strategy is better. In the online activity *To Multitask or Not to Multitask?*, you will design your own simple experiment to solve this very question. Who knows—what you learn could help you actually complete all of those things on your to-do list!

 LaunchPad To complete this activity, visit LaunchPad at launchpadworks.com

Final Thoughts

In this chapter, we moved beyond correlational research designs to begin establishing how one factor *causes* another. The simple two-group experiment allowed us to establish cause and effect by randomly assigning participants to groups and by implementing high degrees of experimental control. Our research question also demonstrated the potential benefits of studying counterintuitive research questions. That is, even though instructors adopt well-intentioned course policies, it may be foolish to blindly trust in their effectiveness. Rather, we should put science to use doing what it does best: testing assumptions.

Who knows—if a smartphone policy could unknowingly undermine learning, could other common course practices or policies be doing the same? Do pop quizzes help or hurt students' scores on larger exams? If a professor requires class attendance, does that impose extrinsic motivations on students, when intrinsic motivation may serve them better? When professors give out their notes ahead of time, do students learn more or less? Does group work help students consider new perspectives, or does groupthink take over and ultimately narrow the range of ideas? You could conduct the research to find out. But before you set out to design a study, be sure to do a thorough literature review. You never know; it could be that others have already researched some of these questions, leaving it up to you to take the next step in broadening our understanding.

CHAPTER 8 Review

Review Questions

1. The local driving school owner, Lorraine, wants to see if her driving school students learn to drive better while listening to jazz music. To test this, she has half of her students listen to loud jazz music, while the other half listen to loud bluegrass music. Everyone learns the driving laws, parallel parking, and the meaning of road signs with music playing. Lorraine then measures the students' performance on their driver's license test. In this study the independent variable is ___, while the dependent variable is ___.

   a. music volume; driving test performance
   b. music volume; type of music
   c. type of music; driving test performance
   d. the driving skills in the lesson; music volume

2. As a TV producer, you are responsible for creating a reality TV show where 20 contestants from a variety of educational and experiential backgrounds and representing a variety of ages compete on physical and mental tasks like solving logic puzzles, building a pyramid, shooting a bow and arrow, completing a trivia quiz, and navigating an obstacle course. To create the two teams, you decide to put everyone's name on a Ping-Pong ball and then draw teams like numbers in the lottery. Which of the following would present a problem to the fairness of your teams?

   a. Four of the contestants are math students from Ivy League schools.
   b. A majority of the contestants have been part of Habitat for Humanity and have building experience.
   c. Eight contestants consider themselves "trivia buffs."
   d. None of the above.

3. Adele thinks the key to weight loss is eating expensive specialty dark chocolate bars that contain 65% cacao, pomegranate extract, and macadamia nuts. In particular, she thinks the pomegranate extract is the key ingredient. She wants to test her idea by comparing a group that eats 4 ounces of this specialty chocolate each day for a week to another group. What would be the best control group to test Adele's belief?

   a. A group that eats 4 ounces of a white chocolate bar.
   b. A group that eats 4 ounces of dark chocolate containing 65% cacao, grape extract, and macadamia nuts.
   c. A group that eats 4 ounces of dark chocolate containing 85% cacao, raspberry extract, and peanuts.
   d. A group that eats macadamia nuts and drinks 4 ounces of pomegranate extract.

4. Eerikki works in human resources and believes that employees at his telemarketing company would be more productive if they took a 30-minute nap each day at 2:30 p.m. at their desks. To test this, he has half of the employees take a nap, while the other half sit quietly for 30 minutes at 2:30 p.m. at their desks. To determine productivity, Eerikki examines log sheets to measure the number of sales each group made. In this study the experimental group is the ___, while the control group is the ___.
   a. nap group; quiet rest group
   b. quiet rest group; nap group
   c. time of day; number of sales
   d. log sheets; number of sales

5. Chip is doing a study on gift-giving around the holidays. He finds that people who received lots of gifts for their birthdays during childhood expect more gifts as adults. In order for Chip to conclude a causal relation, he still needs to establish which of the following?
   a. Covariation
   b. Correlation
   c. Temporal precedence
   d. Elimination of extraneous variables

6. Royale is a tattoo artist at The Ink Spot. He believes that getting a tattoo makes people become more outgoing, brave, and confident. To test this, he finds 60 people who want to get a tattoo and randomly gives half of them a tattoo on their shoulder blade, while the other half get a temporary tattoo in the same spot. Royale asks everyone to keep a daily diary that he will use to determine how outgoing, brave, and confident participants act over the next 3 months. Once the study is underway, Royale becomes worried that some of his participants were already outgoing and finds out that about a dozen already had tattoos. Should Royale be concerned? Why or why not?
   a. Yes, if people were already outgoing, then a tattoo cannot have any effect on them.
   b. Yes, having people who already have tattoos ruins the whole premise of the study.
   c. No, random assignment should balance these types of differences out between groups.
   d. No, a dozen people isn't enough to worry about.

7. Pastora is a club promoter who was hired to increase profitability at The Groove Lounge. Pastora decides to make the lights even dimmer and install oil drums with dry ice to make the entire club foggy. She thinks these changes will lead patrons to experience deindividuation, which will lead them to buy more food and drinks. As people leave the club at night, Pastora asks everyone demographic information, has them complete a deindividuation measure and a self-esteem measure, and asks the club owner how much

money was made each night. Which element of her study was included as a manipulation check?

a. The deindividuation measure

b. The self-esteem measure

c. The amount of money the club made

d. The number of dry ice blocks the club uses each night

8. Dr. Winston is doing a class demonstration where she has half of the class complete a series of 10 math problems, while the rest of the class completes a series of 10 analogies to determine which type of problem promotes greater alertness in her students. She randomly assigns students to groups to complete their problems quietly. Once everyone is finished, she asks everyone in Group 1 to report their current alertness level out loud. She then does the same for Group 2. Which of the following is a problem with Dr. Winston's design?

a. There was a problem with independence such that the groups started out being different.

b. There was a problem with independence such that individuals knew their groups.

c. Participants were not matched up based on math and verbal ability.

d. Some participants may be math or vocabulary geniuses.

9. As a speech pathologist, Flavia always wants to make sure her clients get the best treatment. One day a salesperson for a neurological diagnostic company comes to Flavia's office to share information about the effectiveness of a new diagnostic tool for stuttering to be compared with the current leading technique. The bar chart comparing the two groups looks impressive, but Flavia wants to see the statistical results. The appropriate statistic for comparing two groups is a _____. In those numbers, if Flavia wants to know how big the difference is between the two diagnostic tools, she would focus on the _____.

a. t score; effect size

b. Pearson r; p level

c. p level; Pearson r

d. t score; p level

10. Arielle hypothesizes that the more often a mother interacts with her child, the less distressed the child will be when left with a stranger. This is an example of what type of hypothesis?

a. A nondirectional hypothesis

b. A directional hypothesis

c. A null hypothesis

d. A causal hypothesis

11. Describe the benefits of using confederates in an experiment.

12. Why is using random assignment in experiments important when trying to establish causality?

13. What role does a manipulation check play when interpreting the results of an experiment?

Applying What You've Learned

1. Find a published empirical article that describes an experiment. Evaluate the groups in terms of experimental control. (A) What did they control well? (B) What could they have controlled better?

2. Go to the list of studies on http://psych.hanover.edu/research/exponnet. html. Find a correlational study that interests you and design a two-group experiment to test a similar research question.

3. This chapter's study focused on how overly restrictive smartphone policies can undermine test performance. Design a study to test this basic idea on driving behavior. Be sure your study carefully considers potential harm to participants.

4. Find a product on http://www.asseenontv.com/ and create a two-group experiment to test the "As Seen on TV" product's effectiveness.

5. Texting and technology influence our lives in many ways. Generate five new ideas for studies that have the same focus, but that do not focus on classroom settings or on restrictive smartphone policies. Pick your favorite idea and describe how you would test it with a two-group design.

6. Read the following study: Kay, A. C., Wheeler, S., Bargh, J. A., & Ross, L. (2004). Material priming: The influence of mundane physical objects on situational construal and competitive behavioral choice. *Organizational Behavior and Human Decision Processes, 95,* 83–96. doi:10.1016/j.obhdp. 2004.06.003. As you will see, in Study 1, researchers placed participants into either a business materials group or a neutral control condition, then had them complete a word completion task. (A) For this study, identify the independent variable, levels, dependent variable, and hypothesis. (B) What did the researchers control well? (C) What could they have controlled better?

7. THE NOVICE RESEARCHER: It is important to have experimental control. Playing the role of a novice researcher, design a two-group study that has at least four problems with experimental control. At the end, identify each problem and discuss how a more experienced researcher would have handled it.

8. DIG INTO THE NUMBERS: We have provided your instructor with supplemental data for a two-group design. Analyze that data to build your skills in using the *t*-test for independent means in SPSS. Write an APA-style results section based on your analyses. If you would like even more practice, your instructor also has data that accompanies the study discussed throughout this chapter.

Key Concepts

control group, p. 251

covariation, p. 249

effect size, p. 269

experimental control, p. 252

experimental group, p. 251

experimental hypothesis, p. 257

experimental realism, p. 264

extraneous variable, p. 250

independence, p. 260

independent samples *t*-test, p. 268

internal validity, p. 250

manipulation check, p. 265

matched-pair design, p. 262

mundane realism, p. 251

null hypothesis, p. 269

random assignment, p. 261

researcher notes, p. 264

simple experiment, p. 251

temporal precedence, p. 249

t-test for independent means, p. 268

two-group design, p. 251

Answers to YOUR TURN

Your Turn 8.1: 1. c; 2. d; 3. a

Your Turn 8.2: 1. b; 2. d; 3. c

Your Turn 8.3: 1. d; 2. c; 3. b

Answers to Multiple-Choice Review Questions

1. c; 2. d; 3. b; 4. a; 5. d; 6. c; 7. a; 8. b; 9. a; 10. b

Multigroup Design

I'm Feeling Hot, But Is the Earth Hot, Too?

Michael Runkel/Getty Images

LEARNING OUTCOMES

After reading this chapter, you should be able to:

- Provide operational definitions for key variables.
- Identify key design issues with multigroup research.
- Identify potential confounds in a manipulation.
- Explain the benefits of and uses for multigroup designs.
- Identify the proper statistics to use for multigroup designs.
- Write a results section for a one-way ANOVA and a chi-square.

Something to Think About . . .

Have you seen those images of a polar bear with a sad expression drifting out to sea on a melting ice cap, or paddling around in frigid water, clamoring for the safety of a nearby ice shelf? Unfortunately, these are not just pictures from the Polar Bear X Games. Al Gore, a former U.S. vice president and star of the documentary on climate change *An Inconvenient Truth*, argues that over recent decades the earth has been warming, and that these poor polar bears are innocent victims of climate change. While 97% of the published scientific papers in the field agree that climate change is occurring and is caused by human activity (Cook et al., 2013), 20% of Americans still do not believe that the Earth's temperature is rising (Pew, 2016). Why do people continue to deny climate change in the face of overwhelming evidence? One reason might be that they allow personal experience to override scientific data.

Do *you* believe that climate change is a "truth"? Your own personal experience may determine your beliefs. When you are shoveling out from snow in the freezing cold of winter, it might be difficult to believe in global warming. Yet someone in a part of the world that is experiencing a record heat wave might easily believe that global warming is real. *The Daily Show* once satirized this idea in a segment where one correspondent, pictured standing on a hot beach, passionately argued that global warming was true while the other correspondent, supposedly shivering in a snowstorm, passionately argued that global warming was a hoax. In both cases, the individuals' immediate experiences strongly influenced their attitudes toward the idea of climate change. These examples raise an important issue. Which is it wise to rely upon when deciding what is true: your own immediate experience or scientific evidence?

Regardless of the scientific conclusion, you have probably heard anecdotal assertions about climate change (for or against) based on the current temperature. Of course, these comments may just be flippant, where the person realizes that his or her immediate environment is not directly indicative of climate change. (After all, it is called "global warming," not "neighborhood warming" or "campus warming.") However, it is possible that people unknowingly allow these experiences, or even much less dramatic experiences related to temperature, to influence how they think about climate change.

Introduction to Our Research Question

The purpose of this chapter's study is to explore the following question:

RESEARCH **?** Can the experience of warmth lead you to consider climate change as more problematic, consequently influencing your attitudes and behaviors?

It would be interesting to determine if a person's direct experience of temperature (e.g., hot, average, and cold) influences his or her attitudes and behaviors surrounding climate change. After all, climate change is such a far-reaching phenomenon that we may not recognize how one's immediate experience could have an influence. The best way to begin answering this question is to determine what past research has uncovered on this topic. Let's take a look at whether a person's immediate surroundings can influence attitudes and behaviors.

▶ How do you conduct a literature search?
SEE CHAPTER 2, p. 29

Reviewing the Literature: What Do We Already Know About This Topic?

Given our question, we should look for relevant research in a few key areas: How do people perceive climate change? How can immediate surroundings influence people's thoughts and behaviors? Most importantly, how might temperature influence people? Using PsycINFO, we found some research studies that help us to answer these questions. Here are summaries we created based on reading and taking notes on the articles that we thought were relevant to our research question.

Perception of Climate Change

Lorenzoni, I., Leiserowitz, A., De Franca Doria, M., Poortinga, W., & Pidgeon, N. (2006). Cross-national comparisons of image associations with "global warming" and "climate change" among laypeople in the United States of America and Great Britain. *Journal of Risk Research, 9,* 265–281. doi:10.1080/13669870600613658

In a large sample of British and American citizens, climate change produced negative associations (e.g., heat and ice melting) and was considered an important issue.

Whitmarsh, L. (2008). Are flooding victims more concerned about climate change than other people? The role of direct experience in risk perception and behavioural response. *Journal of Risk Research, 11,* 351–374. doi:10.1080/13669870701552235

To examine whether a direct experience with an environmental event influences perception of risk, researchers interviewed flood victims who had direct experience with an alleged by-product of climate change (i.e., flooding). Results indicated that although flood victims viewed climate change as more personally relevant than those who had not experienced a flood, they were not more concerned, more informed, or more motivated to engage in behavior that would combat climate change.

How Surroundings or the Environment Influence People

Berman, M., Jonides, J., & Kaplan, S. (2008). The cognitive benefits of interacting with nature. *Psychological Science, 19,* 1207–1212. doi:10.1111/j.1467-9280.2008.02225.x

Participants who walked in a park performed better on an attention task than those who walked in a downtown area. In a follow-up study, the researchers replicated the finding simply by having participants either look at pictures of nature or pictures of urban areas.

Liljenquist, K., Zhong, C., & Galinsky, A. (2010). The smell of virtue: Clean scents promote reciprocity and charity. *Psychological Science, 21,* 381–383. doi:10.1177/0956797610361426

A set of studies examining the influence of smell found that participants in a clean-smelling room gave more money to a partner, took more flyers related to volunteering with Habitat for Humanity, and were willing to donate more money than those in a room without a noticeable scent.

The Influence of Temperature on People

Williams, L., & Bargh, J. (2008). Experiencing physical warmth promotes interpersonal warmth. *Science, 322,* 606–607. doi:10.1126/science.1162548

Researchers examined the association between physical warmth and attitudes of interpersonal warmth by examining whether holding a hot cup of coffee (vs. a cold cup) would influence perceptions of another person. Those who held the hot cup rated the other person's personality more favorably. Another study found that those who held a warm (vs. cold) therapeutic pad were more likely to choose a gift for a friend rather than take one for themselves.

IJzerman, H., & Semin, G. R. (2009). The thermometer of social relations: Mapping social proximity on temperature. *Psychological Science, 10,* 1214–1220. doi:10.1111/j.1467-9280.2009.02434.x

This set of studies examined the effect of temperature on a variety of behaviors. Study 1 generally replicated Williams & Bargh (2008) by showing that those who had a warm cup felt close to the experimenter. The follow-up studies looked at the effects of ambient room temperature. Study 2 found that those in a warm room described a film more concretely and felt closer to the experimenter. Study 3 found that participants in the warm room had greater relational focus, as measured by a perceptual task.

Li, Y., Johnson, E. J., & Zaval, L. (2011). Local warming: Daily temperature change influences belief in global warming. *Psychological Science, 22,* 454–459. doi:10.1177/0956797611400913

To determine if fluctuations in daily temperature influenced beliefs in global warming, researchers asked participants in the United States and Australia to report the day's temperature, observe whether it deviated from normal, and then give their assessment of global warming. Those responding on a warm day perceived global warming as more problematic and were more likely to donate money to a global warming charity.

 Thinking Like a Scientist in Real Life

The Smell of Real Estate Success

Realtors commonly suggest baking cookies when selling a house to make it feel more like home. In fact, there is research that suggests the smell of fresh-baked cookies makes people more likely to make unplanned purchases (Li, 2008). Based on this chapter's background research about subtle factors influencing behavior, there are probably other suggestions realtors could make to help sell a house. For example, should a seller borrow a friend's adorable family dog for their open house? When decorating a dorm room, is it better to put up a movie poster from *Fifty Shades of Grey* or a music poster from Slipknot's Prepare for Hell tour? How might these subtle environmental factors influence how people feel about you?

Subtle factors can influence our behavior. If you want to sell a gas-guzzling truck or a fuel-efficient hybrid car, what subtle influences might enhance the sale? *(left: Bloomberg/Getty Images; right: nitinut380/Deposit Photos)*

From Ideas to Innovation

In light of previous research on temperature and climate change, it appears that our research question has merit, and that outdoor temperature influences perceptions of global warming (Li et al., 2011). But we still do not have an answer to our specific question regarding the immediate or subtle experiences of temperature on perceptions of climate change. This is why we need to take the next step, developing a study that not only extends what others have learned but also addresses our research question. As we have done in previous chapters, let's start by clearly defining our terms and developing a testable hypothesis.

Defining Key Terms: What Do You Mean By _____?

If we want our research question to evolve into a testable hypothesis, we will want to be more specific about what we mean by a few of the key ideas. First, we need to develop clear, concise, and repeatable conceptual definitions of our key terms. Looking back at our research question, what do we mean by "warmth"? What does it mean to be "more problematic"? What do we mean by "climate change"? Wait—do we really need to develop a conceptual definition for that last one? Since scientists who study climate change have established its definition, we should probably defer to their expertise. According to the Environmental Protection Agency, climate change involves an increase in the Earth's average temperature resulting from human and natural sources. An existing definition from a credible source is useful because the definition's validity has already been established. Past literature may be less helpful in considering how to define "warmth" and "more problematic" because these ideas are much more specialized in terms of how they could relate to our current hypothesis. So, we are on our own. Thankfully, as the researchers, we have some latitude to craft conceptual definitions that fit how we think of the variables.

To start, it will be helpful to identify the independent variable (IV) and the dependent variable (DV). Based on our phrasing of the research question, which idea do you think influences or causes the other? In our case, we want to see how temperature influences attitudes about climate change, not how attitudes about climate change influence outside temperature (that would be silly, right?). Therefore, temperature is the variable that is having the influence, making it our independent variable. Next, the outcome or the by-product is attitude toward climate change, making it our dependent variable. Differentiating these variables helps because we will want to manipulate the independent variable and measure the dependent variable. Now that we have identified these variables, we can decide how we are going to use them in our study by establishing their operational definitions.

▶ What is the difference between an independent and dependent variable? SEE CHAPTER 2, p. 38

Operationally Defining the DV: Measuring Attitudes Toward Climate Change

If we want to know someone's attitude toward an issue like climate change, what is the easiest way to find out? Well, we could just ask! In our study, we can ask people to self-report how much they agree or disagree with attitudinal statements such as "Climate change is a problem" and "Climate change will negatively impact future generations." Remember, good self-report measures ask multiple questions, so we would want to include several questions just like those. Our participants could then provide their thoughts by indicating how much they agree with each statement on a 5-point scale (1 = strongly disagree; 5 = strongly agree).

Self-report questions are useful because participants can state their own personal views on climate change. But what if some participants feel embarrassed about revealing a politically incorrect attitude toward climate change (e.g., "I am not worried about climate change because I care much more about looking cool in my SUV"), or what if they have never even heard of this issue? In both cases, we

▶ Want further details on how to create quality self-report measures? SEE CHAPTER 7, p. 202

What Do You Think?
What other questions could you ask to determine a participant's attitude toward climate change?

would not know if participants were reporting genuine feelings. They could also succumb to social desirability concerns and simply tell us what they think are the socially acceptable or "right" answers. With controversial issues such as climate change, it may be more politically correct and socially acceptable for an individual to say climate change is a truth when talking to some people (such as Leonardo DiCaprio, who advocated for climate change activism in his acceptance speech for Best Actor at the 2016 Academy Awards) and that it is a hoax when talking to others (such as U.S. Senator James Inhofe from Oklahoma, who brought snowballs into the Senate to "prove" that global warming is a hoax), regardless of what that individual really believes. Given that there are plenty of people who openly mock the "theory" of climate change, the presence of a socially desirable answer may not be a large factor in our study. But you can see how an item such as "preserving the Earth for future generations is important" could place pressure on participants to respond with a socially desirable answer. Can you imagine a person actually saying, "Nope, not important. They're on their own"?

▶ How can demand characteristics impact participants' responses? SEE CHAPTER 4, p. 90

Our self-report measure also may inadvertently introduce demand characteristics. For example, the self-report item itself may make what you are hoping to gather from the study very obvious. Therefore, the participant may think, "They're asking me about climate change, so the researchers likely think it is a problem. They seem nice enough, and I want to help them out, so, yes, I guess climate change may be seen by some as a problem. I'll pick 5, *strongly agree.*" Demand characteristics may be even more of a problem if we ask questions about climate change right after we provide participants with a direct and obvious experience of heat or cold (e.g., "Please put this bag of ice or heat pad on your head").

To help minimize the potential for demand characteristics and, to a lesser degree, social desirability concerns, we can try to disguise the purpose of our study. One way to accomplish this is to include questions that do not relate to our dependent variable. In our study, we could add questions about other social issues (e.g., marriage rights, health care) or environmental issues (e.g., water quality, littering) so that we have a dozen questions with our key climate change questions nestled in with the other issues. These would act as distractor questions to help counteract **hypothesis-guessing,** which occurs when the participant actively attempts to identify the purpose of the research. If the participants do not know which questions are the "real" ones, they will have a harder time figuring out our study's true purpose. While distractors help, participants *could* still be less than totally honest. One way to address this is to assure participants of their anonymity and the confidentiality of their responses, which allows participants to feel more comfortable providing us with their true feelings because we will not know who they are, and we will not be able to link their answers back to them. We may also consider asking the participants during the post-experiment interview, or debriefing, what they were thinking as they read over the self-report items. For example, we could ask them whether or not they determined the purpose of the study, and, if so, how that might have influenced how they answered the questions. Of course, we would still have social desirability concerns during debriefing; hence, we would need to make the process as nonthreatening as possible.

▶ Want to know more about using distractor items in self-report measures? SEE CHAPTER 7, p. 218

▶ Why is confidentiality necessary in human research? SEE CHAPTER 3, p. 58

As you have no doubt seen in your own life, talk can be cheap, and the true measure of a person's beliefs is what that person does, rather than what the

hypothesis-guessing when a participant in a study actively attempts to identify the purpose of the research.

person says. Rather than ask how the participant feels, we could investigate what the participant actually does by measuring his or her behavior.

Weighing Our Options: Identifying Key Behaviors

What actions might reflect a person's attitudes toward climate change? Consider it this way: "A person who perceives climate change as problematic might _____(1)_____, while a person who does not think it is a problem might _____(2)_____." Fill in the blanks.

There are lots of possibilities, but here are some we came up with:

1. attend a rally to support clean air; donate money to an environmental initiative; purchase an ecofriendly bumper sticker
2. drive a gas-guzzling car; sign a petition to support more off-shore drilling for oil; vote against clean energy laws

Looking over these lists, you can see how things in list 1 could apply to list 2 and vice versa. For example, a person who thinks climate change is a problem might not drive an SUV, while a person who does not believe in climate change might drive an SUV. For our study, we do not need to measure all of these behaviors. In fact, for pragmatic reasons, some of these are more feasible than others (e.g., it would be very difficult to provide actual SUVs for people to drive). However, we could easily provide participants with the opportunity to sign a petition in support of a new "Cool Earth" climate change prevention bill. But that opportunity might seem fake. To make it appear more realistic, or increase its mundane realism, we could add a few signatures ahead of time, making sure that each signature appears unique by using different ink colors and handwriting styles, and place the petition on a clipboard.

What Do You Think?
What other behaviors could you investigate in the lab to assess one's attitude toward climate change?

Focus on Ethics: Should We Really Do That?

Okay, so the "Cool Earth" bill does not really exist. Is it wrong for us to tell people it exists to see if they will sign up to support it? We would also need to fake signatures for this contrived petition. Although our study's procedure does involve telling people something that is factually inaccurate, this deception is relatively mild and provides us with a cover story that enables participants to act naturally in this setting. It is hard to imagine that participants would sign the petition knowing that it was fake, which makes the cover story essential. While the addition of fake signatures ahead of time is also deceptive, they have to be fake in order to keep the identity of actual participants hidden. We also should not allow our participants to actually sign the petition. Otherwise, the current participant could read the names of the previous participants, which

What can we infer from behavior? If a car has a bumper sticker like this one, does it necessarily mean the owner is environmentally conscious? *(Jeffrey Coolidge/Photodisc/Getty Images)*

Can you think of more than one reason why a person might sign a petition? *(OLGA MALTSEVA/AFP/Getty Images)*

▶ Is it ever ethical to deceive research participants? SEE CHAPTER 3, p. 71

would compromise their anonymity. Furthermore, each participant would need to receive the exact same sheet so that it is constant for all participants. If it were different for each participant, the number of signatures would be another variable in the study because the number of signatures could influence the decision to sign in and of itself. Therefore, we need to keep this aspect of the study controlled. To resolve these ethical dilemmas, we would debrief participants afterward by telling them the purpose of the study, the nature of the deception, and the reason for its use.

Weighing Our Options: Picking a Measure

Now that we have addressed some ethical concerns, we need to decide whether a self-report or a behavioral measure will best capture a participant's attitude toward climate change. Self-report has the benefit of directly asking participants about their feelings in a quick and simple fashion, but has the downside of participants potentially being less than truthful. The behavioral measure of asking participants to sign a petition can provide more authentic responses, but requires a bit of inference regarding the underlying meaning of the behavior (e.g., a person could sign the petition out of concern for climate change or because they generally like to sign petitions). No research design is perfect; each method has its pros and cons. Therefore, it is best to use **methodological pluralism,** where we employ multiple methods or strategies to answer our question. In most cases, operationally defining attitudes by using self-report and behavioral measurements would be beneficial because the strengths of one will compensate for the weaknesses of the other. To do this, we will operationally define the dependent variable of attitude toward climate change in two different ways: We will measure it behaviorally by giving participants the option to sign a petition, and we will also measure it with self-report using a multiple-item questionnaire that asks about views on various societal problems. Embedded in this questionnaire, shown in **Figure 9.1**, will be four items measuring participants' attitudes toward climate change.

Operationally Defining the IV: Making People Hot

With our dependent variable in place (perceptions of climate change), we can work on identifying an independent variable that may influence those perceptions. If we believe that heat influences attitudes toward climate change, we will need to have people experience heat and then see what they think about climate change and how they behave. People experience heat all the time: sitting at the beach, living close to the equator, taking popcorn out of the microwave, or wrapping up in a blanket. As people naturally experience heat, we could ask them about climate change. However, it would be extremely cumbersome to follow people around, waiting for them to feel hot. We could go to a place where

methodological pluralism the use of multiple methods or strategies to answer a research question.

Societal Concerns Survey

Please rate your level of agreement with the following statements using the scale below.

1	2	3	4	5
Strongly Disagree	Disagree	Neutral	Agree	Strongly Agree

_____ 1. The health care system in the United States is a serious problem.

_____ 2. The lack of equality in marriage rights will have a noticeably negative impact on the environment in which my family and I live.

_____ 3. Climate change is a serious problem*.

_____ 4. The health care system will have a noticeably negative impact on the environment in which my family and I live.

_____ 5. Climate change will have a noticeably negative impact on my health in the next 25 years*.

_____ 6. The rate of unemployment in the United States is a serious problem.

_____ 7. Climate change will have a noticeably negative impact on my economic and financial situation in the next 25 years*.

_____ 8. The lack of equality concerning marriage rights is a serious problem.

_____ 9. The health care system will have a noticeably negative impact on my health in the next 25 years.

_____ 10. Climate change will have a noticeably negative impact on the environment in which my family and I live*.

*We used these items to measure attitudes toward climate change; the other items are distractor items.

FIGURE 9.1 Societal Concerns Survey.

we know people will experience heat, like the beach on a hot day, and give them our measures there. However, this may not be the ideal way to approach our research question either.

Weighing Our Options: Picking a Sample

Our two main options are to use people who are naturally experiencing various temperatures, or to systematically control or manipulate temperature (e.g., make people hot) as part of our study. There are some good reasons to find people at the beach who are already experiencing warmth. It is convenient, since we know there will be many people to provide a large sample, and there are plenty of hot days from which to choose. You could even compare people at the beach on a hot day to people at the beach on a cooler day. Using the exact same beach provides additional control. That seems perfect, right?

Well, let's think about this first. "Beachgoers" are most likely different from people who avoid the beach. For example, everyone in a given country does not have the same chance to visit a beach. In the United States, people who

In what other ways can a person experience the sensation of heat?

(Scott Hortop/Getty Images)

► What is external validity?
SEE CHAPTER 6, p. 164

reside in North Carolina or California are more likely to go to the beach than those living in Iowa or Nebraska. Of those who have more convenient access to the beach, some people are probably more likely to visit the beach than others. Factors such as age, job flexibility, or skin complexion may all influence an individual's affinity for the beach. Speaking of affinity, some people just like the beach and being outside more than others. In terms of feelings about climate change, it is highly probable that people who enjoy being outside have different or stronger opinions about environmental issues like climate change.

These issues are problematic for two reasons. First, beachgoers may possess characteristics that make them different from other people in the world. This creates a sampling bias where we are not gathering information from a certain subset of the population (in this case, people who do not go to the beach). As a result, a study of beachgoers may not generalize to nonbeachgoers, which would hurt our external validity. If our study can only tell us about beachgoers and not about the general population, it may not be worth all the trouble. Second, and even more problematic to our research, is the possibility that beachgoers possess a heightened level of environmental concern that may directly influence their perceptions of climate change. Specifically, beachgoers may be more sensitive to issues surrounding heat, air quality, and rising ocean levels than the average person. This may lead us to overestimate, or possibly underestimate, the impact that situational factors can have on perceptions of climate change. Ideally, we should recruit participants from the general population using random sampling to ensure that we have a good representation of the average person. However, there are pragmatic concerns about the cost of random sampling and the ability to obtain a truly random sample.

As you can see, using people who are naturally experiencing warmth is a poor strategy, so we will use convenience sampling by recruiting people from campus and the surrounding community. To have more confidence about how the experience of temperature (our IV) influences perceptions of climate change (our DV), we could manipulate temperature as part of an experiment instead of relying on actual outdoor temperatures. This would be helpful because it would allow us to establish causation between our variables. At the most basic level, to manipulate temperature we would need one group to experience heat while the other group did not. But, should the nonheat group experience something less hot, like room temperature, or something cold? The best answer hinges on why we think experiencing heat will influence perceptions of climate change. That is, heat could make participants more sensitive to the issue because increasing temperatures globally is a key sign of climate change. However, it is also possible that any deviation from a normal temperature sensitizes people to climate change in the opposite direction (e.g., when people are cold they could be less convinced that climate change exists). Because we have more than two possibilities to test, we should use a design that allows us to have multiple levels of our independent variable. In this case, a **multigroup design,** or an experimental design with three or more groups, would be best and would have a few important benefits.

Benefit of Multigroup Design: Two Studies for the Price of One

To test both hot and cold, we could run two separate two-group designs. The first would compare heat to a control condition of moderate temperature. The second would compare cold to a control condition of moderate temperature. While we could run two studies, it would be simpler if we could make these comparisons all within the same study. Thankfully, we can do exactly that; this is a major benefit of a multigroup design. Instead of two distinct studies, we can run one study where we have three groups (i.e., three levels of our independent variable): hot, cold, and moderate. Being able to use all three in the same study saves us time because it is almost always quicker to run one study than two. It also saves us from having to recruit even more participants because the participants in the control group (moderate temperature) can be compared to both the hot and the cold groups. Most importantly, this approach allows us to make direct comparisons between hot and cold and to test the possibility that experiencing any type of aberrant or different temperature influences attitudes toward climate change.

How could the location of your university influence the results of a climate-change study? *(Reto Stöckli, Nazmi El Saleous, and Marit Jentoft-Nilsen, NASA GSFC)*

multigroup design an experimental design with three or more groups.

Benefit of Multigroup Design: Identifying Relationships

Adding a moderate temperature group also helps us determine the nature of participants' attitudes in the middle of the continuum between hot and cold. This is important because without a moderate condition we would only have two data points, which would lead us to assume a linear relationship between our values, as shown in **Figure 9.2.** That is, we may believe that as temperatures cool, one becomes less concerned about climate change. While it is possible that decreasing the experience of heat results in perfectly corresponding, or linear, changes in the perception that climate change is a problem, it is also possible that perceptions are only negative at higher temperatures (see **Figure 9.3a**), or that high and moderate temperatures lead people to have negative perceptions, but that cold temperatures make it seem less problematic (see Figure 9.3b). Thus,

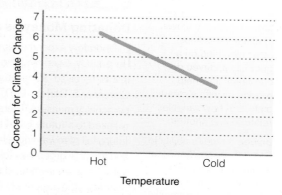

FIGURE 9.2 Perception of Climate Change: Linear Relationship.

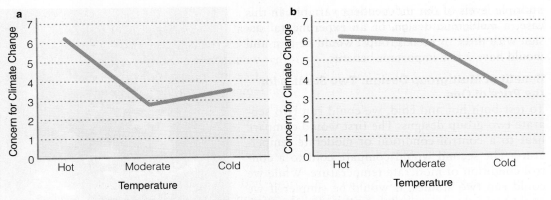

FIGURE 9.3 Two Perceptions of Climate-Change Possibilities.

a major benefit of having more than two groups or levels of the independent variable is that it allows us to identify a potential **nonlinear (or functional) relationship,** which is any association between variables that the use of just two comparison groups cannot uncover. These relationships, often identified on a graph as a curved or curvilinear line, help provide us with a clearer picture of how the independent variable may influence the dependent variable.

Now that we know that we want to test the influence of three temperatures (hot, moderate, cold) on attitudes, we need to determine the mechanics of how to accomplish this. We will want to maximize our study's **power,** or our study's ability to find real differences between our groups. One easy way to do this is to increase the strength of our manipulation. That is, the larger the differences between our groups, the easier it will be to detect whether or not our independent variable influenced the dependent variable. For example, we could manipulate more extreme temperatures and prolong participants' exposure to that temperature.

▶ Want more information on the concept of power?
SEE APPENDIX A, p. 487

nonlinear (or functional) relationships
any association between variables that the use of just two comparison groups cannot uncover. These relationships, often identified on a graph as a curved or curvilinear line, help provide us with a clearer picture of how variables relate to one another.

power a study's ability to find differences between groups when there is a real difference (i.e., when the null hypothesis is false); the probability that a study will yield significant results.

 Research Spotlight

Donating Money as an Indicator of Prosocial Behavior

In laboratory experiments, we often use behavior to assess underlying motivations of attitudes. In a study examining the impact of feeling socially excluded on prosocial behavior, participants received $2 in quarters as payment for participation (Twenge, Baumeister, DeWall, Ciarocco, & Bartels, 2007). Afterward, researchers gave participants feedback based on a personality measure. There were four groups: some participants learned they had a personality linked to a future full of failed relationships and loneliness; others learned they would have a future full of rewarding relationships; others learned they would have a future full of accidents; and the final group was told nothing. At the end of the study, the researcher asked participants to make an anonymous donation to the Student Emergency Fund to help fellow students with unanticipated expenses. The amount donated served as the measure of prosocial behavior. Ultimately, exclusion feedback hindered prosocial behavior, as those who heard that their future was full of loneliness donated less (a fourth of the amount) than those in other conditions.

Focus on Ethics: Should We Really Do That?

Something we need to consider before moving forward is how hot or cold we can make people without them experiencing unnecessary harm. To be safe, we should not expose participants to conditions that would be outside of their typical experience. People do go outdoors in below freezing temperatures (below 32°F/0°C) and go in steam saunas that are set at temperatures as high as 194°F (90°C). Should we make participants sit in a sauna set at 190°F (88°C) or in a meat locker set at 37°F (3°C)? If so, we need to decide for how long participants can safely withstand these temperatures. Also, by exposing participants to such extreme environmental conditions, we run the risk of introducing a potential demand characteristic. If you were a participant sitting in a sauna or meat locker, you might start to think that temperature had something to do with the study. Besides, we would not want to expose participants to unnecessary risks such as heat exhaustion or frostbite by using temperatures at the upper and lower boundaries. We can minimize participant risk as well as potential demand characteristics by using temperatures that more closely conform to everyday experiences. In addition, when considering the participants' length of exposure, it is prudent to use the smallest exposure that will create the desired effect. Therefore, our exposure times should probably be closer to 15 minutes than to 15 hours. We also need to be sure to mention in the study recruitment and informed consent stages that only people in good health should participate in the study.

In light of these concerns, we need to find a way to manipulate temperature in ways that our participants might already experience. One possibility is to have participants in the hot group lie in a tanning bed, while those in the cold group stand in front of an air conditioner set on high. The moderate group could just sit in a temperate room. These approaches would certainly manipulate temperature and are each within participants' everyday experiences. But even assuming we could obtain the necessary equipment to set this up, approval from the IRB to conduct the study, and participants' consent, there is still a problem with these manipulations.

Our question is how temperature influences attitudes about climate change. Since temperature is the intended independent variable, we need to be sure that it is the only thing we manipulate. If we manipulate something else unintentionally, we have introduced a **confound,** which is something that the researcher unintentionally varies along with the manipulation. In our manipulation, we only want to vary temperature, so any other factor that we inadvertently change along with that is a confound. Confounds are problematic because if we discover a difference in attitudes between the three groups, we would not be sure if it was due to temperature or if it was due to other differences that we inadvertently created between those groups.

Do you have any ideas about what some confounds might be within our proposed manipulations? Some possibilities are differences in time exposed to

confound a variable that the researcher unintentionally varies along with the manipulation.

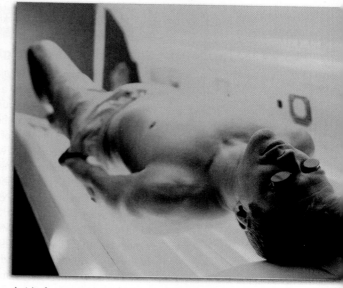

Aside from using a tanning bed, in what other ways could you manipulate the experience of warmth?
(Stockbyte/Getty Images)

light (long vs. short), body position (lying down vs. standing), and the amount of space (enclosed in tanning bed vs. being in an open room). While some factors are more of a stretch than others in terms of whether they might actually influence attitudes, for those lying in a tanning bed, light exposure can improve mood (Terao & Hoaki, 2011) and has even been used as a therapeutic intervention (Privitera, Moynihan, Tang, & Khan, 2010). Happy people are helpful people. Putting some, but not all, of the participants in a better mood may make them more likely to agree with anything we ask them to do, such as signing a petition. Consequently, we must either purposefully manipulate potential confounding factors by adding additional groups (this has the downside of us needing to recruit more participants) or minimize potential confounds by more carefully creating our manipulations.

Rather than reinvent the proverbial wheel, maybe we should look back through our literature review to see how others have dealt with the issue of manipulating the experience of temperature. One of the studies from our review had participants hold a hot, room temperature, or cold cup of coffee (Williams & Bargh, 2008). There is evidence that this manipulation is valid, so we could follow the procedure the authors describe in their study. Digging a bit further into the literature, we find that another potential manipulation involves changing the temperature of the room. One study using this approach had participants sit for 10–15 minutes in a room that was either cold (59–64°F/15–18°C) or warm (71–75°F/22–24°C) to determine that those in the higher temperature demonstrated a greater inclination toward social relations (e.g., stood in closer proximity to another; IJzerman & Semin, 2009). We could adapt this design to suit our own needs by adding a hot condition where participants sit in a room with a higher temperature (81–85°F/27–29°C).

What Do You Think?

Would it ever be ethical to expose participants to a tanning bed given the potential risk of skin cancer?

 Thinking Like a Scientist in Real Life

The Confounds of Weight Loss

Based on the recommendation of her personal trainer, Kate buys an appetite suppressant capsule regimen for $50 a month. Following instructions, she takes two small capsules along with 8 cups of water four times a day. Kate finds that, as the trainer predicted, she is not very hungry on the days she takes the supplement. When she tells her trainer, he reports that over the past 3 months, of his 50 clients, the half who took the capsules experienced suppressed appetite and lost weight, and the half who took nothing did not. Is the supplement responsible for the effect? What else could be responsible for the suppressed appetite? In this case, the amount of water people drink (2 gallons!) along with the supplement. Because people drink water at the same time they take the capsule, the two factors covary, or go together. Since water was not the key ingredient and was not intended to have an effect, it is a potential confound. Consequently, those who took the supplement cannot be sure if their suppressed appetite and weight loss were the result of the capsules, or the by-product of increased water consumption. Some might say that you cannot argue with the results since those on the regimen lost weight. While this is true, if the supplement actually has no effect, those on the regimen have been wasting $50 a month!

Weighing Our Options: Picking a Manipulation

From these two studies, we have two validated ways to manipulate participants' experience of temperature. As is often the case in research design, there really is not a clear-cut best choice. But we do need to make a choice that works for us. Considering our options, the coffee cup manipulation involves direct, tactile temperature experience because participants touch something that is hot or cold (Williams & Bargh, 2008). Manipulating the room temperature involves an ambient experience of temperature because participants experience the temperature all around them (IJzerman & Semin, 2009). Due to the ambient nature of climate change, the room temperature manipulation would seem more likely to influence attitudes toward climate change. For our study, we will operationally define temperature as sitting in a hot (81–85°F/27–29°C), cold (59–64°F/15–18°C), or average (71–75°F/22–24°C) temperature room.

Benefit of Multigroup Design: Additional Groups Help Us Address Alternative Explanations

Before we finalize our hypothesis and plan our procedure, we should consider whether there are any other groups, beyond hot, cold, and average, that would help our study. Remember that we are using a "multigroup" design, so we are not limited to using just three conditions. We can use as many conditions as we want to help us address our research question. For example, we could add an **empty control group,** which is a group that does not receive any form of the treatment and just completes the dependent variable. An empty control group is useful because it shows how participants respond under normal conditions. However, in our study, this group would be difficult to incorporate because we cannot have the absence of temperature. The good news is that our average group (who will sit in a "room temperature" space) already does a good job of determining participants' responses under normal conditions.

Another specialized group to consider adding is a **placebo group,** which is a group where participants believe they are getting the treatment, but, in reality, they are not. A placebo group is useful because we can determine how much participants' responses on the dependent variable are due to their expectations about the independent variable's potential effect. In our study, a placebo would require that participants think they are experiencing a certain temperature when, in reality, they are not. As you can imagine, this would be difficult to incorporate in our study. Fortunately, a placebo group really is not necessary because our manipulation of room temperature is subtle, such that participants may not realize they are receiving a treatment. Rather, they may just think the room happens to be particularly hot or cold without connecting it to the study. Consequently, it will be difficult for them to identify the manipulation and to form expectations about how it might influence the dependent variable.

What Do You Think?
Can you make an argument for why the cup manipulation may have been the better manipulation?

empty control group a group that does not receive any form of the treatment and just completes the dependent variable.

placebo group a group where participants believe they are getting the treatment, but in reality they are not.

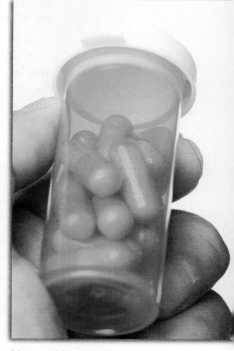

How could researchers use placebos to test the effectiveness of new drugs? *(Nation Wong/First Light/ Getty Images)*

Our Hypothesis

► How does a researcher establish a hypothesis? SEE CHAPTER 2, p. 31

In trying to answer our research question, we have had to consider many issues and make several decisions along the way. Of course, you may have made different decisions than we did, but that is okay! There is no one "right" way to design an experiment. For our independent variable, shown in **Table 9.1**, we decided to manipulate the temperature of the room. We will use two strategies for measuring our dependent variable: We will assess participants' attitudes toward climate change through a self-report questionnaire, and assess their behavior by giving them a chance to sign a petition involving climate change.

TABLE 9.1

Our Multigroup Design		
Temperature Condition		
Hot	Cold	Average

Based on these decisions, we can establish our research hypotheses to formalize our predictions regarding ambient temperature's effect on climate change attitudes and behaviors. Specifically, we will test whether there are general differences between the conditions in our multigroup design by testing the following hypothesis:

There will be a difference between the groups in their reporting of climate change as a problem and in their likelihood of signing a relevant petition.

► What is the difference between a directional and nondirectional hypothesis? SEE CHAPTER 7, p. 217

You will notice that we do not make a specific prediction in this hypothesis, meaning that it is a nondirectional hypothesis. We thought that we would leave that up to you. Given our research question, what other specific hypotheses or comparisons might we want to make concerning the relationship between ambient temperature and attitudes toward climate change? Keep these predictions in mind so that we can test them once we start analyzing our data.

YOUR TURN 9.1

1. All of the following are benefits of multigroup design, *except*:
   a. it allows you to discover functional or curvilinear relationships.
   b. you generally need fewer participants.
   c. you can test several levels of the independent variable in the same study.
   d. you are more likely to have significant findings.

2. To boost morale in the accounting department, the human resources department will place greeting cards on employees' desks. For employees born between January and June, cards will include messages from employees' direct supervisors (e.g., "I know that we can count on you!").

For employees born between July and December, cards will include generic jokes about accounting (e.g., "How many accountants does it take to change a lightbulb? Depends—are they billing by the hour?"). Which of the following is a confound?

a. The source of the message
b. The type of joke
c. The use of greeting cards
d. Month of birth

3. Asa wants to test whether the "boosters" in the smoothies served at the dining hall are effective. She plans on giving one group a strawberry smoothie with a memory booster, and another group a plain strawberry smoothie. After drinking the smoothie, each individual performs a memory test. Her friend Carly, who has taken the research methods course, suggests that she add a(n) _____ group that receives a plain strawberry smoothie, but thinks it has a booster, and a(n) _____ group that does not receive any smoothie. What groups did Carly suggest?

a. control; control
b. empty control; placebo
c. placebo; empty control
d. baseline; placebo

How did you do? Turn to the end of the chapter to check your answers.

Design in Action

Now that we have a plan for our independent and dependent variables, we need to determine how we are going to pull our study off. To give our study the best chance at determining if our hypothesis is correct, we will want to have enough participants. A general rule of thumb is that we should have at least 30 participants per condition for reasonable power. So, for our study, we should recruit at least 90 participants. Most importantly, we will want to maintain experimental control such that each participant has a similar experience, where the only systematic difference is our temperature manipulation.

Assigning Participants to Conditions

Random assignment is key to minimizing systematic differences between our conditions before our study even starts. Because we have three conditions, we cannot simply flip a coin to decide which group to assign each participant, but we do have other options. We could place three slips of paper, each with a condition on it, into a bag and blindly select a slip to tell us each participant's condition assignment. A variant of this technique is to use three coins, all identical (i.e., all quarters) except for the year (e.g., Rind & Bordia, 1995). Beforehand we decide which condition we will associate with each year. We randomly assign participants by reaching into our pocket and drawing out a coin. The year on the coin tells us the participant's condition.

▶ Why is random assignment important to research projects?
SEE CHAPTER 8, p. 261

Another option is to use a random number generator app for our smartphone and generate a random number for each participant. If the last digit in that number is 1, 2, or 3, we assign the participant to the first condition. If the digit is 4, 5, or 6, we place the person into the second condition. Finally, if the last digit is 7, 8, or 9, the participant goes into the third condition. What happens if the last digit is zero? Easy solution: We just generate another random number. One thing we do need to be concerned with is unequal group sizes. We will monitor the situation, and if the groups become too unequal, we will randomly assign participants to the two lower enrolled groups until the conditions are again equal in size.

Developing a Protocol

▶ What should be covered in an informed consent? SEE CHAPTER 3, p. 62

▶ How can the design of a study establish cause and effect? SEE CHAPTER 8, p. 249

To standardize participants' experience, we will develop a protocol that will provide us with directions for what to do and what to say during the course of our study. Our first step will be to obtain informed consent when each participant arrives for our study. Clearly, our manipulation needs to come before our dependent measures, but should participants complete the informed consent in the room with the manipulated temperature? Since temperature is a factor in the study, we will need to handle each step of the process in separate locations, as we cannot expose anyone to the manipulation without consent. Thus, we will have participants arrive at one room for the informed consent. If they consent, the experimenter will take them to another room where the thermostat will be set in the middle of one of the three temperature ranges: hot (81–85°F/27–29°C), cold (59–64°F/15–18°C), or average (71–75°F/22–24°C).

Next, we need to determine how to manipulate the temperature of the room. One solution would be to run one condition each day (e.g., cold on Monday, hot on Tuesday, average on Wednesday, etc.). However, the temperature outside could influence participants and undermine the effectiveness of our manipulation. What if Monday happened to be particularly hot and sunny, while Wednesday was cool and rainy? How we ultimately run the study will depend on where we are able to collect data. The best option would be to run all three conditions each day and alternate between them in a random order that also ensures that we use conditions evenly (e.g., hot/cold/average/cold/average/hot/average/hot/cold, etc.). Doing this would be easiest if we had a waiting room and three identical rooms with one temperature condition in each room. If we only had one room, we could switch back and forth between conditions, but we would need to be sure the room achieved the proper temperature before the next participant.

If we do not have an elaborate room setup, following informed consent, we could ask the participant to wait in another room while we supposedly prepare the study materials, which "may take a couple of minutes—sorry!" In reality, this other room is where we manipulate the independent variable depending on the random assignment. We will ask the participant to wait in a room that is hot, average, or cold. The experimenter will purposely take five minutes to "prepare study materials." Why would the experimenter stall for five minutes? We want to be sure participants fully experience the room temperature. To see if the participants notice the room temperature, we would include a manipulation check in our materials that asks, "Please provide your best guess of the room's current temperature: _____ degrees Fahrenheit." To make it less obvious why we are asking about the room temperature, we will embed our question in a series of distractor questions about the room (e.g., How many square feet do you think are in this room? How many people do you think could fit into this room?). These distractor questions will help minimize hypothesis-guessing and potential demand characteristics.

What if some people show up to our study wearing shorts and a tank top, while others are bundled in sweatpants and a hoodie? What if some people always feel cold or hot, regardless of the temperature of the room? Are some people naturally more agreeable and therefore more likely to sign any petition? Could there be other individual differences such as gender or age that influence these behaviors? Absolutely. However, placing participants into conditions via random assignment will control for potential individual differences because we will place participants in groups based on chance alone. Thus, provided our sample is large enough, we should not end up with one group full of warm-blooded, charitable Earth lovers, and another group full of cold-blooded, miserly petition haters.

For our measures, we could keep it simple and give everyone the self-report and then the petition. But what if answering attitude questions influences the likelihood of signing the petition? In terms of our hypothesis about how temperature influences behavior, because the order of the dependent measures is the same for everyone, the attitude questions' influence on signing behavior would be consistent. That is, since the presentation of materials is the same, we are controlling its influence across conditions. However, if the hot condition had one order, and the cold condition had a different order, it would be a problem (and a confound!). The order of the measures could give us an unrealistic view of petition-signing behavior (either inflated or suppressed) depending on how the attitude questions made participants feel. To solve this problem, we will alternate the order so that odd-numbered participants receive the self-report measure first, while even-numbered participants receive the petition first (we will be sure to number our packets ahead of time). In both cases, participants will complete demographic questions last. Another potential problem avoided!

A self-report measure is fairly straightforward to administer since the participant can simply read the instructions and answer the questions. The petition will be a bit trickier. To make it seem more realistic, we will add the following to our protocol: "There is a new student group on campus that has asked us for some help. The group addresses environmental issues surrounding climate change through educational programs and changes around campus. They are looking for signatures on a petition to support a 5% tuition increase in order to enable the installation of solar panels on all of the buildings around campus. If you support this cause, please consider signing this petition." Next, we will give participants a chance to sign the petition. We want it to look both real and identical for each participant, so we will supply a full first page of fake signatures there already. Participants will then have the opportunity to be the "first" to sign on the top of the next page.

> **What Do You Think?**
> Are there any other ways to determine whether our manipulation worked?

▶ What are the differences between experimental and mundane realism? SEE CHAPTER 8, p. 251

▶ What ethical principle involves confidentiality? SEE CHAPTER 3, p. 57

▶ Why is open science important to the research process? SEE CHAPTER 2, p. 42

After the participants have completed both measures, we will debrief them. During debriefing, we will first ask the participants what they thought the study was really about to see if they suspected its true nature. If some participants tell us that they thought the study had something to do with room temperature and views on climate change, then we may have questions about the study's experimental realism and the effectiveness of the deception.

After we ask for the participant's thoughts, we will then fully explain the nature and purpose of the study, including the need for deception. Our goal is for participants to leave our study confident that they fully understand what the experiment was about and how they helped the scientific process. After recording whether or not the participant signed the petition, we will be sure to destroy the actual signed petition. We always want to protect participants' right to privacy by ensuring their names do not become linked with their responses on the self-report measures in any way.

Focus on Open Science: Preregistering Your Hypotheses, Materials, and Data Analysis Plan

Now that we have made all the key decisions about how to collect data, it is time to preregister the study on an open science website (e.g., http://cos.io/prereg/). There we will share details about the type of experimental design we will use and how we plan to manipulate temperature and measure attitudes toward climate change through both self-report and behavior. We will also share our materials, such as our Societal Concerns Survey and the fictitious petition we intend to use. Once we have a data analysis plan, we will include that, as well, so we know exactly what to do when we finish data collection. For this study, we need to calculate the reliability of our self-report measure, determine if our manipulation of temperature is effective, and test our hypothesis based on how people respond in our survey and whether or not they signed the petition. We will also post our data for others to analyze.

> **YOUR TURN 9.2**

1. If we have a multigroup design with five groups, roughly how many participants should we have for reasonable power in our study?
   a. 30
   b. 50
   c. 90
   d. 150

2. Neil is doing a study on how working in groups influences stress and mood. He has three groups: those who work in a group of 10; those who work in a group of 5; and those who work alone. Afterward, all participants list all of their sources of stress and then answer some questions about their current mood, followed by a few demographic questions. Because he is

keeping the dependent measures in the same order, which of the following is a possible outcome for this study?

a. Mood will be lower for those working in a large group.

b. Those working alone will list more sources of stress.

c. Across all participants, mood may be lower after focusing on stress.

d. Participants will complete the demographics inaccurately.

3. Jessie is studying how watching different types of movies may lead people to have a better sense of humor. She randomly assigns 200 participants to one of three groups: comedies, action movies, and mysteries. She then has them complete an assessment of their sense of humor. Which of the following is a potential problem for her study?

a. Some participants will naturally have a better sense of humor than others.

b. Some participants will not like action movies.

c. Some participants may watch a lot of movies and may have already seen the movies she picked.

d. None of the above, because participants have been randomly assigned.

How did you do? Turn to the end of the chapter to check your answers.

Statistics: In Search of Answers

After we have run our study, we need to enter our data into a spreadsheet for statistical analyses. As seen in **Figure 9.4**, we set up our spreadsheet as we did for our two-group design with one small change. The column representing the independent variable ("condition") now has one of three values to indicate the participant's condition (1 = hot; 2 = cold; 3 = average). With our data entered, we can create our overall climate-change attitude score. We will determine this dependent variable by computing the mean rating given to the four climate-change items in our scale (attitude03, attitude05, attitude07, attitude10). We ignore the other ratings as they are the distractor items. In our spreadsheet, we will name our overall climate-change score "x_gwattitudes" (i.e., "global-warming attitudes"). There is nothing special or magical about the names we use to represent each variable in the spreadsheet. Rather, we use names that make sense to us. We are putting an "x_" in front of this variable name simply to remind us that this is the mean climate-change attitude score (if it were a sum, we would precede the variable name with "s_"). Before calculating the mean attitude score, we compute Cronbach's alpha to evaluate the internal consistency reliability of this four-item scale. Cronbach's alpha for our global-warming scale is .78, which is satisfactory.

▶ What does a Cronbach's alpha tell us? SEE CHAPTER 7, p. 228

We are now ready to answer our research question, "Can the experience of warmth lead a person to consider climate change as more problematic, consequently influencing that person's attitudes and behaviors?" To extract the answer from our data, we will want to compare our three groups to see if they differ in their responses on the self-report measure, as well as in their likelihood of signing the petition. We want to see not just whether average scores for the three conditions differ, but whether they differ enough to be considered

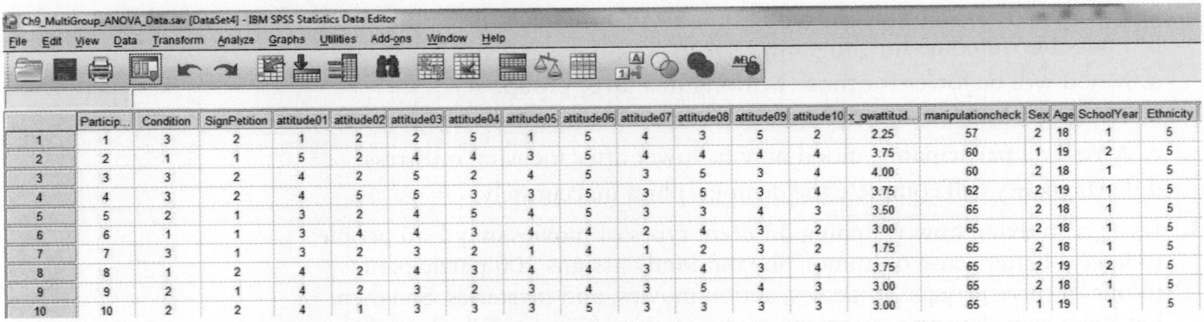

	Particip...	Condition	SignPetition	attitude01	attitude02	attitude03	attitude04	attitude05	attitude06	attitude07	attitude08	attitude09	attitude10	x_gwattitud...	manipulationcheck	Sex	Age	SchoolYear	Ethnicity
1	1	3	2	1	2	2	5	1	5	4	3	5	2	2.25	57	2	18	1	5
2	2	1	1	5	2	4	4	3	5	4	4	4	4	3.75	60	1	19	2	5
3	3	3	2	4	2	5	2	4	5	3	5	3	4	4.00	60	2	18	1	5
4	4	3	2	4	5	5	3	3	5	3	5	3	4	3.75	62	2	19	1	5
5	5	2	1	3	2	4	5	4	5	3	3	4	3	3.50	65	2	18	1	5
6	6	1	1	3	4	4	3	4	4	2	4	3	2	3.00	65	2	18	1	5
7	7	3	1	3	2	3	2	1	4	1	2	3	2	1.75	65	2	18	1	5
8	8	1	2	4	2	4	3	4	4	3	4	3	4	3.75	65	2	19	2	5
9	9	2	1	4	2	3	2	3	4	3	5	4	3	3.00	65	2	18	1	5
10	10	2	2	4	1	3	3	3	5	3	3	3	3	3.00	65	1	19	1	5

FIGURE 9.4 SPSS Spreadsheet for the First 10 Participants. *(SPSS)*

statistically significant. Once we determine if there are overall differences between our groups, we can think about comparing specific groups to one another.

Selecting the Proper Tool

▶ Want to know more about one-way ANOVAs? SEE APPENDIX A, p. 480

To accomplish this, we need to decide which statistical test to use by looking at the key features of our study. We have one independent variable with three levels (or conditions). Because we expose each participant to only one condition, we are employing a between-subjects design. We have one manipulation check using a continuous scale, a continuous dependent variable (an attitude measure that ranges from 1–5), and one categorical measure (signature vs. no signature on the petition).

one-way analysis of variance (one-way ANOVA) a statistical test that determines whether responses from the different conditions are essentially the same or whether the responses from at least one of the conditions differ from the others.

exploratory analyses statistical tests that examine potential differences that were not anticipated or predicted prior to the study.

post-hoc tests statistical tests that examine all of the possible combinations of conditions in a way that statistically accounts for the fact that not all of them were predicted ahead of time.

Let's tackle the continuous measures first because statistics will handle any continuous variable the same way. Based on our independent variable and dependent variables, we should run a **one-way analysis of variance (one-way ANOVA;** see **Figure 9.5**). Generally speaking, an ANOVA tests whether responses from the different conditions are essentially the same or whether the responses from at least one of the conditions differ from the others. The first ANOVA test we should conduct is on our manipulation check. As the name implies, we simply want to "check" on the effectiveness of our manipulation. If everything worked out according to plan, the conditions should report significantly different perceptions of the room temperature. Next, we need to run a one-way ANOVA to test temperature's influence on climate change attitudes. Recall that we hypothesized that *there will be a difference between the groups in their reporting of climate change as a problem.* Our one-way ANOVA only indicates that at least one condition is statistically different from the others.

Unfortunately, a one-way ANOVA does not tell us where the action is in terms of which specific conditions are different from each other (i.e., there could be significant differences between the hot and cold conditions, cold and average conditions, or between all three). As we did not make any predictions about these ahead of time, we will need to do some **exploratory analyses** in which we test for potential differences that we did not anticipate or predict prior to the study. To do this in the context of a one-way ANOVA, we will have to use **post-hoc tests,** which examine all of the possible combinations of conditions (hot vs. cold, hot vs. average, cold vs. average) in a way that statistically accounts for the fact that we did not predict them ahead of time.

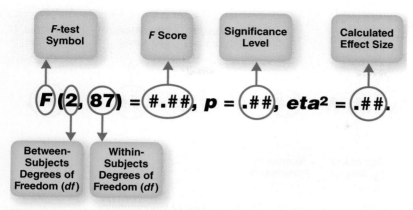

FIGURE 9.5 Anatomy of a One-Way ANOVA.

These analyses address the hypothesis we generated earlier, but neither they nor the hypothesis fully address our primary research question, "Can the experience of warmth lead you to consider climate change as more problematic, consequently influencing your attitudes and behaviors?" Our question focuses on if being hot influences attitudes toward climate change, so we actually have another hypothesis to test. Specifically, we predict that those in the hot condition are the most sensitive to climate change, which means we need a more focused hypothesis:

> *Those sitting in a hot room will report that climate change is more of a problem than those sitting in the cold or average temperature room.*

To test our new and improved hypothesis, we would use **planned contrasts** along with our one-way ANOVA in the statistics program. Planned contrasts are similar to a *t*-test for independent means (in fact, the output is a *t*-test) because they allow us to test comparisons between groups that we predicted ahead of time. They also have the benefit of allowing you to combine two conditions so that you can compare them to a third. In our case, we need to compare the hot condition to the combination of the cold and average temperature conditions.

Now, let's examine the second part of our first hypothesis: *There will be a difference between the groups . . . in the likelihood to sign the petition.* Signing a petition is not a continuous variable. Rather, it is something that you either did or did not do, making it a nominal or categorical variable because the participant can be in one group or the other (i.e., some people are "petition signers" and others are "petition nonsigners"). The question we want to answer is, are there more "petition signers" in some conditions, but not others? To answer this question, we will need to run a **chi-square test of independence** because we have a categorical dependent variable (see **Figure 9.6**). Generally speaking, a chi-square tells us if the distribution of participants across categories deviates from what would be expected if there were no difference between the groups. For there to be a significant difference, there would need to be more participants than expected in some conditions compared to others. Although you may not typically associate chi-squares with multigroup designs, remember that statistics are flexible and the appropriate statistic follows from the type of measurement one is using.

planned contrasts statistical tests that examine comparisons between groups that were predicted ahead of time. These tests have the added benefit of allowing the combination of two conditions to be compared to a third.

chi-square test of independence a statistical test in which both variables are categorical. This test generally examines if the distribution of participants across categories is different from what would happen if there were no difference between the groups.

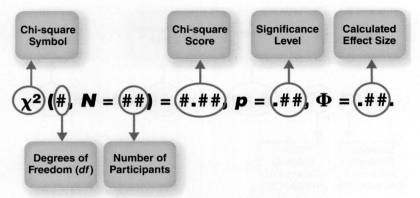

FIGURE 9.6 Anatomy of a Chi-square Test of Independence.

Let's summarize our data-analysis strategy. We will use a one-way ANOVA with post-hoc to test *Hypothesis 1* because the dependent variable is continuous. To test the continuous dependent variable in *Hypothesis 2,* we will use planned contrasts. Finally, we will use a chi-square to test the nominal or categorical variable in *Hypothesis 1.* Next, we will use these statistics to analyze our data. Looking at the results from all of our statistical analyses, we have a mixed bag of good and bad news (which is almost always the case).

Writing the Results in APA Style: One-Way ANOVA (post-hoc/Contrasts) and Chi-Square

Results

Manipulation Check

First, we tested differences between conditions on perceived room temperature. The results of a one-way ANOVA suggest that the participants' perception of room temperature, whether in the hot ($M = 71.07$; $SD = 4.06$), cold ($M = 72.03$; $SD = 4.02$), or average ($M = 71.17$; $SD = 6.02$) condition, was not significantly different, $F(2, 87) = .36, p = .70$.

Attitudes Toward Climate Change (*Hypothesis 1*)

We conducted analyses to determine if there were differences between conditions for attitudes toward climate change. A one-way

ANOVA revealed that there were significant differences between conditions, $F(2, 87) = 3.74$, $p = .028$, $\eta^2 = .09$ (see Table 9.2). post-hoc analyses revealed that the difference between the hot condition ($M = 3.68$; $SD = 0.62$) and the cold condition ($M = 3.38$; $SD = 0.73$) was not significant ($p = .30$). The difference between the cold condition and the average condition ($M = 3.18$; $SD = 0.78$) was also not significant ($p = .91$). However, the difference between the hot condition and the average condition was significant ($p = .024$). Participants in the hot condition had more positive attitudes toward climate change compared to those in the average condition.

Signing the Petition (*Hypothesis 1*)

To determine if room temperature influences participants' willingness to sign a petition, we conducted a chi-square test of independence between conditions (i.e., hot, cold, or average) and recorded whether the participants signed the petition (i.e., yes or no). As expected, participants signed the petition more in some conditions than others ($\chi^2(2, N = 90) = 10.83$, $p = .004$; see Figure 9.7). Those in the hot room were more likely to sign the petition compared to those in the other two rooms ($\chi^2(1, N = 90) = 10.20$, $p < .001$, $\phi = 0.34$).

Attitudes Toward Climate Change (*Hypothesis 2*)

To determine if the hot room temperature uniquely influenced attitudes toward climate change, we conducted a planned contrast comparing the hot condition to both the cold and average conditions. As hypothesized, participants in the hot room reported that climate change was more problematic than did participants in the cold and average rooms combined, $t(87) = 2.53$, $p = .013$, $d = 0.54$.

Don't Just Tell Me, Show Me: Using Figures and Tables

Along with presenting the numerical information in the text of a research report, researchers also report the results of their analyses in tables and figures. These visuals provide a different way to summarize the data analyses. The means of each condition are often represented in figures (see **Figure 9.7**), while details about the analysis itself, such as a one-way ANOVA, are placed in a table (see **Table 9.2**).

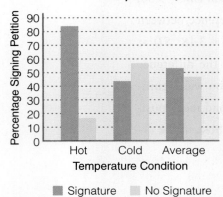

FIGURE 9.7 Percentage of Participants Who Signed Petition for Climate-Change Cause by Condition.

TABLE 9.2

Analysis of Variance for Attitudes Toward Climate Change					
Source	**SS**	**df**	**MS**	**F**	η^2
Between Groups	3.82	2	1.91	3.74*	.09
Within Groups	44.45	87	0.51		
Total	48.27				

Note: N = 90.
$p < .05$.

Our Research Plan at a Glance

What Is Our Research Question? Can the experience of warmth lead you to consider climate change as more problematic, consequently influencing your attitudes and behaviors?

What Is Our Design? We are using a multigroup between-subjects experimental design.

Why Are We Using This Design? This design allows us to test more than two groups in a single study. Having more groups helps to identify nonlinear relationships between variables and gives us a clearer picture of how the independent variable may influence the dependent variable.

What Are Our Variables?
 Independent Variable(s): Temperature
 Hot: 81–85°F/27–29°C
 Cold: 59–64°F/15–18°C
 Average: 71–75°F/22–24°C
 Dependent Variable(s): Attitudes Toward Climate Change
 Participants answer a self-report questionnaire that includes items about climate change. They also have the chance to sign a petition for a climate-change cause as a behavioral measure.

What Are Our Hypotheses? There will be a difference between the groups' perception of climate change as a problem and in their likelihood of signing a relevant petition. More specifically, those sitting in a hot room will consider climate change to be more of a problem than those sitting in a cold or average temperature room.

Who Are Our Participants? Convenience sample of people from campus and the surrounding community.

What Ethical Considerations Do We Need to Keep in Mind?

- We are using deception in the study by presenting participants with a fake petition. We must handle this situation properly by debriefing our participants about the nature of the deception and the reason for it.

- We must not expose participants to temperatures outside their typical experience or for any length of time that might be harmful (i.e., excessive heat or cold).

What Is Our Data Analysis Plan?

1. **Determine the reliability of our measure.** We need to compute a Cronbach's alpha to evaluate the internal consistency of our four-item attitudes toward climate change self-report measure.

2. **Make sure our manipulation is effective.** We compare the three conditions (hot, cold, and average) of our independent variable using a one-way analysis of variance (one-way ANOVA) to determine if the groups had different perceptions of room temperature. This test allows us to assess the differences between 3+ conditions on a continuous dependent variable.

3. **Test our hypothesis.** We compare the three conditions (hot, cold, and average) of our independent variable using a one-way ANOVA to determine if the groups had different responses to the attitudes toward climate change questions in the self-report measure, and complete post-hoc tests. To test the more specific prediction that those in a hot room will report more concern for climate change, we use planned contrasts. We use a chi-square test of independence to examine differences between the three conditions (hot, cold, and average) of our independent variable of likelihood to sign the petition. This test allows us to test for differences with a categorical dependent variable.

Want to practice the analyses for this research yourself? Ask your instructor about the data set that accompanies this study.

Let's Discuss What Happened

In this chapter, the purpose of our study was to use a multigroup design to answer the question, "Can the experience of warmth lead you to consider climate change as more problematic, consequently influencing your attitudes and behaviors?" Now that we have the results from our study, we can focus on determining what we found and what it means. We model this below so that you can see how a researcher might try to make sense of the findings. As you read through, notice how we use previous research and theories to explain our present findings, and how we critically evaluate our own research design to identify possible flaws.

What Did We Find?

Our results indicate that the manipulation check did not reveal perceived temperature differences between conditions. Related to our hypotheses, as

Aside from temperature, what other subtle factors could potentially influence attitudes and behaviors toward climate change? *(artpartner-images/Photographer's Choice/Getty Images)*

predicted, participants' level of concern for climate change varied by condition. Specifically, when participants were in the hot room, they reported that climate change was more problematic and were more likely to sign the petition.

Why These Findings?

Consistent with previous research (Li et al., 2011) and as predicted in our overall hypothesis, the experience of temperature influenced attitudes toward climate change. These results extend previous research on how subtle environmental cues can influence participants (e.g., Berman et al., 2008; Liljenquist et al., 2010).

Our finding related to *Hypothesis 2* regarding the specific influence of heat on climate-change attitudes is consistent with previous research showing that the immediate experience of higher outdoor temperatures positively correlates with belief in climate change (Joireman, Truelove, & Duell, 2010; Li et al., 2011). Our findings extend these studies by showing that heat is primarily responsible for the attitudes and not merely an aberration from the normal or average temperature, which would have also been the case in the cold room condition. We also extended previous work by demonstrating that heat made participants more likely to take action, in addition to altering their reported attitudes.

What Could Be Improved?

Looking at the results, the inconclusive statistical test of our manipulation check is a concern. If participants were not influenced by the manipulation, there really was not an experiment. It just goes to show that experimentation does not always work out in a way that is neat or how we would like. One potential explanation is that, in comparing all three conditions, the average temperature group has a standard deviation (*SD*) that is 2 degrees higher than the other two groups' standard deviations. This indicates that participants in that group gave a wider variety of responses. Sure enough, when looking back at the raw data, participants in the average group gave both the lowest (57°F/14°C) and the highest (90°F/32°C) estimates. This suggests that participants may not be very good at accurately judging a room's temperature. Perhaps there are better ways to assess our manipulation than what we chose. The more important aspect may be how people feel, rather than the numbers on the thermometer, because 70°F may feel warm to some, but cool to others. Thus, we could simply ask for participants' perception of the room's temperature (perhaps with a 1–7 scale ranging from *very cold* to *very warm*). It is also possible that temperature influences participants subconsciously. Although the manipulation check did not produce significant differences, it may be a function of a flawed measure (perceived temperature) rather than a flawed manipulation. Future research in this area should use a different manipulation check, such as one based on a 1–7 scale, in order to be sure that participants' experience of temperature is truly responsible for the outcomes.

What's Next?

The ability of a room's ambient temperature to alter perceptions is consistent with perceptual symbol systems theory, which suggests that various sensori-motor systems help an individual form a simulation of a concept, which subsequently influences how the individual thinks about that concept (Niedenthal, Barsalou, Winkielman, Krauth-Gruber, & Ric, 2005). In our case, feeling hot could lead participants to picture climate change (perhaps a few images of sad polar bears popped into their minds), leading them to think about climate change as more problematic. Future studies should examine why the experience of heat motivates the changes in attitudes and behavior. For example, it is possible that participants are more easily able to mentally simulate climate change, or it could more simply be that heat makes participants more socially consciousness.

YOUR TURN 9.3

1. Juanita randomly assigned 21 participants to think about the past, the present, or the future, then take a creativity test where they had to generate as many unique uses as possible for a brick. Juanita wants to compare the "future" condition with the other two. Which statistic should she use?

   a. A one-way ANOVA

   b. Planned contrasts

   c. post-hoc tests

   d. A priori tests

2. If Juanita ran the same study, but instead wanted to examine the overall differences between groups, which statistic should she use?

   a. A one-way ANOVA

   b. Planned contrasts

   c. post-hoc tests

   d. A priori tests

3. In the discussion, we realized that the manipulation check was not significant. All of the following are potential explanations for our findings, *except*:

   a. there were initial differences between the three conditions based on group assignment.

   b. the actual room temperature may matter less than the participants' subjective interpretation of the temperature.

   c. participants in the average temperature condition gave widely different estimates of temperature.

   d. estimating the temperature in degrees may be too difficult of a task.

How did you do? Turn to the end of the chapter to check your answers.

Research in Action

Dressing for Distress?

One of the many interesting things about psychology is how seemingly inconsequential experiences can subtly change how we think and feel, even in terms of how we see ourselves. Culture exerts a powerful influence over us, and different cultures promote different values. Think about it: To what extent does your culture value independence, materialism, hard work, caring for the less fortunate, or connecting to those around you? Although culture's influence is powerful, the ways that cultural values are communicated can be abstract. Take, for example, the American cultural ideal of being thin and fit. All sorts of things may communicate this message, even the toys that we play with as children. Could playing with dolls that have overly thin or unrealistic bodies, for instance, influence how satisfied girls are with their own body shape?

Using what you know about multigroup designs, maintaining experimental control, picking quality comparison groups, and avoiding confounds, use the online activity ***Dressing for Distress?*** to develop a laboratory study that simulates one way culture may influence how a person views the self.

LaunchPad To complete this activity, visit LaunchPad at launchpadworks.com

Final Thoughts

In this chapter, you have seen how adding groups to a simple two-group experiment can help us answer more complex questions. These extra groups are also beneficial because we can run one multigroup study instead of several separate two-group designs, saving time and requiring fewer participants overall. In our study, having the third group allowed us to reveal a functional relationship between temperature and attitudes. Specifically, hot and cold temperatures yielded similar attitudes, but those who were hot did view climate change as more problematic. If we had only had two groups, we would not have discovered this pattern.

Just think: If something as subtle as a room's temperature has the power to influence your attitudes and behaviors about a worldwide phenomenon such as climate change, it is likely that other seemingly insignificant things in our surroundings are influencing us without our knowing it. For example, could the aroma from vanilla-scented soap or perfume lead to craving sweet desserts? Could pictures of food in a restaurant make you feel hungrier so that you order more? Could the décor of your office influence clients to perceive you as more successful and encourage them to buy more of your product? At this point, these are all empirical questions that require the tools from research to be answered. If you do investigate, we would love to hear what research questions you decided to ask, and how things turned out!

CHAPTER 9 Review

Review Questions

1. Chris designed a study to test children's enjoyment of certain toys. He has a group of 120 children aged 5–7 play with one of the following toys: a jump rope, a remote control car, a doll, or a puzzle. The children then answer three questions about how much they liked the toy, enjoyed playing with it, and would want to play with it again. How many levels does Chris's independent variable have?
   a. 4
   b. 3
   c. 120
   d. 1

2. Rosie has a cold, so her mom gives her hot chicken soup with carrots, noodles, celery, and broth. Rosie's mom explains that the broth will help her feel better. Which of the following is a potential confound in this study?
   a. The carrots
   b. The noodles
   c. The temperature of the soup
   d. All of the above

3. Eliana wants to test the impact of music on time spent running. She plans on having participants listen to Axwell Λ Ingrosso's "More Than You Know" and measuring how long they run on a treadmill. However, Eliana wants to be sure it is not actually the song lyrics that lead to differences in running length. What control group would best address this concern?
   a. A group that walks on the treadmill
   b. A group that reads the song lyrics instead of listening to the music
   c. A group that listens to the music in "More Than You Know" without the lyrics
   d. A group that listens to a different Axwell Λ Ingrosso song

4. LeSean wants to help soldiers returning from overseas acclimate to their home life more easily upon their return by enrolling them in a 4-week life skills course. Since LeSean has taken a research methods course, he knows he should establish a baseline by comparing those who take the course to those who do not. Which of the following best describes the type of group LeSean should include?
   a. Baseline group
   b. Empty control group
   c. Control group
   d. Placebo group

5. If we have a multigroup design with four groups, roughly how many participants do we need in order to ensure we have sufficient power?
   a. 30
   b. 40
   c. 120
   d. 150

6. A financial-planning agency wants to do a study on how exposure to large sums of money can influence decision making among their clients. During study planning, a member of the research team raises the concern that some of their clients routinely handle large sums of money (e.g., some are cashiers, bankers, or already wealthy). What is the best way to solve this issue?
   a. Add an empty control group to the research design
   b. Have the experimenter assign participants to their condition
   c. Use random selection to obtain a representative sample
   d. Use random assignment to place participants into the different conditions

7. Julio believes that drinking iced coffee before his Russian literature class helps him learn the material better. To test this, he runs a study where participants are randomly assigned to either drink iced coffee prepared just how Julio likes it, with 2% milk and 3 packets of sugar, or ice water with 3 packets of sugar mixed in. Which of the following is a confound?
   a. The packets of sugar
   b. The 2% milk
   c. The ice in the drink
   d. All of the above

8. Several research assistants are talking in the Judgment and Decision Making Lab about why their most recent study did not work. The most senior research assistant explains to the others that the study had adequate "power." What is the best explanation for what the senior research assistant means?
   a. The study had enough participants.
   b. The study was able to find a difference (i.e., yield significant results) if one was actually present.
   c. The study had sufficient reliability and validity.
   d. The independent variable had a strong effect on the dependent variable.

9. Florentine wants to determine if males or females are more likely to choose to wear mittens or gloves when it is cold outside. To answer her question, she conducts a phone survey of 400 men and women from across the country and asks them their preference. To answer her original question, which statistical test is most appropriate?
   a. A one-way analysis of variance (ANOVA)
   b. A two-way analysis of variance (ANOVA)
   c. A chi-square test of independence
   d. Correlation

10. Two first-year students, Mary-Kate and Ashley, are out at a party. Knowing that they are underage, the host of the party gives them both nonalcoholic drinks. Mary-Kate knows the drink does not contain alcohol, but Ashley believes there is alcohol in the drink. After they each consume three of these drinks, both Mary-Kate and Ashley proceed to act drunk. In this scenario, Mary-Kate's behavior is most likely due to _____, while Ashley's behavior is most likely due to _____.
    a. social desirability; social desirability
    b. a placebo effect; a placebo effect
    c. a placebo effect; social desirability
    d. social desirability; a placebo effect

11. What advantages does a multigroup design have over a two-group design?

12. Draw a figure of a linear relationship and three different examples of non-linear (or functional) relationships.

Applying What You've Learned

1. Assume that you want to do a study of the effects of violent video games that is similar to the following study: Bushman, B. J., & Anderson, C. A. (2009). Comfortably numb: Desensitizing effects of violent media on helping others. *Psychological Science, 20*(3), 273–277, http://pss.sagepub.com/content/20/3/273.short. Design a study with at least four groups that tests the effect of violent versus nonviolent video games on helping someone in need.

2. Using PsycINFO (or a similar research database), find an empirical research article that uses a multigroup design. Based on the article's method section, generate a protocol that the researcher may have used to run the study.

3. This chapter's study focused on how temperature influences thoughts and behaviors. Generate five new ideas for studies that have the same focus, but that do not focus on climate change. Pick your favorite idea and describe how you would test it with a multigroup design.

4. Television, magazines, and the Internet routinely feature advertisements claiming that a unique treatment (e.g., taking shark cartilage capsules) can help with an illness or other malady (e.g., cancer). These claims are often spurious (if you do a quick Internet search for shark, cartilage, and cancer, you will find more information). How could the placebo effect explain the alleged benefit of shark cartilage on cancer? Look for your own example of a spurious claim and show how the placebo effect may explain that as well.

5. Find an empirical journal article that describes an experimental manipulation. (A) Identify a potential confound. (B) Explain why it may be a confound. (C) Suggest an additional condition that will address the confound.

6. Read the following study: Seltzer, L. J., Prososki, A. R., Ziegler, T. E., & Pollak, S. D. (2012). Instant messages vs. speech: Hormones and why we still need to hear each other. *Evolution and Human Behavior, 33*(1), 42–45.

doi:10.1016/j.evolhumbehav.2011.05.004. As you will see, in the study researchers placed girls into one of the following groups: (1) wait alone with no contact with their mom, (2) talk to their mom in person, (3) talk to their mom via phone, or (4) interact with their mom via instant message. Briefly describe what the researchers could learn by comparing each of the following sets of groups: 2 versus 3; 2 versus 4; 3 versus 4; 1 versus the combination of 2, 3, and 4.

7. THE NOVICE RESEARCHER: Having confounds in your study is problematic, but novice researchers tend to accidentally include them in their studies. Playing the role of a novice researcher, design a multigroup study that includes at least two confounds. At the end, identify the confounds and discuss how a more experienced researcher would have handled them.

8. DIG INTO THE NUMBERS: We have provided your instructor with supplemental multigroup study data. Analyze that data to build your skills in using a one-way ANOVA with either planned contrasts or post-hoc tests in SPSS. Write an APA-style results section based on your results. If you would like even more practice, your instructor also has data that accompanies the study discussed throughout this chapter.

Key Concepts

chi-square test of independence, p. 305

confound, p. 295

empty control group, p. 297

exploratory analyses, p. 304

hypothesis-guessing, p. 288

methodological pluralism, p. 290

multigroup design, p. 293

nonlinear (or functional) relationships, p. 294

one-way analysis of variance (one-way ANOVA), p. 304

placebo group, p. 297

planned contrasts, p. 305

post-hoc tests, p. 304

power, p. 294

Answers to YOUR TURN

Your Turn 9.1: 1. d; 2. a; 3. c
Your Turn 9.2: 1. d; 2. c; 3. d
Your Turn 9.3: 1. b; 2. a; 3. a

Answers to Multiple-Choice Review Questions

1. a; 2. d; 3. c; 4. b; 5. c; 6. d; 7. b; 8. b; 9. c; 10. d

Within-Subjects Design

Can Watching Reality TV Shows Be Good for Us?

(Hoxton/Tom Merton/Getty Images)

LEARNING OUTCOMES

After reading this chapter, you should be able to:

- Develop a literature search plan using specific techniques.
- Describe the purpose and limitations of behavioral diaries.
- Differentiate between pretest-posttest designs and repeated-measures designs.

- Identify the benefits and limitations of within-subjects designs.
- Describe specific threats to the internal validity of a within-subjects design.
- Discuss potential order effects and how to minimize them.
- Write a results section for a pretest-posttest study and a repeated-measures study.

Something to Think About . . .

It has been a long, frustrating day. Tired, you collapse in front of the television and start flipping through channels. As always, there really is not anything worthwhile to watch, but you come across one of those reality shows about the exploits of a dysfunctional group of housewives, celebrity family members, or friends living together. As you watch, you wonder why people share their miserable lives on TV, and why people bother to watch them. Oddly enough, the more you watch, the more you find yourself hooked. As you become increasingly engrossed in the drama, you begin to laugh at their misfortunes, thinking, "Thank goodness I'm not one of these losers!" Although this thought sounds insensitive, it probably makes you feel better about yourself and your awful day. Could the act of taking pleasure in someone else's misery help explain why these types of reality TV shows are so popular? Perhaps these shows are not merely a simple form of entertainment. Maybe there is a psychological benefit to watching reality TV shows. Fortunately, we do not just have to sit on the couch and wonder. We can go out and see if this idea is true for ourselves.

Introduction to Our Research Question

Most of the time we like to feel good about ourselves, and we do whatever we can to protect and increase our feelings of pride and self-worth, or, in other words, our self-esteem. Whenever we experience misfortunes, disappointments,

Might watching reality TV shows such as *The Real Housewives of Beverly Hills* be good for our psychological health? *(Evans Vestal Ward/©Bravo/courtesy Everett Collection)*

failures, or a lousy day, we look for ways to feel better about ourselves. Got a 62% on a midterm exam? Find someone who got a 52%, and suddenly things are not so bad anymore! We seem to feel better about ourselves simply by knowing there is someone who is worse off. Maybe watching others' debacles on television provides a similar psychological benefit. Sounds like we may have our research question:

RESEARCH ?	Is watching reality television good for our self-esteem?

Of course, this question is rather general. Next, we need to search the literature so we can use what others have already learned to refine our research question.

Reviewing the Literature: What Do We Already Know About This Topic?

▶ Need tips on using the literature to write a good research report? SEE APPENDIX B, p. 497

A good literature search always begins with a plan. Simply typing terms into a database without any forethought increases the likelihood that you will miss important research studies on your topic. We suspect that you have had the experience of feeling like you cannot find any research on a particular topic, or of searching for a few terms, only to get back 43,891 results. To avoid these plights, it is best to identify key terms, and then develop a plan to systematically search the literature.

Thinking about our research question, we realize that we have made several assumptions. The first is that people watch reality TV shows for more than just entertainment purposes. In our literature search, we should identify studies investigating people's motivations for watching reality TV. To make our search on this topic as inclusive as possible, we will use the Communication and Mass Media Complete database (http://www.ebscohost.com/academic/communication-mass-media-complete) in addition to psychology databases such as PsycINFO. Our second assumption is that people gain pleasure from observing the misfortunes of others. Finding studies on this topic is tricky because the key terms are not obvious. We first try *pleasure* and *misfortune* as our search terms and immediately find several articles with the word *schadenfreude* in their titles. Schaden-*what?* According to the *Merriam-Webster Dictionary* (http://www.merriam-webster.com), *schadenfreude* is derived from two German words: *schaden,* which means "damage," and *freude,* which means "joy." *Schadenfreude* is defined as the "enjoyment obtained from the troubles of others." Perfect! Maybe it is this feeling that helps boost our self-esteem. We will use *schadenfreude* as one of our key search terms. In our initial search, we also noticed that a researcher named Wilco van Dijk conducted several studies investigating schadenfreude. This suggests that van Dijk is a key researcher on this topic, so we should specifically search for other relevant studies that he coauthored.

Our literature search goal is to find answers to the following questions: What motivates people to watch reality TV shows? Do people watch reality TV for reasons beyond simple entertainment? Can people really experience pleasure from seeing others' misfortunes? If so, what factors influence how much pleasure they may experience? After sifting through multiple studies, we read and summarized the following relevant articles in order to refine our research question.

The term "schadenfreude" refers to the joy experienced from seeing others' misfortunes. Can we feel better about ourselves simply by seeing someone who is worse off? *(Phil Date/Shutterstock)*

Motivations for Watching Reality TV

Baruh, L. (2010). Mediated voyeurism and the guilty pleasure of consuming reality television. *Media Psychology, 13,* 201–221. doi:10.1080/15213269.2010.502871

This study investigated the degree to which voyeurism (i.e., the desire to see what one is not supposed to see) and social comparison (i.e., the process of comparing yourself to others) motivates watching reality TV. Five hundred and fifty adults drawn from a national sample completed an online survey asking about their TV-viewing habits. The researchers found that participants who derived more pleasure from voyeurism tended to prefer watching reality TV.

Papacharissi, Z., & Mendelson, A. L. (2007). An exploratory study of reality appeal: Uses and gratifications of reality TV shows. *Journal of Broadcasting & Electronic Media, 51,* 355–370. doi:10.1080/08838150701307152

Researchers surveyed 157 undergraduate and graduate students about their motivations for watching reality TV shows. The researchers concluded that people watch reality TV not for voyeuristic reasons, but, rather, as a way to pass the time. In addition, it is the entertainment and novelty aspects when compared to fictional TV shows that make reality TV appealing to people.

Factors Influencing the Experience of Schadenfreude

Feather, N. T., Wenzel, M., & McKee, I. R. (2013). Integrating multiple perspectives on schadenfreude: The role of deservingness and emotions. *Motivation and Emotion, 37,* 574–585. doi:10.1007/s11031-012-9331-4

This study tested the impact of perceived deservingness for misfortune and social identity on feelings of schadenfreude. One hundred and seventy undergraduates read two scenarios. One described a college student, either from the same or a different institution, who experienced academic success for either deserving or undeserving reasons. In the second scenario, participants learned that the school rejected the student's application for admission to a prestigious honors program. Participants indicated more pleasure at this rejection when the student's success was undeserved and when the student was from another institution.

van Dijk, W. W., Ouwerkerk, J. W., van Koningsbruggen, G. M., & Wesseling, Y. M. (2012). "So you wanna be a pop star?" Schadenfreude following another's misfortune on TV. *Basic and Applied Social Psychology, 34,* 168–174. doi:10.1080/01973533.2012.656006

This study looked at how one's self-evaluation and the type of feedback one receives influence the experience of schadenfreude. Researchers recruited 53 undergraduate students for two supposedly different studies. In the first study, participants completed a self-evaluation measure and then a performance task allegedly assessing their creative intelligence. Self-threat was manipulated by providing the participants with either positive or negative feedback about their supposed performance on the task. Participants then watched an audition episode from the Dutch television version of *American Idol,* where a woman was ridiculed for her singing abilities. Participants with low self-evaluation who received negative feedback experienced more schadenfreude than those who received positive feedback.

van Dijk, W. W., Ouwerkerk, J. W., Wesseling, Y. M., & van Koningsbruggen, G. M. (2011). Towards understanding pleasure at the misfortunes of others: The impact of self-evaluation threat on schadenfreude. *Cognition and Emotion, 25,* 360–368. doi: 10.1080/02699931.2010.487365

This study examined the impact of self-evaluation on feelings of schadenfreude. In Study 1, 30 undergraduates were recruited for two supposedly unrelated studies. In the first part of this study, participants completed a task described as an assessment of analytic thinking and intellectual abilities. Participants received either negative or positive feedback. In the second part, participants read two interviews. In the first interview, participants read that a student had high potential. In the second interview, participants learned that the student suffered a major academic setback. Participants who had received a negative evaluation experienced more schadenfreude after learning about the student's academic setback.

From Ideas to Innovation

From the literature described above, it seems there are many reasons why people watch reality TV shows. Some are mundane, such as wanting to pass the time, for entertainment, or to see something new (Papacharissi & Mendelson, 2007). Other research reveals that people watch reality TV shows for more psychological reasons, such as voyeurism (Baruh, 2010). Reality TV shows allow us to "see" into other people's lives, which can provide us with opportunities to compare ourselves to other people. Assuming these comparisons involve seeing how we are better off than others, we have some support for our idea that reality TV shows can boost our self-esteem.

The previous schadenfreude research might help explain how reality TV shows benefit the viewer. The research shows that experiencing schadenfreude, or pleasure at the misfortune of others, increases our self-esteem, particularly when we feel negatively about ourselves in general or have recently received negative feedback (van Dijk, Ouwerkerk, van Koningsbruggen, & Wesseling, 2012; van Dijk, Ouwerkerk, Wesseling, & van Koningsbruggen, 2011). Schadenfreude is also more likely when we believe the other person did not deserve the initial success (Feather, Wenzel, & McKee, 2013) or that the person deserved the misfortune (van Dijk et al., 2011). However, it is unclear whether we are more likely to experience schadenfreude when

How often do you chuckle when you see something bad happen to someone else? Do you think that experiencing schadenfreude can increase your self-esteem? *(ColorBlind Images/The Image Bank/Getty Images)*

the other person is similar or dissimilar to us (Feather et al., 2013). Because the research is not clear about its role, similarity makes for an interesting dimension to our research question as well.

We now have the problem of our literature search yielding two good research questions to pursue. The first research question is:

RESEARCH
?   Can watching reality TV shows boost our self-esteem?

The second is:

RESEARCH
?   Do we experience more schadenfreude toward a person who is similar or dissimilar to us?

Which one should we focus on? The good news is that we are not limited to choosing only one. It is common in science to address multiple questions in the same study. Not only does this increase the efficiency of our scientific endeavors, but it also gives us the opportunity to gain a richer understanding of the phenomena under investigation. If watching reality TV shows can improve our self-esteem due to schadenfreude, then it would be interesting to know the types of reality shows that best bring about schadenfreude. We will need to harness our research skills to design a study that allows us to answer both questions.

Defining Key Terms: What Do You Mean By _____?

First, we need to define the key variables. Researchers have conceptually defined schadenfreude as the feelings of pleasure a person experiences after learning about or observing the misfortunes of others (Feather et al., 2013). This closely matches how we have been thinking about the term so far. Researchers typically consider self-esteem to be how positively or negatively we evaluate ourselves (Kassin, Fein, & Markus, 2017), so we will do the same. Defining a "reality TV show" is trickier, as there does not seem to be one single definition (Nabi, Biely, Morgan, & Stitt, 2003). We will focus on TV shows that are unscripted programs about people being themselves in a living or working environment rather than in a TV studio set (Nabi et al., 2003). Finally, we need to conceptualize what we mean by "similar or dissimilar to us." Researchers studying schadenfreude tend to define similarity as whether the person experiencing the misfortune is a member of an in-group or out-group to the person watching (e.g., Feather et al., 2013). Since that definition works well for our purposes, we do not need to create our own definition.

Weighing Our Options: Picking a Design for Our Research Questions

Now that we have defined our key terms, we can determine the best design to answer our research questions. Let's start with our first question, "Can watching reality TV shows boost our self-esteem?" "Boost" is a key word because it implies that a person's self-esteem will increase or improve after watching these types of shows. Ultimately, we want to learn if people feel better about themselves whenever they finish watching a reality TV show.

▶ Want to learn more about survey designs? SEE CHAPTER 7, p. 202

Daily diary smartphone apps allow people to maintain a behavioral diary, or a record of their thoughts, feelings, and/or behaviors as they occur. *(Courtesy Happtic Consulting)*

▶ How do within-subject designs differ from between-subjects designs?
SEE CHAPTER 2, p. 40

behavioral diary a self-report data collection strategy where individuals record their behaviors and associated feelings as they occur.

pretest-posttest design a within-subjects design where participants are measured before and after exposure to a treatment or intervention.

baseline measurement the initial assessment of a participant at the onset of a study, prior to any intervention or treatment.

We could find out if this idea is true by surveying people on whether they feel better about themselves after watching a reality TV show. One pitfall with this approach is that we do not always accurately remember past behaviors and feelings, which is to say we could have retrospective biases. To minimize these potential biases, we could ask people to keep an ongoing record or journal of the reality TV shows they watch each day and how they feel about themselves before and after the show.

This self-report strategy is an example of a **behavioral diary,** where people record their behaviors and associated feelings as they occur (Bolger, Davis, & Rafaeli, 2003). Behavioral diaries are similar to naturalistic observations except that the participant, not an observer, records the person's behavior. Behavioral diary studies typically involve participants recording their own behavior at predetermined times (e.g., right before going to sleep), or when prompted by an electronic device.

While this approach may seem like a good way to evaluate how people feel before and after watching a reality TV show, it will not provide a clear answer to our question. First, if we repeatedly ask participants to keep track of their self-esteem whenever they watch a reality TV show, participants could succumb to demand characteristics and tell us what they think we want to hear. Second, we will have no control over whether participants watch the types of reality TV shows we want to research. It would be better if our design allowed us to have more control over the reality TV shows participants watch and how we assess their self-esteem before and after the show. A **pretest-posttest design,** where we measure the dependent variable before and after exposing participants to a treatment or intervention, will allow us to accomplish this goal. Pretest-posttest designs are an example of a within-subjects design, as we are measuring participants twice on the same dependent variable.

We call the initial assessment in a pretest-posttest design the **baseline measurement** or "pretest." This measurement tells us what participants were like at the onset of our study and prior to any treatment or intervention. We measure participants again after we introduce the intervention (the "posttest"). By comparing participants' pretest and posttest scores, we can evaluate the impact that the treatment had on participants. To test our first research question, we can measure participants' levels of self-esteem before and after they have watched several reality TV shows. If their self-esteem scores are significantly higher on the posttest, we have evidence that reality TV shows may improve self-esteem. To determine how long this improvement lasts, we could measure participants' self-esteem multiple times after exposure to our treatment. This would be an example of a longitudinal design, a type of within-subjects design where we repeatedly measure participants over an extended period of time. For example, we might be interested in seeing what the impact of regularly watching reality TV shows throughout adolescence is on risk-taking behaviors in college. Or, if we wanted to evaluate the effectiveness of early intervention programs such as Head Start, we could conduct a longitudinal study where we track the intellectual, social, and emotional development of a group of children from preschool to middle school.

Now that we have a possible design for our first question, let's consider the second question: Do we experience more schadenfreude toward a person who is similar or dissimilar to us? Simply measuring participants' schadenfreude along with their self-esteem will not answer our second research question because this question requires that an element (similarity) varies, which means we need to have more than one level of the independent variable. Perhaps we can answer this question by embedding another study within our pretest-posttest design. We can systematically vary the reality TV shows participants watch between the initial pretest and final posttest measurements of participants' self-esteem. We would then assess participants' feelings of schadenfreude after watching each show. In other words, we make each type of reality TV show an independent variable and incorporate a **repeated-measures design** into our study. A repeated-measures design is another type of within-subjects design where we expose participants to each level of the independent variable, measuring each participant on the dependent variable after each level. Unlike the pretest-posttest design, there is no baseline measurement.

For an overview of the types of within-subjects designs, see **Table 10.1**.

repeated-measures design a within-subjects design where participants are exposed to each level of the independent variable and are measured on the dependent variable after each level; unlike the pretest-posttest design, there is no baseline measurement.

TABLE 10.1

Types of Within-Subjects Designs	
Type of Design	**Why a Within-Subjects Design?**
Pretest-Posttest Design	Participants are measured twice, once at the beginning of the study and again at the end of the study.
Longitudinal Design	Participants are measured on the dependent variable repeatedly over a period of time.
Repeated-Measures Design	Participants are measured on the dependent variable after exposure to each level of the independent variable.

Advantages of Using Within-Subjects Designs

Within-subjects designs have several advantages over between-subject designs, where we measure each participant only once on the dependent variable. One advantage is that within-subjects designs allow us to answer specific types of research questions. If we want to study changes in behavior or attitudes, or improvements in learning over time, we will naturally want to measure each participant multiple times on the same variables. We would also use a within-subjects design if we wanted participants to compare two or more stimuli relative to one another—similar to what companies do in product comparison tests, such as a Coca-Cola versus Pepsi taste test.

Within-subjects designs do have a statistical power advantage over between-subjects designs. We need fewer participants for a within-subjects design in order to have the same power as a comparable between-subjects design. Suppose we wanted to determine which cold cereal people like the best: Bran Flakes, Corn Flakes, or Sugar Flakes. If we used a multigroup, between-subjects design, we would have 30 participants rate the Bran Flakes, another 30 rate the Corn Flakes, and a final 30 rate the Sugar Flakes. In other words, we would need to recruit at

▶ Why is statistical power important? SEE CHAPTER 9, p. 294

▶ What is a multigroup, between-subjects design? SEE CHAPTER 9, p. 293

least 90 individuals for our study (three levels with 30 participants each). If we used a within-subjects design such as repeated-measures design, we would only need 30 participants, as each of them would rate all three cereals. This design would certainly save us time in both recruiting participants and collecting the actual data, and is particularly advantageous for studies that require recruiting participants from small or difficult-to-access populations.

Within-subjects designs enhance the power of our study because, with the same participants in every condition, we do not have to worry about individual differences between our groups. This factor makes it easier for us to isolate the independent variable's impact on our dependent variable. In between-subjects designs, we use random assignment to minimize these differences between our groups, but they still may be present, making it more difficult to detect how the independent variable influences the dependent variable.

Table 10.2 summarizes the advantages and disadvantages of within-subjects designs, which we continue to discuss below.

TABLE 10.2

Advantages and Disadvantages of Within-Subjects Designs	
Advantages	**Disadvantages**
1. Can address research questions involving change or relative comparisons	1. Potential external validity concerns
2. Fewer research participants needed for adequate statistical power	2. Potential logistical challenges
3. Individual differences are constant across comparison groups	3. Potential threats to internal validity

Disadvantages of Using Within-Subjects Designs

Within-subjects designs do have potential shortcomings, such as lower external validity. Any effects we observe in a within-subjects study could be the cumulative result of multiple exposures rather than a single exposure to the independent variable. It is less common in everyday life for people to experience multiple levels of the same variable in close succession. These aspects could limit our ability to generalize our conclusions to other populations or situations.

Exposing participants to every level of our independent variable can create logistical challenges, especially if the study extends over time. Have you ever tried to schedule a meeting with other classmates to work on a group assignment? No matter how hard you try, there is usually at least one person who cannot make any of the suggested times. Now, imagine the challenge of trying to schedule participants for additional times so they can continue participating in your study. This difficulty can lead to some participants not completing your study. We refer to the differential dropping out of participants from a study as **attrition** or **mortality** (but not in the morbid sense). Participants discontinue studies for many reasons, but if the reason relates in some way to the treatment or

▶ Why is external validity important in a study? SEE CHAPTER 6, p. 164

attrition the differential dropping out of participants from a study; also known as mortality.

independent variable, there is a potential threat to the study's internal validity (Shadish, Cook, & Campbell, 2002).

Suppose we decide to use a pretest-posttest design to evaluate the effectiveness of an after-school antibullying program. The program involves 20 students meeting after school twice weekly for 4 weeks to discuss issues surrounding bullying. For the 9 students who complete the entire program, there is a significant change in their attitudes toward bullying. Before we can endorse the effectiveness of the program, we need to wonder about the 11 students who dropped out of the study. Was it because they thought the program was a waste of time? If so, maybe the program is not as effective as we believe. If they dropped out because they felt such an overwhelming change that they believed they did not need to continue, we may underestimate the program's effectiveness. Attrition can also be a problem in between-subjects designs if participants from one condition are more likely to drop out than those in other conditions. Any differences observed at the end of the study may be due to this uneven dropping out rather than our independent variable. One way to minimize attrition is to make continued involvement in the study appealing or nonthreatening to the participants. It is important to always look at how participants who drop out may differ from those who complete the study in order to identify potential threats to internal validity.

Attrition is not the only threat to the internal validity of a study. Assessing participants multiple times using the same measurement instrument can create its own problems if we are not careful. The more often participants answer the same questions, the more likely they are not only to remember their previous answers but also to figure out the study's purpose. Any changes in participants' scores may be the result of this increased familiarity with the measurements rather than the independent variable, a threat to internal validity known as the **testing effect**. If we keep asking participants how much they enjoyed seeing the cast members get into trouble after watching each TV show, participants will probably begin to guess our study's purpose. In addition, participants may remember their earlier answers to the same questions, possibly influencing their current answers. One strategy for minimizing potential testing effects is to use distractor items in our measurements to make it more difficult to guess what we are studying. Another is to decrease the likelihood of participants remembering their previous answers. We could do this by having participants complete another unrelated distractor task between the experimental conditions. We could also increase the time between the different study conditions (e.g., having participants watch each show on a different day).

Participants' measurement scores could change for another reason: We might inadvertently change how we measure participants on the dependent variable. The result would be that participants' measurement scores would no longer be exactly comparable, and any differences could be due to this change rather than the independent variable. We call this potential threat to internal validity **instrumentation**. Changes in our measurement instrument can be subtle, such as when raters become better or more refined in their observations during the course of the study. Differences in how we administer our measures during the study can also lead to instrumentation problems. Suppose for our baseline measurement that we have participants complete a paper version of the self-esteem measure while waiting for the study to begin. After watching several reality

▶ Why is internal validity critical to good study design?
SEE CHAPTER 8, p. 250

testing effect a threat to the internal validity of a study where participants' scores may change on subsequent measurements simply because of their increased familiarity with the instrument.

instrumentation a threat to the internal validity of a study due to changes in how a variable is measured during the course of a study.

How might your answers to questions in a study differ if you were asked to complete a survey online, then on paper? Would you consider this inconsistency a threat to the study's internal validity? *(German/Getty Images; wdstock/Getty Images)*

▶ How do confounds hurt internal validity? SEE CHAPTER 9, p. 295

TV shows, the participants complete an online version of the same self-esteem measure as the posttest. We now have a potential confound in our study. That is, we may have unintentionally manipulated another variable in addition to our independent variable, meaning that any changes in participants' scores could be due to differences in how we administered the measurement, not from our independent variable, making causal claims difficult to assert. To minimize instrumentation as a potential threat to internal validity, we need to keep our measurement instruments, including how we administer them, consistent throughout the study. Otherwise, we have a plausible alternative explanation for our results, which is not a good thing when trying to evaluate how our independent variable affects our dependent variable.

Maintaining consistency in how we measure variables is within our control as researchers. There are other potential threats to internal validity that are not as easily avoided. For example, the threat of **history,** or an unexpected or unrelated event occurring during our study, could influence our participants' responses. In longitudinal studies, these can be actual historical events like a natural disaster or a nationally significant event (e.g., a terrorist attack). A history threat may also occur on a smaller scale. In our study, imagine that while the participants are watching reality TV, they have to evacuate the building for a fire drill. Now, we cannot be sure whether any changes in self-esteem are due to watching the TV shows or due to some experience related to the fire drill.

Even if external events do not interrupt our study, our participants can experience physiological changes in themselves over time that affect subsequent measurements, a threat known as **maturation.** These changes, which are particularly problematic in longitudinal studies, could be long-term, involving individuals becoming older, wiser, or more mature during the course of the study. The changes can also be short-term, as in the case of participants becoming tired, bored, or hungry as the study progresses. Maturation could be a problem if we had participants binge-watch 6 straight hours of reality TV shows before administering our posttest measure. In this case, if we found no changes in self-esteem, we would not be able to determine if reality TV did not affect participants' self-esteem or if participants simply became so bored they stopped paying attention to the shows.

history a threat to the internal validity of a study due to an external event potentially influencing participants' behavior during the study.

maturation a threat to the internal validity of a study stemming from either long-term or short-term physiological changes occurring within the participants that may influence the dependent variable.

Just because a design has a potential threat to internal validity does not mean that we should avoid using that design. All designs have their strengths and weaknesses, and no one design is superior to another one. Rather, our design choice depends on the question that we are trying to answer. Through careful planning, we can minimize potential threats as we design the best study to answer our research question.

See **Table 10.3** for an overview of potential threats to internal validity.

TABLE 10.3

Potential Threats to Internal Validity		
Threat	**Nature of the Threat**	**Possible Solutions**
Attrition (or Mortality)	The differential dropping out of participants from a study	• Make continuation in the study appealing or nonthreatening
Testing Effect	Participants' scores changing on subsequent measurements simply because of their increased familiarity with the instrument	• Use distractor items or tasks • Increase the time between the different conditions
Instrumentation	Changes in how a variable is measured during the course of a study	• Maintain consistency in the measurement instrument and how it is administered throughout the study
History	An unexpected or unrelated external event occurring during the study that could influence participants' responses	• Difficult to prevent; record in the researcher's notes any unexpected occurrences
Maturation	Physiological changes occurring in participants during the course of the study	• Use a comparison group not exposed to the treatment or intervention to determine if maturation is a potential threat

Operationally Defining the IV: Choosing Our Reality TV Shows

After weighing the pros and cons, we have decided to use within-subjects designs to answer our two research questions. See **Table 10.4** for a summary of our within-subjects study. We will actually utilize two different designs within our one study. We will use a pretest-posttest design to address our first research question and a repeated-measures design to test the second. Next, we need to choose reality TV shows that allow us to manipulate similarity. We already have a conceptual definition to differentiate reality TV shows from other types of programming. Now we need to be more specific, choosing reality TV programs that vary the cast's similarity to the participants in our study. We should avoid shows that involve competitions between individuals or groups of individuals because these shows often feature socially distinct settings such as tropical islands, or require specific talents like singing or dancing that may not provoke the types of social comparisons we want to research. Instead, we will focus on reality TV shows that follow a group of people living in common, everyday situations.

 Research Spotlight

Is It Easier to Kill a Second Time?

Within-subjects designs help us answer questions about how our behavior may change over time or with experience. For example, growing up, did you ever purposely step on a bug to kill it? Did you stop after killing just one, or did it become a game with your friends to see who could step on more bugs? Researchers have examined whether the act of killing once makes it easier for us to kill again with an experimental procedure called the "Bug-Killing Paradigm" (Martens & Kosloff, 2012). What is a "bug-killing paradigm," you ask? The researchers placed a coffee grinder with a funnel and plastic tube attached in front of a participant and gave the participant 20 small cups, each containing a small bug. The participant's task was to drop a bug in the funnel connected to the tube leading into the grinder. Before leaving the room, the researcher told the participant to spend a total of 12 seconds placing bugs into the grinder and then depress the grinder button for at least 3 seconds, ostensibly killing all of the bugs. In reality, the tube was blocked so that no bugs could actually enter the grinder. Each participant performed this "extermination task" twice, making this a within-subjects design. The researchers compared the number of bugs the participants put into the grinder the first and second times, finding that participants put more bugs into the grinder the second time. Another group of participants, who knew beforehand that the grinder did not actually kill bugs, did not show the same increase in bug killings from time 1 to time 2. In this within-subjects design, the researchers concluded that killing once can increase the likelihood of killing again. A sobering thought.

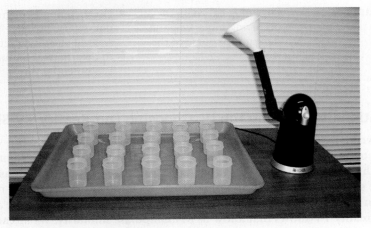

Could you drop a bug into this "bug extermination machine"? If so, could you stop at just one? *(Courtesy Andy Martens)*

TABLE 10.4

Summary of Our Within-Subjects Study									
Pretest Measure*	IV Level 1**	Time 1 Measure	IV Level 2**	Time 2 Measure	IV Level 3**	Time 3 Measure	Posttest Measure*
Self-Esteem Scale	Reality Show #1	Schadenfreude Scale	Reality Show #2	Schadenfreude Scale	Reality Show #3	Schadenfreude Scale	Self-Esteem Scale

*The pretest-posttest measures constitute the pretest-posttest design incorporated into our study.
**The three levels of our independent variable represent the repeated-measures design part of our study.

How do we find noncompetitive reality TV shows to use in our study? This seems like an easy question to answer—just review current reality TV shows and select three that differ in the similarity between the cast and our participants. While simple, this approach may inadvertently create a new problem. Participants may already be familiar with the selected shows and may have even seen the actual episodes we select. Prior exposure could influence participants' reactions to our shows, introducing a potential confound in our study. We should not let this keep us from moving forward with our study, but there are some precautions we should take to minimize this threat. First, we should try to use lesser-known reality shows. Second, we should screen potential participants for their familiarity with the shows we select, choosing those with less familiarity for our study.

The question now is how to find reality TV shows to use in our study. Given our desire to use less well-known reality shows, we googled "cancelled reality TV shows" and obtained a list of reality TV shows that ran for only a single season or episode. We conceptually defined similarity as whether the person experiencing the misfortune is part of the participant's in-group. Because we are going to use college students as our participants, we will want shows that differ in terms of how similar the cast members are to typical college students. Looking through the list of reality TV shows, we notice several shows that track the lives of people in college. These shows would be ideal to use because they allow us to keep the settings for the reality shows we use in our study relatively consistent. More importantly, we identify three shows available on the Internet that have somewhat comparable premises:

What Do You Think?
How might you find reality TV shows with which participants are unlikely to be familiar?

Celebrities Go to College

PREMISE: Follows the exploits of 10 former child celebrities sharing a dorm suite as they navigate the world of college, trying to go from the D-list to the Dean's list.

EPISODE: Raquel goes on a rampage when she must share the bathroom with her suitemates as she gets ready for a fraternity social. Michael confronts the custodian who refuses to clean his room, making it impossible for him to study for his midterm exam.

Babes in College

PREMISE: What happens when 10 single moms live together in a college dorm and try to balance parenting, baby daddies, roommates, classes, and their social lives?

EPISODE: Without money to pay a babysitter, Gina needs to take her screaming baby to class, upsetting both professor and students. Meanwhile, Joyce and Brandi argue over the proper way to handle diaper rash and whether nature or nurture led them to be single moms.

Back in the Day U

PREMISE: Imagine how college was "back in the day," in a world where there are no computers, smartphones, or Internet. Follow 10 college students living together as they try to survive college life without any technology.

EPISODE: Ian and Renee pull an all-nighter at the library writing a history term paper, armed with only a typewriter and access to an old-fashioned card catalog, bound copies of abstract indices, and an encyclopedia. Ben struggles to complete his statistics assignment without the use of a calculator.

These three shows are ideal because although the cast members are college students, they seem to vary in similarity to our intended participants. The people on *Back in the Day U* are probably the most similar to our participants; those in *Celebrities Go to College* are the least similar. The people on *Babes in College* are probably somewhere in between. Using these three shows will allow us to manipulate participants' similarity to the TV show casts while keeping the TV shows as comparable as possible.

Operationally Defining the DVs: Self-Esteem and Schadenfreude

Our next task is to figure out how to measure or operationally define our dependent variables, self-esteem and schadenfreude. Our first question asks whether watching reality TV shows can boost self-esteem. We need a valid and reliable measure of self-esteem. As we learned in Chapter 7, a good first step is to see how other researchers measured self-esteem. Searching the literature, we find that many researchers assessed self-esteem using the Rosenberg self-esteem scale (Rosenberg, 1989), shown in **Figure 10.1**. Since the items match up with how we conceptualized self-esteem, we should use that scale as well. For our second research question, we need to measure participants' feelings of schadenfreude. Again, it is best to see how other researchers measured schadenfreude in their studies. There does not seem to be a well-established scale to assess feelings of schadenfreude, but, as shown in **Figure 10.2**, we can slightly reword a five-item scale used in previous research to fit our study (van Dijk et al., 2012).

Using these self-report measures could present a problem, as participants will have some sense of what we are studying by reading the questions. This is especially true if we ask the same five questions about how much pleasure participants gained from watching others' misfortunes every time they finish watching a reality TV show. Participants could quickly figure out our study's purpose, so we need to minimize the possibility of hypothesis-guessing influencing the participants' responses. We also have the potential for a testing effect, as

▶ What are the advantages of using scales to measure our variables? SEE CHAPTER 7, p. 203

*INSTRUCTIONS: Below is a list of statements dealing with your general feelings about yourself. If you strongly agree, circle **SA.** If you agree with the statement, circle **A.** If you disagree, circle **D.** If you strongly disagree, circle **SD.***

_____ 1.	On the whole, I am satisfied with myself.	SD D A SA
_____ 2.	At times I think that I am no good at all.*	SD D A SA
_____ 3.	I feel that I have a number of good qualities.	SD D A SA
_____ 4.	I am able to do things as well as most other people.	SD D A SA
_____ 5.	I feel I do not have much to be proud of.*	SD D A SA
_____ 6.	I certainly feel useless at times.*	SD D A SA
_____ 7.	I feel that I am a person of worth, at least the equal of others.	SD D A SA
_____ 8.	I wish I could have more respect for myself.*	SD D A SA
_____ 9.	All in all, I am inclined to feel that I am a failure.*	SD D A SA
_____ 10.	I take a positive attitude toward myself.	SD D A SA

Scoring: SA = 3, A = 2, D = 1, SD = 0. Items with an asterisk are reverse scored, that is, SA = 0, A = 1, D = 2, SD = 3. Sum the scores for the 10 items. The higher the score, the higher the self-esteem.

FIGURE 10.1 Rosenberg Self-Esteem Scale. *(Rosenberg, 1989)*

INSTRUCTIONS: Indicate how much you agree or disagree with each statement concerning the TV show that you just watched. Please place your answer in the space next to each item.

1	2	3	4	5
Strongly Disagree	Disagree	Neither Agree Nor Disagree	Agree	Strongly Agree

_____ 1. I enjoy what happened to the people in this show.

_____ 2. I'm satisfied with what happened to the people in this show.

_____ 3. I couldn't resist a little smile as I watched what happened to the people in this show.

_____ 4. I actually had to laugh a little bit at the problems the people were having in this show.

_____ 5. I felt some pleasure at watching the problems the people were having in this show.

FIGURE 10.2 Schadenfreude Scale. *(Copyright © 2006 by the American Psychological Association. Reproduced with permission from van Dijk, W. W., Ouwerkerk, J. W., Goslinga, S., Nieweg, M., & Gallucci, M. (2006). When people fall from grace: Reconsidering the role of envy in schadenfreude. Emotion, 6, 156–160.)*

▶ What are the advantages and disadvantages of using self-report and behavioral measures? SEE CHAPTER 4, p. 88

participants may remember their previous answers if there are only five items per scale. One option might be to use a behavioral measure in lieu of these self-report instruments. But in the instance of our research questions, a behavioral measure may not be ideal, as we want participants to reflect on their psychological state.

Knowing that the better option for our research questions is to use a self-report measure, we should implement strategies for minimizing potential biases and hypothesis-guessing. First, we can tell participants that the study seeks to evaluate students' reactions to various reality TV shows so they will think that we are studying something other than schadenfreude. Second, we can include distractor items within our schadenfreude scale. These distractor items should be other statements about the show, such as, "There was a positive dynamic between the people in this show," "the premise of this show captured my interest," and "the show held my attention the entire time." We will incorporate 10 distractor items so that participants will answer a total of 15 questions after watching each show, and we will vary the order of the 15 items after each show. When computing the participants' overall schadenfreude scores, we will omit their responses to the distractor items.

▶ How important is selecting the best order for the scales in a study? SEE CHAPTER 7, p. 221

Our Hypotheses

Now that we have our design and variables worked out, we are ready to establish the hypotheses for our two research questions. Our first research question is, "Can watching reality TV shows boost our self-esteem?" Based on our literature review, we believe the answer is yes. Because we are predicting an improvement in self-esteem, we have a directional hypothesis.

▶ How do directional and nondirectional hypotheses differ? SEE CHAPTER 7, p. 217

> *After watching several reality TV shows, participants' self-esteem will be higher than it was before watching the shows.*

Our second research question asks whether participants experience more schadenfreude when the other person is similar or dissimilar. Participants will watch three different reality TV shows whose cast members vary in similarity to the participants and will report their feelings of schadenfreude immediately after each show. Because past research is not clear as to whether we experience more schadenfreude when watching the misfortunes of similar or dissimilar others, we will make a nondirectional hypothesis.

> *The three reality TV shows will elicit different amounts of schadenfreude in participants.*

YOUR TURN 10.1

1. A teacher wants to assess how acting concepts out in class influences student learning. The teacher quizzes her students on the topic before and after students act out concepts. What type of design is the teacher implementing?
   a. Pretest-posttest design
   b. Behavioral diary
   c. Two-group design
   d. Longitudinal study

2. Juan is conducting a study to evaluate the effects of music tempo on reaction time while operating a flight simulator. He notices that participants had the quickest reactions for the last song played. Which of the following may represent a threat to the internal validity of Juan's study?
   a. Instrumentation
   b. Maturation
   c. Attrition
   d. Testing effects

3. A physician is evaluating the effectiveness of a new weight-loss strategy involving eating leafy vegetables every 3 hours for 3 weeks. The average weight loss for those who completed the full regimen was 10 pounds. Before concluding that the strategy is an effective method for weight loss, which potential threat to internal validity should the physician consider?
   a. Maturation
   b. Instrumentation
   c. Attrition
   d. History

How did you do? Turn to the end of the chapter to check your answers.

Design in Action

Our study is starting to come together. We have operationally defined our independent and dependent variables and will incorporate two types of within subjects designs to determine whether our participants' self-esteem improves after watching several reality TV shows and whether similarity to the cast members influences participants' schadenfreude.

Weighing Our Options: Which TV Program to Show First?

We know we want participants to watch an episode from three different reality TV shows: *Babes in College*, *Celebrities Go to College*, and *Back in the Day U*. We now need to decide the best order in which to have participants watch them. We could randomly decide which program to show first, second, and last, and then use this order for every participant. However, we could have a problem if that order influences participants' responses in ways unrelated to our independent variable. If the sequence or order of the experimental conditions influences measurements of the dependent variable, we have an **order effect**, which could threaten our study's internal validity.

Types of Order Effects

Earlier we discussed how testing effects can threaten a study's internal validity. Participants' scores may change by the end of the study simply because they have more experience either completing the measures or performing the tasks required in the study. We call this testing effect a **practice effect**. For example, by the last condition, participants may have become better

order effect a threat to the internal validity in a within-subjects design resulting from influence that the sequence of experimental conditions can have on the dependent variable.

practice effect changes in a participant's responses or behavior due to increased experience with the measurement instrument, not the variable under investigation.

at making judgments as they complete the measurement instrument. If you took the SAT or ACT multiple times to improve your test scores, you were trying to use a practice effect to your advantage. In fact, this is one major reason why exam prep classes for college or graduate school focus on having students take several practice tests. For our study, participants will have had practice evaluating the reality TV show they just watched, and may get better at making evaluations as they do more of them. Their experiences may change how they watch subsequent shows. For instance, the participants may start to pay particular attention whenever something bad happens to one of the cast members. In turn, this could influence their feelings of schadenfreude. A possible solution for this problem would be to provide participants with practice at completing our measures or doing the task before starting the actual experiment.

Another potential order effect relates to maturation as a threat to internal validity. We said that physiological changes occurring with participants during the course of the study could be a potential threat to internal validity. The changes could be short-term, as in the case of participants becoming tired, bored, or less enthusiastic the longer a study continues. This change, known as a **fatigue effect**, could lead participants to be less attentive or careful in the study, introducing more error into the measurements. One strategy for countering potential fatigue effects is to make the experimental tasks interesting and relatively brief.

Keeping the order of our reality TV shows the same for all participants can introduce other problems into our study. First, if exposure to an experimental condition influences how participants respond to subsequent conditions, there may be a **carryover effect.** For example, feelings of schadenfreude from the first TV show may linger and influence the amount of schadenfreude participants report after watching subsequent shows. If participants report the most schadenfreude after watching the third show, it is uncertain whether this is a result of watching the third show itself or a cumulative result of watching all three shows in succession. We can try to minimize this problem by giving participants a short break after every TV show.

Exposing participants to each experimental condition may help participants figure out the study's purpose, leading to a **sensitization effect**. This effect becomes more problematic with exposure to each subsequent condition. That is, it may be easier for participants to realize we are interested in schadenfreude after the third TV show than after the first. Such hypothesis-guessing increases the likelihood of demand characteristics and participants changing their behavior accordingly. Reports of increased schadenfreude after watching the third show may simply be the result of demand characteristics rather than the show itself. One strategy for minimizing potential sensitization effects is to mislead participants about the study's purpose. As we decided earlier, we will tell participants that the study's purpose is to obtain their opinions of several reality TV shows, without mentioning that we are really interested in how similarity influences schadenfreude.

Table 10.5 summarizes suggestions for how to reduce potential order effects.

fatigue effect
deterioration in quality of measurements due to participants becoming tired, less attentive, or careless during the course of the study.

carryover effect
exposure to earlier experimental conditions influencing responses to subsequent conditions.

sensitization effect
continued exposure to experimental conditions in a within-subjects study increasing the likelihood of hypothesis-guessing, potentially influencing participants' responses in later experimental conditions.

TABLE 10.5

Order Effects and Potential Solutions		
Order Effect	**The Problem**	**Potential Solutions**
Practice Effect	Participants appear to improve simply because they have more practice completing the dependent variable measures	• Provide participants with extensive training on the task before starting the actual study • Do a trial run so the participants can learn and improve before measurement begins
Fatigue Effect	Participants' performance deteriorates during the study because they become tired, bored, less enthusiastic, etc.	• Make the tasks more interesting • Keep the tasks brief • Keep the tasks from being too taxing
Carryover Effect	Exposure to one treatment changes participants' reactions to another treatment	• Lengthen the time between treatments • Use other strategies that clear the effect before exposing participants to the next condition
Sensitization Effect	With each treatment, participants become more likely to guess the research hypotheses and change their behavior accordingly	• Mislead participants as to the study's purpose • Use other strategies that prevent participants from knowing what you are varying in your study

Minimizing Potential Order Effects

Rather than trying to minimize each order effect in its own unique way, we could vary the sequence of our experimental conditions so that they are not always in the same order for all participants. One way to accomplish this is by randomly selecting which condition comes next for each participant. The hope is that this process will result in all possible sequences being represented in the study and any potential order effects being random errors. However, this proposition can become tenuous as we increase the number of conditions in our study. When we have three conditions, there are only six possible treatment orders. The number of possible treatment sequences grows exponentially with the addition of each new condition. There are 24 possible treatment sequences for a study with four different treatment conditions. Five different conditions result in 120 possible sequences. The problem with randomly selecting the next condition for each participant is that you may select some sequences more frequently and other sequences less frequently or not at all. This will not control for potential biases or order effects as much as we would like.

counterbalancing
identifying and using
all potential treatment
sequences in a within-
subjects design.

Latin square design
a counterbalancing
strategy where each
experimental condition
appears at every position
in the sequence order
equally often.

Rather than leaving things to chance, we can use **counterbalancing,** where we first identify all possible treatment sequences and then randomly assign participants to each one of these sequences. The simplest situation is when we have only two conditions, Condition A and Condition B. We randomly assign half of our participants to receive Condition A first and then Condition B. The other half encounter Condition B first and then Condition A. Complete counterbalancing is still manageable when we have only three conditions. If we had a total of 30 participants, we would randomly assign five participants to each of the six possible sequences, as shown in **Table 10.6.**

TABLE 10.6

Counterbalancing With Three Conditions

Sequence*	First Treatment	Second Treatment	Third Treatment
#1	A	B	C
#2	A	C	B
#3	B	A	C
#4	B	C	A
#5	C	A	B
#6	C	B	A

* We would randomly assign participants to each sequence.

What happens if our repeated-measures design has four experimental conditions and we want at least five participants per sequence? Complete counterbalancing would require at least 120 participants (24 possible sequences; 5 participants per sequence). Adding a fifth condition would require 600 participants for complete counterbalancing. Fortunately, there is a more economical solution for addressing the issue of potential order effects in these situations. Rather than relying on complete counterbalancing to relegate potential order effects to random error, in larger repeated-measures designs we can turn the issue of order effects into a research question: Is it possible that the order sequence influenced the measurements? We can test this by making order sequence its own independent variable with a **Latin square design.** In a Latin square design, displayed in **Table 10.7,** we use only as many possible sequences as we have experimental conditions. If we have four conditions, we will use only four of the 24 possible sequences. When choosing these four sequences, we need to make sure that each experimental condition appears at every position in the sequence order (first, second, third, etc.) equally often. During data analysis, we can specifically test to see if there were differences between these four sequences on our dependent variable. We can also explore whether the effect of a particular level of our independent variable depended on whether participants were exposed to that condition first, second, third, or last. A Latin square design allows us to investigate the potential order effects in our repeated-measures design while still keeping the number of participants we need to recruit manageable.

▶ How do we analyze the data from a study when using a Latin square design? SEE CHAPTER 12, p. 421

TABLE 10.7

Latin Square Design for Four Conditions				
Sequence	Treatment #1	Treatment #2	Treatment #3	Treatment #4
#1	A	B	D	C
#2	B	C	A	D
#3	C	D	B	A
#4	D	A	C	B

 Thinking Like a Scientist in Real Life

Should You Take Back-to-Back Classes?

Order effects can influence you in ways that you might not have previously considered. For example, scheduling classes back-to-back may seem like a good idea during course registration. If you can schedule many classes back-to-back, you will have larger blocks of free time for work and an active social life. But is this schedule good for learning?

Whenever we conduct a within-subjects study, we need to be concerned about potential order effects. Might these order effects also influence how much you learn in back-to-back courses? There is certainly a potential for a fatigue effect, especially if you have an exam in each class, one right after the other. Feeling like you bombed the first exam might result in a carryover effect, as you would feel discouraged, frustrated, or upset before you even took the second exam. But order effects might be to your advantage if you have the same professor for both classes. Questions from the first class's exam might sensitize you to what might be on the second exam, providing you with direction for last-minute studying. Finally, the first exam might give you practice in reading and answering the professor's test questions. The potential for these sensitization and practice effects might give you an advantage when taking the second exam, but could be negated by the potential for fatigue and carryover effects. Something to consider as you select your classes for next semester.

Developing Our Protocol

We have just a few more decisions to make before we start collecting data. One is how participants should watch the reality TV shows. Should we have participants view the shows on a computer screen or on an actual TV? Should participants watch the programs sitting in desk chairs or in more comfortable chairs? To increase the mundane realism of our study, we will want our participants to watch each program on a 32-inch flat screen TV, sitting in comfortable chairs. To reduce potential fatigue effects, we will edit each show so that it is only 30 minutes long. The parts that we will cut include the opening and closing sequences and "commentary scenes,"

▶ What is mundane realism?
SEE CHAPTER 8, p. 251

where the cast members convey their thoughts or explain their actions to the viewer. This will ensure that the participants focus on the events as they unfold, rather than on the cast members' retrospective rationales for their behaviors.

We also need to decide whether to run participants individually or in groups. Running several participants at the same time could be problematic, as participants could influence each other's reactions to what happens in the show. Other people's behavior can be contagious, and one participant laughing at the cast members' exploits may cause other participants to start laughing as well. This group dynamic could influence subsequent ratings of schadenfreude. To minimize the influence of others, we will run participants individually in our study.

Weighing Our Options: Selecting Our Participants

Finally, we need a strategy for recruiting college students for our study. One option is to send out an e-mail to all students and post notices around campus asking for volunteers for our study. While this will certainly satisfy the ethical requirement that all research participation be voluntary, we may have a volunteer subject problem where our study's external validity suffers if people who do and do not volunteer differ in meaningful ways related to our research question. For instance, it is possible that college students who love to volunteer for research studies tend not to experience schadenfreude when witnessing someone else's misfortunes. If we then find no differences in schadenfreude between our reality TV shows, it would be unclear if this finding extends to college students in general, or just to those who volunteer for this type of study. Our goal is to recruit a sample that is representative of all college students without employing overtly coercive tactics to do so.

► What are the different methods for sampling? SEE CHAPTER 4, p. 109

To reduce potential volunteer subject problems, many psychology departments establish a **research participant pool,** or a list of students who receive credit in their psychology class if they participate in a research study. Researchers directly solicit participants for their studies from this group of students. The assumption is that samples obtained from research participant pools are more representative of college students in general because those who do not normally volunteer for psychological studies are more likely to do so to earn course credit. However, this does not mean that potential volunteer biases are not present in research participant pools. When we recruit from the research participant pool at our school, we should remember that students are free to volunteer for only the studies that interest them. Consequently, we do not want to describe our study in a way that appeals to only certain types of people (e.g., "Deviant Sexual Behaviors in College") or inadvertently dissuades people from volunteering (e.g., "Concerns About Dying at an Early Age").

Focus on Ethics: Should We Really Do That?

As we have learned, ethical considerations are paramount when conducting research. One of our ethical obligations is to ensure that individuals are not compelled to participate in research against their will. Establishing a

research participant pool a list of students maintained by a psychology department who will receive credit in their psychology class if they participate in a research study.

research participant pool and requiring students to earn research participation credit as part of a psychology course seems to violate this obligation. However, many psychology professors believe that there are educational benefits to research participation (Rosell et al., 2005). Sometimes the best way to develop an appreciation for the scientific nature of psychology is to actually participate in a research study. Psychology departments try to minimize potential ethical problems while satisfying this educational goal in several ways.

First, no one forces students to participate in specific studies; rather, students are free to volunteer for any study in which they wish to participate. Second, the ethical rules of conducting research remain the same: individuals can terminate their involvement in a study at any point without repercussions. In other words, as soon as a study begins, students have earned their research participation credit, regardless of whether they complete the study. Students cannot be penalized for missing a research appointment, as this may be a subtle indication that they have changed their mind and do not wish to participate in the study. Finally, the department must provide students with opportunities to satisfy their research participation requirement without actually participating in a study. For example, students could read about another research study and write a brief reaction paper. Ultimately, the goal is to ensure that both the researcher and the student benefit from research participation, with the researcher having increased confidence in the representativeness of the sample, and the student experiencing the science of psychology firsthand.

Procedure

To begin conducting our study, we will recruit 30 participants from the departmental research participation pool for a study called "TV Show Opinions." We will prescreen these individuals to ensure that they are not familiar with any of our reality TV shows. We will randomly assign participants to one of the six possible orders for watching our reality TV shows, with the constraint that there be five participants for each sequence. When each participant arrives for our study, we will escort the person to a small room containing the TV and a comfortable chair. After signing the informed consent form, the participant will complete a brief demographics sheet and the Rosenberg self-esteem scale. We will then give the participant a remote control for the TV and tell the person to watch Show A, B, or C, depending on the randomly assigned order sequence, beginning after we leave the room. Once the first show is over, we will enter the room and hand the participant a large manila envelope containing questions for the participant to answer. To minimize carryover effects, we will give participants a 10-minute break to stand, stretch, move around the room, use the restroom, etc., before we ask them to start the next reality TV show in the randomly assigned sequence. The envelope with the questions for the third show will also contain the Rosenberg self-esteem scale for participants to complete again. Upon finishing the study, we will debrief the participant and ensure that the student receives course credit for participating in our study.

▶ In addition to researchers' obligation to act ethically, why is it important for participants to act ethically during the course of a study? SEE CHAPTER 3, p. 71

Focus on Open Science: Preregistering Your Hypotheses, Materials, and Data Analysis Plan

Now that we have planned the study, we should preregister it on an open science website (e.g., http://osf.io/). Here we will describe and upload the details of our study, including our research design, how we are manipulating and measuring our variables, and all of our materials, such as the Rosenberg self-esteem scale and our modified schadenfreude scale. We will provide descriptions and links to the reality TV shows that our participants will watch during the study, and we will register the data analysis plan for testing our hypotheses, including how we are going to determine whether watching reality TV shows can improve self-esteem, and whether similarity between ourselves and another person play a role in our experience of schadenfreude. Once we have run our study, we will share our data on this site so that others can use it to verify our findings and analyze the data in other ways.

▶ Why is open science important to the research process? SEE CHAPTER 2, p. 42

YOUR TURN 10.2

1. George notices that participants are becoming better at solving the word puzzles they are given as his experiment progresses. Which of the following may be a threat to the internal validity of George's study?
   a. Carryover effects
   b. Practice effects
   c. Sensitization effects
   d. Fatigue effects

2. Rupa learns during debriefing that most of the participants in her within-subjects study of sound's impact on memory were able to accurately guess the purpose of her study by the time they encountered her last experimental manipulation. Which of the following order effects may have occurred in Rupa's study?
   a. Sensitization effects
   b. Carryover effects
   c. Practice effects
   d. Fatigue effects

3. Counterbalancing can be used to minimize potential threats to internal validity due to which of the following potential order effects?
   a. Carryover effects
   b. Sensitization effects
   c. Practice effects
   d. All of the above

How did you do? Turn to the end of the chapter to check your answers.

Statistics: In Search of Answers

We have collected our data and are almost ready to test our two research hypotheses. First, we need to enter the data into a spreadsheet for statistical analyses. Each column in our spreadsheet represents a variable; each row represents a participant. Entering the data into a spreadsheet for within-subjects designs is a little different than entering data for between-subjects designs. For each participant, we will have two different self-esteem scores and three different schadenfreude scale scores. We must be certain that we indicate the corresponding time point or condition for each measure. In the case of the Rosenberg self-esteem scale, we need to record whether the total score represents the pretest or the posttest total score. For the schadenfreude scale, we need to specify which reality TV show the participant had just viewed.

When we enter our data into our spreadsheet, each column will represent one of our measurement scores. That is, one column will consist of the participant's self-esteem pretest score (SE_Pretest), the next the self-esteem posttest score (SE_Posttest). The schadenfreude score for each reality TV show will have its own column (Celeb_Schadenfreude, Babes_Schadenfreude, and Back_Schadenfreude). After we enter all of our data, we will need to calculate the overall scores for self-esteem at both pre- and posttest and the schadenfreude measures that correspond to each TV show. For the Rosenberg self-esteem scale, we will first reverse-code the appropriate items and then sum the scores to yield an overall self-esteem score. Self-esteem scores can range from 0 to 40, with higher scores indicating higher levels of self-esteem. Reverse-coding is not necessary for our schadenfreude scale, but we do need to discard the responses to our distractor items when calculating the sum. Summing up participant responses to our five schadenfreude items yields a total score that can range from 5 to 25. The higher the score, the more schadenfreude the participant reported experiencing. **Figure 10.3** provides a screenshot of an SPSS data spreadsheet for our first 10 participants.

Ch10_Data.sav [DataSet5] - IBM SPSS Statistics Data Editor

File   Edit   View   Data   Transform   Analyze   Graphs   Utilities   Add-ons   Window   Help

	Participant	SE_Pretest	SE_Posttest	Celeb_Schadenfreude	Babes_Schadenfreude	Back_Schadenfreude
1	1	24	26	16	7	5
2	2	30	29	11	5	8
3	3	25	23	19	15	10
4	4	24	28	11	6	7
5	5	27	33	21	14	17
6	6	24	23	18	10	13
7	7	22	23	17	13	12
8	8	25	30	19	11	15
9	9	25	24	12	14	10
10	10	20	29	9	10	12

FIGURE 10.3 SPSS Spreadsheet for the First 10 Participants. *(SPSS)*

t-test for dependent means a statistic used to determine if there is a statistically significant difference between two related sets of scores; also known as dependent means *t*-test.

repeated-measures analysis of variance (repeated-measures ANOVA) a statistic used to test a hypothesis from a within-subjects design with three or more conditions.

▶ Curious about which statistical tests we need to use to test our hypotheses and why? SEE APPENDIX A, p. 480

Selecting the Proper Tool

We have two research hypotheses we want to test using our data gathered from two different research designs: a pretest-posttest design and a repeated-measures design. The first hypothesis is that *after watching several reality TV shows, participants' self-esteem will be higher than it was before watching the shows*. Because we used a pretest-posttest design to test this hypothesis, we need to use a statistic that determines whether there is a significant difference between participants' pretest and posttest scores. We can use a **t-test for dependent means** (or **dependent means t-test**) to make this determination. A *t*-test for dependent means evaluates whether the difference between the participants' pretest and posttest scores significantly differs from zero (no difference). If it does, then we would conclude that there was a statistically significant change between pretest and posttest scores.

To test our second hypothesis that *the three reality TV shows will elicit different amounts of schadenfreude in participants,* we will need to use a variant of the one-way analysis of variance test we discussed when conducting a multigroup between-subjects design. A **repeated-measures analysis of variance (repeated-measures ANOVA)** allows us to evaluate whether participants' scores significantly differ across the various levels of the within-subjects independent variable. If we find that there is a significant difference, then we will use post-hoc tests to determine which levels of our independent variable significantly differed from the others.

Writing the Results in APA Style: *t*-Test for Dependent Means and Repeated-Measures ANOVA

Results

We used a *t*-test for dependent means to test the first hypothesis that participants' self-esteem would improve after watching the reality TV shows. As seen in Figure 10.4, the mean self-esteem pretest score was 25.0 ($SD = 2.88$). The mean self-esteem posttest score was 28.3 ($SD = 3.01$). The improvement in self-esteem scores between the pretest and posttest was statistically significant, $t(29) = 4.47, p < .001$ (one-tailed), $d = .82$.

A repeated-measures ANOVA was used to evaluate if feelings of schadenfreude differed among the participants after watching each reality TV show. The groups' means are reported in Table 10.8. Reported feelings of schadenfreude did significantly differ between the three shows, $F(2, 58) = 17.37, p < .001$, eta$^2 = .18$. Post-hoc (LSD) testing revealed that participants experienced more schadenfreude after watching *Celebrities Go to College* than after watching *Babes in College* ($p < .001$) or *Back in the Day U* ($p < .001$). There was not a significant difference in the amount of schadenfreude elicited by *Babes in College* and *Back in the Day U* ($p = .15$).

Don't Just Tell Me, Show Me: Using Figures and Tables

Rather than include the descriptive statistics for the different groups within the text of the results section, researchers often provide this information in a table or a figure. **Figure 10.4** displays the participants' levels of self-esteem before and after watching all three reality TV shows. **Table 10.8** provides the mean reported feelings of schadenfreude associated with each reality TV show.

TABLE 10.8

Means and Standard Deviations for Schadenfreude Scores		
Reality TV Show	Mean	SD
Celebrities Go to College	16.63	3.82
Babes in College	12.63	4.37
Back in the Day U	13.57	4.19

Note: N = 30. Scores could range from 5 to 25. Higher scores indicate a greater schadenfreude.

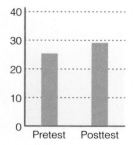

FIGURE 10.4 Self-Esteem Pretest and Posttest Means.

Our Research Plan at a Glance

What Are Our Research Questions?

Question #1: Can watching reality TV shows boost our self-esteem?

Question #2: Do we experience more schadenfreude toward a person who is similar or dissimilar to us?

What Are Our Designs?

Question #1: We are using a pretest-posttest design.

Question #2: We are using a repeated-measures design.

Why Are We Using These Designs?

Question #1: This design allows us to compare participants' self-esteem before and after watching reality TV shows to see if their self-esteem improves.

Question #2: This design allows us to compare participants' experiences of schadenfreude while watching different types of reality TV shows.

What Are Our Variables?

Independent Variable(s):

Question #1: We are not manipulating any variables to test this question.

Question #2: Similarity between the people in the reality TV show and the participants. There are three levels: high similarity, moderate similarity, and low similarity.

Dependent Variable(s):

Question #1: Self-esteem as measured by the Rosenberg self-esteem scale.

Question #2: Feelings of schadenfreude as measured by the modified schadenfreude scale.

What Are Our Hypotheses?

Hypothesis #1: *After watching several reality TV shows, participants' self-esteem will be higher than it was before watching the shows.*

Hypothesis #2: *The three reality TV shows will elicit different amounts of schadenfreude in participants.*

(Continued)

Who Are Our Participants? Thirty undergraduate students recruited from a departmental research participant pool.

What Ethical Considerations Do We Need to Keep in Mind?

• Although research participant pools can be educationally beneficial for students, they must be able to choose the studies in which to participate.

• Students must receive course credit even if they terminate their participation before the study is completed. (They must also be provided with opportunities other than actual research participation in order to satisfy their course requirement.)

What Is Our Data Analysis Plan?

1. **Calculate our data.** We calculate participants' pretest and posttest Rosenberg self-esteem scale scores by reverse-coding the appropriate items, and then summing all of the scores. We calculate participants' schadenfreude scale scores after they have watched each reality TV show, discarding the responses to distractor items before calculating the sum.

2. **Test our hypotheses.** We compare whether there was a significant change in self-esteem between the pretest and posttest scores by using a *t*-test for dependent means. We use a repeated-measures analysis of variance (repeated-measures ANOVA) to determine whether participants' schadenfreude scale scores significantly differed after watching each of the three reality TV shows. If the repeated-measures ANOVA is significant, we follow up with post-hoc tests to determine which reality shows differed in terms of amount of schadenfreude elicited.

Want to practice the analyses for this research yourself? Ask your instructor about the data set that accompanies this study.

Let's Discuss What Happened

We combined two different research designs in our study so we could simultaneously address two different research questions. We used a pretest-posttest design to evaluate whether watching reality TV shows can improve one's self-esteem, and we manipulated participants' similarity to cast members in three different reality TV shows to assess the impact of similarity on the experience of schadenfreude. Using a repeated-measures design, we compared how much schadenfreude a participant experienced after watching each reality TV show. It is now time to discuss our findings in terms of how they contribute to the literature, and to explore possible alternative explanations.

What Did We Find?

We addressed our first question by comparing participants' reported levels of self-esteem when they began our study (before watching any reality TV) with their levels of self-esteem after watching all three reality TV shows. We found that, on average, participants' self-esteem improved by the end of the study, providing support for our first hypothesis. We also found support for our second hypothesis, that each reality TV show would produce different levels of schadenfreude. Specifically, participants experienced significantly more schadenfreude after watching the reality TV show featuring celebrities going to college. We did not find any significant differences between the reality TV shows about single moms and about going to college without the use of technology.

Why These Findings?

Let's first discuss our finding that watching reality TV shows improved participants' self-esteem. Some research suggests that reality TV shows can promote downward social comparisons (e.g., Nabi et al., 2003) or feelings of superiority (e.g., Reiss & Wiltz, 2004), both of which can help enhance self-esteem (Kassin et al., 2017). While our findings seem to provide support for this idea—after all, participants' self-esteem improved from pretest to posttest—we cannot conclude that watching reality TV shows causes people's self-esteem to improve. As discussed in Chapter 8, if we want to establish a causal relation, we need to rule out alternative explanations for our observed results. To do this, we need a comparison or control group. Looking at our pretest-posttest design, we realize that there is no comparison group, which means it is possible that simply watching any type of television, and not just reality TV, can improve our self-esteem over time. Likewise, it is also possible that self-esteem would have naturally improved even more over time if our participants had not watched reality TV. Our results can only tell us that students' self-esteem improved while participating in our study. Without any comparison groups, we are unable to pinpoint the reason this occurred. The lack of a comparison group is a serious limitation when trying to establish causality using pretest-posttest designs.

> ▶ What actions do we need to take to establish causality in a study?
> SEE CHAPTER 8, p. 249

> **What Do You Think?**
> For what other reasons might a person's self-esteem improve in a short time period?

We did find support for our second hypothesis examining how similarity influences feelings of schadenfreude. The research on this question is mixed, with some suggesting that we experience more schadenfreude toward members of an outgroup (e.g., Feather et al., 2013) and others finding that similarity can promote these feelings (e.g., van Dijk, Ouwerkerk, Goslinga, Nieweg, & Gallucci, 2006). Our findings suggest that we experience more pleasure when observing the misfortunes of dissimilar others. Participants probably identified least with the cast members of *Celebrities Go to College* because those individuals likely have experiences outside the show that are not typical for most people. Furthermore, the problems that the *Celebrities Go to College* cast members experienced are mundane for most college students, which may have made the cast members' reactions seem absurd. Participants may have felt more similar to the cast members in the other two shows, which may have made their challenges feel more salient. It is also possible that their struggles in the episodes were more unique and outside students' typical experiences, making them hard for participants to directly compare to themselves.

What Could Be Improved?

We could improve our study in several ways to obtain more confident conclusions. First, we should include a control group to test whether watching a reality TV show can improve self-esteem. One strategy would be to have another group of participants watch scripted shows involving characters and settings similar to our reality TV show. We would evaluate whether participants' self-esteem changed after watching each of these types of shows and whether the two groups significantly differed in their amount of change.

Given that we used three different reality TV shows, each with different cast members, general premises, episodes, directors, etc., it is unclear if cast member similarity was solely responsible for participants' feelings of schadenfreude. At a minimum, we should have included a manipulation check to assess how similar participants perceived the shows' cast members to be to themselves. Another option might be to use one episode from a single reality TV show depicting all of the cast members experiencing misfortune. Through earlier testing, we could determine which cast member each participant was most similar to, and have participants focus either on the most or least similar cast member while watching the episode.

What's Next?

One reason people may like watching reality TV shows is that they provide social comparison opportunities to enhance our self-esteem (Heider, 1958). However, reality TV shows are not our only source of insight into other people's worlds. Social media platforms such as Instagram and Twitter might also boost our self-esteem, especially if we read posts about others' trials and tribulations. Future research is necessary to evaluate whether reality TV shows uniquely affect our self-esteem.

Feelings of schadenfreude have interesting implications when we think about prejudice and discrimination. We may gain some pleasure from observing a member of a stigmatized group struggle, making it less likely we will empathize with that person's plight. This feeling may be even stronger if we believe that the person deserves their misfortunes or problems (van Dijk, Ouwerkerk, & Goslinga, 2009). We also do not know how schadenfreude can influence subsequent behavior toward that individual. Could schadenfreude lead us to engage in aggressive behaviors? Or could it lead us to react with greater empathy because, while we feel better about ourselves, we know the other person feels bad? Sounds like there is much more research for us to do on this topic.

YOUR TURN 10.3

1. During the first month of the season, the players on a baseball team are mired in a terrible hitting slump. The hitting coach believes that the problem is the players' bats being too heavy. One month after switching to lighter bats, the team batting average markedly improves. The hitting coach is now completely convinced that it is better for players to use lighter bats to improve their hitting. Which of the following is the primary problem with this conclusion?

   a. The study did not run long enough to obtain any meaningful conclusions.

   b. The quality of the pitchers the batters faced in this study was not kept constant.

   c. It is unclear if this improvement is statistically significant.

   d. This study lacked any comparison groups.

2. Roxanne is testing the hypothesis that the best-tasting jelly beans are the green ones. Using a within-subjects design, she has participants rate how much they like the taste of four different flavored jelly beans. Which statistical test should Roxanne use to determine if there is a significant difference in participants' ratings of the jelly beans?

   a. A repeated-measures ANOVA

   b. A *t*-test for independent means

   c. A one-way ANOVA

   d. A *t*-test for dependent means

3. Which of the following may have been a confounding variable in our "TV Show Opinions" study?

   a. The order in which the shows were shown

   b. The participants' preferences for watching reality TV shows

   c. The types of misfortunes experienced by the cast members

   d. How comfortable participants were while watching the shows

How did you do? Turn to the end of the chapter to check your answers.

Research in Action

Left Out and Feeling Low

Think back to your days on the school playground. A group of kids are gathering together to play kickball. You do not really care which team you end up on, as long as you get picked to play (and, ideally, are not picked last!). We all know that being included feels good and being left out does not, but are these experiences really that simple? Can experiences of exclusion change how we behave or think?

The only way to know for sure is to design a research study testing this idea. In the online activity *Left Out and Feeling Low,* you will apply what you know about within-subject designs to test whether an individual's self-esteem changes when he or she is included in or excluded from a virtual game of catch.

 LaunchPad To complete this activity, visit LaunchPad at launchpadworks.com

Final Thoughts

It is important to remember that our research question always determines the best design to use. Some research questions require us to measure our participants two or more times on the same variable. In these cases, we need to use a within-subjects design, which has the advantage of allowing us to ask questions about how participants' responses change as the result of an intervention or exposure to different levels of our independent variable.

We began this chapter wondering how watching reality TV shows might be good for our self-esteem. Social comparisons are an important strategy for enhancing and maintaining our feelings of self-worth (Kassin et al., 2017).

However, is there a dark side to such comparisons? Do we ever behave in ways that increase others' misfortunes just for our own psychological benefit? Can schadenfreude make us more susceptible to feelings of prejudice or discrimination toward dissimilar others? Could reality TV shows be good for our self-esteem, but bad for reducing stereotyping and prejudice in society? Fortunately, we have science to help us answer these questions.

CHAPTER 10 Review

Review Questions

1. Bethany is interested in the types of stressors students tend to experience during their first year in college. She has six first-year students download a special app to their smartphone. When the app's alarm goes off, the students must stop and answer a few questions that appear on their smartphone concerning what they are doing at that moment and the level of stress they are currently experiencing. The students complete this task several times a day for one week. Bethany is using a _____ to conduct her study.
   a. within-subjects design
   b. pretest-posttest design
   c. behavioral diary
   d. survey design

(Questions 2–4) Every fall at Life's a Beach U, the Office of Student Life sponsors a hypnotism show to entertain the new first-year students. At the end of the show, the hypnotist always plants the "suggestion" into the new students that they will study hard for their classes. Vicky wonders if this suggestion really works. She asks first-year students to report how much time they spent studying for classes the week before the hypnotism show. She then contacts these same students again a week later. If they had attended the show, she asks them how much time they spent studying during that week. She found that those students increased the time they spent studying by 20% the week after the show.

2. In the above study, what type of design did Vicky use?
   a. A repeated-measures design
   b. A pretest-posttest design
   c. A within-subjects design
   d. A Latin square design

3. In the above study, Vicky assessed how long the participants studied each night the week before the hypnotism show so that
   a. she could minimize potential practice effects.
   b. her study would be completely counterbalanced.
   c. she had a baseline measurement.
   d. testing would not be a potential threat to internal validity.

4. During the course of the study described above, a major hurricane forced the shutdown of the university for several days after the hypnotism show. The number of hours participants reported studying after this unexpected semester break was similar to their study times before the hypnotism show. Which of the following represents a potential threat to the internal validity of Vicky's study?

   a. History

   b. Attrition

   c. Carryover effects

   d. Maturation

5. A professor wants to assess the impact that a newly developed first-year seminar has on the academic perseverance and motivation of new first-year students. The professor measures first-year students' academic perseverance and motivation on the first day of class and again on the last day of class. Which of the following is an obvious threat to the internal validity of this pretest-posttest study?

   a. Attrition

   b. Maturation

   c. Testing effects

   d. Instrumentation

6. A professor notices that students who had her for one course tend to do better in subsequent courses they take with her. Which of the following order effects is most likely *not* a possible reason for this finding?

   a. Sensitization effect

   b. Practice effect

   c. Carryover effect

   d. Fatigue effect

7. Deception might be a useful strategy for minimizing which of the following potential order effects in a repeated-measures design?

   a. Fatigue effects

   b. Sensitization effects

   c. Carryover effects

   d. Practice effects

8. Dixie wants to compare the persuasiveness of three different television commercials using a repeated-measures design. To control for potential order effects, she should

   a. give the participants practice in using the rating scale before starting the study.

   b. use a Latin square design.

   c. implement complete counterbalancing using random assignment.

   d. keep the commercials short to reduce potential fatigue effects.

9. Which of the following is an unethical practice when running a research participant pool?
   a. Requiring students who miss a study appointment to actually participate in that experiment at a later time as a penalty.
   b. Offering students a choice of studies for which they can volunteer.
   c. Providing students with alternative ways for satisfying a course research requirement.
   d. Permitting students to earn their research credit even if they refuse to complete the study.

10. A professor wants to know if students tend to earn the same grades on all three exams in his class. He enters all of the students' exams scores into a spreadsheet. Which statistic should the professor use to answer his question?
    a. A *t*-test for independent means
    b. A *t*-test for dependent means
    c. A one-way ANOVA
    d. A repeated-measures ANOVA

11. Why might one opt to use a within-subjects rather than a between-subjects design when answering a research question?

12. Explain how a within-subjects design is a better option than a pretest-posttest design for establishing causality.

13. Why are order effects of particular concern for within-subjects designs? How can these effects be minimized?

Applying What You've Learned

1. In Chapter 9, we designed a multigroup, between-subjects study to examine how the experience of warmth might influence attitudes and behaviors concerning climate change. How would you redesign this study to be a within-subjects design?

2. Create your own Sprite versus Sierra Mist taste test challenge. Explain how you will minimize threats such as potential practice effects, carryover effects, fatigue effects, and sensitization effects.

3. Search on YouTube for "taste test challenge" videos. Analyze one of the videos in terms of potential threats to internal validity. Redesign the study to eliminate these threats.

4. Read the Martens and Kosloff (2012) study described in the Research Spotlight feature. Why do you think the researchers chose to use a within-subjects rather than a between-subjects design to answer their research questions?

5. Downward social comparison is not the only way that people try to enhance their self-esteem. Think of other methods people use to boost their self-esteem. Describe how you might test the effectiveness of some of these strategies using a within-subjects design.

6. In addition to noncompetitive reality shows, what other types of TV programs might result in the experience of schadenfreude? Design a within-subjects study to see if you are correct.

7. THE NOVICE RESEARCHER: It is important to eliminate potential order effects in a within-subjects design. Playing the role of a novice researcher, design a within-subjects study that suffers from practice, fatigue, carryover, and sensitization effects. Now discuss how a more experienced researcher would eliminate these potential threats to internal validity.

8. DIG INTO THE NUMBERS: We have provided your instructor with data for another within-subjects study. Use that data to build your SPSS skills and to test hypotheses that require repeated-measures ANOVAs. Write an APA-style results section based on your results. If you would like even more practice, your instructor also has the data that accompanies the study discussed throughout this chapter.

Key Concepts

attrition, p. 324

baseline measurement, p. 322

behavioral diary, p. 322

carryover effect, p. 334

counterbalancing, p. 336

dependent means *t*-test, p. 342

fatigue effect, p. 334

history, p. 326

instrumentation, p. 325

Latin square design, p. 336

maturation, p. 326

mortality, p. 324

order effect, p. 333

practice effect, p. 333

pretest-posttest design, p. 322

repeated-measures analysis of variance (repeated-measures ANOVA), p. 342

repeated-measures design, p. 323

research participant pool, p. 338

sensitization effect, p. 334

testing effect, p. 325

t-test for dependent means, p. 342

Answers to YOUR TURN

Your Turn 10.1: 1. a; 2. d; 3. c

Your Turn 10.2: 1. b; 2. a; 3. d

Your Turn 10.3: 1. d; 2. a; 3. c

Answers to Multiple-Choice Review Questions

1. c; 2. b; 3. c; 4. a; 5. b; 6. d; 7. b; 8. c; 9. a; 10. d

Factorial Design

"I Lost My Phone Number, Can I Borrow Yours?" Do Pick-Up Lines Really Work?

Pressmaster/Shutterstock

LEARNING OUTCOMES

After reading this chapter, you should be able to:

- Provide operational definitions for key variables.
- Identify the benefits of a factorial design.
- Understand the nature of interactions.
- Write main effect and interaction effect hypotheses.
- Identify cell and marginal means.
- Write a results section for a two-way analysis of variance (two-way ANOVA).
- Distinguish between synergistic and suppression effects.

Something to Think About . . .

Take a moment to think about this question: What do you care about? On a day-to-day basis, what is important to you? What things do you think about the most? As a college student, you might say a looming deadline for a paper, your classes, your grades in those classes, your future, your career, or how much money you currently lack. You might also list your pets, your friends, your family, and your romantic interests. Nearly everyone's list will contain these last few things because close relationships are a central part of the human experience. They often provide our greatest sources of happiness, as well as despair. College students are no exception to this rule. If you are anything like we were in college, a good deal of your daily mental energy focuses on romantic relationships: getting into them, trying to keep them, trying to strengthen them, trying to get out of them, trying to get into them and then out of them quickly, or perhaps trying to juggle several of them at once.

Certainly, there are numerous things to think about with relationships, but the thought that likely consumes (or consumed, if you are in a relationship) the most mental energy is how to get into a relationship. The process through which two strangers fall in love and form a romantic relationship is no simple matter. Think of everything that goes into it. You have to feel that the other person is physically attractive, reasonably engaging, and intelligent, and that they share your interests and views. You need to feel a sense of connection or chemistry with the person. As if that is not enough, all of these factors have to be in place for the other person to feel attracted to you, as well. On top of everything else, social psychology teaches us that the situation matters, so the spark that gets a relationship started needs to happen in the right situation. If you are both at a party, great, you can proceed with initiating a relationship. If you are both at a funeral . . . not so much. If you are both interested in a relationship, great. If either of you was recently dumped by your supposed soul mate, you should probably continue your search elsewhere.

All things considered, it may seem like studying something as complex as relationship formation is impossible. In fact, one of the major challenges in psychology is to turn complex and seemingly un-study-able phenomena into questions that science can answer. That's where you come in.

Introduction to Our Research Question

By this point in the book, you are a seasoned science veteran. You know that a question such as "What causes relationships to begin?" is too general and vague to study scientifically. Rather, we need to break down this broad question into smaller units, or questions, that we can study using the scientific method. To help us focus on a more specific question, we could identify the earliest moment that a relationship starts to be a relationship. Is it when you notice someone across the room? Probably not—your wandering eyes notice many people, and you would not say that you had relationships with all of those people. A relationship truly begins to blossom when two potential partners first engage in conversation. It could be a simple "Hi," a more casual "How ya doin?," or a funny pick-up line like, "Are you a parking ticket? 'Cause you've got fine written all over you." If you think about it, the sole purpose of this type of pick-up line is to start a relationship. But are pick-up lines really the way to go? Like many things in psychology, it depends. Some pick-up lines might be more effective than others. This idea provides us with an interesting and more specific research question:

RESEARCH

?   When are pick-up lines most effective in starting a relationship?

To study this question, we can start with our own thoughts about what makes pick-up lines effective. After all, you have probably heard or used a few pick-up lines yourself, and you might have some ideas about what makes for good and bad pick-up lines. The obvious thought that comes to mind is that pick-up lines are more effective when the person using the line is cute. The line's effectiveness also depends on what the person says. Some lines are clever ("I seem to have lost my phone number. Can I borrow yours?") while others ("I wanna live in your socks so I can be with you every step of the way") can be creepy. The person's attractiveness and what he or she says both seem like factors that can make pick-up lines more effective, and are worth testing. Because we are predicting how specific factors (attractiveness or type of pick-up line) influence or lead to changes in another factor (starting a relationship), we will need to use an experimental approach. As always, before running out and designing a study, we need to consult the literature to see what other scientists have already discovered in this area.

▶ How do experimental approaches differ from nonexperimental approaches? SEE CHAPTER 2, p. 38

Reviewing the Literature: What Do We Already Know About This Topic?

Since we have already identified two potential factors that could make pick-up lines more effective, let's jump right in and search for articles on both topics. We can decide later which ideas to use in our study. Type "pick-up lines" and "attractiveness" into your research database program and see what you find. When we did this using PsycINFO, the very first article we found was:

Senko, C., & Fyffe, V. (2010). An evolutionary perspective on effective vs. ineffective pick-up lines. *Journal of Social Psychology, 150*(6), 648–667. doi:10.1080/002245 40903365539

Based on the abstract, the researchers had female undergraduates imagine scenarios in which men of different levels of physical attractiveness approached them and used one of three different types of pick-up lines. Wow, this sounds familiar—their study uses not one, but both potential factors we came up with to use in our research! Well, this is a bummer. But not to worry—this happens from time to time and is exactly why it is important to do a literature search before planning a study. This is not a crisis, but rather an opportunity to broaden our literature search into related areas.

Let's think of other things that could influence a pick-up line's effectiveness. Good research ideas are everywhere, and some of the best sources of new research ideas are theories and concepts you have learned about in other classes. Psychology classes are good options, but other classes could relate to your question, as well. Bringing in ideas from a related field has the advantage of making your research interdisciplinary and increasing your study's potential influence. Attraction seems like a basic element of human behavior, so biology may be a good discipline to explore. But "biology" is fairly broad. One way to narrow it down is to get ideas from a Google search. Do a quick search for "biology and attraction." When we did this search, the first article in our results was "The Biology of Attraction" from *Psychology Today*. Now, we know what you are thinking: Articles written for the general public are not appropriate to use as a primary source. You are absolutely right, but these types of sources are helpful tools for generating ideas and identifying research articles. This article discusses several potential factors, one of which is how odor or scent influences attraction. While that might be relevant for ants, bees, and beetles, does it really apply to humans? It would certainly be interesting if it did, especially if it helped explain how relationships begin.

Armed with this new idea for how our two main ideas (pick-up line content and scent) lead relationships to begin, we will limit our search to published research articles from peer-reviewed academic journals. Specifically, we should try to determine answers to the following questions: What types of pick-up lines are there? Is one type more effective than others? Are certain lines always more effective, or does their effectiveness change based on other factors? Can humans communicate through scent well enough to influence each other? Is odor an important factor in human attraction? Due to the biological nature of research on smell, we will need to broaden our search beyond the psychology databases to include databases that focus on other areas of science (e.g., Medline).

Here are some studies that we found after searching these databases. We summarized the studies' main points to guide our thinking on this topic and, ultimately, to help us design our study.

▶ Need tips on how to use databases for searching the literature? SEE APPENDIX B, p. 497

Types of Pick-Up Lines

Weber, K., Goodboy, A. K., & Cayanus, J. L. (2010). Flirting competence: An experimental study on appropriate and effective opening lines. *Communication Research Reports, 27,* 184–191. doi:10.1080/08824091003738149

Over 600 participants viewed videos of five types of pick-up lines: a cute/flippant line ("You must be tired because you've been running through my mind all day"), a humor attempt ("Do you think I look like Johnny Depp?"), a direct compliment ("I had to tell you how fine you are"), a direct introduction ("Hi, my name is Josh. What is your name?"), or a third-party introduction ("Hi Kayla, this is my friend Josh."). After controlling for attractiveness of the person giving the line, participants perceived the direct and third-party introductions as the most effective, while cute/flippant lines, humor attempts, and direct compliments were less effective.

Pick-Up Line Effectiveness

Bale, C., Morrison, R., & Caryl, P. (2006). Chat-up lines as male sexual displays. *Personality and Individual Differences, 40,* 655–664. doi:10.1016/j.paid.2005.07.016

This study tested the effectiveness of pick-up lines/openings by having over 200 undergraduates at a Scottish university read a series of vignettes depicting a man approaching a woman. The man used openings (slightly longer and more involved conversation starters). Women preferred openings that showed the man's wealth, character (e.g., ability to take charge, physical fitness), and culture. The least effective lines involved humor (e.g., "I think you've got something in your eye. Oh never mind, it's just a sparkle.") and sexually suggestive comments (e.g., "I may not be Fred Flintstone, but I bet I can make your Bed Rock.").

Senko, C., & Fyffe, V. (2010). An evolutionary perspective on effective vs. ineffective pick-up lines. *Journal of Social Psychology, 150,* 648–667. doi:10.1080/00224540903365539

Seventy college females imagined a male approaching them and using a pick-up line (cute/flippant, innocuous, or direct). Participants were told that he was attractive, was unattractive, or received no information about him. Participants rated the male on several traits, including intelligence, humor, and trustworthiness, as well as their willingness to speak with him, and whether they would have a long-term or short-term relationship with him. Women indicated that they were less likely to talk with or have a long-term relationship with a male who used a cute/flippant line, regardless of how attractive he was. Generally, women were more likely to talk to him, and have a short-term or long-term relationship with him, if the male was attractive, regardless of pick-up line used. Women perceived males who used the cute/flippant line as less trustworthy and intelligent than if they used a direct or innocuous line.

The Importance of Scent for Communication

Herz, R. S., & Inzlicht, M. (2002). Sex differences in response to physical and social factors involved in human mate selection—the importance of smell for women. *Evolution and Human Behavior, 23,* 359–364. doi:10.1016/S1090-5138(02)00095-8

Data from a survey of 198 college men and women examined the relative importance of several traits for attraction. Results indicated that women considered a partner's body odor more important to attraction than physical attractiveness, and that odor was more important than a majority of social factors (the only exception was pleasantness). Further, in terms of odor, both men and women rated natural body odor as more important to sexual interest than perfume/cologne fragrance.

Wyart, C., Webster, W. W., Chen, J. H., Wilson, S. R., McClary, A., Khan, R. M., & Sobel, N. (2007). Smelling a single component of male sweat alters levels of cortisol in women. *Journal of Neuroscience, 27*, 1261–1265. doi:10.1523/JNEUROSCI.4430-06.2007

Researchers wanted to see if a particular component (androstadienone) of males' sweat could influence women. Twenty-one women smelled both 30 milligrams of the steroidal compound androstadienone and yeast (on separate days) while in a highly controlled air-filtered room that kept temperature and humidity constant. Each participant took 20 sniffs of the jar, then watched some video clips, then provided a saliva sample that researchers used to measure the stress hormone cortisol. Results suggested that smelling androstadienone led to higher levels of cortisol, suggesting that humans are able to influence each other via smell-based chemosignals (i.e., odors or scents).

Scent and Attraction

Thornhill, R., Gangestad, S. W., Miller, R., Scheyd, G., McCollough, J. K., & Franklin, M. (2003). Major histocompatibility complex genes, symmetry, and body scent attractiveness in men and women. *Behavioral Ecology, 14*, 668–678.

This study sought to specify major histocompatibility complex (MHC) genes' role in mate choice. Approximately 200 male and female participants gave a blood sample (to assess their MHC), then slept in a new clean T-shirt for two nights. They did this after washing their bed with unscented soap, not eating pungent food, not having sex or sleeping alongside a partner, and not using any form of deodorant, perfume/cologne, or scented soap. Researchers took each participant's picture, measured right and left side body parts (to assess symmetry), and had participants smell a series of bags containing each other's shirts. Men preferred T-shirts from women with dissimilar MHC and preferred the scent of attractive women and those who had a higher probability of conception. There was no evidence that women preferred T-shirts from men with dissimilar MHC (this did not vary based on women's probability of conception). However, when women not using contraception were in the most fertile part of their menstrual cycle, they preferred symmetrical men's scent over asymmetrical men's.

Pause, B. M. (2004). Are androgen steroids acting as pheromones in humans? *Physiology and Behavior, 83*, 21–29. doi:10.1016/j.physbeh.2004.07.019

Researchers, via a partial replication of Kirk-Smith and Booth (1980), sought to determine whether an androstenone spray could serve as a pheromone (an electrochemical signal to other animals). To test this, researchers had 40 homosexual men and 39 heterosexual women enter a fake waiting room set up in a lab. The participants chose a seat, and then the researchers led them to a side room. After 10 minutes, the participants returned to a larger seating area where the outer leftmost chair (out of four) had a piece of paper treated with androstenone (78 µg 5a-androst-16-en-3-one [Sigma: A8008] diluted in 1 ml propanediol) attached to it. Compared to pretest when no androstenone was present, significantly more participants chose the seat with androstenone at posttest (13.6% vs. 27.8%).

Have you ever thought about how your clothes may capture your natural scent, influencing who is attracted to you? Perhaps you could skip a shower, deodorant, or other scents in the name of science. On second thought, maybe not. *(DAJ/Getty Images)*

From Ideas to Innovation

You may have previously heard of the "art of the pick-up" or people claiming to be "pick-up artists," but now we know there is also "the science of the pick-up," which could make you the next "pick-up scientist." From that research, cute/flippant (i.e., funny and sexually suggestive), innocuous (i.e., nonovert pick-ups that sound like typical conversation starters), and direct (i.e., blunt and to the point) pick-up lines seem to be the most standard (Senko & Fyffe, 2010). However, researchers have sought to broaden those categories to focus on other types of lines (Weber, Goodboy, & Cayanus, 2010), and on slightly more in-depth pick-up attempts or "openings" that go beyond a single line (Bale, Morrison, & Caryl, 2006).

As much as the initial idea that humans communicate through smell, and that scent may influence attraction, seems far-fetched, the research says otherwise. Not only do people self-report that smell is important (Herz & Inzlicht, 2002), but humans clearly communicate through scent (Wyart et al., 2007), and these scents influence attraction (Pause, 2004; Thornhill et al., 2003).

It appears as though previous research has covered each of our original ideas (types of pick-up lines and scent). Some research has looked at how different types of pick-up lines combine with other factors, such as gender (Weber et al., 2010) and attractiveness (Senko & Fyffe, 2010). However, no one seems to have looked at our two ideas together. By testing two factors at once that researchers have only tested individually, not only are we building on previous researchers' works, but we are exploring a previously unstudied facet of relationship initiation. Thus, our research question has become:

RESEARCH **?** How do pick-up lines and a person's scent influence relationship initiation?

Defining Key Terms: What Do You Mean By _____?

Since research on pick-up lines exists, we will not have much work to do in terms of defining them. Studies use a variety of names for the techniques people use to initiate or begin relationships, including terms such as chat-up lines, pick-up lines, opening lines, opening gambits, and openers. Some researchers study these techniques delivered as single lines (e.g., Weber et al., 2010), while others study them in the context of a broader conversation (e.g., Bale et al., 2006). Of the various terms, there appear to be several synonyms for single lines (e.g., "pick-up line," "chat-up line," "opening gambit," and "opening line"); an "opener" seems to focus more on the longer, more conversational approach. Regardless of the exact term, for simplicity we can classify them all as pick-up attempts that aim to begin a conversation that could lead to a romantic relationship.

In terms of a person's scent, the research is clear that natural scents are more important than manufactured scents such as perfume or cologne (Herz & Inzlicht, 2002), so we will want to stick with natural scents. A person's natural scent is complex and contains several compounds, including indicators of major histocompatibility complex, or MHC (e.g., Thornhill et al., 2003), and androstadienone (Wyart et al., 2007). The research indicates that MHC varies inherently from individual to individual, while androstadienone can be administered via a spray (Pause, 2004). We already know that some people are better at starting a relationship than others, so it might be more interesting to identify a scent that can help those who have trouble initiating relationships increase their success rate. Given the research showing androstadienone's influence on attraction, the idea to administer it seems promising.

Next, we need to pinpoint what we mean by "relationship initiation." According to the *Handbook of Relationship Initiation,* a relationship begins when both partners have an awareness of the relationship or think of it as a relationship (Sprecher, Wenzel, & Harvey, 2008). These relationships can be close (e.g., friendships, family relationships) or intimate (close relationships that also have a romantic or sexual element). It seems odd that a person would use a pick-up line or opening to establish a friendship, so, for our purposes, we should focus on the formation of an intimate relationship. Interestingly, much of the pick-up line research focuses on participants' ratings of the pick-up lines themselves (e.g., Was it funny? Did it make the person seem trustworthy?) and not on how the participant might respond to the actual pick-up attempt (e.g., smile, walk away, etc.). In order to detect whether an intimate relationship will begin, we will want to focus on behaviors that indicate a romantic relationship is forming.

Weighing Our Options: Picking a Design

As in previous chapters, our research question clearly identifies a **factor,** or independent variable, that causes or changes an outcome, or dependent variable. In cases when you are trying to identify why something happens, an experimental design is the best choice. However, unlike in previous chapters, we have more than one factor (pick-up line and scent) that could influence our outcome (relationship initiation). We could run two separate studies, investigating each independent variable in isolation, but doing so would not allow us to test our research question about how pick-up lines and scent may work together, or combine, to influence relationship initiation. To look at how variables may interact with each other, we can use a **factorial design,** which is the most frequently used experimental design for a study that has more than one independent variable, or factor.

Anatomy of a Factorial Design

Factorial designs can take many forms, depending on the number of independent variables we are including in our study. For example, when reading journal articles, you may have seen factorial designs described with a set of numbers: "a 2×2 factorial design" or "a $4 \times 2 \times 3$ factorial design." These descriptions indicate the number of independent variables in the study and the number of levels of each independent variable. In these descriptions, how many numbers there are indicates how many independent variables the design includes. In a 3×4

factor something that can influence an outcome or dependent variable; also known as an independent variable.

factorial design an experimental design that has more than one independent variable.

TABLE 11.1

Anatomy of a Factorial Design			
Design	Number of Independent Variables	Levels in the First Independent Variable	Levels in the Second Independent Variable
2 × 2	2	2	2
2 × 3	2	2	3
2 × 2 × 4	3	2	2
3 × 3 × 2	3	3	3
4 × 3 × 2 × 3 × 2 × 2	6	4	3

factorial design, there are two numbers, so there are two independent variables. In a 2 × 2 × 4 factorial design, there are three numbers, so there are three independent variables. See **Table 11.1** for an explanation of the anatomy of a factorial design.

The value of the numbers themselves indicates how many levels or conditions each independent variable has. In a 3 × 4 factorial design, the first independent variable has 3 levels, while the second independent variable has 4 levels. While the number of independent variables, or factors, we can have in a study is unlimited, the more we include, the more complex and confusing our results may become. For example, if we wanted to conduct a 5 × 3 × 2 × 4 × 2 factorial design, we would have five different independent variables. This sounds useful—until we realize that with five independent variables, we would have to make sense of 31 different combinations of your factors! Remember that a good experiment should stay focused. While a 5 × 3 × 2 × 4 × 2 factorial design is theoretically possible, it is not advisable. For this reason, you will commonly see either 2 × 2 or 2 × 3 factorial designs in the literature.

In their most basic form, factorial designs are true experiments, where the researcher manipulates all of the independent variables, which are between-subjects, such that each participant only gets one level of each independent variable. However, if any one of the independent variables is a within-subjects variable, the factorial design becomes a mixed design (more on this in Chapter 12). If one of the independent variables is a quasi-independent variable, or something the researcher cannot truly manipulate (e.g., gender), we consider it a **hybrid design**, as we are limited in the causal conclusions we can make involving the quasi-independent variable. Since we have two independent variables, we know that we will use a factorial design, but our decisions about how we operationalize those independent variables will determine which type of factorial design we will have.

Benefits of Factorial Designs

Like other experimental designs, factorial designs have the benefit of being able to establish cause and effect, allowing the researcher to run multiple experiments for the price of one. For example, in a 2 × 2 factorial design, there are actually

▶ What is the difference between true experiments and quasi-experiments? SEE CHAPTER 4, p. 86

▶ How do between-subjects and within-subjects variables differ? SEE CHAPTER 10, p. 323

hybrid design any factorial design that has at least one quasi-independent variable.

two different simple experiments, or two-group designs. The first 2 represents one independent variable with two levels. A 2 × 3 factorial design, meanwhile, would be like combining a two-group design with a multigroup design. To test our research question, we could first run a study to determine how different pick-up attempts influence relationship initiation, and then run a separate study to determine how scent influences relationship initiation. A factorial design, like a researcher's version of "buy one/get one free," allows us to accomplish both, all within the same study. This design saves us time, requires fewer participants, and allows us to see how the two independent variables work together to influence the dependent variable.

▶ How do simple experiments and multigroup experiments differ? SEE CHAPTER 9, p. 293

Overall, the most important benefit of factorial designs is the ability to examine how the combination of the independent variables affects the dependent variable. This allows us to determine whether there is an **interaction**, which is when one independent variable's influence on the dependent variable changes depending on the level of the other independent variable(s). In other words, when one independent variable alters how the other independent variable influences the dependent variable, an interaction has occurred. You can also think of an interaction as a unique effect that occurs when combining two or more factors. When it comes to interactions, it may be easier to explain with an example.

As you might know, drinking alcohol initially heightens mood (i.e., gives you a buzz), but, as the quantity of alcohol increases, the drinker becomes less alert and often sedated or tired (i.e., buzz kill). In this case, alcohol is an independent variable that influences the dependent variable of alertness. If another variable causes this association to change, then we have an interaction. For example, if your second independent variable was an energy drink, that could change the alcohol's effect on alertness. That is, alcohol on its own may produce an alertness of 3 on a 10-point scale, where higher numbers indicate greater alertness, while the energy drink produces an alertness of 7. Taken together, these would average to a 5. However, in an interaction, the result is an effect that is different than the sum of the two main effects. In this case, an interaction between alcohol and an energy drink might produce an alertness of a 2 (low) or a 9 (high).

interaction when one independent variable's influence on the dependent variable changes depending on the level of the other independent variable(s).

You might guess that energy drinks change how alcohol influences alertness by making the drinker more alert and less likely to get tired. In fact, research in this area has shown that energy drinks lead people to feel less drunk than they actually are (Marczinski, Fillmore, Bardgett, & Howard, 2011). The interaction between alcohol and energy drinks is serious because it can lead the drinker to consume more alcohol than intended and more than is safe. Other research has shown that alcohol decreased performance on a motor coordination task, but when alcohol was combined with the energy drink, participants had increased feelings of stimulation and increased confidence in their performance, although it was actually worse (Marczinski, Fillmore, Henges, Ramsey, &

By themselves, baking soda and vinegar are both inert. However, when combined, they produce a classic interaction from seventh-grade science classes, known more commonly as a "volcano." *(busypix/E+/Getty Images)*

When alcohol is combined with the ingredients in an energy drink, the resulting interaction is very different than if you had consumed either one of the drinks alone.
(Joe Raedle/Getty Images)

Young, 2012). The interaction goes the other way, as well. If you were to consume too much of an energy drink, you would become hyperalert, edgy, and jittery. But combined with alcohol, the effect of the energy drink on these outcomes is different. One independent variable (Red Bull) alters how the other independent variable (alcohol) influences the dependent variable (alertness).

Another benefit of studying interactions is that they more closely approximate how our everyday lives play out. In your life, you will rarely encounter a situation where one single independent variable is responsible for a particular outcome. Rather, anytime you examine an outcome, there are numerous variables that are responsible, and many causes and combinations of causes that produce any effect. Human experience is complex, which makes psychology research challenging, but also intriguing. Using factorial designs that allow us to examine interactions puts us one step closer to understanding the world around us.

Operationally Defining the IVs: Pick-Up Attempts and Scent

Our independent variables are pick-up attempts and scent because we expect them to influence or create differences in our dependent variable, relationship initiation. To operationally define pick-up attempts, we should think about how these experiences typically unfold in everyday life. When you meet someone for the first time, it can be intimidating. Someone has to say *something* just so you both avoid enduring an awkward silence. Previous research has most often studied these encounters in the context of three main types of pick-up lines: cute/flippant, innocuous, and direct (e.g., Cunningham, 1989; Kleinke, Meeker, & Staneski, 1986). Yet, how often in your everyday dating life have you heard or used a single line that then determines whether that relationship begins? A single line may get things started, but typically, there needs to be a more substantive back-and-forth exchange. You know—a conversation. So, while our research question asks about the effectiveness of pick-up *lines,* it seems more natural to focus on openers or conversation starters as the basis for pick-up attempts.

What combinations of variables interact to produce the outcomes you see on your report card? *(Lisa Kyle Young/Getty Images)*

Next, we need to decide what types of openers we think will be most effective. Whenever possible, it is best to build on previous research so that you

Thinking Like a Scientist in Real Life

Everyday Interactions Between Variables

One of the main benefits of studying interactions is that combinations of variables more closely resemble how things happen in real life. There is rarely a single, isolated cause for any effect. Instead, there are many causes working together that produce an outcome. You can see what we mean if you look at a typical day in your life. How tired you are when you wake up is the result of an interaction between how many hours you slept, how much stress you have experienced, where you slept, if you slept alone, the temperature of the room, and so on. Each factor influences your tiredness on its own, but as they start to combine in various ways, each variable interacts with the others so that the end result goes beyond what each factor would contribute on its own. Your everyday interactions do not end there: A toothbrush by itself can clean your teeth, as can toothpaste. But when you combine them, they interact to clean your teeth above and beyond the cleaning capacity of each. When getting dressed, you may consider a favorite shirt and a favorite pair of jeans that look good separately, but when you pair them together in an outfit . . . not so much. Similarly, you may use a variety of scented products while getting ready in the morning, each of which has a pleasant smell. A lemon and sage face scrub, an ocean-scented body wash, and a designer perfume or cologne all clearly enhance your smell on their own. But what about when they are combined? There is a distinct possibility that these three pleasant scents may interact in a way that leaves you smelling quite repugnant. When you wake up tomorrow, pay attention throughout the day to the various interactions you experience and how rare it is for you to experience one variable working in isolation as a main effect. We think you will be surprised at how many interactions you experience every day and how important interactions are to consider as you propose answers to your research questions.

---

have a theoretical basis for your predictions. In our case, there has been a lot of research on cute/flippant, innocuous, and direct pick-up attempts. Our best bet is to use these as the basis of our research, while mixing in a new twist. The existing research seems to agree that cute/flippant lines are the least effective (e.g., Bale et al., 2006; Cunningham, 1989; Senko & Fyffe, 2010). Cute lines often use humor, while simultaneously incorporating a sexual element (e.g., "You look familiar . . . did we take a class together? I could've sworn we had chemistry"). Perhaps we could compare a cute pick-up attempt with a direct or innocuous pick-up attempt that also includes a sexual component.

Focus on Ethics: Should We Really Do That?

Before we go too far down the path of using sexual pick-up attempts in our research, we need to fully consider whether we can do so ethically and in a way that helps us answer our research question. One complication we have is that some pick-up lines have the potential to make participants highly uncomfortable. Fortunately, our research question does not require that the pick-up attempt be sexual. If something is not crucial to our research and increases participants' risk, we cannot justify including it in our study. Instead, we should always make decisions that protect participants by using an approach that is less costly, but still allows us to answer our research question. Let's rethink things.

Previous research found that cute/flippant lines were least effective. But, if we focus on more conversational openings instead of individual lines, cute/flippant lines may not be so bad. For example, we could start cute, then shift to direct and innocuous lines, which are similarly effective (e.g., Cunningham, 1989; Senko & Fyffe, 2010).

Based on this line of thought, we could test two conversational openings. The first opening can start with a cute/flippant line, followed by a direct approach. As we develop our openings, we cannot be absolutely certain what the person being approached (who researchers call "the target") will say, but we can take our best guess.

INITIATOR: I must be a snowflake, because I've fallen for you.

TARGET: *Umm, okay.*

INITIATOR: That was a clever pick-up line that you're supposed to find cute and/or funny, leading you to think that I'm outgoing and confident. You should in no way think that was corny or potentially creepy.

TARGET: *Oh yeah?*

INITIATOR: Really what I wanted to say was, "Hi, my name's Josh. What's your name?"

That opening does a good job of starting out cute, but then quickly becomes a direct approach by addressing the situation, and then ultimately uses a standard direct line where the initiator gives his name. If we use an introduction like that, the second opening should stay as similar as possible to maintain experimental control, but use the direct approach the entire time. In doing so, we can use a combination of several direct lines from previous research (e.g., Kleinke et al., 1986; Senko & Fyffe, 2010; Weber et al., 2010).

▶ Why is control important in an experimental study? SEE CHAPTER 8, p. 251

INITIATOR: I saw you across the room and knew I had to meet you.

TARGET: *Umm, okay.*

INITIATOR: That was a direct pick-up line that you are supposed to find appealing, leading you to think that I'm outgoing and confident. You should in no way think that was corny or potentially creepy.

TARGET: *Oh yeah?*

INITIATOR: Really what I wanted to say was, "Hi, my name's Josh. What's your name?"

That solves the pick-up attempt independent variable, and results in two levels: cute-direct and direct-direct.

For the scent, we have already decided to use androstadienone. Next, we need to think about how to use it. Previous research has had people smell androstadienone in a jar (Wyart et al., 2007). However, that seems a bit unnatural for a dating context ("Hi. What's your name? Smell my jar."). Other research has involved spraying it on a piece of paper and sticking it to a chair (Pause, 2004).

The spray approach is more promising because it is a bit like those special pheromone colognes and perfumes advertised on late-night television. Just imagine if we could identify a sprayable compound that increases the chances of people starting a relationship. Certainly, there would be a strong market for such a product. We can use the androstadienone as a pheromone-like spray in our study, and should use the exact concentrations that were used in previous research (e.g., Pause, 2004).

Weighing Our Options: Between Versus Within Subjects

At this point in our study, we have our two independent variables, each with two levels. This makes our study a 2 × 2 factorial design. We also know that we do not have a hybrid design because we have two true independent variables that we will manipulate. However, we still need to decide whether we should use a between-subjects or within-subjects approach for each independent variable. As with all decisions, we must think about the best way to answer our research question.

▶ How do between-subjects and within-subjects designs differ? SEE CHAPTER 2, p. 40

If we use a within-subjects design, each participant would be assigned both types of pick-up lines and both levels of the spray. Having heard both pick-up lines, participants would easily see the difference between them. As a result, participants might engage in hypothesis-guessing, or not act as naturally as they would if they had only heard one of the pick-up lines. Thus, it seems that a between-subjects approach where each participant only receives one type of pick-up attempt is best. For the spray, there might be large individual differences in how sensitive each participant is to the scent of androstadienone. While a within-subjects approach could control for individual variation, previous research is not clear about how long the effects of androstadienone last, so we cannot be sure how long we need to wait between levels. Given that uncertainty, it is safest to use a between-subjects approach where each participant only receives one level of the scent.

Our final design, then, will be a between-subjects 2 × 2 factorial design. Most importantly, because we are combining independent variables, we will have four potential combinations of our independent variables:

a) cute-direct + no spray
b) cute-direct + spray
c) direct-direct + no spray
d) direct-direct + spray

Often, the easiest way to see the combinations is by creating a table where one independent variable is on the left with each level in a row, and the other independent variable at the top with each level in a column. **Table 11.2** displays our factorial design.

TABLE 11.2

Our Factorial Design			
		Scent	
		No Spray	Spray
Pick-Up Attempt	Cute-Direct	a	b
	Direct-Direct	c	d

Operationally Defining the DV: Relationship Initiation

With our independent variables in place, we now need to decide how we will measure the dependent variable. Much of the previous work on pick-up lines has used dependent variables that focus on the target's perception of the pick-up line. Specifically, researchers have asked about the line's desirability (Kleinke et al., 1986), or about perception of the initiator's traits, such as honesty, kindness, intelligence, and humor (Senko & Fyffe, 2010). Research conducted in a naturalistic setting had raters judge the target's response based on facial expressions, behaviors (e.g., walking away), and comments the target made (Cunningham, 1989). Other research looked at likelihood of continuing the conversation, either in terms of judgments about another person's behavior (Bale et al., 2006) or a prediction of one's own behavior (Senko & Fyffe, 2010).

Although it would be ideal for us to use the same dependent variables that were used in other studies, previous research has not focused specifically on behaviors or responses that might indicate a desire to start a relationship. We can use the idea of "continuing a conversation," but we should think of questions that tap into other, related behaviors. For example, we could ask whether responses included "being polite," "smiling," "asking questions," "talking to the other person for more than 5 minutes," "giving the other person their phone number," "agreeing to meet for coffee," "going out to dinner," "hugging the other person," or "kissing the other person." We could also measure desire to start a relationship if a person reports that he or she would not engage in behaviors such as "ignoring the other person," "mocking or laughing at the other person," "telling the other person to leave you alone," or "walking away." If we combine these types of behaviors together, we can determine the measurement of a "receptivity to relationship initiation" dependent variable, or how receptive participants are to starting a relationship.

Our Hypothesis

We started with the question, "When are pick-up lines most effective in starting a relationship?" Based on our literature search, that question evolved into "How do pick-up lines and a person's scent influence relationship initiation?" To answer that question, we needed multiple independent variables, which will also mean that we will need multiple hypotheses. **Main effect hypotheses** focus on the effect of a single independent variable on the dependent variable, ignoring all other independent variables. In our study, we have two potential main effect hypotheses, one for pick-up approach and one for scent. Multiple independent variables also mean that we can propose an **interaction effect hypothesis**. This hypothesis is our prediction about how the levels of one independent variable will combine with another independent variable to impact our dependent variable in a way that extends beyond the sum of the two separate main effects. In our study, we believe pick-up attempt and scent combined can influence relationship receptivity, so we have a potential interaction between our two independent variables.

What Do You Think?
What other behaviors could you measure that might indicate whether a person wants to initiate a relationship?

main effect hypothesis a prediction that focuses on the effect of one independent variable on the dependent variable at a time, ignoring all other independent variables.

interaction effect hypothesis a prediction about how the levels of one independent variable will combine with another independent variable to impact the dependent variable in a way that extends beyond the sum of the two separate main effects.

In factorial designs, you have as many potential main effect hypotheses as you have independent variables, and as many potential interaction hypotheses as you have combinations of independent variables. Note that we say "potential" because whether you predict a difference between levels of each independent variable or that the independent variables interact is up to you as a researcher. However, it is rare not to predict an interaction since this is one of the main benefits of a factorial design. Also, it is important to note that the main effect and interaction hypotheses are not dependent on one another. That is, you can have an interaction hypothesis without predicting differences for either main effect. Or you can have a main effect hypothesis for one independent variable without having a main effect hypothesis for the other independent variable. **Table 11.3** shows all of the possible outcomes you can have with a factorial design involving two independent variables.

To determine whether we want to make specific hypotheses about possible main effects and/or interaction effects, we need to predict how our study will turn out. Even though research shows that cute pick-up lines are not effective, because we have included a direct approach along with the cute pick-up line, it is possible that this approach will combine the best qualities of both types. That is, a cute pick-up line can make the person seem outgoing and funny, but the direct pick-up line as a follow-up can compensate for any negative reactions the cute pick-up line may have initially created. The direct-direct opening should be effective, but

TABLE 11.3

Potential Outcomes for a Factorial Design with Two Independent Variables		
Independent Variable One (IV1)	**Independent Variable Two (IV2)**	**Interaction (IV1 × IV2)**
Significant Main Effect	Significant Main Effect	Significant Interaction Effect
Significant Main Effect	Significant Main Effect	No Significant Interaction Effect
Significant Main Effect	No Significant Main Effect	Significant Interaction Effect
Significant Main Effect	No Significant Main Effect	No Significant Interaction Effect
No Significant Main Effect	Significant Main Effect	Significant Interaction Effect
No Significant Main Effect	Significant Main Effect	No Significant Interaction Effect
No Significant Main Effect	No Significant Main Effect	Significant Interaction Effect
No Significant Main Effect	No Significant Main Effect	No Significant Interaction Effect

Research Spotlight

Are They Interested?

While it might seem easy to judge our own interest in starting a relationship, how good are we at judging whether another person is receptive to starting a relationship with someone? Have you ever spent time "people watching," noticed two people sitting alone and talking, and thought, "I bet that they want to be a couple"? Researchers tested participants' ability to assess romantic interest by having males and females watch short video clips of couples during a date (Place, Todd, Penke, & Asendorpf, 2009). Participants were from the Midwestern United States, but watched interactions between German-speaking couples. Why? This way, the participants could not rely on what the partners were saying, and instead had to focus on nonverbal cues. The clips were of actual dates, so the researchers knew the actual level of interest between the partners in the video. Participants viewed clips of different lengths (10 vs. 30 seconds) and from different parts of the date (beginning, middle, end). The researchers also tested whether the participants' own genders or relationship statuses improved judgment accuracy. The results revealed that, overall, participants were better than chance at judging romantic interest, with men and women showing similar levels of proficiency. However, it was easier for participants to judge males in the video more accurately than females. Participants had higher accuracy when judging clips from the middle or end of the date, though length of clip did not influence accuracy. This study suggests that people can make judgments about others' receptivity to beginning a relationship even when judging strangers for less time than it takes to watch a TV commercial.

perhaps less so than the cute-direct approach because too much directness may sound unnatural and robotic. Thus, we can test the following hypothesis:

> *Main Effect 1: The cute-direct pick-up approach will lead to more relationship receptivity than the direct-direct approach.*

Since we believe cute-direct pick-up lines will be more effective, users of these lines are the experimental group, while the direct-direct line users serve as the control group.

▶ What is the difference between an experimental group and a control group? SEE CHAPTER 8, p. 251

Past research is fairly clear that an androstadienone spray influences participants, so it makes sense to predict that it influences receptivity in our study:

> *Main Effect 2: The presence of androstadienone spray will lead to more relationship receptivity than no spray.*

In this case, the spray condition is the experimental group, while no spray is the control group.

Finally, we need to think about how our independent variables will affect each other. In our main effect hypotheses, we think that cute-direct openings and spray individually will be effective in promoting relationship receptivity. When considering a potential interaction, we need to decide whether the androstadienone spray will make each type of opening more effective, less effective, or have no influence. We also need to think about whether the effect will be the same for each level, or if we have a **crossover interaction** (or **disordinal interaction**), which occurs when the influence of one independent variable on the other reverses across levels of the other independent variable. In our case, a crossover interaction would mean the spray helped the effectiveness of one type of opening, but hurt the other. It seems unlikely at this point that spray would have opposite effects on the openings, since both openings should be fairly effective. Rather, we could have an **ordinal interaction,** where one independent variable has an influence on a particular level of the other independent variable, but not on all of its levels. That is, the spray helps (or hurts) the effectiveness of one type of opening line, but has no effect on the other type of opening line.

Previous research indicates that cute pick-up lines make the initiator seem less trustworthy (Senko & Fyffe, 2010), but that the presence of androstadienone spray leads participants to engage in approach behavior (Pause, 2004), which should increase feelings of trust. Thus, we can predict that the spray will have a bigger influence on the cute-direct approach than on the direct-direct approach, where the effect should be similar, but much smaller.

> *Interaction Effect: The impact of the spray condition on the attractiveness effect will be enhanced for those in the cute-direct condition, but reduced for those in the direct-direct condition.*

In looking back at the interaction effect hypothesis, you could also say that cute-direct approaches are especially effective when combined with scent, while scent hurts the effectiveness of direct-direct approaches more. In essence, and as shown in the summary of our hypotheses in **Table 11.4,** scent supercharges the cute-direct approach, but diminishes the direct-direct approach.

TABLE 11.4

Summary of Hypotheses		
Effect	Independent Variable	Hypothesis
Main Effect 1	Pick-Up Attempt	*The cute-direct pick-up approach will lead to more relationship receptivity than the direct-direct approach.*
Main Effect 2	Scent	*The presence of androstadienone spray will lead to more relationship receptivity than no spray.*
Interaction	Pick-Up Attempt × Scent	*The impact of the spray condition on the attractiveness effect will be enhanced for those in the cute-direct condition, but reduced for those in the direct-direct condition.*

crossover interaction when the influence of one independent variable on the other reverses across levels of the other independent variable; also known as a disordinal interaction.

ordinal interaction when one independent variable has an influence on one level, but not all levels, of the other independent variable.

YOUR TURN 11.1

1. Elsie designs a study to determine if media influences body image. In her study, she will give participants either a magazine to read or a short 5-minute video clip to watch. There will be two types of magazines (news and fitness) and three video clips (sports, news, and nature). Each participant only receives one combination. Which of the following accurately describes this design?

   a. 2 × 2 Hybrid Design

   b. 2 × 3 Mixed Design

   c. 2 × 3 Factorial Design

   d. 2 × 3 × 2 Factorial Design

2. In a 4 × 3 × 2 × 2 factorial experiment, you have _____ independent variables and potentially _____ main effect hypotheses.

   a. 11; 4

   b. 4; 4

   c. 4; 11

   d. There is not enough information to tell.

3. Each of the following is an example of an interaction *except*:

   a. How well you do on a test depends on whether you read the textbook and the quality of your class notes.

   b. Your tiredness is influenced by the number of hours you sleep, but only when you sleep at home.

   c. The ability for certain jokes to make you laugh depends on who is telling the joke.

   d. How much you like each of your friends is similar whether they text you a lot or not.

How did you do? Turn to the end of the chapter to check your answers.

Design in Action

We have a basic idea of our independent variables (pick-up attempt and scent) and dependent variable (receptivity to relationship initiation). Although we now know what we want to manipulate and measure, we need to think about how we will do this in our actual study.

Weighing Our Options: The Lab Versus the Real World

Settings influence relationships. If setting or context did not matter, you could have an equally romantic dinner with your partner by candlelight or under a spotlight. For our study, the most ideal place to examine how relationships begin is in a place where relationships typically begin. Like Cunningham (1989), we could test participants in a bar, or we could try other meeting places, like a bookstore, coffee shop, out on the quad, or a party. Each setting closely matches the participant's typical real-life experience, which gives any of these approaches a high degree of mundane realism. However, these natural environments pose a significant obstacle to our scent independent variable. Each natural setting likely has other smells in the air that could overpower the smell of the androstadienone spray. Natural settings also present practical challenges, like how to keep outside influences (e.g., music, other people) and what participants say to each other well-controlled. In any natural environment, it is much more difficult to ensure internal validity due to extraneous factors, which are potential confounds.

▶ What types of validity and realism might we consider in our experimental design? SEE CHAPTER 8, p. 250

If we do the study in a lab, we can have more control, which will increase our internal validity, or our confidence that our independent variables are responsible for changes in the dependent variable. The downside, of course, is that we lose out on mundane realism. How many people have really started their relationship in a lab? However, it may be possible to strengthen our study's experimental realism by creating an experience in the lab that participants believe is a real pick-up attempt.

Weighing Our Options: Manipulating the Pick-Up Attempt

To manipulate our pick-up attempt in a lab setting, we could have participants read a **vignette**, which is a description of a hypothetical situation, event, or scenario to which participants react. Vignettes can be useful, especially if you are studying situations that you cannot actually re-create in a laboratory setting for practical or ethical reasons. Vignettes also provide a great deal of experimental control because the researcher can dictate exactly what the participant sees. However, for our research, we want our pick-up attempt to resemble an opening conversation, which will be difficult to convey on paper. We also want participants to react to an actual pick-up attempt (because the last time someone started a relationship via a piece of paper was in the fifth grade).

To mimic a real pick-up attempt, we need a real person to approach the participant and start a conversation. The easiest solution is to have the initiator be a confederate, someone who is secretly part of the study and will act however we want. This way, we can eliminate many extraneous factors by keeping the situation more consistent. Our confederate's attractiveness and pick-up ability will naturally remain fairly stable over time. We can also make sure that the confederate dresses similarly, and we can train the confederate extensively to help ensure consistency in responses and behaviors across participants.

Weighing Our Options: Manipulating the Scent Independent Variable

Now that we have a solution for manipulating our pick-up attempt independent variable, we need to figure out how to manipulate scent. Previous research had participants purposefully smell T-shirts in a bag (e.g., Thornhill et al., 2003), or passively exposed participants to a sprayed piece of paper attached to a chair (Pause, 2004). The problem with those approaches is that they are not realistic in an everyday dating context ("Really what I wanted to say was, 'Hi, my name is Josh. Also, please smell this T-shirt that I keep in a bag.'"). If that does not

vignette a description of a hypothetical situation, event, or scenario to which participants react.

sound like an awkward exchange to you, nothing will! The best solution may be to spray the confederate. This way, the participant would only smell the scent in the confederate's presence, making the participant much more likely to directly associate the scent with the confederate. A set-up like this also more closely parallels everyday life, where an androstadienone scent is part of a person's natural scent (Wyart et al., 2007).

In order to have the androstadienone be the only scent emanating from our confederate, we will want the confederate to follow some fairly stringent steps to help eliminate competing odors. Here we can borrow procedures from previous research that outline foods and behaviors to avoid (e.g., no spicy or pungent foods, no smoking), while providing new, clean clothing and unscented soap for the confederate to use (Thornhill et al., 2003). We will want our confederate to shower right before arriving to our study and to put on clean clothes we provide. Then, depending on the condition or level of the independent variable, we will spray the confederate's shirt with the androstadienone, or with nothing.

Weighing Our Options: Measuring Receptivity to Relationship Initiation

We decided earlier that we could measure receptivity to relationship initiation with a series of self-report questions about the participants' anticipated behavior. This approach is reasonable, but, given our current plan for manipulating the independent variables, if we want the confederate's pick-up attempt to feel realistic, we cannot follow the pick-up attempt by giving the participant a self-report measure. Doing so would immediately reveal that the pick-up attempt is part of the study. Consequently, we are going to have to scrap using a self-report measure for our dependent variable. It is alright that our initial idea will not work—good researchers remain flexible and stay true to whatever provides the best answer to the original question. The important thing is that we weigh our options appropriately before conducting the study. A self-report of what a person *might do* is okay, but looking at what that person actually *does* is much better, and, in this case, avoids hypothesis-guessing.

Instead, as has been done in previous research (Cunningham, 1989), we should use the participants' actual responses to the pick-up attempt. Although the nature of our measure changed, generating self-report items was not a waste of time because we can incorporate those behaviors into ratings of observed behaviors. Specifically, we will have coders focus on participant behaviors (e.g., being polite, smiling, continuing the conversation, eye contact, laughing, not being rude). Coders will give a 1–5 rating for each, where 1 = behavior indicates no interest in beginning a relationship and 5 = behavior indicates strong interest in beginning a relationship.

▶ What are the best ways to record observations? SEE CHAPTER 6, p. 173

We will train impartial raters to pick out the behaviors we specify in our list. To minimize the raters' biases, we will not tell them the study's purpose nor its hypotheses. To further minimize potential bias, as well as random error or mistakes, we should have more than one rater. This way, if one rater has a bias (e.g., she or he always thinks blondes have romantic interest) or is more error prone (e.g., she or he tends to miss social cues), the presence of the other rater will help balance and improve the reliability of our ratings. To allow raters to thoroughly review the interactions, we will set up a video camera behind a two-way mirror. Having the interactions on videotape will also allow us to return to and rate additional aspects of the interaction if necessary.

▶ How can we minimize observer biases?
SEE CHAPTER 6, p. 176

Focus on Ethics: Should We Really Do That?

With our variables firmly in place, we should take a moment to assess the ethics of what we plan to do in our study. Perhaps the broadest ethical concern is that our study uses deception to influence participants' emotions and love lives. This means that our study will undergo a more thorough review by the Institutional Review Board prior to approval. Regardless, we should weigh the relevant issues ourselves to make sure that we have done everything possible to protect our participants.

▶ Why are Institutional Review Boards an important part of the research process?
SEE CHAPTER 3, p. 72

By attempting to create relationships in the lab, we run the risk of having participants feel flattered, desirable, and hopeful about beginning a real relationship, only to later tell them that it was all fake and part of the study. Although we cannot completely rule out hurt feelings, previous research reported that ". . . several (participants) expressed good-humored disappointment" (Cunningham, 1989, p. 32) when they learned that the pick-up attempt was part of a study. We can further avoid awkwardness by recruiting only participants who are currently not in a relationship. Also, if we use college students as our participants, we are incorporating a sample with a high likelihood of experiencing pick-up attempts (both welcomed and unwelcomed) in everyday life. Familiarity with pick-up attempts helps limit the potential risk of discomfort that our study poses to our participants.

While we are on the topic of participants, we should decide whether our study should focus on males and females, or only one or the other, and how we want to handle sexuality. It is not ethical to exclude anyone based on convenience or the researcher's whim; we must have a strong theoretical and/or empirically based reason to focus on one group. Looking back at our literature review, the research on scent suggests that women report that natural smell is especially important to attraction (Herz & Inzlicht, 2002). Not surprisingly, much of the research in this area focuses on heterosexual female participants smelling males' scents (e.g., Thornhill et al., 2003; Wyart et al., 2007), and shows that androstadienone spray effectively altered women's behavior (Pause, 2004). Based on these findings, we have enough justification to limit our study to heterosexual women and to use a male confederate.

Because the confederate is such an important part of our study, we will want to carefully select the person playing that role. Specifically, we will want someone who is comfortable carrying out a pick-up attempt with a female college student. We also want someone who is familiar with basic research principles so that he will understand the importance of treating all participants the same and maintaining consistency throughout the study. We should also find a confederate who is moderately attractive, because if he is too attractive or too unattractive, he may overly influence participants, making our independent variables less effective. Rather than relying on our own judgments of attractiveness, we will pilot test pictures of potential confederates with college students to find the right person.

▶ Why is pilot testing important?
SEE CHAPTER 6, p. 178

Developing a Protocol

Good experimentation often relies on devising a procedure that allows you to manipulate your independent variables and measure your dependent variables seamlessly. For our study, we need to start the procedure by focusing on the setting so that we can maximize the potential impact of the scent. We should also borrow some of the ideas from previous research (e.g., Wyart et al., 2007) by using a highly controlled lab that filters the air and keeps humidity and temperature constant. We will also make sure that there are no air fresheners or other scents present.

Assigning Participants to Conditions

Because this is a 2 × 2 factorial design, our study has four conditions: cute-direct + no spray; cute-direct + spray; direct-direct + no spray; direct-direct + spray. We should randomly assign participants to one of these four conditions before they arrive for our study. One way to do this is to use a random number generator (e.g., http://www.random.org), where we randomly generate numbers between 1 and 4, which represent each of our four conditions. We will assign each participant to the condition corresponding to the randomly generated number, and we should generate a random number for at least 120 participants since we will ideally have at least 30 participants per condition. It may be safer, however, to generate codes for at least 200 participants, because we would like to collect as much data as possible to ensure we have enough statistical power to detect our hypothesized interaction. The participant's randomly assigned number will be on the researcher's note sheet, which will also include a space to note any problems or abnormalities that occurred during the session.

Before moving on, we should think about who the researcher should be. Although it would be nice to run the study ourselves and see our data coming in, we could unconsciously influence the pick-up attempts because we know the hypotheses. Thus, we will use a research assistant who we will train on the procedure, but to whom we will not reveal the specific hypotheses. Just in case having another male's scent in the room influences the results, we will make sure our research assistant is a female.

Next, we need to structure the experiment so that participants feel like their experience is a real pick-up attempt. When the participant arrives, the researcher can text the confederate (who should be in a nearby research lab, out of sight) the pick-up attempt he should use. There is no way to hide each participant's pick-up condition from the confederate, as he needs to know which type of line to deliver. However, we will not reveal our hypotheses to him, especially about which type of line we expect to yield more receptivity. We will also avoid telling him which spray condition he is delivering so that he can remain unbiased. Instead, we will have two different outfits for the confederate to wear and will let him know whether to wear the shirt in bag A or B, along with newly washed jeans and socks we provide, each time. Taking these steps, along with using a spray that is unscented and unconscious in its influence, will minimize the confederate's ability to knowingly or unknowingly influence the results.

Procedure

We will post two studies online that are both titled "Attitudes Toward Print Media," one for females who are not currently in a romantic relationship and one for males that we will keep closed. (The study for males will not actually be a study, but posting the "study" will help preserve our cover story.) On the registration page, the females will see that two people can sign up for the same timeslot, but we will arrange it so that the first spot is always occupied by a person with a gender neutral name, leading participants to anticipate the presence of a fellow participant at their study session.

Participants will report to the lab for their 30-minute timeslot. When the participant arrives, we will have three chairs set up on one side of the room and will direct the participant to select a seat. We will then give the participant the informed consent form on a clipboard to read and sign. Then, we can have the confederate arrive a few minutes late to the study, and, upon entering the room, ask, "Am I in the right place? That online sign-up thing is suuuper confusing." (We want to include this type of detail to make the situation seem more realistic, because participants commonly communicate in this way.) The researcher will treat the confederate exactly the same as the participant, directing him to the chairs to complete the same informed consent.

After they have both completed the informed consent, the researcher will say, "Thanks. As you were filling those out, I realized that I left the study materials in the other room. I'm sorry about this! It's just been one of those days. I'll be back in a few minutes." Having the researcher leave gives the confederate the chance to deliver the pick-up attempt in a setting that makes more sense (it would not be realistic for a student to hit on a fellow participant with the researcher present). After leaving the pair alone, the researcher will turn on the video camera in the next room. The confederate will sit and appear bored for a minute, and will then deliver the randomly assigned pick-up attempt. Three minutes later, the researcher will return to the lab. Three minutes should be enough time to provoke a range of verbal and nonverbal reactions, but short enough to prevent the interaction from having real ramifications for the participant.

Whenever possible, it is a good idea to include a manipulation check to ensure we properly manipulated the independent variable. However, since we want to capture the participant's natural reaction, we cannot easily obtain a self-reported manipulation check. Once we ask the participant to reflect on how she felt, she inevitably will realize the pick-up attempt was not real, which will change how she felt about it. So, when the researcher returns, we will simply have the confederate end the conversation. At that point, the researcher will give both the participant and the confederate a demographic sheet to complete, to maintain the premise that the confederate is a real participant.

The demographic sheet will contain standard information (age, sex, ethnicity), as well as a question about contraceptive use. This information is important to ask about because previous research suggests that androstadienone's effects are most potent, and may only work, for women who are not taking hormonal contraceptives (e.g., Thornhill et al., 2003). After the

▶ How can manipulation checks tell us if we actually manipulated the independent variable(s)? SEE CHAPTER 8, p. 265

participant completes these measures, the researcher will debrief the participant by revealing the extent of the deception, as well as why it was necessary. The confederate will explain that he is part of the experiment and the nature of his participation, including the two different types of lines and the two different spray conditions. The researcher will ensure that the participant knows that the pick-up attempt was part of the study, and that it was natural to not realize it was fake, with the goal being that the participant leaves the study in a similar state as when she arrived. In addition, the researcher will emphasize that it would be best if the participant did not discuss the specifics of the study with other potential participants. After each participant leaves, we will have the confederate return the experimental clothes and change back into his own clothes.

Focus on Open Science: Preregistering Your Hypotheses, Materials, and Data Analysis Plan

It seems like we are ready to run our study, right? However, there is one more thing that we need to do. We should preregister our research plan on an open science website (e.g., http://osf.io/), where we will share our plan, including how we will manipulate our independent variables and measure our dependent variables. We will describe the pick-up lines to be used in the study, and how we will manipulate scent using the two types of T-shirts. Additionally, we will include the list of behaviors that the observers will focus on, the scale to be used for coding the degree of interest in beginning a relationship, our main effect and interaction effect hypotheses, and our data analysis plan. Once we have run our study, we will share our data on this site so that others can use it to verify our findings and analyze the data in other ways.

▶ Why is open science important to the research process? SEE CHAPTER 2, p. 42

YOUR TURN 11.2

1. Jack wants to conduct a study on how music influences students' memory of a lecture. Which of the following settings would be the best for optimizing mundane realism?

   a. A research laboratory

   b. A classroom

   c. A library

   d. A dorm room

2. Using a confederate in our study is important for which of the following reasons?

   a. It allows us to maximize experimental control.

   b. It allows us to maximize external validity.

   c. It is the only way we can be sure to have a reliable measure.

   d. It is the only way we can be sure to have a valid measure.

3. When determining who can participate in your study, you can ethically exclude people for which of the following reasons?

   a. You can exclude them because you think other types of participants will benefit the most from the treatment.

   b. You can exclude them because you believe that you will more likely obtain statistical significance by excluding that one type of participant.

   c. You can exclude them because previous research indicates that one type of participant is most appropriate.

   d. Both A and C are ethical reasons to exclude participants.

How did you do? Turn to the end of the chapter to check your answers.

Statistics: In Search of Answers

After we have finished collecting data from our participants in the lab, we will give the videotapes of each participant to our three coders, who will independently rate the videos. Each coder will rate each behavior (eye gaze, smiling, etc.) and will then average all behaviors to create each participant's receptivity score. Next, we will check that we have strong inter-rater or inter-observer reliability, which is the extent to which the coders agree in their assessment of the videos. For the purpose of our data here, we will assume that we had high inter-observer reliability and can average across the three coders' receptivity scores for each participant. That is, every participant had three receptivity scores (one from each coder) that we averaged to create one score that represents each participant's receptivity to relationship initiation.

▶ Why do we need to worry about inter-observer reliability? SEE CHAPTER 6, p. 179

To create the data set, we will have columns for the participant number, the independent variables, the dependent variable, and the demographic information. It is important to note that there are two independent variables, so we will need separate columns for each. We will name one independent variable "Pick-Up" and identify the groups as follows: 1 = Cute-Direct (Experimental Condition), 2 = Direct-Direct (Control Condition). We will name the other independent variable "Scent" and identify the groups as follows: 1 = Spray (Experimental Condition), 2 = No Spray (Control Condition). In each case, we label the group that, based on our hypothesis, we think will have a greater effect on the dependent variable. We will name the dependent variable column "Receptivity." If this were real data, we would enter each participant's data in one row, aligning the information with the proper column as in **Figure 11.1**.

Selecting the Proper Tool

To answer our research question, we need to do the following:

- Include only those participants who reported that they do not use hormonal contraceptives.

- Test the hypothesis about pick-up attempts.

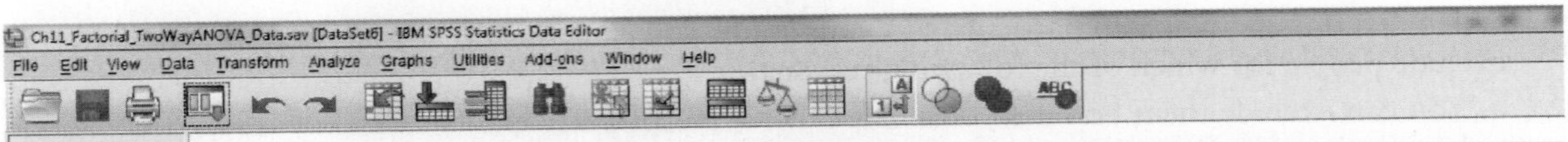

	ParticipantNumber	PickUp	Scent	Receptivity	Sex	Age	Ethnicity	YearInSchool	Contraceptive
1	1.00	Cute-Direct (Experimental Condition)	No Spray (Control Condition)	3.25	female	21.00	white or eu...	sophomore	Yes
2	2.00	Cute-Direct (Experimental Condition)	Spray (Experimental Condition)	4.44	female	19.00	white or eu...	junior	No
3	3.00	Cute-Direct (Experimental Condition)	Spray (Experimental Condition)	4.44	female	21.00	white or eu...	freshman	No
4	4.00	Cute-Direct (Experimental Condition)	Spray (Experimental Condition)	3.92	female	19.00	white or eu...	junior	Yes
5	5.00	Direct-Direct (Control Condition)	No Spray (Control Condition)	3.99	female	20.00	eastern or ...	sophomore	No
6	6.00	Cute-Direct (Experimental Condition)	No Spray (Control Condition)	2.96	female	22.00	white or eu...	freshman	No
7	7.00	Cute-Direct (Experimental Condition)	Spray (Experimental Condition)	3.99	female	21.00	white or eu...	junior	Yes
8	8.00	Direct-Direct (Control Condition)	No Spray (Control Condition)	2.96	female	20.00	white or eu...	sophomore	No
9	9.00	Cute-Direct (Experimental Condition)	No Spray (Control Condition)	3.51	female	20.00	black or afr...	freshman	No
10	10.00	Direct-Direct (Control Condition)	No Spray (Control Condition)	3.49	female	20.00	eastern or ...	sophomore	No

FIGURE 11.1 Example of an SPSS Data Spreadsheet. *(SPSS)*

- Test the hypothesis about scent.
- Test the hypothesis about the interaction between pick-up attempts and scent.

To accomplish the first task, we will need to exclude from the analysis anyone who reported using hormonal contraceptives. Then, we need to test our three hypotheses. With three hypotheses, you might assume that we need to run three separate analyses. However, when we have more than one independent variable, we use a **two-way analysis of variance** (also known as a **two-way ANOVA** or **factorial ANOVA**), which is a statistical test that allows us to simultaneously test how two separate nominal or categorical independent variables (or factors) influence the dependent variable, and how those independent variables interact to influence the dependent variable. In a 2 × 2 factorial design, you can think of this statistical test as a combination of two independent samples *t*-tests (one for each independent variable that has 2 levels) that provides a bonus test of the interaction between the two independent variables. If you had a 2 × 3 factorial design, it would be similar to combining an independent samples *t*-test with a one-way ANOVA. As with other statistical tests, the significance, or *p* level, represents how likely it is that the groups differ in a way that cannot be accidental or by chance.

▶ What is an analysis of variance? SEE CHAPTER 9, p. 304

two-way analysis of variance a statistical test that allows us to simultaneously test how two separate nominal or categorical independent variables (or factors) influence the dependent variable, and how those independent variables interact to influence the dependent variable; also known as a two-way ANOVA or factorial ANOVA.

A two-way ANOVA tests for any main or interaction effects. In our study, since we have two independent variables, we have two main effects and one interaction effect to test. It just so happens that we have hypotheses for each of these potential effects and will need to test each. Unlike in a two-group or multigroup design, where there is a single mean for each level of the independent variable, a factorial design has several different means. As you know from previous chapters, once we are aware that there is a significant difference, we need to find out what this difference is by determining which level or group is higher on the dependent variable than the other(s). In factorial designs, a two-way ANOVA examines how levels

TABLE 11.5

Combinations of Independent Variables and Levels			
		IV2	
		Level 1	Level 2
IV1	Level 1	IV1 (Level 1) × IV2 (Level 1)	IV1 (Level 1) × IV2 (Level 2)
	Level 2	IV1 (Level 2) × IV2 (Level 1)	IV1 (Level 2) × IV2 (Level 2)

of each independent variable combine with levels of other independent variables (see **Table 11.5**). These combinations result in the **cell mean**, which is the average on the dependent variable for participants with a specific combination of the levels of the independent variables. We look at the pattern of the cell means to understand how the two independent variables interact or combine to influence the dependent variable. In our study, we would look at how receptivity to cute-direct pick-up attempts across spray and no spray conditions differs from receptivity to direct-direct pick-up attempts across spray and no spray conditions.

In addition, a two-way ANOVA provides **marginal means**, which are the averages of all participants on each level of the independent variable, ignoring the other independent variable. In our study, one set of marginal means would focus on the spray versus no spray condition without accounting for or acknowledging the differences in the pick-up attempt levels, while the other set would focus on pick-up attempts ignoring spray. Often, you will see cell and marginal means depicted in a table, as in **Table 11.6**.

If you have trouble remembering which effect goes with which means, remember M&Ms: Marginal Means with Main Effects. *(FADEDink.net/Shutterstock)*

cell mean the average on the dependent variable for participants with a specific combination of the levels of the independent variables.

marginal mean the average of all participants on one level of the independent variable, ignoring the other independent variable.

TABLE 11.6

Cell and Marginal Means in a Factorial Design			
		IV2	
		Level 1	Level 2
IV1	Level 1	Cell Mean	Cell Mean	Marginal Mean
	Level 2	Cell Mean	Cell Mean	Marginal Mean
		Marginal Mean	Marginal Mean

Writing the Results in APA Style: Two-Way Factorial ANOVA

Results

We computed a two-way factorial analysis of variance with the pick-up attempt (cute-direct or direct-direct) and the presence of the androstadienone scent (spray or no spray) as the independent variables and receptivity to relationship initiation as the dependent variable. Means and standard deviations for the four combinations (cute-direct/spray, direct-direct/spray, cute-direct/no spray, direct-direct/no spray) of the independent variables on receptivity to relationship initiation appear in Table 11.7. The pick-up attempt main effect was significant, $F(1, 116) = 5.30$, $p = .023$, eta^2 = .044, such that cute-direct openings led to greater receptivity than direct-direct openings. However, the androstadienone scent main effect was not significant, $F(1, 116) = 1.08$, $p = .30$, eta^2 = .009. The interaction effect was significant, $F(1, 116) = 6.81$, $p = .01$, eta^2 = .055, such that the spray made cute-direct pick-up attempts more effective, but made direct-direct pick-up attempts less effective.

Don't Just Tell Me, Show Me: Using Tables and Figures

Rather than including all of the cell means and marginal means within the text of the results section, researchers will often provide them either in a table or visually as a figure. This helps with the interpretation of any significant main or interaction effects. See **Figure 11.2** for a partial graphic depiction of **Table 11.7**, the influence of type of pick-up attempt and scent on receptivity to starting a relationship. See **Figure 11.3** for the anatomy of a two-way (factorial) ANOVA.

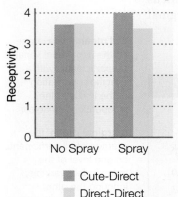

FIGURE 11.2 Pick-Up Attempts and Scent's Influence on Receptivity.

TABLE 11.7

Means and Standard Deviations for Pick-Up Attempts and Scent on Receptivity			
	Scent		
Pick-Up Attempt	**No Spray**	**Spray**	**Overall Mean**
Cute-Direct	3.69 (0.34)	4.03 (0.57)	3.86
Direct-Direct	3.72 (0.55)	3.56 (0.58)	3.64
Overall Mean	3.70	3.80	

Note: N for each cell = 30. The main effect for pick-up attempt was significant $F(1, 116) = 5.30$, $p = .023$, effect size = .044, and the interaction effect was significant, $F(1, 116) = 6.81$, $p = .01$, effect size = .055. The main effect for scent was not significant.

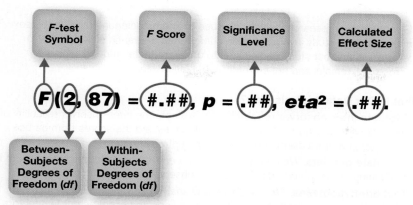

FIGURE 11.3 Anatomy of a Two-Way (Factorial) ANOVA.

Our Research Plan at a Glance

What Is Our Research Question? How do pick-up lines and a person's scent influence relationship initiation?

What Is Our Design? We are using a 2×2, between-subjects factorial design.

Why Are We Using This Design? This design allows us to test potential interactions between independent variables. We not only want to know the influence that pick-up lines and a person's scent can have on relationship receptivity, but also how the combination of the two may influence this receptivity.

What Are Our Variables?

    Independent Variable(s):

        Type of Pick-Up Line: Cute-Direct or Direct-Direct

        Scent: Presence of Androstadienone or Nothing

    Dependent Variable(s): Receptivity to starting a relationship

What Are Our Hypotheses?

    Main Effect for Pick-Up Line: The cute-direct pick-up approach will lead to more relationship receptivity than the direct-direct approach.

    Main Effect for Scent: The presence of androstadienone spray will lead to more relationship receptivity than no spray.

    Interaction Effect: The impact of the spray condition on the attractiveness effect will be enhanced for those in the cute-direct condition, but reduced for those in the direct-direct condition.

Who Are Our Participants? 120 heterosexual female undergraduate students not currently in a relationship.

What Ethical Considerations Do We Need to Keep in Mind?

▪ The pick-up lines we choose should not be overtly sexual or inappropriate, as this could lead to participants feeling uncomfortable.

▪ Because we want our participants to act naturally in this situation, we need to use deception. We ask the Institutional Review Board to approve our use of deception and make sure that when we debrief our participants, they do not depart from the study feeling embarrassed or duped by this deception.

(Continued)

- Given that past research involving the use of androstadienone used heterosexual females, and our study involves a male confederate delivering pick-up lines to a female, we limit our study participants to undergraduate students who are heterosexual, female, and not currently in a relationship.

What Is Our Data Analysis Plan?

1. **Evaluate inter-observer reliability.** We evaluate the inter-observer reliability of the observers' coding for receptivity, and then discard the scores from participants who reported using hormonal contraceptives.

2. **Calculate our data.** We create an overall receptivity score for each participant by calculating the mean ratings given by the observers.

3. **Test our hypotheses.** We use a two-way analysis of variance (i.e., a factorial ANOVA) to test our predictions, with pick-up lines and scent as our two factors and relationship receptivity as our dependent variable.

Want to practice the analyses for this research yourself? Ask your instructor about the data set that accompanies this study.

Let's Discuss What Happened

We set out to determine how two factors (pick-up attempt and scent) influenced a woman's receptivity to relationship initiation. Based on previous research, we tested a lengthier pick-up attempt that either combined elements of cute and direct pick-up lines or combined several direct methods. We also wanted to see if the scent of androstadienone influenced receptivity and if pick-up attempts and scent combined to produce greater receptivity. We were able to test all three effects at the same time by using a 2 × 2 factorial design where we randomly assigned each participant to receive one combination of the independent variables. Now, as we begin to discuss and interpret our results, we should be careful to stay organized, and, as we did with other designs, relate our study back to previous research, evaluate our strengths and limitations, and discuss some directions that future research could take.

What Did We Find?

Based on ratings of the videotaped interactions between the confederate and participants, we found that female participants were more receptive to cute-direct openings than direct-direct openings. Contrary to our hypothesis, the presence of the androstadienone spray alone did not result in greater receptivity. Our analyses, however, revealed a significant interaction effect. As predicted, the spray made cute-direct pick-up attempts more effective. But contrary to our prediction that the spray would not influence the direct-direct approach's effectiveness, the spray made direct-direct pick-up attempts less effective. In other words, the interaction revealed that when there was no spray, the two types of pick-up attempts were equally successful. But the presence of the spray made the cute-direct attempts more successful than the direct-direct attempts.

When evaluating interactions, there are two common ways that variables combine. A **synergistic effect** is an effect where two variables combine to produce an outcome that is greater than what each individual variable contributes. In essence, the whole is greater than the sum of the parts. When looking at our results, the presence of the androstadienone scent appears to amplify the effectiveness of the cute-direct approach so that it is even more effective than we would expect by simply adding the cute-direct approach and spray's effectiveness. This interaction is consistent with a synergistic effect.

It is also possible to have a **suppression effect**, which is the opposite of synergy, where two variables combine to produce an outcome that is smaller than what each individual variable contributes. In essence, the sum is less than the parts. In our study, the spray's effect on the direct-direct approach appears to be a case of suppression because the combination of spray and the direct-direct approach is less effective than the direct-direct approach by itself. This interaction indicates that the addition of the spray limits or holds back the influence of the direct-direct approach on receptivity.

synergistic effect an effect where two variables combine to produce an outcome that is greater than what each individual variable contributes.

suppression effect an effect where two variables combine to produce an outcome that is smaller than what each individual variable contributes.

Thinking Like a Scientist in Real Life

A Dangerous Interaction?

Life is all about what happens when two or more variables interact. Who doesn't love eating candy and drinking soda? Who hasn't washed down some chocolates with their root beer, or drank some Coca-Cola through a Twizzler or licorice straw? Certainly, when you put two great things together, you *must* get even more greatness, right? It is also possible that combining two things that are delicious on their own (e.g., candy and soda) is not good for you, or could even be deadly. Sure, you could get diabetes, but there are even more immediate concerns. Take, for example, the urban legend of Pop Rocks and soda. For the uninitiated, Pop Rocks are a candy that gently explodes and pops in your mouth. As the legend goes, when you combine the gaseous effects of Pop Rocks with the fizziness of soda, your stomach could explode, resulting in possible death. Where some see a cautionary tale about the hazards of sweet combinations, we, however, see a synergistic interaction between two independent variables. That is, both main effects result in high levels of the dependent variable, enjoyment. But, according to legend, when an innocent youth combines these independent variables, the result is anything but enjoyment. If you are curious about the veracity of this urban legend, Google search "Pop Rocks Soda Mythbusters" and check out the video.

Why These Findings?

Female participants were more receptive to beginning a relationship when the male confederate used a cute-direct pick-up attempt than when he used a direct-direct pick-up attempt. This finding contradicts previous research showing that cute/flippant pick-up lines are less effective than direct approaches (Bale et al., 2006; Cunningham, 1989; Senko & Fyffe, 2010). However, that research looked at cute pick-up lines by themselves and not in the context of a more complex opening. The cute-direct opening could have been successful because it portrays the male as a "fun/sexy guy" who, similar to a bad boy, is interesting, exciting, and charming (McDaniel, 2005). Consistent with our findings, previous research found that this type of guy had an increased likelihood of a second date. Although we did not test for it, females may perceive a guy who uses a cute-direct approach as more dominant, assertive, and confident, all qualities that women potentially value in mates (Bryan, Webster, & Mahaffey, 2011).

Contrary to our hypothesis and to some previous research, the androstadienone spray did not increase receptivity. It is possible that we did not find an effect because we put the spray on the confederate's T-shirt, whereas previous research delivered the spray in more controlled ways (e.g., Pause, 2004; Wyart et al., 2007). Although we made sure that the confederate sat close to the participant, it is possible that the participant did not detect the androstadienone spray. However, the spray did interact with pick-up attempts, which suggests that participants were able to detect it. Thus, it may be that the spray by itself is not powerful enough to influence receptivity, and only has an impact when combined with another factor.

The significant interaction between spray and pick-up line attempts is interesting because the use of a cute-direct approach suggests dominance, which is generally attractive to women (Vacharkulksemsuk et al., 2016). However, it may also suggest some negative "bad boy" traits like insensitivity, selfishness, and a macho disposition (Urbaniak & Kilmann, 2003). On the other hand, our data suggest that the spray may counteract some of these perceptions and lead women to focus more on the desirable aspects, such as the confederate's confidence. The spray appears to have had the opposite effect on direct-direct pick-up attempts, resulting in those openings being even less effective than they were without spray. It is possible that the androstadienone spray created a stress response similar to previous research (Wyart et al., 2007), and that this response, combined with the confederate's very direct approach, led participants to feel threatened or uncomfortable. In contrast, the same stress response could have led females to find the cute-direct approach friendlier and more welcoming, leading to greater receptivity to a relationship. Because the influence of one independent variable on the other independent variable differed across levels (i.e., the spray helped one type of opening, but hurt the other), this is a crossover (disordinal) interaction.

What Could Be Improved?

Our study improved on previous relationship initiation research by observing participants' actual receptivity in a controlled lab environment, rather than relying on self-reported reactions to hypothetical scenarios. Ours is also the first study that we know of that incorporated a biologically based variable like androstadienone.

As with all studies, we also had some limitations. First, our procedure attempted to keep the confederate and the research assistants who rated the videotapes in the dark about the condition to avoid bias. However, we were

What Do You Think?

What other factors could help explain the findings from this study?

Research Spotlight

Does Biology Influence Clothing Choices?

This chapter's research question focuses on how biology influences our behavior. As humans who like to believe that we control our own destiny, we often think that our biology does not influence us much. As an evolved species, we would rather believe that we use our intellect to make informed choices. Yet, as you can see in this chapter's research, our basic biology can influence us in ways we may not even realize. As research technology improves, this type of research is becoming more prevalent, often with fascinating implications. In this vein, researchers have sought to determine how women's ovulatory cycle influences their behavior. One study examined whether women dress differently across their ovulatory cycle (Durante, Li, & Haselton, 2008). Specifically, the researchers sought to determine if women favored sexier and more provocative clothing during highly fertile times of the month. To test this, 88 undergraduate women from a large university in the southern United States reported on their normal ovulation cycles. None were using hormonal contraceptives. The women came into the lab twice: once on a high-fertility day of their cycle, and once on a low-fertility day, both determined via a urine sample. At each session, researchers photographed the participant's full body and the participants completed self-report measures about their attractiveness, previous sexual experience, and sociosexuality (i.e., how willing they were generally to have sex without being in a committed relationship). At the end of each session, participants drew an outfit they would likely wear to a party where there would be a lot of attractive single people. The results indicated that highly fertile (i.e., ovulating) women planned on wearing more revealing clothing to the party than less-fertile women. Follow-up analyses revealed that this was especially true for sexually experienced women. Although there were not any differences for the participants' photographs based on fertility overall, when researchers accounted for the participants' sociosexuality, they found that women who were more able to have sex without commitment wore more revealing clothes to the experiment on high versus low fertility days. Women with lower sociosexuality did not show this difference.

---

not able to conceal the pick-up attempt condition, meaning that the cute-direct pick-up attempt could have been more effective because either the confederate and/or the research assistants thought it would be more effective. If the confederate thought it was more effective, it could have created a self-fulfilling prophecy in which participants became more receptive due to the confederate's behaviors (Snyder et al., 1977). But it is not clear that the confederate or the research assistants would have had clear expectations that one type of opening would have superior effectiveness, because both types of openings should have been effective.

Although we controlled the confederate for competing scents, we did not do the same with participants, which could have made it difficult for some participants to identify the androstadienone spray over other smells, such as their own perfume, lingering cigarette smoke on their clothing, or scented hygiene products.

We could have improved our chances of identifying a significant difference between the scent conditions if we had made sure participants came into the study "scent free," perhaps via a different cover story. Finally, due to our desire to capture natural reactions, we were unable to ask participants how each pick-up attempt made them feel or how it influenced their perceptions of the confederate.

What's Next?

Our results are encouraging for those who hope to identify ways to help people develop romantic relationships. However, we would caution against extrapolating or extending our results into a real-life context. We conducted our study in a highly controlled environment that does not provide an exact parallel to natural situations, such as people meeting in a bar or a club. Thus, future research is necessary to determine if the same results are possible outside of the lab.

We also limited our study to women who were not taking hormonal contraceptives. Future research could examine our variables in women who take hormonal contraceptives to see if results differ. Also, in light of research showing that ovulation influences how women dress (Haselton, Mortezaie, Pillsworth, Bleske-Recheck, & Frederick, 2007) and women's preference for masculine men (Penton-Voak & Perrett, 2000), future research on scent and pick-up attempts could consider how a woman's ovulatory cycle influences receptivity.

> **What Do You Think?**
>
> What other variables could future research study in order to investigate what might influence receptivity to relationship initiation?

> **YOUR TURN 11.3**
>
> 1. Javier wants to see if the environment influences how much his pet guinea pig eats. He decides to manipulate whether or not there are people in the room, whether or not the television is on, and the guinea pig's type of food (pellets vs. lettuce). Which statistical test should he use to analyze his data?
>   **a.** A *t*-test for independent means
>   **b.** A one-way ANOVA
>   **c.** A two-way ANOVA
>   **d.** A three-way ANOVA
>
> 2. Boyd has signed up for a weight-control group at his company. He can select which plan he wants to participate in and has a choice of diet only, exercise only, or a diet and exercise combination. The literature says that over the next year, Boyd can expect to lose 5 pounds with diet only, 7 pounds with exercise only, and 20 pounds with the diet and exercise combination. Which of the following best describes this effect?
>   **a.** Main effect
>   **b.** Interaction effect
>   **c.** Suppression effect
>   **d.** Synergistic effect

3. In the discussion, we noted that our confederate knew which pick-up attempt condition was taking place. We could potentially solve this issue by having one confederate for each condition. Which of the following are problems with that proposed solution?

a. Having one confederate for each condition introduces a confound because there is something (i.e., who the confederate is) that systematically varies between conditions.

b. It compromises experimental control because one confederate may be more attractive than the other.

c. It compromises experimental control because one confederate may be a more natural pick-up artist than the other.

d. All of the above are potential problems.

How did you do? Turn to the end of the chapter to check your answers.

 Research in Action

Can the News Influence Our Implicit Prejudice?

Today we get the news from a variety of sources. Although we can still watch the nightly news, we are also likely to get news from comedy shows, Twitter feeds, and Facebook posts. Each of these news sources may present slightly different information about the same event. Although these variations may seem harmless, the differences can influence us in subtle ways. For example, the news could influence your attitudes toward particular groups. Which factors might strengthen or weaken your implicit and potentially prejudicial attitudes?

In the online activity ***Can the News Influence Our Implicit Prejudice?***, you will develop a factorial design to examine whether the nature of the crime and the race of the suspect reported in a news story can separately, and in combination, influence racial prejudices that participants may unknowingly harbor.

LaunchPad To complete this activity, visit LaunchPad at launchpadworks.com

Final Thoughts

In this chapter, we built on our knowledge of experiments by utilizing an experimental design that allowed us to essentially combine several experiments into one design. Factorial designs save us time and give us the ability to determine how independent variables combine or interact with each other to influence the dependent variable. Overall, this design allowed us to use many of the skills we developed in previous chapters to find an answer to our research question in a way that was creative, but also scientific.

Our research question touches on a fundamental question about human existence: Are we really in control of our own behavior? Certainly, we would like to think that if we have a choice in anything at all, we can choose our romantic partners. Remember that we did not find any research showing that scent or pheromones influence relationship initiation in everyday settings. But if scent could influence relationship initiation, what other factors might influence who you fall in love with? Do your friends' or family's opinions influence you? Could stress or the amount of sunshine on a particular day change how likely you are to give out your phone number? What if you frequently listen to romantic music, read love stories, or watch sappy movies? There might not be a topic that people spend more time thinking about than relationships. As a result, most people are full of opinions and may feel some degree of expertise. But as you now know, it is only after testing theories and assumptions scientifically that you can have confidence in the claims.

CHAPTER 11 Review

Review Questions

1. Modesto is a member of the student government and is in charge of the midterm De-Stress Festival. He wants to do a study to determine the best stress reliever. For his study, he will have participants do either 5 minutes or 10 minutes of deep breathing. While students do this, they will hear either a wind chime or the sound of waves on a beach. Each participant will experience only one combination. Everyone will have their stress levels and relaxation levels measured. Which of the following accurately describes this design?
   a. $2 \times 2 \times 2$ hybrid design
   b. $2 \times 2 \times 2$ mixed design
   c. $2 \times 2 \times 2$ factorial design
   d. 2×2 factorial design

2. Caron has designed a $3 \times 2 \times 2$ factorial experiment. Based on this information, you know that she has _____ independent variables and potentially has as many as _____ main effect hypotheses.
   a. 7; 3
   b. 3; 3
   c. 3; 7
   d. There is not enough information to tell.

3. Ed's senior project used a factorial design. He hypothesized a main effect for his first independent variable and achieved significance. Now he wants to determine the direction of the effect (i.e., which level of his independent variable is higher than the other). Where should he look for this information?
   a. Marginal means
   b. Cell means
   c. Significance level
   d. Effect size

4. Kaci is the president of the Math and Science Club on campus and wants to see if eating chocolate and drinking coffee helps members solve more math problems. She manipulates her independent variables by giving members a piece of either dark, milk, or white chocolate, and a cup of either caffeinated or decaffeinated coffee. Everyone gets one combination. She then gives everyone the same set of 100 problems to see which group solves the most. Which statistical test should she use to analyze her data?

    a. A one-way ANOVA

    b. A two-way ANOVA

    c. A three-way ANOVA

    d. A *t*-test for independent means

5. Dinorah has been a teacher at the town's preschool for 27 years. Based on her experience, she knows what makes kids happy. For example, she knows that giving a kid a lollipop increases happiness by 2 points (if you were measuring on a 10-point scale). Dinorah also knows that if you read a funny story, it increases happiness by 5 points. A new teacher suggests that on the last day of school, the staff give all of the kids lollipops and read them stories. However, Dinorah explains that when you combine lollipops and stories, the kids' happiness will actually decrease by 1 point. Which of the following best describes this effect?

    a. Synergistic effect

    b. Interaction effect

    c. Suppression effect

    d. A crossover interaction

6. Genevie conducted a 2×2 factorial study examining the maze completion ability of rats and found that the main effect for her second independent variable was significant. Based on this finding, what do we expect the rest of her results will be?

    a. The main effect for the first independent variable will also be significant.

    b. The main effect for the first independent variable will not be significant.

    c. The interaction effect will be significant, but the main effect for the first independent variable will not be significant.

    d. There is not enough information to tell.

7. Which of the following statements is true?

    a. In a factorial design, there is always just one main effect and one interaction effect in total.

    b. If you have a significant interaction, you will also have at least one significant main effect.

    c. A major benefit of a factorial design is that it allows researchers to guarantee that they find significance.

    d. All of the previous statements are false.

8. Each of the following is an example of an interaction *except*:
   a. How much you like going to the mall is similar regardless of the day of the week that you go.
   b. The quality of your relationship depends on the time you spend together and what you do during that time.
   c. Who you are with and the quality of the band determines how much you enjoy a concert.
   d. The quality of a haircut depends on the stylist you go to and the humidity that day.

9. Lanelle works for a market research company and is in charge of a project focusing on video-game sales. The software company wants to know if enjoyment of types of video games differs for teenage boys and girls. To test this idea, Lanelle solicits male and female participants from the local mall to play one of three game types: driving, role play, or sports. Lanelle then asks each participant a series of questions about his or her enjoyment of the game. Which of the following accurately describes this design?
   a. 2 × 3 hybrid design
   b. 2 × 2 mixed design
   c. 2 × 2 factorial design
   d. 2 × 3 factorial design

10. A research group in a memory lab wanted to see how rats who grew up in an enriched environment (i.e., with lots of things to interact with) compared on a memory test to rats who grew up in an impoverished environment (i.e., nothing to do). The researchers also wanted to see if verbal encouragement (e.g., "You can do it, Rat!") improved performance compared to no encouragement. The results of their study indicate that verbal encouragement improved performance for rats from an impoverished environment, but it hurt performance for rats from an enriched environment. Which of the following best describes this effect?
    a. A crossover interaction
    b. Synergistic effect
    c. Interaction effect
    d. Suppression effect

11. Describe the benefits of using a factorial design.

12. In this chapter's study, it is possible that some participants will always be highly receptive to starting a relationship, while others will be perpetually hesitant. Is this a problem for the study? Why or why not?

13. Create a table (like we did in Table 11.2) that depicts the following study:

A marketing agency wants to test advertisements' effectiveness for watches. The agency creates three different ads: one that shows just the watch, one that features a single model wearing the watch, and one that shows a group of people admiring the watch. They place the ads in two types of magazines: news and lifestyle. All ads feature a QR code for readers to scan with their cell phone. The agency counts the number of visits from each code to determine effectiveness.

Applying What You've Learned

1. Find a published empirical article that describes a factorial design. Evaluate the groups in terms of experimental control. What did they control well? What could they have controlled better?

2. This chapter's study focused on relationship initiation. Design a study that uses two entirely different independent variables to test the same dependent variable.

3. Visit the following site: http://greatergood.berkeley.edu/. There you will find several core themes (e.g., gratitude, altruism, etc.) that help people lead a meaningful life. Use a 2 × 2 factorial design to test two independent variables that could help a person improve on the core theme of your choice.

4. Relationships are responsible for much of your life's happiness. Generate five new ideas for studies that focus on relationships. Pick your favorite idea and describe how you would test it with a factorial design.

5. Generate three different variables that could fill in the blank. That is, what other variable could you add that would interact with the first independent variable?

   a. The presence of a Tattoo × _____ → How Much You Trust the Person
   b. Amount of Suntan Lotion × _____ → How Much Sunburn You Get
   c. Quality of the Professor × _____ → Students' Interest in a Class

6. Read the following study: Guéguen, N. (2013). Weather and courtship behavior: A quasi-experiment with the flirty sunshine. *Social Influence, 8*, 312–319. doi:10.1080/15534510.2012.752401

   As you will see, the researcher examines how sunshine influences receptivity to pick-up lines (hint: it makes women more likely to give out their phone number). It is a quasi-experiment because we cannot manipulate sunshine. Using a factorial design, test a similar idea. Bonus: Design two different studies, one that you can conduct in a lab and one that you conduct outside the lab.

7. Have you ever gone camping and made s'mores from marshmallows, chocolate, and graham crackers? Explain how a s'more represents an interaction.

8. THE NOVICE RESEARCHER: Write an interaction hypothesis that mistakenly does not predict an interaction. Also write a main effect hypothesis that mistakenly does not focus on only one independent variable. For each, describe what is wrong, and then provide a correct hypothesis.

9. DIG INTO THE NUMBERS: We have provided your instructor with data for another factorial design study. Use that data to build your skills using SPSS to test hypotheses which require two-way ANOVAs. Write an APA-style results section based on your results. Be sure to interpret any statistically significant main and interaction effects. If you would like even more practice, your instructor also has data that accompanies the study discussed throughout this chapter.

Key Concepts

cell mean, p. 379

crossover interaction, p. 369

disordinal interaction, p. 369

factor, p. 359

factorial ANOVA, p. 378

factorial design, p. 359

hybrid design, p. 360

interaction, p. 361

interaction effect hypothesis, p. 366

main effect hypothesis, p. 366

marginal mean, p. 379

ordinal interaction, p. 369

suppression effect, p. 383

synergistic effect, p. 383

two-way analysis of variance, p. 378

two-way ANOVA, p. 378

vignette, p. 371

Answers to YOUR TURN

Your Turn 11.1: 1. c; 2. b; 3. d

Your Turn 11.2: 1. b; 2. a; 3. c

Your Turn 11.3: 1. c; 2. d; 3. d

Answers to Multiple-Choice Review Questions

1. d; 2. b; 3. a; 4. b; 5. c; 6. d; 7. d; 8. a; 9. a; 10. a

Mixed Design

Which Therapy Is Best for Treating Eating Disorders?

Nataliia Petrovska/Shutterstock

LEARNING OUTCOMES

After reading this chapter, you should be able to:

- Provide operational definitions for key variables.
- Identify key design issues with single-subject designs.
- Discuss key design issues with mixed design research.

- Explain the benefits of and uses for mixed designs.
- Discuss ethical and methodological issues related to clinical research.
- Choose the proper statistic to use for mixed designs.
- Write a results section for a mixed design ANOVA.

Something to Think About . . .

When was the last time you ate? Perhaps it was dinner at the dining hall or breakfast at home this morning. Maybe you are munching on a snack as you read this chapter. Now, think about why you ate. It could be that you were hungry, but it is also possible that you ate because the clock says it is mealtime, because you happen to have free time between classes or work, or just because you want something to do. Although we need food to survive, food is also part of our culture and social interactions. We eat when celebrating at birthdays and grieving after funerals. We share food with family and friends to bond. We may also eat because we are bored, stressed, happy, or sad. Do you ever find yourself eating more junk food and fewer salads during finals? Or bringing food to your less interesting classes, just so you have something to do?

There are many reasons why people eat, but there are also reasons why people avoid eating. Some people avoid gluten, dairy, or carbs as part of a fad diet or because of food allergies, while others cut calories to lose weight. For some people, restricted eating can become a serious problem. Millions of people in the United States suffer from eating disorders, in which the basic act of eating can become complicated, maladaptive, and even life-threatening. One disorder, anorexia nervosa, involves the refusal to maintain a healthy body weight, a fear of gaining weight, and an altered experience of one's own body weight

Why do we eat when we are not hungry? What emotions may be underlying this behavior? *(Comstock Images/Getty Images)*

(Adenzato, Todisco, & Ardito, 2012). Most people with this disorder exercise excessively and starve themselves to lose weight.

To help gain insight into what contributes to eating disorders like anorexia nervosa, we can look at some of our own eating behaviors. What triggers you to eat? You might find yourself anxiously sharing a bowl of chips with the guys as you watch the big game. Perhaps you are experiencing mild stress while listening to your friend cry about her failed career plans over a couple of hot fudge sundaes. Or you might eat candy out of boredom while watching *Wonder Woman* for the fifth time. What triggers you to *not* eat? Some people avoid eating in times of stress or negative emotion, like during those weeks when all of your classes have tests and papers due on the same day. When we look at all the reasons you might or might not eat, there may be a common thread in what can trigger eating behavior: emotions.

Introduction to Our Research Question

Perhaps the same types of events that trigger a nondisordered eater to eat may also lead a person with anorexia to avoid eating. Think about the last time you were really happy, angry, sad, or nervous. Chances are that your emotion was associated with particular behaviors or thoughts. Could particular emotions trigger the maladaptive behaviors or thoughts associated with anorexia nervosa? To develop this idea into a research question, we must search the literature to learn how external or situational factors might impact anorexia nervosa. We also need to see if existing research suggests that emotional triggers are a viable option for our research. If we find support for our idea, we can try to answer this question: "How do emotional triggers impact anorexia nervosa?"

Anorexia nervosa is a serious mental health disorder that requires professional help. People who suffer from this disorder have a pattern of engaging in unhealthy behaviors to lose weight, an intense fear of gaining weight, and a distorted body image (American Psychiatric Association, 2013). There are multiple approaches to treating the disorder, such as cognitive-behavioral, psychodynamic, family, and expressive therapies, and many mental health professionals adopt a particular approach in their practice. Knowing the strengths and weaknesses of each approach would help patients select the mental health professional who is best suited for treating them. A literature search will help us understand whether one form of therapy is better than the other based on empirical data. Since therapy is vital to the treatment of anorexia nervosa, perhaps our research question should be, "How do types of treatment impact anorexia nervosa?"

We now have two potential research questions. We could consider how real-world emotional triggers impact people who struggle with anorexia nervosa, or we could study the effectiveness of particular treatment types. How do we choose which research question to pursue? Maybe we do not have to choose just one. By studying both, we have the most to gain and learn. One type of treatment may be better when people with anorexia encounter an emotional trigger, while another treatment may be best when no emotional trigger exists. In other words, one treatment might not always be best; what is best may depend on the emotional triggers a person encounters. As you learned in Chapter 11, you can have more than one factor involved in a single study.

▶ How do you include more than one independent variable in a study? SEE CHAPTER 11, p. 359

As we are interested in the impact of both emotional triggers and treatment type on anorexia nervosa, the best research question for us would be:

RESEARCH ?   How do treatment types and emotional triggers impact anorexia nervosa?

This research question allows us to investigate both emotional triggers and treatment for anorexia nervosa, as well as the combination of the two.

What Do You Think?
What other variables that might influence anorexia nervosa could future research study?

Reviewing the Literature: What Do We Already Know About This Topic?

Before we go any further, we need to see what researchers already know about the treatment of anorexia and the role of emotional triggers in the disorder by investigating the following questions: What factors influence anorexia nervosa, and, in particular, what role does emotion play? What is the effectiveness of therapeutic treatments for anorexia nervosa? With these questions in mind, we will search the literature to determine if our research question is both novel and grounded in theory. Because we do not yet know much about these topics, and could benefit from an overview, it would be helpful to find at least one research article that includes a **meta-analysis**. A meta-analysis is a quantitative statistical analysis that compares and integrates the results from multiple studies on the same research question to summarize what they say collectively on that topic.

Below are summaries we wrote on empirical research articles we found that were relevant to our questions, including a meta-analysis on the topics of eating disorders, emotion, and therapy.

Anorexia Nervosa and Emotion

Adenzato, M., Todisco, P., & Ardito, R. B. (2012). Social cognition in anorexia nervosa: Evidence of preserved theory of mind and impaired emotional functioning. *PLOS ONE, 7*(8). doi:10.1371/journal.pone.0044414

To study the social cognition of those suffering from anorexia nervosa, researchers compared 30 women diagnosed with anorexia nervosa and 32 healthy control participants matched for age and education. Those with anorexia nervosa had poorer emotional functioning.

Lavender, J. M., De Young, K. P., Wonderlich, S. A., Crosby, R. D., Engel, S. G., Mitchell, J. E., . . . Le Grange, D. (2013). Daily patterns of anxiety in anorexia nervosa: Associations with eating disorder behaviors in the natural environment. *Journal of Abnormal Psychology, 122,* 672–683. doi:10.1037/a0031823

Researchers studied 118 women with anorexia nervosa to examine the association between daily anxiety and eating disorder behavior. Over a 2-week period, participants recorded details about their life six times throughout the day. Each time, they recorded

meta-analysis
a quantitative statistical analysis that compares and combines the results of individual, but similar, studies.

their anxiety levels and eating disorder behaviors, such as body checking, binge eating, skipping meals, excessive exercise, or self-induced vomiting. There were distinct patterns in the types of anxiety experienced throughout the day and the particular eating disorder behaviors. Daily anxiety may trigger particular eating disorder behaviors.

Therapy for Eating Disorders

Couturier, J., Kimber, M., & Szatmari, P. (2013). Efficacy of family-based treatment for adolescents with eating disorders: A systematic review and meta-analysis. *International Journal of Eating Disorders, 46,* 3–11. doi:10.1002/eat.22042

The authors conducted a meta-analysis to summarize the effectiveness of family-based treatment (FBT) compared to individual treatment for eating disorders among adolescents. At the end of treatment, the remission rates for those in FBT and individual therapy were the same. Follow-ups 6 to 12 months after treatment, however, indicated that FBT produced higher remission rates than individual therapy.

Grave, R. D., Calugi, S., Doll, H. A., & Fairburn, C. G. (2013). Enhanced cognitive behaviour therapy for adolescents with anorexia nervosa: An alternative to family therapy? *Behaviour Research and Therapy, 51,* R9–R12. doi:10.1016/j.brat.2012.09.008

Forty-six adolescent anorexia nervosa patents participated in 40 weeks of individual "enhanced" cognitive-behavioral therapy. General cognitive-behavioral therapy addresses dysfunctional emotions and maladaptive behaviors and cognitions. The "enhanced" therapy used in this study emphasized participants' processing the disorder and their current state, developing pros and cons of treating their disorder, regaining weight, and modifying their concerns about body shape and weight. Researchers assessed body weight, BMI, and eating disorder features at the start and end of treatment, as well as 60 weeks after treatment. Those who completed treatment displayed improvements in weight and eating disorder psychopathology. The effects were stable 60 weeks after treatment completion. This study indicates that "enhanced" cognitive-behavioral therapy is a promising treatment approach for anorexia nervosa.

Murphy, S., Russell, L., & Waller, G. (2005). Integrated psychodynamic therapy for bulimia nervosa and binge eating disorder: Theory, practice and preliminary findings. *European Eating Disorders Review, 13,* 383–391. doi:10.1002/erv.672

This research examined the effectiveness of psychodynamic therapy, which is a psychotherapy focusing on unconscious content and past experiences. This study specifically examined bulimia nervosa and binge eating disorder. Researchers recorded the body mass index (BMI) and frequency of bulimic behaviors at the start of treatment, the end of treatment, 3 months later, and 6 months later in 21 women (14 with bulimia nervosa and 7 with binge eating disorder). Participants received between 20 and 40 weekly individual therapy sessions. The therapy was an adapted psychodynamic model that integrated cognitive-behavioral interventions. The frequency of bulimic behaviors dropped significantly during treatment for both types of disorders, and this reduction remained 3 and 6 months after treatment. BMI was stable throughout treatment and after. Psychodynamic therapy integrated with cognitive-behavioral interventions may be a helpful treatment for eating disorders.

Poulsen, S., Lunn, S., Daniel, S., Folke, S., Mathiesen, B., Katznelson, H., & Fairburn, C. (2014). A randomized controlled trial of psychoanalytic psychotherapy or cognitive-behavioral therapy for bulimia nervosa. *American Journal of Psychiatry, 171,* 109–116. doi:10.1176/appi.ajp.2013.12121511

This study compared psychoanalytic psychotherapy and cognitive-behavioral therapy for the treatment of bulimia nervosa. Seventy participants received either 2 years of weekly psychoanalytic psychotherapy or 20 sessions of cognitive-behavioral therapy over 5 months. Researchers assessed participants after 5 months and again after 2 years. At both assessments, a higher percentage of the cognitive-behavioral therapy group had stopped binging and purging compared to the psychoanalytic psychotherapy group. Overall, cognitive-behavioral therapy was faster and more effective at reducing bulimic behaviors.

From Ideas to Innovation

Based on the literature, we learned that emotion plays a role in eating disorders. This means that our research question may be on to something. People with an eating disorder have lower emotional functioning (Adenzato et al., 2012) and daily anxieties that can trigger disordered eating behaviors (Lavender et al., 2013), so our hunch that particular emotions trigger maladaptive behaviors or thoughts associated with anorexia nervosa is still on target. However, there are many other emotions that previous research has not yet examined. It seems we have a novel research question grounded in what we already know about the disorder, which is exactly what we hoped for when we first had the idea.

When it comes to therapy type, a meta-analysis revealed that family-based therapy was superior to individual therapy in the long-term treatment of eating disorders (Couturier et al., 2013). Still, many people who suffer from anorexia nervosa may seek out individual therapy. The most effective type of individual therapy for treating the disorder is still unclear: The research on cognitive-behavioral therapy indicates it can be effective (Grave et al., 2013), while psychodynamic therapy seems to significantly help women suffering from bulimia nervosa, a psychopathology that overlaps with anorexia nervosa (Murphy et al., 2005). Likewise, the only study in our literature review involving a direct comparison between pure cognitive-behavioral therapy and pure psychodynamic psychotherapy addressed sufferers of bulimia nervosa (Poulsen et al., 2014). We do not yet know if similar results would occur in those suffering from anorexia. When it comes to evaluating the efficacy of different treatments, it seems there is still more work to do, and we are just the people to do it! Even better, we did not find any studies combining therapy type with specific emotional triggers to determine whether a particular treatment approach helps prepare those with anorexia nervosa to deal with such triggers. This is great news because it shows that our study could make an important contribution to what the psychological community already knows about treating anorexia nervosa.

This study, and this type of research, could be the most important we discuss in this textbook, as it is the one that could most directly save lives. Anorexia nervosa is a complex disorder that is difficult to treat (Isserlin & Couturier, 2012) and impacts about 3 of every 1,000 young women (Morris & Twaddle, 2007). Sadly, eating disorders can lead to mortality, with a death rate of about 5 in every 1,000 people with the disorder (Arcelus, Mitchell, Wales, & Nielson, 2011), which demonstrates how vital it is to find ways to treat those who suffer from them. For successful treatment, it is essential for mental health professionals to understand all the situational factors that might exacerbate the disorder, as well as the best form of treatment. Knowing the triggers and causes of anorexic behavior can help health professionals and sufferers better manage the disorder.

Defining Key Terms: What Do You Mean By _____?

▶ Why is defining
key terms critical to
your study?
SEE CHAPTER 2, p. 38

To start, we must determine what we mean by each key concept in our study. Obviously, we need a clear definition for *anorexia nervosa,* as well as for *treatment.* We also need to pinpoint the types of emotional triggers we want to study.

The American Psychiatric Association (APA) recognizes anorexia nervosa as a clinical disorder, so there is no need for us to define it ourselves. Instead, we can use the fifth edition of the *Diagnostic and Statistical Manual of Mental Disorders (DSM-5;* American Psychiatric Association, 2013b) as a basis for our definition. The *DSM-5* defines anorexia nervosa as three specific features: The first is a significantly lower than medically expected body weight based on the limiting of calorie consumption. The second is severe anxiety about weight gain that leads to behaviors to prevent it. The third is a distorted view of one's body weight and shape, an overemphasis of body shape and weight to one's self-concept, or a denial of the seriousness of one's low body weight.

"Treatment" is a broad term that could mean various forms of psychotherapy and/or pharmacological treatment. With just a little digging, we find that treatment for anorexia nervosa may include medication, but only after weight is back to a healthy level to help prevent relapse, and only to address comorbid issues, such as anxiety or depression, not the eating disorder itself (Gorla & Mathews, 2005). This means that pharmacological treatment is not a logical choice for our research question. Psychotherapy, on the other hand, is a generic term that describes any therapeutic interaction between a health professional and a client, patient, family, couple, or group that focuses specifically on psychological problems. Because there is a wide range of psychotherapeutic techniques and approaches within psychotherapy, later, when we operationalize our variables, we will need to decide which therapy type or therapeutic approach makes the most sense in our study.

The therapeutic community does not clearly define emotional triggers the way they do therapeutic approaches and anorexia nervosa, so we will need to define this idea in our own terms. Remember that we began thinking about this topic by brainstorming reasons we eat and realizing that sometimes we eat when we feel a particular emotion, such as stress, sadness, or happiness. We also recognized that a particular emotion may automatically activate particular thoughts or behaviors (Geliebter & Aversa, 2003; Ozier et al., 2008), which is what we mean by an emotional trigger. We want to test whether a particular emotional experience or trigger will incite a particular behavior in those with anorexia nervosa.

The *Diagnostic and Statistical Manual of Mental Disorders, Fifth Edition (DSM-5)* is the main reference tool for clinicians, researchers, health insurance companies, the legal system, and policy makers. The American Psychiatric Association adds and removes mental disorders with each revision. *(Maia Rosenfeld)*

Research Spotlight

Pro-Anorexia Websites

This chapter's study focuses on helping people recover from anorexia, but you do not need to work with a clinical sample to conduct research on this topic. For example, you could examine how people portray the illness online, including websites promoting anorexia as a lifestyle choice. These sites, known as pro-anorexia, pro-ana, or simply ana, post photographs and tips designed to inspire others to lose weight. They also have forums where people can share and support positive views of anorexia. Clearly, ana websites are problematic, but there are other websites that advocate for healthier lifestyles by promoting recovery from eating disorders. To understand the dynamics of both pro-anorexia and pro-recovery communities on Flickr, an Internet photo sharing site, researchers categorized users of public accounts as either pro-anorexia or pro-recovery based on the types of pictures they posted and the comments associated with the pictures (Yom-Tov, Fernandez-Luque, Weber, & Crain, 2012). Pro-recovery users posted more pictures overall, including more pictures of themselves, than pro-anorexia users. However, pro-anorexia users posted more pictures with tags referring to body image (e.g., doll, skinny, sexy) than pro-recovery users. Based on picture comments, pro-recovery users commented on pro-recovery pictures and pro-anorexia commented on pro-anorexia ones, which indicates that the messages portrayed by pro-recovery users to live healthier lives are not crossing over into the pro-anorexia community. Unfortunately, the pro-recovery communities have little impact on the pro-anorexia ones. This example illustrates, however, that there are many aspects of clinical disorders that you can study without a clinical sample, thus advancing the understanding and treatment of the disorder.

What emotional impact do you think pro-anorexia websites have?
(GaudiLab/Shutterstock)

Weighing Our Options: Picking a Design

▶ What is the difference between experimental and nonexperimental research?
SEE CHAPTER 2, p. 38

Our research question ("How do treatment types and emotional triggers impact anorexia nervosa?") undoubtedly implies a cause-and-effect relationship. We want to know how both treatment type and emotional triggers cause a change in the experience of anorexia nervosa. Therefore, our research question is experimental in nature.

The Single-Subject Design

It is highly likely that you know, or know of, someone with an eating disorder such as anorexia nervosa. To make things simple, we could just ask that person to be our sole research participant and focus on the person in depth. In a clinical experiment like ours, researchers sometimes use a **single-subject design** (also referred to as a **single-case experimental design** or **single-n design**). This is a special type of within-subjects design using one subject (human or animal) or perhaps a single group to assess changes within that individual or group. The subject or participant in the design serves as his or her own control. There are several different ways that researchers make comparisons with this basic design (see Table 12.1).

▶ What makes a research study a within-subjects design?
SEE CHAPTER 10, p. 322

TABLE 12.1

Summary of Single-Subject Designs			
A-B Design	Phase A baseline measurement taken	Phase B intervention introduced and measurement taken	
A-B-A Design	Phase A baseline measurement taken	Phase B intervention introduced and measurement taken	Phase A intervention removed and measurement taken
A-B-A-B Design	Phase A baseline measurement taken	Phase B intervention introduced and measurement taken	Phase A intervention removed and measurement taken	Phase B intervention reintroduced and measurement taken

single-subject design a special type of within-subjects design using one participant (human or animal) or one group to assess changes within that individual or group; also known as a single-case experimental design or single-n design.

A-B design a single-subject design in which researchers take a baseline measurement (A), then introduce the intervention, and then measure the same variable again (B).

The simplest single-subject design is the **A-B design**. To establish a cause-and-effect relationship, the researcher takes a baseline measure before intervention, noted as the A phase of the study, and then introduces an intervention or experimental treatment, known as the B phase. Afterward, researchers measure the same variable again within the same participant, hence the within-subjects nature of this design. For example, we might monitor someone with anorexia nervosa by measuring the number of calories they consume over the course of a week to establish a baseline pattern (phase A) and then introduce an emotional trigger and assess caloric intake again (phase B). A change in measurement from the A phase to the B phase might suggest a causal relation. In this case, we would look for a change in caloric intake after the emotional trigger.

Of course, in the A-B design, the second measure of caloric intake could be higher because the participant may naturally become better and eat more over time. To evaluate this possibility, the researcher may decide to add another A phase in which the intervention or treatment is removed and the researcher takes a third measurement, resulting in an **A-B-A design.** In our example, this means assessing caloric intake again after removing the emotional trigger. This time, we would hope to see a reversal in the effect, or the caloric intake returning to what it was in the baseline measurement in the absence of the intervention (emotional trigger). This design helps to establish covariation by showing that behavior systematically changes as researchers introduce and remove the treatment.

To obtain even more proof of causality, you could use an **A-B-A-B design,** in which the researcher takes a measurement before exposure to treatment (A), after exposure to treatment (B), after the treatment has been removed (A), and again after the treatment has been reinstituted (B). But given that we are working with a vulnerable population of people with an eating disorder, would it be ethical to execute *any* single-subject design in order to study the impact of an emotional trigger? If emotional triggers do cause changes in caloric intake for better or for worse, we would not want to go back and forth in exposing and then removing the emotional trigger. Doing so could have major implications for the participant's health and well-being.

In addition to the ethical ramifications for our research question, there are some other notable weaknesses with single-subject designs. First, as we discussed with pretest-posttest designs in Chapter 10, there is no control group, which limits our ability to establish cause and effect. (Arguably, however, the participant serves as the control group whenever the treatment is removed in A-B-A designs.) Another weakness of this design is external validity, or our ability to generalize our findings beyond the study. With this type of design, it is hard to discern if the single subject or group in our study is representative of the population at large. The single subject or group could be systematically different than others at the onset, meaning that the same treatment may not have the same impact on other individuals or groups. Our participant with anorexia might have a unique and atypical response to the emotional trigger intervention. Therefore, the results may not be very useful, especially if our goal is to help others. In addition, the single-subject design allows us to introduce and remove only one level of the same treatment, and our research question involves two factors to test: treatment type and emotional triggers. Although this design may be useful for other research questions, a single-subject design is not the best choice for our research question.

A-B-A design a single-subject design in which researchers establish a baseline (A), introduce the intervention and measure the same variable again (B), then remove the intervention and take another measurement (A).

▶ What is covariation? SEE CHAPTER 8, p. 249

A-B-A-B design a single-subject design in which researchers establish a baseline (A), introduce the intervention (B), remove the intervention (A), and then reintroduce the intervention (B), measuring the dependent variable each time.

▶ What role do control groups play in establishing cause and effect? SEE CHAPTER 10, p. 345

▶ How does representative sampling help with external validity? SEE CHAPTER 6, p. 164

Research Spotlight

An A-B Single-Subject Design in Sports Psychology

Single-subject designs are a type of within-subjects design that psychologists use in their research programs. One study in particular used an A-B design to examine the impact of hypnosis on a professional golfer's performance during the Senior European Tour (Pates, 2013). In the A (baseline) phase, the researcher recorded the golfer's average strokes to complete 18 holes of golf. In the B (intervention) phase, the golfer experienced 40 minutes of hypnosis followed by 7 days of listening to an audio recording of the live hypnosis session. Then the researcher recorded the golfer's average strokes to complete 18 holes of golf again. Compared to the baseline, the participant improved his performance by 4.2 fewer strokes during the intervention phase. These findings suggest that hypnosis may help improve the personal performance of elite athletes. Since professional athletes are not a large population from which to sample, using a single-subject design may be the best way to study strategies for improving their performance.

If hypnosis administered as treatment in an A-B single-subjects design can cause a professional golfer to perform better, how might it help you? *(Amy Allcock/Getty Images)*

The Mixed Design

Before we decide on the best design to use, we should think about each factor in our research question more closely. First, we want to know the impact of treatment type on anorexia nervosa. We could analyze this in two different ways, using either a within-subjects or a between-subjects design. If we decide to do a within-subjects design, our participants will receive one type of treatment and then the other. But wait—in real life, people would not receive two different types of therapy, one after the other. Besides, if one therapy is effective, there would be no reason for the person to undergo additional therapy for a disorder that is already under control. Receiving two different forms of therapy not only lacks mundane realism, but might be confusing and detrimental to our participants. Therapy is intended to be a long-lasting remedy, meaning that carryover effects between the first and second therapy types are practically inevitable. A better idea is to keep the therapy type factor between-subjects so that half of our participants receive one type of therapy, while the other half receive a different therapy.

Now consider our other factor, emotional triggers. Are we more interested in how emotional triggers influence different groups of people or how they influence the same person differently? If we think about real-life situations again, we might have an answer. In life, we do not encounter just one type of emotional trigger. Rather, in one day alone we typically encounter multiple triggers. If we make emotional triggers a within-subjects factor by exposing each participant to multiple levels of emotional triggers, we will not only make our study truer to real life, but will also be able to observe how different emotional triggers impact the same individual. Although we will need to be careful to design our experiment so that the emotional triggers are short-term in nature, thus minimizing potential carryover effects, we should make emotional triggers a within-subjects factor. Because we are more interested in how emotional triggers change the experience of anorexia nervosa within one individual, we should use a within-subjects, rather than a between-subjects, design for this factor.

Can we design a study that allows us to assign treatment type as a between-subjects factor and emotional triggers as a within-subjects factor? Fortunately, there is a design that combines the elements of between-subjects and within-subjects designs. A **mixed design** has all participants receive every level of the within-subjects factor, but only one level of the between-subjects factor. Essentially, it is a factorial design with multiple independent variables, but with at least one within-subjects independent variable and at least one between-subjects independent variable. For our purposes, we can use a mixed design to assign different therapy types to our participants while still exposing them to all levels of emotional triggers. See **Table 12.2** for a summary of within-subjects and between-subjects designs.

▶ What are the differences between within-subjects and between-subjects designs?
SEE CHAPTER 2, p. 40

▶ How can you avoid carryover effects?
SEE CHAPTER 10, p. 334

TABLE 12.2

Summary of Within-Subjects and Between-Subjects Designs	
Type of Design	Methodology
Two-group design	Between-subjects
Pretest-posttest design	Within-subjects
Multigroup design	Between-subjects
Factorial design	Between-subjects
Repeated measures design	Within-subjects
Mixed design	Between-subjects and within-subjects

mixed design an experimental design that combines within-subjects and between-subjects methods of data collection.

Benefits of Mixed Designs

Researchers use a mixed design for the same reason they use any design: because it is the best way to answer their specific research question. No design is perfect, but a nice feature of a mixed design is that the strengths of the within-subjects aspects help compensate for the weaknesses of the between-subjects aspects and vice versa. See **Table 12.3** for a comparison of the strengths and weaknesses of within-subjects and between-subjects designs.

TABLE 12.3

Comparison of Within-Subjects and Between-Subjects Designs		
	Between-Subjects	**Within-Subjects**
Method	Expose participants to one level of treatment	Expose participants to all levels of treatment
Random Assignment	Randomly assign participants to one condition	Randomly assign participants to a sequence of treatment conditions
Strengths	Internal and external validity	Power
Weaknesses	Power	Internal and external validity

▶ How do within-subjects designs increase statistical power? SEE CHAPTER 10, p. 323

While within-subjects designs can have internal validity concerns such as potential order effects, they can also increase the power of your study. Because participants serve as their own control, we can eliminate random error due to individual differences. We also have an increase in power because a within-subjects design naturally increases the number of measurements we obtain from each participant. The more measurements we have, the more likely it is that random error will cancel out, increasing power. Although we can still have satisfactory power in a between-subjects design, it takes more participants to increase the number of observations. However, between-subjects designs using random assignment have stronger internal validity. If conducted well, there is less chance in between-subjects designs that anything other than the independent variable causes the changes we see in the dependent variable. A between-subjects design also has higher external validity because, in real life, people usually only get one level of treatment instead of a sequence of treatments. By combining between and within factors in a mixed design, we can rely on the strengths of both designs while compensating for some of the weaknesses.

▶ How do between-subjects designs impact the internal validity of a study? SEE CHAPTER 8, p. 250

Another nice feature of a mixed design is that it allows us to answer three research questions at the same time. Within the same study, we can investigate the impact of each independent variable individually on the dependent variable. We can see how treatment type impacts anorexia nervosa, as well as how emotional triggers impact anorexia nervosa. This design requires fewer participants and less time, as the only other way to test both ideas would be to run two completely separate studies. Better yet, we can also test for an interaction effect to determine whether the combination of independent variables results in something different than each individual impact on the dependent variable. The interaction effect will tell us if a particular therapy type is more beneficial in combination with a particular emotional trigger.

▶ What is an interaction effect? SEE CHAPTER 11, p. 366

Ultimately, the research question determines the best design to use. While mixed designs have many benefits, they will not be ideal for every research question.

Operationally Defining the IV: Treatment Type and Emotional Triggers

We anticipate that both treatment type and emotional triggers will influence anorexia nervosa, so these are our independent variables. While we have determined what we mean conceptually for each of these factors, we will need to figure out how to make them work in our specific study. That is, we need to operationally define our variables.

To start, we should consider which treatments or psychotherapies we want to compare in our study. While our literature review revealed that professionals use numerous approaches to treat eating disorders, two approaches appeared multiples times: cognitive-behavioral therapy and psychodynamic psychotherapy (Grave et al., 2013; Murphy et al., 2005). Cognitive-behavioral therapy seeks to address dysfunctional emotions and maladaptive behaviors and cognitions (Schacter, Gilbert, & Wegner, 2010). In the case of anorexia nervosa, this therapy focuses on the person's cognitions about body image and eating behaviors, including identifying and managing these issues through goal-oriented procedures. In psychodynamic psychotherapy, the focus is on identifying and resolving the unconscious content of a client's psyche, as well as determining how past experiences are responsible for the client's symptoms (Whitbourne & Halgin, 2013). This form of therapy relies heavily on the interpersonal relationship between client and therapist. Although these two types of therapy are very different in their approaches, we will investigate them in our study because both have demonstrated effectiveness in treating eating disorders. According to our literature review, researchers have not directly compared their effectiveness in treating anorexia nervosa, meaning our study could contribute to the advancement of science. As we have already decided, therapy type will be between-subjects because we already know we do not want our participants to receive both therapy types.

To operationally define emotional triggers, we should think about the goals of our research study. We want to determine whether exposure to particular emotions will reduce or exacerbate anorexia nervosa, so we should consider emotions we encounter on a daily basis, specifically those that might trigger a specific, eating-related behavioral response. Earlier we explored how happiness, boredom, and sadness might impact eating and how nervous energy might lead to eating when we feel anxious or stressed. That last idea relates to some of the research on anxiety in our literature review (Lavender et al., 2013). Perhaps we should focus on anxiety in particular. Remember that we want to see changes within the individual, so we will be using a within-subjects methodology for this factor. That means we need to determine several triggers that would produce different levels of anxiety, and expose participants to each trigger during our study.

Focus on Ethics: Should We Really Do That?

Before making any final decisions about how to manipulate our variables, we should consider our ethical obligations to our participants. After all, we are

What Do You Think?
What other types of emotion do you think might impact anorexia nervosa?

working with a special and potentially vulnerable population. Your first thought might be that research like ours cannot be done with this population because potential participants have a mental disorder. Yet our literature review showed that researchers often focus on this population, which is possible because they make sure to uphold each of the ethical principles. The researchers in those studies guaranteed that they assigned participants to groups in fair and just ways, made sure that participants were healthy enough to freely give informed consent, and demonstrated that their studies had more potential benefit than harm. A deeper understanding of this population could allow us to provide better care and treatment for the disorder. As long as we are ethical in how we conduct the study, the IRB should allow us to do it.

Next, we need to determine whether undergraduate students have the necessary qualifications to research a clinical population. In general, a professional who has experience and training with this population should lead this sort of clinical research, but an undergraduate could still be involved in the research by forming a partnership with a professional in the field. We could find someone who has training and experience in treating eating disorders to help us develop an ethical protocol and conduct the therapeutic part of the study.

Weighing Our Options: Identifying Manipulations

Next we need to consider how best to ethically manipulate our independent variables, given our vulnerable population. We have already established that we want to compare cognitive-behavioral therapy and psychodynamic therapy, but what about using a control group? We could have a placebo group, or a group in which participants think that they are receiving therapy, but are not actually receiving treatment. Although a placebo group helps determine if just the act of believing that one is receiving therapy helps, there could be serious ethical problems with including a placebo group in our study. What if a person in our study knows his anorexia nervosa symptoms are becoming more severe, but believes he is already receiving therapy, and thus does not need to seek additional help? Besides increasing his suffering, this could result in potentially life-threatening conditions for him. The use of a placebo group in this situation is not ethically sound. In fact, some argue that placebo controls are inappropriate for use in medical studies because they may cause unnecessary suffering (Enserink, 2000).

We could have a control group that receives no therapy at all instead. In clinical research like ours, researchers often examine the effect of no treatment through a **waiting-list control group**. Initially, the researcher assesses the participants who are not exposed to the treatment on the dependent variable. After the results of the study become clearer and researchers identify the best form of intervention, participants in the waiting-list control group receive the better treatment at no cost. Still, it is ethically questionable to identify people who need treatment and then purposely withhold treatment from them for even a short period of time. With a life-threatening illness like anorexia nervosa, the costs could far exceed the potential benefits. Another option is to have a **treatment-as-usual group,** or a group that receives an already established treatment throughout the study. Researchers then compare this group to the experimental intervention group to determine if the experimental treatment is more effective than the established

---

▶ How do we protect vulnerable populations in human research? SEE CHAPTER 3, p. 60

▶ What is a placebo group? SEE CHAPTER 9, p. 297

waiting-list control group a control group often used in clinical research; participants in this group do not receive treatment or intervention until after the completion of the study.

treatment-as-usual group a comparison group in clinical studies in which already established treatment is administered for comparison to experimental treatment.

one. Although using this type of control group would allow us to avoid the questionable ethics of people in need receiving no treatment throughout the study, we are not empirically investigating a new type of treatment in our study. Rather, we are comparing two established types of treatment to see which is better and how the different treatments might interact with emotional triggers.

▶ When should you use a control group?
SEE CHAPTER 8, p. 251

Consequently, we should avoid using either a control or a placebo group when manipulating treatment. Instead, we will manipulate our independent variable using types of treatment: cognitive-behavioral therapy and psychodynamic psychotherapy. That way, we can be sure everyone will receive an already established treatment. While this is the best decision ethically, it does limit what questions we can answer with our data. The lack of a control group prevents us from determining whether receiving any treatment is better than no treatment. By just comparing the two types of treatment without a control group, we can only compare the efficacy of the two treatments. This limitation is a good reminder that each design decision we make has specific consequences and that it is difficult to accomplish everything we want to in a single study.

We already know that people with anorexia nervosa experience compromised emotional functioning (Adenzato et al., 2012), so ethically we cannot create too much emotional distress in our participants. Remember that the potential benefits of our study need to outweigh the potential costs. We can seek to limit participants' risk by using a milder form of emotional trigger. While anxiety may be ideal for our research question, it might be too intense for our clinical sample. Instead, we can ethically manipulate stress. We could vary the stress level we expose participants to in an attempt to learn whether they are able to handle mild forms of stress versus more extreme forms, focusing on various forms of everyday stress. Everyone encounters mild stressors in day-to-day life, so experiencing stress in our study would not go beyond our participants' typical daily lives. In fact, we can be sure to introduce the types of mild stress that our participants are most likely to encounter.

Think about the types of stress you experience on a daily basis. Does your schoolwork cause you stress? Have you ever worried about finishing assignments on time or completing them well enough to get a good grade? Perhaps you have experienced stress in your relationships with others. Maybe your roommate left the kitchen a mess again or your sister is driving you crazy. You might also feel stress about what the future holds for you. Have you ever felt anxious about what classes you should take next semester, whether you are making enough money, or what you are going to do after graduation? These are all potential stressors related to your future. Since work, relationships, and the future are all common stressors, perhaps we should use them as inspiration for the emotional triggers in our study. We can see how each individual responds to work stress, relationship stress, and stress about their future.

Another precaution we can take is to make sure our participants complete their designated therapy before we introduce our emotional triggers. That way we do not expose them to the emotional trigger at their most vulnerable time, but, rather, when they should be more resilient, thus reducing the potential negative impact of our trigger. The result is a 2 × 3 mixed design to help us answer our research question. A combination of our independent variables in a mixed design is shown in **Table 12.4.**

TABLE 12.4

Combination of Our Independent Variables in a Mixed Design				
		IV2 (Within) Stressor		
		Level 1 **Work Stress**	**Level 2** **Relationship Stress**	**Level 3** **Future-Related Stress**
IV1 **(Between)** **Therapy** **Type**	**Level 1** **Cognitive-** **Behavioral**	Cognitive-Behavioral × Work Stress	Cognitive-Behavioral × Relationship Stress	Cognitive-Behavioral × Future-Related Stress
	Level 2 **Psychodynamic**	Psychodynamic × Work Stress	Psychodynamic × Relationship Stress	Psychodynamic × Future-Related Stress

Operationally Defining the DV: Anorexia Nervosa

In our study, we are exploring two factors that might impact anorexia nervosa, making anorexia nervosa our dependent variable. While we have decided how to operationally define both our independent variables, we still need to determine how we will assess anorexia nervosa. As we know from the *DSM-5* (American Psychiatric Association, 2013b), specific behaviors and thoughts are associated with anorexia nervosa. As part of our study, we could ask family or friends if they have noticed the participant engaging in behaviors such as excessively exercising or skipping meals. However, loved ones may not be around our participants enough to know that a trip to the gym was actually a 5-hour run on the treadmill. We could assess anorexic tendencies by asking participants to self-report on anorexia-related thoughts and behaviors. If we went this route, we would not need to design a measure since several already exist, such as the Yale-Brown-Cornell Eating Disorder Scale (YBC-EDS; Mazure, Halmi, Sunday, Romano, & Einhorn, 1994) or the Eating Disorder Inventory-3 (EDI-3; Clausen, Rosenvinge, Friborg, & Rokkedal, 2011).

However, if we used a self-report, we could not be certain that our participants were being truthful in their responses, because they might not want to be forthcoming about their struggles. For this reason, there are clinical diagnostic tools that only mental health professionals are qualified to use, as the results may indicate a need for hospitalization or other extreme interventions. Since we are not mental health professionals, we will need to find another way to assess our dependent variable. A better option might be to focus on behaviors related to anorexia nervosa that we can easily observe, such as restricted eating and excessive exercising.

▶ When is using
self-reports
appropriate?
SEE CHAPTER 7, p. 202

Weighing Our Options: Identifying Key Behaviors

Should we measure restricted eating, exercise, or both? We should use the behavior that makes the most sense theoretically and practically. Overexercising is a behavioral symptom of anorexia nervosa that therapy would attempt to remediate or improve. We could give participants the opportunity to exercise (e.g., running on a treadmill) after exposure to one of the emotional triggers, but there would be a number of precautions we would have to take to ensure our participants' safety. For example, we would need to make sure they are healthy enough for aerobic activity based on screening by a medical doctor, have the proper shoes and enough water, and sign waivers in case they sustain an injury, etc. Instead, we could just ask participants to report how many minutes they would like to exercise. In this case, they would not have to actually exercise, since we would only need to know how long they would like to do it. The complication with this type of self-report is that what they report wanting to do may not be what they actually would do if given the opportunity.

A different approach would be to focus on undereating, another behavioral symptom of the disorder that therapy aims to address. This idea has more theoretical support than exercise. Even for those with nondisordered eating, emotions sometimes lead to excessive or restricted eating (Geliebter & Aversa, 2003). We could again use a behavioral choice and ask participants if they want to eat after exposure to an emotional trigger, or we could actually give them the opportunity to eat, presenting participants with a taste test where they could eat a particular food. We could ask them to eat enough to fully and accurately judge the taste and quality of a food we provide. Later, we could determine how much, if any, of the food the participant consumed.

▶ Is self-report a dependable way to measure behavior? SEE CHAPTER 4, p. 88

Our Hypothesis

Now that we have defined the individual pieces of our study, it is time to make predictions about how the independent variables will affect the dependent variable. Our research question necessitated using multiple independent variables, which means we will need multiple hypotheses as well. In all, we need two main effect hypotheses, as well as an interaction effect hypothesis. Each main effect hypothesis focuses on only one independent variable, while the interaction hypothesis is a prediction of how the two independent variables might combine to have a unique impact on the dependent variable.

First, we should consider our main effect hypothesis regarding treatment type. No studies in our literature review provided a direct comparison of these two therapy types. The *DSM-5* (American Psychiatric Association, 2013b) clearly notes that there are maladaptive thoughts and behaviors associated with anorexia nervosa. The overall goal of cognitive-behavioral therapy is to identify and change problematic thoughts and behaviors, while psychodynamic psychotherapy focuses on resolving unconscious content and past experiences. For this particular disorder, cognitive-behavioral therapy might help our participants more because it more directly addresses the key aspects of the disorder. This therapy may result in a willingness to eat when asked to do a taste test in our study. Remember that our prediction should reflect the comparison between our two groups of participants. Thus, we can test the following hypothesis:

> **Main Effect 1:** *Those completing cognitive-behavioral psychotherapy will be more likely to eat than those completing psychodynamic psychotherapy.*

Second, we need to consider our main effect hypothesis for emotional triggers. We decided that our participants would experience mild forms of stress after treatment. In particular, we decided to test stress related to work life, relationships, and the future. We next need to consider which forms of mild stress might impact our dependent variable differently than the others. While everyone might feel stress in each of these circumstances, relationship stress might be the toughest. One can often take action, such as better time management, to solve work stress. One can also reduce future-related stress by taking concrete steps toward improving in the future, such as by seeking out more job experience.

What Do You Think?
What other behaviors could we use to measure anorexia nervosa?

▶ What types of experimental designs lead to interaction hypotheses? SEE CHAPTER 11, p. 366

In both cases, there is some control over the situation. Relationships by definition involve another person, which provides less overall control and perhaps higher stress. Therefore, relationship stress may result in exacerbated anorexic behaviors, such as a reduced desire to eat, compared to the other two levels of stress. This time our prediction should reflect the within-subjects nature of the independent variable. Hence, we will test the following hypothesis:

Main Effect 2: After exposure to relationship stress, participants will be less likely to eat compared to after exposure to either future-related stress or work stress. There will be no difference in eating behavior between work stress and future-related stress.

Last, we need to think about how each of our independent variables will affect one another. In our main effect hypotheses, we made predictions about each independent variable separately. When hypothesizing an interaction, we need to think about how treatment type and emotional triggers will jointly influence eating behavior. Given the logic we have already used for our main effect predictions, we might predict that psychodynamic psychotherapy and relationship stress will combine to reduce eating while the other combinations will lead to more eating. We can predict the following:

Interaction Effect: Participants completing psychodynamic psychotherapy will be less likely to eat when exposed to relationship stress than any other combination of treatment and stress.

YOUR TURN 12.1

1. Etta wants to determine whether Fourth of July fireworks or parades make people feel more patriotic. All of her participants first attend a parade and then, 8 hours later, a fireworks display in the same town. After each event, research assistants offer flag stickers for participants to wear on their clothes. Etta assumes those feeling patriotic will be more likely to wear the sticker. What type of methodology is Etta using?
   a. Between-subjects
   b. Within-subjects
   c. Correlational
   d. Mixed

2. Professor Inquisitive wonders if using PowerPoint during a lecture helps students take better class notes. To test this idea, she first gives a lecture without PowerPoint and then evaluates the accuracy of the students' class notes. The next day, she adds a PowerPoint to her lecture and assesses their note accuracy again. On day three, she returns to lecturing without the PowerPoint and assesses note accuracy for a third time. Which type of design is she using?
   a. A-B design
   b. A-B-A design
   c. A-B-A-B design
   d. Mixed design

3. Vernon wants to know the best dessert to make for the psychology club's next bake sale, as he wants the club to make the most money possible. He specifically wants to know the influence of both chocolate flavor and type of dessert on the price he can charge for the dessert, so he designs a study to test each variable. He assigns half of his participants to the chocolate condition and half to the nonchocolate condition. Those in the chocolate condition try some chocolate cookies, a chocolate cake, and a chocolate pie. After each one, the participants write down how much they would pay for that dessert. Those in the nonchocolate condition also sample nonchocolate cookies, cake, and pie, writing down how much they would pay for each of those desserts. What type of design is Vernon using?

   a. Between-subjects
   b. Within-subjects
   c. Correlational
   d. Mixed

How did you do? Turn to the end of the chapter to check your answers.

Design in Action

We have decided how to manipulate our independent variables (treatment type and emotional triggers) and measure our dependent variable (anorexia nervosa). However, we still need to think through how to turn these pieces into a viable research design.

Weighing Our Options: Manipulating Treatment Type

While we know we want to compare cognitive-behavioral therapy and psycho-dynamic psychotherapy, we still have to decide who will administer therapy to our participants (since we are not qualified) and for how long. We could search for local therapists with expertise in eating disorders, finding one who specializes in treating anorexia nervosa with cognitive-behavioral therapy and another who specializes in psychodynamic psychotherapy. We would want to maximize experimental control by attempting to match the two therapists on level of education (e.g., MA or PsyD), experience in the field (e.g., 10 years after licensure), age, gender, and personality. However, even with all of this matching, we could not be sure that the therapy type was the only difference between the therapists. By using two different therapists, we introduce a potential confound because we would have something other than the treatment (i.e., differences between the therapists) systematically varying over conditions. If we were to find differences in the dependent variables at the conclusion of our study, we would have no way to discern if the type of therapy or a difference between the two therapists impacted the results. To avoid this potential confound, we need to find one therapist who has experience with eating disorders and has training and experience using both types of therapy.

Can you identify potential confounds in a study? SEE CHAPTER 9, p. 295

We also need to decide how long the treatment phase of our experiment should last. We want our study's treatment to mirror the same treatment our participants would receive in real life, so we should investigate the average length of treatment that others use. In one study using cognitive-behavioral therapy, participants received weekly 45-minute one-on-one sessions over a 40-week period (Grave et al., 2013). Similarly, a study employing psychodynamic therapy treated participants between 20 and 40 weeks through weekly individual sessions (Murphy et al., 2005). Based on this information, we should have our participants receive individual therapy for 45 minutes weekly for a total of 40 weeks.

Weighing Our Options: Manipulating Emotional Triggers

For ethical reasons, we decided to use relationship stress, work stress, and stress about the future as emotional triggers. Next we need to figure out how we are going to induce these different types of stress. We could create stress by having participants watch a short video clip of others in stressful situations related to work, relationships, or the future. Although watching someone else's stress might vicariously elevate our own stress, it is not the same as feeling the stress ourselves. Instead, we could ask participants to read scenarios or vignettes in which they imagine themselves feeling stress due to work, relationships, or the future. Still, we want the experience of stress to have strong ecological validity so that the research situation mimics the real-life psychological experience of stress in our study. Can we find a way to have participants genuinely experience mild stress? Perhaps we can have them think about their own concerns about their current relationships, work situations, and futures. We could have participants describe a specific concern they have about each stressor and why the issue concerns them. This method allows the participants to personalize each type of stressful experience and, hopefully, feel real stress as they write about each situation.

▶ How can one increase ecological validity in a study?
SEE CHAPTER 6, p. 164

Are movies or video clips an effective way to alter emotions in a research study? Are the emotions you feel watching a movie the same as they would be if you were experiencing the event yourself? *(uniquely India/Getty Images)*

Weighing Our Options: Measuring Anorexia Nervosa

We have already decided to use the behavioral measure of food consumption to assess behaviors associated with anorexia nervosa. But how will we make this happen? We want to use food that is easy to quantify or count in order to measure consumption. For this reason, something like a sandwich would not work well. We could offer participants Skittles or M&Ms with the supposed purpose of providing a taste rating for potential use in a future experiment, starting the study with a specific number of candy pieces in a bowl, and then counting the number of remaining pieces after the participant completes the study. However, considering our sample, asking our participants to eat unhealthy food such as candy may add unintentional stress or additional risk to participants. This may also lead a majority of participants to refuse to eat any, which would result in a floor effect where we are not able to differentiate participants because the scores are all so low (e.g., eating zero pieces of candy). To avoid these problems, we should use a healthier food, such as grapes. Once again, we can count individual grapes both before and after the taste test portion of the study. The number of grapes participants eat out of the, say, 30 we provide will indicate their interest in eating. By providing a healthy food and giving them the choice of how much to eat, we can create an ethical way to measure eating behavior.

Because we cannot be confident that we have eliminated the potential for a floor effect entirely (we could still have many participants who choose not to eat anything), we should have a second behavioral measure that might also indicate interest in eating. One strategy for reducing the temptation to eat is to keep the food out of reach. To incorporate this idea into our study, when we give the participants the grapes, we could hand them the grapes in a bowl and ask the participants to take it over to where they will sit to do the taste test. The participant would then have to set the bowl down to complete the taste test, allowing us to measure how far away from themselves they place the bowl of grapes on the table. Placing the bowl farther away from the seat, as measured in inches, would suggest less desire to eat. By including this measure, we are operationalizing our dependent variable using two different behavioral measures without taking much time or further burdening our participants.

Weighing Our Options: Obtaining Participants

How will we obtain participants for our study? Ideally, we would use a random sample; however, that would mean selecting participants at random from the entire population of people with anorexia nervosa, which would be very time consuming and expensive to do. For ease, we will use a convenience sample by getting referrals from local general practitioners who, based on yearly checkups, suspect a patient may have an eating disorder. To determine whether or not these patients qualify for the study, the therapist we have partnered with will do a psychiatric assessment on potential participants. Prospective participants must meet the *DSM-5* (American Psychiatric Association, 2013b) diagnostic criteria for anorexia nervosa. To ensure as much similarity as possible between participants before the study begins, we will only accept participants who have not undergone formal treatment for their disorder. Prior treatment might interfere with the treatment we provide throughout the study and could complicate the results of our study later. Similarly, to avoid the complication of other disorders playing a role in our study, we will only accept those with no comorbid mental health disorders. We also want to make sure that participants are medically stable enough to receive outpatient treatment, so we will not accept participants who are at a life-threatening point in the disorder, as those people should be under the constant care of an inpatient facility. We have to be certain our participants are medically and mentally stable enough to fully understand the risks, benefits, and requirements of the study, and to give their informed consent.

There are still two more requirements we should consider in our list of restrictions about participation: age and gender. Although many adolescents suffer from anorexia nervosa, the average onset occurs at age 19 (Hudson, Hiripi, Pope, & Kessler, 2007). Our research question does not speculate about a particular age group. While those younger than 18 years of age can give assent and their legal guardians can give consent, this could be an unnecessary complication to our research project. Therefore, we will only recruit participants who

▶ How do researchers detect a floor effect? SEE CHAPTER 4, p. 104

▶ Why does psychological research often use convenience sampling? SEE CHAPTER 4, p. 111

▶ Can researchers
ethically use minors in
human research?
SEE CHAPTER 3, p. 65

are 18 years of age or older for our study. We also need to consider gender. The majority of people with anorexia nervosa are female, with only 0.3% of males in the population suffering from the disorder (Hudson et al., 2007). This means that recruitment of male participants will be more difficult. Still, there may be significant differences between males and females in the manifestation of the disorder. As the focus of our study does not include gender differences, and it will be difficult to obtain enough males in our sample, it is best to include only females in our study. Thus, we are offering study enrollment to medically stable people who have anorexia nervosa and are female, are 18 years of age or older, and have no coexisting mental health problems.

With such strict criteria, we should expect that we will have to turn away some participants who would have been otherwise willing to participate in our study. We may also have participants who become medically unstable and need to discontinue the study to receive more intense inpatient treatment. During the study, it may become apparent that some are also suffering from another mental health issue and no longer fit our criteria. Attrition is a concern, too, given that our study requires 40 weeks of treatment. Some participants may stop therapy before the 40 weeks is over because they feel the treatment is too taxing or takes too much time. Alternately, some may decide they are feeling better 20 weeks into the study and stop their treatment, and some may move or have other reasons they can no longer participate. Remember, participants can leave our study at any time without penalty or judgment. For this reason, we may need to offer participation to more people than we think we actually want to have in the study. That way, we can still be sure our study has enough power to adequately test our hypotheses, even if we lose a few participants.

▶ Why does attrition
represent a potential
threat to internal validity?
SEE CHAPTER 10, p. 324

▶ What role does sample
size play in power?
SEE CHAPTER 9, p. 294

Focus on Ethics: Should We Really Do That?

While research on clinical populations like ours is common and important, we have to be especially careful in how we conduct these studies. For example, we have to be sure participation is entirely voluntary. Potential participants may feel coerced to volunteer for a potentially dangerous study if the payment or reward for participation is too enticing. You may be thinking that this is not a concern for us since we are not offering any rewards or inducements to participate in our study. However, you must think about this study from the potential participants' perspectives. An underlying benefit of their participation is free therapy for 40 weeks. For one reason or another, participants may be desperate for help they cannot afford. The benefit of free therapy for an extended period of time might cross the line into coercion for some potential participants. To combat this, we must offer information about free treatment that does not require participation in our study. That way, we can be certain participants give their consent freely and not out of desire for the free therapy associated with our study.

▶ What ethical principle
does coercion violate?
SEE CHAPTER 3, p. 61

We have already decided for ethical reasons not to have a waiting-list or placebo control, so everyone in our study will receive therapy. Currently, health professionals use both cognitive-behavioral therapy and psychodynamic therapies to treat the disorder (Grave et al., 2013; Leichsenring, 2005), so there is no reason to believe that either therapy will hurt our participants. In a sense, we are comparing two treatment-as-usual groups. Still, we must monitor participants for any potential adverse effects and be ready to act if we see any sign that our participants are suffering. If at any point we have evidence that one form of therapy is detrimental to our participants, we must immediately stop that form of treatment to minimize harm, and offer those participants other treatment. Additionally, if we find that one type of therapy is clearly more effective, it will be inappropriate to allow participants to continue receiving inferior treatment when we know the other therapy is more helpful. In this case, we will stop the study early and switch our participants to the more beneficial treatment as soon as possible. If we do not know the benefit of one treatment over another until the conclusion of our study, we should offer the better treatment for free to the participants in the inferior treatment group after the study concludes.

Considering the medical danger of anorexia nervosa, we certainly have an ethical obligation to monitor the physical safety of our participants throughout our study. Each week during therapy, we should have our partner therapist weigh our participants. If at any point we notice a dramatic decline in BMI, suggesting that the disorder is worsening, or a consistent lack of increase in BMI, indicating that treatment is not working, we will drop the affected participant from our study and immediately place them in inpatient therapy.

Developing a Protocol

We have already made some basic design decisions about how to manipulate and measure our variables, as well as who we will recruit as our participants. Next, we need to develop a procedure for administering the study, starting with how we will assign participants to conditions.

Assigning Participants to Conditions

Our first independent variable, treatment type, will be a between-subjects variable, meaning that half of our participants will receive cognitive-behavioral therapy, while the other half will receive psychodynamic psychotherapy from the same therapist. We could allow participants to decide for themselves which therapy they want to receive. Although this freedom is very accommodating to participants, it could bias our results. Allowing participants to select or even know which treatment group they are in could create a situation where participants go into the therapy expecting it to be effective (or ineffective). This could lead to a self-fulfilling prophecy, where participants act in ways that result in the expected outcome. For instance, if a participant believes a particular therapy will be effective, she may be more motivated to actively engage in the therapy, resulting in a more positive outcome than would otherwise occur without this additional motivation. If participants feel strongly about participating in our study only if they receive a certain type of treatment, then we will refer them to free therapy options outside our study.

We need a way to balance participants' individual differences—such as age, duration of illness, extent of illness, and so on—between both groups. The best way to do this is through random assignment. Random assignment ensures that these individual differences have an equal chance of making it into the cognitive-behavioral therapy group and psychodynamic psychotherapy group. If our sample is large enough and our assignment is truly random, individual

▶ How does random assignment diminish the impact of individual differences?
SEE CHAPTER 8, p. 261

What Do You Think?

What other individual differences might participants in our study have?

▶ How do we incorporate counterbalancing into our study?
SEE CHAPTER 10, p. 336

differences will not greatly influence our results, and the two therapy groups should be comparable at our study's onset.

We still have another independent variable to consider: emotional triggers. We decided to evoke three different forms of mild stress as a within-subjects factor. This time, we do not need to worry about randomly assigning participants to one group or another, because all participants will receive all three levels of the independent variable. For ease, we could determine an order of exposure and keep it consistent for everyone in the study (e.g., each person would always be exposed to the relationship stress first, the work stress second, and the future-related stress last). But as you learned in Chapter 10, order effects make this approach problematic. If the order remains constant, each emotional trigger's impact may depend on whether it appears first, second, or last, and not based on the emotion itself. For example, let's assume we find that relationship stress exacerbates anorexia nervosa more than the other types of stress. If we always presented relationship stress first, our finding may actually be that the first type of stress participants encounter is always the most troublesome. To avoid having order influence our results, we will use counterbalancing. With this method, we will determine every possible sequence of exposure to future-related stress, work stress, and relationship stress and then randomly assign each participant to a sequence. This method ensures we represent all sequences equally throughout the study.

Procedure

Now that we know how we will assign participants to the conditions, we need to consider the participant experience, starting with consent and ending with debriefing. After initial screening for study qualification, we will inform potential participants about the study and invite them to join it. Participants who give their informed consent will move into the treatment phase of the study. We will randomly assign each participant to receive either cognitive-behavioral therapy or psychodynamic psychotherapy in individual sessions with the same therapist for 45 minutes a week for 40 consecutive weeks. Each week, the therapist will weigh the participants and calculate their BMI to determine that they are physically healthy enough to proceed in the study.

One week after the treatment concludes, we will expose participants to the emotional triggers. For this phase of the study, we will ask participants to minimize eating for 3 hours before the study because we do not want a recent meal to prevent our participants from sampling the assigned food. To make this request easier for participants, we will schedule data collection between meal times, such as at 3 p.m.

Based on the randomly assigned sequence, we will expose the participant to the first emotional trigger. To do this, we will have participants recall and describe a specific concern they have about work, their future, or a relationship in their life, and why the issue is a concern for them. Should we let participants take as much time as they need to complete the assigned writing prompt? Does it really matter if it takes some people 5 minutes to write about the event and others 20 minutes? Remember that this is our stress manipulation, so we want the writing experience to be as similar as possible for each person. If one person only spends 5 minutes writing and another spends 15 minutes writing, the one taking 15 minutes might experience the associated stress more intensely or for longer. To help keep this part of the study consistent, we will give everyone 15 minutes to complete each writing prompt. If people finish earlier, we will ask them to reread their story until the 15 minutes is over. This way, we can keep how long everyone is thinking about the concern fairly consistent. To be sure the writing prompt is inducing stress the way we hope it will, we should include a manipulation check that asks participants how stressed they feel after each writing prompt. After the 15 minutes of writing concludes, participants will move on to the eating portion of the study.

▶ What important information can a manipulation check provide?
SEE CHAPTER 8, p. 265

Our plan is to mildly deceive participants about the nature of the eating task by saying we would like them to taste test the food for potential use in another study. Given the within-subjects nature of this independent variable, we need to offer the participants food on three different occasions as we expose them to each of the different emotional triggers. This means we need to tweak our cover story. We will further explain that participants will receive one of three types of white grapes to taste test, so we can determine which is best. However, in reality, the grapes will all be the same to keep that aspect controlled. We will tell participants they are free to eat as many or as few grapes as they need to complete a short questionnaire about the quality and taste of the grapes. Our dependent variables are the number of grapes each participant eats and where participants place the bowl on the desk in front of them. For this part of the study, we will need to move participants into a new room after the stress induction and hand them the bowl of grapes as they enter the room. We will ask them to have a seat at the desk across the room. This will encourage them to walk across the room with the bowl and place it where they like. We will give them as much time as they need to sample the grapes and complete a short survey about the taste of the grapes.

Next we need to decide when we will expose participants to the other two levels of emotional triggers. Logistically, it would be easiest to wait just a few minutes before moving on to the next type of stress and next tasting, as we could finish each participant's data collection in a single day. However, this would be problematic for several reasons. First, our stress induction may last a while. If it does, we could have carryover effects, with the stress from one trigger still lingering when we move on to the next trigger. Another concern is the food assessment. We ask participants to freely eat so we can determine food consumption. Offering participants bowl after bowl of grapes all in one sitting, however, is not ideal. Participants might eat some from the first bowl and then be too full to eat more right away, which would be problematic because their lack of eating would be due to basic satiation and not due to symptoms of their disorder.

▶ What factors hurt internal validity?
SEE CHAPTER 10, p. 324

Based on these concerns, we should space out the emotional triggers, but for how long? The longer it takes to run our study, the more likely it is we will run into potential problems with attrition, history, or external events that might influence eating. We have to balance out these competing issues. After 40 weeks of therapy, our participants will be in a routine where they come in once a week for our study. Sticking with this pattern might help increase the odds that participants continue to come to the study and will provide enough time for carryover effects to subside. So, we will have participants continue to come in for three more weeks, exposing them to one type of stress each week, followed by the taste test. Before the study is complete, we should also gather demographic information about our participants (e.g., age, ethnicity, etc.) so we can describe our sample to others.

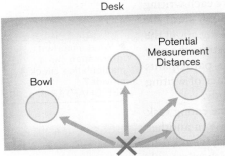

Desk

Potential Measurement Distances

Bowl

Starting Point for Measurement

Participant Chair

FIGURE 12.1. Measuring Bowl Distance.

▶ What is a demand characteristic? SEE CHAPTER 4, p. 90

experimenter-expectancy effect occurs when a bias causes a researcher to unconsciously influence the participants of an experiment; also known as expectancy bias or experimenter effect.

double-blind procedure both the participants and the administrators of treatment are unaware of, or blind to, the types of treatment being provided in order to reduce the likelihood that expectancies or knowledge of condition will influence the results.

single-blind procedure participants are unaware of, or blind to, the types of treatment they are receiving, but the administrator knows.

Do not forget that we need to fully debrief each participant about the variables, hypotheses, and cover story deception after we have finished collecting all the data on that particular participant. Each week, after we release participants from the study, we will record how many of the 30 grapes the participant ate and the distance in inches between the table's edge (from the point centered in front of the participant's chair) to the nearest top edge of the bowl, as shown in **Figure 12.1**.

Double- and Single-Blind Procedures

Now that we have considered the participant experience in our study, we need to think about the researcher's experience. The therapist we are partnering with will have an ongoing relationship with our participants for 40 weeks. While the participants may not know the type of therapy they receive, the therapist will have to know this information. The concern from a research design perspective is that the therapist might introduce demand characteristics, or cues about what we expect from the participant, potentially biasing our results. Similarly, as the administrator of the emotional triggers, you might display an **experimenter-expectancy effect**, also known as an **expectancy bias** or **experimenter effect**. This occurs when a bias leads a researcher to unconsciously influence the participants of an experiment. You might expect the relationship stress condition to eat less, and thus unconsciously do things to encourage less eating, such as being less friendly with participants in this condition. For this reason, many studies often develop a **double-blind procedure**. In these studies, both the participants and the treatment administrators are unaware of, or blind to, the types of treatment they provide to participants. This is easy to manage in medical studies, where the medication and placebo are virtually identical, such that the patient and the nurse or physician cannot easily differentiate between the experimental drug and the placebo. A double-blind procedure helps to reduce the likelihood that expectancies or knowledge of condition will influence the results.

In our study, we cannot use a double-blind procedure with our therapist. Our therapist will have to know which form of therapy he or she is giving to participants. When the administrators of a study know which treatment they are assigning, but the participants do not, it is a **single-blind procedure**. We can try to minimize bias by not revealing our hypothesis about therapy type to the therapist. That way, the therapist cannot unintentionally bias the results to confirm the hypothesis. Likewise, when we administer the emotional triggers to participants, we will stay blind to the type of therapy the participant received. We can go one step further and make the researcher's role in the study double-blind by coding each emotional trigger condition. We could have a research assistant label each condition with a code, such as relationship stress as condition A, work stress as B, and future-related stress as C. Through counterbalancing, we will know the sequence of exposures (e.g., B, A, C), but not know what each letter represents. Instead of telling the participants the instructions for the writing prompt out loud, we should also have the research assistant put the writing prompt in an envelope that the participants open in privacy. Then, the research assistant will not know the participants' emotional trigger conditions while interacting during the experiment.

Thinking Like a Scientist in Real Life

How to Trust an Opinion

The single-blind procedure is not limited to lab research. This is a technique you have likely employed in your everyday life. Ever had a decision to make and sought out others for advice? Suppose you are looking to buy a new smartphone. Without expressing your opinion and without telling them why you are asking, you ask a few friends or family members what they think of the latest iPhone. In this case, you want to make sure what they tell you is their true viewpoint, not simply what they think you want to hear. Imagine that you ask your dad how he likes his new iPhone, and he starts raving about it. After telling him that you are thinking of purchasing one, he immediately backtracks, saying the iPhone is really not that great, especially considering the expense, because he is worried about your finances. Which of your dad's opinions about the new iPhone are we more likely to believe? The first one, of course! We are more likely to trust his unbiased response, before he knew the reason you were asking about the iPhone, over the biased one. When your source of information has no idea why you are asking your questions, you are mimicking the single-blind procedure that researchers use in their studies. Both you and the researchers are trying to avoid potential bias by minimizing or eliminating any information that could alter an honest response.

Focus on Open Science: Preregistering Your Hypotheses, Materials, and Data Analysis Plan

Now that we have made key decisions about our study, we can preregister it on an open science website (e.g., http://clinicaltrials.gov). We will share our decisions about the independent variables involved, as well as the levels of each, and describe our choice to use a mixed design. We will also explain the two ways we will behaviorally assess the dependent variable. Given that we plan to use writing prompts to manipulate stress in our study, we will post them as well. Once we have a data analysis plan, we will post it for others to review along with our data set.

YOUR TURN 12.2

1. To avoid order effects in her study, Roshini determines the order of all potential treatment sequences of her within-subjects independent variable. She then places all the sequences into a hat and draws out a sequence for each participant. What method is she using?
   a. Randomization
   b. Counterbalancing
   c. Latin square
   d. Random selection

2. In a study examining the effectiveness of a new antidepressant, Nurse Rory administers all the study participants' medications. Because both the active medication and placebo are the same size, shape, and color, neither Nurse Rory nor the participants know the condition in which they are participating. What type of study is this?

a. Mixed design study

b. Single-subject design study

c. Single-blind study

d. Double-blind study

3. Carl studies compassion and wants participants in his study to really experience the act of nurturing. Instead of having participants recall a time when they were nurturing, he has them take care of a kitten for 5 minutes. Carl is trying to ensure his study has good

a. ecological validity.

b. external validity.

c. reliability.

d. sensitivity.

How did you do? Turn to the end of the chapter to check your answers.

Statistics: In Search of Answers

We started with a question about how therapy type and emotional triggers impact anorexia nervosa. Now that we have collected data, we have information indicating each participant's therapy type, which emotional trigger she experienced, and how many grapes she consumed, as well as where she placed her bowl after each emotional trigger. With the help of statistics, this information will tell us if therapy, emotional triggers, and/or their combination influence participants' eating behaviors.

As we create our data set, shown in **Figure 12.2**, we need to include the participant numbers, demographic variables, and information about our independent and dependent variables. Remember that we have two independent variables, one between-subjects variable and one within-subjects variable, which means that

	Participant_num	Therapy	Rel_grapes	Work_grapes	Future_grapes	Rel_distance	Work_distance	Future_distance	Gender	Age	Ethnicity
1	33.00	Psychodynamic	.00	.00	.00	12.75	7.00	14.75	female	28.00	European Ancestry
2	39.00	Psychodynamic	.00	.00	.00	10.75	14.00	11.50	female	22.00	Asian or Eastern Ancestry
3	61.00	Psychodynamic	.00	.00	.00	11.25	8.50	9.66	female	20.00	Black or African Ancestry
4	63.00	Cognitive-Behavioral	.00	.00	.00	12.66	7.75	8.25	female	27.00	European Ancestry
5	2.00	Psychodynamic	.00	5.00	5.00	14.33	16.50	12.25	female	19.00	Black or African Ancestry
6	35.00	Psychodynamic	.00	7.00	9.00	7.50	9.50	8.00	female	40.00	European Ancestry
7	13.00	Cognitive-Behavioral	.00	8.00	6.00	15.00	6.00	6.33	female	18.00	European Ancestry
8	49.00	Psychodynamic	.00	9.00	5.00	10.25	10.25	10.00	female	20.00	European Ancestry
9	25.00	Cognitive-Behavioral	1.00	1.00	3.00	12.33	10.50	12.25	female	23.00	Hispanic, Latino, or of Spanish Ancestry
10	52.00	Psychodynamic	1.00	5.00	3.00	11.00	13.33	12.33	female	18.00	European Ancestry

FIGURE 12.2 Example of an SPSS Data Spreadsheet. *(SPSS)*

we need to handle each differently in our data set. For the independent variable of therapy type, we will create a column named "Therapy" and represent group assignment as follows: 1 = Cognitive-behavioral and 2 = Psychodynamic. Our other independent variable is emotional triggers, or, more specifically, three different origins of stress. Because this variable is within-subjects, we have dependent variable measurements for each stress condition (relationship stress, work stress, and future-related stress). For this reason, we cannot create a "stress" variable with three levels like we do for between-subjects independent variables, and then an additional variable to indicate the dependent variable measurement for that stress level. Instead, we need to create a column in the data where we will record the dependent variable measurement for that stress level. First, we need three columns to represent the combination of the three emotional triggers and the dependent variable of number of grapes consumed. We will label them as "rel_grapes," "work_grapes," and "future_grapes" to represent the number of grapes consumed after each stress type. Next, we will do the same for bowl distance by adding another three columns, "rel_distance," "work_distance," and "future_distance," and entering the bowl distance measurements we took after each stress type. As we enter data, we should enter one participant at a time, with each participant's information occupying a single row, aligning the information with the proper column.

Selecting the Proper Tool

Now that we have the data properly entered, we are ready to test our three hypotheses. As you recall, we have one hypothesis about therapy type, one about emotional triggers, and one about the interaction between therapy and emotional triggers. Although we have three hypotheses, we do not need to run three different analyses. This is because there is one statistical analysis that tests all three hypotheses of a mixed design at once. A **mixed design analysis of variance (mixed design ANOVA)** tests for differences between two or more independent variables, where at least one is a between-subjects variable and another is a within-subjects variable. This ANOVA will simultaneously test all three of our predictions by testing for a main effect for treatment, a main effect for origin of stress, and an interaction effect for the two. Essentially, our mixed design ANOVA is a combination of a repeated-measures ANOVA and a factorial ANOVA. As always, we will look for the significance, or p-value, in our study to be below .05. Because we have two dependent variables, we will test each hypothesis twice, once for each dependent variable, as shown in **Table 12.5**.

mixed design analysis of variance (mixed design ANOVA) a statistical analysis that tests for differences between two or more categorical independent variables, where at least one is a between-subjects variable and another is a within-subjects variable.

TABLE 12.5

Combinations of Independent Variables and Levels				
		IV2 (Within)		
		Level 1	**Level 2**	**Level 3**
IV1 (Between)	**Level 1**	IV1 (Level 1) × IV2 (Level 1)	IV1 (Level 1) × IV2 (Level 2)	IV1 (Level 1) × IV2 (Level 3)
	Level 2	IV1 (Level 2) × IV2 (Level 1)	IV1 (Level 2) × IV2 (Level 2)	IV1 (Level 2) × IV2 (Level 3)

Writing the Results in APA Style: Mixed Design ANOVA

Results

Grapes Consumed

A 2 therapy type (cognitive-behavioral therapy vs. psychodynamic psychotherapy) × 3 emotional trigger (relationship stress, work stress, and future-related stress) mixed design ANOVA on the number of grapes consumed revealed a main effect for type of treatment, $F(1, 61) = 12.10$, $p = .001$, eta$^2 = .166$. Those in the cognitive-behavioral therapy condition ($M = 14.43$, $SD = 8.06$) consumed more grapes overall compared to participants who received psychodynamic therapy ($M = 8.27$, $SD = 7.36$). The main effect for stress was also significant, $F(2, 122) = 14.62$, $p < .001$, eta$^2 = .193$. Post hoc testing (Bonferonni) indicated that participants in the relationship stress condition ($M = 9.19$, $SD = 7.73$) ate significantly fewer grapes than participants in either the work stress ($M = 12.65$, $SD = 8.64$, $p < .001$) or future-related stress conditions ($M = 12.36$, $SD = 8.45$, $p = .001$). Grape consumption did not differ between the work and future-related stress conditions ($p = 1.00$). The interaction between treatment type and stress was not significant, $F(2, 122) = 1.18$, $p = .312$, eta$^2 = .019$. The number of grapes participants consumed in each therapy condition did not depend on which emotional trigger they experienced. See Table 12.6 for means and standard deviations for the number of grapes consumed.

Bowl Distance

A 2 therapy type (cognitive-behavioral therapy vs. psychodynamic) × 3 emotional trigger (relationship stress, work stress, and future-related stress) mixed design ANOVA on bowl distance did not reveal a main effect for treatment, $F(1, 61) = 1.00$, $p = .320$, eta$^2 = .016$. Participants in the cognitive-behavioral therapy condition ($M = 9.67$, $SD = 3.05$) placed their bowls a similar distance away from themselves as those in the psychodynamic condition ($M = 9.09$, $SD = 2.80$). The main effect for type of emotional trigger was also not significant, $F(2, 122) = 1.38$, $p = .254$, eta$^2 = .022$. Participants did not differ in where they placed their bowls after exposure to the relationship stress condition ($M = 9.78$, $SD = 2.70$), work stress condition ($M = 9.22$, $SD = 3.03$), or future-related stress condition ($M = 9.17$, $SD = 3.10$). The interaction between treatment type and stress was not significant, $F(2, 122) = 1.73, p = .182$, eta^2 = .016, indicating that where participants placed the bowl did not depend on what treatment they received or what emotional trigger they had experienced.

Don't Just Tell Me, Show Me: Using Tables and Figures

Just as discussed in Chapter 11, researchers often include cell means and marginal means in a table instead of in the text of a results section. One can convey cell means more easily in a table than describing them in the text. See **Table 12.6** for means and standard deviations for the number of grapes consumed. See **Figure 12.3** for the effect of treatment types and emotional triggers on bowl distance, and refer to **Figure 12.4** for the anatomy of a mixed design ANOVA.

TABLE 12.6

Means and Standard Deviations for Number of Grapes Consumed			
	Emotional Trigger		
Therapy Type	Relationship Stress	Work Stress	Future-Related Stress	Overall Mean
Cognitive-Behavioral Therapy	11.63 (7.73)	16.10 (8.58)	15.55 (7.88)	14.43
Psychodynamic Therapy	6.68 (7.00)	9.08 (7.24)	9.05 (7.84)	8.27
Overall Mean	9.19	12.65	12.36	

Note: N for each cell = 31–32. The main effect for treatment was significant $F(1, 61) = 12.10$, $p = .001$, eta^2 = .166, and the main effect for stress was significant, $F(2, 122) = 14.62, p < .001$, eta^2 = .193. The interaction was not significant.

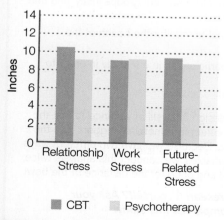

FIGURE 12.3 Treatment Type and Emotional Triggers on Bowl Distance.

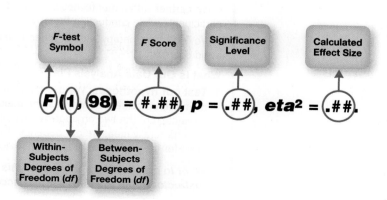

FIGURE 12.4 Anatomy of a Mixed Design ANOVA.

Our Research Plan at a Glance

What Is Our Research Question? How do treatment types and emotional triggers impact anorexia nervosa?

What Is Our Design? We are using a 2 × 3 mixed experimental design.

Why Are We Using This Design? This design allows us to combine between-subjects and within-subjects methods. The strengths of the within-subjects aspects compensate for the weaknesses of the between-subjects aspects and vice versa.

What Are Our Variables?
  Independent Variable(s):
    Treatment Type: Cognitive-Behavioral Therapy or Psychodynamic Psychotherapy
    Emotional Triggers: Work Stress, Relationship Stress, Future-Related Stress
  Dependent Variable(s): Anorexia Nervosa (more specifically, the number of grapes participants eat during a "taste test" and how far away they place the bowl of grapes from themselves)

What Are Our Hypotheses?
  Main Effect for Therapy: Those completing cognitive-behavioral therapy will be more likely to eat than those completing psychodynamic psychotherapy.
  Main Effect for Emotional Trigger: After exposure to relationship stress, participants will be less likely to eat compared to after exposure to either future-related stress or work stress. There will be no difference in eating behavior between work stress and future-related stress.
  Interaction Effect: Participants completing psychodynamic psychotherapy will be less likely to eat when exposed to relationship stress than any other combination of treatment and stress.

Who Are Our Participants? A convenience sample of medically stable females over the age of 18 who have anorexia nervosa, no coexisting mental health problems, and no history of treatment.

What Ethical Considerations Do We Need to Keep in Mind?
- We are using a vulnerable population and therefore must ensure that participants are able to consent freely, that we assign them to treatment groups justly, and that our study has more potential benefit than harm.
- We partner with a mental health professional to monitor the health of the participants while conducting therapy.
- We offer free therapy without a need for participation in our study in order to avoid coercion.

What Is Our Data Analysis Plan?
1. **Test our hypotheses.** We use a mixed design analysis of variance to test the main effect for treatment types, the main effect for emotional triggers, and the interaction of the two on anorexia nervosa. Because we have two different ways to behaviorally measure our dependent variables, we conduct this analysis twice, once for the number of grapes consumed and once for the distance of the bowl.

Want to practice the analyses for this research yourself? Ask your instructor about the data set that accompanies this study.

Let's Discuss What Happened

Our study sought to determine the most effective treatment for anorexia nervosa. Based on past literature, we decided to specifically test cognitive-behavioral therapy and psychodynamic psychotherapy. Due to the role of emotion in eating behavior, we also tested whether emotional triggers, specifically types of stress, would exacerbate symptoms of anorexia nervosa after treatment, and whether the combination of therapy and stress would combine to uniquely impact participants. We conducted a 2 × 3 mixed design study in which we randomly assigned participants to one of the two therapy types and to a sequence of three different emotional triggers (work stress, relationship stress, and future-related stress). Our dependent variables measured anorexic eating with two behavioral measures: grapes consumed and bowl placement. Next, we need to interpret our results to determine if our three hypotheses have support, consider the weaknesses of the study, and make some recommendations about further research on this topic and how to apply what we have learned in order to help others.

What Did We Find?

For eating behavior, in terms of grapes consumed, we found two main effects. As we predicted, participants who had 40 weeks of cognitive-behavioral therapy ate more grapes than those who had 40 weeks of psychodynamic psychotherapy, indicating a greater willingness to consume calories. Given cognitive-behavioral therapy's effectiveness, we will offer all our participants in the psychodynamic condition 40 weeks of cognitive-behavioral therapy.

As predicted, we found that relationship stress influenced eating behavior more than either work stress or future-related stress. When exposed to relationship stress, participants ate significantly fewer grapes than when exposed to either of the other two forms of stress, indicating that relationship stress might exacerbate symptoms of anorexia nervosa compared to the other forms of stress. The interaction between therapy and stress was not significant, which means these two factors did not combine to influence eating behavior in a unique way. Unfortunately, the results for bowl distance were less conclusive. Neither of the two main effects nor the interaction was significant, indicating that these did not significantly influence where participants placed the bowl of grapes.

Why These Findings?

We found that those with anorexia nervosa who had completed 40 weeks of cognitive-behavioral therapy ate more grapes overall, regardless of the emotional trigger they experienced. This finding is consistent with the results of a study using enhanced cognitive-behavioral therapy (Grave et al., 2013). Cognitive-behavioral therapy's goal is to identify and change problematic thoughts and behaviors. Perhaps cognitive-behavioral therapy is a better approach for the particular nature of anorexia nervosa, which includes maladaptive thoughts about eating and body image and maladaptive behaviors involving eating and exercising (American Psychiatric Association, 2013b).

Regarding emotional triggers, different types of stress do not seem to have the same impact on people who have anorexia nervosa. Our study revealed that relationship stress led to less eating, indicating that our participants might have been falling back to maladaptive eating behaviors after exposure to that particular type of stress. We can take action to reduce some forms of stress more than others, but stress in our relationships may be the least controllable. Consistent with this interpretation, those who have anorexia nervosa have extremely high self-control in various areas of their life (Steinglass et al., 2012). Given the inability to fully control every aspect of relationship stress (e.g., another person's behavior), our participants may have coped by focusing on their eating, something they could control. We originally thought that treatment type might interact with emotional triggers to influence eating behaviors more than each factor did by itself. However, we did not find that to be the case. While psychodynamic psychotherapy was less effective for grape consumption, it was similarly effective across all three types of stress. While each factor has its own impact on eating behavior, our study indicates that therapy type does not influence how a person with anorexia nervosa will react to different types of stress. Our results may be due to our focus on eating behaviors rather than maladaptive thoughts. We cannot rule out the possibility that therapy type might have interacted differently with various stressors if we focused on maladaptive thoughts instead. Future research should investigate this possibility using maladaptive thinking as the dependent variable instead of anorexic behavior.

Bowl distance was our second dependent variable because we were concerned that participants might not eat any grapes, which would result in a floor effect and prevent us from properly testing our hypothesis. Interestingly, we did not get a floor effect on the grape consumption dependent variable. Of our 63 participants, only 4 participants (or 6.34%) chose not to eat any grapes. Across all conditions, the overall mean of grapes consumed was 11.40 ($SD = 7.63$), and of those who ate grapes, the number of grapes consumed ranged from 1 to 30, which further indicates that we did not have a floor effect.

We thought that the distance participants placed the bowl from themselves would indicate their desire to avoid eating the grapes. Yet our analysis of bowl distance revealed that neither treatment nor origin of stress impacted bowl placement. These findings also did not match the pattern of results we found for the independent variables' influence on actual eating. When selecting behavioral measures, it can be difficult to know exactly which underlying psychological process (if any) produces a specific behavior. In this case, participants may have placed the bowl based on other factors, such as moving it out of their way to complete paperwork instead of out of the desire to avoid the thought of food.

What Could Be Improved?

Our study was the first that we are aware of that directly compared two common forms of treatment for anorexia nervosa and tested the impact of daily stressors in a controlled experimental environment. Yet our study was not perfect. One problem was our bowl-distance measure. While we established a clear method of measuring bowl distance at the end of the study, we did not account for how the participants might move the bowl throughout the study. Some participants placed the bowl on the desk and never moved it again. Others moved the bowl back and forth each time they took a grape. Our study would have benefited from establishing a better procedure for assessing bowl distance or perhaps using a different behavioral measure altogether.

We also had some attrition in our study. Although we ended the study with enough participants ($N = 63$), we lost a handful of participants before the study concluded. Two participants fell below our physical health minimum or never improved and were dropped from the study and encouraged to seek immediate inpatient treatment. Another five participants failed to complete the study. Four of them stopped coming to therapy, and one completed therapy, but did not return for the emotional trigger portion of the study. Attrition is a potential threat to internal validity. There may be something different about the people who dropped out of our study compared to those who completed it, and that difference might have impacted our dependent variable instead of our independent variables. Some people might have dropped out of the study because they were getting worse; some might have dropped out because they were better and did not think they needed more treatment. Although the various reasons that people did not complete the study might balance out with a large enough sample, we cannot rule out the possibility of a systematic difference between those who completed the study and those who did not. Of particular concern would be if there was more attrition in one treatment group than the other. This might indicate that one of the treatment groups might not be very effective (e.g., "This study doesn't work, so I quit") or that it was highly effective (e.g., "I'm feeling a lot better, so I don't need to go back"). Attrition, however, does not seem to be a major concern in our study, as the seven participants who did not complete the study were distributed fairly evenly across all conditions.

For ethical reasons, we decided not to include a control group, but this decision created another weakness in our study. Without a control group that did not receive treatment, we do not know how our participants might have progressed over time without therapeutic intervention. In short, we cannot rule out the influence of maturation. Although unlikely, it is possible that people with anorexia nervosa could naturally improve over time without therapy. Thus, it is possible that those without therapy could have done similarly, if not even better, than those in our therapy conditions in our emotional trigger task. Of course, it is also possible, and, given past research, more likely, that the no-therapy control group would have had worse outcomes. However, without a control group, we have no way of knowing for sure.

▶ What is maturation?
SEE CHAPTER 10, p. 326

What's Next?

Our results indicate that cognitive-behavioral therapy is better at improving eating behavior in people with anorexia nervosa, but we only tested two of the various types of therapy used to treat anorexia nervosa. Future work in this area should focus on the efficacy of other types of therapy, such as family therapy, group therapy, or therapy techniques that combine different therapeutic approaches. Future research could also test other types of emotional triggers (e.g., anger, sadness, fear), or focus on thoughts instead of behaviors. Our study does confirm that everyday situational influences, like stress, affect recovery. Understanding these everyday situational triggers is critical to overcoming this disorder.

In addition to furthering this line of research, we also need to consider our obligation to share our research findings with the clinical community. We now

What Do You Think?
What other situational variables that might *reduce* the symptoms of anorexia nervosa can you think of for future research to study?

know that cognitive-behavioral therapy is more effective than psychodynamic psychotherapy for eating behaviors in our controlled setting. This might influence how therapists approach treatment or how potential clients seek help. We also know that relationship stress is a specific emotional trigger that may reduce a person with anorexia's willingness to eat. Therapists can address this specific trigger in therapy, helping their clients to better cope with it. Likewise, client awareness that relationship stress might trigger disordered eating could help them avoid it. As scientists, we have an ethical obligation to share what we know by communicating our findings to others through writing a research report, publishing or presenting our findings, and posting the details of our study on open science websites.

▶ How can we communicate scientific findings? SEE APPENDIX B, p. 492

YOUR TURN 12.3

1. Caleb conducts an experiment on frustration and varies how much the lights flicker in the room. Participants sit in a room where either the lights do not flicker or they flicker twice a minute. Caleb also has all participants answer both math and verbal Graduate Record Exam questions while they sit in either the flickering or flicker-free room. Which of the following statistical analyses should Caleb use to test his research hypotheses?
   a. A mixed design ANOVA
   b. A factorial ANOVA
   c. A repeated ANOVA
   d. A one-way ANOVA

2. You conduct a mixed design ANOVA and find the following outcome: $F(1, 58) = 10.21$, $p = .021$, eta^2 = .18. Which number represents the significance level?
   a. 10.21
   b. .18
   c. .021
   d. 58

3. Athena has 100 people return a completed survey about political attitudes through the mail. She sends each of them a follow-up survey 4 weeks later, but only 72 participants return the follow-up survey. Which of the following is a potential problem with Athena's study?
   a. Demand characteristics
   b. Maturation issues
   c. Attrition
   d. Ecological validity

How did you do? Turn to the end of the chapter to check your answers.

Research in Action

Do Speed Daters Become Pickier the Later It Gets?

There are more and more ways to meet new romantic partners. Whether it is in person or online, today's dating approaches rely on presenting potential daters with many options quickly. Speed dating accomplishes this by having daters experience very brief encounters with multiple people in a single evening. How does getting to know so many people throughout the night influence whom a speed dater finds appealing? Are people pickier early on, or do they get pickier after they've seen some of the available options? Does it work the same for everyone?

In the online activity ***Do Speed Daters Become Pickier the Later It Gets?,*** use your design skills to help unlock the mysteries of speed dating.

LaunchPad To complete this activity, visit LaunchPad at launchpadworks.com

Final Thoughts

This chapter introduced the last of the experimental designs that you will learn in this textbook. Mixed designs build upon what you already knew from between-subjects designs and within-subjects designs to demonstrate how all of their components can coalesce. We used a mixed design to test the effectiveness of two types of treatment and the role that emotional triggers play in the eating behavior of those with anorexia nervosa. We were able to answer several research questions through one data collection procedure and statistical analysis while thinking through the many and diverse ethical considerations necessary for working with a clinical sample. Now, you have a full toolbox that will serve you well in answering any research question you want to explore.

There is still much to learn about the treatment of anorexia nervosa. Sufferers have 5-year recovery rates of approximately 67% (Keski-Rahkonen et al., 2007), which indicates that there is much room for improvement in the treatment of this disorder. As scientists, we have an ethical obligation to help others, so hopefully someone will use science to improve recovery rates. Perhaps someday that person will be you.

CHAPTER 12 Review

Review Questions

(Questions 1–3) Based on an article he read in a men's magazine, Brendan wants to see if alcohol impacts the perceived attractiveness of a female. He thinks two factors may be involved: the type of alcohol the male participant drinks and the type of alcohol the woman drinks. He first assesses the preferred type of alcohol of his male participants and categorizes them as beer, wine, or liquor drinkers. He then shows each male participant the same set of female pictures four different times. Each time, the pictures remain the same, but the associated information about the woman in the picture changes, indicating whether she prefers to drink beer, wine, or liquor. Each time, the men rate how attractive the woman is on a 9-point scale.

1. In the above study, what is the dependent variable?
   a. The type of alcohol the male participant likes to drink
   b. The type of alcohol the woman in the picture likes to drink
   c. Attractiveness of the woman
   d. The pictures of the woman

2. In the above study, what is the between-subjects independent variable?
   a. The type of alcohol the male participant likes to drink
   b. The type of alcohol the woman in the picture likes to drink
   c. Attractiveness of the woman
   d. The pictures of the woman

3. In the above study, what is the within-subjects independent variable?
   a. The type of alcohol the male participant likes to drink
   b. The type of alcohol the woman in the picture likes to drink
   c. Attractiveness of the woman
   d. The pictures of the woman

4. Rosalind wants to study how a specific intervention might help gifted children develop intellectually. In the first phase of the study, Rosalind reads a story to a gifted 5-year-old, asking simple memory questions throughout. In phase two of the study, Rosalind reads another story to the same 5-year-old while asking higher order questions (i.e., questions that require critical thinking and more than simple recall). In the third phase of the study, Rosalind reads a third story, but returns to asking simple memory questions. After each phase of the study, Rosalind records the complexity of the child's answers. Which type of design did Rosalind utilize?
   a. A multigroup design
   b. A single-subject design
   c. A mixed design
   d. A repeated measures design

5. Your friend tells you that the Beatles' version of *Free as a Bird* contains a hidden verbal message when you play it backward. With this new information, you listen to the song very closely as you play it backward and think you hear several messages. Your sister doesn't know what to listen for and thinks it is just random sounds. Which of the following concepts are you displaying that your sister is not?
   a. Experimenter-expectancy effect
   b. Inter-observer reliability
   c. Power
   d. External validity

6. Clayton is terminally ill and has the chance to participate in a promising drug trial that may save his life. The promising medication is only available through the drug trial, as the Food and Drug Administration (FDA) has not yet approved it for the market. Clayton knows that, through random assignment, he may receive a placebo instead of an active drug. What ethical issue does this study potentially have?

   a. Clayton does not have an equal chance to receive the potential costs and benefits of the new drug.

   b. The potential benefits of the experimental drug do not outweigh the potential costs.

   c. Clayton may not really feel like he can refuse consent to participate, considering his terminal diagnosis.

   d. All of the above

7. Minnie is trying to determine the best treatment for anxiety. She includes a group of participants in her study who do not receive any treatment. After the conclusion of the study, she takes the best treatment type and gives it to this group. What is the name of this type of control group?

   a. Waiting-list control group

   b. Empty control group

   c. Placebo control group

   d. Treatment group

8. Casey wants to see if there are gender differences between the way adult men and women describe newborn babies. Casey shows each person in the study two pictures of the same newborn. In one picture, the baby is wearing pink clothes. In the other, the baby is wearing blue clothes. After seeing each picture, the adults rate how much the babies in the pictures possess a number of both feminine and masculine characteristics. Which of the following statistical analyses is appropriate given the study design?

   a. A one-way ANOVA

   b. A two-way ANOVA

   c. A repeated measures ANOVA

   d. A mixed design ANOVA

(Questions 9–10) As a summer camp counselor, you want to design a study to find the most effective way to get your campers to have fun. You decide to have half of your campers work in groups of three and half of your campers work alone to catch a butterfly, lightning bug, and ladybug. After the campers catch each bug, they rate on a 9-point scale how much fun they had doing it. A 2 activity condition (group vs. alone) $\times$ 3 bug types (butterfly, lightning bug, and ladybug) mixed design ANOVA on happiness revealed the following:

- Main effect results for activity condition: $F(1, 60) = 7.28, p = .04,$ eta$^2 = .233$
  - Group condition: $M = 7.89, SD = 4.05$
  - Solo condition: $M = 4.25, SD = 3.95$

- Main effect results for bug type: $F(2, 120) = 11.76$, $p < .001$, eta^2 = .193
  - Butterfly condition: $M = 6.28$, $SD = 2.47$
  - Lightning bug condition: $M = 8.78$, $SD = 2.64$
  - Ladybug condition: $M = 5.64$, $SD = 2.79$
- Interaction effect results: $F(2, 120) = 1.89$, $p = .264$, eta^2 = .007

9. Which of the following is an accurate conclusion based on the results of the study?
   a. The information provided does not allow me to make a conclusion about whether working alone or in a small group impacts happiness.
   b. There was no main effect for activity condition. Whether they did the activity alone or in small groups did not impact their enjoyment of the activity.
   c. There was a main effect for activity condition, with campers working alone enjoying the activity more.
   d. There was a main effect for activity condition, with campers who worked in a small group enjoying the activity more.

10. Which of the following is a correct conclusion based on the results of the study?
    a. Bug type did not impact happiness.
    b. Activity condition (whether campers worked alone or in a small group) did not impact happiness.
    c. There was no interaction between bug type and activity condition.
    d. Campers liked catching butterflies as a group, but preferred to catch lightning bugs alone.

11. Describe the benefits of using a mixed design.

12. Describe the pros and cons of using a single-subject design to answer a research question.

13. List and describe at least two ethical issues that are of particular concern when conducting research on a clinical sample.

Applying What You've Learned

1. Find a published empirical article that describes a between-subjects factorial design. Describe how you could change the study to make one of the independent variables within-subjects. Describe how this methodological change would impact the type of information the study would provide and whether the change would be beneficial.

2. Test the idea that stimulus-free environments lead to better sleep using a single-subject design. Be sure to explain the specifics of your procedure.

3. Take the premise of the single-subject design study about hypnosis and golf featured in the Research Spotlight on p. 402 (Pates, 2013) and create your own mixed design to test an additional hypothesis. Be sure to explain the specifics of your procedure.

4. Debate with yourself about the inclusion of a control group in clinical research. What is the ethical implication of some participants not receiving treatment? What is the cost to the research process to not include a control group? Which is more important? Think of a study where a control group would be ethical and useful to include.

5. Read the following information about fad diets: webmd.com/diet/guide/the-truth-about-fad-diets. Create a mixed design study that compares the effectiveness of a fad diet with a nonfad diet. (Hint: First, consider whether diet should be a within-subjects or between-subjects factor, then use your own ideas for a second independent variable.)

6. Clinical psychologists and other mental health professionals routinely conduct research to help improve treatment options for those with mental illnesses. Generate five new ideas for studies that focus on clinical research. Pick your favorite idea and describe how you would test it with a mixed design.

7. THE NOVICE RESEARCHER: Describe a study that fails to properly implement a double-blind procedure. Next, describe what the researcher did wrong and how to fix it.

8. DIG INTO THE NUMBERS: We have provided your instructor with supplemental mixed design study data. You can analyze that data to build your skills in using a mixed design ANOVA in SPSS. Write an APA-style results section based on your analyses. If you would like even more practice, your instructor also has data that accompanies the study discussed throughout this chapter.

Key Concepts

A-B design, p. 400

A-B-A design, p. 401

A-B-A-B design, p. 401

double-blind procedure, p. 418

expectancy bias, p. 418

experimenter effect, p. 418

experimenter-expectancy effect, p. 418

meta-analysis, p. 395

mixed design, p. 403

mixed design analysis of variance (mixed design ANOVA), p. 421

single-blind procedure, p. 418

single-case experimental design, p. 400

single-n design, p. 400

single-subject design, p. 400

treatment-as-usual group, p. 406

waiting-list control group, p. 406

Answers to YOUR TURN

Your Turn 12.1: 1. b; 2. b; 3. d

Your Turn 12.2: 1. b; 2. d; 3. a

Your Turn 12.3: 1. a; 2. c; 3. c

Answers to Multiple-Choice Review Questions

1. c; 2. a; 3. b; 4. b; 5. a; 6. c; 7. a; 8. d; 9. d; 10. c

Program Evaluation

Applying Your Skills in the Real World

Rawpixel.com/Shutterstock

LEARNING OUTCOMES

After reading this chapter, you should be able to:

- Identify when and why to use a program evaluation.
- Articulate the various types of program evaluations.

- Understand the various steps in the program evaluation process.
- Implement a focus group.
- Write a program evaluation report.
- Convey complex statistical information in nontechnical formats.

Something to Think About . . .

Why did you choose to go to college? If you are like us, you may have wanted to go to college to jump-start a successful career and a fulfilling life. College helps us achieve these goals by providing opportunities to broaden our knowledge and to develop important marketable skills. There is probably no class where this is truer than in the psychology research methods course, where you build critical-thinking, decision-making, analytical, and written communication skills, as well as a healthy dose of time management skills in order to get all of that done. According to a national survey by the Association of American Colleges and Universities (AACU) and Hart Research Association, "More than 75% of employers say they want *more emphasis* on 5 key areas including: critical thinking, complex problem-solving, written and oral communication, and applied knowledge in real-world settings" (AACU & Hart Research Associates, 2013, p. 12). The same survey also found that "employers consistently rank outcomes and practices that involve application of skills over acquisition of discrete bodies of knowledge," and that employers value "practices that require students to a) conduct research and use evidence-based analysis; b) gain in-depth knowledge in the major and analytic, problem solving and communication skills; and c) apply their learning in real-world settings" (p. 13). Clearly, your research skills are in high demand by a wide variety of employers, and these skills will increase your marketability and chances of getting a job after graduation. Or, if you are interested in pursuing a graduate degree, these skills could lead to employment opportunities in academic research, such as research assistant or research analyst positions (Jones, 2017).

As a student who has an interest in psychology, you likely also have a deep interest in helping people. Although many students see psychology as a way of helping others only in the context of the various counseling professions (e.g., therapy, psychiatry), you can also help others by using your research training to conduct applied research, which has practical implications and can solve real-world problems. Applied research is possible in a variety of settings. For example, you can use your research skills in market research to determine which products consumers prefer and what influences their preferences. You can conduct usability research to help make products easier to use (one of the keys to Steve Jobs and Apple's success). You can conduct industrial/organizational research to help companies maximize employee productivity. You can also do research to help nonprofit organizations better serve their clients. There are a variety of organizations and programs (e.g., Head Start, local counseling centers, residential care centers for abused women, crisis hotlines, etc.) that have an explicit purpose of helping those in need.

▶ Want to learn more about how to use your research training in your career? SEE CHAPTER 1, p. 16

As you can see, there are many opportunities for your research skills to make a difference in peoples' everyday lives. With so many ways to help others, you may feel some uncertainty about which career to pursue, especially when deciding between research and counseling interests. One way to help your decision is to seek out real-world experience, which will also better prepare you for life after graduation. Some of the best experience comes through internships. According to a survey from the National Association of Colleges and Employers (NACE), "63.2 percent of graduating seniors from the Class of 2013 reported having taken part in an internship, co-op, or both" (NACE, 2013). Another survey found that 32% of students from the Class of 2013 completed two or more internships (Eye of the Intern, 2014). Internships, which can be paid or unpaid, provide students with the opportunity to apply knowledge and skills from the classroom to a real-world setting. Given statistics about many recent graduates being unemployed or underemployed, it is clear that internships are important, as they have become "the 'new interview' in the job search process for students and employers alike" (Smith, 2013). An article from CNN states it more bluntly: "Graduating students with paid or unpaid internships on their résumé have a much better chance at landing a full-time position upon graduation" (Hering, 2010). Looks like you should add "completing at least one internship" to your college bucket list.

What Do You Think?

In what other settings will you be able to use your research skills?

As a savvy and career-minded student, you decide to look for an internship using your school's career services website, which advertises available internships. As you scan the list, you realize that not all internships are created equal. Many are unpaid, and several sound like you would get low-level experience entering data, filing, or answering phones at best. However, one internship possibility, shown in **Figure 13.1**, is particularly intriguing because it requires training in research design and statistics and is a paid position. Your research skills may be paying off already! While the position sounds great, there is one aspect of the announcement that concerns you, namely "experience with program evaluation preferred." Unsure of exactly what that means, you decide to talk to your advisor.

When you meet with your advisor, she commends you for taking the initiative to seek out an internship and for finding one where you can use your

> ### DRUG/ALCOHOL TREATMENT PROGRAM INTERN
> *Posted 7/15–Internship in Psychology, Sociology, Social Work, Mental Health Counseling, Social Science, or related fields*
>
> *Agency Description*
>
> *Programulation* is an independent research company specializing in program evaluations of nonprofit organizations. We help key stakeholders determine where their program or service meets the established objectives and where there are opportunities for improvement.
>
> *Job Description*
>
> *Programulation* seeks a hard-working and detail-oriented intern to join our staff for the upcoming semester for a paid internship position for a program evaluation. This particular evaluation will focus on a small nonprofit organization that assists adults dealing with alcohol or prescription drug dependencies. To qualify, you must be able to receive college credit for the experience. Primary duties include performing a program evaluation of the organization's services, along with collaborating with all levels of staff and interacting with clients. The successful applicant will be compassionate, be able to work with diverse groups of people, and have a background in research design and statistics. Experience with program evaluation preferred, but not required. This position is ideal for a self-starter who will take advantage of the autonomy and flexible hours that come with the position.
>
> *To Apply*
>
> Please submit a resume to director@programulation.com. Background check and drug test required.

FIGURE 13.1 Internship Posting for a Student with a Research Background.

research skills. According to your advisor, a **program evaluation** involves using the scientific method to assess whether an organized activity is achieving its intended objectives. In other words, a program evaluation helps determine whether a program accomplishes what it hopes to and whether it is really helping the people it intends to help. Your advisor explains that program evaluations are a bit like a progress check, similar to how you might check your grades during the semester to see how you are doing, or how you look at the display on the treadmill to see how far you have run. In each case, you start with a goal in mind, such as keeping your GPA above a 3.5 or running 4 miles, and then you evaluate the extent to which you are achieving those goals. These evaluations are useful because they tell you how well your current strategy is working, and whether you need to alter your approach to achieve the desired goal. Program evaluations take place in a variety of fields, such as business (e.g., for improving customer service), criminal justice (e.g., to optimize post-incarceration outcomes), health care (e.g., for improving maternal nutrition), education (e.g., to enhance the quality of advisement on campus), or government (e.g., for assessing food stamp programs). In fact, the U.S. government

program evaluation using the scientific method to assess whether an organized activity is achieving its intended objectives.

has an office within the Centers for Disease Control and Prevention (CDC) specifically tasked with program evaluation (http://www.cdc.gov/eval/).

Even though you have never done a program evaluation, your advisor views this as a wonderful opportunity to strengthen your research and statistical skills and develop a new skill that will make you more marketable after graduation. She offers to be your faculty internship advisor and provide you with the necessary guidance and support for doing a quality program evaluation at the placement site. It may be a challenge, but you know that such experiences are often the most valuable ones, so you apply for the internship. Fortunately for you, there are very few students who share your level of research training, so you get an interview with the organization.

From Ideas to Innovation

During your internship interview, you meet with the project lead at Programulation to discuss the internship responsibilities. During the meeting, you learn that the evaluation will focus on *The Sanctuary Under the Palms,* a private boutique treatment center for those who are able to afford the very best care. The program's mission is to help individuals achieve personal growth through holistic life changes as they overcome their addictions and pursue a meaningful and balanced future. The center is unique in that it does not offer therapy. Rather, the focus is on self-guided discovery through reflection. The project lead explains that one way the center achieves their goals is by posting quotes around the facility, such as *"Life can only be understood backwards; but it must be lived forwards."* ~ *Søren Kierkegaard*, and, *"In a word, each man is questioned by life; and he can only answer to life by answering for his own life; to life he can only respond by being responsible."* ~ *Viktor E. Frankl.* The center has a simple organizational structure, with a 10-member Board of Trustees, a director, and just over a dozen coaches who are responsible for case management and program implementation. After telling you a bit more about the program, the project lead asks about your research qualifications and how this position fits into your career plans. You describe your research training in psychology and how your college advisor will supervise you throughout the internship experience. When the project lead asks if you have any questions, you pose the one that has been plaguing you since you submitted your résumé: "What do you hope to accomplish with this program evaluation?" The project lead explains that The Sanctuary Under the Palms Board of Trustees mandated that the center conduct a program evaluation to document how well they are indeed helping people recover from their drug and alcohol addictions. Basically, the Board of Trustees wants to be sure that the center's approach "works," even though there is a very long waitlist of people wanting to enter the program. You wonder if the program staff assumes their program works and merely wants to confirm that this is the case.

However, we are taking a scientific approach that tries to remain fair and objective, and must ask and answer the question, "Does it work?" honestly. This is not to say that we think the treatment center's motivations are unethical. Rather, it is simply human nature to seek confirmation that we are doing a good job by focusing on the positives and avoiding indications that suggest otherwise. When you think like a scientist, you know to mitigate these types of confirmation biases by designing a set of studies, or, in our case, a program evaluation, to address a research question. Science does not seek to confirm existing beliefs by designing studies that support our preconceived notions. Rather, we must devise a plan that provides the best test of the program so that we have confidence in our conclusions. Although the program coaches are all convinced that the program's long waitlist is proof of its effectiveness, the Board wisely acknowledges that popularity does not qualify as sufficient evidence.

The Board knows that tested evidence of effectiveness will help The Sanctuary's pursuit of **grants,** or monetary gifts given to help organizations meet a specific goal or objective. Granting agencies, or those who provide the financial support, commonly have affiliations with the government, private foundations, or corporations. Granting agencies require that organizations engage in **grant writing,** which involves submitting an application in which the organization provides specific information about the program's goals, along with evidence of the program's effectiveness. The organization would also like to use the program evaluation results to help with future program advertisements and client recruitment.

▶ Want to learn more about the characteristics of a good scientist? SEE CHAPTER 1, p. 9

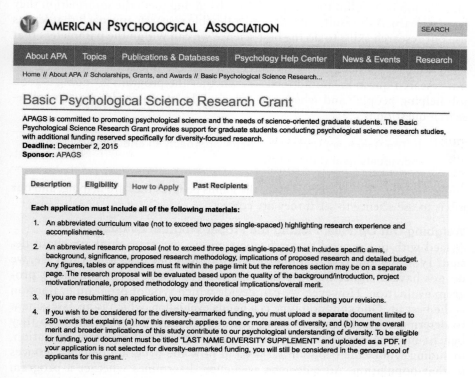

AMERICAN PSYCHOLOGICAL ASSOCIATION

SEARCH

About APA | Topics | Publications & Databases | Psychology Help Center | News & Events | Research

Home // About APA // Scholarships, Grants, and Awards // Basic Psychological Science Research...

Basic Psychological Science Research Grant

APAGS is committed to promoting psychological science and the needs of science-oriented graduate students. The Basic Psychological Science Research Grant provides support for graduate students conducting psychological science research studies, with additional funding reserved specifically for diversity-focused research.
Deadline: December 2, 2015
Sponsor: APAGS

Description | Eligibility | How to Apply | Past Recipients

Each application must include all of the following materials:

1. An abbreviated curriculum vitae (not to exceed two pages single-spaced) highlighting research experience and accomplishments.

2. An abbreviated research proposal (not to exceed three pages single-spaced) that includes specific aims, background, significance, proposed research methodology, implications of proposed research and detailed budget. Any figures, tables or appendices must fit within the page limit but the references section may be on a separate page. The research proposal will be evaluated based upon the quality of the background/introduction, project motivation/rationale, proposed methodology and theoretical implications/overall merit.

3. If you are resubmitting an application, you may provide a one-page cover letter describing your revisions.

4. If you wish to be considered for the diversity-earmarked funding, you must upload a **separate** document limited to 250 words that explains (a) how this research applies to one or more areas of diversity, and (b) how the overall merit and broader implications of this study contribute to our psychological understanding of diversity. To be eligible for funding, your document must be titled "LAST NAME DIVERSITY SUPPLEMENT" and uploaded as a PDF. If your application is not selected for diversity-earmarked funding, you will still be considered in the general pool of applicants for this grant.

Many social services agencies rely on grant funding to keep their programs going. Program evaluations are essential to the grant application process. *(APA)*

grants monetary gifts given to help organizations meet a specific goal or objective.

grant writing developing an application in which an organization provides specific information regarding a program's goals along with evidence of the program's effectiveness in order to gain monetary gifts.

The Sanctuary Under the Palms needs to conduct an independent program evaluation to demonstrate effectiveness, but no one in the organization has a clue about how to do one—hence the decision to hire Programulation to do it for them. Three days after your interview, you receive a phone call from the project lead at Programulation saying that you are the right person for the job. They were impressed with your research and communication skills and are confident in your abilities, especially since you will be working under the guidance of a faculty advisor who has experience completing program evaluations. Congratulations on landing your first paid internship! Because of your research training in psychology, the project lead informs you that you will be able to work independently to develop a plan that you will then present to the team at Programulation. If all goes well, you will then share your results directly with The Sanctuary Under the Palms.

Introduction to Our Research Question

Based on what you learned from the project lead, it is already clear that doing a program evaluation will be different from the other types of research you have done so far. In the past, we started with our own research question, completed a literature review, and then identified our key variables and best design to use. With a program evaluation, the organization provides the research question and our job is to fulfill their expectations by giving them the information they hope to learn. As a result, we will need a flexible research approach that lets us use our research skills to do the best science we can within the parameters that Programulation and The Sanctuary Under the Palms establish for us. From what we have gathered from the interview and the internship advertisement, our research question should focus on whether the program is "doing a good job helping people" and whether it "works." In other words, the general research question is,

---

RESEARCH ? Is The Sanctuary Under the Palms' approach an effective way to help individuals deal with addiction?

Essentially, The Sanctuary Under the Palms believes they are helping, and our job is to use science to see if they are correct.

Weighing Our Options: Picking the Proper Program Evaluation

Armed with our general research question, we can start thinking about design. Typically, our research question determines our design. In this case, we do not have a choice because the organization wants us to conduct a program evaluation. However, we can decide which type of program evaluation is the best fit. One common type is a **needs evaluation**, which is an assessment to determine which features of a program are most valuable and who they benefit most. A **process evaluation** assesses the general program operation, including whom the program serves and how the program delivers services to that population. An **outcomes evaluation** determines whether a program effectively produces outcomes that are consistent with the stated objectives or goals.

needs evaluation an assessment to determine which features of a program are most valuable and who they benefit most.

process evaluation an assessment of a general program operation, including who the program serves and how the program delivers services to that population.

outcomes evaluation an assessment that determines whether a program effectively produces outcomes that are consistent with the stated objectives or goals.

Of these options, a needs evaluation does not seem appropriate because the organization has an established program and a clearly defined population that it serves. They do not require much program planning at this stage. We also know that The Sanctuary Under the Palms has a long waiting list, which generally indicates that clients see value in the program, have few concerns about the services provided, and believe the program meets their needs. Thus, a process evaluation does not seem like the best choice. Perhaps most importantly, the Board of Trustees' mandate is to determine if the program actually helps people with their drug and alcohol addictions. This maps nicely to the purpose of an outcomes evaluation, which is to see if the organization is effectively achieving its program goals.

There are many programs supported by the U.S. government. All three types of program evaluations help determine the best ways to use funding. Needs evaluations help determine what new programs need to be developed. Process evaluations can help determine how to help programs run more smoothly. Outcomes evaluations assess the effectiveness and, therefore, the fundability of existing programs. *(Uschools University Images/Getty Images)*

Benefits of Program Evaluation

Completing a quality program evaluation has many benefits. First, a good program evaluation forces members of an organization to clarify the program's purpose and intended outcomes. Clearly articulating the organizational "mission" can help identify program priorities and eliminate less important initiatives. Program evaluations can also provide the organization with evidence of the program's benefits or knowledge that the program is using its resources efficiently. In addition, program evaluations allow an organization to evaluate a new approach or resource in order to determine if it should continue or if it warrants additional funding and resources.

Program evaluations give those running the program confidence that their efforts are worthwhile and making a difference. They allow the program to provide external constituencies, such as granting agencies, with tangible evidence that the program's goals have merit, that the program achieves its objectives, and that the program uses its resources wisely. Making data-based claims, rather than opinion-based claims, enables the organization to promote the program's merits to potential clients in a more convincing fashion, which can also help with public relations. Finally, program evaluations encourage organizations to identify areas for improvement. Identifying underdeveloped or deficient areas allows an organization to allocate the necessary resources to produce better outcomes. Program evaluations should not result in useless numbers or information simply for the sake of learning something new. Rather, a quality evaluation provides actionable information that should directly improve the program and, more importantly, has the potential to make an immediate improvement in the lives of the people the program serves.

Table 13.1 summarizes the types and benefits of program evaluation.

TABLE 13.1

Types of Program Evaluation		
Evaluation Type	**Description**	**Purpose**
Needs Evaluation	Determines which features of a program are most valuable and who they benefit most.	To identify program features to continue or discontinue and to determine potential new components to add. Helpful for program planning.
Process Evaluation	Assesses the general program operation, including whom the program serves and how the program delivers services to that population.	To determine ways to improve program implementation and delivery. Also seeks to ensure a match between program goals and those serviced.
Outcomes Evaluation	Determines whether a program effectively produces outcomes that are consistent with the stated objectives or goals.	To identify unmet goals and outcomes the program can improve in order to better serve the clients, or to establish evidence for program effectiveness.

Key Considerations for Program Evaluation

In order to optimize our evaluation's impact, we need to consider several issues. Foremost, we need to keep our purpose in mind. Program evaluation is different from other types of research in that we are not trying to build upon or advance a theory by adding to accumulated knowledge, though if we did so that would be an added bonus. Rather than to advance scientific understanding of a phenomenon, our job is to provide a specific organization with actionable information that can have immediate implications that benefit their specific program. For this reason, we may not be able to implement the design we think is best.

For example, because program evaluation occurs in real-world contexts rather than a research laboratory, we will have less control of extraneous variables that may bias our findings. We also must be sensitive to our role as researchers. Similar to when we need to be careful of interviewer bias, evaluators need to monitor ways they can potentially influence the evaluation's findings. For this reason, although a person within the organization has more intimate knowledge of a program than an outsider, an outside consultant may be the best evaluator in order to avoid personal agendas and limit potential biases. In terms of identifying program benefits, we need to realize that a program's outcomes are not always immediately obvious, and will need to account for this when deciding how to measure the program's benefits. Finally, although program evaluations seek to help improve programs and their

▶ Why should we be concerned about interviewer bias? SEE CHAPTER 5, p. 137

clients' experiences, we have an ethical obligation to pay attention to potential unanticipated consequences of our evaluation. For example, if our evaluation is too intrusive, we could undermine clients' trust or limit the program's effectiveness.

The Program Evaluation Process

The general process of a program evaluation, as displayed in **Figure 13.2**, involves developing a plan, gathering and analyzing the data, and communicating the results.

Step 1: Planning Phase

- *Identify Key Stakeholders*—We determine the individuals who will use the evaluation and who will benefit from it by engaging organizational leadership, as well as those with less influence (e.g., program staff and clients).

- *Describe the Program*—We collect information about the program's mission and specific goals, the nature of the program and services delivered, and whom the program serves.

- *Clarify the Evaluation's Goals*—We identify what the evaluation hopes to accomplish, the steps needed to do so, and how the organization hopes to use the evaluation's results.

- *Create an Evaluation Plan*—We formulate and describe a plan that outlines our evaluation's design.

FIGURE 13.2 The Program Evaluation Process.

Step 2: Execution Phase

- *Gather the Data*—Based on our design, we collect information via interviews, focus groups, and surveys.

- *Analyze Data*—We use the appropriate statistics to summarize information we collected and put it in a form that will be most useful for the program.

Step 3: Communication of Results

- *Form Conclusions*—We evaluate findings from the data analyses to determine which conclusions have empirical support.

- *Make Recommendations*—We interpret the findings as they relate to the program's goals to identify areas of strength or areas of improvement. We also make suggestions for how the data should inform potential program modifications.

- *Report the Results*—We communicate our findings to the various stakeholders in a clear, nontechnical, and easy-to-use format.

Research Spotlight

A Program Evaluation of "Comics for Health"

A major benefit of program evaluation is that it can help us identify effective intervention programs that address health concerns. One such program, "Comics for Health," uses comic books and comic strips as part of a childhood obesity prevention intervention in 12 after-school programs (Branscum, Sharma, Wang, Wilson, & Rojas-Guyler, 2013). Each week of the program focuses on a different lifestyle behavior associated with healthy eating habits, including the making and reading of comic books. A program evaluation that collected data on the program's effectiveness included surveys, field notes, and open-item questionnaires. The researchers were interested in program fidelity (how strictly lessons were followed), dose (the number and length of lessons), and program reach (child attendance). Results indicated that program implementation had an almost perfect rate of fidelity, and dosage was at recommended levels. The majority of children (70%) attended the entire program, so reach was as expected. In addition, staff members reported that the program was well received by children, and recommended program replication in the future. With this program evaluation evidence, we can be more confident that after-school programs can conduct the program as intended.

There are hundreds of after-school programs across the United States. Each has their own goals, but how do we know if any of these programs work? Program evaluations scientifically determine which programs children should participate in after school. *(The Washington Post/Getty Images)*

Focus on Ethics: Should We Really Do That?

Before continuing, we should consider the ethical implications of doing our program evaluation. Specifically, are there possible negative effects or unintended consequences of doing this evaluation? One possibility is that critically evaluating the program may lead staff and clients to question the efficacy of the program's unique approach. Simply having doubts about the program may make some coaches less effective in helping their clients, and these doubts may give some clients less confidence, which could undermine their dedication to the program. Collectively, this could undermine the program's effectiveness.

If this were the case, one might wonder if the program's effectiveness results from its perceived, rather than true, effectiveness. In other words, the apparent success of the program could be the result of a placebo effect, suggesting that the program is not supporting its claims. Our evaluation may also find that the program is ineffective and that clients are wasting their time and money by staying at The Sanctuary for 30 days. Although the Board of Trustees may consider this conclusion a potential negative outcome of the evaluation, it is not an ethical concern. In fact, learning that the program does not work is a potential benefit of the program evaluation; it would be unethical *not* to evaluate the program just because some stakeholders thought the evaluation might produce unfavorable results. No one wants to be the person to tell the boss the negative aspects of a program, however. For this reason, many programs that receive grant funding hire an external evaluator to conduct their program evaluations in order to avoid the pressure to report only positive results. Overall, the benefits of doing this evaluation outweigh the costs, so we can proceed.

Planning Our Program Evaluation

Looking at the steps for program evaluation, our first objective is to identify key stakeholders. From your internship interview, we know that The Sanctuary Under the Palms is a small organization. It is clear that the Board of Trustees is the main driver behind this evaluation and will be the group most likely to use the results. However, we should also engage other levels of the organization, including the director, coaches, and current and former clients, to obtain the most comprehensive snapshot of the program possible. Next, before we create a specific evaluation plan, we need to "Describe the Program" and "Clarify the Evaluation's Goals."

Previously, whenever we wanted to learn about a topic, we conducted a literature search. That approach does not make sense in this context because our focus is specifically on The Sanctuary Under the Palms. Yet we still need a way to learn more about the program. We could simply walk around the organization and strike up casual conversations with people to get their thoughts. If this sounds like a bad option, you are thinking like a scientist. As scientists, we want to be comprehensive and empirically based, which means that we should have a systematic way to gather information that is as unbiased as possible. Our need for detailed information presents an ideal situation for using qualitative methods, which focus on gaining in-depth information on a few individuals with the goal of developing a more thorough understanding of their perspectives and experiences. As you recall from Chapter 5, there are several qualitative methods from which to choose. We could use an interview again, but rather than use the method that is most familiar, we must pick the best method for our research. An interview or series of interviews is not ideal because we are interested in how the organization operates as a whole, including how the staff works together to deliver the program and how clients receive the program. A focus group may be more suitable.

▶ Interested in learning more about the different types of qualitative methods? SEE CHAPTER 5, p. 130

Focus Groups

Focus groups involve assembling several individuals to discuss a specific topic. They provide participants with the opportunity to react to each other's contributions, thus providing richer information to the researcher. Ideally, focus groups include 6–12 participants to optimize individual member participation. Focus groups have the advantage of providing a high volume of insightful content using participants' own words in a quick and efficient manner, while capturing group members' interactions. They allow the facilitator to ask follow-up questions to clarify meaning, which can elicit additional information that participants did not think to volunteer initially. Although there are some disadvantages, notably the inability to generalize to other populations, we are only concerned with learning about The Sanctuary Under the Palms and not about how our findings relate to others, so this is not a major concern for us. As we did in Chapter 5, we will also be sure to avoid interviewer bias that may influence participants' responses. In light of these considerations, a focus group seems ideal for learning more about The Sanctuary Under the Palms' program and what the Board would like to discern from the program evaluation.

Next, we need to put our design into action by deciding who to include in our focus group. It is ideal to include focus group members who do not know each other, but given the small size of our potential population, that is an unrealistic goal. To determine who will be in the group, we should use what we know about sampling. Whenever possible, we should first identify the population to whom we hope to apply the results. In our case, the population is all of the stakeholders, which includes three main groups: Administration (Board of Trustee members, the director; 11 people total), Staff (program coaches; 15 total), and Clients (current and former; 100+). The simplest approach would be to lump everyone together into one focus group. However, that would create potential problems with power differentials. That is, would staff members feel comfortable giving their honest opinion in the presence of board members or their director? Similarly, clients might not feel comfortable offering constructive feedback that their current or former coach could hear. Staff might also not want to say anything in front of clients that could potentially undermine their progress.

To address this problem, we can run three different focus groups, one for each type of stakeholder (Administration, Staff, Clients). By conducting three separate focus groups, we can aim to include the entire population for the Administration and Staff groups since those groups have only 11–15 members each. The population of the Client group is much bigger (over 100), so we will have to select a smaller, ideally random sample. It is not always feasible or necessary to use random sampling when running a focus group, but it is best to use this and other sound research practices whenever possible. Ultimately, our goal is to have three focus groups, each with 9–12 members.

▶ Why is sampling important? SEE CHAPTER 4, p. 109

With three distinct groups, each with different levels of involvement at The Sanctuary, we could tailor our questions to each subgroup. However, asking each subgroup unique questions would not allow us to directly compare the subgroups' responses. Then we could not be sure if any differences between their responses were due to varying perspectives or having been asked different questions. Thus, we should use the exact same questions for each group, which will allow us to make comparisons more easily across groups. Within each group, we will also want to assess how and why group members agree or disagree with each other's perspectives, which is one of the primary benefits of conducting a focus group (Stewart, Shamdasani, & Rook, 2007).

So what should we ask during each discussion? We could simply see where the conversation with each group takes us. Our experience with conducting interviews, however, has taught us that this is probably not the best approach. Instead, we should create a protocol, similar to an interview schedule, which outlines our questions and their order. Having a protocol will help keep the group discussion on track, allowing us to obtain the information we need.

One other decision to make as we develop our protocol is the number of questions to ask. The purpose of focus groups is to discuss specific issues, so we will want to keep the number of questions manageable and address a basic idea: What do we want to learn from the focus groups? Although each person may not be able to comment fully on every question, the participants' interactions will help us determine the extent to which their perspectives resonate with each other. With manageability and our basic idea in mind, here are the six key questions we came up with to ask during our focus groups:

▶ Want to learn more about developing and sequencing interview questions?
SEE CHAPTER 5, p. 138

- What are the program's goals?
- What are the key features that the program uses to achieve these goals?
- How effective is the program as it is now?
- What current measures are in place to determine the program's effectiveness?
- What is the goal of the program evaluation?
- What do you hope the program evaluation accomplishes?

With our questions in place, we can plan how we will conduct the focus groups. To maximize participation, we should conduct the groups in a familiar and convenient location that we can keep consistent for all three groups. The conference room at the facility would be an ideal setting. Focus groups also require a **moderator,** or a person who asks the questions and facilitates the discussion. An ideal moderator has a thorough understanding of the focus group's topic, has a strong foundation in research methods, and understands group dynamics, or the behaviors and psychological processes of a social group. Although you may not have a strong background in group dynamics, your qualifications on the other criteria make you well-suited to serve as the moderator. In this role, you will want to remain neutral and bias-free during the discussions. Across all three groups, you should treat all members equally and respectfully and avoid agreeing or disagreeing with their responses. You should be willing to manage the group discussion, such as by keeping overly talkative or verbose members from dominating the conversation, and calling on shy members if needed.

As you prepare to conduct the focus groups, you will need an audio recorder to capture the discussion for later transcription. You will want a notepad where you can take notes regarding members' nonverbal or other behaviors that the audio may not reveal. Finally, you should have a watch placed in front of

What Do You Think?
What other questions could we ask in the focus group in order to learn about the program?

moderator the person who asks the questions and facilitates discussion in a focus group.

This scene from *Mad Men*, which depicts women giving their opinions on a product, has the same features of any focus group. The scene includes several participants, typically strangers, gathered together to discuss a topic with a moderator. *(Mike Yarish/© AMC/Courtesy: Everett Collection)*

▶ Why is debriefing important to the research process? SEE CHAPTER 2, p. 43

you during the conversation. Out of respect for the participants, you should not allow the focus groups to extend beyond the established (90-minute) time frame.

You will follow the same procedure for all three groups. As the participants arrive, you will provide each with an informed consent form, being sure to point out that you will audio-record their responses and will identify participants only by number in any subsequent reports. Following consent from all participants, you will follow your protocol that outlines what you will say to participants. For example, you will open the discussion by saying, "Thanks for coming. We're meeting today to discuss the program offered here at The Sanctuary Under the Palms. Let's start by having everyone introduce themselves. I'll go first . . ." Next, you will establish the basic guidelines for the group: "There are a few simple rules that we should all follow: What you say here stays here, there are no wrong ideas or opinions, I may call on individuals, and you should be respectful of each other." To increase group members' comfort level, you can start with a general or fun question, such as, "If you could be any color in a box of crayons, what color would you be, and why?" Like we had in Chapter 5, you will want to have a few follow-up questions and phrases prepared (e.g., "Please tell me more about that," "What does everyone else think about that?") to help you elicit more information and obtain the rest of the group's feedback. After asking your key questions, you should pose a general wrap-up or exit question, such as, "Was there anything that we did not touch on that you'd like to discuss?" At the end of each focus group, you will thank everyone for their participation, answer any additional questions, and let them know how to access a copy of the final report when it is available.

To aid our search for answers, we must first transcribe the audio recording of each focus group session. We will then analyze the data by conducting a content analysis of participant responses to each question. The content analysis will allow us to identify key themes that emerged from administration, staff, and clients' answers to each question. Using those themes, we will create a summary table with quotes from the groups that are representative of each major theme, shown in **Table 13.2**. To help preserve each respondent's relative anonymity, we should not identify the source of the quotes in the table (e.g., board member, staff, director, client, etc.). Although we have compiled the results in a table, we are not going to write up an APA-style results section. Instead, we will use the focus group data to help us plan the actual program evaluation. Our final report will also include an easy-to-use summary of the findings.

Our final data came from 8 people in the Administration group, 10 in the Staff group, and 11 in the Client group (8 were current clients and 3 were former).

TABLE 13.2

Focus Group Results: Representative Responses	
Question	**Representative Statements**
What are the program's goals?	**Administration:** "To help clients achieve personal growth by guiding them through the process of making holistic life changes that lead to feeling empowered." "To increase the number of clients we serve and to provide those clients with the highest level of care." **Staff:** "To work with clients who suffer from dependency on alcohol or prescription drugs to detoxify their mind and body in order to overcome their addiction." "To change lives by addressing the total person intellectually, biologically, and spiritually." **Clients:** "To help me grow as a person to overcome my addiction so that I can have a better life." "To help me grow as a human being, mind, body, and soul, so that when I walk out of here after 30 days, I can get back on track and just be happy." "Having a meaningful life and becoming my own person."
What are the key features that the program uses to achieve these goals?	**Administration:** "We are an inpatient facility that offers a unique 30-day comprehensive holistic treatment plan focused on self-guided discovery rather than therapy, paired with comprehensive nutrition and mindful exercise." "Wrap-around care in a secure, wellness-promoting environment full of dedicated and highly qualified staff." **Staff:** "A combination of hot yoga, personalized smoothie supplements based on an analysis of each individual client's metabolism, as well as daily solitary reflection times." "Clients solve their existential crisis through insightful self-discovery in combination with organic food, and a spa-like experience. Our program uniquely engages the whole person by engaging mind, body, and soul. We cover it all." **Clients:** "There isn't any therapy, but there is a lot of alone time to think, reflect, and renew." "Lots of quotes, time to myself, too much hot yoga, and not enough comfort food." "There are quotes everywhere that force you to really think. Plus they help you out by controlling everything you do, including what you eat, but all in a way that doesn't lose that resort spa feel."

(Continued)

TABLE 13.2 (*Continued*)

Question	Representative Statements
How effective is the program as it is now?	**Administration:** "*The program is extremely effective. The waiting list for people to enter the program continues to grow.*" "*Our numbers speak for themselves.*" **Staff:** "*We turn lives around. I've been here since we started and have never seen a client come back needing help.*" "*After getting the full experience of our program, clients leave as a brand new person. There is no better evidence of effectiveness than that.*" **Clients:** "*I'm doing well, much better than when I entered the program. I have a whole new perspective on life thanks to The Sanctuary.*" "*The program isn't cheap and you get what you pay for. I know that it changed my life.*" "*I'm guessing that it is very effective considering how hard it is to get into this place.*"
What current measures are in place to determine the program's effectiveness?	**Administration:** "*We aren't doing anything formal.*" "*We recognize the importance of high-quality assessment to gain program-based insights.*" **Staff:** "*We continually check in on clients' progress and monitor them.*" "*We see every day that the program works . . . just look at the smiles on our clients' faces.*" **Clients:** "*They always ask if I'm happy and finding balance, and if I need anything.*" "*I'm really not sure.*" "*Why do they need to? I'm doing much better.*"
What is the goal of the evaluation?	**Administration:** "*An easy-to-understand report that shows the wonderful program we offer here.*" "*Evidence of the high-quality service we provide and identification of potential growth opportunities.*" **Staff:** "*We just want to know that we're doing a good job.*" "*To figure out what we should do more, and what we should do less.*"

	Clients: *"To tell them what they already know. This place is the best."* *"To see if they can charge more."* *"Probably to help advertise and increase their popularity."*
What do you hope the program evaluation accomplishes?	**Administration:** *"We'd like to have empirical evidence of program effectiveness that we can share with external agencies to secure potential funding."* *"Validation of the good work we are doing at The Sanctuary."* **Staff:** *"To affirm the good that we are doing, but also to improve anything we can."* *"It is clear that we are helping people, but to have some evidence of that would be great."* **Clients:** *"I'm really not sure."* *"I'd like to see just how good the treatment I'm getting is."* *"To practice what they preach."*

Looking more closely at the focus group data, we learned about several key aspects of the program. The Sanctuary Under the Palms' program uses a unique, self-guided style of treatment to help clients overcome their addictions. The program requires an inpatient stay at their West Palm Beach facility for 30 consecutive days during which clients cannot leave or have visitors. Clients of the program suffer from alcohol or substance dependency involving painkillers or prescription drugs. The program also states that benefits should only be evident after a client completes the full 30-day program cycle.

Based on the focus group transcripts and subsequent coding, several themes emerged that help us summarize the program. The Sanctuary Under the Palms' "unique treatment" appears to involve "self-guided discovery rather than therapy," "quotes," "daily solitary reflection times," "personalized smoothie supplements based on an analysis of each individual client's metabolism," "organic food," and "hot yoga." "Successful outcomes" involve "overcome my addiction," "personal growth," "feeling empowered," "having a meaningful life," and "being happy." Instead of discussing the implications of our findings as we have in the past, the focus group data is merely the first step in our program evaluation. At the end of the full evaluation, we will discuss the focus group findings as part of our overall report, rather than writing separate reports following each step. Now that we have completed the first three steps in our program evaluation by identifying stakeholders, describing the program, and establishing goals for the evaluation, we can take the next step.

What Do You Think?
What other outcomes would it make sense for a program evaluation to assess?

Thinking Like a Scientist in Real Life

Are News "Focus" Groups Informative?

If you regularly watch the news, you most likely have seen a reporter moderating a discussion among a small focus group of "ordinary" people or "experts" on an upcoming election or social issue facing the country. Have you ever considered whether these "made for TV" focus groups are really that informative or unbiased? To help make this determination, you should ask yourself several questions. First, who does the group include? It seems likely that those willing to express their opinions on television hold strong, and some may say biased, views concerning the topic under discussion. Good focus groups should represent all relevant constituencies and incorporate a variety of opinions and viewpoints. Second, what role is the moderator playing in the group? It is possible that the moderator poses leading questions that encourage responses that convey a particular opinion. Similarly, the moderator could let some individuals dominate the discussion at the expense of those with contrary views. In a good focus group, the moderator should remain objective and value-free. Finally, what group dynamics do you observe among participants? There could be evidence of subtle pressure to agree with certain viewpoints or opinions. Participants' body language can also suggest that they have disengaged themselves from the conversation or are quietly disagreeing with others' statements, rather than actively contributing. Remember: A focus group's purpose is to inform, not to entertain, create artificial conflict, or confirm preexisting opinions. The next time you see the news asking for thoughts from a group, we hope that you will ask these questions and think about what you see differently.

Weighing Our Options: Taking the Next Step

We know from Chapter 5 that researchers use mixed methods research, or a blend of qualitative and quantitative methods, to capitalize on the strengths of each method when examining a research question from multiple perspectives. We should do the same for our program evaluation plan because it will help us obtain higher-quality information.

By gathering data on program effectiveness from the focus groups, we have essentially completed "Study 1." This qualitative information provides us with a strong foundation, and allows us to make informed decisions about the following steps of our program evaluation, but is from a relatively small number of participants. We should determine if the themes that emerged from the focus groups hold in a larger sample, perhaps by treating the themes as the key variables we want to explore in a descriptive research design. As we learned in Chapter 6, observation is a useful way to obtain descriptive information. Yet, in our case, many of the key outcome variables for evaluating the program's effectiveness (e.g., personal growth, having a meaningful life, empowerment) do not lend themselves easily to direct observation. Given that the individual is the person with the most information about each of these variables, a survey relying on self-report is a more appropriate form of descriptive research and a better choice for our second study. To design our survey, we can let the focus group themes and individual responses guide how we operationalize the variables. Specifically, these themes can help us generate survey questions or identify established measures in the literature that address key variables.

Once we conduct our survey and obtain the results, it would be ideal for us to track clients over a year or two as part of a longitudinal study to determine if the program's effectiveness changes over time. Unfortunately, Programulation and the Board of Trustees want our report to them by the end of the semester, making a longitudinal design impossible. In addition, our limited research budget precludes such an extensive investigation. Though this does not seem ideal in terms of employing the best research design possible, in fairness to the Board's desires, a program evaluation needs to be timely and cost-effective in order to be maximally beneficial. That is, The Sanctuary does not want to go another year or two without knowing whether they are doing a good job, could do a better job, or, worse, are harming clients in some fashion. Despite not including a longitudinal design in our program evaluation plan, we will suggest in our final report that The Sanctuary Under the Palms continue to monitor its program and consider implementing a longer-term evaluation.

▶ Interested in learning more about longitudinal designs?
SEE CHAPTER 10, p. 322

YOUR TURN 13.1

1. Amelia wants to open a community center in her neighborhood where students can go after school instead of being home alone. She needs to determine who would benefit most from the community center and what would be the most valuable services to offer. Which type of program evaluation should she conduct?

   a. A needs evaluation

   b. A process evaluation

   c. An outcomes evaluation

   d. A focus group

2. Bart has finished the planning phase of a program evaluation on the first-year experience at his university. What is his next step after gathering and analyzing the data?

   a. Identifying stakeholders

   b. Describing the program

   c. Communicating his results

   d. Clarifying the goals of the evaluation

3. For your senior capstone project, you plan on conducting a focus group at your former high school to learn about the effectiveness of recent education reforms. You would like information from administrators, teachers, parents, and students, and want to be mindful of power differentials. Which groups make the most sense?

   a. Group 1 (Administrators/Teachers); Group 2 (Parents/Students)
   b. Group 1 (Administrators/Teachers); Group 2 (Parents); Group 3 (Students)
   c. Group 1 (Administrators); Group 2 (Teachers); Group 3 (Parents/Students)
   d. Group 1 (Administrators); Group 2 (Teachers); Group 3 (Parents); Group 4 (Students)

How did you do? Turn to the end of the chapter to check your answers.

Design in Action

Putting our program evaluation into action requires us to conduct two studies: Study 1 = Focus Group and Study 2 = Survey. We have already completed Study 1, which provided qualitative information about the program's effectiveness. Utilizing a survey design for Study 2 will enable us to gather quantitative information about program outcomes. We can use what we learned from the focus groups to develop our survey.

Weighing Our Options: Conducting a Survey to Test Treatment Effectiveness

Whereas our focus groups helped us identify how various stakeholders felt about the program, a survey can help us quantify the extent to which a person holds a particular perspective. For example, in the focus groups, someone may have said, "The program worked for me." A survey will tell us whether it worked just a little, moderately well, or really well. It will also let us see if the program worked for many other clients, or just a few. While the focus groups provided a large amount of detailed information on several different questions from a broad cross-section of stakeholders, a survey will allow us to gather more specific information about our research question from a larger group of stakeholders.

Defining Key Terms: What Do You Mean By _____?

To plan our survey study, we first need to determine what our key variables should be. Here, we should take full advantage of our focus group findings, asking specifically about the "unique treatment" and the "successful outcomes" that emerged as key themes. For the treatment, themes included "self-guided discovery rather than therapy," "quotes," "daily solitary reflection times," "personalized smoothie supplements based on an analysis of each individual client's metabolism," "organic food," and "hot yoga." In terms of program effectiveness, we should ask participants how much each individual aspect contributed to their personal outcomes. We can use these themes as individual items on our survey, asking participants, "How much has each of the following helped you while in this program?" using a 1–7 scale (1 = not at all; 7 = a great deal).

We also need to take the focus group themes regarding successful outcomes and turn them into variables. Our focus group participants used their own terms to describe psychological constructs, so we will need to identify those constructs by carefully reviewing the focus group transcripts and considering what the participants meant by their statements. For example, the statement "overcome my addiction" probably refers to the person's addiction recovery or a lack of dependency and ability to function normally on a daily basis. "Feeling empowered" relates to being in control of one's own outcomes or having an internal locus of control. "Having a meaningful life" refers to a person whose life satisfaction is high. Other themes from the focus group such as "personal growth" and "happiness" map directly onto established psychological constructs.

The scales or measures we include in our survey ultimately determine how we operationalize each construct or variable. That is, how we operationally define happiness depends on the scale we find or the measure we create. Although creating a measure is sometimes necessary, it is always best to use measures with established reliability and validity if possible. To find such measures for our key variables, we should conduct a literature search.

Reviewing the Literature: Finding Scales to Measure Our Variables

Throughout this book, we have used a literature search to help us learn more about the topics related to our research question. We did not need to do that this time because the focus groups provided the background information. Now, however, we can use a literature search to help us find articles where researchers describe the scales they created to measure a particular variable. To do this, we will use the search boxes in a research database to our advantage. We search for "Personal Growth" in the "TI Title" field and "Scale" in the "KW Keywords" field in both PsycINFO and PubMed and find the following articles that discuss measures related to our key variables. From each article we extract information about what the scale intends to measure, example items, Cronbach's alpha, and how to score the scale.

Addiction Recovery

Butler, S. F., Budman, S. H., McGee, M. D., Davis, M. S., Cornelli, R., & Morey, L. C. (2005). Addiction severity assessment tool: Development of a self-report measure for clients in substance abuse treatment. *Drug and Alcohol Dependency, 80,* 349–360. doi:10.1016/j.drugalcdep.2005.05.005

Total Items = 27; Purpose = allows adults to self-report their dependence severity, recovery effectiveness, daily and relationship functioning, and negative feelings; Example Items = "I can't ignore my cravings for alcohol or drugs" and "I am able to do the things I need to do each day (reverse-scored)"; Scale = four-point scale (1 = not at all true; 4 = very true) with higher scores (mean of items) indicating more addiction; Alpha = .93.

Personal Growth

Robitschek, C. (1998). Personal growth initiative: The construct and its measure. *Measurement and Evaluation in Counseling and Development, 30,* 183–198.

> **What Do You Think?**
> What additional concepts could we measure to determine the effectiveness of treatment?

Total Items = 9; Purpose = Measure individual's involvement in her/his own personal growth enhancing experiences; Example Items = "I have a good sense of where I am headed in life" and "I know what I need to do to get started toward reaching my goals"; Scale = six-point scale (0 = disagree strongly; 5 = agree strongly) with higher scores indicating more personal growth initiative (scores range from 0–45); Alpha = .93.

Locus of Control

Rotter, J. B. (1966). Generalized expectancies for internal versus external control of reinforcement. *Psychological Monographs, 80,* 609. doi:10.1037/h0092976

Total Items = 29; Purpose = Measures whether a person believes outcomes are contingent upon her/his own behavior or external forces; Example Items = Participants select from two options: "a. Becoming a success is a matter of hard work, luck has little or nothing to do with it. b. Getting a good job depends mainly on being in the right place at the right time"; Scale = one point for each option that indicates external locus of control, with higher scores indicating more external locus of control (scores range from 0–29); Scale reliabilities from several samples ranged from .65 to .79.

Life Satisfaction

Diener, E., Emmons, R. A., Larsen, R. J., & Griffin, S. (1985). The Satisfaction with Life Scale. *Journal of Personality Assessment, 49,* 71–75. doi:10.1207/s15327752jpa4901_13

Total Items = 5; Purpose = To assess global life satisfaction; Example Items = "In most ways my life is close to my ideal" and "I am satisfied with life"; Scale = seven-point scale (1 = strongly disagree; 7 = strongly agree) with higher scores indicating more satisfaction; Alpha = .87.

Happiness

Lyubomirsky, S., & Lepper, H. S. (1999). A measure of subjective happiness: Preliminary reliability and construct validation. *Social Indicators Research, 46,* 137–155. doi:10.1023/A:1006824100041

Total Items = 4; Purpose = To measure an individual's current level of happiness; Example Item = "Some people are generally very happy. They enjoy life regardless of what is going on, getting the most out of everything. To what extent does this characterization describe you?"; Scale = seven-point scale with anchors that vary by item and higher scores indicating more happiness; Scale reliabilities from several samples ranged from .79 to .94.

With this information in hand, we need to decide if we will use the measures "as is" or if it is better for us to adapt them slightly to fit our needs. For example, in thinking ahead to how we will present findings in our report, it would be best if we reported all measures in the same way. That is, for consistency, rather than having some sum scores and some mean scores, we will calculate means for the personal growth and locus of control scales rather than using sums as the authors did. Similarly, for the addiction recovery scale, it is more intuitive and consistent with other measures to have high scores indicate the more positive outcomes.

The scale information from the articles will also help us describe the measures in our final report so that the Board of Trustees can see that we used quality measures. For example, we would describe the Addiction Severity Assessment

Tool (ASAT) as a 27-item measure that assesses a person's dependence on drugs or alcohol. Example items include "I can't ignore my cravings for alcohol or drugs," and "I am able to do the things I need to do each day (*reverse-scored*)." We would explain that we modified the scale to make interpretation of the results easier for the program. Specifically, participants respond to each statement using a four-point scale (1 = very true; 4 = not at all true), with higher scores indicating less addiction. The scale is reliable (Cronbach's alpha = .93).

The measures we found through our literature search cover most of what we need. However, the literature did not have a scale that asks specifically about clients' perceptions of the program itself. We will need to create our own measure. One option is to simply ask clients about their satisfaction with the program (e.g., "Were you happy with your experience in the program?"). But this type of question is laden with demand characteristics that may lead participants to tell us what they think we want to hear ("Of course I'm happy."). More importantly, this question does not specifically address program effectiveness. That is, a person could be very happy with an ineffective program, while another person could be unhappy with a highly effective program. Instead, we could ask, "Was The Sanctuary Under the Palms' approach effective in helping you deal with addiction?" and have them respond using a six-point scale (1 = extremely ineffective; 2 = ineffective; 3 = somewhat ineffective; 4 = somewhat effective; 5 = effective; 6 = extremely effective). This question also has the benefit of having high face validity because it directly addresses our research question. The downside is that it is a **single-item indicator,** meaning that we measure a variable with only one question. This can present several problems. One concern is reliability, as these types of measurements can fluctuate more due to random error. The second issue is that this item only measures effectiveness in the general sense and is not able to tap into each of the specific outcomes. We will need to be aware of these issues as we analyze our findings. Finally, we will include in our survey general demographic questions (e.g., age, sex, and ethnicity), as well as questions about the client's addiction history (program status, days in the program, days sober, and substance of abuse).

In terms of putting our survey into action, we need to consider which of our stakeholders are in the best position to assess program effectiveness. Although we included the program staff in the focus group, staff members have a vested interest in the program's effectiveness (e.g., if the program is not effective, they may be out of a job) and may not be able to provide unbiased answers. Clients, however, should be much more honest in their assessment, so we will use both past and current clients as our participants, just as we did with the focus groups. More specifically, we should focus on current clients who have been in the program for a long enough period of time to have an informed opinion concerning its effectiveness. We will only survey current clients who have been in the program for at least 10 days.

We will administer the survey using a "paper and pencil" format, meaning that we will provide participants with printed copies that they will complete by writing in the answers. Before we actually distribute the survey, we should first share the survey and our planned protocol with Programulation and the Board

▶ Want to learn more about scale item construction? SEE CHAPTER 7, p. 203

single-item indicator only one item or question being used to measure a variable.

of Trustees. Under normal circumstances, we would have our study reviewed by an Institutional Review Board. However, because our study is part of a program review for a specific organization, we do not require IRB approval. This does not mean that we do not have to worry about ethics. Asking our project lead and the Board of Trustees to review and approve our study will help minimize potential ethical problems that we may not have fully considered.

The Board is fine with our protocol, but asks that we take greater steps to ensure the participants' confidentiality given patient privacy concerns. We assure the Board that we will not include any identifying information as part of the survey and that we will have no direct contact with respondents. We will also use implied consent, which means that rather than having participants sign and include an informed consent with their response, we will note at the beginning of the survey that returning it implies the participant's consent to being part of the study. To address confidentiality concerns, and because our research focuses on providing internal feedback for this particular program, we will skip the steps we typically take regarding open science (e.g., preregistration).

To distribute the survey, we place a copy in current clients' in-house mailboxes and mail former clients the survey to their home addresses, along with a stamped return envelope. To facilitate our data collection efforts, the center has committed to offering all survey participants their choice of a $50 gift card from several popular stores in exchange for their participation. The program is currently in its 5th year and averages 80 clients per month, though in the first 4 years they only averaged 5–10 per month. This gives us a potential data set of approximately 1,100 former clients. However, response rates on these types of mailed surveys are notoriously low, so we will hope to have a final data set of around 100 participants.

▶ Want more information about response rates? SEE CHAPTER 7, p. 223

As we receive the completed surveys, we enter the data and then lock the actual surveys in a cabinet to keep the survey responses confidential. Our data set has a column for each place on the survey where a participant could provide a response. For example, each item from the Addiction Severity Assessment Tool (ASAT) will have a column (e.g., ASAT01, ASAT02, etc.). Each participant's data will appear on its own row. To analyze our data, we first create means for each of the scales, as shown in **Figure 13.3**. To answer our central question about the program's effectiveness with helping addiction, we will run descriptive statistics on our outcome variables. To see if perceptions of each program feature and outcome are significantly higher than the scale midpoint, we will conduct **single sample t-tests**, which evaluate whether a sample mean statistically differs from a specific value. Scores significantly higher than the midpoint would indicate that the clients fall at the positive end of a particular measure.

Typically, we would write up the results of our analyses using APA style. For now, we only need to determine our findings so that we can use them as part of the overall program evaluation report. Often the best way to quickly make sense of data is with tables. The results of our analysis are in **Table 13.3**. As you can see from the table, clients report significantly high outcomes for all variables except locus of control. We also asked clients how individual features of the program's treatment contributed to their successful outcomes. Clients rated every aspect of treatment as almost uniformly highly

single sample t-tests a statistic to evaluate whether a sample mean statistically differs from a specific value.

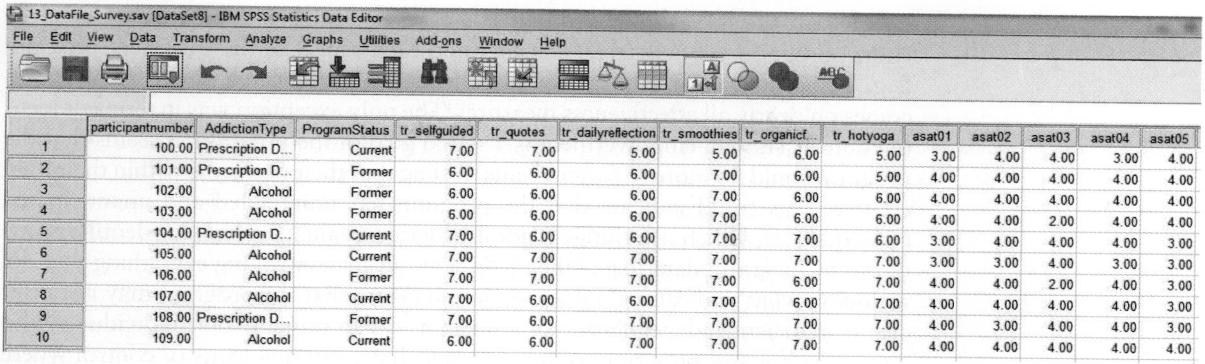
13_DataFile_Survey.sav [DataSet8] - IBM SPSS Statistics Data Editor
File Edit View Data Transform Analyze Graphs Utilities Add-ons Window Help

	participantnumber	AddictionType	ProgramStatus	tr_selfguided	tr_quotes	tr_dailyreflection	tr_smoothies	tr_organicf...	tr_hotyoga	asat01	asat02	asat03	asat04	asat05
1	100.00	Prescription D...	Current	7.00	7.00	5.00	5.00	6.00	5.00	3.00	4.00	4.00	3.00	4.00
2	101.00	Prescription D...	Former	6.00	6.00	6.00	7.00	6.00	5.00	4.00	4.00	4.00	4.00	4.00
3	102.00	Alcohol	Former	6.00	6.00	6.00	7.00	6.00	6.00	4.00	4.00	4.00	4.00	4.00
4	103.00	Alcohol	Former	6.00	6.00	6.00	7.00	6.00	6.00	4.00	4.00	2.00	4.00	4.00
5	104.00	Prescription D...	Current	7.00	6.00	6.00	7.00	7.00	6.00	3.00	4.00	4.00	4.00	3.00
6	105.00	Alcohol	Current	7.00	7.00	7.00	7.00	7.00	7.00	3.00	3.00	4.00	3.00	3.00
7	106.00	Alcohol	Former	7.00	7.00	7.00	7.00	6.00	7.00	4.00	4.00	2.00	4.00	3.00
8	107.00	Alcohol	Current	7.00	6.00	6.00	7.00	6.00	7.00	4.00	4.00	4.00	4.00	3.00
9	108.00	Prescription D...	Former	7.00	6.00	7.00	7.00	7.00	7.00	4.00	3.00	4.00	4.00	3.00
10	109.00	Alcohol	Current	6.00	6.00	7.00	7.00	7.00	7.00	4.00	4.00	4.00	4.00	4.00

FIGURE 13.3 Survey Data Set Spreadsheet. *(SPSS)*

effective (on a seven-point scale): self-guided discovery ($M = 6.50$, $SD = .52$), quotes ($M = 6.63$, $SD = .50$), daily reflection ($M = 6.52$, $SD = .52$), smoothies ($M = 6.75$, $SD = .51$), organic food ($M = 6.49$, $SD = .50$), and hot yoga ($M = 6.74$, $SD = .54$). Single sample *t*-tests confirm that clients rated each significantly above the scale midpoint (all *t*'s > 59.29).

Although these analyses answer our key research question regarding program effectiveness, our data can give us other information for our final report that may interest the Board of Trustees. For example, we can run a *t*-test for independent means to compare current clients to former clients who completed the program on the various outcomes. The results indicate that former clients report significantly higher outcomes for all variables compared to current clients except for locus of control and satisfaction with life. Similarly, a *t*-test for independent means comparing clients by addiction type on outcomes revealed that addiction type only influenced locus of control, such that those dealing with alcohol addiction reported more empowerment (i.e., had higher internal locus of control) than those dealing with prescription drug addiction. We will be sure to include figures depicting all of these results in the final report.

▶ When should we use *t*-tests to test our hypotheses?
SEE CHAPTER 8, p. 268

TABLE 13.3

Descriptive Statistics and Differences From Scale Midpoint on Key Outcome Variables

Variable	*M*	*SD*	*t*	*P*
Addiction Recovery	3.61	0.23	72.71	<.001
Personal Growth	4.56	0.31	67.75	<.001
Locus of Control	0.48	0.17	–1.01	.313
Satisfaction with Life	6.20	0.48	57.49	<.001
Happiness	61.15	0.53	61.15	<.001
Effective Approach (single item)	5.70	0.57	39.57	<.001

Note: $n = 106$. Higher scores indicate a greater magnitude of each variable.

Overall, the survey indicated that 106 clients consider The Sanctuary Under the Palms' program very effective. Clients rated each aspect of the treatment program (e.g., smoothies, yoga, etc.) as equally effective, and indicated above-average outcomes on nearly all effectiveness measures. The only exception was in terms of locus of control. Though empowerment is a stated goal of the program, it seems that the program could do more to foster clients' feeling that their destiny is within their own control. This could indicate that the program has unintended and unanticipated consequences, which are things a good program evaluation should identify. Some of the focus group data (e.g., "they help you out by controlling everything you do, including what you eat . . .") does seem to indicate that the program may not offer clients sufficient independence. Of course, it is also possible that individuals who abuse alcohol and prescription drugs tend to have external locus of control where they believe uncontrollable factors outside of themselves control their destiny. Temporal precedence is an aspect that The Sanctuary can examine in the future.

Our survey results also revealed that former clients who have graduated from the program reported higher ratings than current clients on all outcomes except locus of control and life satisfaction. This finding is consistent with how the program describes itself (i.e., that clients should see benefits upon completing the full 30-day program cycle) and with focus group findings where program staff and clients mentioned the importance of the "full experience." As one former client from the focus group put it, "During the program I had my doubts, but after getting the full experience, I know that it changed my life." Although not significant, there was a trend for current clients to have a greater sense of empowerment (i.e., greater internal locus of control) than former clients. The lack of significance on life satisfaction may reflect the fact that the former clients who responded to the survey had not been out of the program for very long ($M = 13.34$ days; $SD = 11.97$, $range = 2$–60 days).

YOUR TURN 13.2

1. Neville decides to simply ask, "How anxious do you currently feel?" instead of using several questions as a measure of anxiety in his study. This is an example of which of the following?
   a. Triangulation
   b. A single-item indicator
   c. Methodological pluralism
   d. An experimenter bias

2. Professor Snape redesigns his chemistry class to make much more of the learning interactive. He wants to know if his new method of teaching has improved students' learning from last year. What statistical test would he use to determine if the current class has significantly better grades than the class average last year?
   a. A single sample t-test
   b. An independent samples t-test
   c. A correlation
   d. A one-way ANOVA

3. What could an experiment tell us that Study 2 (the survey) cannot?
   a. Whether the treatment program helps people recover from addiction more effectively than no treatment.
   b. Whether clients are significantly higher than the midpoint on addiction recovery.
   c. Whether clients are not higher than the midpoint on locus of control.
   d. Whether clients perceive the program as beneficial to their recovery.

How did you do? Turn to the end of the chapter to check your answers.

The Program Evaluation Report: In Search of Answers

Now that we have completed the two studies in our program evaluation plan, we can pull together the key findings to address Programulation and the Board of Trustee's fundamental question: "Is The Sanctuary Under the Palms' approach an effective way to help individuals deal with addiction?" Each study provides some unique insight that answers that question, but the systematic nature of the studies also helps us identify which findings are most consistent and reliable. Our final report—an example anatomy of which can be found in **Figure 13.4**—should include both types of information when discussing the findings.

Writing the Results in a Program Evaluation Report

Typically, psychology researchers present their findings in an APA-style results section that includes APA-style tables and figures. However, we need to consider our intended audience and communicate our findings in the format that is most useful to potential future clients, the director, staff, and Board of Trustees. As a result, we will avoid jargon by using nontechnical and straightforward language. We will try to avoid discussion of complex statistics in our report, and we will present information in tables or figures that are easy to interpret. In addition, we will provide Programulation and The Sanctuary with all of our findings and materials as supplemental material in the appendices.

Program Evaluation Report

Program Goals and Objectives
   A. Program Context
   B. Program Participants
   C. Program Goals

Evaluation's Procedure and Methods
   A. Identify Stakeholders/Information Sources
   B. Gather Information to Describe Program
   C. Gather Information to Clarify Evaluation's Goals
   D. Evaluation Plan and Procedures

Summary of Key Findings
   A. Study 1
   B. Study 2

Conclusion and Program Recommendations
   A. Overall Comments (Program Goals vs. Outcomes)
   B. Program Strengths and Weaknesses
   C. Recommendations for Program Improvement
   D. Recommendations for Continued Evaluation

Appendices
   A. Research Measures/Materials Used for the Evaluation
   B. Data (Transcripts, Data Files, etc.)
   C. Full Report of Analyses and Findings
   D. References

FIGURE 13.4 Anatomy of a Program Evaluation Report.

Program Evaluation Report: Summary of Key Findings

Study 1: Focus Groups

- Three groups—Administration (8 people); Staff (10 people); Clients (11; 8 current and 3 former)—responded to the question, "How effective is the program as it is now?"

Key Findings

- Administration, program staff, and clients were unanimous in their belief in program effectiveness.
- Clients expressed a range of benefits: addiction recovery, growth, happiness, a better life, and empowerment.
- Key evidence of effectiveness includes:
  - (administration) number of people on the program's waitlist
  - (staff) clients not returning to the program for additional help;
  - (staff) being able to see the difference in clients;
  - (clients) feeling better than when they entered; and
  - (clients) difficulty getting into the program.
- Example Administration Response: *"The program is extremely effective; it is obvious when people leave that they are doing better. The waiting list for people to enter the program continues to grow."*

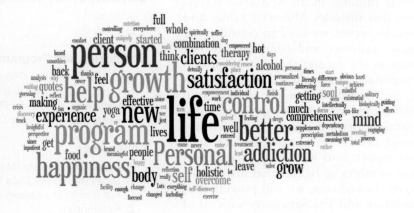

(wordle.net)

- Example Staff Response: *"After getting the full experience of our program, clients leave as a brand new person. There is no better evidence of effectiveness than that."*
- Example Client Response: *"I can feel that I'm a better person than when I started."*

Summary

We created a **word cloud** by entering all of the focus group transcripts into an online app (www.wordle.net) that visually conveys the frequency that certain words were used. The larger the word in the word cloud, the more frequently it was used. Less frequent words are smaller in size. As you can see, the vast majority of the largest words are positive, which reflects administrators', staff's, and clients' feelings about program effectiveness.

Study 2: Survey

- A group of 106 current and former clients completed measures designed to assess program effectiveness.

Key Findings and Summary Figures

- Clients considered all facets of the program (e.g., quotes, smoothies, etc.) to be valuable. (See **Figure 13.5.**)

Program Feature	Percentage	Grade
Self-Guided Discovery	92.86%	A-
Quotes	94.71%	A
Daily Reflection	93.00%	A
Smoothies	96.43%	A+
Organic Food	92.71%	A-
Hot Yoga	96.29%	A+

Note: Percentage indicates where each scale's mean fell relative to the highest possible scale score.

FIGURE 13.5 Treatment Report Card.

word cloud a visual representation of the frequency with which certain words are used in a qualitative assessment; larger words indicate higher frequency of use.

- Clients reported high outcomes pertaining to addiction recovery, personal growth, life satisfaction, and happiness, but did not report high levels of empowerment. (See **Figure 13.6.**)

Outcome	Percentage	Grade
Addiction Recovery	90.25%	A−
Personal Growth	91.09%	A−
Locus of Control	51.69%	F
Satisfaction with Life	88.57%	B+
Happiness	94.71%	A
Effective Approach	95.00%	A

Note: Percentage indicates where each scale's mean fell relative to the highest possible scale score.

FIGURE 13.6 Outcomes Report Card.

- Clients reported that the program effectively helped them deal with their addiction. (See **Figure 13.7.**)

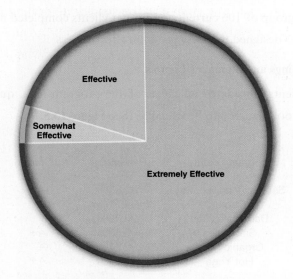

FIGURE 13.7 Program Effectiveness by Percentage.

- The program was more effective for former clients than current clients on all outcomes except locus of control and life satisfaction. (See **Figure 13.8.**)

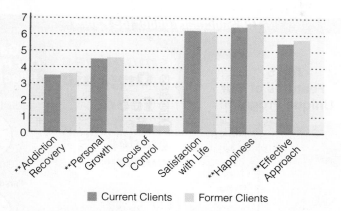

Current Clients   **Former Clients**

Note: Variables designated with ** are those for which there is a significant difference between conditions.

FIGURE 13.8 Outcomes on Key Variables by Client Type.

- The program was more effective for clients dealing with alcohol addiction in terms of locus of control. The program was equally effective for both addiction types for all other outcomes. (See **Figure 13.9.**)

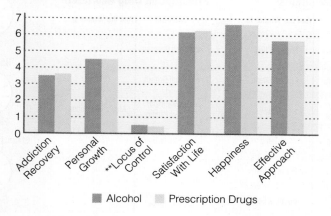

Alcohol   **Prescription Drugs**

Note: Variables designated with ** are those for which there is a significant difference between conditions.

FIGURE 13.9 Outcomes on Key Variables by Addiction Type.

▶ Curious to learn more about infographics?
SEE CHAPTER 1, p. 18

Finally, given The Sanctuary Under the Palms' desire to use findings as a way to advertise their program's effectiveness to future clients, we can present key findings in an infographic. Although not something that we could do in an APA-style paper, an infographic can quickly convey a lot of information in an engaging and easy-to-understand format.

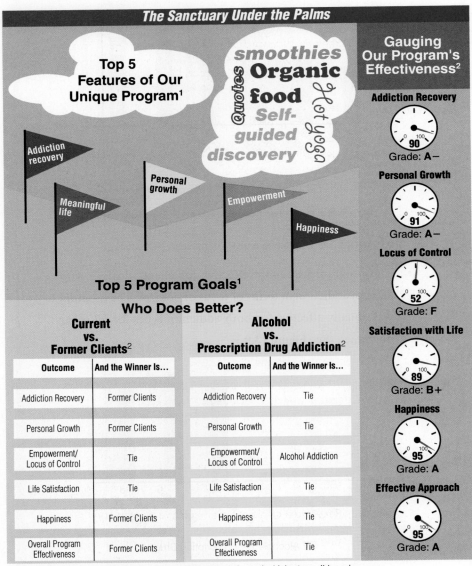

Note: Percentage indicates where each scale's mean fell relative to the highest possible scale score.
[1] Data taken from Study 1 (Focus Group)
[2] Data taken from Study 2 (Survey)

Program Evaluation Results for The Sanctuary Under the Palms.

Our Research Plan at a Glance

What Is Our Research Question? Is The Sanctuary Under the Palms' approach an effective way to help individuals deal with addiction?

What Is Our Design? We are using an outcomes evaluation (a type of program evaluation) consisting of two studies: focus groups and a survey.

Why Are We Using This Design? An outcomes evaluation is a framework for determining whether a program produces results that are consistent with stated objectives or goals. Study 1, the focus groups, allows us to determine if three types of stakeholders (administration, staff, and clients) have similar ideas about the program's goals and effectiveness. Study 2, the survey, builds on this qualitative information by soliciting ratings from current and former clients to quantify program effectiveness.

What Are Our Variables?

> **Study 1:** Because of the type of design we are using, there are no true independent or dependent variables.

> **Study 2:** We have the following variables, none of which we manipulate: perceived effectiveness of program features and program outcomes (addiction recovery, personal growth, locus of control, satisfaction with life, happiness, overall effectiveness). We use scales adapted from the relevant literature to assess each variable except overall effectiveness, which we assess using a self-developed, single-item scale.

What Are Our Hypotheses? With this design, we do not have pre-established hypotheses to test. We take a bottom-up approach and allow the information that we collect to inform our conclusions. However, we do establish a protocol of guiding topics for our focus groups in Study 1, and use the key themes that emerge to inform our survey questions in Study 2.

Who Are Our Participants?

> **Study 1:** Administration, staff, and current and former clients.

> **Study 2:** Current and former clients.

What Ethical Considerations Do We Need to Keep in Mind?

- Are there possible negative effects or unintended consequences for administration, staff, and/or clients from doing this evaluation?

What Is Our Data Analysis Plan?

1. **Complete our content analysis (Study 1).** We assess the content of responses from our three focus groups to determine key themes and create a word cloud.

2. **Calculate our data (Study 2).** Using data collected from our survey, we determine if participants' perceptions of program features and reported outcomes are higher than the scale midpoint using a single sample t-test. We compare outcomes for current versus former clients with a t-test for independent means, and compare outcomes for addiction type (alcohol vs. prescription drugs) with an additional t-test for independent means.

Want to practice the analyses for this research yourself? Ask your instructor about the data set that accompanies this study.

The Program Evaluation Report: Conclusions and Program Recommendations

By this point, we have unpacked the results of our two studies, and presented some overall findings. If we were writing an APA-style paper with multiple studies, we would have a section for "General Discussion" to interpret the overall themes and place the findings in context. We would also discuss the strengths and weaknesses of our studies, and suggest future research directions. For a program evaluation, we essentially want to do the same thing. However, the "Conclusion and Program Recommendations" section of our report (see Figure 13.4) focuses more specifically on how the outcome findings match up with the program goals, what the findings indicate about the program's strengths and weaknesses, and what steps the program should take for improvement, as well as subsequent evaluation. As we write these sections, we should be mindful that readers of this report likely do not have the same research background as we do, so we should be sure to help them avoid potential misinterpretations of the data.

In addition to our written report, we will schedule a series of presentations—first with the team at Programulation, then with key stakeholders at The Sanctuary—where we can discuss our findings. When communicating findings in either format, we should anticipate stakeholders expressing "we knew it all along," hindsight-biased reactions to our findings by reminding them about the benefits of having data to support assumptions. Before our program evaluation, it may have seemed like their program was effective, but now they know it with greater certainty. It is also worth pointing out that the program was not universally effective, and that some of their assumptions about the program's impact on clients were inaccurate and overconfident. When program evaluation findings disagree with prevailing opinions, we will likely find stakeholders expressing reactions like, "Numbers are useless; I know from my own experience what's accurate." In these cases, we can incorporate information about natural flaws in thinking into our presentations.

▶ Want to learn more about common flaws in thinking? SEE CHAPTER 1, p. 3

Why These Findings?

One indicator of program effectiveness is if the program's outcomes align with its goals. We learned from the staff in our focus group that The Sanctuary Under the Palms' goal is to provide a 30-day inpatient, holistic mind–body treatment program that fosters clients' addiction recovery, growth, empowerment, life satisfaction, and happiness. In each of our two studies, clients reported outcomes consistent with these program goals. The survey data confirmed the center's perspective on the importance of completing the full 30-day program for the best treatment outcomes. The focus groups revealed that administration, staff, and clients were unanimous in their view of the program's effectiveness. The groups' participants based their views on circumstantial evidence, such as size of the waitlist, program expense, and personal feelings about clients' progress, while the broader sample of clients in the survey revealed similar levels of belief in the program's effectiveness, with empowerment as a glaring exception. In addition, the survey allowed us to dig a bit deeper and revealed that the program generally helped former clients more than current clients, and the program helped empower those dealing with alcohol addictions.

Taking Studies 1 and 2 together, the overall program evaluation results demonstrate The Sanctuary Under the Palms' effectiveness. Unfortunately, without an experiment, we cannot pinpoint which aspect of the program is most responsible for its positive outcomes. The program's daily reflection component resembles the idea of mindfulness, which facilitates relaxation, increases positive affect, and reduces cravings among those undergoing treatment (Fernandez, Wood, Stein, & Rossi, 2010; Witkiewitz, Lustyk, & Bowen, 2013). Given the research showing the benefits of yoga for helping people overcome nicotine addiction/smoking (Bock et al., 2012), it is also possible that the yoga portion of The Sanctuary's program is at least partially responsible for the positive outcomes. Additional research would be beneficial in this area.

What Could Be Improved?

Based on our program evaluation, The Sanctuary Under the Palms' program has several strengths. First, the program administration, staff, and clients are all "believers" in the program and what it tries to accomplish. This type of "buy-in" should only help program effectiveness. Second, there is a high level of agreement between program staff and clients in terms of program goals and methods, which indicates that the program does a good job of communicating its objectives. Third, while serving two different populations (alcohol and prescription drug abusers) within the same program can present problems, our survey data found both populations reported the program was effective for them.

One weakness of the program is the presence of such a long waitlist. Though program administrators, staff, and, to some extent, clients, view this as a sign of the program's effectiveness (e.g., "The program is extremely effective. The waiting list for people to enter the program continues to grow"), it suggests a need for more resources to expand the program in order to accommodate more clients. Based on some comments from the focus group (e.g., "The program isn't cheap and you get what you pay for"), cost also may be a barrier for potential clients. In terms of the program's effectiveness, the program appears to be ineffective in terms of helping clients feel like they are leading a meaningful life. The lack of findings could be the result of how we measured life satisfaction or because changes on that variable are only evident over a longer period of time. Finally, focus group data where clients stated their success was "thanks to The Sanctuary" and that "they help you out by controlling everything" suggest that the program could perhaps do more to empower clients.

What's Next?

Our program evaluation for Programulation and The Sanctuary Under the Palms reveals a treatment program that provides many benefits for its clients. As such, one recommendation would be for The Sanctuary to broaden its reach by offering the program on an outpatient basis. Program administrators and staff should reevaluate if program improvements could better address clients' feelings about leading a meaningful life. For example, the program could incorporate training that emphasizes character strengths such as gratitude, enthusiasm, and optimism, which research demonstrates improves life satisfaction (Proyer, Ruch, & Buschor, 2013). It is also possible that clients could feel more empowered if clients and coaches engaged in more shared decision making regarding their treatments and schedules. Researchers have found such efforts increase client autonomy and feelings of control in inpatient settings (Joosten, De Jong, de Weert-van Oene, Sensky, & van der Staak, 2011).

The other major recommendation we can make is for The Sanctuary Under the Palms to use this initial program evaluation to build a culture of assessment that continuously provides feedback to help the program improve. First, future program evaluations should seek to replicate the present findings, increasing our confidence that our results were not simply due to chance factors. As part of the replication, the evaluations should include individual interviews with key stakeholders. It is possible that the clients, staff, and administration were not entirely forthcoming in expressing their honest views of the program because of group dynamics. Through one-on-one interviews, individuals may be more willing to honestly assess the program and suggest opportunities for improvements without feeling the need to censor their views due to power differentials in the group. Future evaluations should also explore which treatment features (e.g., hot yoga, quotes, solitary reflection, etc.) are most and least responsible for the program's successes. Finally, future program evaluations should include a longitudinal component to see if the program's effectiveness extends beyond the short term. In all cases, the center should consider seeking out a partnership with a research institution and taking steps to receive IRB approval for their research so that they can potentially publish their findings.

 Research Spotlight

To Toke or Not to Toke?

Just as good science is necessary for demonstrating the effectiveness of programs designed to improve people's lives, good science is equally important for helping to guide important governmental policy decisions. The legalization of cannabis (marijuana) is certainly a controversial issue that science can help inform. To evaluate the neurological impact of cannabis, a research team examined brain function among recent heavy cannabis users who smoked at least seven times per week (Kanayama, Rogowska, Pope, Gruber, & Yurgelun-Todd, 2004). Twelve long-term cannabis users and 10 nonusers performed a spatial working memory task while a functional magnetic resonance imaging (fMRI) machine monitored their brain activity. The heavy cannabis users displayed greater and more widespread brain activation than nonusers, suggesting that they needed more areas in their brain to do the same tasks. Maybe there is truth to the idea that regular cannabis use can lead to neurophysiological deficits, something that policy makers should weigh as they wrestle with the legalization issue and its potential long-term consequences.

YOUR TURN 13.3

1. Which of the following is *not* a recommendation made based on the outcome of our program evaluation?

   a. Clients and coaches should engage in more shared decision making regarding their treatment and schedules.

   b. A continuation of assessment is necessary to continue to improve the program.

   c. The Sanctuary Under the Palms should compare its treatment to other local addiction treatment centers.

   d. The Sanctuary Under the Palms should identify which treatment features are the most effective.

2. Which of the following is a way to visually represent the frequency of specific words used by participants in a qualitative study?

   a. A frequency polygon

   b. A word histogram

   c. A frequency distribution

   d. A word cloud

3. In a program evaluation report, where does one indicate the strengths and weaknesses of the program and what steps the program should take to improve?

   a. In the introduction of the program report

   b. In the "Conclusions and Program Recommendations" section of the program evaluation report

   c. In the evaluation's "Procedure and Methods" section of the program evaluation report

   d. In the appendices of the program evaluation report

How did you do? Turn to the end of the chapter to check your answers.

Research in Action

Why Did You Buy THAT?

What influences your willingness to buy a product? Perhaps it is quality, price, brand name, or a glowing endorsement from your best friend or favorite celebrity. Maybe it is a combination of these factors. Many people have made careers out of market research that answers questions just like these.

By now, you have learned about a number of nonexperimental and experimental designs that psychology researchers commonly use to answer their research questions. How do you know which design to use? The answer is that there is no one right answer—this is just another decision you must make as a researcher. Often the best decision is to create a program of research that uses multiple designs to learn about a topic from different perspectives. In the online activity **Why Did You Buy THAT?**, explore how you can address the same research using a variety of research designs.

 LaunchPad To complete this activity, visit LaunchPad at launchpadworks.com

Final Thoughts

When you learn about psychology, you learn things that empower you to help others. Learning how to conduct quality scientific research—whether during a hands-on internship or in the university lab—is no exception. Psychologists generally post their research procedures on open science websites and publish their findings in scientific journals so that they can eventually improve people's lives. Applied, real-world research endeavors like program evaluations offer a way to help people more directly.

Although the benefits are more immediately obvious, real-world research is messy. We cannot control or manipulate everything that we want. We cannot always use the best design for our questions due to logistical or ethical reasons. However, we can still do high-quality science when addressing real-world problems or trying to answer questions with real-world implications. As long as we exhibit flexibility and creativity as we use our research skills, we can work toward making the world a better place.

CHAPTER 13 Review

Review Questions

1. Professor Sanderson wants to know if his sophomore research methods class prepares his students to successfully complete their senior thesis. What type of program evaluation would help Professor Sanderson answer this question?

   a. A needs evaluation

   b. An outcomes evaluation

   c. A focus group evaluation

   d. A process evaluation

2. The principal at a local charter school wants to demonstrate that the school's alternative curriculum and general approach to education is enabling under-prepared students to succeed in school and beyond. To accomplish this goal, the principal should

   a. pursue programmatic research on the effectiveness of alternative education strategies.

   b. hold focus groups involving current students and their parents.

   c. survey graduates of the charter school.

   d. conduct a program evaluation of the curriculum.

3. As part of the planning stage for a program evaluation she is conducting of a nonprofit group, Camille systematically reviews the organization's website and print publications. What is Camille's goal at this stage of her program review?

   a. To describe the program

   b. To make recommendations for improvement

   c. To create a program evaluation plan

   d. To clarify the program evaluation goals

4. As Camille continues preparing for her program evaluation of a nonprofit group, she asks the director for an organizational chart. Why does Camille want this information?

   a. It will help her clarify the goals for the program evaluation.

   b. She can use the chart to identify potential stakeholders in the program evaluation.

   c. This information will suggest how detailed her program evaluation plan should be.

   d. The program cannot be described without this information.

5. Officials have asked a nearby counseling center to establish a program to provide long-term help to victims of a natural disaster in their community. To get started, the counseling center should

   a. pursue grants to support their efforts.

   b. do a process evaluation.

   c. conduct a needs evaluation.

   d. engage in an outcomes evaluation.

6. Rekha consults with a local food bank to help them improve and expand their delivery of services to the local community. Rekha's first task should be to

   a. pursue grants to support the food bank's new initiatives.

   b. do a process evaluation of the food bank's operations.

   c. conduct a needs evaluation of the local community.

   d. engage in an outcomes evaluation of the food bank's impact in the surrounding area.

7. A university wants to learn how it can better serve the needs of its international students. The director of global initiatives invites several groups of international students to discuss how well the university serves their needs. What data collection strategy is the director employing?

   a. A focus group

   b. Programmatic research

   c. A survey

   d. A program evaluation

8. Wanting to reduce bullying in schools, Dr. Rivera conducts several studies to identify potential factors that influence students' perceptions of bullying. Due to space constraints, she measures bullying perceptions with a single item ("How problematic is bullying in your school?") for students to rate on a six-point scale (1 = not at all problematic; 6 = extremely problematic). Which of the following issues is most likely?

   a. You cannot use a six-point scale with that type of measure.

   b. The measure has low face validity.

   c. The measure cannot distinguish between different types of bullying.

   d. Students may not know what a single-item indicator is.

9. Word clouds can be useful when
   a. interpreting the data from a program evaluation.
   b. writing an APA-style results section.
   c. making recommendations based on a program evaluation.
   d. sharing the results from a program evaluation.

10. After hearing that this year's freshman class is the brightest class ever admitted to his university, Dr. Fung decides to evaluate this claim by comparing mean SAT score for the incoming class against the average new student SAT score from the previous 10 years. Which statistical test should Dr. Fung use?
   a. A single sample t-test
   b. A t-test for dependent means
   c. A t-test for independent means
   d. An independent samples t-test

Applying What You've Learned

1. Find a published empirical article that describes a program evaluation. Evaluate their research design. (a) What could they have done better? (b) What other study could they have run? Why would that extra study help?

2. Find a treatment program on the Internet. Read about the program's goals and program details. Create a set of focus group questions that would help you learn more about the program, and describe how you would carry it out.

3. When writing program evaluation reports, it is important to convey results clearly because your readers may not share your research background. Find a recently published study (i.e., in the last 12 months) on a topic that interests you. In 150 words or less, describe what they did, what they found, and what it means, being sure to avoid technical words and jargon.

4. This chapter's program evaluation included a focus group and a survey. We're giving you a chance for a "do-over." That is, design the best possible experiment to help determine the program's effectiveness without worrying about potential logistical limitations. Just make sure your study is ethical.

5. Using your favorite areas of psychology, generate five new ideas for research questions. Pick your favorite idea and describe how you would use a programmatic research approach to plan three studies that would answer your research question.

6. Read the following study: Milliken, R. (2008). Intervening in the cycle of addiction, violence, and shame: A dance/movement therapy group approach in a jail addictions program. *Journal of Groups in Addiction & Recovery, 3*, 5–22. doi:10.1080/15560350802157346. As you will see, the article provides anecdotal evidence to support their approach. Take on the role of program evaluation intern and help them design a program evaluation plan to assess their program's effectiveness. Be sure to explain the benefits of your plan compared to their current approach.

7. THE NOVICE RESEARCHER: It is common for individuals to have a high degree of confidence in their own effectiveness and for them to provide "proof." Generate three pieces of shaky evidence that someone in a helping profession (i.e., a program director, a counselor, a teacher, etc.) may provide to demonstrate that they are helping people. For each piece, explain why that "proof" does not really prove anything.

8. DIG INTO THE NUMBERS: We have provided your instructor with data that accompanies the study discussed throughout this chapter. Use that data to build your skills in using SPSS to evaluate the program. Write an APA-style results section based on your results.

Key Concepts

grants, p. 439

grant writing, p. 439

moderator, p. 447

needs evaluation, p. 440

outcomes evaluation, p. 440

process evaluation, p. 440

program evaluation, p. 437

single-item indicator, p. 457

single sample *t*-test, p. 458

word cloud, p. 463

Answers to YOUR TURN

Your Turn 13.1: 1. a; 2. c; 3. d

Your Turn 13.2: 1. b; 2. a; 3. a

Your Turn 13.3: 1. c; 2. d; 3. b

Answers to Multiple-Choice Review Questions

1. b; 2. d; 3. a; 4. b; 5. c; 6. b; 7. a; 8. c; 9. d; 10. a

Statistical Tools for Answering Research Questions

Rawpixel.com/Shutterstock

LEARNING OUTCOMES

After reading this Appendix, you should be able to:

- Develop a data analysis plan for answering your research question.
- Differentiate between the four types of measurement scales.
- Choose the appropriate statistic to use based on design elements.

- Utilize descriptive statistics to summarize the data collected.
- Measure associations between variables.
- Explain how statistical hypothesis testing is used to answer research questions.

You were interested in finding an answer to your research question, so you designed a quality study and collected your data. Now what? How do you make sense out of the data? To do this, you need to know the best way to describe how people tended to answer your questions and which variables appear related to one another. You also need to determine if the data support your research hypothesis and what level of confidence you should have in your research conclusions, given the data. This is where the wonderful world of statistics enters into the research process. We use statistics to summarize and analyze our collected data as we try to answer our question. Once we understand how best to use statistics to analyze our data, we can finally find an answer to our research question.

What Is Your Plan?

It is important to make good design choices when answering our research questions. A crucial part of the decision process is the creation of a data analysis plan. This plan helps us determine how we will use the collected data to answer our research question. If we do not use the best statistical tests for our research design, our conclusions might be erroneous or misleading. This is why undergraduate psychology programs often require students to take a statistics course. Rather than focusing on the "nuts and bolts" of statistical analyses that are typically taught in a statistics course, we will review the series of decisions you need to make to develop a quality data analysis plan to answer your research question.

Is Our Goal to Describe the Data or to Make Inferences?

The first factor to consider when determining what statistic to use is our general research goal. There are two broad goals we can have for our data analysis plan. One goal may be to summarize or describe our measurements to provide better information about the variable. We can use descriptive statistics to accomplish this task. Our other goal may be to use the data to draw conclusions about how our variables relate in the population. That is, do our data suggest that our answer to our research question is correct? In this case, we engage in statistical hypothesis testing, where we essentially ask the question, "What are the chances we would obtain this data if our variables were unrelated in the population?" To evaluate this likelihood, we use inferential statistics.

What Measurement Scale Are We Using?

▶ When might we use a categorical variable? SEE CHAPTER 6, p. 184

Our first decision is to identify the **measurement scale,** or classification system, we are using for each of our variables. The four scales or levels of measurement are: nominal, ordinal, interval, and ratio, or NOIR (the French word for black). The key difference between the scales is the way in which each scale assigns numerical values to our observations.

A **nominal scale** uses numbers simply as a substitute for category names. This is why we often call variables measured using this scale categorical variables. Sex, ethnicity, and relationship status are common examples of nominal scale variables.

We assign numbers to these types of variables using a process called **dummy coding.** For example, we can indicate a participant's sex in our data set using a "1" if the participant is a female and a "2" if the participant is a male. We assign these numbers arbitrarily to each category. They do not imply a hierarchy or ordering to our measurements (we could have just as easily used "77" to indicate males and "89" to indicate females). While there is no limit to the number of categories we can have for a nominal level variable, if there are only two categories, we call the variable a **dichotomous variable.**

If we measure our variable by ranking our observations, we are using an **ordinal scale.** Here you might assign the value of "1" to the participant with the "most" of the variable, a "2" to the one with the second "most," and so on. In this case, the numbers let us know which observations have more or less of the variable. It does not tell us how much "more" or "less" the observations have compared to other observations. Consider the top 50 songs on Spotify. We know that the song in the number 1 position is currently the most popular song on Spotify as measured by number of plays. What we do not know is how much more popular the top song is than the second, third, and fourth songs. It is possible that the first song had slightly more plays than the second song listed, but both had many more plays than the other songs on the list. This type of measurement scale limits us to statistics appropriate for ranked data.

For **interval scales,** we assume that numbers represent order and that the quantitative difference between each number is the same. For example, if we have participants rate their self-confidence on a 1 to 9 scale, we assume that the difference in confidence between a score of a 3 and a 4 is equal in magnitude to the confidence difference between a score of an 8 and a 9 (i.e., they have equivalent

measurement scale a classification system used to measure a variable.

nominal scale a measurement scale where numbers are used as a substitute for category names.

dummy coding the process of assigning numbers to represent categories when measuring nominal scale variables.

dichotomous variable a nominal scale variable with only two categories.

ordinal scale a measurement scale where numbers are used to rank the variable on some dimension.

interval scale a measurement scale where numbers indicate an ordering to the measurements, and the difference between each measurement value is the same.

interval differences). IQ tests use an interval scale to measure intelligence. An IQ score of 100 indicates that the person is 10 points "more intelligent" than someone with a score of 90. Likewise, this person is 10 points "less intelligent" than someone with a score of 110. One limitation of an interval scale is that it does not have a true zero point indicating the total absence of the measured variable. In terms of IQ, there is no score indicating the complete lack of intelligence. Without a true zero point, we cannot say that a person with a score of 100 on an IQ test is twice as smart as someone with a score of 50. Similarly, if participants rate themselves as a 6 on our self-confidence scale, it does not mean they are twice as confident as those participants with a 3 on the same scale.

If we want to make these types of comparisons, we need to use a **ratio scale**. This measurement scale conveys order, has equal differences between scale points, and has a true zero point. On a ratio scale, a score of zero indicates a total absence of the measured variable. With a true zero, we can say a score of 6 is twice as much as a score of 3. Because there is a true zero point, it is impossible to have a negative value for this measurement scale. In psychology, we use a ratio scale when we measure frequency of behaviors, such as how many times a parent spanks his or her child each week. Here, we have a true zero point, as some parents never spank their children. We can also say that parents with a score of 4 spank their children twice as often as parents with a score of 2 do. The battery life meter on your cell phone is another ratio scale. If you have ever forgotten to charge your phone, you know what a true zero is. **Table A.1** summarizes the four types of measurement scales.

The type of scales or levels of measurement we use while collecting data has a direct impact on the types of statistics we can use later to determine what is happening in our study. Incidentally, the interval scale is the most commonly

▶ Why does a Likert scale represent an interval scale? SEE CHAPTER 7, p. 205

▶ When might we use a ratio scale to measure a variable? SEE CHAPTER 6, p. 174

TABLE A.1

Comparison of the Four Types of Measurement Scales		
Type of Scale	**What the Measurement Value Represents**	**Examples**
Nominal	The category name for the observation	• Sex • Ethnicity • Religious preference
Ordinal	The ordering or ranking of the observation on some dimension	• High school class ranking • Socioeconomic class • Most "top 10" lists
Interval	The ordering of the observation where there are equal differences between each value	• IQ and SAT scores • Year in school • Satisfaction ratings
Ratio	The ordering of the observation where there are equal differences between each value and a true zero point	• Income • Number of children • Frequency of behavior scores

ratio scale a measurement scale where numbers indicate an ordering to the measurements, the difference between each measurement value is the same, and there is a true zero point.

used measurement scale in psychology. It is difficult to describe a psychological construct as having a true zero point. That is, a person cannot ever really have zero anxiety, depression, happiness, intelligence, motivation, etc. We need to keep this in mind whenever we want to compare the magnitude of our participants' measurements. We refer to interval or ratio scale variables as continuous variables because they can theoretically take on any value within a specified range of scores. When choosing what statistic will best answer our research question, we usually use the same statistics for both types of continuous variable.

How Often Do We Measure Each Participant?

▶ When would we want to statistically compare different groups of participants? SEE CHAPTER 8, p. 251

What statistic we use to analyze our data is also determined by the number of times we measure each participant. We need to consider whether we have the same participants or different participants in each of our comparison groups. When each group has different participants, we are employing a between-subjects design. This means we need to use a statistical test appropriate for comparing the measurements between different groups of participants.

▶ When would we evaluate changes within participants? SEE CHAPTER 10, p. 323

Sometimes we use a within-subjects (or repeated measures) design to test our research question. In a within-subjects design, we measure our participants on the same measure more than once. We test our hypothesis by looking for changes within the individual as a result of exposure to various levels of the independent variable. In this case, we need to use a statistic that specifically allows us to test for these changes within each participant.

How Many Comparison Groups Does the Study Have?

▶ Want an example of a study that uses an independent *t*-test? SEE CHAPTER 8, p. 269

▶ Want an example of a study that uses a one-way ANOVA? SEE CHAPTER 9, p. 306

▶ Want an example of a study that uses a repeated measures ANOVA? SEE CHAPTER 10, p. 342

The last consideration in determining the correct statistic to use is the number of comparison groups in our study. As you learned in the design chapters of this book, the researcher determines the number of independent variables and the number of levels based on the specific research question. In part, the statistic we use ultimately depends on how many different groups we have in our research design. If our study is between-subjects with one independent variable and two groups, we use an independent *t*-test. If the study has three or more groups, then we use a one-way analysis of variance (ANOVA). Alternatively, if our study is within-subjects with one independent variable and two levels, we use a *dependent t-test;* if it has three or more groups, we use a repeated-measures ANOVA.

Choosing the Right Statistical Test for Your Research Design

As you can see, the design decisions we make before collecting data determine which statistic will help us make sense of our data. It starts with the overall goal of our research (to describe or draw conclusions), but we must also consider the types of measurements involved in our study, the number of times we measure each participant, and the number of comparison groups we have in our design. In **Table A.2**, we provide you with a "cheat sheet" to help you identify which statistic you should use based on these considerations. It is critical to remember that if you choose the wrong statistic, your research conclusions will be incorrect or misleading. When we use statistical software such as SPSS to do our computations, it is particularly easy to do unnecessary or incorrect analyses.

The software does not know if you are using the correct statistic to test your research hypothesis, but it will give you an answer regardless. If we make a poor decision in our choice of statistic, then our research conclusions will be wrong.

TABLE A.2

Determining Which Statistic to Use

Design Elements	Which Statistic Should You Use?	Example Research Question	Chapter of Statistic Introduction
Measurements of the same variable	Measure of central tendency; measure of variability	What is the average age of my sample? How much do the ages in the sample vary from one another?	Chapters 5 & 6
Several scale items designed to measure the same construct	Cronbach's alpha	Are the items in my created love scale reliably measuring the same thing?	Chapter 7
2 Continuous Variables	Bivariate correlation (Pearson r)	What is the association between intelligence and GRE scores?	Chapter 7
Two-Group/Simple Experiment: 1 IV; 2 levels (Between-Subjects); 1 Continuous DV	t-test for independent means	Is practice better than no practice on a performance task?	Chapter 8
2 Categorical Variables	Chi-square	Do the number of males and females in the study differ by year in school?	Chapter 9
Multigroup Design: 1 IV; 3+ levels (Between-Subjects); 1 Continuous DV	One-way analysis of variance (ANOVA)	Which type of therapy is most effective in treating depression?	Chapter 9
Two-Group/Pretest-Posttest Design: 1 IV; 2 levels (Within-Subjects); 1 Continuous DV	t-test for dependent means (also called a paired samples t-test)	Does one's mood improve after exercising?	Chapter 10
Multigroup/Repeated Measures Design: 1 IV; 3+ levels (Within-Subjects); 1 Continuous DV	Repeated-measures ANOVA	Which type of coping style is most effective in reducing stress level over time?	Chapter 10
Factorial Design: 2+ IV; 2+ levels each (Between-Subjects); 1 Continuous DV	Factorial or two-way ANOVA	What effect do different types of product advertising have on sales? What about product cost? Do they interact?	Chapter 11
Mixed Design: 1 IV; 2+ levels (Between-Subjects) 1 IV; 2+ levels (Within-Subjects) 1 Continuous DV	Repeated-measures ANOVA	Can listening to a public service message lead to a change in willingness to help? Does message length influence the amount of change? Do they interact?	Chapter 12

Descriptive Statistics: Tell Me About My Data

Simply having numerous measurements does very little to help us answer our research question. To make that information useful, we need to summarize the data in an easy-to-read format. One way to accomplish this is by depicting our data in the form of a graph or chart. We can also use several different statistics to represent the typical score in our data, as well as how much our measurements differ from one another.

Creating a "Picture" of Our Data

There is the saying "a picture is worth a thousand words." This is certainly true when we analyze our data. By visually representing the data, we can easily see the answers to certain questions. For example, we can see if the data clump around a few scores or if they are spread out. We can decide whether any of our participants' measurements are extreme scores, or outliers, compared to other participants' scores. We have several options for displaying our data.

▶ When might we want to represent data using a graph? SEE CHAPTER 6, p. 187

One option is the frequency distribution, which is essentially a table with two columns (see **Table A.3**). In the first column is every possible measurement score or category we could have. In the second is the actual number of observations, or the percentage of the sample that had that particular measurement. Another way to visualize data is to create a graph. If we are graphing a categorical variable, we would use a bar chart, shown in **Figure A.1**. In this type of graph, the height of the bar represents the frequency of that score in our measurements. The bars do not touch one another and the order of the categories is interchangeable, as they have no implicit ordering. If our variable is continuous, then we create a **histogram** where the categories are in a logical sequence (e.g., lowest score to highest score) and the bars touch each other, such as in **Figure A.2**.

TABLE A.3

Example of a Frequency Distribution	
Where Participants Live	**Frequency**
Rural	8
Urban	6
Suburban	15

histogram a type of chart used to graph continuous variables; the frequency of a measurement is represented with bars that touch to indicate that a continuous variable is being graphically displayed.

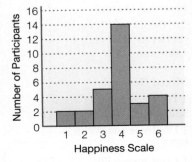

FIGURE A.1 Example of a Bar Chart.

FIGURE A.2 Example of a Histogram.

This touching immediately tells us that the variable is continuous and not categorical. For continuous variables, we can also use a **frequency polygon** where, as shown in **Figure A.3**, we represent the frequency of our different measurements with a line rather than the height of a bar. In this case, we mark the frequency of a measurement with a point, then connect the points with a line.

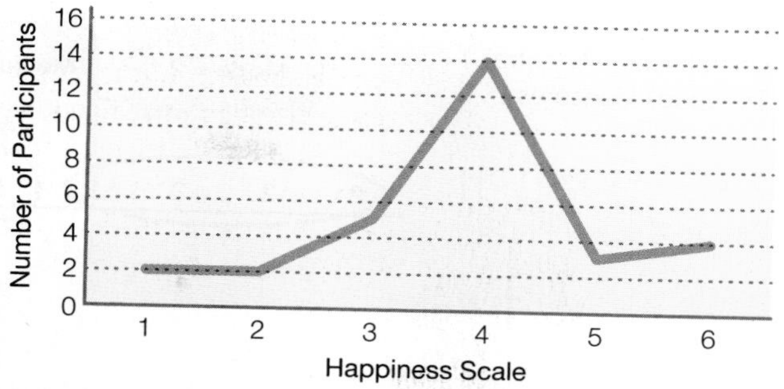

Histograms and frequency polygons are useful for showing us whether the distribution of our measurements resembles a **normal distribution.** A normal distribution looks like a bell-shaped curve in that it is symmetrical with a single peak. If there are a few outliers, our scores will be bunched up on one end of the scale so that the distribution no longer looks like a bell-shaped curve. We call these **skewed distributions.** A skewed distribution can mean several things. One possibility is that you made a mistake entering those scores into your data set. Another possibility is that there is a confound variable in your study that influenced the scores of some of your participants. A skewed distribution can also indicate a possible ceiling effect or floor effect in your measurements. Whenever you have a skewed distribution, you should carefully examine your data so that you are confident that they accurately reflect what you are intending to measure. See **Figure A.4** for an example of normal versus skewed distributions.

Measuring Central Tendency

When trying to summarize a large group of numbers, it is helpful to identify the "typical" or "average" score, also known as the measure of central tendency. The specific measure of central tendency that we use depends on our measurement scale. For interval and ratio measurement scales, we use the mean (or arithmetic mean; symbolized M) to represent the average score. We calculate the mean by summing up all of the scores and dividing this total by the number of observations we have.

When we have ordinal or ranked data, we use the median (symbolized Mdn) as our central tendency measure. The median represents the middle score in the distribution. This means that half or 50% of the scores in our data set are higher than the median, and 50% are lower. Sometimes we will use the

FIGURE A.3 Example of a Frequency Polygon.

▶ What is the difference between a ceiling effect and a floor effect? SEE CHAPTER 4, p. 104

frequency polygon a type of chart used to graph continuous variables; the frequency of a measurement is represented with a point in the graph and these points are connected with a line; similar to the histogram.

normal distribution a distribution of scores that resembles a bell-shaped curve, is symmetrical with one peak, and shows an equivalent mean, median, and mode.

skewed distribution a distribution of scores that is nonsymmetrical because some scores are more extreme than the majority of the other scores.

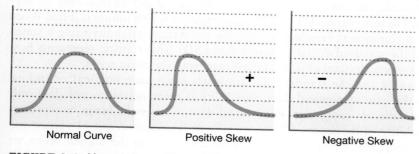

Normal Curve   Positive Skew   Negative Skew

FIGURE A.4 Normal Versus Skewed Distributions.

FIGURE A.5
Comparison of Central
Tendency Measures.

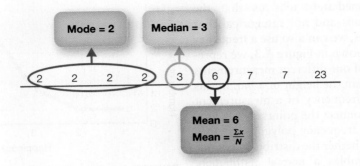

median in conjunction with the mean to describe the central tendency of a continuous variable when we have a few outliers. Suppose you want to summarize the age of your research participants. While many of your participants may be between 18 and 21, it is possible you will have a few older participants (e.g., 67) in your sample. The median would be your best choice in that it does not give undue weight to these extreme scores in your data, providing a false impression of the data. You might find yourself in the same situation if you are recording the total household income of your participants, with many participants citing a salary between $40,000 and $60,000, and only a few citing a salary of $100,000 or more.

When we have nominal-level data, our only option is to use the mode (symbolized Mo). The mode represents the most frequently occurring category or categories in our data. If we wanted to know the typical religious affiliation of our participants, the mode is simply the category with the most participants. One limitation of using the mode is that we might have more than one mode. That is, we might have two religions that occur with equal frequency, such that we have 50 people who are Christian and 50 who are Muslim. Refer to **Figure A.5** for a comparison of central tendency measures.

► How can we use
measures of central
tendency to answer our
research question? SEE
CHAPTER 6, p. 184

Measuring the Variability of the Data

While identifying the central tendency of a variable is important, it does not tell us the full story. For example, if we have three scores, such as 4, 5, and 6, the mean is 5 (4 + 5 + 6 = 15; 15/3 = 5). We can also have a mean of 5 with a completely different set of three scores, such as 2, 12, 1 (2 + 12 + 1 = 15; 15/3 = 5). In the first case, the scores are very similar, while in the second case, they are very different. The term variability refers to the degree to which numbers differ. When we have a continuous variable, we describe the data's variability using a statistic called the standard deviation (symbolized SD). This statistic represents how much the scores deviate, or differ, on average from the mean score.

► Why is it important
to assess our data's
variability? SEE
CHAPTER 7, p. 229

We cannot use the standard deviation when we have nominal or ordinal data. In the case of nominal data, variability is meaningless, as our data only represent different categories. For ordinal data, we use the **range** to represent the variability of the scores. The range tells us how spread out or variant our measurements are. By subtracting the lowest score from the highest score, we can convey the range within our ranked data.

range a measure of
variability in the data
computed by subtracting
the lowest score from
the highest score.

Measuring Associations Between Variables

We usually do not measure variables in isolation. Our research question typically involves asking how two or more variables relate to one another, or the tendency for the variables to covary or change together. A common statistic to use when we want to describe this relation is the correlation coefficient. The value of the correlation coefficient can range from 0 to 1. The larger the value, the stronger the relation is between the two variables. The sign of this value tells us the direction of the relationship. A positive sign means that higher scores on one variable are associated with higher scores on the other variable. The relation between humor and leadership effectiveness is an example of a positive correlation. Research suggests that the more humorous a supervisor is, the more satisfied the workers are with their job (Decker, 1987). Likewise, the less humorous the supervisor is, the less satisfied the workers are. A correlation coefficient with a negative sign indicates that there is an inverse relationship between the two variables. High scores on one variable correspond with low scores on the other variable. For example, students who frequently text during class tend to have a lower overall grade point average compared to those who text less often (Harman & Sato, 2011). A correlation coefficient tells us whether several variables vary together, as well as the strength and nature of that relationship. You can see the anatomy of a correlation in **Figure A.6**.

There are different types of correlations, depending on the type of variables you are using. The most common correlation is the **Pearson product moment correlation coefficient**, or **Pearson r**. We use Pearson r when both variables are continuous variables. We use other types of correlations for different kinds of variables, but they are essentially variations on Pearson r and are interpreted in the same way. For more information on which correlation coefficient to use given the types of data we are working with, see **Table A.4**.

Regardless of the specific correlation coefficient, what we learn remains the same: the strength and direction of the association between the two variables based on our measurements. However, we do not know which variable is possibly causing changes in the other variable. In addition, we do not know

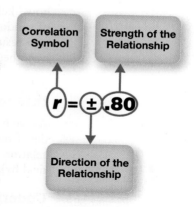

FIGURE A.6 Anatomy of a Correlation.

▶ Want an example of a study that uses a correlation coefficient? SEE CHAPTER 7, p. 230

TABLE A.4

Types of Correlation Coefficients		
Correlation Coefficient	**Symbol**	**When Typically Used**
Pearson r	r	Both variables are continuous
Point Biserial	r_{pb}	One variable is dichotomous; the other variable is continuous
Phi	Φ (Greek letter phi)	Both variables are dichotomous
Spearman's rho	ρ (Greek letter rho)	Both variables are ordinal

Pearson product moment correlation coefficient (or Pearson r) the correlation coefficient used when both variables are continuous.

how likely it is that this observed relationship is a "real" one or simply the result of random error or chance alone. Anytime we want to find out the likelihood of a result being "real" versus happening by chance, we need to use statistical hypothesis testing.

Inferential Statistics: Going Beyond Our Sample

As we have learned, error is part of any measurement. This can lead us to wonder if our obtained result is primarily due to an error or if it represents a real relation between our variables. To make this decision, we need to include statistical hypothesis testing in our data analysis plan.

Understanding the Logic Behind Statistical Hypothesis Testing

▶ How do we use statistical hypothesis testing to answer our research question? SEE CHAPTER 8, p. 269

When we analyze our data, we try to determine if there is support for our research hypothesis. To find this support, we have to engage in some counterintuitive thinking. In statistical hypothesis testing, we start with the premise that the null hypothesis is correct. The null hypothesis typically is that there is no relation or difference between our variables. We use our hypothesis-testing statistic to evaluate the probability that this null hypothesis is correct. If we decide that the null hypothesis is unlikely, we "reject" it in favor of the **alternative hypothesis**. The alternative hypothesis is, generally speaking, our research hypothesis. When we reject the null hypothesis, we are concluding that our results are statistically significant, meaning that we are reasonably sure that something real is happening in our study. We refer to this probability value as our statistic's **p-value**, or **significance level**, symbolized as p.

alternative hypothesis the hypothesis that is tested against the null hypothesis when engaging in statistical hypothesis testing.

p-value the probability that something real is happening in our study; also known as the significance level.

significance level the probability of making a Type I error; also known as the p-value.

Type I error the mistake we make when we decide to reject the null hypothesis when, in reality, we should not reject it; considered an "error of gullibility."

Type II error the mistake we make when we fail to reject the null hypothesis when, in reality, it should be rejected; considered an "error of blindness."

beta the probability of making a Type II error; symbolized as β.

Identifying Potential Errors in Statistical Hypothesis Testing

Because we base our decision to either reject or accept the null hypothesis on probability, we must recognize that sometimes our decision is incorrect and we have made an error. When we decide to reject the null hypothesis when it is actually true, then we have made a **Type I error**. This is an error of gullibility where we believe or claim that a relationship exists when it does not. The p-value of our statistic is roughly the probability of making a Type I error. If we set this value at 5%, as is typical in psychology, we are essentially stating that there is no more than a 5% chance that we have made a Type I error when we decide to reject the null hypothesis.

The other mistake we might make is accepting the null hypothesis when, in fact, it should be rejected. We call this a **Type II error**. This error is an error of blindness where we are not able to see that there is a difference or association between our variables, even though one truly exists. We call the probability of making a Type II error **beta** (symbolized as β). The statistical power of a test is simply the probability of avoiding a Type II error or rejecting the null hypothesis when we should reject it. See **Table A.5** for an overview of statistical hypothesis-testing outcomes.

TABLE A.5

Possible Statistical Hypothesis-Testing Outcomes		
	Null Hypothesis Is True	**Null Hypothesis Is False**
Reject the Null Hypothesis	Type I error *False positive; error of gullibility*	Correct *True positive*
Accept the Null Hypothesis	Correct *True negative*	Type II error *False negative; error of blindness*

The number of research participants in our study determines our statistical power. The more participants we have, the less likely it is that we will make a Type II error because our study will have greater power. The problem is that the more participants we have in our study, the costlier in time and other resources our study becomes. The question is then, How many participants do we need in order to have a reasonable chance of being able to reject the null hypothesis when it should be rejected (i.e., not making a Type II error) without the study becoming burdensome or costly? The answer to this question is, "It depends." We realize that this answer is unsatisfactory, but it really does depend on the magnitude of difference we believe there to be between the groups in our study. If there truly is a large difference between the groups, then we will not need as many participants to observe this difference in our study. Suppose we wanted to see if the heights of two groups of children significantly differed from one another. If one group consisted of 2-year-olds and the other of 10-year-olds, we would need to measure very few from each group to quickly identify that their heights significantly differed. However, suppose we wanted to know if the height of women significantly differed from that of men. In this case, there is a much smaller, but still meaningful, difference between our two groups that will be harder to detect. Therefore, we will need to measure more participants in each group.

Unfortunately, it is difficult to know beforehand how large of a difference there is between the groups, especially as one of the reasons for doing our study is to see if a difference exists! Nevertheless, through our literature search, we can develop a sense of how large this difference might be based on similar research studies. Armed with this knowledge, we can consult what are referred to as "power tables" (see, for example, Cohen, 1988) to estimate how many participants we will need if we want to conduct a study with a specified level of power.

▶ What are some ways we can increase the power of our study? SEE CHAPTER 9, p. 294

Measuring the Size of the Effect

There is certainly a thrill of excitement whenever we conclude that our results are "statistically significant," meaning that we are reasonably confident that any connections between variables or differences between groups are real and not due to error. We now have evidence that our research hypothesis may be correct. Still, there is one thing we cannot tell from our *p*-value: the strength of our

▶ Why is it important to evaluate the effect size associated with our statistical test? SEE CHAPTER 8, p. 269

experimental effect or association. We need to determine if the independent variable had a large or small impact on the dependent variable. To help us estimate this, we can calculate the effect size associated with our statistical significance test result. The effect size is an estimate of the strength of the relationship or association between our variables. The greater the impact or association, the larger our effect size will be.

There are different ways we can represent the effect size, depending on the statistical test we are using and the number of comparison groups we have. One common measure of effect size is **Cohen's *d***, which represents the standardized difference between our conditions' means. If Cohen's *d* is .50, then we are stating that exposing a group to one of the levels of the independent variable increases that group's mean by one half of a standard deviation. As a guide for helping us interpret *d*, Cohen (1992) described a *d* of .20 as representing a small effect. A *d* of .50 might be considered a medium effect and a *d* of .80 a large effect. These interpretations are subjective, as small effects can be very meaningful or important, depending on the research question.

Another common effect size measure is **effect size *r***. This effect size is equivalent to the correlation between the independent and dependent variable, as measured using a point-biserial correlation. Because this is a correlation, effect size *r* can range from 0 to 1.0. In this case, .10 is considered to be a small effect size, .30 a medium effect size, and .50 a large effect size (Cohen, 1992). When you have two categorical variables, each with two levels, you can use the phi-coefficient as your measure of effect size. See **Table A.6** for examples of effect size measures.

In addition to estimating the size of the impact that our independent variable had on our dependent variable, effect sizes are useful when examining the statistical power of our study. If we failed to reject the null hypothesis (i.e., $p > .05$), but we calculate an effect size that suggests there is a strong relationship between our two variables, then we are alerted to the possibility that we have made a Type II error. In this case, we can modify our research design by either strengthening our manipulation or recruiting more participants. This increases the likelihood of finding a relationship that may exist between our variables.

Cohen's *d* a measure of effect size that represents the standardized difference between the means of two conditions.

effect size *r* a measure of effect size that represents the correlation between the independent and dependent variables in comparisons involving two conditions.

TABLE A.6

Examples of Effect Size Measures		
Effect Size Measure	**When Typically Used**	**What It Indicates**
Cohen's *d*	Two comparison groups	Standardized difference between sample means
Effect size *r*	Two comparison groups	Correlation between the independent variable and the dependent variable
Phi (Φ)	Two dichotomous, categorical variables	Correlation between the two dichotomous variables

Final Thoughts

A good scientist always starts with a plan. To develop the best way to test your research hypothesis, you need to consider all of your design options and strategies for measuring your variables. The same is true when developing a data analysis plan. You need to consider the purpose of your study, the research design decisions you have made, and the type of data you have collected. By making both good research design and data analysis strategy decisions, you can have confidence in your research conclusions.

Key Concepts

alternative hypothesis, p. 486

beta, p. 486

Cohen's *d*, p. 488

dichotomous variable, p. 478

dummy coding, p. 478

effect size *r*, p. 488

frequency polygon, p. 482

histogram, p. 482

interval scale, p. 478

measurement scale, p. 478

nominal scale, p. 478

normal distribution, p. 482

ordinal scale, p. 478

Pearson product moment correlation coefficient (or Pearson *r*), p. 485

p-value, p. 486

range, p. 484

ratio scale, p. 479

significance level, p. 486

skewed distribution, p. 482

Type I error, p. 486

Type II error, p. 486

Communicating the Science of Psychology

Hero Images/Getty Images

LEARNING OUTCOMES

After reading this Appendix, you should be able to:

- Explain the importance of developing strong communication skills.
- Effectively and clearly convey science through writing.
- Develop strategies for searching the scientific literature using databases.
- Take quality notes when reading a scientific article.
- Avoid plagiarism when summarizing previous research.
- Properly cite previous research using APA style.
- Write an APA-style research report.
- Effectively share scientific findings through poster and paper presentations.

You decided to go to college for many reasons, but perhaps the main reason is to develop the knowledge and skills that are necessary for your future career. Lucky for you, a research methods course provides a variety of opportunities to develop marketable skills, including critical-thinking skills, analytical skills, and the ability to communicate ideas clearly and effectively. These skills are inextricably linked within the scientific process, and, as we discussed in Chapter 2, communication is the essential final step of this process. As scientists, not only do we have an obligation to communicate our findings, but we need to do so in a way that makes these findings useful to others.

Beyond its importance for science, communicating effectively in your writing and presentation of information is one of the most important skills that you can cultivate. Employers value effective communication and rank it as one of the top skills students should develop in college (Hart Research Associates, 2015). Professionals spend much of their day writing e-mails, reports, and memos that require clear and succinct writing. In this Appendix, we further develop your communication skills by helping you improve your technical writing style, facilitate the writing process, and understand the "nuts and bolts" of how to communicate in a variety of formats, including an American Psychological Association (APA)-style paper, poster presentation, and paper/oral presentation. To help you master these communication skills and APA style, the APA publishes the *Publication*

▶ What skills can you build in the research methods course? SEE CHAPTER 1, p. 16

Manual, now in its 6th edition. This Appendix highlights key information, and we identify where you can find more information in the manual with the following symbol: ψ APA Manual.

The Importance of Communication

The APA has recognized the importance of communication skills in its *Guidelines for the Undergraduate Psychology Major* by making "communication" one of the main goals for psychology majors. This goal specifies that students should be able to write and present information effectively for different purposes. You have likely heard the saying "know your audience," and this is necessary when communicating about science. The tricky part, however, is that scientific writing can serve several different purposes and can have at least two very distinct audiences. First, you have your professional peers or fellow scientists, who need to know what you found and how you found it so that they can use your study in their research. Communicating with other scientists typically takes place via open science websites, through published research in academic journals, and during research conferences through poster or paper presentations. Writing scientifically is a skill and, as with any skill, takes time and practice to perfect.

Although it is not the focus of this Appendix, it is worth acknowledging that a second audience that scientists increasingly need to effectively communicate with is the general public. This audience can include your nonscientist friends, family members, neighbors, and anyone who may be able to use the scientific findings in psychology to improve their lives. When writing for this purpose, the trick is to stay true to the science by not overstating or oversimplifying findings, and to write in a way that avoids jargon and complex explanations that will lose readers' interest. Popular writers like Malcolm Gladwell and Dan Ariely make this look easy, but this type of writing is much more difficult to craft than it appears to be.

▶ What are the different ways that scientists communicate their findings? SEE CHAPTER 2, p. 45

General Writing Tips

To write effectively and clearly about science, there are a few things to keep in mind.

ψ APA Manual
(Writing Tips)

Chapters 3 and 4 provide suggestions for writing style and grammar use.

It's a Whole New World

In what may come as good news to some people and bad news to others, writing in a scientific field is quite different from writing in a literary field such as English. Scientific writing is a formal style of technical writing, meaning that you should avoid writing in a casual style similar to how you talk with your friends in person, over e-mail, or via text. You should also avoid overly descriptive writing or flowery language like you might use in a creative writing class. The key goal in scientific writing is to clearly convey information. If you can state something simply, do it. Avoid complicated sentences, long paragraphs, big words, or anything else that may come across as "trying to sound smart." It is not smart to write in a way that is hard to understand. Whether you are writing for an English or psychology class, academic writing also requires that you give credit to your sources and format your paper appropriately. While you may have used MLA style in your liberal arts and humanities courses, in psychology we use APA style. You can see the difference between the two for yourself in **Table B.1**.

TABLE B.1

APA Style Versus MLA Style: A Comparison

	APA Style	MLA Style
Abstract	Yes	No
Quotes	Generally avoided. Instead it is preferable to paraphrase.	Generally okay to use.
Giving Credit	References	Works Cited
Reference (Book)	Last Name, First Initial. (Year). *Title of book.* Place of Publication: Publisher. **Example →** Seligman, M. E. P. (2002). *Authentic happiness.* New York, NY: Free Press.	Last Name, First Name. <u>Title of Book</u>. Place of Publication: Publisher, Year of Publication. **Example →** Seligman, Martin. <u>Authentic Happiness</u>. New York: Free Press, 2002.
Reference (Journal)	Author(s). (Year). Title of article. *Title of Journal, Volume(Issue),* pages. doi:# (if applicable) **Example →** Diener, E., & Seligman, M. (2002). Very happy people. *Psychological Science, 13*(1), 81–84. doi:10.1111/1467-9280.00415	Author(s). "Title of Article." <u>Title of Journal</u> Volume (Year): pages. **Example →** Diener, Edward, and Martin Seligman. "Very Happy People." <u>Psychological Science</u> 13 (2002): 81–84.
Parenthetical Citations	Author last name, comma, date of publication. **Example →** (Baker, 2008)	Author last name and page number. No comma. **Example →** (Baker 58)
Where to Cite	First use of information from another source. **Example →** Sentence 1 (CITE). Sentence 2. Sentence 3. Sentence 4. Sentence 5.	Last use of information from another source. **Example →** Sentence 1. Sentence 2. Sentence 3. Sentence 4. Sentence 5 (CITE).
Headers	Abbreviated version of the title and page number	Author's name and page number
Use of Author's First Name	Generally not used. First initials of first names appear in the References.	Used in the Works Cited.

Note. This table represents key differences between the two styles. It does not include how the styles are similar, and is not meant to be an exhaustive list.

ψ **APA Manual (Succinctness)**
Page 67

Say It Succinctly

In technical writing, there are no bonus points for length. A research report only needs to be long enough to convey the necessary information. Adding extra words or long-winded explanations makes the science harder to understand. As you write, make sure that every sentence has a purpose and supports your point. Sometimes a whole sentence can be eliminated with the use of a single word.

Example →

Bad: Participants were college students. Those who spent more time in a hot classroom used more profanity.

Better: College students who spent more time in a hot classroom used more profanity.

Often a single word from an extraneous sentence can convey the entire point. Similarly, you should avoid extraneous words and aim for an economy of expression. If the sentence can retain its meaning without certain words, remove them. Saying less can help you say things more clearly. There are several common phrases you can typically omit without changing the meaning of sentences.

Example →

"it was found that"   "shown to be"   "study that was done"

"research done in the past"   "a previous study"   "previous research has found that"

Choose Your Words Wisely

Your writing should be specific and precise. For example, you should avoid saying a study was "interesting" because this word is subjective. What is interesting to you could be boring to someone else. Also avoid saying what a study "intended" to find. Science tests hypotheses, and lets the data determine the rest. Similarly, it is never appropriate to say a study can "prove" something. Due to the nature of science and statistics, we are unable to state anything as 100% factual. Instead, when we decide that a finding is statistically significant, we are at least 95% sure it is a real effect. This means that there is a 5% chance we are wrong. As a result, we must avoid absolute declarations in our writing and instead use hedge wording that helps make this uncertainty clear.

Example →

"It seems"   "It is likely"   "It is possible"

"It could be"   "This could indicate"   "This suggests"

"One possibility is that . . ."

You should also ensure that you are using psychological terms appropriately. For example, avoid using the word "correlate" unless you really mean a statistical correlation. Similarly, you must be sure to avoid overstating your claims. If your study was correlational, you must avoid using causal language.

Example →

Nonexperimental Terms = correlates, associates, relates, coincides, corresponds

Experimental Terms = causes, predicts, leads to, creates

Bad: A survey of 596 college freshmen found that poor class attendance caused lower grades.

Better: A survey of 596 college freshmen reported that poor class attendance related to lower grades.

Choose Your Verb Tense Wisely

One tricky element of writing a scientific paper is that the time frame of events varies. You first say what you think will happen, then describe how you did it, and conclude by explaining what happened in the past. These differences mean that your verb tense will vary over the course of your paper. You should use the past tense to describe what past studies found, the details of data collection in Methods, and what you found. You should use the present tense when describing findings that continue to be true, discussing current findings, explaining the implications of findings, and drawing conclusions.

Example →

For Previous Findings = ". . . jealousy positively correlated with . . ."

For Present Findings = ". . . jealousy positively correlates with . . ."

Writing is clearer when it uses the active voice, where the actor or subject precedes the action. In the previous sentence, writing (the subject) comes before the action (uses). When we describe things in the context of science, the theory explains the outcomes, and the cause produces the effect. Contrast this with the nonpreferred passive voice, where the outcomes are explained by the theory or the effect was produced by the cause. Not only is passive voice more cumbersome, but it requires extra, unnecessary words. Phrases like "were taken" or "was given" typically indicate the passive voice.

Example →

Passive Voice = The book was written by the author.

(Here the action [writing] precedes the actor [the author].)

Active Voice = The author wrote the book.

(Here the actor [the author] precedes the action [writing].)

Passive Voice = The ratings of physical attractiveness were significantly influenced by the attractiveness of the photograph.

Active Voice = The attractiveness of the photograph significantly influenced ratings of physical attractiveness.

Keep Things Clear and Organized

In contrast with other types of writing, where the author will purposely keep information hidden from the reader for dramatic effect, technical writing strives to make things as easy to follow as possible. You should always be clear about the nature and direction of the findings, by explaining, for example, how groups differ.

Example →

Bad: Many experiments have tested self-reference, which have shown significant results.

Better: Studies of the self-reference effect show that memory is better for self-relevant words compared to non-self-relevant words.

Another way to do this is by clearly labeling sections of a paper with headings, and by having clear guidelines about what type of information goes where. In psychology, we call this APA style (there will be much more information on this topic in the next section).

The goal of technical writing is to make a fact-based case to justify a study. To accomplish this, authors need to write with a clear focus supported by a logical and intuitive organization of ideas. Each idea should flow naturally into the next through smooth transitions between sentences and between paragraphs. In organizing your paper, it is best to make general points first, with more specific points to follow.

Example →

Bad: Among college students involved in serious intimate relationships, 75% of men and 68% of women are unfaithful. Several studies indicate that men are more likely than women to commit infidelity.

Better: Several studies indicate that men are more likely than women to commit infidelity. Among college students involved in serious intimate relationships, 75% of men and 68% of women are unfaithful.

 Research in Action

The Editor's Studio

Any good writer will tell you that first drafts of anything usually are not very good. The secret to good writing is revising, revising again, and then revising some more. As your writing improves, so will your ability to identify and fix common grammatical issues. Although learning how to write in APA style is important, the formatting (e.g., when to use a comma, "&" or "and," or when to use "et al.") and structure (e.g., do tables go before or after the references?) of APA style are not the most important things this style can teach you. Rather, the APA style of writing is a form of technical writing, which aims to explain things as clearly and directly as possible.

To help you build this skill, the online activity **The Editor's Studio** will ask you to edit sentences in order to say things succinctly, choose words and verb tenses wisely, and describe things clearly. Here is your chance to play the role of editor to make sure the writing clearly communicates the ideas.

📔 LaunchPad To complete this activity, visit LaunchPad at launchpadworks.com

The Writing Process

The writing process involves many different steps and skills. First, you need to be able to read and comprehend the research in order to state the findings in your own words. You also need to determine an overall structure for your paper that clearly integrates your ideas in an organized manner, while giving others appropriate credit for their ideas and research. After that, you still need to proof-read several times to ensure you have a polished product.

Tips for Searching Databases

As we have modelled in every chapter, developing a high-quality research project starts with reviewing the literature. The goal is to become familiar with peer-reviewed research on topics similar to yours and with how others did those studies. Learning how to find relevant articles in databases that catalogue scientific literature in psychology, such as PsycINFO and PsycARTICLES, is a skill in and of itself. The best way to start a search is with an article that you are already aware of and that focuses closely on some aspect of your topic. You can then use details from this article, such as its keywords, the authors' names, or the journal name, to help locate other relevant articles. Once you have found an article that is relevant to your research project, be sure to read the full abstract to determine if the article fits your needs. Finding relevant articles is often more difficult than you might assume, so be persistent and give yourself plenty of time. Waiting until the night before a deadline to begin your search will guarantee that you will not be able to do a quality job.

Here are some techniques to help you start your search. You can use these one at a time or in combination to find what you need.

- **By Key Concepts:** You can search for articles using words that are relevant to your research topic. At first, you might not be familiar with the appropriate scientific jargon to search to find what you need by key concept. When you find a good article, pay attention to the keywords listed with the article. These can help you find better subject terms to search. Using Key Concepts will truly help you target the literature that is most relevant to your topic.

- **By Author:** You can use the last name of any researcher you know who does research on your topic. As you begin to familiarize yourself with your topic's relevant literature, you will likely see some of the same authors listed multiple times. Be sure to do a literature search on the authors of each of your most related articles.

- **By Source:** If there is a particular journal that is dedicated to your research topic, you can search for articles appearing in that journal.

- **By Title:** If you see an article you would like to read, you can search the title of the article to find it.

Each time you identify a superstar article for your project, be sure to look through all of the research your article cites. Similarly, in the research database, there is typically a link that identifies other articles that have cited your superstar article. In both cases, whether your superstar article cites a study, or some other study cites your superstar article, they will provide you with worthwhile leads to track down. One last tip: As the entire literature search process unfolds, create a system that will help you keep track of which leads you have followed and which ones you have yet to pursue.

Tips for Taking Notes on Articles

Taking good notes on research articles that provide a background for your research ideas will greatly facilitate your comprehension of the material and the eventual writing of your paper. Having a good system for taking notes will allow you to organize information in an easily accessible fashion, which is especially useful when you have several articles that are similar. Further, taking good notes in your own words will ensure that accidental plagiarism does not occur. If you write from your notes instead of the article, it is harder to accidentally use the author's words. Taking quality notes may seem like it is a waste of time, but doing so will actually save you time in the long run by helping you understand your topic better, making you aware of key references, and making the writing of the paper much easier. Here are some tips on how to read and take notes on research articles:

1. Read each article *at least* twice. As you read through the article for the first time, highlight parts of sentences instead of whole sentences or paragraphs. Also make notes in the margins about the thoughts you have, how things may relate to your paper, and so on. As you read the article for the second time, transfer your highlighting and notes to a typed document that is designed to organize and summarize the article's essential information (see **Figure B.1**). As you do this, avoid copying any text word for word. Instead, put things into your own words, which will help you learn the information better and make you less likely to plagiarize unintentionally.

2. Keep your notes as short and succinct as possible. The goal is to create a source for yourself that is easier to use than the original article. It is much easier to read 1 page of notes than 10–20 pages of an article.

3. Remember, your notes are a reference for you. If there is a lot of information you find useful (e.g., information about a scale), describe it briefly, then include a page number. Ultimately, you will be using your notes along with the original article.

4. Save your work on a computer and be consistent in your style and organization. You should generally include the information listed below. (Note that the specific types of information you include may vary depending on whether you are reading an empirical versus a review article or chapter.)

- **Citation**—APA style (this way you can copy it into your References section later)
- **General Topic**—What does this source focus on? (be as specific as possible)
- **Subtopic(s)**—Are there any key subtopics? (be as specific as possible)

Note Sheet Template for an Empirical Article

Reference: Give the proper APA reference citation for this work.

General Topic:

Subtopic(s):

Reference for Key Research Cited in Article: List any article that is central to the one you are reading here. Make a small note about why the article is a key article and give the proper APA reference for it, so you can easily find the article later.

Independent Variable(s): What variable(s) are researchers comparing for changes in the dependent variable?

Dependent Variable(s): What are researchers measuring?

Hypotheses (number them): What is predicted about how the independent variable(s) will influence the dependent variable(s)?

Participants:

Design Elements:

Key Results Specifically Related to Each Hypothesis (number them): You should have at least one key finding for each hypothesis.

Other Key Findings Related to Your Topic:

Overall Thoughts: What is this article's main contribution? What can you use from it for your Introduction?

---

*Save this to your computer and modify it to accommodate your own style/needs.

FIGURE B.1 An Example Note Sheet for Empirical Articles.

- **Key Research Cited in Article**—Do the authors mention any research that is relevant to yours? Describe it briefly and give the brief citation. Keep in mind that you should *not* use this information as something your article found. Rather, you can use this information to find other useful sources later. Also, check the references! Look through and highlight any key references so that you can track them down if you need them.

- **Overall Thoughts**—What are your thoughts on the research? What could be improved? What else could be considered, like other variables, measures, or interactions, etc.? The Discussion section of the paper might get you started here.

For Empirical Articles:

- **Hypotheses/Research Question**—What was the research testing? (use these to organize results; there should be a result for each hypothesis)
- **Participants**—Who was in the study? Were they college-aged? Married couples? Friends?
- **Design Elements**—What type of design did the researchers use? What was the procedure for data collection?
- **Variables**—What were the IVs/DVs? What did the researchers manipulate? How did they measure variables?
- **Key Results**—What were the key findings? Give a written summary in your own words. There is no need to include the actual statistics or numbers in your notes.

For Review Articles/Chapters:

- **Key Theories and Ideas**—This should be a summary of the central ideas in the article/chapter.

The purpose of reviewing articles or chapters is typically to summarize previous research to advance our understanding of a particular research area or question. The focus is on synthesizing previous research rather than empirically testing specific hypotheses.

The Powers of Paraphrasing and Avoiding Plagiarism

When writing about other studies' findings, you should paraphrase by restating the authors' words in a way that is different, but still retains the original meaning. More simply, you should put things in your own words. In scientific papers, there is a strong preference for paraphrasing and for avoiding the use of quotes.

Paraphrasing is powerful because it helps you master the material. It is very hard to put things into your own words if you do not fully understand the concepts. Paraphrase the essential pieces of a research article as you read and take notes on it and you will find that, because you are using your own words, you are less likely to plagiarize. Plagiarism can occur simply by using a string of three or more words from the original source. Properly paraphrasing avoids this form of plagiarism while still conveying the same overall meaning of the original source.

▶ What is plagiarism?
SEE CHAPTER 3, p. 78

Example →

Original:	". . . parents' negative emotionality was a relatively robust predictor of child problem behaviors and negative emotion word use in everyday life . . ." (Slatcher & Trentacosta, 2012, p. 938)
Plagiarized: (Severe)	Parents' negative emotionality was a relatively robust predictor of child problem behaviors and negative emotion word use in everyday life (Slatcher & Trentacosta, 2012).

Plagiarized: (Moderate)	When parents had a negative temperament it was a relatively robust predictor of child problem behaviors and children's negative emotion word use, like "mad" and "sad" to describe their emotions (Slatcher & Trentacosta, 2012).
Paraphrased:	When parents have a neurotic temperament, their children are more likely to use negative words like "mad" and "sad" to describe their emotions (Slatcher & Trentacosta, 2012).

Many faculty have access to web-based systems that check for plagiarism, such as Turnitin.com. These services help determine the originality of your papers and prevent plagiarism by comparing papers against other materials stored in the system (e.g., Internet documents, journal articles, previously submitted papers) and scanning for matching text. Seeing how your writing may match too closely with sources can help you understand what constitutes plagiarism, learn how to write better, and ensure academic integrity.

Creating an Outline

Making an outline before you jump into writing your paper is useful for several reasons. First, it helps you begin the paper without actually writing it. Very few students like the idea of starting a paper, and the outline helps ease you into the process. Most importantly for the writing itself, the outline helps you organize your ideas and develop the logic behind your study and each part of your paper. Because it is organized around a logical flow of ideas, a good outline will naturally help you formulate transitions between ideas. Writing an outline will also reveal areas where your paper may be short on references. But perhaps the best reason to create an outline is that it saves time by decreasing the number of drafts you need to finalize your paper, increasing the chances that you will write a focused paper from the outset of the writing process.

The section that benefits the most from an outline is the Introduction. When creating an outline for your Introduction, you should first determine the general topics you will cover and the most logical order for them. When determining the organization, be sure to focus on topics and not articles. That is, it is likely that one article covers several different ideas and consequently will appear in several different topics or sections of your Introduction. There is no magic number of topics that you should have. However, you should try to organize ideas so there are a few main topics with subtopics, as needed, under each larger topic. Within topics, be sure to set your articles up in a coherent manner that will "tell a story." Your overall Introduction should flow from one topic area to another in such a way that the reader feels as though the majority of the previous literature naturally points to your study as the next logical step.

The Building Blocks of Your Paper

The more narrative parts of an APA-style paper (i.e., the Introduction and Discussion) will rely heavily on your ability to clearly convey ideas in an organized manner. To do this, each paragraph should focus on conveying a single idea rather than several different ideas. It is helpful to think of each paragraph as a "mini-paper" that sets up the topic in the first sentence or two, provides supporting information in the next few sentences, and then ends with a conclusion. Paragraphs focus on ideas, not articles, such that most of the time you will use several articles to form your paragraphs. Each article will have a slightly different focus, so it will be up to you to synthesize and integrate the different ideas to reveal a common theme.

Tying It All Together

ψ **APA Manual (Transitions)** *Page 65*

When writing your paper, you will want to stick to the facts. However, your paper will not be very persuasive if it reads like a long list of disconnected pieces of information. To avoid this, you will want to incorporate transition statements to show the reader how information is related. These transitions should appear both between and within paragraphs. To write good transitions, think about how you would explain one topic flowing into another as if you were talking to someone. You would not just list the information. Rather, you would say, "The previous study talked about ____ and this next finding is similar or different because it talks about ____." Sure, this structure is a bit formulaic, but it illustrates the general idea. When transitioning, avoid vague connections such as "Another study . . ." because every study is "another study." Instead, focus on how the next study adds to the previous one. Even if there might be 98% similarity between the studies, you should use transitions to highlight their differences. Basic transition phrases for within paragraphs include "Further, . . ." "Similarly, . . ." "In contrast, . . ."

Example →

"A study with similar methods found the basic effect of X, but also found Y."

Giving Credit Where Credit Is Due

ψ **APA Manual (Citations)** *Pages 169–192*

Science's goal is to add to our existing knowledge by building on findings from previous studies. Any time you write a scientific paper in psychology, you will need to paraphrase other studies' findings. When you do, you must properly give credit to the researchers by using citations. In fact, you should cite any portion of the paper that is not your own original thought. Citations correspond to articles that should appear in the References (more on that section below). When writing a paragraph, you should cite at the *first* instance of using information from another source. You then cite again any time you change sources.

In terms of formatting, here are some general "rules" for APA-style citations:

1. Purge other styles (e.g., MLA) from your brain. APA style has a unique format.

2. Always refer to the current APA manual instead of relying on the citation format being used in journal articles, websites, PsycINFO, textbooks, or other sources. The APA manual is always the most up to date.

3. Citations follow the general "Author, Author, & Author, Year" format.

4. Do not use first names. Initials are included only if two authors have the same surname.

5. Do not bold or underline anything.

6. The Author and Year always stay together. Do not put the year at the end of a sentence by itself.

7. Cite each time you use information from a source.

8. It is preferable to cite at the end of sentences so that your sentence focuses on the ideas and not the authors.

9. Do not write citations into the sentences.

Example →

Bad: According to an article by Klohnen and Lau, which appeared in the 2003 *Journal of Relationships,* those who scored high on avoidance were more attracted to fearful and dismissing partners (Klohnen 2003).

Better: In a study conducted by Klohnen and Luo (2003), those who scored high on avoidance were more attracted to fearful and dismissing partners.

Best: Those who scored high on avoidance were more attracted to fearful and dismissing partners (Klohnen & Luo, 2003).

 Research in Action

Giving Credit Where Credit Is Due

Science advances by building upon the findings of others, an idea captured by the saying that we are always "standing on the shoulders of giants." The findings in past studies inspire and serve as the basis for future studies. APA-style writing provides us with a structure for how to consistently acknowledge these contributions.

Here is your chance to try out several online activities that will help you practice properly citing, referencing, and **Giving Credit Where Credit Is Due.** These skills will prove useful as you help to advance science in the pursuit of knowledge with your own research papers.

LaunchPad To complete these activities, visit LaunchPad at launchpadworks.com

Proofreading and the Revision Process

Read the following:

Tihs is my fvaoirte txebtook eevr. Cmomnuicaioitn is an ipomtrnat slikl and APA sylte is asbluoelty fnatstaic. I lvoe tcnehical wnritig and hpoe to laenr mroe aobut it. Wehn APA sylte is msisnig form my lfie, my lfie is msisnisg maennig.

How many typos or spelling errors were there? Too many! But, you could read it nonetheless. Similarly, when you reread your own papers, you will have a tendency to skip over obvious errors without noticing them—that is, unless you take your time and review your writing with a conscientious eye.

Ultimately, good writing is all about revisions. No one, not even an accomplished scientist, can write a paper or even a sentence perfectly for grammar or content the first time. The journal articles you read have likely been through numerous revisions. Similarly, you should not expect to sit down and write a high-quality paper in one sitting. Instead, you should plan on writing several drafts, editing your paper for content and checking for grammatical mistakes and typos as you go along. Sure, this sounds time-consuming, and it is to some degree. However, it is liberating because you have the freedom to write the first few drafts without worrying about perfecting each sentence. You can always "wordsmith" things in a later draft, ensuring then that every sentence has a clear purpose and your writing is succinct and direct. Getting into the habit of proofreading and revising will make you a better and more productive writer.

The APA-Style Research Report

In psychology, research reports conform to APA style. As we mentioned in Chapter 4, the APA manual (American Psychological Association, 2010) provides guidelines regarding two key types of information for each section of the paper: formatting and content. With APA style, there is little mystery to the reader or the author about how things should look and what types of information should appear in each section of the paper. In this section, we provide a series of checklists that aim to help simplify APA style for each section. For more detailed information, consult the APA manual (we provide page number references where appropriate).

▶ What is the purpose
of each section of an
APA-style report?
SEE CHAPTER 2, p. 45

Title Page Formatting and Content

- **Title Page appears on page 1 of the paper**
- **Running head**
  - After the words "Running head:" keywords from the title appear in ALL CAPS (50 characters max), followed by the page number at the far right on page 1.

    Example → Running head: THE ROLE OF AROUSAL 1

  - All other pages contain the same information, but omit "Running head:".
- **Title**
  - Summarizes the main idea of your paper in 10–12 words maximum.
  - For an experimental study, it mentions the general relationship between the IV and DV.

    Example → The Effects of (Independent Variable) on (Dependent Variable).

    Example → The Role of Arousal on the Interpersonal Attraction Between Strangers

**ψ APA Manual
(Running Heads)**
Page 41 (example)

**ψ APA Manual
(Titles)**
Page 23

- o If you used a nonhuman sample, did you mention it in the title?
- o The title should be centered on the page, capitalizing the first letter of important words only.

- **Author Name(s)**
  - o Your name should appear centered on the page, under the title.
  - o If you are collaborating on this paper with others, list the names in order of contribution to the article. For example, the person who contributed the most should be listed as the first author.

- **Affiliation**
  - o Under each author's name, provide the person's institutional affiliation. Only provide the institution's name. Do not include the name of the person's department within the institution.

> ψ **APA Manual**
> **(Author Names)**
> *Page 23*

> ψ **APA Manual**
> **(Affiliation)**
> *Page 23*

Abstract

Formatting

- The abstract appears on page 2 of the paper.
- The word "Abstract" is centered on the top of the page, without formatting (such as bold or italics).
- Typing starts on the *next* double-spaced line (using normal paragraphs).
- First line is NOT indented.
- Avoid referencing other authors where possible.
- The text is a brief (150–250 words) comprehensive summary of the study.

> ψ **APA Manual**
> **(Abstract)**
> *Pages 25–26, 41 (examples)*

Content

- The abstract should include the following key information:
  - o What is being studied? (topic, hypotheses)
  - o Who was in the study? (participant information)
  - o How was it studied? What methodology was used? (methods)
  - o What did you find? What was/was not significant? (results)
  - o What does it mean? (discussion)

Introduction

Formatting

- The Introduction starts on page 3 of your paper.
- Page starts with your *exact title from the title page* (centered), not the word "Introduction."
- Typing starts on the *next* double-spaced line (using normal paragraphs).

> ψ **APA Manual**
> **(Introduction)**
> *Page 27*

Content

- **Opening Paragraph(s)**
  - ○ Attention Grabber—Starts with an engaging opening that will interest readers.
  - ○ Justification—Explains why the reader should care about this topic. Why is this important?
  - ○ Defines any relevant constructs that may be ambiguous.
  - ○ Purpose—Gives an indication of what your paper is trying to accomplish.

    Example → "The purpose of this paper is to . . ." "This study seeks to . . ."

- **Review of the Relevant Literature Paragraph(s)**
  - ○ Gives the reader a sense of the most important past research conducted on your topic.
  - ○ The review makes it seem as though the majority of previous literature naturally points to your study/topic as the next logical step.
  - ○ Order of the articles presented demonstrates an underlying organization. This is where the outline helps tremendously.
  - ○ The organization follows a general theme of going from general to progressively more specific topics.
  - ○ The topics covered in the articles are interrelated such that they form a cohesive story (i.e., there are not any articles that do not fit in with your topic).
  - ○ The order and organization of your articles funnel toward (naturally lead to) your specific topic/hypotheses.
  - ○ Has transitions between paragraphs that link the last idea in the previous paragraph to the first idea in the next paragraph (i.e., there is an explicit connection between the ideas).
  - ○ For any article that is central to your study, has it been thoroughly described? (What were the hypotheses? How were they studied? What did the researchers find?)
  - ○ Summarizes articles through paraphrasing.
  - ○ Avoids using quotes (except where 100% necessary).
  - ○ The results/conclusions from each article are interpreted within the context of your paper's organization.

- **Concluding Paragraph(s)**
  - ○ Paper has a short paragraph right before the hypotheses explicitly linking past literature to the current research.
  - ○ Emphasizes the importance of what you are doing and demonstrates how your research fits into a long line of other important/interesting work.
  - ○ Makes a connection between what you think will happen (hypotheses) and why you think it will happen (basis for this provided by review of relevant literature).
  - ○ Uses the general idea of "One area that past research has failed to address is __."

- **Hypotheses**
  - Gives a general idea of how you will attempt to solve the problem.
  - Explains why you expect results that will confirm the hypotheses.
  - Hypotheses are stated in a *clear and specific* manner.
  - Hypotheses make clear predictions about how you think the independent and dependent variables will relate to each other.
  - All relevant constructs are clearly defined (i.e., what is the IV, what is the DV, are there any levels?).

Method

Formatting

- The Method starts right after the Introduction (not on a new page).
- The word "Method" is centered and bolded at the start of the section and is double-spaced with everything else.
- Typing starts on the *next* double-spaced line (using normal paragraphs).
- The section is organized into the following sections: Participants, Materials (Measures), Design, and Procedure.
- Each subsection has a heading but does not start on a new page. Bold the headings and align them to the left.
- Avoid unnecessary details throughout that are not directly relevant to the problem under examination.

ψ **APA Manual
(Method: Formatting)**

*Page 29; page 44
(example); page 62
(for heading information)*

Content

- **Participants**
  - Gives number of participants (and they are referred to as participants, not subjects, unless you are describing animal research).
  - Gives gender distribution (# males, # females).
  - Gives mean, standard deviation, and range of participants' ages. Remember to *italicize* statistical symbols.

    Example → (M = ##.##, SD = ##.##, range = ##–##)
  - Gives generalization about the whole group (e.g., college sophomores, married couples, preschool children, etc.).
  - Gives where participants or subjects are from.
  - Gives the method the researcher used to select participants or subjects (random or convenience sampling).
  - Gives information regarding incentive (money, class credit, etc.) for participation.

ψ **APA Manual
(Method: Participants)**

Page 29

- **Materials (Measures)**
  - Lists all measures.
  - For each measure, provides any available info on the following: reliability information (alpha), convergent/discriminant validity, example items, scoring, and a relevant citation.

ψ **APA Manual
(Method: Materials)**

Page 31

o For each scale, italicizes the scale anchors.

  Example → (1 = *not at all*; 7 = *extremely*).

o Provides a description for each piece of equipment (e.g., computers, software used), including the model number, company, and state abbreviation of company location.

o Gives dimensions (and other descriptive details) of any important items used in the study.

o Do not describe procedures here (i.e., how things were used or administered).

- **Design**

ψ **APA Manual (Method: Design)**

Page 31; page 249 (the information that should be reported for an experiment)

o Describes the overall experimental design that you have used.

o Describes key variables of interest. Distinguishes independent variables (including levels) and dependent variables.

o Describes variables that were controlled, and gives why this was necessary.

o Further operationalizes variables where needed.

o Describes the groups that comprise your design in detail, noting the control group.

o Describes how researchers assigned participants to groups.

- **Procedure**

ψ **APA Manual (Method: Procedure)**

Page 32

o Describes where the study took place.

o Gives a step-by-step summary of the steps needed to run the study.

  Example → "After participants gave consent, . . ." "Next, the researcher . . ."

o Indicates what a typical test, trial, or session involved.

o Describes any phases that the study had or any instructions that the participants received.

o Makes use of descriptive labels when referring to groups.

Results

Formatting

ψ **APA Manual (Results)**

Page 32; page 46 (example); page 62 (for heading information)

- The Results section starts right after the Method (not on a new page).
- The word "Results" is centered and bolded at the start of the section and is double-spaced with everything else.
- Typing starts on the *next* double-spaced line (using normal paragraphs).
- Section is organized based on the hypotheses that were tested.

Content

- For each hypothesis:

  o Provides descriptive statistics by groups (mean, standard deviation, percentages).

  o Describes how you analyzed your data (the test/procedure used).

  o Describes the results of the statistical tests (the actual numbers).

○ Gives a very basic statement of the results (what this indicates in terms of the hypotheses).

• Uses and refers to tables and/or figures that help make the data easier to understand.

• Avoids going into detail about the implications of the tests (this is saved for the Discussion).

• Avoids using "prove" and "disprove" terminology.

▶ How do you determine what statistical analysis will address your research question? SEE APPENDIX A, p. 480

Discussion

Formatting

• The Discussion starts right after the Results section (not on a new page).

• The word "Discussion" is centered and bolded at the start of the section and is double-spaced.

• Typing starts on the *next* double-spaced line (using normal paragraphs).

Content

• This section is organized into the following sections: Restatement of Hypotheses, Implication/Interpretation of Results, Strengths/Limitations, Future Directions, and Conclusion.

• Restatement of Hypotheses

○ Gives a brief review of what you were trying to accomplish (i.e., what was the purpose?).

○ Summarizes the hypotheses that the study tested, including whether they were supported.

    Example → "Contrary to the hypothesis . . ." "As hypothesized . . ."

• Implication/Interpretation of Results

○ Section avoids statistical jargon and explains results in plain wording.

○ Gives the major findings related to the hypotheses (i.e., whether hypotheses were supported or not).

○ Explains what these findings mean to the topic in general.

○ Connects findings with literature reviewed in the Introduction.

    Example → "The present study suggests X. In contrast, previous research found Y (cite)."

○ Connects new areas of research (related to the findings).

○ Uses theory to help explain the present findings.

    Example → "The present study found X. This may be due to the fact that A, B, C, and D."

• Strengths of Study

○ Note strong points in the design (e.g., sampling, procedure) using proper terminology.

ψ APA Manual (Discussion)

Page 35; page 47 (example); page 62 (for heading information)

- Limitations of Study
  - o Mention the obvious shortcomings of your study (i.e., the main things that might qualify your results).
  - o Note limitations of the design (sampling, procedure, etc.) using proper terminology.
- Future Directions of This Research Area
  - o Discusses things that future studies on this topic should examine, above and beyond addressing any limitations in your design. Focus on the ideas!
- Conclusion
  - o Provides a very general summary of research accomplishments by generally addressing what was looked at, what was found, and how knowledge has been advanced.
  - o Last sentence provides a general "take-home message."

References

ψ **APA Manual (References)**

Formatting for other types of sources appears on pages 193–224.

- Starts on a new page with the word "References" centered on the page (not Works Cited).
- "References" is *not* in ALL CAPS, **bold**, *italics*, or underline format.
- References appear in alphabetical order based on the first author's last name.
- Everything after the first line is indented for each reference.
- The entire page is double-spaced with no extra spaces between references.
- There are no first names in the citation, only initials.
- You have a sufficient number of acceptable references (i.e., scholarly journals, edited academic books, etc.).
- You have reference-citation agreement. That is, all research cited throughout your paper is referenced and all references are referred to in your paper as citations.
- Be sure your sources follow the proper format.

Example (Journal Article) →

Baker, T., McFall, R., & Shoham, V. (2008). Current status and future prospects of clinical psychology: Toward a scientifically principled approach to mental and behavioral health care. *Psychological Science in the Public Interest, 9*(2), 67–103. doi:10.1111/j.1539-6053.2009.01036.x.

Example (Book Chapter) →

Wolitzky, D. (2011). Psychoanalytic theories of psychotherapy. In J. C. Norcross, G. R. Vandenbos, & D. K. Freedheim (Eds.), *History of psychotherapy: Continuity and change* (2nd ed., pp. 65–100). Washington, DC: American Psychological Association.

Example (Book) →

Leary, M., & Tangney, J. (2003). *Handbook of self and identity*. New York, NY: Guilford Press.

Tables and Figures

- Qualities of Good Tables and Figures
  - The Tables/Figures augment, rather than duplicate, the text.
  - Convey essential facts.
  - Omit visually distracting detail.
  - Are easy to read.
  - Are easy to understand (purpose is readily apparent).
  - Are consistent in style to other tables and figures in article (lettering, etc.).
  - Are carefully planned and organized.
  - Figures are properly scaled (start at 0 if appropriate) and consistent with other figures.

> **ψ APA Manual (Tables)**
> *Page 52 (example); pages 125–150; (examples); page 150 (checklist)*

> **ψ APA Manual (Figures)**
> *Page 53 (example); pages 150–167; page 167 (checklist)*

 Research in Action

The Structure of an APA-Style Paper

When you walk into your local grocery store, you know right where to head to find the items you need. This familiarity makes the experience easy and efficient. Alternatively, when you are shopping at an unfamiliar grocery store, you can get easily frustrated at the slow process of walking through every aisle to find that last item on your list. The same is true of APA-style papers: To make it easier to find the information you want, the APA dictates the order in which information appears in journal articles.

The online activity ***The Structure of an APA-Style Paper*** will help you practice structuring an APA-style title page, as well as the paper as a whole. Soon you will know right where to look in an APA-style research paper for the information that you need!

LaunchPad To complete this activity, visit LaunchPad at launchpadworks.com

Tips for Effective Poster Presentations

As we introduced in Chapter 2, a research poster presentation summarizes a study, most commonly on a 3-foot x 4-foot (0.91 meter x 1.22 meter) sheet of paper that the researcher affixes to a bulletin board. Posters typically have many of the same sections as an APA-style research paper. However, because space is at a premium, it is common to see posters omit the Abstract, References, and some parts of the Discussion (e.g., strengths, future directions). As you read above, APA style focuses on stating things succinctly. This is even more important in a poster presentation because of the limited space. Here are several tips to keep in mind when preparing a poster presentation:

1. **Size Matters**—You should make sure that everything on your poster is readable from a distance. With any luck, you will have several interested readers of your poster at the same time, so you want to be sure everyone can read the content while standing a few feet away. Generally, the minimum font size for text on a poster is 24 point in a professional and readable font such as Times New Roman or Garamond.

2. **Less Is More**—Poster presentation sessions are often crowded, which means attendees want to see a lot of posters, but cannot afford to spend a great deal of time at any one poster. To help out, you should keep text on your poster at a minimum. Rather than including large blocks or paragraphs of text, which are time-consuming to read, try to use bulleted lists that feature quick statements of important information.

3. **Get Visual!**—Whenever possible, use charts, diagrams, graphs, figures, and pictures to convey information. These types of visuals provide information much more efficiently than text, and add visual interest to your poster.

4. **Aesthetics Matter**—Because posters are such a visual medium, you will want to pay attention to the overall aesthetics of your poster. Make your poster easy to read by featuring a black text on a white background. You can (and should) add color so that your poster is not all black and white. As you select colors, avoid visually jarring combinations (e.g., yellow and red). Finally, spend extra time making sure that objects and sections in your poster line up and that you are consistent in your use of font size. Things may appear "close enough" on your computer screen, but when your poster is full size, small differences will be very noticeable.

5. **A Quick Rundown**—Often the people who visit your poster will skip reading altogether and will simply ask you to personally summarize what you did. When you summarize, aim for a quick 1- to 2-minute description that includes the key points (the purpose, the basic method, and the findings) right up front. From there allow the person to ask questions or to give their thoughts. In other words, avoid giving a 20-minute story of your research journey. As with all forms of public speaking, practice your 1- to 2-minute summary ahead of time. Know that you may not have the answer to every question a visitor asks, and that is all right. Sometimes these conversations with others inspire the next research question.

6. **Have Handouts**—Some visitors may not have time to read your poster during the session or may want to have specific details about your study after the conference. For this reason, you should provide a handout that summarizes your research project. Be sure to include your contact information in case someone would like to contact you about your research.

Figure B.2 is an example of a research poster.

Tips for Effective Paper Presentations

A paper presentation involves giving a speech about your study. Your presentation will include the same basic components as an APA-style research report (i.e., background, hypotheses, methodology, results, discussion, and references). These presenta-

FIGURE B.2 An Example Research Poster *(David B. Strohmetz and Jessica Ketch)*

tions typically last from 15 to 30 minutes and almost universally incorporate a slide (e.g., PowerPoint, Google Slides, Prezi) presentation. Here are tips related to three key areas: presenting your information, formatting your slides, and choosing content.

Presentation

1. Avoid reading information off of the slides. The audience reads more quickly than you speak, so they will ignore what you are saying and will lose focus while they wait for the next slide of information to appear.

2. Similarly, avoid reading information from your notes. Reading notes inhibits the connection you can have with the audience. When you break away from your notes, it makes the conversation seem more natural, and opens up the possibility of a more flexible and lively discussion.

3. Avoid having a full slide of information on the screen at once. Rather, animate each piece of information (e.g., fade in, appear, wipe) so that it appears as you discuss it. This way, the audience will focus on what you are saying, rather than trying to read the slides.

4. If at all possible, walk around and use a wireless presentation remote clicker to advance your slides. Being a moving target will help you engage the audience and appear more dynamic.

Format

1. Create visual interest by using a slide background that has some color (i.e., avoid plain white). However, keep the background simple so that it is not too distracting. Backgrounds that are primarily white can provide enough light in the room that you are able to keep the lights off, which also helps slide readability.

2. Make sure font colors contrast well enough with the background (e.g., avoid red on blue, gray on black, etc.). Also be sure to account for how a projector or different screen may distort colors. Generally, you will be safe with blue/black/red on white backgrounds. Yellow can be especially tricky.

3. Whenever possible, use fonts that are easy to read. However, avoiding the standard fonts that people see all the time (e.g., Times New Roman, Courier, Arial) will help your presentation stand out.

Content

1. Avoid putting too much text on your slides. Audience members will read whatever you put on the slides, often at the expense of listening to you.

2. Use simple visuals, diagrams, tables, graphs, and animations to help the audience understand concepts. With that said, if visuals and animations are gratuitous or overly detailed, they could distract or overwhelm the audience.

3. When including pictures, animate them along with the associated content. Similarly, if you have a picture of something especially funny or visually interesting, have it disappear so the audience does not focus their attention on it for an extended period of time.

4. Neatness and attention to detail matter. Everything on your slides should line up, font sizes should be consistent, and your presentation should be free of typos. The audience spends a lot of time looking at your slides and will notice all of these things.

5. Becoming familiar with the "Slide Master" function in PowerPoint and Google Slides is priceless. It is much better to make changes there than to make changes on each individual slide. You can also create one slide, copy/paste it, and then edit it to keep things consistent.

6. When in doubt, add more slides (rather than piling more onto one slide). Having more slides helps keep the flow of information manageable, and makes it easier to make changes later. Besides, the audience can't tell if you have 5 or 50 slides.

Student Example of an APA-Style Manuscript

Now that you have seen the elements involved in writing an APA-style research report, we would like you to see a model of how to put it all together. The following is an example of an APA-style research report written by an undergraduate student. You will see all of our general writing tips, as well as the formatting and context of an APA-style research report, in this example.

Running head: WHAT DOES IT TAKE TO DATE? 1

What Does It Take to Date?:

The Effects of Ego Depletion on Dating Choices

Victoria Dunlap

Monmouth University

> The title page has very specific formatting, so you need to pay attention to details such as the running head. The words "Running head:" only appear on the first page, while the actual running head and page number appear on every page in all capital letters. The title of the paper, authors, and the affiliation of the authors are each centered on their own double-spaced line.

Author Note

We would like to thank Amanda Pollifrone for conducting an engaging senior thesis study and providing an excellent example of student writing that we altered into a flawed one as a resource for teaching others.

> Author notes are not necessary for theses or dissertations. They include more information about the authors and acknowledgements.

WHAT DOES IT TAKE TO DATE? 2

Abstract

This study examines how depletion of self-control influences dating choices. A sample of 43 single (32 females, 11 males) college undergraduates completed an ego depletion task, looked at pictures of potential dating partners, and filled out a first date goals questionnaire. As hypothesized, depletion significantly influenced selectivity of dating partner choices. Individuals depleted of self-control had a higher likelihood to date a greater number of people than those who were non-depleted. Also as hypothesized, depletion significantly influenced certain first date goals, particularly in relation to sexual activity. Depleted participants had a higher likelihood to go on a first date for the purpose of engaging in sexual activity than those who were non-depleted. These findings help advance the understanding and awareness of how moments of depletion influence important decisions in our lives, such as whom and why we choose to date.

Keywords: self-control, depletion, selectivity, dating choices, first date goals

The abstract is a very important part of the research paper. It needs to be a concise and accurate summary of the research. Others will read the abstract of your article to decide if it is useful background for their own research project.

The abstract has specific formatting. For example, you do not indent the first sentence as you would normally.

You can add keywords to your paper which are used to catalog your paper in search engines for articles.

WHAT DOES IT TAKE TO DATE?   3

What Does It Take to Date? The Effects of Ego Depletion on Dating Choices

On a daily basis, we make many choices whether we are mentally worn-out or not. In fact, people have a limited amount of self-control available and when self-control deteriorates, following thoughts and behaviors are affected (Baumeister, Bratslavsky, Muraven, & Tice, 1998). Some important decisions and thoughts most individuals face are why and whom they would like to date. Among all the available potential dating partners, people have to go through and pick ones who might be suitable for them. Individuals also have to think about what reasons they would like to date, such as just to have fun or to look for love. Dating is an essential part in relationship formation, which relationships are ultimately one of the most important aspects of our lives. This study seeks to advance the understanding of our limited amount of self-control on the influence of how selective we are in making dating partner choices and the dating goals in which we are interested.

Dating

Dating is a major way that people develop and initiate romantic relationships (Henningsen, Henningsen, McWorthy, & McWorthy, 2011; Morr & Mongeau, 2004). Some people date for specific reasons or for a variety of different goals (Mongeau, Serewicz, & Therrien, 2004). For example, people date to have fun, to socialize, to impress others, to experiment sexually, for satisfaction, for companionship, for romantic potential, and for intimacy (Clark, Shaver, & Abrahams, 1999; Roscoe, Diana, & Brooks, 1987). According to past research, the most prevalent reasons among these are to have fun, to get to know someone better (reduce uncertainty), to engage in sexual activity, to form a friendship, and to form a romantic relationship (Mongeau et al., 2004.) In heterosexual dating, men evolutionarily choose to date more for physical attractiveness

---

Annotations (margin callouts):

The opening paragraph of your Introduction should start with an attention grabber that will interest readers.

The next part of your opening paragraph, known as the justification piece, should explain why the reader should care about this topic.

The opening paragraph should end with a purpose statement in which you indicate what the paper is trying to accomplish.

Your Introduction should include several topics that connect to your research project. Each topic should give the reader a sense of the most important research on this topic.

Headings like this are a great way to reveal your organization to the reader.

Avoid unnecessary or extra words that don't add meaning. Omit these words and start this sentence with "The most prevalent..."

WHAT DOES IT TAKE TO DATE? 4

and sexual activity, while women date more for earning potential and relational escalation (Buss & Schmitt, 1993; Finkel & Eastwick, 2008; Mongeau et al., 2004). Considering that men and women may have different first date goals suggests individuals engage in thoughtful decision making when dating. It may also suggest that individuals naturally look for something specific in a mate (Buss & Schmitt, 1993). Though research supports the instinctive gender differences among males and females, this may not be the case in all situations. Situational factors, such as how a person feels at the moment, may also influence dating preferences.

Self-Control

Self-control is the capacity to alter one's own responses, especially when involving morals and social expectations (Baumeister, Vohs, & Tice, 2007), while the term self-regulation refers to one's ability to exert restraint over impulses, emotions, and behaviors (Baumeister et al., 1998). Self-control suggests the idea of willpower or some type of internal strength and energy resource. Even Freud anticipated that the ego depended on the self's capacity of an inner resource (Freud, 1961). He believed that the ego needed energy to accomplish tasks. This supports the term of "ego-depletion," which suggests that engaging in tasks involving self-control, such as decision making, dieting, and emotion regulation, will weaken later use of self-control (Vohs & Heatherton, 2000; Vohs, Schmeichel, Nelson, Baumeister, Twenge, & Tice, 2008). A depleted level of self-control will influence subsequent thoughts and behaviors, which is potentially how self-control may relate to making choices in dating (Baumeister et al., 1998). Though decision making is one of the many factors that deplete self-control, depleted self-control may also influence our decision making.

Margin annotations:

Say it more succinctly by simplifying when possible. This could read "Men and women's different first date goals . . ."

Use transitions like this to show how the previous section's topic links logically to the next section's topic.

Notice how the author paraphrases the definition of self-regulation using her own words.

Omit extra or unnecessary words. Taking out "the idea of" doesn't change the sentence's meaning.

This an example of "hedge-wording" to make it clear this is the author's speculation.

WHAT DOES IT TAKE TO DATE?   5

Self-Control and Decision Making

Depleted individuals are likely to make different choices than those who are non-depleted. For example, depleted individuals are more passive in the decisions that they make (Baumeister et al., 1998). This is potentially because of their exhausted mental state and their low level of availability to make an effortful decision. Previous research has found that depletion also leads to taking shortcuts in the decision-making process, and it negatively influences decision making because individuals may not have the resources or effort to fully process information (Baumeister, Muraven, & Tice, 2000; Baumeister, Sparks, Stillman, & Vohs, 2008). It is quite possible that individuals may only want to date for low mental effort reasons (sexual activity, to reduce uncertainty, and to have fun) rather than high mental effort reasons (relationship potential or companionship). Relationship potential and companionship may require more effort and dedication than the first interactions of getting to know someone better on a first date or to just date for fun or sexual activity. Depleted individuals may also be too mentally exhausted to make a decision about whom they would like to date.

Depleted individuals are more cautious when deciding to take a risk (Unger & Stahlberg, 2011), which may also influence dating decisions. One could decide that dating is ultimately a risk because of its potential for rejection (Haselton & Buss, 2000). If an individual is more open in their selectivity of dating partner choices (Baumeister et al., 1998), then there is a larger possibility of potential partners reciprocating their interest. Just as men and women give thought to what they want from a first date, this research further suggests that individuals think through their dating decisions.

To even be aware of risk and taking precaution when it comes to dating may be distinctly human (Vohs et al., 2008). The ability to process

> Say it more succinctly: "make decisions more passively."

> Omit extra words. This sentence could start with "Depletion also leads . . ."

> Throughout this section the author makes connections between the past research findings and her research ideas. This helps make the current research topic seem like the next logical step.

WHAT DOES IT TAKE TO DATE?

6

certain information and to actually make a decision is a major component to human social life. It takes a certain amount of effort to contemplate a possible selection of choices. According to Baumeister and colleagues (1998) depletion has prevented people from clearly seeing their original planned aspirations and goals for themselves. If individuals are unable to put forth an effortful decision or visibly see their life aspirations, then they may also lose sight of their original dating goals. In dating relationships, individuals tend to make different situational choices when it comes to the very beginning stages of dating with pick-up lines to the very late stages of relationships with infidelity (Ciarocco, Echevarria, & Lewandowski, 2012; Lewandowski, Ciarocco, Pettanato, & Stephan, 2012).

Self-Control and Relationships

Relationship initiation sometimes begins with pick-up lines (Lewandowski et al., 2012). Depletion can change how individuals perceive initiation attempts. Specifically, cute, cheesy pick-up lines were less well received by depleted individuals. This further supports the low level of mental effort because individuals may not have the resources left after depletion to have tolerance for such an obvious type of pick-up line. In the later context of relationships, depleted individuals may also not have the resources necessary to control themselves when it comes to infidelity (Ciarocco et al., 2012). Depleted individuals in committed relationships were more likely to accept a coffee date and give out their phone number than non-depleted individuals.

Their loss of self-control proves there is a lack of ability to resist desire and awareness of their original situation (Baumeister et al., 1998; Ciarocco et al., 2012; Hofmann, Baumeister, Förster, & Vohs, 2012). Depletion has a significant influence on relationship aspects, such as pick-up lines and infidelity, and this may further suggest it affects the decisions people make in the dating world.

Whenever possible, avoid writing citations into sentences. It is much easier for the reader if citations are at the ends of sentences. In this case you could put "... (Baumeister et al., 1998)." at the end of the sentence.

When you have more than one article that supports your point, you should cite all of them. To do this, you alphabetize the citations based on the last name of the first author (C comes before L).

This citation uses et al., because it has been cited before and has 3 + authors.

Use active voice—where the actor engages in the action—versus passive voice—where the action was engaged in by the actor. To use active voice, revise this to, "Specifically, depleted individuals were less receptive to cute, cheesy opening pick-up lines."

Here the author summarizes an article through paraphrasing.

Avoid saying "prove." Instead use less definitive wording here such as "suggests."

The Present Study

In dating and relationships, research supports that depleted individuals are more likely to commit infidelity and are much less willing to put up with cute opening pick-up lines. Individuals who are depleted are more likely to be passive, less likely to take a risk, and less likely to put effort forth in decision making. Though studies have examined depletion of self-control in many aspects of interpersonal relationships, they have yet to take a look at how depletion influences selectivity in dating. Therefore, this study will attempt to advance research by learning about how moments of depleted self-control may influence dating choices. In the present study, the researcher will manipulate self-control to see the influence of depleted self-control on selectivity of dating partner choices and first date goals. The researcher predicted that individuals depleted of self-control will have a higher willingness to date a greater number of people than those who are non-depleted. The researcher also hypothesized that those depleted of self-control will have a higher likelihood to go on a first date for purposes related to low mental effort, such as engaging in sexual activity, than those who are non-depleted.

Method

Participants

The participants in this study included 32 single female and 11 single male college undergraduates from a private university in the northeast of the United States. They ranged from 18 to 25, with a mean age of 19.21 ($SD = 1.32$). The participants were European-American (81.4%), African American (7.0%), Hispanic/Latino(a) (7.0%), Multiracial (2.3%), and Arab/Arab-American (2.3%). A majority of the participants were heterosexual (93.0%). Researchers recruited participants using a convenience sample from the undergraduate research participation pool. The participants received credit toward a class assignment for participating in this experiment.

This is a logical way to conclude your Introduction. This paragraph links the past research covered in the Introduction to the current research study in three pieces, ending with the hypotheses.

Here is the link between past research and the current research.

In this section the author points out what is still unknown about this topic. You want this section to set you up as the research hero in that you should point out a gap in the literature that your study will attempt to fill.

In this section the author is giving a general idea of how the study will attempt to fill the research gap.

Here the author provides a prediction about how the independent variable and dependent variables will be related.

In this section the author describes her sample by identifying the sample size, breakdown of sex, ethnicity, and class rank, as well as relationship status of her participants. This section also includes the sources of the sample.

You should include any additional demographic information relevant to your study here as well.

WHAT DOES IT TAKE TO DATE? 8

Materials

This experiment included a demographic questionnaire, a dating partner selectivity measure, a first date goals questionnaire, and a manipulation check.

Demographics. The demographics questionnaire asked the participants their sex, sexual orientation, age, academic standing, relationship status, and ethnicity/race.

Dating partner selectivity measure. To measure the how discerning participants were when making choices about whom to date, participants viewed seven pictures of either males or females, based on their sexual preference. The pictures were selected based on level of attractiveness (7 out of 10) from hotornot.com. Participants looked at these pictures and answered the question, "How many of these men/women would you consider going on a date with? Please check off whoever interests you."

First date goals questionnaire. This measure assesses participants' reasons for going on a first date (Mongeau et al., 2004). Participants answered the question, "For what reasons would you like to go on a first date?" on a 27-item measure of first date goals with subscales of reducing uncertainty (Cronbach's alpha = .89), engaging in sexual activity (Cronbach's alpha = .95), and having fun (Cronbach's alpha = .91). Participants answered on a 5-point scale (1 = *strongly disagree;* 5 = *strongly agree*).

Manipulation check. The manipulation check assessed whether crossing off the letter "e" depletes individuals' self-control. Participants answered questions such as "To what extent did you have to concentrate on crossing off the letter *e*?" and "To what extent did you want to give up during the task?" on a 7-point scale (1 = *not at all; 7 = very much*).

Design

This experiment used a two-group, between-subjects design. The independent variable was ego depletion (depletion and non-depletion).

Margin notes (left side):

In this section you want to list and then describe in detail each material you used in the study.

Describe the measure using terminology that isn't part of the heading or the measure's name.

Be careful with passive voice, because here it isn't clear who did the selecting (participants? the researcher?). It would be better to write, "The researcher selected pictures . . ."

When describing an established measure, you should be sure to cite the original scale publication.

Be sure to give the reader direct quotes of example items in your survey.

When describing a survey used in your study, you should also include information about the inter-item reliability of the survey.

Provide the response scale, including key anchors.

WHAT DOES IT TAKE TO DATE? 9

The dependent variables were dating partner selectivity (7 pictures per participant) and first date goals (to reduce uncertainty, to engage in sexual activity, and to have fun).

Depletion manipulation. To deplete the participants, they completed a regulatory-depletion task (Baumeister et al., 1998). The researcher gave participants a typewritten sheet of paper with text on it (a page from a statistics book). The photocopy of the text was lightened. The researcher instructed participants to cross off the letter "*e*" only if it is not next to another vowel or not one extra letter away from another vowel. The non-depleted condition required that participants completed a similar task, but the photocopy of text was not lightened and the participants were told to cross off every single letter "*e*". The researcher placed participants into conditions using random assignment.

> If your study is an experiment that includes a manipulation, you should describe the manipulation in the design subsection as you see here.

> This section should describe the typical participant's experience in chronological order.

Procedure ◦

Participants signed up online for a time slot of twenty minutes through the research participation pool. Data collection occurred on an individual basis. After participants read and signed an informed consent, they filled out the demographic questionnaire. After the demographic questionnaire, the researcher placed participants into either a depletion condition or non-depletion condition based on random assignment. Next, the participants in both conditions completed the dating selectivity measure. Before looking at the pictures, the researcher asked participants which set of pictures (male or female) at which they would like to look. Next, participants completed the manipulation check. Once they finished, the researcher debriefed them.

> Because the author described the depletion task above, there is no need to repeat the information here. As a general rule, you should avoid repetition in APA style.

> Try to write succinctly, using as few words as possible to express your ideas.

> If you conducted an experiment with a manipulation check, you want to begin the results section discussing it. The results of the manipulation check put the rest of the results in context.

Results

Manipulation Check ◦

To test if the depletion task felt depleting, the researcher conducted an independent samples *t*-test comparing the depletion and non-depletion groups on the manipulation check for depletion. Means

> State what you sought to do.

> State the statistical test you conducted.

WHAT DOES IT TAKE TO DATE?   10

Describe what the statistics mean in plain wording.

and standard deviations for the depletion manipulation check were: depletion ($M = 4.97$, $SD = 1.56$), non-depletion ($M = 4.39$, $SD = 1.13$). The analysis was not significant and had a weak effect size; $t(41) = 1.39$, $p = .17$ (two-tailed), $d = .21$. This indicates that there is no significant difference between depletion and non-depletion conditions. Participants in the depletion condition did not report feeling depleted compared to the non-depletion condition.

Selectivity of Dating Partner Choices

To test the selectivity hypothesis, the researcher used an independent samples t-test comparing the depletion and non-depletion groups on selectivity of dating partner choices. The means and standard deviations for the two conditions were: depletion ($M = 3.05$, $SD = .86$), non-depletion ($M = 2.36$, $SD = 1.22$). The analysis was significant and had a weak effect size, $t(41) = 2.12$, $p = .04$, $d = .31$. This indicates that there is a significant difference between conditions. As hypothesized, depleted individuals had a higher likelihood to date a greater number of people than those who were non-depleted (see Figure 1).

Italicize all statistic symbols (t, F, p, d, r). There is also spacing around each side of mathematical symbols, such as = and <.

You should always report an effect size, so the reader knows the importance of the findings.

First Date Goals

To test first date goals, the researcher used an independent samples t-test comparing depletion and non-depletion conditions on the likelihood to go on a first date for sexual reasons. The means and standard deviations for the two experimental conditions were: depletion ($M = 2.61$, $SD = 1.08$), non-depletion ($M = 2.02$, $SD = .71$). The analysis was significant and had a moderate effect size, $t(41) = 2.11$, $p = .04$, $d = .31$. This indicates that there is a significant difference between conditions. As hypothesized, depleted individuals were more likely to go on a first date to engage in sexual activity than non-depleted individuals (see Figure 2).

In APA-style research reports, you explain your findings in part with the use of figures and tables.

It is important to tie the results of the analysis back into the original research hypothesis addressed by this analysis.

Exploratory Analyses of Sex Differences on First Date Goals

A two-way factorial analysis of variance was computed with the sex (male or female) and the ego depletion condition (depletion or non-depletion) as the independent variables and the likelihood to go on a first date for sexual activity as the dependent variable. See Table 1 for the means and standard deviations of the four combinations. The results of the two main effects were: sex, $F(1, 39) = 13.51$, $p = .001$, effect size $r = .26$, and ego depletion condition, $F(1, 39) = 13.67$, $p = .001$, effect size $r = .26$. Males had a higher likelihood to go on a first date for sexual activity than females. Also, depleted individuals had a higher likelihood to go on a first date for sexual activity than non-depleted individuals. The results show that the interaction between sex (male or female) and ego depletion condition (depletion or non-depletion) was significant, $F(1, 39) = 7.78$, $p = .008$, effect size $r = .17$. The results supported that there was an interaction between sex and ego depletion condition for the likelihood to go on a first date for sexual activity.

> Be sure you refer to any tables or figures you have created in the text of the appropriate part of the results section.

Discussion

The purpose of this study was to examine if depletion of self-control influences dating choices. As hypothesized, depleted individuals were more willing to date a greater amount of people than those who were non-depleted. Also as hypothesized, those depleted of self-control were more likely to go on a first date to engage in sexual activity than those who were non-depleted.

> No need to repeat the hypotheses. Rather, you should focus on the findings in the context of the hypotheses (i.e., whether they were confirmed or not).

Depletion Manipulation

Participants in the depletion condition did not self-report feeling any more depleted than participants in the non-depletion condition. This is important to examine especially because this ego-depletion manipulation has worked in past studies (Baumeister et al., 1998). The issue may

> Specify which finding you're discussing.

WHAT DOES IT TAKE TO DATE? 12

Discussions often identify differences or potential issues with the methods.

be that the present study used a time limit for the manipulation. The researcher gave participants in both the depletion and non-depletion condition five minutes to complete the "*e*" task. The majority of participants used the full five minutes. This may have been an issue because participants in both conditions used the same amount of time to complete the task, and it is possible that there was not enough time for depletion to be distinguished. It is also possible that manipulation check questions on the follow-up questionnaire were not strong enough to pick up what participants were really feeling or that participants did not want to admit that they felt depleted.

Have headings here match headings in the Results for easy cross-reference.

Selectivity of Dating Partner Choices

The following paragraphs provide interpretations of the results as well as their implications. The goal of this section of the Discussion is to put the results of the study into the context of the general topic.

As hypothesized, individuals depleted of self-control had a higher likelihood to date a greater amount of people than individuals who were non-depleted. This may possibly be due to the effects of depletion on decision making. Depleted individuals tend to be more passive in the decisions that they make, and this might be because of their exhausted mental state and their low level of availability to make an effortful decision (Baumeister et al., 1999). Depletion also leads to taking shortcuts when making a decision because they do not have the resources or effort left available to fully process information (Baumeister et al., 2000; Baumeister et al., 2008). Depleted individuals may ultimately be too mentally exhausted to make a decision about whom they would like to date. Also, depleted individuals are more cautious when deciding to take a risk (Unger & Stahlberg, 2011). Dating is a risk because of its potential for rejection (Haselton & Buss, 2000). Individuals may choose a large amount of potential dating partners because this may reduce the likelihood of experiencing rejection. If an individual is more open and passive in their selectivity of dating partner choices (Baumeister et al., 1998), then there is a larger possibility of garnering interest back. As supported, depleted individuals were less selective in their dating partner choices than non-depleted individuals.

Use past research findings to support your thoughts.

Remember, if you've cited a study with 3+ authors anywhere in the paper, you cite it using et al. every time after the first cite.

WHAT DOES IT TAKE TO DATE? 13

First Date Goals

As expected, individuals depleted of self-control had a higher likelihood to go on a first date to engage in sexual activity than individuals who were non-depleted. This may be due to the lack of mental effort once again (Baumeister et al., 2000; Baumeister et al., 2008), but it may also be because depletion has prevented people from clearly seeing their original planned aspirations and goals for themselves (Baumeister et al., 1998). If individuals are unable to put forth an effortful decision or visibly see their life aspirations, then it may be possible that they also lose sight of their original dating goals, which might be something more like relationship potential rather than sexual activity for a first date. First dates also mark one point where relationships might turn from friendly to romantic, and this may be distinct by sexual engagement (Mongeau, 2004).

> Here the author is connecting her research findings to the literature on the topic and using it to explain her results, which places the results into context.

Related to this, alcohol intoxication, which is representative of situational low self-control, suggests a lack of strength to resist desire (Hofmann, Baumeister, Förster, & Vohs, 2012). This shows that depleted individuals may have a harder time resisting sexual activity and desire. As supported, those who depleted had a higher likelihood to go on a first date to engage in sexual activity than individuals who were non-depleted.

> If it helps makes sense of the findings, feel free to bring in new research.

Sex Differences

As exploratory analyses revealed, males had a higher likelihood to go on a first date for the purpose of engaging in sexual activity than females. It seems that while females focused more on serious potential first date goals, such as relationship potential, males focused more on enjoyable goals, such as engaging in sexual activity (Mongeau, 2004). Depleted males had the highest likelihood to go on a first date for the purpose of engaging in sexual activity. This relates to males' high interest in physical attractiveness (Eastwick & Finkel, 2008). Research finds that men's view of sexual intent is higher than women's and that men

> You want to be sure to address and explain every hypothesis in your study, whether the hypotheses were supported or not.

WHAT DOES IT TAKE TO DATE?   14

also report a sex goal more frequently than women (Mongeau, 2004; Clark et al., 1999). This all further supports why depleted males are the ones who have the highest likelihood to go on a first date to engage in sexual activity.

Strengths and Limitations

> You may be able to use literature from your Introduction to help you interpret your results, but oftentimes you need to go back to the literature to find studies that help explain your results, especially if they are unexpected.

One major limitation was that the manipulation check did not work. Though there were evident effects of the manipulation considering that both of the hypotheses in this study found significance, the manipulation check was not significant. Another major limitation was the laboratory setting of this study. It is important to realize that what people say and actually do is very different. Being in a laboratory really constrains this research from discovering what true real life results would look like. The relatively small sample size of only 43 participants was also a limitation in the present study that constrained the study's power.

> In this section you want to note the strengths and shortcomings of your research.

> Throughout this section you want to focus on the design elements that may have influenced the findings.

Despite the limitations of the present study, there were strengths to note. The use of random assignment was a major strength of this study. Placing participants into conditions using random assignment increased the validity of the experiment by minimizing the influence of subject variables. Another important strength to note was that the researcher collected data on an individual basis. This ensured comfort, honesty, and confidentiality, especially during the selectivity of dating partner choices part of the procedure when the researcher asked the participant about his or her sexual orientation.

> It is important to use proper terminology.

> Be sure to not only identify a strength (e.g., increased validity), but also say why that would be the case. That is, in the Discussion, you should explain things and not leave them up to the reader to figure out.

Future Directions

> Spend a short time explaining how future research on this topic can correct for problems with the original study.

Researchers who wish to expand on this research may want to consider fixing any problems within this study. They may want to remove the time limit for the manipulation to allow for a stronger manipulation. By removing the time limit, the participants may feel the strain of ego-depletion more consciously. Also, future researchers may want to conduct this study outside of the laboratory to allow for more real life results. By trying this study through speed dating or at a bar, it may be more possible to see the truth in people's actions rather than what they think they want.

Another suggestion for future researchers to consider is attempting the first hypothesis regarding selectivity of dating partners in a different way. Instead of just using pictures of equal attractiveness, the potential dating partners could range in their physical looks. There can also be different descriptions of each of the potential partners including different jobs, hobbies, morals, etc. This would be a really strong way to determine the actual selectivity of depleted individuals versus non-depleted individuals. Future researchers could also consider using trait self-control instead of state self-control as an independent variable to see how the natural level of self-control individuals have influences their dating choices.

> You also want to offer ideas for new research studies on this topic. Imagine this is a program of research. What would the next study be?

Conclusion

The purpose of the present study was to determine the influence of ego depletion on dating choices. As hypothesized, individuals depleted of self-control had a higher willingness to date a greater amount of people than those who were non-depleted. Also as hypothesized, individuals depleted of self-control had a higher likelihood to go on a first date for the purpose of engaging in sexual activity. Dating is an essential part of relationship formation and relationships are ultimately some of the most important aspects of our lives. This research has helped to advance the understanding of self-control in dating. The current study indicates that moments of depletion influence the decisions we make about dating.

> The conclusion paragraph should start with a recap of the hypotheses and a reiteration of whether they were supported or not.

> This paragraph should also include how knowledge on this topic advanced through this research.

> This is the "take-home message" of this research study. This is what we know now that we did not know before.

WHAT DOES IT TAKE TO DATE? 16

References

It is important to make sure that every article you cited in the paper appears in the References section and that anything listed in the References section is cited in the paper. In other words, you need your citations and references to match.

Your References should appear on a new page after the end of your Discussion.

Baumeister, R. F., Bratslavsky, E., Muraven, M., & Tice, D. M. (1998). Ego depletion: Is the active self a limited resource?. *Journal of Personality & Social Psychology, 74*(5), 1252–1265.

Baumeister, R. F., & Muraven, M. (2000). Ego depletion: A resource model of volition, self-regulation, and controlled processing. *Social Cognition, 18*(2), 130–150.

Baumeister, R. F., Sparks, E. A., Stillman, T. F., & Vohs, K. D. (2008). Free will in consumer behavior: Self-control, ego depletion, and choice. *Journal of Consumer Psychology, 18*(1), 4–13. doi:10.1016/j.jcps.2007.10.002

Articles should appear in alphabetical order, based on the last name of the first author in the citation.

Always insert a comma before the & symbol.

Baumeister, R. F., Vohs, K. D., & Tice, D. M. (2007). The strength model of self-control. *Current Directions in Psychological Science, 16*(6), 351–355. doi:10.1111/j.1467-8721.2007.00534.x

You want to use a hanging indent when creating your reference page.

Baxter, L. A., & Bullis, C. (1986). Turning points in developing romantic relationships. *Human Communication Research, 12,* 469–493.

This represents the year the journal article appeared in publication.

Buss, D. M., & Schmitt, D. P. (1993). Sexual Strategies Theory: An evolutionary perspective on human mating. *Psychological Review, 100*(2), 204–232. doi:10.1037/0033-295X.100.2.204

This is the name of the article itself.

Ciarocco, N. J., Echevarria, J., & Lewandowski, G. W. (2012). Hungry for love: The influence of self-regulation on infidelity. *Journal of Social Psychology, 152*(1), 61–74. doi:10.1080/00224545.2011 .555435

This is the name of the journal in which the article appeared and should appear in italics.

Clark, C. L., Shaver, P. R., & Abrahams, M. F. (1999). Strategic behaviors in romantic relationship initiation. *Personality and Social Psychology Bulletin, 25,* 707–720.

This represents the volume number of the journal in which the article appeared and should appear in italics.

If the author includes his or her middle initial on the publication you must make sure it appears in the reference. Remember to add a period and a space between initials. Never use first names, only initials.

WHAT DOES IT TAKE TO DATE? 17

Eastwick, P. W., & Finkel, E. J. (2008). Sex differences in mate preferences revisited: Do people know what they initially desire in a romantic partner? *Journal of Personality & Social Psychology, 94*(2), 245–264.

Finkel, E., & Eastwick, P. (2008). Speed-dating. *Current Directions in Psychological Science, 17,* 193–197.

Freud, S. (1961). New introductory lectures on psycho-analysis. In J. Strachey (Ed. and Trans.), *The standard edition of the complete psychological works of Sigmund Freud* (Vol. 22, pp. 7–182). London: Hogarth Press. (Original work published 1933)

Haselton, M. G., & Buss, D. M. (2000). Error management theory: A new perspective on biases in cross-sex mind reading. *Journal of Personality and Social Psychology, 78,* 81–91.

Henningsen, D., Henningsen, M., McWorthy, E., McWorthy, C., & McWorthy, L. (2011). Exploring the effects of sex and mode of presentation in perceptions of dating goals in video-dating. *Journal of Communication, 61*(4), 641–658. doi:10.1111/j.1460-2466.2011.01564.x

Hofmann, W., Baumeister, R. F., Förster, G., & Vohs, K. D. (2012). Everyday temptations: An experience sampling study of desire, conflict, and self-control. *Journal of Personality & Social Psychology, 102*(6), 1318–1335. doi:10.1037/a0026545

Lewandowski, G. W., Ciarocco, N. J., Pettenato, M., & Stephan, J. (2012). Pick me up: Ego depletion and receptivity to relationship initiation. *Journal of Social and Personal Relationships.* doi:10.1177/0265407512449401

Mongeau, P. A., Serewicz, M., & Therrien, F. (2004). Goals for cross-sex first dates: Identification, measurement, and the influence of contextual factors. *Communication Monographs, 71*(2), 121–147. doi:10.1080/0363775042331302514

These numbers are the page numbers on which the article appeared in the journal.

Notice the differences in a book chapter citation.

Author names should remain in the same order that they appear in the research article. Authorship order is very important to researchers as it is based on contribution to the work. There is no need to alphabetize authorship of a reference.

The DOI is the "digital object identifier." It is a unique alphanumeric string that helps provide a link to the article on the Internet. You can often find the DOI on the first page of a research article.

WHAT DOES IT TAKE TO DATE? 18

Roscoe, B., Diana, M. S., & Brooks, R. H. (1987). Early, middle, and late adolescents' views on dating and factors influencing partner selection. *Adolescence, 85,* 59–68.

Unger, A., & Stahlberg, D. (2011). Ego-depletion and risk behavior: Too exhausted to take a risk. *Social Psychology, 42*(1), 28–38. doi:10.1027/1864-9335/a000040

Vohs, K. D., Schmeichel, B. J., Nelson, N. M., Baumeister, R. F., Twenge, J. M., & Tice, D. M. (2008). Making choices impairs subsequent self-control: A limited-resource account of decision making, self-regulation, and active initiative. *Journal of Personality & Social Psychology, 94*(5), 883–898. doi:10.1037/0022-3514.94.5.883

WHAT DOES IT TAKE TO DATE? 19

Table 1

Means and Standard Deviations for Sex and Ego Depletion on Sexual Activity

Sex	Ego-Depletion		
	Depleted	Non-Depleted	Overall Mean
Male	3.91 (1.23)	2.19 (1.19)	2.97
Female	2.20 (0.63)	1.96 (0.47)	2.08
Overall Mean	2.61	2.02	

Note. $N = 5$ to 16. The main effect for sex was significant $F(1, 39) = 13.51$, $p = .001$, effect size $r = .26$. The main effect for ego depletion was significant $F(1, 39) = 13.67$, $p = .001$, effect size $r = .26$. The interaction was significant $F(1, 39) = 7.78$, $p = .008$, effect size $r = .17$.

Researchers use tables and figures to augment what is in the text. Tables begin on a new page after your references. If you have multiple tables, each table is on a separate page.

Instead of listing each mean in the text, the author refers to the table that provides this information.

Figures appear on a new page after your tables. Like the tables, there is only one figure per page.

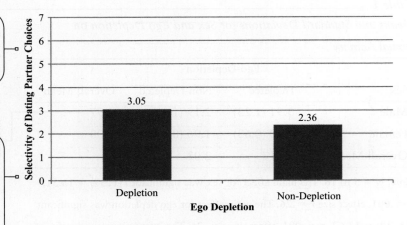

Figures should be easy to read and understand. You should clearly label the y-axis and x-axis based on the variables in your study. The x-axis should represent the independent variable, while the y-axis represents the dependent variable of the analysis.

Figure 1. Means for Depletion and Non-Depletion on Selectivity of Dating Partner Choices.

WHAT DOES IT TAKE TO DATE? 21

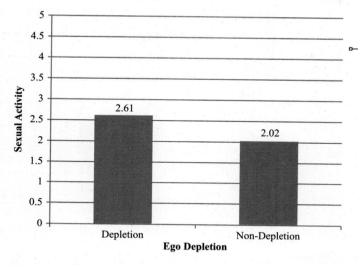

Be sure the numbers on the y-axis represent the range of the dependent variable. Sometimes graphing programs like to automatically adjust these number to make the bars look more different than they actually are. This can be a misrepresentation of the data.

Figure 2. Means for Depletion and Non-Depletion on the First Date Goal of Sexual Activity.

Glossary

A-B-A-B design a single-subject design in which researchers establish a baseline (A), introduce the intervention (B), remove the intervention (A), and then reintroduce the intervention (B), measuring the dependent variable each time.

A-B-A design a single-subject design in which researchers establish a baseline (A), introduce the intervention and measure the same variable again (B), then remove the intervention and take another measurement (A).

A-B design a single-subject design in which researchers take a baseline measurement (A), then introduce the intervention, and then measure the same variable again (B).

abstract a short summary of an entire research report that addresses the research topic, methodology used, findings, and conclusions.

acquiescent response set a response bias where a participant tends to agree with most, if not all, of the items on a scale, regardless of what questions are asked.

alternative-form reliability a form of reliability that evaluates how well a measure correlates with a similar, but different, measure of the same variable.

alternative hypothesis the hypothesis that is tested against the null hypothesis when engaging in statistical hypothesis testing.

altruistic perspective the perspective that ethical decisions should be based on helping without personal benefit.

anonymity a guarantee in research studies that individual responses cannot be linked back to individual participants.

APA Publication Manual a publication of the American psychological association that details how to write research reports in APA style.

APA style a format for writing a research report, addressing both content and formatting, that was established by the American Psychological Association and that researchers in psychology and many other social sciences use.

applied research research dedicated to solving a problem and helping people by improving their quality of life.

archival data data that have already been collected in a naturally occurring setting, such as newspapers, health records, or social media.

area probability sampling a sampling strategy where the researcher first divides the population into subgroups based on geographic area and then randomly selects participants from each geographical subgroup.

assent an active affirmation of a desire to participate from a person who does not have the ability to consent themselves; consent must also be sought from the legal guardian.

attrition the differential dropping out of participants from a study; also known as *mortality.*

autonomy freely making an informed decision about participation in research.

availability heuristic a mental shortcut strategy for judging the likelihood of an event or situation occurring based on how easily we can think of similar or relevant instances.

bar chart a figure with rectangular bars that represent the values of a variable.

Barnum effect the tendency of people to believe that general descriptions of their personality are highly accurate and tailored specifically for them.

baseline measurement the initial assessment of a participant at the onset of a study, prior to any intervention or treatment.

basic research research dedicated to expanding the existing knowledge on a topic.

behavioral choice a behavioral measure involving participants making a purposeful selection from several options.

behavioral diary a self-report data collection strategy where individuals record their behaviors and associated feelings as they occur.

behavioral measure a measure of participants' actions in a research design.

behavioral observation a behavioral measure that relies on directly seeing or observing behavior.

behavioral trace a behavioral measure that relies on evidence left behind by a participant who is no longer present.

belief perseverance maintaining a belief despite encountering contradictory factual information; often accomplished by interpreting information in a way that does not invalidate the original belief.

beneficence actively promoting the welfare of others; an ethical obligation to maximize benefits in research studies.

beta the probability of making a Type II error; symbolized as β.

better-than-average effect the tendency to overestimate our skills, abilities, and performance when comparing ourselves to others.

between-subjects design a data collection method in which each participant or subject is only assessed on the dependent variable once.

bias error that consistently pushes scores in a given direction; also known as systematic error.

blind observation an observational data collection technique in which observers are trained to look for particular behaviors, but are uninformed about study expectations or the overall purpose of the research investigation.

bottom-up approach an approach where the researcher develops a theory by exploring a topic using information provided from participants' direct experiences.

carryover effect exposure to earlier experimental conditions influencing responses to subsequent conditions.

case study a comprehensive description of a specific organization, group, or person studied over a period of time that contains information from a variety of sources.

categorical variable a way to classify data into distinct groupings.

ceiling effect occurs when the upper boundary of a measurement tool is set too low, leading most to select the highest response.

cell mean the average on the dependent variable for participants with a specific combination of the levels of the independent variables.

central tendency a value that summarizes all of the other obtained measurements or values for a particular variable.

chi-square test of independence a statistical test in which both variables are categorical. This test generally examines if the distribution of participants across categories is different from what would happen if there were no difference between the groups.

closed-ended question a question that participants answer using a predetermined set of response options.

cluster random sampling dividing the total population into groups (or clusters), then using simple random sampling to select which clusters participate; all observations in a selected cluster are included in the sample.

coding system a set of rules to help guide how the researcher classifies and records behaviors under observation.

Cohen's d a measure of effect size that represents the standardized difference between the means of two conditions.

Cohen's kappa coefficient a statistical measure of interobserver agreement between two observers for categorical items.

concealed observation an observational data collection technique in which participants do not know that their behaviors are being recorded.

conceptual definition defining a variable in theoretical terms.

concurrent validity the degree to which a measurement corresponds with an existing outcome or behavior; used to establish the criterion validity of a measurement.

confederate an accomplice of the experimenter.

confirmation bias a bias in which we only look for evidence that confirms what we already believe, thereby strengthening the original belief.

confound a variable that the researcher unintentionally varies along with the manipulation.

constant a factor that does not change and remains consistent.

construct validity the degree to which the scale actually measures the desired construct; established by evaluating the convergent and discriminant validity of the measurement.

content analysis an analysis technique that involves the systematic examination of communication where researchers organize responses in order to summarize the substance of the communication.

content validity the degree to which the items on a scale reflect the range of material that should be included in a measurement of the target variable.

continuous recording documenting all of the behaviors of a target individual during a specified observation period.

continuous variable a variable with an infinite number of different values between two given points.

contrived observation an observational data collection technique in which the researcher artificially introduces a variable of interest and unobtrusively records what happens.

control group any condition that serves as the comparison group in an experiment.

convenience sampling nonrandom selections of participants who are readily available to the researcher to serve as the sample.

convergent validity the degree to which scores on a measurement correspond to measures of other theoretically related variables; used to help establish the construct validity of a measurement.

conversation analysis an analysis technique that involves an examination of the natural patterns of dialogue and focuses on features such as turn taking, gaze direction, and how speakers sequence speech.

correlation a measure of the linear relationship between two variables; can range from −1.0 to +1.0; typically represented by the symbol r.

correlational design a design in which there is no control or manipulation of the independent variable; cause-and-effect relationships between variables cannot be established; also known as a *nonexperimental design*.

correlational study a research approach that focuses on how variables relate to one another.

cost-benefit analysis an ethical principle of research in which a researcher weighs all the potential and known benefits against all the potential and known risks before conducting a study.

cost of not doing the research considering the potential beneficial application of study findings when doing a cost-benefit analysis.

counterbalancing identifying and using all potential treatment sequences in a within-subjects design.

covariation when changes in one variable are associated with changes in another variable; part of determining causality.

criterion validity the degree to which a measurement relates to a particular outcome or behavior; established by evaluating the concurrent and predictive validity of the measurement.

criterion variable the outcome variable in non-experimental designs; also known as a *response variable*.

critical incident technique an interview technique where the researcher purposefully has the interviewee focus on a key event or specific behavior.

critical-thinking skills the process of actively evaluating, applying, analyzing, and synthesizing information.

Cronbach's alpha a statistic used to evaluate the internal consistency reliability of a scale; can range from 0 to 1.0.

crossover interaction when the influence of one independent variable on the other reverses across levels of the other independent variable; also known as a *disordinal interaction.*

data distinct pieces of information.

debriefing a part of standard ethical procedures at the end of a research study; contains an explanation of the purpose of the study and disclosure of deception, and gives participants a chance to ask questions.

deception intentionally misleading participants in some fashion.

demand characteristic a cue that potentially makes participants aware of what the experimenter expects.

dependent means *t*-test a statistic used to determine if there is a statistically significant difference between two related sets of scores; also known as a *t-test for dependent means.*

dependent variable (DV) the variable measured in association with changes in the independent variable; the outcome or effect. In nonexperimental studies it is referred to as the *criterion* or *response variable.*

descriptive research a research design that describes what is happening.

descriptive statistics statistics that describe or summarize quantitative data in meaningful ways.

dichotomous variable a nominal scale variable with only two categories.

directional hypothesis a hypothesis that makes a specific prediction as to the exact nature of the relationship between two variables.

discriminant validity the degree to which a measurement does not correspond to measures of unrelated variables; used to help establish the construct validity of a measurement.

discussion the portion of an APA-style research report in which the researcher interprets, explains, and applies the results of the study.

disordinal interaction when the influence of one independent variable on the other reverses across levels of the other independent variable; also known as a *crossover interaction.*

distractor items items included in a scale to mislead participants as to the real purpose of the scale.

double-blind procedure both the participants and the administrators of treatment are unaware of, or blind to, the types of treatment being provided in order to reduce the likelihood that expectancies or knowledge of condition will influence the results.

dummy coding the process of assigning numbers to represent categories when measuring nominal scale variables.

duration recording documenting the time elapsed during which a behavior occurs.

ecological validity the degree to which the research situation recreates the psychological experiences that participants would have in real life.

effect size a statistical measure of the magnitude of the difference between groups.

effect size *r* a measure of effect size that represents the correlation between the independent and dependent variables in comparisons involving two conditions.

egoism the perspective that ethical decisions should be based on acting in accordance with one's own self-interest.

empirical an approach in which the experimenter uses direct and indirect observations or experiences to test the research question.

empirical research gaining knowledge with the use of systematic observation, experience, or measurement.

empty control group a group that does not receive any form of the treatment and just completes the dependent variable.

equivalent-form reliability another name for *alternative-form reliability.*

error extraneous influences that cause the raw score to deviate from the true score.

error of central tendency a response bias where a participant tends to avoid using the extreme response alternatives on a scale.

ethics the application of moral principles to help guide one's decisions and behavior.

evaluation apprehension anxiety or concern that participants may experience about how their answers or behaviors appear to the researcher.

experimental control the ability to keep everything between groups the same except for the one element we want to test in an experiment.

experimental design a research method in which the experimenter controls and manipulates the independent variable, allowing the establishment of cause-and-effect relationships between the independent and dependent variables.

experimental group the group or condition that gets the key treatment in an experiment.

experimental hypothesis a clear and specific prediction of how the independent variable will influence the dependent variable.

experimental realism the degree to which a study participant becomes engrossed in the manipulation and truly influenced by it.

experimental research a research design that explores why a phenomenon occurs.

experimenter-expectancy effect occurs when a bias causes a researcher to unconsciously influence the participants of an experiment; also known as *expectancy bias* or *experimenter effect*.

explanatory variable a potential causal variable in nonexperimental designs; also known as a *predictor variable*.

exploratory analyses statistical tests that examine potential differences that were not anticipated or predicted prior to the study.

external validity the extent to which study findings are applicable or generalize outside the data collection setting to other persons, in other places, at other times.

extraneous variable a factor other than the intended treatment that might change the outcome variable.

face validity the degree to which a scale appears, on the surface, to measure the intended variable.

factor something that can influence an outcome or dependent variable; also known as an *independent variable*.

factorial ANOVA a statistical test that allows us to simultaneously test how two separate nominal or categorical independent variables (or factors) influence the dependent variable, and how those independent variables interact to influence the dependent variable; also known as a *two-way ANOVA* or *two-way analysis of variance*.

factorial design an experimental design that has more than one independent variable.

fatigue effect deterioration in quality of measurements due to participants becoming tired, less attentive, or careless during the course of the study.

file drawer problem a bias in the scientific community to only publish findings that confirm a researcher's hypothesis.

floor effect occurs when the lower boundary of a measurement tool is set too high, leading most to select the lowest response.

focus group a data collection format where several participants, typically strangers, gather together to discuss a topic.

focusing effect a bias in which we emphasize some pieces of information while undervaluing other pieces.

forced choice scale a scale where a person must choose between only two response alternatives for each item.

frequency-count recording documenting each time a target behavior occurs.

frequency distribution a summary of how often the individual values or ranges of values for a variable occur.

frequency polygon a type of chart used to graph continuous variables; the frequency of a measurement is represented with a point in the graph and these points are connected with a line; similar to the histogram.

grants monetary gifts given to help organizations meet a specific goal or objective.

grant writing developing an application in which an organization provides specific information regarding a program's goals along with evidence of the program's effectiveness in order to gain monetary gifts.

grounded theory technique an approach where the researcher does not have any explicit theories or hypotheses to test prior to the research, but instead uses information from participants to generate the categories and build a theory.

hindsight bias a sense that we "knew it all along" after we learn the actual outcome.

histogram a type of chart used to graph continuous variables; the frequency of a measurement is represented with bars that touch to indicate that a continuous variable is being graphically displayed.

history a threat to the internal validity of a study due to an external event potentially influencing participants' behavior during the study.

holistic analysis an approach where the researcher examines how numerous properties contribute to patterns within the larger and more complex system.

hybrid design any factorial design that has at least one quasi-independent variable.

hypothesis an educated prediction that provides a testable explanation of a phenomenon.

hypothesis-guessing when a participant in a study actively attempts to identify the purpose of the research.

independence the assumption that each participant represents a unique and individual data point.

independent samples *t*-test a statistical test comparing groups' means to see if the groups differ to a degree that could not have happened accidentally or by chance; also known as a t-*test for independent means*.

independent variable (IV) the variable that influences the dependent variable. In experiments the researcher manipulates or controls this variable. In nonexperimental studies, it is the *explanatory* or *predictor variable* and is not manipulated by the researcher.

infographic a graphic that synthesizes statistical information with aesthetically appealing visuals.

informed consent a part of standard ethical procedures at the beginning of a research study in which the participant learns about the expectations of the study, is told the risks and benefits of participating, and then freely makes the choice about whether he or she wants to be in the study.

Institutional Animal Care and Use Committee (IACUC) a board that reviews the ethical merit and research procedures for all animal research conducted within an institution and ensures research animals have proper living conditions.

Institutional Review Board (IRB) a board that reviews the ethical merit of all the human research conducted at an institution.

instrumentation a threat to the internal validity of a study due to changes in how a variable is measured during the course of a study.

interaction when one independent variable's influence on the dependent variable changes depending on the level of the other independent variable(s).

interaction effect hypothesis a prediction about how the levels of one independent variable will combine with another independent variable to impact the dependent variable in a way that extends beyond the sum of the two separate main effects.

internal consistency reliability the degree to which the individual items in a scale are interrelated.

internal validity the degree to which we can rule out other possible causal explanations for an observed relationship between the independent and dependent variables.

inter-observer reliability the level of agreement between two observers' coding of the same phenomenon; also known as *inter-rater reliability*.

interval recording breaking down an observational period into equal, smaller time periods and then documenting whether a target behavior occurred during each time period.

interval scale a measurement scale where numbers indicate an ordering to the measurements, and the difference between each measurement value is the same.

interview a data collection technique that can mimic a conversation where the researcher elicits self-report data directly from the participant.

interview agenda see *interview schedule.*

interviewer bias any way that the interviewer influences the participant's responses (e.g., through leading questions).

interview schedule a type of protocol that includes the questions to ask and anticipated order in which the interviewer should ask them; also called an *interview agenda.*

intra-observer reliability the extent to which an observer consistently codes a phenomenon.

introduction the portion of an APA-style research report that provides background literature on the topic under investigation, as well as a justification of importance for the work and the hypotheses.

introspection reflecting on our own thoughts and experiences to find relevant evidence.

justice fairness in selecting study participants and in determining which participants receive the benefits of participation and which bear the burden of risk.

laboratory observation an observational data collection technique in which the researcher witnesses and systematically records behaviors as they occur in a controlled setting.

Latin square design a counterbalancing strategy where each experimental condition appears at every position in the sequence order equally often.

law of small numbers extreme outcomes are more likely when considering a small number of cases.

levels different variations of the independent variable determined by the researcher.

Likert scale another name for a *summated ratings scale.*

longitudinal design the collection of data on participants over a set period of time.

loss of confidentiality a failure to protect the privacy of individuals; a potential risk to participants.

main effect hypothesis a prediction that focuses on the effect of one independent variable on the dependent variable at a time, ignoring all other independent variables.

manipulation check a measure that helps determine whether the manipulation effectively changed or varied the independent variable across conditions.

marginal mean the average of all participants on one level of the independent variable, ignoring other independent variables.

matched-pair design a design in which one creates a set of two participants who are highly similar on a key trait and then randomly assigns individuals in the pair to different groups.

maturation a threat to the internal validity of a study stemming from either long-term or short-term physiological changes occurring within the participants that may influence the dependent variable.

mean (*M*) the mathematically calculated average of a set of scores; a measure of central tendency.

measurement scale a classification system used to measure a variable.

median (*Mdn*) the value found at the exact middle of the set of scores; a measure of central tendency.

meta-analysis a quantitative statistical analysis that compares and combines the results of individual, but similar, studies.

method the portion of an APA-style research report in which the researcher provides details about the sample, materials, and procedure of collecting data.

methodological pluralism the use of multiple methods or strategies to answer a research question.

mixed design an experimental design that combines within-subjects and between-subjects methods of data collection.

mixed design analysis of variance (mixed design ANOVA) a statistical analysis that tests for differences between two or more categorical independent variables, where at least one is a between-subjects variable and another is a within-subjects variable.

mixed methods research a blend of qualitative and quantitative methods that capitalizes on the strengths of each to examine a research question from multiple perspectives.

mode (*Mo*) the most frequently occurring value in a set of scores; a measure of central tendency.

moderator the person who asks the questions and facilitates discussion in a focus group.

mortality the differential dropping out of participants from a study; also known as *attrition*.

multigroup design an experimental design with three or more groups.

mundane realism the degree to which a study parallels everyday situations in the real world.

naturalistic observation an observational data collection technique in which the researcher witnesses and systematically records behaviors as they occur in their original, unaltered setting.

needs evaluation an assessment to determine which features of a program are most valuable and who they benefit most.

nominal scale a measurement scale where numbers are used as a substitute for category names.

nonconcealed observation an observational data collection technique in which participants know that their behaviors are being recorded.

nondirectional hypothesis a hypothesis that does not make a specific prediction as to how two variables are related.

nonempirical research gaining knowledge with the use of nonsystematic methods such as the examination of personal experiences and opinions.

nonexperimental design a design in which there is no control or manipulation of the independent variable; cause-and-effect relationships between variables cannot be established; refer to the independent variable as the *explanatory* or *predictor variable* and the dependent variable as the *criterion* or *response variable;* also known as a *correlational design.*

nonlinear (or functional) relationships any association between variables that the use of just two comparison groups cannot uncover. These relationships, often identified on a graph as a curved or curvilinear line, help provide us with a clearer picture of how variables relate to one another.

nonmaleficence do no harm; an ethical obligation to mitigate or eliminate risks to study participants.

nonprobability sampling everyone in the population does not have an equal chance of being sampled, therefore creating a bias in the sample.

nonresponse bias a potential systematic difference between those who refused to participate in a study and those who participated.

normal distribution a distribution of scores that resembles a bell-shaped curve, is symmetrical with one peak, and shows an equivalent mean, median, and mode.

null hypothesis the hypothesis of no difference; usually the hypothesis the researcher is trying to statistically reject.

observation schedule a paper-and-pencil or electronic form in which the observers note the particulars of the behavior or phenomenon that they observe.

observer or scorer bias misinterpreting an observation based on the researcher's existing beliefs, previous experiences, or expectations.

Occam's razor refers to the cutting away of the unnecessary; important in hypothesis development; named after William of Ockham, a 14th-century English philosopher.

one-way analysis of variance (one-way ANOVA) a statistical test that determines whether responses from the different conditions are essentially the same or whether the responses from at least one of the conditions differ from the others.

open-ended question a question that participants answer using their own words.

open science the practice of freely sharing our scientific work along all stages of the research process.

operational definition determining how we will use variables in our study.

order effect a threat to the internal validity in a within-subjects design resulting from influence that the sequence of experimental conditions can have on the dependent variable.

ordinal interaction when one independent variable has an influence on one level, but not all levels, of the other independent variable.

ordinal scale a measurement scale where numbers are used to rank the variable on some dimension.

outcomes evaluation an assessment that determines whether a program effectively produces outcomes that are consistent with the stated objectives or goals.

outlier a case or instance that is distinct from the majority of other cases; an oddball.

overconfidence phenomenon the tendency to be overly confident in the correctness of our own judgments.

paper presentation a formal oral research presentation explaining key features of the study and the results.

paraphrase summarizing others' ideas in our own words while providing a proper citation.

participant observation an observational data collection technique in which the researcher interacts with those being studied while systematically recording their behavior.

participant reactivity participants act differently or unnaturally because they know someone is watching them.

Pearson product moment correlation coefficient (or Pearson r) the correlation coefficient used when both variables are continuous.

peer review the process by which other scientific experts in the field review and evaluate the quality of research before it is reported in a publication.

phenomenological approach an approach that seeks to understand a human experience and the meaning of experiences based on how those involved view that situation.

physical harm a physical toll that study participation may have; a potential risk to participants.

pilot testing a trial run used to refine the design, methods, and instruments for a study prior to carrying out the actual research.

placebo group a group where participants believe they are getting the treatment, but in reality they are not.

plagiarism representing others' work or ideas as our own, or without giving proper credit.

planned contrasts statistical tests that examine comparisons between groups that were predicted ahead of time. These tests have the added benefit of allowing the combination of two conditions to be compared to a third.

pleasure paradox when an introspective analysis regarding a positive experience results in it becoming less enjoyable.

population the entire group of interest in a research study from which the researcher draws the sample.

post-hoc tests statistical tests that examine all of the possible combinations of conditions in a way that statistically accounts for the fact that not all of them were predicted ahead of time.

power a study's ability to find differences between groups when there is a real difference (i.e., when the null hypothesis is false); the probability that a study will yield significant results.

practice effect changes in a participant's responses or behavior due to increased experience with the measurement instrument, not the variable under investigation.

predictive validity the degree to which a measurement corresponds with a particular outcome or behavior that occurs in the future; used to establish the criterion validity of a measurement.

predictor variable a potential causal variable in nonexperimental designs; also known as an *explanatory variable*.

pretest-posttest design a within-subjects design where participants are measured before and after exposure to a treatment or intervention.

probability sampling a sampling approach in which everyone in a given population has an equal chance of selection for participation.

process evaluation an assessment of a general program operation, including who the program serves and how the program delivers services to that population.

program evaluation using the scientific method to assess whether an organized activity is achieving its intended objectives.

programmatic research a systematic and planned sequence of related studies where subsequent studies build directly on a previous study's findings to provide a more comprehensive understanding of a phenomenon.

pseudoscience claims or beliefs that are misrepresented as being derived from the use of the scientific method.

psychological harm a psychological toll that study participation may have such as stress, negative emotions, or loss of self-esteem; a potential risk to participants.

purposive sampling the researcher chooses the sample based on who they think would be appropriate or qualified for the study; used when a limited number of people have expertise in the area under investigation.

p-value the probability that something real is happening in our study; also known as the significance level.

qualitative research a generic term representing a variety of methodologies that focus on obtaining an in-depth account of participants' perspectives on their own worlds and their experiences of events.

quantitative research a generic term for methods that seek to objectively examine associations between variables, predict outcomes, and make comparisons.

quasi-experimental designs designs in which the researcher cannot manipulate the independent variable or use random assignment.

quasi-independent variables variables treated as if they were independent variables in the experimental design even though the researchers did not manipulate them.

quota sampling freely choosing any participant as long as they help meet predetermined targets for the sample's characteristics.

random assignment any method of placing participants in groups that is nonsystematic and nonbiased, and that ensures each participant has an equal chance of being in any group.

random error variation from the measure's true score due to unsystematic or chance factors.

range a measure of variability in the data computed by subtracting the lowest score from the highest score.

ratio scale a measurement scale where numbers indicate an ordering to the measurements, the difference between each measurement value is the same, and there is a true zero point.

raw score the actual score, comprised of a true score and error.

reactivity when individuals alter their performance or behavior due to the awareness that they are under observation.

reference page the part of an APA-style research report in which referenced literary works are given credit.

reflexivity a practice through which the researcher monitors and records his or her role in the data collection on a continuous basis during the study, which allows for a more accurate assessment of the researcher's influence.

reliability the stability or consistency of a measure.

repeated-measures analysis of variance (repeated-measures ANOVA) a statistic used to test a hypothesis from a within-subjects design with three or more conditions.

repeated-measures design a within-subjects design where participants are exposed to each level of the independent variable and are measured on the dependent variable after each level; unlike the pretest-posttest design, there is no baseline measurement.

replication recreating another person's study to see if the findings are the same.

representativeness heuristic a mental shortcut strategy for determining the likelihood of an event by how much it resembles what we consider to be a "typical" example of that event.

representative sample a sample with specific features that characterize the population of interest.

researcher notes a place to keep track of anything out of the ordinary that happens during a study.

research journal a periodical containing articles by experts in a particular field of study.

research participant pool a list of students maintained by a psychology department who will receive credit in their psychology class if they participate in a research study.

research poster a formal visual research presentation.

research protocol a detailed series of steps that describes the order in which to administer the study and provides a script of what the researcher should say and do.

response rate the proportion of the invited sample that actually completes a survey.

response set a response bias where a participant tends to give the same answer to most, if not all, of the items on a scale, regardless of what questions are asked.

response variable the outcome variable in non-experimental designs; also known as a *criterion variable*.

results the portion of an APA-style research report that provides information about how the hypotheses were tested, explaining through statistical language, narrative, and reference to tables and graphs.

retrospective bias when participants view or interpret past events in an inaccurate way.

reverse-coding a scoring strategy where more negative response alternatives are assigned higher numerical values and more positive response alternatives are assigned lower numerical values; used to minimize the potential for an acquiescent response set.

sample a subset of the population from which the researcher collects data.

sampling plan the explicit strategy used for recruiting participants from the population.

scale a measurement strategy for assigning a number to represent the degree to which a person possesses or exhibits the target variable.

scientific integrity a commitment to intellectual honesty and adherence to ethical principles in scientific research.

scientific law a statement based on repeated experimental observation that describes some aspect of the world.

scientific method a systematic approach for addressing questions of interest.

scientific theory a well-substantiated explanation of some aspect of the natural world confirmed through repeated observation and experimentation.

script a written set of instructions that the researcher reads to the participant while collecting data.

self-report any measurement technique that directly asks the participant how they think or feel.

semistructured interview a combination of structured and unstructured interview approaches where some questions and portions of the order are preplanned, but the interviewer remains flexible to probe via additional questions that allow the participant to provide further information.

sensitivity the range of data a researcher can gather from a particular instrument.

sensitization effect continued exposure to experimental conditions in a within-subjects study increasing the likelihood of *hypothesis-guessing*, potentially influencing participants' responses in later experimental conditions.

significance level the probability of making a *Type I error*; also known as the *p-value*.

simple experiment an experimental design that compares two groups or conditions and is the most basic way to establish cause and effect; also known as a *two-group design*.

simple random sampling a probability sampling method in which a subset of individuals are randomly selected from population members.

single-blind procedure participants are unaware of, or blind to, the types of treatment they are receiving, but the administrator knows.

single-item indicator only one item or question being used to measure a variable.

single sample *t*-test a statistic to evaluate whether a sample mean statistically differs from a specific value.

single-subject design a special type of within-subjects design using one participant (human or animal) or one group to assess changes within that individual or group; also known as a *single-case experimental design* or *single-n design*.

situated analysis an approach where the researcher examines a topic while it is embedded within its naturally occurring context.

skewed distribution a distribution of scores that is nonsymmetrical because some scores are more extreme than the majority of the other scores.

snowball sampling existing study participants recruit future participants from among their acquaintances.

social desirability the tendency for respondents to give answers that make them look good.

standard deviation a statistic used to indicate how much, on average, an individual score differs from the arithmetic mean of the scores; represented with the symbol SD.

standardization keeping the experimental situation the same for everyone and as free from variation as possible.

statistical hypothesis testing a procedure for evaluating the probability of obtaining one's results given the researcher's prediction; this probability is represented with the symbol p.

statistically significant the conclusion a researcher makes when the probability is that one's hypothesis is likely to be correct given the data collected.

stratified random sampling includes dividing the population into strata or subpopulations and using simple random sampling to select participants from each strata in proportion to the population at large.

structured interview an interview style where the researcher prepares specific questions prior to the interview and asks them in a standardized, fixed order with little or no probing.

summated ratings scale a scale where a participant evaluates a series of statements using a set of predetermined response options, and the responses are summed to represent the overall measurement for the variable; commonly referred to as a *Likert scale*.

suppression effect an effect where two variables combine to produce an outcome that is smaller than what each individual variable contributes.

survey a quantitative research strategy for systematically collecting information from a group of individuals; the information is then generalized to a larger group of interest.

synergistic effect an effect where two variables combine to produce an outcome that is greater than what each individual variable contributes.

systematic error error that consistently pushes scores in a given direction; also known as *bias*.

systematic observational research the viewing and recording of a predetermined set of behaviors in an organized way.

temporal precedence when changes in the suspected cause (treatment) occur before changes in the effect (outcome).

testing effect a threat to the internal validity of a study where participants' scores may change on subsequent measurements simply because of their increased familiarity with the instrument.

test-retest reliability the temporal stability of a measure.

title page the first page of an APA-style report that identifies the title of the work as well as the authors and their institutional affiliations.

top-down approach a deductive approach where the researcher tests preconceptions and previously established theories with the collected data.

treatment-as-usual group a comparison group in clinical studies in which already established treatment is administered for comparison to experimental treatment.

triangulation a research strategy that involves using multiple techniques and/or samples to assess the same information to provide a more comprehensive examination.

true experiments designs in which the researcher manipulates all of the independent variables and randomly assigns participants to groups.

true score what the score would be if the test were a perfect measure of the attribute being tested and were uninfluenced by any extraneous factors.

t-test for dependent means a statistic used to determine if there is a statistically significant difference between two related sets of scores; also known as *dependent means t-test.*

t-test for independent means a statistical test comparing groups' means to see if the groups differ to a degree that could not have happened accidentally or by chance; also known as an *independent samples t-test.*

two-group design an experimental design that compares two groups or conditions and is the most basic way to establish cause and effect; also known as a *simple experiment.*

two-way analysis of variance a statistical test that allows us to simultaneously test how two separate nominal or categorical independent variables (or factors) influence the dependent variable, and how those independent variables interact to influence the dependent variable; also known as a *two-way ANOVA* or *factorial ANOVA.*

Type I error the mistake we make when we decide to reject the null hypothesis when, in reality, we should not reject it; considered an "error of gullibility."

Type II error the mistake we make when we fail to reject the null hypothesis when, in reality, it should be rejected; considered an "error of blindness."

unit of analysis major entity under investigation or type of data (e.g., individual or group, etc.) that is the focus of the study.

unobtrusive measures strategies that allow for observation and assessment without the participant's awareness.

unstructured interview an interview style where the researcher may anticipate potential topics but does not plan specific questions or the order of topics so that the interview is conversational and allows participants to describe their own views, share stories, and determine the interview's structure; allows the interviewer to probe to promote elaboration.

utilitarian perspective the perspective that ethical decisions should be based on doing the greatest good for the greatest number of people.

validity the degree to which a tool measures what it claims to measure.

variability the degree to which individual measurements of a variable differ from one another.

variables elements that we expect to change or vary, or that can have several different values.

vignette a description of a hypothetical situation, event, or scenario to which participants react.

waiting-list control group a control group often used in clinical research; participants in this group do not receive treatment or intervention until after the completion of the study.

"what you see is all there is" phenomenon a failure to see the limitations of our immediate experience, making it difficult to predict alternative outcomes.

within-subjects design a data collection method in which each participant or subject is assessed on the dependent variable more than once.

word cloud a visual representation of the frequency with which certain words are used in a qualitative assessment; larger words indicate higher frequency of use.

References

Adenzato, M., Todisco, P., & Ardito, R. B. (2012). Social cognition in anorexia nervosa: Evidence of preserved theory of mind and impaired emotional functioning. *PLOS ONE, 7(8)*. doi:10.1371/journal.pone.0044414

Adriaanse, M. A., van Oosten, J. F., de Ridder, D. D., de Wit, J. F., & Evers, C. (2011). Planning what not to eat: Ironic effects of implementation intentions negating unhealthy habits. *Personality and Social Psychology Bulletin, 37,* 69–81. doi:10.1177/0146167210390523

Ajzen, I., & Fishbein, M. (2005). The influence of attitudes on behavior. In D. Albarracin, B. T. Johnson, & M. P. Zanna (Eds.), *The handbook of attitudes* (pp. 173–221). Hillsdale, NJ: Erlbaum.

Allwood, C. M. (2012). The distinction between qualitative and quantitative research methods is problematic. *Quality & Quantity: International Journal of Methodology, 46(5),* 1417–1429. doi:10.1007/s11135-011-9455-8

Altmann, E. M., & Trafton, J. (2007). Timecourse of recovery from task interruption: Data and a model. *Psychonomic Bulletin & Review, 14,* 1079–1084. doi:10.3758/BF03193094

American Psychiatric Association. (2013). *Diagnostic and statistical manual of mental disorders* (5th ed.). Washington, DC: Author.

American Psychological Association. (2010). *Publication manual of the American Psychological Association* (6th ed.). Washington, DC: APA.

American Psychological Association. (2013). *APA guidelines for the undergraduate psychology major: Version 2.0.* Retrieved from http://www.apa.org/ed/precollege/undergrad/index.aspx

American Psychological Association. (2017). *Ethical principles of psychologists and code of conduct* (2002, Amended June 1, 2010, and January 1, 2017). Retrieved from http://www.apa.org/ethics/code/index.aspx

Anderson, C. A., Anderson, K. B., & Denser, W. E. (1996). Examining an affective aggression framework: Weapon and temperature effects on aggressive thoughts, affect, and attitudes. *Personality and Social Psychology Bulletin, 22,* 366–76. doi:10.1177/0146167296224004

Anderson, C. A., & Bushman, B. J. (2001). Effects of violent video games on aggressive behavior, aggressive cognition, aggressive affect, physiological arousal, and prosocial behavior: A meta-analytic review of the scientific literature. *Psychological Science, 12,* 353–359. doi:10.1111/1467-9280.00366

Anonymous. (1998). A serial killer's perspective. In R. Holmes & S. Holmes (Eds.), *Contemporary perspectives on serial murder* (pp. 123–136). Thousand Oaks, CA: Sage.

Appleby, D. C. (2014). A skills-based academic advising strategy for job-seeking psychology majors. In R. Miller & J. Irons (Eds.), *Academic advising: A handbook for advisors and students, Volume 1: Models, students, topics, and issues* (pp. 143–156). Retrieved from http://www.teachpsych.org/Resources/Documents/ebooks/advising2014Vol1.pdf

Arcelus, J., Mitchell, A. J., Wales. J., & Nielsen, S. (2011). Mortality rates in patients with anorexia nervosa and other eating disorders: A meta-analysis of 36 studies. *Archives of General Psychiatry, 68(7),* 724–731.

Arnett, J. J. (2008). The neglected 95%: Why American psychology needs to become less American. *American Psychologist, 63,* 602–614. doi:10.1037/0003-066X

Aronson, E., Wilson, T. D., & Brewer, M. B. (1998). Experimentation in social psychology. In D. T. Gilbert, S. T. Fiske, & G. Lindzey (Eds.), *The handbook of social psychology* (4th ed., Vol. 1, pp. 99–142). New York, NY: McGraw-Hill.

Asch, S. E. (1951). Effects of group pressure upon the modification and distortion of judgment. In H. Guetzkow (Ed.), *Groups, leadership, and men* (pp. 177–190). Pittsburgh, PA: Carnegie.

Associated Press. (1990, August). Judas Priest's lead singer testifies. *The New York Times.* Retrieved from http://www.nytimes.com/1990/08/01/arts/judas-priest-s-lead-singer-testifies.html

Association of American Colleges and Universities & Hart Research Associates. (2013). *It takes more than a major: Employer priorities for college learning and student success*. Retrieved from http://www.aacu.org/leap/presidentstrust/compact/2013SurveySummary.cfm

Atlas, G., & Morier, D. (1994). The sorority rush process: Self-selection, acceptance criteria, and the effect of rejection. *Journal of College Student Development, 35*, 345–353.

Bain, K. (2004). *What the best college teachers do.* Cambridge, MA: Harvard University Press.

Baldwin, W. (2000). Information no one else knows: The value of self-report. In A. A. Stone, J. S. Turkkan, C. A. Bachrach, J. B. Jobe, & H. S. Kurtzman (Eds.), *The science of self-report: Implications for research and practice* (pp. 3–7). Mahwah, NJ: Lawrence Erlbaum Associates.

Bale, C., Morrison, R., & Caryl, P. (2006). Chat-up lines as male sexual displays. *Personality and Individual Differences, 40*, 655–664. doi:10.1016/j.paid.2005.07.016

Baltaci, S., & Gokcay, D. (2016). Stress detection in human–computer interaction: Fusion of pupil dilation and facial temperature features. *International Journal of Human-Computer Interaction, 32*(12), 956–966. doi:10.1080/10447318.2016.1220069

Bartlett, T. (2010, August 19). Document sheds light on investigation at Harvard. *The Chronicle of Higher Education.* http://chronicle.com/article/Document-Sheds-Light-on/123988/

Baruh, L. (2010). Mediated voyeurism and the guilty pleasure of consuming reality television. *Media Psychology, 13*, 201–221. doi:10.1080/15213269.2010.502871

Baumeister, R. F., Bratslavsky, E., Muraven, M., & Tice, D. M. (1998). Ego depletion: Is the active self a limited resource? *Journal of Personality and Social Psychology, 74*, 1252–1265. doi:10.1037/0022-3514.74.5.1252

Baumeister, R. F., & Leary, M. R. (1995). The need to belong: Desire for interpersonal attachments as a fundamental human motivation. *Psychological Bulletin, 117*, 497–529. doi:10.1037/0033-2909.117.3.497

Baumeister, R. F., Vohs, K. D., & Funder, D. C. (2007). Psychology as the science of self-reports and finger movements: Whatever happened to actual behavior? *Perspectives on Psychological Science, 2*, 396–403.

Beatty, J. (1986). The pupillary system. In G. H. Coles, E. Donchin, & S. W. Porges (Eds.), *Psychophysiology: Systems, Process, and Applications* (pp. 43–50). New York, NY: Guilford Press.

Bem, D. J. (2011). Feeling the future: Experimental evidence for anomalous retroactive influences on cognition and affect. *Journal of Personality and Social Psychology, 100*, 407–425. doi:10.1037/a0021524

Benedetto, A., Calvi, A., & D'Amico, F. (2012). Effects of mobile telephone tasks on driving performance: A driving simulator study. *Advances in Transportation Studies, 26*, 29–44. doi:10.4399/97888548465863

Berg, S. (2006). Snowball sampling—I. In S. Kotz, C. Read, N. Balakrishnan, & B. Vidakovic (Eds.), *Encyclopedia of statistical sciences* (pp. 7817–7821). Hoboken, NJ: John Wiley and Sons, Inc.

Berger, R. (2015). Now I see it, now I don't: Researcher's position and reflexivity in qualitative research. *Qualitative Research, 15*(2), 219–234. doi:10.1177/1468794112468475

Berlin, L. J., Ispa, J. M., Fine, M. A., Malone, P. S., Brooks-Gunn, J., Brady-Smith, C., Ayoub, C., & Bai, Y. (2009). Correlates and consequences of spanking and verbal punishment for low-income White, African American, and Mexican American toddlers. *Child Development, 80*, 1403–1420. doi:10.1111/j.1467-8624.2009.01341.x

Berman, M., Jonides, J., & Kaplan, S. (2008). The cognitive benefits of interacting with nature. *Psychological Science, 19*, 1207–1212. doi:10.1111/j.1467-9280.2008.02225.x

Bock, B. C., Fava, J. L., Gaskins, R., Morrow, K. M., Williams, D. M., Jennings, E., Becker, B. M., Tremont, G., & Marcus, B. H. (2012). Yoga as a complementary treatment for smoking cessation in women. *Journal of Women's Health, 21*, 240–248. doi:10.1089/jwh.2011.2963

Bolger, N., Davis, A., & Rafaeli, E. (2003). Diary methods: Capturing life as it is lived. *Annual Review of Psychology, 54*, 579–616. doi:10.1146/annurev.psych.54.101601.145030

Branscum, P., Sharma, M., Wang, L., Wilson, B., & Rojas-Guyler, L. (2013). A process evaluation of a social cognitive theory–based childhood obesity prevention intervention: The comics for health program. *Health Promotion Practice, 14*, 189–198.

Brett, P. (2011). Students' experiences and engagement with SMS for learning in higher education. *Innovations in Education & Teaching International, 48,* 137–147. doi:10.1080/14703297.2011.564008

Bronkhorst, A. W. (2000). The cocktail party phenomenon: A review of research on speech intelligibility in multiple-talker conditions. *Acustica, 86,* 117–128.

Bryan, A. D., Webster, G. D., & Mahaffey, A. L. (2011). The big, the rich, and the powerful: Physical, financial, and social dimensions of dominance in mating and attraction. *Personality and Social Psychology Bulletin, 37,* 365–382. doi:10.1177/0146167210395604

Buhrmester, M., Kwang, T., & Gosling, S. D. (2011). Amazon's Mechanical Turk: A new source of inexpensive, yet high-quality, data? *Perspectives on Psychological Science, 6,* 3–5.

Bushman, B. J., & Anderson, C.A. (2009). Comfortably numb: Desensitizing effects of violent media on helping others. *Psychological Science, 20*(3), 273–277, http://pss.sagepub.com/content/20/3/273.short

Butler, S. F., Budman, S. H., McGee, M. D., Davis, M. S., Cornelli, R., & Morey, L. C. (2005). Addiction severity assessment tool: Development of a self-report measure for clients in substance abuse treatment. *Drug and Alcohol Dependency, 80,* 349–360. doi:10.1016/j.drugalcdep.2005.05.005

Callaghan, S., & Joseph, S. (1995). Self-concept and peer victimization among schoolchildren. *Personality and Individual Differences, 18,* 161–163. doi:10.1016/0191-8869(94)00127-E

Camic, P. M., Rhodes, J. E., & Yardley, L. (2003). Naming the stars: Integrating qualitative methods into psychological research. In P. M. Camic, J. E. Rhodes, & L. Yardley (Eds.), *Qualitative research in psychology: Expanding perspectives in methodology and design* (pp. 3–15). Washington, DC: American Psychological Association.

Campbell, D. T., & Fiske, D. W. (1959). Convergent and discriminant validation by the multitrait-multimethod matrix. *Psychological Bulletin, 56,* 81–105. doi:10.1037/h0046016

Campbell, J. D. (1990). Self-esteem and clarity of the self-concept. *Journal of Personality and Social Psychology, 59,* 538–549. doi:10.1037/0022-3514.59.3.538

Campbell, J. D., Trapnell, P. D., Heine, S. J., Katz, I. M., Lavallee, L. F., & Lehman, D. R. (1996). Self-concept clarity: Measurement, personality correlates, and cultural boundaries. *Journal of Personality and Social Psychology, 70,* 141–156. doi:10.1037/0022-3514.70.1.141

Campbell, J. H., & DeNevi, D. (2004). Interviewing techniques for homicide investigations. In J. H. Campbell & D. DeNevi (Eds.), *Profilers: Leading investigators take you inside the criminal mind* (pp. 109–114). Amherst, NY: Prometheus Books.

Canter, D. V., Alison, L. J., Alison, E., & Wentink, N. (2004). The organized/disorganized typology of serial murder: Myth or model? *Psychology, Public Policy, and Law, 10,* 293–320. doi:10.1037/1076-8971.10.3.293

Capaldi, D. M., Pears, K. C., Kerr, D. R., & Owen, L. D. (2008). Intergenerational and partner influences on fathers' negative discipline. *Journal of Abnormal Child Psychology, 36,* 347–358. doi:10.1007/s10802-007-9182-8

Carey, B. (2011, November 2). Fraud case seen as a red flag for psychology research. *The New York Times.* Retrieved from http://www.nytimes.com/2011/11/03/health/research/noted-dutch-psychologist-stapel-accused-of-research-fraud.html

Carmines, E. G., & Zeller, R. A. (1979). *Reliability and validity assessment.* Newbury Park, CA: Sage.

Carneval, A. P., Strohel, J., & Melton, M. (2011). *What's it worth? The economic value of college majors.* Retrieved from http://cew.georgetown.edu/whatsitworth-the-economic-value-of-college-majors/

Carney, D. R., Cuddy, A. J. C., & Yap, A. J. (2010). Power posing: Brief nonverbal displays affect neuroendocrine levels and risk tolerance. *Psychological Science, 21,* 1363–1368. doi:10.1177/0956797610383437

Chan, M. S., Jones, C. R., Jamieson, K. H., & Albaraccin, D. (2017). Debunking: A meta-analysis of the psychological efficacy of messages countering misinformation. *Psychological Science.* Online. doi:10.1177/0956797617714579

Cialdini, R. B. (2009). We have to break up. *Perspectives on Psychological Science, 4,* 5–6.

Cialdini, R. B., & Baumann, D. J. (1981). Littering: A new unobtrusive measure of attitude. *Social Psychology Quarterly, 44,* 254–259.

Clausen, L., Rosenvinge, J. H., Friborg, O., & Rokkedal, K. (2011). Validating the eating disorder inventory-3 (EDI-3): A comparison between 561 female eating disorders patients and 878 females from the general population. *Journal of Psychopathology and Behavioral Assessment, 33,* 101–110. doi:10.1007/s10862

Cohen, A. H., & Krueger, J. S. (2016). Rising mercury, rising hostility: How heat affects survey response. *Field Methods, 28*(2), 133–152. doi:10.1177/1525822X15627974

Cohen, J. W. (1988). *Statistical power analysis for the social and behavioral sciences* (2nd ed.). Hillsdale, NJ: Erlbaum.

Cohen, J. W. (1992). A power primer. *Psychological Bulletin, 112,* 155–159.

Colbert, S. (Writer) (2008, December 15). Great president . . . or greatest president? From *The Colbert Report.* http://thecolbertreport.cc.com/videos/d5rh5f/great-president---or-greatest-president-

Constantine, M. G., & Ponterotto, J. G. (2006). Evaluating and selecting psychological measures for research purposes. In F. T. L. Leong & J. T. Austin (Eds.), *The psychology research handbook* (pp. 104–113). Thousand Oaks, CA: Sage.

Cook, J., Nuccitelli, D., Green, S. A., Richardson, M., Winkler, B., Painting, R., Way, R., Jacobs, P., & Skuce, A. (2013). Quantifying the consensus on anthropogenic global warming in the scientific literature. *Environmental Research Letters, 8*(2), 1–7. doi:10.1088/1748-9326/8/2/024024

Couturier, J., Kimber, M., & Szatmari, P. (2013). Efficacy of family-based treatment for adolescents with eating disorders: A systematic review and meta-analysis. *International Journal of Eating Disorders, 46,* 3–11. doi:10.1002/eat.22042

Cronbach, L. J. (1951). Coefficient alpha and the internal structure of tests. *Psychometrika, 16,* 297–334. doi:10.1007/BF02310555

Cronbach, L. J., & Meehl, P. E. (1955). Construct validity in psychological tests. *Psychological Bulletin, 52,* 281–302. doi:10.1037/h0040957

Cunningham, M. (1989). Reactions to heterosexual opening gambits: Female selectivity and male responsiveness. *Personality and Social Psychology Bulletin, 15,* 27–41. doi:10.1177/0146167289151003

Darley, J. M., & Latané, B. (1968). Bystander intervention in emergencies: Diffusion of responsibility. *Journal of Personality and Social Psychology, 8,* 377–383. doi:10.1037/h0025589

Decker, W. H. (1987). Managerial humor and subordinate satisfaction. *Social Behavior and Personality, 15,* 225–232.

De Leeuw, E. D., Hox, J. J., & Dillman, D. A. (2008). The cornerstones of survey research. In E. D. de Leeuw, J. J. Hox, & D. A. Dillman (Eds.), *International handbook of survey methodology* (pp. 1–17). New York, NY: Lawrence Erlbaum Associates.

Diener, E., Emmons, R. A., Larsen, R. J., & Griffin, S. (1985). The Satisfaction with Life Scale. *Journal of Personality Assessment, 49,* 71–75. doi:10.1207/s15327752jpa4901_13

Dillman, D. A., Smyth, J. D., & Christian, L. M. (2009). *Internet, mail, and mixed-mode surveys: The tailored design method.* Hoboken, NJ: Wiley.

Dollard, J. (1953, September 13). The Kinsey report on women: "A strangely flawed masterpiece." *The New York Herald Tribune,* Section 6, p. 3.

Drouin, M. A. (2011). College students' text messaging, use of textese and literacy skills. *Journal of Computer Assisted Learning, 27,* 67–75. doi:10.1111/j.1365-2729.2010.00399.x

Durante, K. M., Li, N. P., & Haselton, M. G. (2008). Changes in women's choice of dress across the ovulatory cycle: Naturalistic and laboratory task-based evidence. *Personality and Social Psychology Bulletin, 34,* 1451–1460. doi:10.1177/0146167208323103

Dyer, J. (2001, June 10). Ethics and orphans: The "monster study." *San Jose Mercury News.* http://www-psych.stanford.edu/~bigopp/stutter2.html

Eisner, E. W. (2003). On the art and science of qualitative research in psychology. In P. M. Camic, J. E. Rhodes, & L. Yardley (Eds.), *Qualitative research in psychology: Expanding perspectives in methodology and design* (pp. 17–29). Washington, DC: American Psychological Association.

Ellard, J. H., & Rogers, T. B. (1993). Teaching questionnaire construction effectively: The ten commandments of question writing. *Contemporary Social Psychology, 17,* 17–20.

England, D. E., Descartes, L., & Collier-Meek, M. A. (2011). Gender role portrayal and the Disney princesses. *Sex Roles, 64,* 555–567. doi:10.1007/s11199-011-9930-7

Enserink, M. (2000). Helsinki's new clinical rules: Fewer placebos, more disclosure? *Science, 290,* 418–419.

Eye of the Intern. (2014, January 23). Infographic: Internship survey and 2014 internship trends [Web log post]. Retrieved from http://www.internships.com/eyeoftheintern/

Fanelli, D. (2012). Negative results are disappearing from most disciplines and countries. *Scientometrics, 90,* 891–904. doi:10.1007/s11192-011-0494-7

Feather, N. T., Wenzel, M., & McKee, I. R. (2013). Integrating multiple perspectives on schadenfreude: The role of deservingness and emotions. *Motivation and Emotion, 37,* 574–585. doi:10.1007/s11031-012-9331-4

Federal Bureau of Investigation. (2008). *Serial murder: Multi-disciplinary perspectives for investigators.* Retrieved from http://www.fbi.gov/stats-services/publications/serial-murder/serial-murder-1/

Fernandez, A. C., Wood, M. D., Stein, L. R., & Rossi, J. S. (2010). Measuring mindfulness and examining its relationship with alcohol use and negative consequences. *Psychology of Addictive Behaviors, 24,* 608–616. doi:10.1037/a0021742

Feurer, C., Burkhouse, K. L., Siegle, G., & Gibb, B. E. (2017). Increased pupil dilation to angry faces predicts interpersonal stress generation in offspring of depressed mothers. *Journal of Child Psychology and Psychiatry, 58*(8), 950–957. doi:10.1111/jcpp.12739

Finke, J. B., Deuter, C. E., Hengesch, X., & Schächinger, H. (2017). The time course of pupil dilation evoked by visual sexual stimuli: Exploring the underlying ANS mechanisms. *Psychophysiology, 54*(10), 1444–1458. doi:10.1111/psyp.12901

Fletcher, A. C., Walls, J. K., Cook, E. C., Madison, K. J., & Bridges, T. H. (2008). Parenting style as a moderator of associations between maternal disciplinary strategies and child well-being. *Journal of Family Issues, 29,* 1724–1744. doi:10.1177/0192513X08322933

Forer, B. R. (1949). The fallacy of personal validation: A classroom demonstration of gullibility. *Journal of Abnormal and Social Psychology, 44,* 118–123. doi:10.1037/h0059240

Fridlund, A., Beck, H. P., Goldie, W. D., & Irons, G. (2012). Little Albert: A neurologically impaired child. *History of Psychology.* doi:10.1037/a0026720

Fritsche, I., & Linneweber, V. (2006). Nonreactive methods in psychological research. In M. Eid & E. Diener (Eds.), *Handbook of multimethod measurement in psychology* (pp. 189–203). Washington, DC: American Psychological Association. doi:10.1037/11383-014

Furnham, A., Chamorro-Premuzic, T., & Callahan, I. (2003). Does graphology predict personality and intelligence? *Individual Differences Research, 1,* 78–94.

Gabbiadini, A., Riva, P., Andrighetto, L., Volpato, C., & Bushman, B. J. (2014). Interactive effect of moral disengagement and violent video games on self-control, cheating, and aggression. *Social Psychological and Personality Science, 5*(4), 451–458. doi:10.1177/1948550613509286

Gallrein, A. B., Webels, N. M., Carlson, E. N., & Leising, D. (2016). I still cannot see it—A replication of blind spots in self-perception. *Journal of Research in Personality, 60,* 1–7. doi:10.1016/j.jrp.2015.10.002

Geddes, D. P. (Ed.). (1954). *An analysis of the Kinsey reports.* New York, NY: New American Library.

Geliebter, A., & Aversa, A. (2003). Emotional eating in overweight, normal weight, and underweight individuals. *Eating Behavior, 3,* 341–347. doi:10.1016/S1471-0153(02)00100-9

Gershoff, E. T. (2002). Corporal punishment by parents and associated child behaviors and experiences: A meta-analytic and theoretical review. *Psychological Bulletin, 128,* 539–579. doi:10.1037/0033-2909.128.4.539

Gershoff, E. T. (2008). *Report on physical punishment in the United States: What research tells us about its effects on children.* Columbus, OH: Center for Effective Discipline.

Gershoff, E. T., & Grogan-Kaylor, A. (2016). Spanking and child outcomes: Old controversies and new meta-analyses. *Journal of Family Psychology, 30*(4), 453–469. doi:10.1037/fam0000191

Gershoff, E. T., Grogan-Kaylor, A., Lansford, J. E., Chang, L., Zelli, A., Deater-Deckard, K., & Dodge, K. A. (2010). Parent discipline practices in an international sample: Associations with child behaviors and moderation by perceived normativeness. *Child Development, 81,* 487–502. doi:10.1111/j.1467-8624.2009.01409.x

Gescheider, G. A. (1997). *Psychophysics: The fundamentals* (3rd ed.). Mahwah, NJ: Lawrence Erlbaum Associates.

Gilbert, D. T. (2006). *Stumbling on happiness.* New York, NY: Vintage.

Glaser, B. G., & Strauss, A. L. (1967). *The discovery of grounded theory: Strategies for qualitative research*. Chicago, IL: Aldine.

Goodenough, F. L. (1931). *Anger in young children*. Minneapolis, MN: University of Minnesota Press.

Goodman, H. (1998, July 21). Studying prison experiments; Research: For 20 years, a dermatologist used the inmates of a Philadelphia prison as the willing subjects of tests on shampoo, foot powder, deodorant, and later, mind-altering drugs and dioxin. *The Baltimore Sun*, 8B.

Gorla, K., & Mathews, M. (2005). Pharmacological treatment of eating disorders. *Psychiatry (Edgmont), 2*(6), 43–48.

Gosling, S. (2008). *Snoop: What your stuff says about you*. New York, NY: Basic Books.

Gosling, S. D., Vazire, S., Srivastava, S., & John, O. P. (2004). Should we trust web-based studies? A comparative analysis of six preconceptions about Internet questionnaires. *American Psychologist, 59*, 93–104. doi:10.1037/0003-066X.59.2.93

Grave, R. D., Calugi, S., Doll, H. A., & Fairburn, C. G. (2013). Enhanced cognitive behaviour therapy for adolescents with anorexia nervosa: An alternative to family therapy? *Behaviour Research and Therapy, 51*, R9–R12. doi:10.1016/j.brat.2012.09.008

Grove, W. M., Zald, D. H., Lebow, B., Snitz, E., & Nelson, C. (2000). Clinical versus mechanical prediction: A meta-analysis. *Psychological Assessment, 12*, 19–30. doi:10.1037/1040-3590.12.1.19

Guéguen, N. (2013). Weather and courtship behavior: A quasi-experiment with the flirty sunshine. *Social Influence, 8*(4), 312–319. doi:10.1080/15534510.2012.752401

Haggerty, K. D. (2009). Modern serial killers. *Crime, Media, Culture, 5*, 168–187. doi:10.1177/1741659009335714

Halpern, D. F. (Ed.). (2009). *Undergraduate education in psychology: A blueprint for the future of the discipline*. Washington, DC: American Psychological Association Books.

Hamilton, L. (2013). More is more or more is less? Parental financial investments during college. *American Sociological Review, 78*, 70–95. doi:10.1177/0003122412472680

Hancock, J. T., Woodworth, M. T., & Porter, S. (2013). Hungry like the wolf: A word-pattern analysis of the language of psychopaths. *Legal and Criminological Psychology, 18*, 102–114. doi:10.1111/j.2044-8333.2011.02025.x

Harman, B. A., & Sato T. (2011). Cell phone use and grade point average among undergraduate university students. *College Student Journal, 45*, 544–549.

Harmon-Jones, E., & Sigelman, J. (2001). State anger and prefrontal brain activity: Evidence that insult-related relative left-prefrontal activation is associated with experienced anger and aggression. *Journal of Personality and Social Psychology, 80*, 797–803. doi:10.1037/0022-3514.80.5.797

Hart Research Associates. (2015). Falling short? College learning and career success. *Association of American Colleges and Universities*. Retrieved from https://www.aacu.org/sites/default/files/files/LEAP/2015employerstudentsurvey.pdf

Harwood, T. G., & Garry, T. (2003). An overview of content analysis. *The Marketing Review 3*, 479–498. doi.org/10.1362/146934703771910080

Haselton, M. G., Mortezaie, M., Pillsworth, E. G., Bleske-Recheck, A. E., & Frederick, D. A. (2007). Ovulation and human female ornamentation: Near ovulation, women dress to impress. *Hormones and Behavior, 51*, 40–45. doi:10.1016/j.yhbeh.2006.07.007

Heider, F. (1958). *The psychology of interpersonal relationships*. New York, NY: Wiley.

Henrich, J., Heine, S. J., & Norenzayan, A. (2010a). The weirdest people in the world? *Behavioral and Brain Sciences, 33*, 61–135. doi:10.1017/S0140525X0999152X

Henrich, J., Heine, S. J., & Norenzayan, A. (2010b). Most people are not WEIRD. *Nature, 446*, 29.

Hering, B. B. (2010). Why are internships so important? *CNN*. Retrieved from http://www.cnn.com/2010/LIVING/worklife/04/14/cb.why.internships.important/index.html

Herz, R. S., & Inzlicht, M. (2002). Sex differences in response to physical and social factors involved in human mate selection—the importance of smell for women. *Evolution and Human Behavior, 23*, 359–364. doi:10.1016/S1090-5138(02)00095-8

Hofstee, W. K. B. (1994). Who should own the definition of personality? *European Journal of Personality, 8*, 149–162. doi:10.1002/per.2410080302

Holmes, R., & DeBurger, J. (1985). Profiles in terror: The serial murderer. *Federal Probation, 39*, 29–34.

Holmes, R. M., & Holmes, S. T. (2009). *Serial murder* (3rd ed.). Thousand Oaks, CA: Sage Publications, Inc.

Hornblum, A. M. (1998). *Acres of skin.* New York, NY: Routledge.

Hudson, J. I., Hiripi, E., Pope, H. G., & Kessler, R. C. (2007). The prevalence and correlates of eating disorders in the National Comorbidity Survey Replication. *Biological Psychiatry, 61*, 348–358.

Humphreys, L. (1975). *Tearoom trade: Impersonal sex in public places* (2nd ed.). Chicago, IL: Aldine.

IJzerman, H., & Semin, G. R. (2009). The thermometer of social relations: Mapping social proximity on temperature. *Psychological Science, 10*, 1214–1220. doi:10.1111/j.1467-9280.2009.02434.x

IJzerman, H., van Dijk, W. W., & Gallucci, M. (2007). A bumpy train ride: A field experiment on insult, honor, and emotional reactions. *Emotion, 7*, 869–875. doi:10.1037/1528-3542.7.4.869

Inbar, Y., & Lammers, J. (2012). Political diversity in social and personality psychology. *Perspectives on Psychological Science, 7*, 496–503. doi:10.1177/1745691612448792

Isserlin, L., & Couturier, J. (2012). Therapeutic alliance and family-based treatment for adolescents with anorexia nervosa. *Psychotherapy, 49*, 46–51. doi:10.1037/a0023905

Jackson, L. A., von Eye, A., Witt, E. A., Zhao, Y., & Fitzgerald, H. E. (2011). A longitudinal study of the effects of Internet use and videogame playing on academic performance and the roles of gender, race and income in these relationships. *Computers in Human Behavior, 27*, 228–239. doi:10.1016/j.chb.2010.08.001

Janisse, M. P., & Bradley, M. T. (1980). Deception, information and the pupillary response. *Perceptual and Motor Skills, 50*, 748–750. doi:10.2466/pms.1980.50.3.748

Joireman, J., Truelove, H. B., & Duell, B. (2010). Effect of outdoor temperature, heat primes and anchoring on belief in global warming. *Journal of Environmental Psychology, 30*, 358–367. doi:10.1016/j.jenvp.2010.03.004

Jones, S. M. W. (2017, January). Research careers with a bachelor's degree in psychology: Academic research opportunities for psychology majors. *Psychology Student Network, 5*(1). Retrieved from http://www.apa.org/ed/precollege/psn/

Joosten, E. G., De Jong, C. J., de Weert-van Oene, G. H., Sensky, T., & van der Staak, C. F. (2011). Shared decision-making: Increases autonomy in substance-dependent patients. *Substance Use & Misuse, 46*, 1037–1048. doi:10.3109/10826084.2011.552931

Kahneman, D. (2011). *Thinking, fast and slow.* New York, NY: Farrar, Straus and Giroux.

Kahneman, D., Krueger, A. B., Schkade, D., Schwarz, N., & Stone, A. A. (2006). Would you be happier if you were richer? A focusing illusion. *Science, 312* (5782), 1908–1910. doi:10.1126/science.1129688

Kakalios, J. (2010). *The amazing story of quantum mechanics: A math-free exploration of the science that changed our world.* London: Duckworth.

Kalton, G. (1983). *Introduction to survey sampling.* Newbury Park, CA: Sage.

Kanayama, G., Rogowska, J., Pope, H. G., Gruber, S. A., & Yurgelun-Todd, D. A. (2004). Spatial working memory in heavy cannabis users: A functional magnetic resonance imaging study. *Psychopharmacology, 176*, 239–247. doi:10.1007/s00213-004-1885-8

Kassin, S., Fein, S., & Markus, H. R. (2017). *Social psychology* (10th ed.). Boston, MA: Cengage.

Kay, A. C., Wheeler, S., Bargh, J. A., & Ross, L. (2004). Material priming: The influence of mundane physical objects on situational construal and competitive behavioral choice. *Organizational Behavior and Human Decision Processes, 95*, 83–96. doi:10.1016/j.obhdp.2004.06.003

Keski-Rahkonen, A., Hoek, H. W., Susser, E. S., Linna, M. S., Sihvola, E., Raevuori, A., Bulik, C. M., Kaprio, J., & Rissanen, A. (2007). Epidemiology and course of anorexia nervosa in the community. *The American Journal of Psychiatry, 164*(8), 1259–1265. doi:10.1176/appi.ajp.2007.06081388

Kinsey, A. C., Pomeroy, W. B., & Martin, C. E. (1948). *Sexual behavior in the human male.* Philadelphia, PA: Saunders.

Kinsey, A. C., Pomeroy, W. B., Martin, C. E., & Gebhard, P. H. (1953). *Sexual behavior in the human female.* Philadelphia, PA: Saunders.

Kirk-Smith, M. D., & Booth, D. A. (1980). Effect of androstenone on choice of location in others' presence. In H. van der Starre (Ed.), *Olfaction and taste* (pp. 389–392). London: IRL Press.

Kisilevsky, B. S., Hains, S. M. J., Brown, C. A., Lee, C. T., Cowperthwaite, B., Stutzman, S. S., & Wang, Z. (2009). Fetal sensitivity to properties of maternal speech and language. *Infant Behavior & Development, 32*, 59–71. doi:10.1016/j.infbeh.2008.10.002

Kleinke, C., Meeker, F., & Staneski, R. (1986). Preference for opening lines: Comparing ratings by men and women. *Sex Roles, 15,* 585–600. doi:10.1007/BF00288216

Klomek, A. B., Marrocco, F., Kleinman, M., Schonfeld, I. S., & Gould, M. S. (2007). Bullying, depression, and suicidality in adolescents. *Journal of the American Academy of Child & Adolescent Psychiatry, 46,* 40–49. doi:10.1097/01.chi.0000242237.84925.18

Knee, C. R., Lonsbary, C., Canevello, A., & Patrick, H. (2005). Self-determination and conflict in romantic relationships. *Journal of Personality and Social Psychology, 89,* 997–1009. doi:10.1037/0022-3514.89.6.997

Knight, Z. G. (2006). Some thoughts on the psychological roots of the behavior of serial killers as narcissists: An object relations perspective. *Social Behavior and Personality, 34,* 1189–1206. doi:10.2224/sbp.2006.34.10.1189

Kornell, N. (2009). Optimizing learning using flashcards: Spacing is more effective than cramming. *Applied Cognitive Psychology, 23,* 1297–1317. doi:10.1002/acp.1537

Kreiner, D. S., Altis, N. A., & Voss, C. W. (2003). A test of the effect of reverse speech on priming. *Journal of Psychology: Interdisciplinary and Applied, 137,* 224–232. doi:10.1080/00223980309600610

Krueger, R. A., & Casey, M. A. (2008). *Focus groups: A practical guide for applied research.* Thousand Oaks, CA: Sage.

Kvale, S. (1996). *InterViews: An introduction to qualitative research interviewing.* Thousand Oaks, CA: Sage.

Kvale, S., & Brinkmann, S. (2008). *InterViews: Learning the craft of qualitative research* (2nd ed.). Thousand Oaks, CA: Sage.

LaBrode, R. (2007). Etiology of the psychopathic serial killer: An analysis of antisocial personality disorder, psychopathy, and serial killer personality and crime scene characteristics. *Brief Treatment and Crisis Intervention, 7,* 151–160. doi:10.1093/brief-treatment/mhm004

Landrum, R. E., & Harrold, R. (2003). What employers want from psychology graduates. *Teaching of Psychology, 30,* 131–133.

Lansford, J. E., Wager, L. B., Bates, J. E., Pettit, G. S., & Dodge, K. A. (2012). Forms of spanking and children's externalizing behaviors. *Family Relations: An Interdisciplinary Journal of Applied Family Studies, 61,* 224–236. doi:10.1111/j.1741-3729.2011.00700.x

Larson, C. (2011, March 25). Mark Zuckerberg speaks at BYU, calls Facebook "as much psychology and sociology as it is technology." *Deseret News.* Retrieved from http://www.deseretnews.com/article/700121651/Mark-Zuckerberg-speaks-at-BYU-calls-Facebook-as-much-psychology-and-sociology-as-it-is-technology.html

Lavender, J. M., De Young, K. P., Wonderlich, S. A., Crosby, R. D., Engel, S. G., Mitchell, J. E., Crow, S. J., Peterson. C. B., & Le Grange, D. (2013). Daily patterns of anxiety in anorexia nervosa: Associations with eating disorder behaviors in the natural environment. *Journal of Abnormal Psychology, 122,* 672–683. doi:10.1037/a0031823

Lavie, N. (2010). Attention, distraction, and cognitive control under load. *Current Directions in Psychological Science, 19,* 143–148. doi:10.1177/0963721410370295

Lee, L. A., & Sbarra, D. A. (2013). The predictors and consequences of relationship dissolution: Breaking down silos. In C. Hazan & M. I. Campa (Eds.), *Human bonding: The science of affectional ties* (pp. 308–342). New York, NY: Guilford Press.

Leichsenring, F. (2005). Are psychodynamic and psychoanalytic therapies effective?: A review of empirical data. *The International Journal of Psychoanalysis, 86,* 841–868. doi:10.1516/RFEE-LKPN-B7TF-KPDU

Lenhart, A., Ling, R., Campbell, S., & Purcell, K. (2010). Chapter two: How phones are used with friends—What they can do and how teens use them. In *Teens and mobile phones.* Retrieved from http://www.pewinternet.org/Reports/2010/Teens-and-Mobile-Phones/Chapter-2/Why-teens-text.aspx

Levitt, S. D., & Dubner, S. J. (2005). *Freakonomics: A rogue economist explores the hidden side of everything.* New York, NY: William Morrow.

Lewandowski, G. W., Jr., & Nardone, N. (2012). Self-concept clarity's role in self-other agreement and the accuracy of behavioral prediction. *Self and Identity, 11,* 71–89. doi:10.1080/15298868.2010.512133

Lewandowski, G. W., Jr., Nardone, N., & Raines, A. J. (2010). The role of self-concept clarity in relationship quality. *Self and Identity, 9,* 416–433. doi:10.1080/15298860903332191

Lewandowski, G. W., Jr., & Strohmetz, D. B. (2009). Actions can speak as loud as words: Measuring behavior in psychological science. *Social and Personality Psychology Compass, 3*(6), 992–1002. doi:10.1111/j.1751-9004.2009.00229.x

Lewin, K. (1952). *Field theory in social science: Selected theoretical papers by Kurt Lewin.* London: Tavistock.

Lewis, M. (2003). *Moneyball.* New York, NY: Norton.

Li, X. (2008). The effects of appetitive stimuli on out-of-domain consumption impatience. *Journal of Consumer Research, 34,* 649–656. doi:10.1086/521900

Li, Y., Johnson, E. J., & Zaval, L. (2011). Local warming: Daily temperature change influences belief in global warming. *Psychological Science, 22,* 454–459. doi:10.1177/0956797611400913.

Likert, R. A. (1932). A technique for the measurement of attitudes. *Archives of Psychology, 140,* 1–55.

Liljenquist, K., Zhong, C., & Galinsky, A. (2010). The smell of virtue: Clean scents promote reciprocity and charity. *Psychological Science, 21,* 381–383. doi:10.1177/0956797610361426

Loftus, E. F., & Pickrell, J. E. (1995). The formation of false memories. *Psychiatric Annals, 25,* 720–725.

Lohmann, A., Arriaga, X. B., & Goodfriend, W. (2003). Close relationships and placemaking: Do objects in a couple's home reflect couplehood? *Personal Relationships, 10,* 437–449. doi:10.1111/1475-6811.00058

Lopez, N. L., Schneider, H. G., & Dula, C. S. (2002). Parent discipline scale: Discipline choice as a function of transgression type. *North American Journal of Psychology, 4,* 381–393.

Lorenzoni, I., Leiserowitz, A., De Franca Doria, M., Poortinga, W., & Pidgeon, N. (2006). Cross-national comparisons of image associations with "global warming" and "climate change" among laypeople in the United States of America and Great Britain. *Journal of Risk Research, 9,* 265–281. doi:10.1080/13669870600613658

Luangrath, A., & Hiscock, H. (2011). Problem behaviour in children: An approach for general practice. *Australian Family Physician, 40*(9), 678–681.

Lyubomirsky, S., & Lepper, H. S. (1999). A measure of subjective happiness: Preliminary reliability and construct validation. *Social Indicators Research, 46,* 137–155. doi:10.1023/A:1006824100041

Macan, T. (2009). The employment interview: A review of current studies and directions for future research. *Human Resource Management Review, 19*(3), 203–218. doi:10.1016/j.hrmr.2009.03.006

Madill, A. (2007). Survey of British Psychological Society qualitative methods in psychology section members 2006. *British Psychological Society Qualitative Methods in Psychology Section Newsletter, 3,* 9–14.

Madill, A., & Gough, B. (2008). Qualitative research and its place in psychological science. *Psychological Methods, 13,* 254–271. doi:10.1037/a0013220

Marczinski, C. A., Fillmore, M. T., Bardgett, M. E., & Howard, M. A. (2011). Effects of energy drinks mixed with alcohol on behavioral control: Risks for college students consuming trendy cocktails. *Alcoholism: Clinical and Experimental Research, 35,* 1282–1292. doi:10.1111/j.1530-0277.2011.01464.x

Marczinski, C. A., Fillmore, M. T., Henges, A. L., Ramsey, M. A., & Young, C. R. (2012). Effects of energy drinks mixed with alcohol on information processing, motor coordination and subjective reports of intoxication. *Experimental and Clinical Psychopharmacology, 20,* 129–138. doi:10.1037/a0026136

Marecek, J. (2003). Dancing through the minefields: Toward a qualitative stance in psychology. In P. M. Camic, J. E. Rhodes, & L. Yardley (Eds.), *Qualitative research in psychology: Expanding perspectives in methodology and design* (pp. 49–69). Washington, DC: American Psychological Association.

Martens, A., & Kosloff, S. (2012). Evidence that killing escalates within-subjects in a bug-killing paradigm. *Aggressive Behavior, 38,* 170–174. doi:10.1002/ab.21412

Maslow, A. H., & Sakoda, J. M. (1952). Volunteer-error in the Kinsey study. *Journal of Abnormal and Social Psychology, 47,* 259–262. doi:10.1037/h0054411

Mazure, C., Halmi, K., Sunday, S., Romano, S., & Einhorn, A. (1994). The Yale-Brown-Cornell eating disorder scale: Development, use, reliability and validity. *Journal of Psychiatric Research, 28,* 425–445. doi:10.1016/0022-3956(94)90002-7

McDaniel, A. K. (2005). Young women's dating behavior: Why/why not date a nice guy? *Sex Roles, 53,* 347–359. doi:10.1007/s11199-005-6758-z

McGuire, W. J. (1997). Creative hypothesis generating in psychology: Some useful heuristics. *Annual Review of Psychology, 48,* 1–30. doi:10.1146/annurev.psych.48.1.1

McNemar, Q. (1946). Opinion-attitude methodology. *Psychological Bulletin, 43,* 289–374. doi:10.1037/h0060985

Meehl, P. E. (1954). *Clinical versus statistical prediction: A theoretical analysis and a review of the evidence.* Minneapolis, MN: University of Minnesota Press. doi:10.1037/11281-000

Milgram, S. (1974). *Obedience to authority.* New York, NY: Harper.

Miller, T. M., & Geraci, L. (2011). Unskilled but aware: Reinterpreting overconfidence in low-performing students. *Journal of Experimental Psychology: Learning, Memory, and Cognition, 37*(2), 502–506. doi:10.1037/a0021802

Milliken, R. (2008). Intervening in the cycle of addiction, violence, and shame: A dance/movement therapy group approach in a jail addictions program. *Journal of Groups in Addiction & Recovery, 3,* 5–22. doi:10.1080/15560350802157346

Miyajima, T., & Naito, M. (2008). Conformity under indirect group pressure in junior high school students: Effects of normative and informational social influences and task importance. *Japanese Journal of Developmental Psychology, 19*(4), 364–374.

Moore, R. S., & Ames, G. M. (2002). Survey confidentiality vs. anonymity: Young men's self-reported substance use. *Journal of Alcohol and Drug Education, 47*(2), 32–41.

Morris, J. & Twaddle, S. (2007). Anorexia nervosa. *British Medical Journal, 334,* 894–898.

Murphy, S., Russell, L., & Waller, G. (2005). Integrated psychodynamic therapy for bulimia nervosa and binge eating disorder: Theory, practice and preliminary findings. *European Eating Disorders Review, 13,* 383–391. doi:10.1002/erv.672

Myers, D. G. (2013). *Social psychology* (11th ed.). New York, NY: McGraw-Hill.

Nabi, R. L., Biely, E. N., Morgan, S. J., & Stitt, C. R. (2003). Reality-based television programming and the psychology of its appeal. *Media Psychology, 5,* 303–330. doi:10.1207/S1532785xmep0504_01

Najmi, S. (2013). Thought suppression. In D. E. Carlston (Ed.), *The Oxford handbook of social cognition* (pp. 417–432). New York, NY: Oxford University Press.

Najmi, S., Reese, H., Wilhelm, S., Fama, J., Beck, C., & Wegner, D. M. (2010). Learning the futility of the thought suppression enterprise in normal experience and in obsessive compulsive disorder. *Behavioural and Cognitive Psychotherapy, 38,* 1–14. doi:10.1017/S1352465809990439

Nathan, D. (2011). *Sybil exposed: The extraordinary story behind the famous multiple personality case.* New York, NY: Free Press.

Nathan, R. (2006). *My freshman year: What a professor learned by becoming a student.* New York, NY: Penguin Books.

National Association of Colleges and Employers. (2013). *Class of 2013: Majority of seniors participated in internships or co-ops.* Retrieved from http://www.naceweb.org/press/releases/internship-co-op-participation.aspx

Niedenthal, P. M., Barsalou, L. W., Winkielman, P., Krauth-Gruber, S., & Ric, F. (2005). Embodiment in attitudes, social perception, and emotion. *Personality and Social Psychology Review, 9*(3), 184–211. doi:10.1207/s15327957pspr0903_1

Nisbett, R., & Wilson, T. (1977). Telling more than we can know: Verbal reports on mental processes. *Psychological Review, 84,* 231–259. doi:10.1037/0033-295X.84.3.231

Oishi, S., & Diener, E. (2003). Culture and well-being: The cycle of action, evaluation and decision. *Personality and Social Psychology Bulletin, 29,* 939–949. doi:10.1177/0146167203252802

Orne, M. T. (1962). On the social psychology of the psychological experiment: With particular reference to demand characteristics and their implications. *American Psychologist, 17,* 776–783. doi:10.1037/h0043424

Ozier, A. D., Kendrick, O. W., Leeper, J. D., Knol, L. L., Perko, M., & Burnham, J. (2008). Overweight and obesity are associated with emotion- and stress-related eating as measured by the eating and appraisal due to emotions and stress questionnaire. *Journal of the American Dietetic Association, 108,* 49–56.

Paasche-Orlow, M. K., Taylor, H. A., & Brancati, F. L. (2003). Readability standards for informed-consent forms as compared with actual readability. *The New England Journal of Medicine, 348,* 721–726.

Papacharissi, Z., & Mendelson, A. L. (2007). An exploratory study of reality appeal: Uses and gratifications of reality TV shows. *Journal of Broadcasting & Electronic Media, 51,* 355–370. doi:10.1080/08838150701307152

Park, A., Sher, K. J., & Krull, J. L. (2008). Risky drinking in college: Changes as fraternity/sorority affiliation changes: A person-environment perspective. *Psychology of Addictive Behaviors, 22,* 219–229. doi:10.1037/0893/0893-164X.22.2.219

Parmentier, F. R., Elsley, J. V., & Ljungberg, J. K. (2010). Behavioral distraction by auditory novelty is not only about novelty: The role of the distracter's informational value. *Cognition, 115,* 504–511. doi:10.1016/j.cognition.2010.03.002

Pates, J. (2013). The effects of hypnosis on an elite senior European tour golfer: A single-subject design. *International Journal of Clinical and Experimental Hypnosis, 61,* 1–12. doi:10.1080/00207144.2013.753831

Patterson, M. L. (2008). Back to social behavior: Mining the mundane. *Basic and Applied Social Psychology, 30,* 93–101. doi:10.1080/019735 30802208816

Pause, B. M. (2004). Are androgen steroids acting as pheromones in humans? *Physiology and Behavior, 83,* 21–29. doi.org/10.1016/j.physbeh.2004.07.019

Penton-Voak, I. S., & Perrett, D. I. (2000). Female preference for male faces changes cyclically: Further evidence. *Evolution and Human Behavior, 21,* 39–48. doi:10.1016/S1090-5138(99)00033-1

Pew. (2016). *Public views on climate change and climate scientists.* Pew Research Center. Retrieved from: http://www.pewinternet.org/2016/10/04/public-views-on-climate-change-and-climate-scientists/

Pinderhughes, E. E., Dodge, K. A., Zelli, A., Bates, J. E., & Pettit, G. S. (2000). Discipline responses: Influences of parents' socioeconomic status, ethnicity, beliefs about parenting, stress, and cognitive-emotional processes. *Journal of Family Psychology, 14,* 380–400. doi:10.1037/0893-3200.14.3.380

Place, S. S., Todd, P. M., Penke, L., & Asendorpf, J. B. (2009). The ability to judge the romantic interest of others. *Psychological Science, 20,* 22–26. doi:10.1111/j.1467-9280.2008.02248.x

Potegal, M., & Davidson, R. J. (2003). Temper tantrums in young children: Behavioral composition. *Journal of Developmental and Behavioral Pediatrics, 24,* 140–147. doi:10.1097/00004703-200306000-00002

Potter, J., & Hepburn, A. (2005). Qualitative interviews in psychology: Problems and possibilities. *Qualitative Research in Psychology, 2,* 281–309.

Poulsen, S., Lunn, S., Daniel, S., Folke, S., Mathiesen, B., Katznelson, H., & Fairburn, C. (2014). A randomized controlled trial of psychoanalytic psychotherapy or cognitive-behavioral therapy for bulimia nervosa. *American Journal of Psychiatry, 171,* 109–116. doi:10.1176/appi.ajp.2013.12121511

Privitera, M. R., Moynihan, J., Tang, W., & Khan, A. (2010). Light therapy for seasonal affective disorder in a clinical office setting. *Journal of Psychiatric Practice, 16,* 387–393. doi:10.1097/01.pra.0000390757.19828.e0

Proyer, R. T., Ruch, W., & Buschor, C. (2013). Testing strengths-based interventions: A preliminary study on the effectiveness of a program targeting curiosity, gratitude, hope, humor, and zest for enhancing life satisfaction. *Journal of Happiness Studies, 14,* 275–292. doi:10.1007/s10902-012-9331-9

Przybylski, A. K., & Weinstein, N. (2013). Can you connect with me now? How the presence of mobile communication technology influences face-to-face conversation quality. *Journal of Social and Personal Relationships, 30,* 237–246. doi:10.1177/0265407512453827.

Reiss, S., & Wiltz, J. (2004). Why people watch reality TV. *Media Psychology, 6,* 363–378. doi:10.1207/s1532785xmep0604_3

Rentfrow, P. J., & Gosling, S. D. (2003). The do re mi's of everyday life: The structure and personality correlates of music preferences. *Journal of Personality and Social Psychology, 84,* 1236–1256. doi:10.1037/0022-3514.84.6.1236

Ressler, R. K. (2004). How to interview a cannibal. In J. H. Campbell & D. DeNevi (Eds.), *Profilers: Leading investigators take you inside the criminal mind* (pp. 135–177). Amherst, NY: Prometheus Books.

Ressler, R. K., Douglas, J. E., Groth, A. N., & Burgess, A. W. (2004). The men who murdered. In J. H. Campbell & D. DeNevi (Eds.), *Profilers: Leading investigators take you inside the criminal mind* (pp. 73–81). Amherst, NY: Prometheus Books.

Rind, B., & Bordia, P. (1995). Effect of server's "thank you" and personalization on restaurant tipping. *Journal of Applied Social Psychology, 25,* 745–751. doi:10.1111/j.1559-1816.1995.tb01772.x

Robinson, J. P., Shaver, P. R., & Wrightsman, L. S. (Eds.). (1991). *Measures of personality and social psychological attitudes.* San Diego, CA: Academic Press.

Robitschek, C. (1998). Personal growth initiative: The construct and its measure. *Measurement and Evaluation in Counseling and Development, 30,* 183–198.

Rosell, M. C., Beck, D. M., Luther, K. E., Goedert, K. M., Shore, W. J., & Anderson, D. D. (2005). The pedagogical value of experimental participation paired with course content. *Teaching of Psychology, 32,* 95–99. doi:10.1207/s15328023top3202_3

Rosen, L. D., Lim, A. F., Carrier, M., & Cheever, N. A. (2011). An empirical examination of the educational impact of text message-induced task switching in the classroom: Educational implications and strategies to enhance learning. *Educational Psychology, 17,* 163–177.

Rosenberg, M. (1989). *Society and the adolescent self-image* (Rev. ed.). Middletown, CT: Wesleyan University Press.

Rosenberg, M. J. (1969). The conditions and consequences of evaluation apprehension. In R. Rosenthal & R. L. Rosnow (Eds.), *Artifact in behavioral research* (pp. 279–349). New York, NY: Academic Press.

Rosenberg, M. J. (2009). The conditions and consequences of evaluation apprehension. In R. Rosenthal and R. L. Rosnow, *Artifacts in behavioral research: Robert Rosenthal and Ralph L. Rosnow's classic books* (pp. 211–263). Oxford, England: Oxford University Press. (Original work published 1969).

Rosenthal, R., & Rosnow, R. L. (2009). *Artifacts in behavioral research: Robert Rosenthal and Ralph L. Rosnow's classic books. A re-issue of Artifacts in behavioral research, Experimenter effects in behavioral research, and the volunteer subject.* New York, NY: Oxford University Press.

Rosnow, R. L., & Rosenthal, R. (1997). *People studying people: Artifacts and ethics in behavioral research.* New York, NY: W. H. Freeman.

Rosser, J. C., Jr., Lynch, P. L., Cuddihy, L., Gentile, D. A., Klonsky, J., & Merrell, R. (2007). The impact of video games on training surgeons in the 21st century. *Archives of Surgery, 142,* 181–186. doi:10.1001/archsurg.142.2.181

Rotter, J. B. (1966). Generalized expectancies for internal versus external control of reinforcement. *Psychological Monographs, 80,* 609. doi:10.1037/h0092976

Santelices, M. V., & Wilson, M. (2010). Unfair treatment? The case of Freedle, the SAT, and the standardization approach to differential item functioning. *Harvard Educational Review, 80,* 106–142.

Sartori, R. (2010). Face validity in personality tests: Psychometric instruments and projective techniques in comparison. *Quality & Quantity: International Journal of Methodology, 44,* 749–759. doi:10.1007/s11135-009-9224-0

Schacter, D. L., Gilbert, D. T., & Wegner, D. M. (2010). *Psychology* (2nd ed.). New York, NY: Worth.

Schmaltz, R., & Lilienfeld, S. O. (2014). Hauntings, homeopathy, and the Hopkinsville Goblins: Using pseudoscience to teach scientific thinking. *Frontiers In Psychology, 5,* 336.

Schreier, A., Wolke, D., Thomas, K., Horwood, J., Hollis, C., Gunnell, D., Lewis, G., Thompson, A., Zammit, S., Duffy, L., Salvi, G., & Harrison, G. (2009). Prospective study of peer victimization in childhood and psychotic symptoms in a non-clinical population at age 12 years. *Archives of General Psychiatry, 66,* 527–536. doi:10.1001/archgenpsychiatry.2009.23

Schröder-Abě, M., Rudolph, A., Wiesner, A., & Schütz, A. (2007). Self-esteem of discrepancies and defensive reactions to social feedback. *International Journal of Psychology, 42,* 174–183. doi:10.1080/00207590601068134

Schuman, H., & Presser, S. (1996). *Questions and answers in attitude surveys: Experiments on question form, wording, and context.* Thousand Oaks, CA: Sage.

Sears, D. O. (1986). College sophomores in the laboratory: Influences of a narrow base on social psychology's view of human nature. *Journal of Personality and Social Psychology, 51,* 515–530. doi:10.1037/0022-3514.51.3.515

Sedikides, C., & Spencer, S. J. (Eds.). (2007). *The self.* New York, NY: Psychology Press.

Seltzer, L. J., Prososki, A. R., Ziegler, T. E., & Pollak, S. D. (2012). Instant messages vs. speech: Hormones and why we still need to hear each other. *Evolution and Human Behavior, 33*(1), 42–45. doi:10.1016/j.evolhumbehav.2011.05.004

Senko, C., & Fyffe, V. (2010). An evolutionary perspective on effective vs. ineffective pick-up lines. *Journal of Social Psychology, 150*(6), 648–667. doi:10.1080/00224540903365539

Shadish, W. R., Cook, T. D., & Campbell, D. T. (2002). *Experimental and quasi-experimental designs for generalized causal inference.* Boston, MA: Houghton Mifflin.

Shaw, M. E., & Wright, J. M. (1967). *Scales for the measurement of attitudes.* New York, NY: McGraw-Hill.

Shepperd, J., Malone, W., & Sweeny, K. (2008). Exploring causes of the self-serving bias. *Social and Personality Psychology Compass, 2,* 895–908. doi:10.1111/j.1751-9004.2008.00078.x

Simmons, J. P., Nelson, L. D., & Simonsohn, U. (2011). False-positive psychology: Undisclosed flexibility in data collection and analysis allows presenting anything as significant. *Psychological Science, 22,* 1359–1366. doi:10.1177/0956797611417632

Simons, D. A., & Wurtele, S. K. (2010). Relationships between parents' use of corporal punishment and their children's endorsement of spanking and hitting other children. *Child Abuse & Neglect, 34,* 639–646. doi:10.1016/j.chiabu.2010.01.012

Sizemore, O. J., & Lewandowski, G. W., Jr. (2009). Learning might not equal liking: Research methods course changes knowledge but not attitudes. *Teaching of Psychology, 36*(2), 90–95. doi:10.1080/00986280902739727

Skierkowski, D., & Wood, R. M. (2012). To text or not to text? The importance of text messaging among college-aged youth. *Computers in Human Behavior, 28,* 744–756. doi:10.1016/j.chb.2011.11.023

Smith, J. (2013). Internships may be the easiest way to a job in 2013. *Forbes.* Retrieved from http://www.forbes.com/sites/jacquelynsmith/2012/12/06/internships-may-be-the-easiest-way-to-a-job-in-2013/

Smith, J. K. (1983). Quantitative versus qualitative research: An attempt to clarify the issue. *Educational Researcher, 12*(3), 6–13.

Smith, T., Isaak, M. I., Senette, C. G., & Abadie, B. G. (2011). Effects of cell-phone and text-message distractions on true and false recognition. *CyberPsychology and Behavior & Social Networking, 14,* 351–358. doi:10.1089/cyber.2010.0129

Song, J., & Oh, I. (2018). Factors influencing bystanders' behavioral reactions in cyberbullying situations. *Computers in Human Behavior, 78,* 273–282. doi:10.1016/j.chb.2017

Spector, P. E. (1992). *Summated rating scale construction: An introduction.* Newbury Park, CA: Sage.

Sprecher, S., Wenzel, A., & Harvey, J. (2008). *Handbook of relationship initiation.* New York, NY: Psychology Press.

Stanovich, K. E. (2010). *How to think straight about psychology* (9th ed.). Boston, MA: Pearson.

Steering Committee of the Physicians' Health Study Research Group. (1988). Preliminary report: Findings from the aspirin component of the ongoing physicians' health study. *New England Journal of Medicine, 318,* 262–264.

Steinberg, L. (2008). *Adolescence* (8th ed.). New York, NY: McGraw-Hill.

Steinglass, J. E., Figner, B., Berkowitz, S., Simpson, H., Weber, E. U., & Walsh, B. (2012). Increased capacity to delay reward in anorexia nervosa. *Journal of the International Neuropsychological Society, 18,* 773–780. doi:10.1017/S1355617712000446

Stewart, D. W., Shamdasani, P. N., & Rook, D. W. (2007). *Focus groups: Theory and practice* (2nd ed.). Thousand Oaks, CA: Sage.

Strauss, B. (2002). Social facilitation in motor tasks: A review of research and theory. *Psychology of Sport and Exercise, 3*(3), 237–256. doi:10.1016/S1469-0292(01)00019-X

Streiner, D. L. (2003). Starting at the beginning: An introduction to coefficient alpha and internal consistency. *Journal of Personality Assessment, 80,* 99–103. doi:10.1207/S15327752JPA8001_18

Strohmetz, D. B. (2008). Research artifacts and the social psychology of psychological experiments. *Social and Personality Psychology Compass, 2,* 861–877. doi:10.1111/j.1751-9004.2007.00072.x

Struch, N., & Schwartz, S. H. (1989). Intergroup aggression: Its predictors and distinctness from in-group bias. *Journal of Personality and Social Psychology, 56,* 364–373.

Tajfel, H. (1970). Experiments in intergroup discrimination. *Scientific American, 223,* 96–102.

Taleb, N. N. (2010). *The black swan: The impact of the highly improbable.* New York, NY: Random House.

Tavris, C., & Aronson, E. (2007). *Mistakes were made (but not by me): Why we justify foolish beliefs, bad decisions, and hurtful acts.* Orlando, FL: Harcourt.

Taylor, S. E. (2009). Publishing in scientific journals: We're not just talking to ourselves anymore. *Perspectives on Psychological Science, 4,* 38–39. doi:10.1111/j.1745-6924.2009.01101.x

Terao, T., & Hoaki, N. (2011). Light can ameliorate low mood in healthy people. *Psychopharmacology, 213,* 831. doi:10.1007/s00213-010-2046-x

Thompson, J. G., Jr., Oberle, C. D., & Lilley, J. L. (2011). Self-efficacy and learning in sorority and fraternity students. *Journal of College Student Development, 52,* 749–753. doi:10.1353/csd.2011.0078

Thornhill, R., Gangestad, S. W., Miller, R., Scheyd, G., McCollough, J. K., & Franklin, M. (2003). Major histocompatibility complex genes, symmetry, and body scent attractiveness in men and women. *Behavioral Ecology, 14,* 668–678.

Tindell, D. R. (2012). The use and abuse of cell phones and text messaging in the classroom: A survey of college students. *College Teaching, 60,* 1–9. doi:10.1080/87567555.2011.604802

Twenge, J. M., Baumeister, R. F., DeWall, C., Ciarocco, N. J., & Bartels, J. (2007). Social exclusion decreases prosocial behavior. *Journal of Personality and Social Psychology, 92,* 56–66. doi:10.1037/0022-3514.92.1.56

Twenge, J. M., Baumeister, R. F., Tice, D. M., & Stucke, T. S. (2001). If you can't join them, beat them: Effects of social exclusion on aggressive behavior. *Journal of Personality and Social Psychology, 81,* 1058–1069. doi:10.1037/0022-3514.81.6.1058

Underwood, M. K., Rosen, L. H., More, D., Ehrenreich, S. E., & Gentsch, J. K. (2012). The BlackBerry project: Capturing the content of adolescents' text messaging. *Developmental Psychology, 48,* 295–302. doi:10.1037/a0025914

University of Notre Dame. (2011). Want smarter children? Space siblings at least two years apart, research shows [Press release]. Retrieved from http://newsinfo.nd.edu/news/27408-want-smarter-children-space-siblings-at-least-two-years-apart-new-research-shows/

Urbaniak, G. C., & Kilmann, P. R. (2003). Physical attractiveness and the "nice guy paradox": Do nice guys really finish last? *Sex Roles, 49,* 413–426. doi:10.1023/A:1025894203368

U.S. Department of Health and Human Services. (2009). Title 45: Public welfare, part 46, protection of human subjects. Revised January 15, 2009. http://www.hhs.gov/ohrp/humansubjects/guidance/45cfr46.html

Vacharkulksemsuk, T., Reit, E., Khambatta, P., Eastwick, P. W., Finkel, E. J., & Carney, D. R. (2016). Dominant, open nonverbal displays are attractive at zero-acquaintance. *Proceedings of the National Academy of Sciences of the United States of America, 113*(15), 4009–4014. http://doi.org/10.1073/pnas.1508932113

Van den Bos, K., Euwema, M. C., Poortvliet, P. M., & Maas, M. (2007). Uncertainty management and social issues: Uncertainty as an important determinant of reactions to socially deviating people. *Journal of Applied Social Psychology, 37,* 1726–1756. doi:10.1111/j.1559-1816.2007.00235.x

van Dijk, W. W., Ouwerkerk, J. W., & Goslinga, S. (2009). The impact of deservingness on schadenfreude and sympathy: Further evidence. *Journal of Social Psychology, 149,* 290–292. doi:10.3200/SOCP.149.3.390-392

van Dijk, W. W., Ouwerkerk, J. W., Goslinga, S., Nieweg, M., & Gallucci, M. (2006). When people fall from grace: Reconsidering the role of envy in schadenfreude. *Emotion, 6,* 156–160. doi:10.1037/1528-3542.6.1.156

van Dijk, W. W., Ouwerkerk, J. W., van Koningsbruggen, G. M., & Wesseling, Y. M. (2012). "So you wanna be a pop star?" Schadenfreude following another's misfortune on TV. *Basic and Applied Social Psychology, 34,* 168–174. doi:10.1080/01973533.2012.656006

van Dijk, W. W., Ouwerkerk, J. W., Wesseling, Y. M., & van Koningsbruggen, G. M. (2011). Towards understanding pleasure at the misfortunes of others: The impact of self-evaluation threat on schadenfreude. *Cognition and Emotion, 25,* 360–368. doi:10.1080/02699931.2010.487365

Van Kempen, L. (2004). Are the poor willing to pay a premium for designer labels? A field experiment in Bolivia. *Oxford Development Studies, 32,* 205–224. doi:10.1080/13600810410001699957

Verschueren, K., Dossche, D., Marcoen, A., Mahieu, S., & Bakermans-Kranenburg, M. (2006). Attachment representations and discipline in mothers of young school children: An observation study. *Social Development, 15,* 659–675. doi:10.1111/j.1467-9507.2006.00363.x

Vohs, K. D., & Schooler, J. W. (2008). The value of believing in free will: Encouraging a belief in determinism increases cheating. *Psychological Science, 19,* 49–54. doi:10.1111/j.1467-9280.2008.02045.x

Vokey, J. R., & Read, J. (1985). Subliminal messages: Between the devil and the media. *American Psychologist, 40,* 1231–1239. doi:10.1037/0003-066X.40.11.1231

Wainer, H. (1999). The most dangerous profession: A note on nonsampling error. *Psychological Methods, 3,* 250–256. doi:1082-989X/99

Walter, M. (2012). Human experiments: First, do harm. *Nature, 482,*148–152. doi:10.1038/482148a

Watson, J. B., & Rayner, R. (1920). Conditioned emotional reactions. *Journal of Experimental Psychology, 3,* 1–14. doi:10.1037/h0069608

Webb, E. J., Campbell, D. T., Schwarz, R. F., Sechrest, L., & Grove, J. B. (1981). *Nonreactive measures in the social sciences* (2nd ed.). Boston, MA: Houghton Mifflin.

Weber, K., Goodboy, A. K., & Cayanus, J. L. (2010). Flirting competence: An experimental study on appropriate and effective opening lines. *Communication Research Reports, 27,* 184–191. doi:10.1080/08824091003738149

Wegner, D. M. (1994). Ironic processes of mental control. *Psychological Review, 101,* 34–52. doi:10.1037/0033-295X.101.1.34

Whitaker, J. L., Melzer, A., Steffgen, G., & Bushman, B. J. (2013). The allure of the forbidden: Breaking taboos, frustration, and attraction to violent video games. *Psychological Science, 24,* 507–513. doi:10.1177/0956797612457397

Whitbourne, S. K., & Halgin, R. P. (2013). *Abnormal psychology: Clinical perspectives on psychological disorders* (7th ed.). New York, NY: McGraw Hill.

Whitmarsh, L. (2008). Are flooding victims more concerned about climate change than other people? The role of direct experience in risk perception and behavioural response. *Journal of Risk Research, 11,* 351–374. doi:10.1080/13669870701552235

Wilder, D. H., Hoyt, A. E., Surbeck, B. S., Wilder, J. C., & Carney, P. I. (1986). Greek affiliation and attitude change in college students. *Journal of College Student Personnel, 27,* 510–519.

Williams, L., & Bargh, J. (2008). Experiencing physical warmth promotes interpersonal warmth. *Science, 322,* 606–607. doi:10.1126/science.1162548

Willig, C. (2008). *Introducing qualitative research in psychology* (2nd ed.). New York, NY: Open University Press.

Wilson, F. A., & Stimpson, J. P. (2010). Trends in fatalities from distracted driving in the United States, 1999 to 2008. *American Journal of Public Health, 100,* 2213–2219. doi:10.2105/AJPH.2009.187179

Wilson, T. D. (2002). *Strangers to ourselves.* Cambridge, MA: Harvard.

Wilson, T. D., Centerbar, D. B., Kermer, D. A., & Gilbert, D. T. (2005). The pleasures of uncertainty: Prolonging positive moods in ways people do not anticipate. *Journal of Personality and Social Psychology, 88,* 5–21. doi:10.1037/0022-3514.88.1.5

Witkiewitz, K., Lustyk, M. B., & Bowen, S. (2013). Retraining the addicted brain: A review of hypothesized neurobiological mechanisms of mindfulness-based relapse prevention. *Psychology of Addictive Behaviors, 27,* 351–365. doi:10.1037/a0029258

Wolfe, J. (2014). Theoretical and behavioral aspects of selective attention. In M. S. Gazzaniga & G. R. Mangun (Eds.), *The cognitive neurosciences* (5th ed., pp. 167–176). Cambridge, MA: MIT Press.

Wyart, C., Webster, W. W., Chen, J. H., Wilson, S. R., McClary, A., Khan, R. M., & Sobel, N. (2007). Smelling a single component of male sweat alters levels of cortisol in women. *Journal of Neuroscience, 27,* 1261–1265. doi:10.1523/JNEUROSCI.4430-06.2007

Yom-Tove, E., Fernandez-Luque, L., Weber, I., & Crain, S. P. (2012). Pro-anorexia and pro-recovery photo sharing: A tale of two warring tribes. *Journal of Medical Internet Research, 14,* 85–96. doi:10.2196/jmir.2239

Zajonc, R. B. (1965). Social facilitation. *Science, 10,* 224–228. doi:10.1126/science.149.3681.269

Zell, E., & Krizan, Z. (2014). Do people have insight into their abilities? A metasynthesis. *Perspectives on Psychological Science, 9*(2), 111–125. doi:10.1177/1745691613518075

Zimbardo, P. G., Haney, C., Banks, W. C., & Jatle, D. (1973, April 8). A Pirandellian prison. *The New York Times Magazine, 66,* 38–60.

Name Index

Subject Index